D0224674

The Global West
Connections & Identities
Third Edition

Volume II: Since 1550

Frank L. Kidner
San Francisco State University

Maria Bucur
Indiana University

Ralph Mathisen
University of Illinois at Urbana-Champaign

Sally McKee
University of California, Davis

Theodore R. Weeks
Southern Illinois University, Carbondale

Australia • Brazil • Mexico • Singapore • United Kingdom • United States

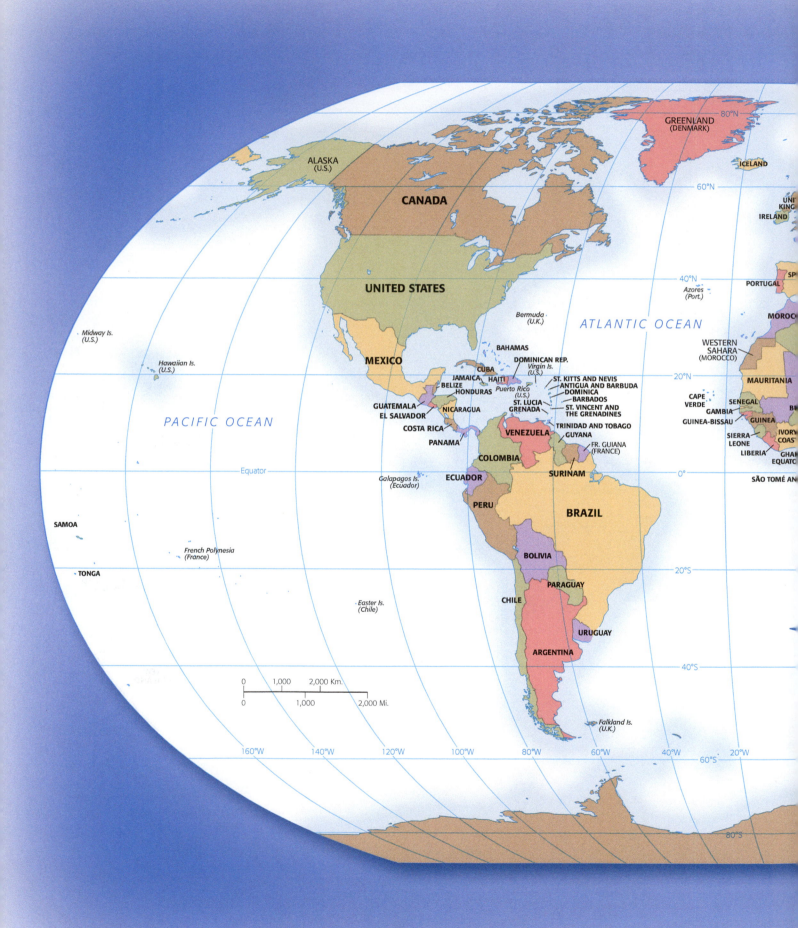

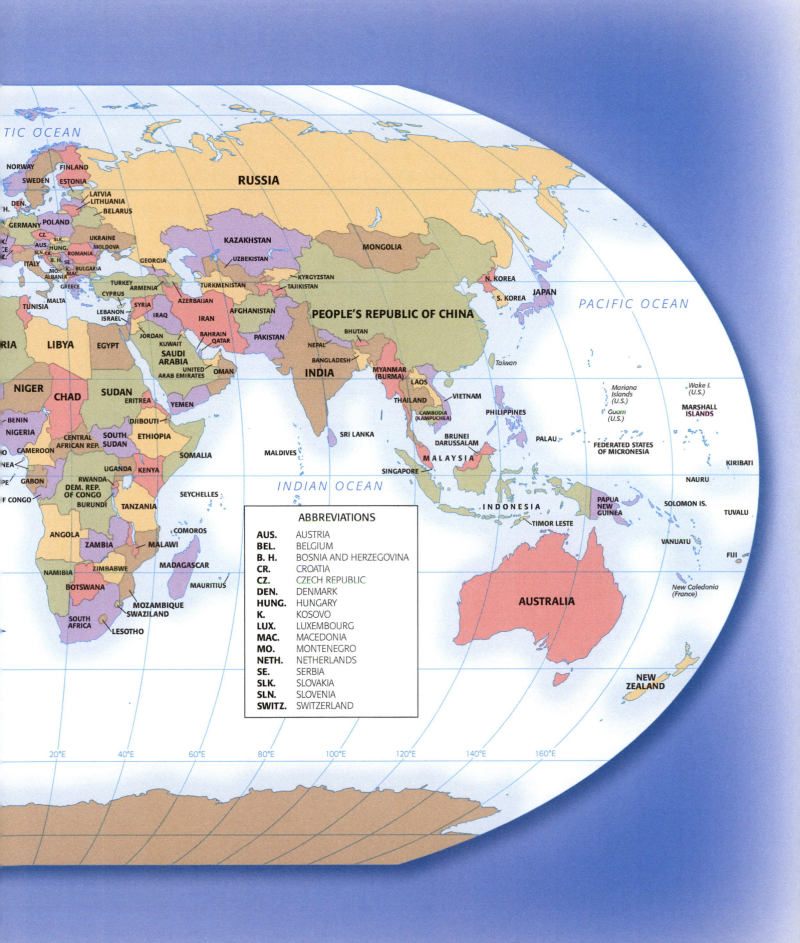

The Global West: Connections & Identities,
Volume II: Since 1550, Third Edition
Frank L. Kidner/Maria Bucur/
Ralph Mathisen/Sally McKee/
Theodore R. Weeks

Product Director: Paul Banks

Product Manager: Richard Lena

Senior Content Developer: Erika Hayden

Associate Content Developer: Emma Guiton

Product Assistant: Alexandra Shore

Senior Marketing Manager: Valerie Hartman

Senior Content Project Manager: Carol Newman

Manufacturing Planner: Julio Esperas

IP Analyst: Alex Ricciardi

IP Project Manager: Erika Mugavin

Production Service: SPi Global

Senior Art Director: Cate Rickard Barr

Text and Cover Designer: Studio Montage

Cover Images: *Top left to right*: Olaudah Equiano:
National Portrait Gallery, Smithsonian Institution/
Art Resource, NY; Portrait of Fyodor Dostoyevsky
(1821-81) 1872 (oil on canvas), Perov, Vasili
Grigorevich (1833-82) / Tretyakov Gallery, Moscow,
Russia / Bridgeman Images; Garibaldi: Alinari
Archives/The Image Works; Aleksandra Kollontai :
HIP / Art Resource, NY. *Bottom*: Map: Wagons-Lits
Simplon Orient Express brochure, 1934. Collection
Arjan den Boer, http://retours.eu

About the Cover Map The cover of this volume
features a map of the Simplon Orient Express'
route from about 1932. The famous luxury train
made her maiden voyage from Paris in 1883,
and by 1888, the track system provided a direct
connection between Paris and Constantinople
(Istanbul), with associated lines that branched to
points as far east as the Persian Gulf and as far
south as Cairo. Throughout the heyday of the
Orient Express, brochures that advertised the
journey made the train's destinations seem exotic
and overpromised on the accessibility of many of
the cities noted along the route.

For product information and technology assistance, contact us at
Cengage Customer & Sales Support, 1-800-354-9706.

For permission to use material from this text or product, submit all
requests online at **www.cengage.com/permissions.**
Further permissions questions can be emailed to
permissionrequest@cengage.com.

Library of Congress Control Number: 2017952994

Student Edition: ISBN: 978-1-337-40139-5

Loose-leaf Edition: ISBN: 978-1-337-40370-2

Cengage
20 Channel Center Street
Boston, MA 02210
USA

Cengage is a leading provider of customized learning solutions with
employees residing in nearly 40 different countries and sales in more than
125 countries around the world. Find your local representative
at **www.cengage.com.**

Cengage products are represented in Canada by Nelson Education, Ltd.

To learn more about Cengage platforms and services, visit **www.cengage.com.**

Purchase any of our products at your local college store or at our preferred
online store **www.cengagebrain.com.**

Printed in the United States of America
Print Number: 01   Print Year: 2019

Brief Contents

Contents

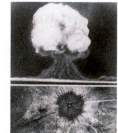
Photo credits: "Women of Britain Say - Go!," recruitment poster, 1915 (litho), Kealey, E.P. (20th century) / Private Collection / Photo © Bonhams, London, UK / Bridgeman Images; Ullstein Bilderdienst/The Image Works; Granger, NYC — All rights reserved

28 Europe Divided, 1945–1968 790

29 Lifting the Iron Curtain, 1969–1991 822

30 Europe in a Globalizing World, 1991 to the Present 852

Maps

Features

Preface

For years, we five professors from across the country have taught Western Civilization courses without the textbook we really wanted to have—a textbook with a coherent strategy for helping students to study and learn. In 1999, we began to develop such a text. This book is the result.

The five of us bring to this book a variety of backgrounds, interests, and historical approaches, as well as a combined total of nearly one hundred years of teaching. Two of us completed graduate degrees in literature before turning to history. We have all studied, worked, or lived on three continents; we are all American citizens, but not all of us were born in the United States. Although we come from different parts of the country and have different historical specializations, all of us teach in large state university systems. We have a strong commitment to the kinds of students who enroll in such schools, and in community colleges—first-generation college students from richly diverse cultural and ethnic backgrounds who are enthusiastic and prepared to work but have little knowledge of history and few formal skills in historical analysis. We were gratified to be developing a new kind of textbook to meet their needs.

We conceived of a textbook that would be lively and absolutely up-to-date, but did not presume a great deal of prior knowledge of Western civilization. We also wanted to include new types of learning aids that were fully integrated into the text itself. Our greatest hope is that students who use this book will come to understand how the West has developed within a global context and, at the same time, to see the importance of the past for the present. In other words, we want to help them value the past as well as understand it, and thus to think historically.

Approaches and Themes

This textbook introduces the cultural unit we call "the West," from its beginnings in the ancient Near East to the present. It is focused around five themes: politics, religion, social history, biography and personality, and individual and collective identity.

Politics This book's first theme centers on Western politics, states, and the state system, from the emergence of civilization in Mesopotamia and Egypt down to the twenty-first century. Politics provides the underlying chronological backbone of the text. Our experience has taught us that a politically centered chronology is the most effective way to help inexperienced students get a sense of what came before, what came after, and why. Political chronology helps them perceive trends and recognize the forces behind historical continuity and change.

If there are sensible reasons for organizing the text around a political chronology, there are pitfalls as well. Chief among them is the disaffection many students may have felt in the past with a history that seems little more than a list of persons, reigns, and wars (Kings and Things) needing to be memorized. To avoid this pitfall, we have adopted an approach that centers on dynamic exchanges between states and political elites on the one hand, and citizens or subjects on the other. In this textbook, students will read and think about the ways taxation, the need for armies, and judicial protection affect ordinary people and vice versa—how the marginal and unrepresented affect the politically powerful. Our approach focuses both on what states and their political elites want from the people who live in them and on what benefits they provide to those people. In turn, we also consider what ordinary people do or do not want from the state, and what kinds of people benefit and do not benefit from the state's policies. When relevant, we also examine the state's lack of impact.

Religion Our second theme takes up the history of Western religion. We have aimed for an expansive treatment of religious activity that includes its institutions and beliefs, but is not confined to them. This textbook ranges widely over issues of polytheism, monotheism, civic religion, philosophically inspired religion, normative religion, orthodoxy and heresy, popular practices, ultimate spiritual values, and systematically articulated agnosticism or atheism. Since from beginning to end we emphasize religious issues, this book is set apart from most Western Civilization texts, which treat religious matters fairly consistently up through the sixteenth century, then drop them.

This text's distinctive post-1600 emphasis on religion arises from our sense that religious beliefs, values, and affiliations have continued to play a central role in European life up to and including the twenty-first century. Although in part compartmentalized or privatized in the last several centuries as states pursued various secularizing agendas, religious sensibilities have still had a considerable impact on economic behavior, social values, and political action, while simultaneously adjusting to or resisting changes in other aspects of life. In addition, of course, they regularly influenced European activity in colonies and empires.

In our treatment of religion, we do not focus simply on the dominant religion of any time or place. Judaism, for example, is discussed throughout the text, while Islam, introduced in Chapter 8, is discussed again in connection with such issues as the Moriscos of Spain, the Habsburg re-conquest of Hungary, tension in Russian Central Asia and the Balkans before World War I, Soviet campaigns against religion, the arrival of Muslim immigrants in post-World War II Europe, and the dissolution of Yugoslavia. In addition, an emphasis on religious pluralism in European life leads to discussions of the variety of subcultures found in the West, many of which believe that their religious and ethnic identity is integral to their other values and practices. Indeed, our belief that religion continues to play an important role in modern European history rests in large part on the abundant evidence showing it to be a core component of life for subcultures within the larger Western context. Catholic and Protestant Irish, Protestant northern Germans and Catholic southern Germans, Orthodox Russians, and Bosnian Muslims stand as examples of communities whose values and actions have been significantly shaped by ongoing religious allegiances, and whose interactions with those practicing other religions have had lasting repercussions. Our intention is to present the religious past of the West in all its complex, multifold voices to students who are more and more self-consciously aware of racial, cultural, and ethnic diversity in their own world.

We also believe attention to religion reflects the current public debate over values, using students' experience of this contested territory to stimulate their interest. Their awareness of current values-based programs can serve as a springboard for a study of the past. Does one choose aggression, persuasion, or passive resistance and nonaggression?

Social History The theme of social history is integrated into the text as consideration is given to the way politics and religion affect people and societies. Discussions of daily lives and family structures are illuminated through occasional spotlights on the experience of a single, typical individual. We also pay close attention to issues of gender norms and roles in the past, drawing on the work of a generation of historians concerned with the history of ordinary men, women, and children. We see many possibilities for engaging the interest of students in this approach. We hope this book will stimulate productive classroom discussions of what it meant to live as a citizen in the Athenian city-state, as a peasant or a landlord in the relatively stateless world of the early Western Middle Ages, as a man or woman during the French Revolution, or as a soldier or nurse in the trenches of World War I.

Biography and Personality To give focus and immediacy to the themes we emphasize, we have chosen to highlight the biographies of important or representative figures in the past and, when possible, to give students a sense of their personalities. We want key figures to live for students through their choices and actions and pronouncements. Each chapter contains a feature, "Profiles in Change," that focuses on biography and personality. The person discussed in this box is integrated into the chapter narratives.

Identity An emphasis on individual and collective identity is another distinctive feature of this book. By addressing matters of identity for each era, we believe that we can help students see themselves in—or as against—the experiences of those who preceded them. To this end, the relationship between the individual and the group is examined as well as changing categories of identity, such as religion, class, gender, ethnicity, nationality, citizenship, occupation or profession, generation, and race. In a real sense, this emphasis flows from the preceding four themes. It means the political narrative is personalized; history is not only an account of states, institutions, and policies, but also of people.

The West and the World

In addition to emphasizing the themes outlined above, we have adopted a view of the West that shapes this volume. It derives from a rejection of the tendency to treat the West as a monolithic entity, or to imply that the West is "really" western Europe after 500 and, after 1500, specifically northwestern Europe. We define the West more broadly. Throughout the book, students remain informed about developments in eastern Europe, western Asia, and Africa. We show that, far from being homogeneous, the West represents a diversity of cultures. By taking this approach, we hope to be able to engage students in a way that will lead them to understand the causes, effects, and significance of the cultural diversity that exists in the modern world.

We also address the issue of cultural diversity by looking at the impact of the non-Western world on the West, from antiquity to the present. We discuss both Western knowledge and Western fantasies about non-Western peoples, the actual contact or lack of contact with non-Western societies, and the growing global impact of Europe and Europeans during the last five hundred years. The emphasis is on the West—on how the West did or did not make contact with other societies and, in the case of contacts, on the consequences for everyone involved. Thus we place the West in its larger global context as one of humanity's many cultural units. From the beginning, the global contextualization of the West has been a central point in our approach. In this third edition of our book, we decided to underscore this by opting for a title change. "Making Europe," the title of the book in its two previous editions, always implied a global dimension to the history of the West. Now we make the implication explicit with the new title, *The Global West: Connections and Identities*. The themes and emphases of the previous editions remain in this one, but we believe the global contextualization of the West is now clearer.

Pedagogy and Features

One of the most common questions our students ask is: "What's important?" This textbook aims to help them answer that question for themselves. We have found students can profit from a text that takes less for granted, provides a consistent and clear structure for each chapter, and incorporates primary documents. For both teachers and students, "Western Civ" is often the most difficult history course in the curriculum. With this textbook, we hope to change that reputation. In the life of this title, we have developed a strong pedagogy, based on feedback from more than five hundred instructors and students. This pedagogy is realized through a series of innovative features that will assist students in understanding the book's content and help them master it. The book and the accompanying MindTap become a complete study tool for students to ensure they are able to read and understand the material. We also kept instructors in mind, because we believe carefully constructed chapters that convey basic information are the best support for teaching. Instructors may then build on the text or modify it to meet specific needs.

Chapter Openers Every chapter begins with a list of focus questions previewing the content covered within that chapter. These questions direct students' attention to the central concerns and issues about to be examined. The new edition includes a more thoroughly integrated chapter-opening image that expresses a topical focus of the chapter.

Section Opening Questions Before students begin reading the chapter sections, they will see focus questions related to the material they will read. These questions invite students to remain focused while going through the material.

Connections New to this edition, these brief feature boxes can be found throughout each chapter to help illustrate how topics and themes from one period or region relate to those from another. In many cases, the Connections are supported with cross-references that let students know where to find additional related information in the text. In some cases, the features are designed to spur students to connect historical themes of the past with today's social and political landscape.

Profiles in Change As noted earlier in this Preface, each chapter contains an account of an individual making a crucial choice that mattered, that had important consequences, and that can be used to highlight the chapter's central concerns. Our intention in this feature is to foreground human agency and to spark the interest of students. Thus Chapter 12, which introduces students to the Renaissance in Italy and Northern Europe, features Michelangelo Buonarotti as a new kind of artist who changed the way the public viewed art and creativity. Chapter 22, which discusses the "triumph" of the nation-state in the late nineteenth century, contains an account of Theodor Herzl's endorsement of Zionism as a way to discuss the impact of nationalist ideology and to carry out the book's emphasis on religious diversity in the West.

Learning from a Primary Source Each chapter also features a document from an individual who lived during the era of the chapter, sometimes from the same individual featured in "Profiles in Change." An explanatory headnote sets the context for the document. Students are then helped to analyze and interrogate it historically through a series of numbered marginal notes and questions, which are also designed to aid instructors seeking to integrate primary sources into their classrooms.

Analyze & Compare Dispersed throughout this edition are also five features that provide an opportunity for comparative analysis of two primary sources that address a common issue or theme. In each pairing, one of the readings offers a Western perspective, and the other offers a global perspective. An explanatory headnote sets the context for the comparison; marginal annotations and questions help to support their interrogation and analysis. This feature helps students to place the history of the West in a global context.

In addition, we have built into each chapter a strong framework of pedagogical aids to help students navigate the text. All of the maps are partnered with critical thinking questions. Most photo captions have been enriched with questions for students to ponder.

A distinctive feature of this text is the glossary—a system whereby boldfaced names, terms, organizations, concepts, and events are explained or defined on the same page on which they are introduced. These definitions support students whose vocabulary and knowledge of history are weak, enhance the background a better-prepared student may have, and serve as a convenient review and study aid.

Chapter Review An enhanced end-of-chapter section provides students with a number of ways to review the chapter. This thorough review features a bulleted summary and a more comprehensive boxed chronology table of events, which includes a mix of Western and non-Western developments for global context. Critical thinking questions are broken down by section, allowing students to easily refer back to the sections or concepts they need to review. Instructors can use these questions to gauge student understanding of each major chapter division.

New to This Edition

The third edition of *The Global West: Connections & Identities* has been updated in a myriad of ways. The most significant of these revisions are:

- Chapter 1 includes a new *Analyze & Compare* feature that presents two versions of a mutual defense treaty between the Egyptians and the Hittites, which requires students to consider issues of perspective and repetition of themes.
- Chapter 2 features a new primary source—"The Victory Stele of Piankhi"—a record of the Nubian ruler's successful military campaign against opposition seeking to gain territory in Upper Egypt.
- Chapter 6 includes a new *Profiles in Change* feature on the Apostle Paul.
- Chapter 7's *Profiles in Change* focuses on Hypatia, thus increasing coverage of the role of women in the early Christian Church. In a new *Learning from a Primary Source* feature, students will read an excerpt of Bishop Augustine of Hippo's monumental work *The City of God*, which covers the Visigothic Sack of Rome.
- Chapter 9 has a new *Learning from a Primary Source*, a letter from Pope Gregory I to a missionary traveling to Britain to help St. Augustine of Canterbury establish Roman Christianity there. There is now also a greater emphasis on Charlemagne's reliance on nobles and clergy as imperial agents in governance. The section on the Vikings and Norse migrations has been updated with new research.
- Chapter 10 covers the climatic and environmental changes over the tenth and eleventh centuries that contributed to changes in agriculture and the economy. A new *Analyze & Compare* section features two documents that shed light on trade among Roman and Eastern Christian merchants and traders from Muslim lands.

- Chapter 11 includes more material on the climatic and environmental changes around the turn of the fourteenth century.
- Chapter 12 has been reorganized for better reader comprehension. More material on humanist education in the fifteenth century has been added. The role and contributions of women, especially intellectual women, receive more attention.
- Chapter 13 features a new *Profiles in Change* on Francis I of France allying with the Turks and addresses European world expansion using three plays of Willaim Shakespeare to examine Europeans' understanding of non-Europeans.
- Chapter 15 expands the discussion on Europe's Jewish communities in a period of prolonged warfare, including a discussion of the messianic claims of Sabbatai Sevi.
- Chapter 17 includes the new *Analyze & Compare* feature using Voltaire's attack on Christianity and an eightenth century Japanese account of an anatomical dissection to compare Western and non-Western attitudes toward tradition. It also offers an expanded discussion of religion that includes a section on Methodism and a section on Jews in Europe, which looks at hasidism, traditional rabbinic Judaism, and the Jewish Enlightenment.
- Chapter 19 includes a new *Learning from a Primary Source* box using Thomas Paine's *The Rights of Man*, and an expanded discussion of Toussaint L'Ouverture.
- Chapter 24 has new material on imperialism in Africa and Asia, including an *Analyze & Compare* feature presenting views on European imperialism from Cecil Rhodes and Lin Zexu, a Chinese official writing to Queen Victoria to protest the opium trade.
- Chapter 25 includes a revised *Learning from a Primary Source* on Lenin, leader of the Russian Revolution.
- Chapter 26 provides more connections between the photographs and the themes covered in the respective sections, such as asking students to identify important aspects of Kemal Ataturk's nationalism by examining a propaganda poster. New images and content provide more vivid connections with colonial non-European territories and the tensions after World War I.
- Chapter 27 offers more discussion of the impact of the Great Depression and European political developments in Asia and Latin America.
- Chapter 28 provides more discussion of the anti-colonial movements after World War II, with an *Analyze and Compare* feature offering perspectives by two prominent individuals, Wangari Maathai and Franz Fanon. New images of the civil rights movement in the United States and violence

in Europe ask students to compare these new trends.

- Chapter 29 includes a new *Learning from a Primary Source* feature from Fatema Mernissi about Islamic feminism which asks students to consider the changes in Muslim communities from this perspective.
- Chapter 30 includes an extended profile of Angela Merkel. This chapter also includes a discussion of the Arab Spring, and the most recent developments in the Middle East, with a rich accompanying map. Developments in the European Union have been updated, including a discussion of the recent Brexit vote and presidential elections in France. A substantial update on Russian politics under Vladimir Putin has also been added, as well as a new primary source , a section of the *Paris Climate Agreement*.

MindTap

MindTap 2-semester Instant Access Code:
ISBN 9781337401913
MindTap 2-semester Printed Access Card:
ISBN 9781337401920
MindTap 1-semester Instant Access Code:
ISBN 9781337403566
MindTap 1-semester Printed Access Card:
ISBN 9781337403573

MindTap for *The Global West*, 3e is a flexible online learning platform that provides students with an immersive learning experience to build and foster critical thinking skills. Through a carefully designed chapter-based learning path, MindTap allows students to easily identify learning objectives; draw connections and improve writing skills by completing unit-level essay assignments; read short, manageable sections from the e-book; and test their content knowledge with timeline-based critical thinking questions.

MindTap allows instructors to customize their content, providing tools that seamlessly integrate YouTube clips, outside websites, and personal content directly into the learning path. Instructors can assign additional primary source content through the Instructor Resource Center and Questia primary- and secondary-source databases that house thousands of peer-reviewed journals, newspapers, magazines, and full-length books.

The additional content available in MindTap mirrors and complements the authors' narrative, emphasizing the global connections that have been central to the history of the West. It also includes research and writing support, recommended secondary sources, additional primary source content, and assessments not found in the printed text. To learn more, ask your Cengage Learning sales representative to demo it for you—or go to www.Cengage.com/MindTap.

Supplements for *The Global West*, 3e

Instructor's Companion Website The Instructor's Companion Website, accessed through the Instructor Resource Center (login.cengage.com), houses all of the supplemental materials you can use for your course. This includes a Test Bank, Instructor's Manual, and PowerPoint Lecture Presentations. The Test Bank for *The Global West*, 3e is offered in file formats that can be seamlessly integrated with and delivered through your LMS or the accompanying MindTap from your classroom, or wherever you may be, with no special intalls or downloads required. It contains multiple-choice, identification, true or false, and essay questions for each chapter. The Instructor's Resource Manual includes chapter summaries, suggested lecture topics, map exercises, discussion questions for the primary sources, topics for student research, relevant websites, suggestions for additional videos, and online resources for information on historical sites. Finally, the PowerPoint Lectures are ADA-compliant slides collating the key takeaways from the chapter in concise visual formats perfect for in-class presentations or for student review.

Cengagebrain.com Save your students time and money. Direct them to www.cengagebrain.com for a choice in formats and savings and a better chance to succeed in your class. Cengagebrain.com, Cengage Learning's online store, is a single destination for more than 10,000 new textbooks, eTextbooks, eChapters, study tools, and audio supplements. Students have the freedom to purchase à la carte exactly what they need when they need it. Students can save 50 percent on the electronic textbook, or can purchase individual eChapters for as little as $1.99.

Doing History: Research and Writing in the Digital Age, 2e ISBN: 9781133587880 Prepared by Michael J. Galgano, J. Chris Arndt, and Raymond M. Hyser of James Madison University. Whether you're starting down the path as a history major or simply looking for a straightforward, systematic guide to writing a successful paper, this text's "soup to nuts" approach to researching and writing about history addresses every step of the process: locating your sources, gathering information, writing and citing according to various style guides, and avoiding plagiarism.

Writing for College History, 1e ISBN:9780618306039 Prepared by Robert M. Frakes of Clarion University. This brief handbook for survey courses in American, Western, and world history guides students through the various types of writing assignments they may encounter in a history class. Providing examples of student writing and candid assessments of student work, this text focuses on the rules and conventions of writing for the college history course.

The Modern Researcher, 6e ISBN: 9780495318705 Prepared by Jacques Barzun and Henry F. Graff of Columbia University. This classic introduction to the techniques of research and the art of expression thoroughly covers every aspect of research, from the selection of a topic through the gathering of materials, analysis, writing, revision, and publication of findings. They present the process not as a set of rules, but through actual cases that put the subtleties of research in a useful context. Part One covers the principles and methods of research; Part Two covers writing, speaking, and getting one's work published.

Reader Program Cengage Learning publishes a number of readers. Some contain exclusively primary sources, others are devoted to essays and secondary sources, and still others provide a combination of primary and secondary sources. All of these readers are designed to guide students through the process of historical inquiry. Visit www.cengage.com/history for a complete list of readers.

Custom Options Nobody knows your students like you, so why not give them a text that is tailor-fit to their needs? Cengage Learning offers custom solutions for your course—whether it's making a small modification to *The Global West,* 3e, to match your syllabus or combining multiple sources to create something truly unique. Contact your Cengage Learning representative to explore custom solutions for your course.

Acknowledgments

It is a pleasure to thank the many instructors who read and critiqued this text through its development:

James (Brett) Adams, Collin College
William Bolt, Francis Marion University
Ian Campbell, University of California at Davis
Holly Dawson, Erie Community College
Korcaighe Hale, Ohio University - Zanesville
Stephen Hebert, Tidewater Community College
Frederic Krome, University of Cincinnati Clermont College
Barbara Newton, Longwood University
Ginger Smoak, University of Utah
Rebecca Woodham, Wallace Community College

The following instructors helped to shape the unique pedagogy offered in the third edition by participating in interviews, focus groups, reviews, or class tests:

Stephen Andrews, Central New Mexico Community College
Ingrid Arguelles, Florida SouthWestern State College
Pat Artz, Bellevue University
Rebecca Baird, Porterville College
Jordan Bauer, University of Alabama-Birmingham

Wayne Bowen, Southeast Missouri State University
Kevin Brady, Tidewater Community College
Chrystal Bucchioni, Thomas Nelson Community College
Curtis Burchfield, Itawamba Community College
Matthew Cain, College of Southern Maryland
Rocco Campagna, Finger Lakes Community College
Amanda Carr Wilcoxson, Pellissippi State Community College
Elizabeth Collins, Triton College College
Scott Corbett, Ventura College
Holly Dawson, Erie Community College
Annika Frieberg, San Diego State University
Anthony Heideman, Front Range Community College
Riley Holt, Tri-County Tech College
Adam Howard, George Washington University
David Kiracofe, Tidewater Community College
Stacy Kowtko, Spokane Community College
James McIntyre, Moraine Valley Community College
Jennifer McNabb, Western Illinois University
Gregory Miller, Hillsborough Community College
Brandon Morgan, Central New Mexico Community College
Anthony Nardini, Widener University
Eric Nelson, Missouri State University
Chris Powers, Fort Hays State University
Malcolm Purinton, Northeastern University
Kim Richardson, University of South Carolina
Sarah Shurts, Bergen Community College
Kate Staples, West Virginia University
Natalia Starostina, Young Harris College
Allison Stein, Pellissippi State Tech Community College
Gary Steward, Colorado Christian University
Chris Thomas, Reynolds Community College
Ronald Traylor, Southeastern Louisiana University
Della Vanhuss, Tri-County Tech College
Greg Vitarbo, Meredith College
Ronald Young, Florida SouthWestern State University

And a big thank you to the dozens of students who contributed to the development of the third edition by participating in focus groups and class tests.

Frank Kidner wants to thank his fellow authors and the many students who over thirty years taught him much about teaching. He also wishes to thank Fred Astren, San Francisco State University, and Frederic Krome, University of Cincinnati Clermont

College for their advice on specific chapters. And thanks Jody Jurgens and Ben Garcia for help with photographs for this edition.

Maria Bucur wishes to thank her husband, Daniel Deckard, for continued support and inspiration in matters intellectual and musical, and her children Dylan and Elvin, for putting up with the many hours she had to be away from them, and for reinvigorating her in the hours she was lucky to be with them.

Ralph Mathisen wishes to thank Frank Kidner for getting this project going and keeping it on track, as well as the thousands of students who have always kept him on his toes.

Sally McKee wishes to thank her fellow authors for their mutual support, epicurean disposition, and good cheer over the years.

Ted Weeks would like to thank his history department colleagues at SIUC for intelligence, a sense of humor, and solidarity in the face of adversity. The same appreciation goes to his students, whether in their first or tenth semester—you make it all worthwhile!

We are indebted to the following for creating the instructor and student resources for *The Global West,* 3e: Jennifer Black, Misericordia University Daniel Clinkman, Indian Springs School; and Ty Robinson, San Francisco State University.

We also want to offer our warmest thanks to all who have worked to make this third edition possible and especially to Paul Banks, Product Director; Scott Greenan, Product Manager; Sayaka Kawano and Alex Shore, Product Assistants; Carol Newman, Senior Content Project Manager; Erika Mugavin, Alex Ricciardi, and Julie Tesser for help with photographs and permissions; Mohanarengan Dilli for his work in preparing page proofs; and Cate Barr and Charlotte Miller for interior, cover, and art design. Finally, we want to thank Erika Hayden, our editor and guiding light. Thank you Erika for all your hard work!

F. L. K.
M. B.
R. M.
S. M.
T. R. W.

About the Authors

Frank L. Kidner is Professor of History Emeritus at San Francisco State University, where he taught from 1968 until his retirement in 2006. He has also taught in the Western Civilization program at Stanford University and at Amherst College. His courses include Western Civilization, undergraduate and graduate courses in Early Modern Europe, and the history of the Christian Church, as well as a graduate course in historical methodology. He has authored articles on topics in Late Antiquity and co-edited *Travel, Communication and Geography in Late Antiquity*.

Maria Bucur is John V. Hill Professor in Eastern European History and Professor of Gender Studies at Indiana University, where she has taught an undergraduate course on "The Idea of Europe" and other topics in nineteenth- and twentieth-century eastern Europe. Her research focus is on social and cultural developments in eastern Europe, with a special interest in Romania (geographically) and gender (thematically). Her publications include *Eugenics and Modernization in Interwar Romania* and *Heroes and Victims: Remembering War in Twentieth-Century Romania*. When not writing and reading history or administrative memos, Maria is following her dream of being in a band (violin and bass) with her husband and children. You can find them jamming at a campground near you.

Ralph Mathisen is Professor of History, Classics, and Medieval Studies at the University of Illinois at Urbana-Champaign. He is a specialist in the ancient world with a particular interest in the society, culture, and religion of Late Antiquity. His teaching experience includes Western Civilization and topics in the Ancient Near East, Greece, Rome, Byzantium, coinage, and Roman law. He has written more than seventy scholarly articles and written or edited ten books, the most recent of which is *People, Personal Expression, and Social Relations in Late Antiquity*. He also is the founding editor and editor emeritus of the *Journal of Late Antiquity* and editor of *Oxford Studies in Late Antiquity*. He enjoys traveling, running, and ballroom dancing.

Sally McKee is Professor of History at the University of California at Davis, where she teaches courses on Western Civilization and medieval history. Her research focus has been Venice and its colonies and Mediterranean slavery, but her new project centers on nineteenth-century France and Italy. She is the author of numerous articles, one of which has won a prize and been anthologized, and she has also published a three-volume edition of Venetian-Cretan wills and a monograph, *Uncommon Dominion: Venetian Crete and the Myth of Ethnic Purity*. When she is not teaching, she travels the world in search of archives, modern art museums, and great street food.

Theodore R. Weeks is Professor of History at Southern Illinois University at Carbondale, where he teaches Western Civilization and World and European history. His research centers on nationality, inter-ethnic relations, and antisemitism in eastern Europe. He is the author of *Nation and State in Late Imperial Russia* and *From Assimilation to Antisemitism: The "Jewish Question" in Poland, 1850–1914*, and his articles have appeared in several languages, including Estonian and Hebrew.

The Global West

CHAPTER 15

A Century of Crisis, 1550–1650

Chapter Outline

As you read, consider the following questions:

❱ What were the causes and consequences of Europe's economic downturn and population stagnation after 1550?

❱ How did political and religious issues shape the nature of the European states covered in this chapter?

❱ How did the meaning of community change during a century of crisis?

❱ How did religious conflict affect the everyday lives of Europeans?

EUROPE IN 1550 was troubled and turbulent. Rulers fought increasingly expensive and destructive wars and, not content with battling their enemies at home, carried the struggles overseas. The Spanish and Portuguese fought to maintain their empires, while the French, English, and Dutch attempted to seize their rivals' wealth or establish competing empires of their own in the Western Hemisphere and Asia. Treasure fleets that consisted of galleons transporting precious metals and other valuables from the New World to Spain, like the example seen here, were targeted by colonial rivals.

After 1550, the prosperity Europeans had experienced since the mid-fourteenth century ended. In both town and country, the numbers of the poor grew, while a small, well-to-do elite struggled to maintain control over the increasingly restless and riot-prone masses. Hard times produced widespread anxiety. People became obsessed with witches, who were feared as agents of the Devil bent on ruining society. Many believed that the troubles they were experiencing were a prelude to Christ's Second Coming to judge the world.

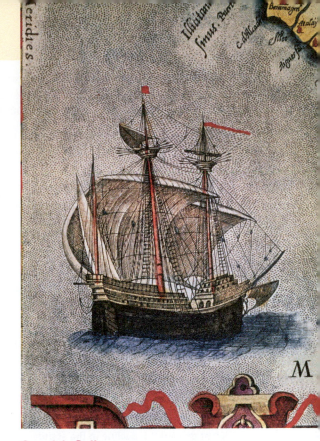

Spanish Galleon
Spanish Atlantic trade ship carrying silver from South America to Spain. Album/Art Resource, NY

The church reforms of the sixteenth century had created two mutually hostile religious communities in western Europe. Neither the Protestants nor the Catholics accepted that religious unity had been shattered, and both fought ferociously to impose their own ways on their opponents. Philip II of Spain, the son of Charles V, took the lead in the fight for Catholicism. His extensive European territories positioned him to champion the cause of Catholicism throughout Europe as did a flood of new wealth from silver mines in Spanish America, carried annually across the Atlantic to Spain in ships like the one depicted at the opening of this chapter. The Netherlands, France, Germany, and the British Isles all saw religious warfare. In some wars, all Protestants joined to fight Catholics; in others, different types of Protestants fought each other. Both Protestants and Catholics committed terrible atrocities. The fierceness of the fighting shows how central the principle of religious unity was for the culture of early modern Europe.

Warfare accelerated economic decline, producing widespread famine and disease. In parts of Europe, population dropped by 50 percent. In the end, neither Protestants nor Catholics succeeded in eliminating their opponents, and religious disunity prevailed. By 1650, most Europeans had accepted it, often unwillingly, as a fact of life. Also by 1650, Spain, having exhausted its resources in the fight against Protestantism, had lost its preeminent position in Europe. France, weathering the crisis of its religious wars, now emerged as the dominant European power (see Map 15.1).

Although the Jews were not directly involved in disputes between Christians, they, too, experienced hard times when wars broke out in the lands where they lived. Nevertheless, the Jews' condition improved in western Europe, where they settled once again and often prospered. Yet, as a despised minority, Jews were sometimes subjected to terrible attacks.

15-1 Europe's Economy and Society

» **What were the effects of overseas empire building and global trading on Europe's economy?**

» **What caused the decline in the standard of living for most Europeans, and what effect did this decline have on society?**

Between 1550 and 1650, Europe's economy, which had boomed in the previous hundred years, began to stagnate. Silver from Spanish mines in the Americas caused inflation, which, combined with overpopulation, reduced the standard of living for most Europeans. Hardship was widespread, evident in protests and riots. As communities' traditional sense of solidarity crumbled, the well-to-do became obsessed with maintaining social order. Panic over witches was another symptom of the hard times that struck after 1550.

15-1a Europe's Continuing Overseas Expansion

During the sixteenth century, Portuguese and Spanish success in creating empires stirred similar ambitions in France and England. At first, the French and English were content to conduct raids against Spanish shipping. In 1523, a French ship seized three ships loaded with Moctezuma's personal treasure and the booty collected by Hernán Cortés's army. Since France and Spain were at war for most of the sixteenth century, this attack was considered part of the larger struggle. In the late sixteenth century, when relations between England and Spain deteriorated, Queen Elizabeth I commissioned the **privateer** Sir Francis Drake to seize Spanish treasure. These raids constituted the first phase of France's and England's entry into empire building in the New World, and by the early seventeenth century permanent English and French colonies were being established.

English, French, and Dutch Colonies in the New World In 1607, businessmen financed the first permanent English settlement in North America at Jamestown in present-day Virginia. In 1625, the English colonized the Caribbean island of Barbados and imported African slaves to work sugar plantations there. The French state also sponsored colonial ventures in America. In 1608, Samuel de Champlain founded the city of Quebec on the Saint Lawrence River as the center of the new colony of Canada.

In 1683, a French nobleman, Robert Cavalier, Sieur de La Salle, led an expedition from the Great Lakes down the Mississippi River to the Gulf of Mexico and claimed the lands along the river for France, naming them **Louisiana** in honor of the French king, Louis XIV. At the very end of the century, France claimed the western half of the island of Hispaniola and established sugar plantations there.

The Dutch also established sugar plantations in the Caribbean as, like the English and French, they seized islands originally claimed by Spain. In Asia, the Dutch attacked the Portuguese and gradually replaced them as the major power in the spice trade.

Establishing colonies and attacking empires were costly adventures involving large investments and high risks. To raise the necessary money, Europeans developed a new form of business organization, the **joint-stock company**, in which individuals pooled their capital and received stock shares in proportion to the size of their investment. The joint-stock technique raised huge sums of money but limited the risk factor for each investor. Jamestown was founded by a joint-stock venture, the Virginia Company. The English **East India Company**, founded in 1600, established

privateer Private vessel commissioned by a state to attack the commercial and naval ships of another country.

Louisiana French colony in the Mississippi valley named after King Louis XIV.

joint-stock company Company in which individuals pool their capital and receive stock shares in proportion to the size of their investment.

East India Company English joint-stock company founded in 1600 to establish trading posts on the Indian subcontinent.

Map 15.1 **Europe in the Age of the Religious Wars** From 1550 to 1650, Europe was engulfed in a series of religious wars. One of the last was the Thirty Years' War, fought from 1618 to 1648 in the Holy Roman Empire. It pitted the Catholic Habsburgs and their German allies against the Protestants of the empire. During the war Sweden, Denmark, the Dutch Republic, Spain, and France were drawn into the fighting.

1. Consult the map legend and identify the "Spanish Habsburg Lands" and the "Austrian Habsburg Lands."
   a. Why do mapmakers make this distinction for the years after 1550?
   b. Trace the boundary of the Holy Roman Empire. Which lands of the Austrian Habsburgs lie outside the empire? Why are the Spanish Netherlands inside the empire and the United Provinces outside of it?
2. Does the position of the empire in relation to the other states of Europe suggest why so many European states were drawn into the Thirty Years' War?

trading posts on the subcontinent of India, and the Dutch United East India Company, founded in 1602, was profitable for more than a century.

New Foods and New Goods Nowhere were the effects of trade and colonization more far reaching than in the exchange between Europe and the Western Hemisphere. In the century after Columbus's voyages, many new food items were introduced into Europe: chili peppers, beans, pumpkins, squashes, tomatoes, peanuts, chocolate, maize, and potatoes. Maize and potatoes were to become staples in the diets of southern and northern Europeans, respectively.

These strange foods provoked doubt and debate. Some argued that people should eat only foods mentioned in the Bible. Others wondered if potatoes and peanuts, which grew underground, should be fed to animals but not to humans, who were higher up in the ladder of creation. Tobacco, cultivated early in Virginia, provided a satisfying New World smoke, sniff, or chew after a New World turkey dinner, washed down with rum, an alcoholic drink made from American-grown sugar.

The exchange brought even more dramatic changes to the Americas. On his second voyage, Columbus brought wheat, melons, onions, radishes, grapevines, sugarcane, cauliflower, cabbages, lemons (originally from Asia), and figs to the Western Hemisphere, along with the European rat. Horses, cattle, pigs, goats, dogs, sheep, and chickens came as well, changing forever the animal population of the Americas.

Later European arrivals unknowingly brought weed seed with them in the form of Kentucky bluegrass, daisies, and dandelions, as well as the European honeybee. The European ox pulled plows through soils that had been too heavy to turn over with the Indians' handheld tools.

Trade with Asia also brought more new products to Europe. The first shipment of tea from China arrived at the beginning of the seventeenth century, and rice, a staple in some Asian diets, was soon widely grown in Italy. By the end of the century, coffee, native to the Arabian peninsula, was grown in the East Indies and then shipped to Europe. Soon it would also be grown in the Americas. The rich prized Asian ebony wood for furniture and delicate Chinese porcelains for their collections of rare items. At a less exotic level, Chinese zinc and Indian tin were imported in ever-increasing quantities.

Thus, the entry of new states and private companies into Europe's overseas trade expanded the global trading networks linking America, Europe, and Asia that had begun in the sixteenth century. The result was the beginning of a new era in Europe's economic life based on commerce.

15-1b A River of Silver

Spain's silver mines in the Americas, opened in the 1540s, produced huge quantities of precious metal that flowed to Europe and Asia. Contemporary official estimates of silver exports from the Spanish Empire place the figure at some 17,800 tons, but smuggling and unofficial exports may have pushed it as high as 29,000 tons. This amount would have tripled silver supplies in Europe, where the metal was used mainly as money; when news of silver's discovery reached Europe, Charles V's credit rating soared. The most productive mine was in present-day Bolivia at San Luis de Potosí. The other main source was at Zacatecas (zah-cah-TAY-cahs) in northern Mexico. Gold and emeralds were also mined.

From Mines to Markets The silver of Potosí was either minted into coins or melted into bars and then transported to the Peruvian port of Lima. From there it went by ship to Panama, where it was hauled overland to the Caribbean for transfer to Spain. Some silver from northern Mexico was also carried to the Caribbean while the rest went to Acapulco on the Pacific, where it was loaded onto the **Manila galleon**, a large, square-rigged sailing ship sent to the Philippine Islands to purchase Chinese silks and porcelains. The galleon's annual round trip was the single most profitable voyage in the Spanish Empire, and the millions of silver coins used to pay for trade goods flooded Southeast Asia, where they became the standard international currency.

The silver for Europe, along with goods from China, was collected once a year by armed Spanish ships that arrived in the Caribbean in late summer. After wintering there, they joined up in Havana for the voyage home. This was the most perilous part of the trip because the fleet's valuable cargo made it subject to seizure by independently operating pirates or privateers commissioned by the governments of Spain's enemies.

Silver and the Spanish Monarchy If the Spanish fleet managed to dodge attacks and survive storms at sea, it headed for **Seville**, Spain's largest and richest city. In theory, all precious metals from the Americas had to be registered with the port authorities and then taxed, but smuggling, bribery, false declarations of value, and other techniques were routinely used to evade this requirement. Nevertheless, the government *quinto*, or fifth tax on gold and silver, made up a quarter of the royal income. Other goods were stored on the wharves, but few merchants gathered there to buy them. Instead, goods were shipped north to the trading centers of Antwerp and Amsterdam. Thus, Seville never became a major hub in the global commercial network, but served simply as a transit point for Spanish overseas riches.

Despite the sizable sum provided by the royal quinto, Charles V and then his son, **Philip II**, found that

Manila galleon Spanish sailing ship that carried Spanish silver from Mexico to exchange for Chinese silks and porcelains in the Philippine Islands.

Seville Spain's largest city and government-mandated port for all goods going to or coming from the Spanish Empire.

ruling their lands created costs even the river of silver from the New World could not completely pay. So Philip, like his father, borrowed. During his reign, he overextended himself, borrowing more than he could repay and declaring bankruptcy four times. Each bankruptcy created a financial crisis throughout Europe. Lenders disappeared, and expenses piled up until a renegotiation of Spain's debt was worked out. The crisis solved, lenders returned—until the next bankruptcy.

15-1c A Revolution in Prices

Around the middle of the sixteenth century, Europe experienced **inflation**, a sharp rise in prices for land, food, and other basic necessities that had major effects on Europeans' day-to-day lives. Several factors explain this **price revolution**.

Silver and the Price Revolution The New World silver flowing into Spain soon spread through Europe as the Spanish government sent it out of the country in the form of coins to pay for the costs of warfare in Italy, the Netherlands, and elsewhere, which never seemed to stop. As silver coins became more and more common, the value of the metal in them declined, and their purchasing power diminished. To counteract the declining value of silver, people with things to sell raised their prices.

Population Growth and the Price Revolution The continuing rise in Europe's population after 1450 also caused the price revolution. At first, population growth stimulated the economy and led to increased agricultural and commercial activity, which benefited many urban and rural workers. By the mid-sixteenth century, however, as population continued to grow, Europe was experiencing a crisis of overpopulation that put pressure on the ability of people to sustain themselves. For example, in agriculture, the growing population required that more and more land had to be cultivated. By about 1550, good land was running out, and cultivation moved to marginal, less productive land. The result was an inadequate food supply and a rise in food prices.

Hard Times The rise in the price of food led, in turn, to two other developments: First, fierce competition for food-producing acreage caused land prices to rise sharply; and second, a glut of workers in need of jobs caused wages to decline. The impact of declining wages might have been offset if rural workers could

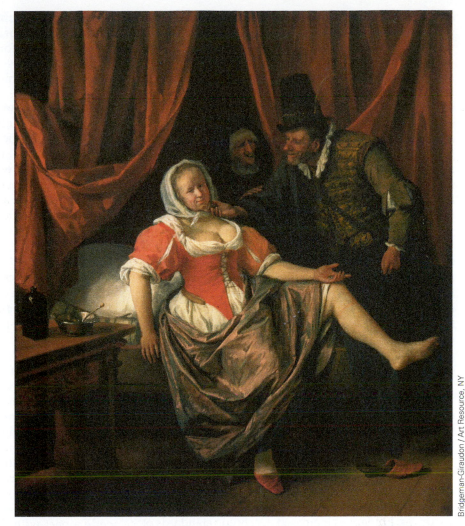

Bridgeman-Giraudon / Art Resource, NY

Jan Steen Painting of a Trollop

Steen presents the viewer with three persons in his painting:

》 *How does Steen present visual evidence of stereotypes about women's disorderliness in his image of the trollop?*

》 *What do you make of the customer?*

》 *Who is the older woman and why is she there?*

》 *What seems to be Steen's understanding of the reasons women might have for choosing prostitution?*

Philip II (r. 1556–1598) King of Spain, the most powerful ruler in late sixteenth-century Europe and leader of the Catholic crusade against Protestantism.

inflation Process by which the cost of goods and services increases and the value of money declines.

price revolution Rise in prices for land, food, and other basic necessities in mid-sixteenth-century Europe.

have raised enough food for themselves on their own plots, but most could not because their landholdings were too small.

To make ends meet, peasants borrowed from local moneylenders. As collateral, they would put up their land or anything else they owned. If they defaulted on the loan, the lender would seize the collateral. So, another problem was rising peasant debt. Over the hundred years from 1550 to 1650, rural communities were gradually polarized between a few rich peasants who managed to keep or increase their landholdings and a mass of poor small-scale landowners, landless wage laborers, and sharecroppers who paid rent for the land they farmed by sharing its produce with their landlord.

Urban workers also suffered from rising prices and declining wages brought on by overpopulation. Guild members in the textile industry, which employed thousands in cities across Europe, were particularly hard hit because they faced fierce competition from merchants who hired needy peasants to weave in their homes for low wages and to produce cloth that was not subject to guild regulations. The result was a growing gap between the urban rich and poor that strained relief agencies.

The Little Ice Age To make matters worse, Europe was experiencing a period of climate change known as the Little Ice Age (see also Section 11-1 Famine and Plague, for a discussion of how this climate change manifested in the fourteenth century). Winters were colder and longer than previously; glaciers in the Alps advanced to cover inhabited land; in England, the Thames froze over. Colder, wetter years damaged crops, causing food shortages. Epidemics increased. Declining standards of living, vulnerability to disease, and the growing polarization between rich and poor weakened both rural and urban communities' sense of solidarity and mutual responsibility. The needy protested and rioted more frequently, while the well-off became obsessed with maintaining order among the masses.

15-1d The Hunt for Witches

Local political leaders shared the concern for maintaining popular order. In addition to economic hard times and social unrest, they also faced religious turmoil and spiritual anxiety as Europe split permanently into hostile Protestant and Catholic camps. Religious uncertainty lay behind rising beliefs that the world was coming to an end and that the Devil's attempt to destroy good Christians was intensifying. These fears led in turn to a search for scapegoats who could be blamed for the troubled times.

For centuries, Europeans thought that some people possessed magical skills that allowed them to cast harmful or helpful spells.

witches People, usually women, who were believed to have made a pact with the Devil, whom they worshiped.

These so-called cunning men and women were consulted by people at all levels of society. Both Catholic and Protestant reformers considered them nuisances and tried to draw their followers away from their "superstitious" practices, usually with little effect.

The Stereotype of the Witch By the sixteenth century, however, a belief spread that these cunning folk were not just magicians, but Devil worshippers. As it did, authorities in many parts of Europe inaugurated a crusade against **witches**.

Belief in witches was long standing, but it was only in this period that a sustained campaign against them was launched. After 1550, a stereotype of the witch emerged. Witches were said to be cunning folk who sold their souls to the Devil. In their obscene night rituals, called witches' Sabbaths, they sacrificed infants to Satan, engaged in cannibalism, and performed disgusting sexual acts. In a world where most people's lives were increasingly insecure, fear of bad magic skyrocketed, encouraging people to accuse their neighbors of satanic witchcraft.

Witchcraft Trials As many as 200,000 witchcraft trials were held all over Europe, most leading to convictions. The number of trials varied from place to place. Where lawyers and church officials had strict standards for accepting accusations or were skeptical of them, there were fewer trials. In England, for example, legal procedures prohibiting torture to procure confessions lowered the rates of self-incrimination. Rates were also low in Spain, where the Inquisition doubted that those accused of witchcraft had really made a pact with the Devil. The greatest number of trials—three-quarters of all known cases—occurred in the Holy Roman Empire, in areas where local officials, rather than state or church authorities, were in charge of the process. There, community leaders, clergymen, and other members of the local social elite, fearing social disorder and panicked by their belief in Satan's subversion of society, carried out wholesale prosecutions of people accused of witchcraft.

Women and Witchcraft The vast majority of those accused were older women, most of whom were widowed or single and therefore lacked male protection. Some had served as midwives. Most were poor, but some controlled their own property. Those who were quarrelsome or sexually independent were seen as transgressors against prevailing patriarchal values. Women accused of witchcraft were, therefore, associated with dangerous activities, or seen as an economic burden to their communities, or envied for their material wealth, or despised as violators of the community's norms of behavior.

Trials and Torture Witchcraft trials often involved torture to get the accused to confess their activity and then more torture to force them to name accomplices. In cities, torture often produced a chain reaction of accusations. As the numbers of accused grew, the victims bore less and less resemblance to the stereotypical poor-woman witch: men, the rich, and children were named. On average, half of those convicted were executed, and the rest were imprisoned or subjected to other forms of punishment.

The Decline in Trials Beginning in 1650, witch trials declined dramatically, as more and more centralized states took jurisdiction away from local authorities. Lawyers also worked to end persecutions. Although most lawyers still believed in witches, they also believed that legal standards for accusing and trying them had been too lax. Some people also believed in newly proposed scientific views of the world that questioned the Devil's active intervention in human affairs. Thus, a sense of fairness, along with doubts about Satan's power, won out over the fear of the Devil's subversion of society by means of witchcraft.

CONNECTIONS: The marginalization of groups through stereotyping and the creation of scapegoats has occurred repeatedly in human history. (See, for example, Section 22-4a Integral Nationalism, Racism, Anti-Sematism, and Zionism.)

15-2 The Fate of Spain and the Flourishing of the Netherlands

» **What were Philip II's successes and failures?**

» **What explains the success of the Dutch economy?**

Museo Nacional del Prado, Madrid/Art Resource, NY

Portrait of Philip II by Sanchez Coello, 1583
This portrait of Philip II shows the king in the somber dress favored at the Spanish court.

» *How does this style of royal portrait compare with the one of his father, Charles V, in Chapter 13. "Resurgent Monarchies— Charles I of Spain, Charles V of the Holy Roman Empire"?*

» *Can you identify anything in this portrait that would emphasize Philip's role as the champion of Roman Catholicism?*

In 1550, Spain, with its silver and empire, was the most powerful state in Europe. Philip II dominated international affairs, making war on Muslims and attempting to eliminate Protestantism throughout his lands. Philip also sought to defend the western Mediterranean from the Ottomans while making war on his own Moriscos and laying the grounds for their expulsion from the Iberian Peninsula. His greatest failure came in the Netherlands, where his attempt to crush Protestantism provoked a rebellion during which the northern provinces declared their independence. These provinces, now organized as the Dutch Republic, soon dominated the European economy.

15-2a Philip II

In 1556, Philip II succeeded his father, Charles V, as head of the Habsburg dynasty. Despite Charles's grant of the Holy Roman emperorship to his younger brother, Ferdinand I, Philip ruled over a vast assembly of territories: Castile, Aragon, and Granada in Spain; the Netherlands; Franche-Comté on the Rhine; Naples,

Sicily, and Milan on the Italian peninsula; Spanish America; and the Philippine Islands (named after him) in East Asia. His global empire was the wonder of the world, and he was the most powerful ruler of his age.

"His Most Catholic Majesty" By the time Philip became king, Protestantism was challenging the Catholic Church throughout central and northern Europe, and Philip undertook its defense, using both military and diplomatic means. He also continued Christian Spain's attack on the Muslim world, now dominated in the West by the **Ottoman Turks**. In Spain, he adopted the title of His Most Catholic Majesty and supported Teresa of Ávila's reform of the Carmelites while collecting manuscripts of her religious writings for his library. He also built a residence, just outside Madrid, the new Spanish capital. Called the **Escorial**, it housed both

Ottoman Turks Muslims who captured Constantinople in 1453, ending the Byzantine Empire and founding the Ottoman Empire.

Escorial Philip II's palace and monastery complex outside of Madrid.

the royal palace and a monastery where Philip frequently prayed and meditated with the monks. His most important advisers were the priests who heard his confessions and the theologians he kept at his side.

In appearance, Philip hardly looked like the self-appointed leader of the Catholic world. Short and soft-spoken, he presided over a somber court and rarely left the area around Madrid because he thought that "traveling about one's kingdom is neither useful nor decent." In this he unwisely rejected the policy of his predecessors, whose frequent travels throughout their lands kept them in touch with their subjects. Cautious by nature, he kept tight personal control over government, making every important policy decision and spending hours alone in his office pouring over the mountains of memoranda that had to be prepared for his approval.

Before his death, Charles V had urged Philip to fight heresy and to hold onto the lands God had given him. Philip followed this advice. The money he amassed through taxes and borrowing was spent in pursuit of these aims.

15-2b The Spanish War Against the Moriscos and the Turks

In the early sixteenth century, the Ottoman Turks continued to push into Christian territory. Hungary fell in 1521, and in 1529 a Turkish army laid siege, unsuccessfully, to Vienna. When the Ottomans conquered Christian peoples in the Balkans, they organized them as a **millet**, or non-Muslim subject people. Millet Christians had to pay special taxes and accept that some of their boys would be recruited into the army as janissaries. But they were allowed to practice their religion, and conversion to Islam was discouraged because the taxes Christians paid were an important source of state revenue. Nevertheless, many Christians did convert to improve their position in society. The Christian millet was dominated by Greeks in Constantinople, headed by the Orthodox patriarch there. Jews under the Ottomans were not organized into a millet but were encouraged to immigrate to Turkish lands when western Christian states expelled them.

The Moriscos The Turks also established contact with the Moriscos. Following Ferdinand and Isabella's conquest of Granada in 1492, its Muslim population, now called Moriscos, had been forced to convert to Christianity. Then Christians seized their lands and sought to stamp out their culture along with their religion. Speaking Arabic and bathing on Fridays, along with traditional dancing and eating couscous, were forbidden as signs of heresy. Faced with this repression, the Moriscos rose up in 1569. The revolt lasted two years and involved 30,000 rebels joined by 4,000 Turks and North Africans. The revolt was put down in 1571, but hatred remained on both sides.

In 1609, Philip's son, Philip III, ordered all 300,000 Moriscos expelled from Spain. Many went to North Africa, while some went to northern Greece and Constantinople. The expulsion of the Moriscos was the last step in the dismantling of the cultural and religious diversity that had characterized medieval Spain. Some Spaniards hailed the expulsion as a purification of the land, but others, like the great novelist **Miguel de Cervantes**, condemned it. In *Don Quixote*, Ricote, an expelled Morisco, laments, "Wherever we are, we weep for Spain, because we were born there and it is our native land."

The Turks In 1571, the last year of the Morisco revolt, Philip destroyed the Turkish navy at **Lepanto** (leh-PAN-to) off the coast of Greece; 195 ships in the Turkish fleet of 230 were captured or sunk, 30,000 Turks were killed or wounded, and 3,000 were taken prisoner. Although the Turks assembled another fleet in 1572 and continued to harass the coasts of Italy and Sicily, their dominance of the Mediterranean had been weakened. Then, in 1580, Philip became ruler of Portugal and its empire when the Portuguese king disappeared on a crusade in Morocco against the Muslims. Philip was now at the height of his power.

15-2c The Revolt in the Netherlands

Even as Spanish might awed Europe, Protestant forces in England and the Netherlands were rising to challenge it. Protestantism had not spread to Spain, but it had to the Netherlands, the Habsburgs' richest territory. Charles V had tried without success to eliminate it there, and Philip tried as well, with even worse results. Philip viewed his Protestant subjects as heretics, but at first he recognized that their growing numbers required a political solution. Therefore, in 1566, on the advice of his court theologians, he granted religious **toleration** to the Protestants. Shortly thereafter, militant Calvinists went on a rampage across the country, destroying Catholic churches and religious images. Philip now decided on a military solution.

War and Revolt In 1567, a Spanish army marched north to subdue the Protestants. Its commander, the duke of Alba, then tried and executed more than a thousand people. To pay for his army, Alba also imposed a tax on the Netherlanders. Both Protestants and Catholics condemned it and rebelled when it was not withdrawn. Then, in 1572, Calvinist exiles in England returned home and joined the rebellion, seizing the country's northern

millet Legally defined community for non-Muslims living within the Ottoman Empire.

Miguel de Cervantes (ser-VAHN-tehs) (1547–1616) Spanish writer and critic of Philip II who wrote *Don Quixote*.

Lepanto Naval battle won by Spain over the Ottomans in October 1571.

toleration Recognition of the right to hold dissenting beliefs.

Hulton Archive / Stringer/Getty Images

Fluteships

This engraving from 1647 shows fluteships in a Dutch harbor. The fluteship's deck is narrower than the bulging hull below it, which will be filled with the goods shipped in what the Dutch called the "mother trade" between Dutch ports and Baltic ports in the east.

provinces and electing **William of Orange** as their leader. The general rebellion in the Netherlands forced Philip to recall Alba in 1573.

In 1575, Philip declared a bankruptcy that delayed pay for his troops in the Netherlands. In response, his army mutinied and sacked Antwerp, destroying property and leaving 8,000 dead. This "Spanish Fury" signaled the end of Antwerp as Europe's leading commercial hub. Finally, in 1579, Philip's new military governor was able to consolidate Spain's rule in the southern provinces, thereafter known as the Spanish Netherlands. But the northern provinces were lost when rebels there forced the Spanish army to retreat by opening the dikes that kept the sea out, flooding large parts of the country. Having declared their independence from Spain, the northern provinces reconstituted themselves as the **United Provinces**, or **Dutch Republic**.

The Armada of 1588 Queen Elizabeth I of England had aided the Dutch Protestants, and Philip decided to attack her. In 1588, he sent the **Spanish Armada**—130 ships and 30,000 men—to join with his loyal forces in the Spanish Netherlands and then conquer the island kingdom. The Spanish met a slightly larger and much faster English fleet in the English Channel, where stormy weather and superior English cannon

fire broke up the Armada. Only half the Spanish ships returned to their ports.

The defeat was the beginning of Spain's decline. The failure to stamp out Protestantism in the Netherlands, followed by the loss of the northern provinces, was a bitter blow to Philip, who grieved that he had betrayed his father's trust.

15-2d The Dutch Miracle

It would take decades for Spain to acknowledge Dutch independence, but from the 1590s on, the breakaway provinces were free from serious invasion. Distracted by other wars, Spain was never able to conquer the north. Finally, in 1609, the Spanish signed the Twelve Years' Truce with the rebels (see Map 15.2).

A Limited Religious Toleration The Dutch Republic was founded by Calvinists

William of Orange (1533–1584) Calvinist nobleman, also known as William the Silent, who led the Protestant rebellion against the Spanish in the Netherlands.

United Provinces (Dutch Republic) Northern Netherlands provinces that successfully threw off Spanish rule.

Spanish Armada Unsuccessful armed fleet sent by Philip II in 1588 to conquer England.

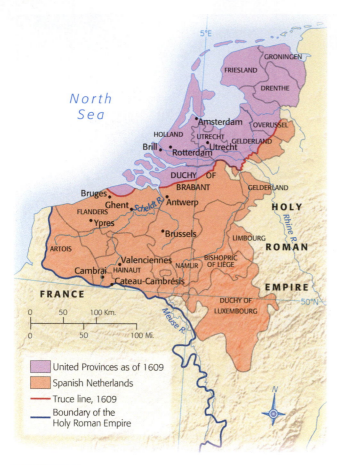

North
Sea

Map 15.2 **The Netherlands** When the Twelve Years' Truce was signed in 1609, the seven northern provinces of the Netherlands, along with parts of the duchy of Brabant (BRAH-bant) and the county of Flanders, were put under Dutch control. Spain continued to control the remaining southern provinces.

1. Refer to Map 15.1 at the beginning of this chapter and place the northern provinces (the United Provinces) in the larger context of European states.
   a. How large do you imagine the largest and smallest provinces of the Dutch Republic were?
   b. Were there any states in Europe smaller than the United Provinces?
2. What does this tell you about the "Dutch miracle?"

who sought to reform church and state. But William of Orange and his successors feared that the rebellion's success would be jeopardized if the Catholics of the north, who made up a third of the population, were alienated. So, a policy of partial toleration was instituted. Calvinism was recognized as the state

calling Calvinist belief that ordinary work was a means for serving God.

religion, but the church was not allowed to control state policy. Although Catholics were forbidden to worship publicly, they were allowed unofficially to open private chapels. Anabaptists, Lutherans, and Jews also had their places of worship. None of these communities really welcomed the others; each tended to mix socially and marry only with its own kind. But a grudging live-and-let-live attitude prevailed in the country.

The Calling Although Calvinist church members were a minority of the Dutch population, Calvinist values were widely shared. Chief among them was the idea of the **calling**. Calvin had rejected Catholic practices such as renouncing the sinful world by joining religious orders or giving one's wealth to the church or the poor. Like Luther, he believed these acts were useless for salvation. Instead, he urged people to treat their ordinary work as a divine calling through which they could serve God with diligence and to avoid sinful idleness, luxury, and waste.

When giving this advice, Calvin did not have a particular economic agenda in mind, but his ideal of a sober and serious attitude toward one's calling in the world encouraged attentive, thrifty behavior among the merchants, manufacturers, and artisans who heeded it. This attitude was one of the factors behind the Dutch economic miracle of the late sixteenth century.

An Economic Boom The revolt against Spain hurt the economy of the southern Netherlands and hastened the decline of Antwerp. But while the economy faltered in the south, it boomed in the north. Unlike most of Europe, which experienced hard times after 1550, the Dutch Republic flourished (see Map 15.3). As both population and workers' wages rose, the Dutch economy became the wonder of the age. Its success rested on an adequate grain supply from Poland that prevented the food shortages plaguing other parts of Europe.

With the grain supply assured, Dutch farmers were free to specialize in other foodstuffs: butter, cheese, hops for beer, and livestock for meat. In addition, the North Sea provided catches of nutritious herring. Half the labor force was engaged in agriculture, the rest in a variety of industries. There was a need for labor, and workers' wages rose as a consequence. Men worked on large reclamation projects as coastal land was pumped dry with windmills for agricultural use.

Dutch cities grew and with them a demand for servants, carpenters, masons, and other urban workers. High literacy rates and lax censorship created a demand for books, news sheets, and pamphlets offering a wide range of opinions on often-controversial subjects like religion. These, in turn, called for printers and engravers. Shipyards employed others, and the ships they built needed

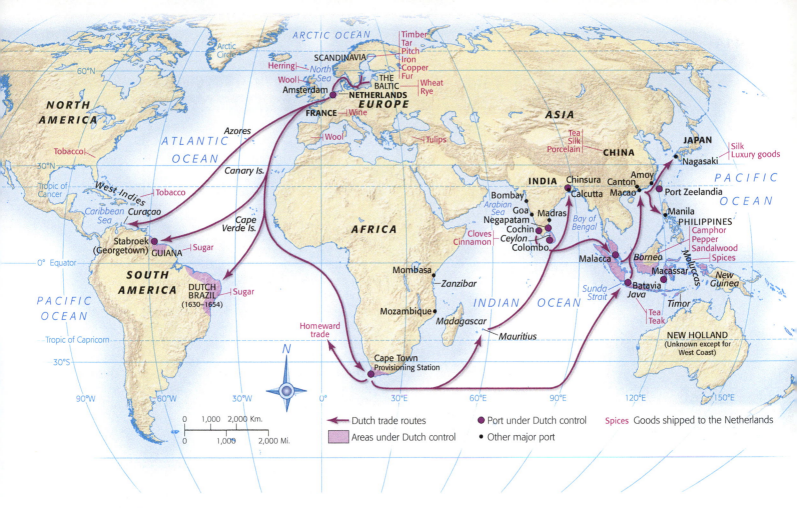

Map 15.3 **Dutch Commerce in the Seventeenth Century** By the seventeenth century, the Dutch had developed a complex global trading network. They took over Europe's East Asia trade from the Portuguese, dominated the European seaborne trade routes, traded with their New World colonies, and became the major trading partner with the Portuguese in Brazil.

1. Locate Amsterdam and the United Provinces on this map.
2. Trace Dutch trading routes and estimate the overall size of the "Areas under Dutch control." Is it larger or smaller than the United Provinces?
3. Where on the globe was Dutch trading activity the most intense?
4. Look back at Map 13.4 in Chapter 13:
   a. Compare the relative size of Spain and Portugal to their overseas possessions.
   b. Do the same patterns hold for these states and their possessions that hold for the Dutch and theirs?

crews. In fact, ships and shipping did the most to stimulate the economy.

Shipbuilding and Trade After 1550, the Dutch became the best shipbuilders in Europe. They also created an international trading network and used their ships to move their goods. The success of Dutch shipbuilding and trade rested on the **fluteship**, a large-hulled boat with a shallow draft. Fluteships carried salt, herring, and cloth east to Poland and other Baltic ports and brought back grain and timber. Some of the imports were used locally, while the rest were sold abroad.

Interestingly, Spain was one of the Dutch Republic's best customers. Although at war with the rebels for much of the time, Spain could not do without

Dutch-shipped timber for its navy and grain for its food-hungry territories in Italy. So, the Spanish swallowed their principles and traded.

The Dutch also entered the East Asian trade. In 1602, the government licensed the United East India Company to set up trading posts from Persia to Japan. Because Portugal was ruled by Spain after 1580, the Dutch aimed to reduce Spanish power by supplanting Portuguese traders in Asia. After the Portuguese were driven out, the company dominated the spice trade with Europe. It also dominated the inter-Asian trade, picking up cotton cloth in India and trading it

fluteship Merchant ship with an enlarged cargo hold and shallow draft used in Dutch trade with eastern Europe.

Musee Cantonal des Beaux-Arts de Lausanne, Switzerland/The Art Archive at Art Resource, NY

Saint Bartholomew's Day Massacre

The Huguenot François Dubois's painting of the Saint Bartholomew's Day Massacre, August 24, 1572, graphically depicts the chaos and violence of this event.

❯❯ *How might Dubois's fellow Huguenots read the pictorial message of the painting?*

❯❯ *What might have motivated the artist to include a leaping dog in the lower right-hand corner of his painting near a group of armed horsemen?*

elsewhere for goods like porcelain and silk that were then sold in Europe.

After the Japanese government began persecuting Japanese Christian converts and shut off contact with the outside world, the Dutch alone were allowed a trading post there. In 1621, the Dutch government also chartered the Dutch West India Company, which set up posts in Curaçao on the Caribbean and Surinam on the South American coast. Soon the Dutch were trading with Brazil, exporting European goods to the colony, and importing African slaves in return for sugar. Dutch settlers also founded the colony of New Amsterdam on Manhattan Island at the mouth of the Hudson River.

The hub of Dutch life was **Amsterdam** in the province of Holland. By the early seventeenth century, Amsterdam had replaced Antwerp as Europe's chief commercial and banking center. Because the republic's commercial activity spread across Europe and the world, involving people in complex, long-distance economic activity, the Dutch can be seen as the creators of the first truly modern economy.

Amsterdam Capital of the Dutch province of Holland and commercial center of the Dutch Republic.

15-3 Political Contests and More Religious Wars

❯❯ **What explains the violence of Europe's political contests and religious wars?**

❯❯ **What were the outcomes of the wars?**

In 1562, France was plunged into religious warfare between Catholics and Protestants that lasted for nearly seventy years. In the end, the Protestants were granted limited religious toleration, but their attempts to create their own semi-independent political communities within France failed. The Holy Roman Empire also experienced a religious war. The German war lasted fewer years than the war in France, but it brought non-German states into the fighting, and its destruction was far greater (see Profiles in Change: Jacques Callot Publishes "The Miseries and Misfortunes of War"). The peace settlement ending the war granted religious toleration to Calvinists, Lutherans, and Catholics and reduced the emperor's power. Like the French, the Germans had to learn to live with a new religious pluralism. The conflict also accelerated Spain's decline and France's rise as the most powerful state in Europe.

15-3a France's Wars of Religion

When Henry II died in 1559, he left his fourteen-year-old son Francis II to succeed him. In the confusion following Henry's death, the powerful **Guise (Gheez) family**, utterly committed to the extermination of Protestantism, seized control of the government. For the next thirty years, as three of Henry's young sons ruled France in succession, plots and fighting broke out between the Catholic Guises and the Protestant Huguenots.

The Saint Bartholomew's Day Massacre In 1572, a Catholic attack on the Huguenots that began in Paris on Saint Bartholomew's Day—thus known as the **Saint Bartholomew's Day Massacre**—spread to the provinces. Some 5,000 people died as violence reached extraordinary levels—heads, hands, and genitals were cut off; pregnant women were stabbed in the stomach; and bodies were burned. The massacres put an end to the growth of Protestantism in France.

The brutality of religious conflict demonstrated that both sides believed a fundamental issue was at stake—the belief that all members of a community had to share a common religious commitment for the community to function properly. In early modern Europe, religion was more a matter of community solidarity than of individual belief. Therefore, all religious dissent had to be stamped out to restore communal unity and win God's favor, especially since the Second Coming and Last Judgment were believed to be near at hand. Thus, Huguenots and Catholics saw each other not simply as different, but as dangerous polluters of the community. Killing as a rite of purification was not enough; the very bodies of the enemy had to be degraded.

Henry IV and the Edict of Nantes In 1589, the last of Henry II's sons, Henry III, died, assassinated by a fanatical Catholic monk. Since Henry III had no children, the Crown passed to a cousin, **Henry IV of Navarre** (nah-VAHR), a Huguenot. Henry was eager to end the fighting, but he faced a dilemma. The law of royal succession made him king, but his coronation oath would require him to attack non-Catholic heretics. In 1593, Henry resolved the issue by converting to Catholicism, supposedly saying that "Paris is well worth a Mass." In 1595, when the pope absolved Henry of his Huguenot errors, Henry was able to win over all but the die-hard Catholics.

Henry reassured the Huguenots by issuing the **Edict of Nantes** (nahnt), granting official toleration, in 1598. This edict brought an uneasy religious peace to France, but at a high price to community unity. The Huguenots were permitted to worship undisturbed, and they were also granted some two hundred fortified towns, along with troops to defend them. These towns were effectively independent from royal control and became a Huguenot state within the state.

To rally support for the edict, Henry showered powerful Catholic and Huguenot nobles with high government positions and large pensions. He also insisted that the king, who was the source of all law and order, should be obeyed regardless of his religion. Henry's emphasis on the importance of law and order vested in the king's authority became one of the basic principles of **absolutism**, which guided French kings' rule for the next two centuries.

15-3b The Resurgent French Monarchy

At the grassroots level, Henry IV built on an expansion of government begun by his predecessors, who had sold administrative offices to middle-class lawyers and then forced them to loan the government money. This strategy raised additional revenue and built loyalty, as the new officeholders had a compelling reason to see that the monarchy remained strong. Henry IV used this expanded administrative force to consolidate royal power and initiated tax reform to erase the royal debt and build up a treasury surplus.

Henry's chief minister, the Huguenot duke of Sully, lowered direct taxes while raising indirect ones. The direct tax of the taille took one large bite out of incomes whereas indirect taxes on commodities nibbled slowly away at them, so the pain of taxation was obscured. Most important, Sully imposed the annual *paulette* tax on all officials who had bought their offices. Because their numbers were now so large, paulette payments raised revenues that eventually rivaled the taille as the chief source of royal income.

Guise family Powerful Catholic nobility committed to eliminating Protestantism in France during the French religious wars of 1559–1588.

Saint Bartholomew's Day Massacre Catholic massacre of Protestants in Paris and throughout France in 1572 that ended the growth of Protestantism in the kingdom.

Henry IV of Navarre (r. 1589–1610) Protestant king of Navarre who became king of France, converted to Catholicism, and started to end the religious wars.

Edict of Nantes Decree issued by Henry IV in 1598 that allowed the Huguenots to practice their religion and gave them two hundred fortified towns.

absolutism Doctrine that a king was the sole source of all law in his realm.

Jacques Callot Publishes "The Miseries and Misfortunes of War"

IACOBVS CALLOT
CALCOGRAPHVS AQVA FORTI NANCEII IN LOTHARINGIA.
NOBILIS.

Portrait of Jacques Callot

In 1633, Jacques Callot (kal-lo), nearing the end of his life and suffering from a painful stomach disorder, published eighteen large etchings depicting "The Miseries and Misfortunes of War." Military scenes had always been part of his artistic repertory, but the "Miseries" were something different. With them, the respected portrayer of elite life in early-seventeenth-century Europe revealed himself as one of the most powerful protesters against the dark side of war.

Callot was born in 1592 into a noble and devout Roman Catholic family in the duchy of Lorraine. His artistic talent was apparent at an early age, and in his teens he joined a band of gypsies heading south to Rome, where he worked as an assistant in a print shop specializing in religious images at a time when the campaign against Protestantism gripped the city. The papacy urged the Catholic faithful to come to Rome to reinforce their faith through visits to the tombs of saints and the city's magnificent churches. When they left, these pilgrims were eager to take home souvenirs, and prints like Callot's of the famous paintings they had seen in churches were especially prized.

In 1611, Callot moved to Florence to serve the grand duke Cosimo II and his mother, the grand duchess Christine, who, like Callot, was from Lorraine. Cosimo's court was one of the most brilliant and intellectually distinguished in Europe, and Florence was filled with artists and scientists in the grand duke's employ. Here Callot perfected his etching technique using the extra-hard varnish Italian violin makers put on their instruments. This varnish allowed Callot to prepare his copper printing plates by cutting fine, clear lines with his etching needle. The result was a remarkably detailed and precise etching ready to pick up ink for printing. In Florence, Callot continued to produce religious prints, but he also documented the lives

---

Although Henry IV won many Huguenots and Catholics over to his policies of religious toleration and administrative consolidation, in 1610, he was stabbed to death by a deranged ex-monk obsessed with the continuing presence of heretics in the kingdom. Henry's heir was his nine-year-old son, **Louis XIII**, who, once king in his own right, resumed war against the Huguenots. In 1629, he issued the **Peace of Alès** (ah-LES), which dismantled the Huguenots' fortified towns and ended France's Wars of Religion.

Louis XIII (r. 1610–1643) King of France who made war on the Huguenots and took France into the Thirty Years' War to weaken France's political rival, Spain.

Peace of Alès Treaty in 1629 that ended France's religious wars, allowed Huguenots freedom of worship, but took away their fortified towns.

But the religious toleration granted to the Huguenots in 1598 was reaffirmed.

15-3c The Habsburg War Against the Turks

Charles V had put his younger brother Ferdinand in charge of the Holy Roman Empire before his abdication in 1556. Thirty years earlier, Ferdinand had also been elected king of Hungary and Bohemia after the previous king died fighting the Ottoman Turks. While Ferdinand had full control of Austria and Bohemia, the Turks conquered most of Hungary, leaving only the northern part in Habsburg hands. Even that was threatened when the Turks, marching up the Danube River, tried in 1529 and again in 1532 to seize all of Hungary and the city of Vienna in Austria. For Ferdinand, a devout Catholic, the Turks posed a greater threat than the Protestants.

of the grand dukes and their lavish court—scenes of operas, precision marching, and tournaments. Soldiers also figured prominently in these works because the rulers of the time were expected to project an image of warrior power. Callot's soldiers were dashing and heroic, mounted on prancing horses and glittering with finely polished armor.

In 1621, Cosimo II died, and the grand duchess Christine, reducing state expenditures, dismissed Callot and other court artists. Callot returned to his father's house in Lorraine, which, in 1630, the French invaded. They invaded again in 1632 and in 1633, when they finally annexed the duchy to France and demanded an oath of loyalty from all locally prominent people, including Callot.

The invasion of Lorraine brought the harsh facts of warfare directly into Callot's family. Plague swept through the duchy, brought in by French soldiers, and Callot's father fell victim to it. It was in this context that Callot decided to create his "Miseries and Misfortunes of War." The series of prints were published in 1633. The first shows an army recruiter luring men to sign up with promises of good pay. A fierce battle scene follows, and then come five prints showing the cruelty of soldiers against civilians as troops pillage a farm, attack a monastery, burn a village, and seize a stagecoach. In these scenes, people are stabbed, shot, and burned alive. The next prints show the tables turned on the soldiers, who are tortured and killed by their commanders for military crimes such as desertion. Here, men are tied to a rope and hurled earthward from a great height, shot by a firing squad, torn apart on a rack, or burned at the stake, while others hang by their necks like human fruit on the branches of a great tree. We then see wounded and mangled soldiers crowding a hospital, people dying by a roadside, and peasants attacking soldiers in revenge for their atrocities. The series ends with a conqueror rewarding his troops, implying that the horrors, now celebrated as a "victory," will start all over again. Callot presented his prints without any commentary, intending that his artistic skill alone should carry his bitter message; the moralizing lines now seen on many of them were added later.

In 1635, at the age of forty-three, Jacques Callot died in a Lorraine that was ravaged by wartime disease and famine. But his prints endured. They struck home to many of his generation who, like him, were deeply committed Christians, whether Catholic or Protestant, and who were also appalled by the horror and futility of the warfare that had torn Europe apart for nearly a century.

Thus, during Ferdinand's reign, and that of his son Maximilian II (r. 1564–1576), various kinds of Protestants increased their followings in all Habsburg lands. Lutherans predominated in Austria, Lutherans and Calvinists flourished in Bohemia, and Calvinists and **Unitarians** gained converts in Habsburg Hungary. "In affairs of religion everyone does as he pleases," one Catholic complained. After Maximilian died in 1576, effective Habsburg rule declined, as a contest between his two sons encouraged the great nobles who controlled the representative assemblies, or **diets**, to seek increased political independence.

The nobles' model for good government was **Poland-Lithuania**, where the nobility elected the king and had the right to rebel against him if he violated his coronation oath. In the Polish Diet, each noble had the right to veto a measure and thus "explode" the diet. They were also free to govern their serfs without royal interference and to choose between Catholicism and some form of Protestantism. When new war with the Turks broke out in 1593, the nobility in the Habsburg lands demanded more religious freedom and greater local control of government in return for funds for the war.

15-3d The Thirty Years' War

As Protestantism grew in Habsburg lands, the Catholics launched a counteroffensive. As early as the 1590s, Jesuits from Italy rallied Catholic communities, which soon established a militant anti-Protestant movement. Catholics found their leader in the new emperor, **Ferdinand II**, a fervent Catholic. His determination to put an end to Protestantism launched the **Thirty Years' War**, the most devastating conflict of the seventeenth century. At first confined to Bohemia, it soon engulfed the Holy Roman Empire and drew in many European states as it went through Bohemian, Danish, Swedish, and French phases. (See Learning from a Primary Source: *Simplicius Simplicissimus* Encounters Some "Merry Cavalrymen.")

The War Begins in Bohemia In 1617, after he was elected king of Bohemia, Ferdinand II ordered Protestant churches closed in two Bohemian towns. Enraged Protestants confronted two of Ferdinand's officials in Prague, the capital of the kingdom, and threw them out of an upper-story window. Surprisingly, they survived. Catholics claimed they had been wafted gently

---

Unitarians Christians who denied the traditional doctrine of the Trinity.

diets In the Holy Roman Empire under Habsburg rule, representative assemblies dominated by the great nobility that sought increased control of government.

Poland-Lithuania Kingdom formed in 1569 from two previously independent states; included modern Poland, the Baltic states, Belarus, and most of Ukraine.

Ferdinand II (r. 1619–1637) Habsburg emperor who reestablished Catholicism in Bohemia and Austria but failed to do so in the empire as a whole.

Thirty Years' War General war, 1618–1648, between German Protestant princes and their foreign allies against the Habsburgs, who were allied with Catholic princes.

Erich Lessing/Art Resource, NY

Jacques Callot's *Miseries of War*

Thieving soldiers are executed in this etching from Jacques Callot's *Miseries of War*. A priest blesses the men as they are led up a ladder to be hung. A caption describes the executed as "infamous lost souls . . . hung like unhappy fruit."

》 *Hanging was a common form of execution in early modern Europe. What gives Callot's etching its particular power?*

》 *Do you know of any other instance in which people hanged from a tree branch are referred to as the fruit of the tree?*

to Earth on angels' wings, while Protestants protested that a pile of dung had broken their fall. This "defenestration of Prague" prompted a Bohemian rebellion, which Ferdinand subdued with help from the Spanish Habsburgs. Ferdinand seized rebel lands and gave them to Habsburg supporters. Believing that religious dissent polluted society and offended God, he banned Protestant worship, ordering Protestants to convert or leave. In 1627, a subdued Bohemian Diet declared that the Crown was no longer elective, but rather hereditary in the Habsburg family. The abolition of elective monarchy marked the high point in Ferdinand's reconquest of Bohemia.

The Danes and the Swedes Enter the War The Habsburg victory in Bohemia had repercussions throughout Europe. The Spanish branch of the family used it to seize the Palatinate, a state on the Rhine River, and thereby expand its control of the "Spanish Road" that led north from Habsburg, Italy, to the Spanish Netherlands. Soon, the king of Denmark entered the war as leader of the Protestants. But he was defeated and driven out of the empire in 1629. Victorious, Ferdinand II supposedly reaffirmed the 1555 Peace of Augsburg, but in reality sought to strengthen

Gustavus II Adolphus (r. 1594–1632) King of Sweden who led Protestant forces against the Habsburgs until his death in battle in 1632.

Cardinal Richelieu (1585–1642) Louis XIII's chief minister, who persuaded Louis to enter the Thirty Years' War against Ferdinand II.

Catholicism, not only in Habsburg lands but also throughout the empire.

At this point, the Swedish phase of the war began, when the Lutheran king of Sweden, **Gustavus II Adolphus**, assumed leadership of the Protestant cause.

Gustavus Adolphus was a seasoned warrior, having already fought the Danes, the Russians, and the Poles. His chief concern was to expand Swedish power in the Baltic, as he feared that a Catholic Habsburg victory in Germany would threaten his interests. But his death in battle in 1632 spread confusion. When Ferdinand, realizing he would never be able to eradicate Protestantism, offered toleration for Lutherans, the war entered its French phase.

France Enters the War Although Louis XIII and his chief minister, **Cardinal Richelieu**, were devout Catholics, they feared that Ferdinand's reconciliation with the Protestants would increase the power of France's long-standing Habsburg enemy. They, therefore, entered the war, and for the next eleven years, French and Swedish troops continued to fight the Habsburgs. Almost all the fighting was done on German soil, and the devastation was terrible. The Thirty Years' War made the region's economic decline immeasurably worse.

Overall, the population of the empire fell between 15 and 20 percent as the warring armies disrupted agriculture, sacked villages and cities, and spread disease among the civilian population. In areas of the worst fighting, such as Bohemia and the southern Baltic coast, population declined by 50 percent as people died or fled. Cities fell into debt because of the huge bribes they paid the warring armies, whether friend or foe, in hopes of averting pillaging by the troops.

15-3e The Peace of Westphalia

The war finally came to an end in 1648 with the **Peace of Westphalia**. It amended the 1555 Peace of Augsburg to allow rulers to choose Catholicism, Calvinism, or Lutheranism as their state religion. Thus, Ferdinand II's dream of reestablishing Catholic dominance in the empire died forever. Like the Peace of Alès in France almost twenty years earlier, the Peace of Westphalia ratified a grudging recognition that the state's religious unity had been shattered and that new ways of forming community and community identity would have to be found.

Important political changes also occurred. The empire's boundaries were altered: The Swiss Confederation and the Dutch Republic were now placed outside the empire and recognized as independent states. Within the empire, states were granted the right to develop their own foreign policies without the emperor's approval. Both France and Sweden took imperial territory. Sweden gained control of the southern Baltic shore, and France received three important bishoprics on its eastern frontier.

The French Fight On Although France ended its war in Germany in 1648, war against the Habsburgs continued, with fighting between France and Spain along the borders of the Spanish Netherlands and the Pyrenees Mountains. In 1659, the two countries signed the **Treaty of the Pyrenees**. France extended its rule along the eastern Pyrenees and took important cities in the Spanish Netherlands. To celebrate the peace, the king of Spain agreed to the marriage of his eldest daughter, Anne, to the young king of France, Louis XIV, who had succeeded Louis XIII in 1643. Spain, exhausted by decades of warfare, never regained the position it held under Philip II. France was now the most powerful state in Europe.

Europeans were to fight many more wars after the Treaty of Westphalia, but religious motivations for conflict were never again as strong as they had been in the century before 1648. Now, states formed diplomatic and military alliances to advance their political and economic agendas while curbing those of their rivals, thereby creating an unstable and ever-shifting **balance of power** that prevented any one state from overwhelming the others.

CONNECTIONS: The Treaties of Westphalia and the Pyrenees were attempts to address relations between states on a European-wide basis. In the future, similar attempts were made to restore international order after major conflicts. (See for example, Section 20-1a The Congress of Vienna.)

15-4 Reformation and Revolution in the British Isles

» **How did the expectations of the English people change, or remain the same, from 1558 to 1660?**

» **What were the relations among the English, Scots, and Irish in this period?**

England experienced a golden age during the reign of Elizabeth I, the last Tudor monarch. But during the seventeenth century, the British Isles experienced religious wars when different Protestant groups fought to control state churches. Like their counterparts on the continent, Protestant Scots and English believed that their communities should be united by a single church. Gradually, however, a party formed that called for toleration of different forms of Protestantism, but not of Catholicism. In Ireland, where Catholics predominated, English and Scots prejudice led to a brutal conquest of the island that established Protestant control. Conflict over religion also involved a struggle between the English monarch and Parliament for control of policy, which led to revolution in England, the execution of the king, and the establishment of a republic. In 1660, the republic came to an end and the monarchy was restored.

15-4a Elizabeth I

Elizabeth I was one of England's ablest and most popular rulers. At five feet ten inches, she was exceptionally tall for her time, and her flaming red hair, along with her trim, athletic body, caught everyone's attention. Elizabeth was a shrewd ruler who played on her womanhood, challenging contemporary views about women's weakness with her own force of will and political skill while instilling fear in anyone who challenged her. She was exceptionally well educated, speaking French, German, and Italian as well as reading Latin and Greek with ease. When Philip II, anxious to continue his English alliance, proposed marriage, the "virgin queen" turned him down, as she did everyone else, saying, "I am wedded to England." Her subjects hailed her as Good Queen Bess.

Peace of Westphalia Peace in 1648 ending the Thirty Years' War, allowing states in the Holy Roman Empire to establish their own foreign policies and state religion.

Treaty of the Pyrenees Treaty in 1659 ending the wars between France and Spain and leaving France the most powerful state in Europe.

balance of power Long-time European diplomatic aim for a distribution of power among several states that would prevent the dominance of any one state.

Simplicius Simplicissimus Encounters Some "Merry Cavalrymen"

Jacques Callot was not alone in commenting on seventeenth-century warfare. In 1669, a German inn-keeper, Johann von Grimmelshausen, who had fought as a soldier in the Thirty Years' War, published *Simplicius Simplicissimus* (Simplest of Simpletons), a tale that mixes humor and horror in equal measure. It went through three editions in 1669 alone. In the excerpt that follows, young Simplicius/The Simpleton, while working as a shepherd for his father, meets a band of cavalrymen and accompanies them to his home. Here, he tells us what happened next.

❶ Why does the author use these remarks to set up what follows?

❷ What effect in the reader does the author try to create when he mixes his account of pillaging with humor?

❶ Though I hadn't intended to take the peace-loving reader into my father's home and farm along with these merry cavalrymen, the orderly progress of my tale requires me to make known to posterity the sort of abysmal and unheard-of cruelties occasionally perpetrated in our German war, and to testify by my own example that all these evils were necessarily required for our own good by the kindness of our Lord. For, my dear reader, who would have told me that there is a God in heaven if the warriors hadn't destroyed my [father's] house....

❷ The first thing these horsemen did in the nice black rooms of the house was to put in their horses. Then everyone took up a special job, a job having to do with death and destruction. Although some began butchering, heating water, and rendering lard, as if to prepare for a banquet, others raced through the house, ransacking upstairs and down.... Still others bundled up big bags of cloth, household goods, and clothes, as if they wanted to hold a rummage sale somewhere. What they did not intend to take along they broke up and spoiled. Some ran their swords into the hay and straw, as if there hadn't been hogs enough to stick.... Some shook the feathers out of beds and put bacon slabs, hams, and other stuff in the ticking,

The Twin Problems of Spain and Ireland In addition to promoting a moderate form of Protestantism in England, Elizabeth faced two problems—the power of Spain and opposition in Ireland. Philip II's attempt to assert strong Spanish and Catholic control over the Netherlands threatened English economic interests there as the Netherlands had long been the main market for English wool exports. Thus, in 1585, Elizabeth sent an army to aid the Dutch rebels against Philip. The next year, she sanctioned Sir Francis Drake's raids on Spanish colonial shipping. The English now identified themselves as pro-Protestant, anti-Catholic, and anti-Spanish. Thus, religious, economic, and political issues deepened the rift between

Spain and England, thereby ending the medieval alliance between the two countries that had led to the marriage of Catherine of Aragon to Henry VIII.

Rivalry with Spain also influenced developments in Ireland. Like her father and grandfather, Elizabeth was determined to strengthen English control of the island. But her attempts were met with a local rebellion led by Catholics, who received Spanish help, including the failed Spanish Armada of 1588. In the end, Elizabeth triumphed and transferred vast tracts of Irish land to loyal English Protestants, thus consolidating the conquest of the kingdom.

The English Renaissance Elizabeth's England saw a flowering of literature, known as the **English Renaissance**. William Shakespeare wrote many of his plays during her reign, performing them at court and in his own theater, the Globe. Shakespeare's contemporary, **Christopher Marlowe**, wrote equally popular plays, including *The Massacre at Paris*, about

English Renaissance Flowering of English literature during Elizabeth I's reign.

Christopher Marlowe (ca. 1564–1593) Playwright in Elizabeth I's reign, author of the play *Doctor Faustus* and a contemporary of William Shakespeare.

3 Why does Grimmelshausen order the details of the pillaging in the way he does?

4 What is the point of this sentence?

5 Why would Grimmelshausen choose to describe the destruction of a clearly prosperous, well-supplied peasant household?

6 Grimmelshausen knew that his description of soldiers in war would be read by contemporaries who had lived through the same events he had. In summing up, what opportunities did this knowledge offer him? And what constraints did it place on him?

as if they might sleep better on these. **3** They flattened out copper and pewter dishes and baled the ruined goods. They burned up bedsteads, tables, chairs, and benches, though there were yards and yards of dry firewood outside the kitchen. Jars and crocks, pots and casseroles, all were broken, either because they preferred their meat broiled or because they thought they'd eat only one meal with us. In the barn, the hired girl was handled so roughly that she was unable to walk away, I am ashamed to report. They stretched the hired man out flat on the ground, stuck a wooden wedge in his mouth to keep it open, and emptied a milk bucket full of stinking manure drippings down his throat; they called it a Swedish cocktail. He didn't relish it and made a very wry face. By this means they forced him to take a raiding party to some other place where they carried off men and cattle and brought them to our farm.... I can't say much about the captured wives, hired girls, and daughters because the soldiers wouldn't let me watch their doings. But I do remember hearing pitiful screams from various dark corners and I guess that my mother and our Ursula had it no better than the rest. **4** Amid all this horror I was busy turning a roasting split and didn't worry about anything, for I didn't know the meaning of it. **5** In the afternoon I helped water the horses and that way got to see our hired girl in the barn. She looked wondrously messed up and at first I didn't recognize her. In a sickly voice she said, "Boy, get out of this place, or the soldiers will take you with them." **6**

Source: *The Adventures of Simplicius Simplicissimus* by Hans Jacob Christoffel van Grimmelshausen. A modern translation with an introduction by George Schultz-Behrend, second revised edition. Rochester, New York: Camden House, 1993. Reprinted with permission.

the Saint Bartholomew's Day slaughter during France's religious wars. Marlowe's greatest play is *Doctor Faustus*, about a man who sells his soul to the Devil in return for power and knowledge.

Poetry also flourished in Elizabeth's reign. **Edmund Spenser** continued the tradition of epic poetry that stretched back to Dante Alighieri, Virgil, and Homer in his *Faerie Queene*, an elaborate allegory celebrating Protestant England's struggle with Catholicism and Spain. Spenser's friend and fellow poet **Sir Walter Raleigh** also extolled Elizabeth and Protestant England in verse. Both Raleigh and Spenser actively pursued politics.

As a young man at court, Raleigh became a favorite of the queen, who commissioned him to attack Spanish shipping. In 1587, he founded a short-lived colony on Roanoke Island off present-day North Carolina, and in 1595 he led the first English expedition into South America, sailing up the Orinoco River in search of a fabled kingdom ruled by El Dorado, a man covered in gold. No gold was found, but his account of the expedition established him as a master of the literature of discovery and exploration. When Elizabeth began her conquest of Ireland, both Raleigh and Spenser joined her forces and were rewarded with estates confiscated from the rebels.

Mary Stuart, Queen of Scots Elizabeth's refusal to marry was based more on political calculation than on personal preference; she feared the challenges to her power and independence that submission to a husband might bring. As the years passed, however, the problem of succession became acute because her heir was her cousin, **Mary Stuart, Queen of Scots**, the Catholic widow of King Francis II of France and a relative of the Guises. After Francis's death, Mary had returned to Scotland, where she married a Scots nobleman and had a son, James.

Mary's religion caused problems in newly Calvinist Scotland, and in 1568 she fled to England after nobles deposed her and seized James. Elizabeth promptly imprisoned Mary because her Catholicism made her a magnet for those who favored the old church. Rumors of Catholic plots swirled around Mary for years. In 1587, when the rumors seemed to stick, Elizabeth had her beheaded.

Edmund Spenser (1553–1599) Poet and author of the epic poem *The Faerie Queene*.

Sir Walter Raleigh (ca.1554–1618) Privateer, explorer, poet, and favorite of Elizabeth I.

Mary Stuart, Queen of Scots (r. 1542–1587) Cousin of Elizabeth I and heir to the English throne whose Catholicism led to her execution.

15-4b The Early Stuart Monarchs

In 1603, Mary Stuart's son, **James VI** of Scotland, succeeded the virgin queen as **James I** of England and Ireland, and, for the first time, the separate kingdoms of Scotland and England were ruled by the same person. James had an excellent mind and published ten works, including a *Counterblast to Tobacco* that denounced smoking as "loathsome to the eye, hateful to the nose, harmful to the brain, [and] dangerous to the lungs." His greatest literary achievement was to sponsor a new translation of the Christian Bible for use in the Anglican Church. Published in 1611 and known as the **King James Version**, it has shaped the English language down to the present.

King and Parliament Two issues dominated James's reign and that of his son, **Charles I**: religion and relations between king and Parliament. Henry VIII and Elizabeth had used Parliament to implement the English Reformation, thereby giving it a permanent place in the country's political life. But the exact nature of Parliament's authority was disputed. Both James and Charles believed that God appointed kings to rule and that they were accountable to Him alone. But they also knew that Parliament had a traditional right to raise taxes. For its part, Parliament believed the king could formulate state policy, but it claimed the right to criticize policy. James rejected this right. Parliament, he said, was no place "for every rash and hair-brained fellow to propose new laws of his own invention."

At stake in these conflicts was a fundamental political issue: should Parliament simply express opinions, or Should it have a voice in policy making? Traditions of strong kingship, stretching back to the Middle Ages, favored the king, but Parliament's power to grant or withhold taxes enabled it to assess the policies its taxes would finance. James and Charles leaned toward royal absolutism, whereas Parliament favored a theory of limited royal rule.

James VI/James I (r. 1567/1603–1625) Son of Mary, Queen of Scots, king who ruled in Scotland as James VI from 1567 and in England and Ireland as James I from 1603.

King James Version Translation of the Bible sponsored by King James I for use in the Church of England and published in 1611.

Charles I (r. 1625–1649) King of England, Ireland, and Scotland who was beheaded by order of Parliament in 1649.

Puritans Calvinists who wanted to eliminate bishops and favored more sermons, policing of people's behavior, and a strong Protestant foreign policy.

Ulster Northeastern part of Ireland colonized by Scots and English Protestants after England's defeat of the local Catholics.

William Laud (1573–1645) Archbishop of Canterbury who enforced Charles I's unpopular religious policies through royal courts.

Religion regularly divided king and Parliament. Like Elizabeth, James was a moderate Protestant, but he was married to a Catholic. His moderation and his wife raised suspicions among the **Puritans**, Calvinists who thought that the Anglican Church was not completely reformed. Puritans wanted no bishops, no church ceremony, more sermons, policing of people's behavior, and an effective Protestant foreign policy. Their suspicions of James were overcome in 1605 when the government discovered a Catholic plot to blow up the king, along with Parliament. Thereafter, James followed Elizabeth in treating English Catholics as traitors.

Colonization: Ulster and America Anti-Catholicism also shaped English policy in Ireland. In 1597, another rebellion broke out in **Ulster**, in the northeastern part of the island. It ended just as the plot to blow up the king and Parliament was discovered. In the anti-Catholic backlash, the lands of the rebel Catholic leaders were confiscated and given to English owners, who then colonized them with some 100,000 Scottish Protestants. The Catholic Irish, viewed as "savages," were driven onto marginal lands. Later, habits learned in Ireland were transferred to North America, where settlers drove Indian "savages" off the lands they then farmed. Ulster was England's first successful colony.

In North America, the Virginia Colony boomed when tobacco was grown for export. James I may have hated the "pernicious weed," but his subjects loved it and Virginia's economic success was assured. Beginning in the 1620s, other colonies were founded, this time by religious dissidents upset with the monarchy's support of Anglicanism and persecution of Catholics.

The Pilgrims, Protestant Separatists who, like the Anabaptists, believed that the church should be a voluntary association, founded Plymouth Colony in 1620. In 1629, Puritans founded the Massachusetts Bay Colony, and English Catholics emigrated to Maryland in the 1630s. Unlike the colonies of Spain and Portugal, the English settlements were not directly sponsored by the state. Instead, they began as commercial ventures, like the Virginia Colony, or as religious havens.

Charles I James died in 1625, and his son became king as Charles I. Like his father, Charles had an unshakeable belief in his right to rule as he pleased. He also shared his father's views about Parliament. Between 1625 and 1629, the king clashed with parliamentary leaders who criticized his policies and refused to grant him money for his wars against Spain and in support of the Huguenots, questioning the success of his campaigns and criticizing the men in charge of them. Finally, in 1630, Charles decided to govern without Parliament and did not convene it for ten years.

Ruling Without Parliament: Charles and Laud Charles ruled well enough on his own for most of the 1630s. One policy, however, provoked growing opposition—reform of the Anglican Church. In 1633, the king appointed **William Laud** archbishop of Canterbury;

Hulton Archive/Getty Images

Execution of Charles I

In this woodcut print of the execution of Charles I, the blindfolded king, his hat set to the side, puts his neck on the chopping block and waits for the executioner's ax. An Anglican clergyman prays while armed guards and a crowd look on.

›› *Thinking back to the portraits of sixteenth- and seventeenth-century rulers that have appeared in this text, how do you imagine people in Charles's lifetime, whether English or not, would react to this woodcut?*

Laud introduced new church ceremonies and ordered the clergy to adhere strictly to Elizabeth's 1559 Book of Common Prayer. The Puritans were outraged, seeing Laud's program as an attempt to reintroduce Catholic practices. Some of them left for North America, where they joined their fellow Puritans in Massachusetts.

Others waited for a chance to turn on Laud. Laud's position was further weakened when he stated that the clergy alone, not the local laity, would control church affairs. He also ordered the restoration of church lands that the laity had taken over. These policies angered a large group of landowners with seats in Parliament, who now had economic and political reasons, as well as religious ones, for opposing the king and his archbishop.

Parliament Reconvened Charles and Laud were not content to revamp the Church of England. In 1637, the king imposed the Book of Common Prayer, along with bishops, on the Presbyterian Church of Scotland. In response, in 1639, the Scots rebelled. Charles, now at war with his Scottish subjects, needed funds for an army. In 1640, he resummoned the English Parliament and demanded money from it.

15-4c Civil War, Revolution, and the Commonwealth

The new **Long Parliament** was filled with men angry at Laud and the king. It passed a bill stating that the king could not dissolve Parliament without its own permission (which Charles signed, probably inadvertently). Parliament removed Archbishop Laud and sent him to prison. It also passed an act requiring the king to call Parliament into session on a regular basis. In 1641, Charles was forced to sign a treaty with the Scots that gave the Scottish parliament a role in the appointment of royal ministers and conceded the Scottish parliament's right to oversee policy. The English Parliament promptly demanded the same concessions, and when Charles refused, it proposed a bill abolishing bishops in the Church of England.

At this point, another Catholic rebellion broke out in Ireland, and several thousand Protestants were massacred in Ulster. In 1642, Charles demanded money from Parliament for an army to subdue the Irish. When Parliament refused and started to form its own army, Charles declared war on Parliament.

Civil War England had now fallen into civil war. For the next seven years, the king and his supporters fought Parliament's army. Troops of both sides damaged crops and disrupted trade, and cold temperatures ruined the harvests of the late 1640s. By war's end, popular rebellions against both sides had broken out in various parts of the country.

In 1643, Parliament reorganized the Church of England along Presbyterian lines and then executed Laud. In 1645, Charles, finally defeated in battle, surrendered to the Scots, who turned him over to the English Parliament in 1647. In 1648, the army purged Parliament of those favoring monarchy.

The King's Trial and Execution The remaining members of Parliament brought the king to trial on charges of treason and murder for his role in the civil

Long Parliament English Parliament that sat from 1640 until 1660.

war. Charles denied the court's legitimacy, proclaiming that "the king cannot be tried by any superior jurisdiction on earth." But Charles was convicted and publicly beheaded in London on January 30, 1649. When the executioner's ax fell on his neck, a huge groan went up from the crowd surrounding the scaffold, for it was a momentous event. Never before had an English court of law removed a monarch or the English people killed their king. Civil war had become revolution. England was now a republic.

Political Ferment and Debate Even as the civil war raged, the English engaged in an unprecedented debate over the nature of the state and the role of ordinary people in political life. Charles's growing unpopularity led many to go beyond older arguments about the king's relation to Parliament. The Levellers wanted to establish a democratic republic in England and allow all men to vote. Women activists supporting the Levellers petitioned Parliament on their behalf.

Even more radical were the Diggers. Responding to economic hard times, they rejected the institution of private property and supported a form of communal ownership. Levellers and Diggers were always in a minority, but the very fact that they gave public voice to their ideas for reform stimulated popular thought about the nature of England's social order and raised questions about the political and economic identities of English men and women.

15-4d Oliver Cromwell

One of Parliament's generals in favor of Charles's execution was **Oliver Cromwell**. In 1649, Cromwell led an army to put down the rebellion in Ireland, where disruptions from fighting and crop failures had produced widespread famine; the Irish population fell by almost 40 percent. Cromwell's invasion delivered the final blows. His army massacred thousands, 80 percent of agricultural land was transferred to the Protestant minority, Catholicism was outlawed, and 12,000 rebels were deported as penal slaves to Barbados and other English colonies in the West Indies. For the next two hundred years, English Protestant control of Ireland was assured.

With Ireland subdued, Cromwell turned to Scotland. Despite their differences with Charles I, most Scots favored the continuation of monarchy. After the king's execution, **Charles II**, Charles I's elder son, was summoned from exile and crowned Scottish king in 1650. Cromwell then invaded Scotland, forced Charles to flee, and established the rule of the English Parliament there.

When Cromwell returned from Scotland, he quickly dominated the new English **Commonwealth**, as the republic was called. Cromwell believed that God had called him to leadership and guided his actions. In this, he was exactly like the king he had helped to execute.

Attacks on Dutch Trading In 1651, Parliament attempted to break the Dutch shipping monopoly with the **Navigation Act**, which required overseas goods destined for England to be carried in English ships or ships of English colonies. The next year, Cromwell supported a war against the Dutch, telling them that "the Lord has declared against you." The war was short, and the act did little to limit Dutch trade, but it signaled England's rise as a commercial power and marked the beginning of government control of the emerging English Empire.

In 1653, Cromwell took the title of Lord Protector. Parliament continued to meet, but Cromwell and the army actually ruled. In 1655, after suppressing a royalist rebellion, Cromwell established a military dictatorship. Press censorship was instituted, and traditional local officials were replaced by major generals who ran local government and carried out a moral reform of society along strict Calvinist lines.

Although Cromwell ruled as a Calvinist-inspired dictator, he abolished the requirement that everyone attend Calvinist church services, proclaiming, "I meddle not with any man's conscience." He did, however, ban Anglican and Catholic services for political reasons. By the 1650s, growing numbers of Protestants shared Cromwell's embrace of limited toleration.

Cromwell was offered a crown by some followers who wanted him to become King Oliver. He refused it.

The Restoration of the Stuart Kings When Cromwell died in 1658, his son Richard became the new lord protector. Richard, however, did not have his father's political skills and soon retired to his country estates. His departure left England leaderless. Once again, a general stepped in; George Monck marched his army on London and negotiated the return of King Charles II, along with the House of Lords, the Church of England, and all its bishops. Oliver Cromwell's corpse was dug up and publicly hanged.

In 1660, it seemed that England's troubles had come full circle. Anglican monarchists viewed the post-1660 regime as a simple "restoration" of older ways. But in the wake of the Anglican Church being outlawed, a king executed, and a republic created, the merits of absolutist monarchy and limited constitutional government had been debated. There had been calls for democracy, communal ownership of property,

Oliver Cromwell (1599–1658) General on Parliament's side in English civil war who eventually established a military dictatorship in England.

Charles II (r. 1650/1660–1685) Son of Charles I, crowned king of Scotland in 1650 but ruled there only after 1660, when he was crowned king of England as well.

Commonwealth Name of the English republic from 1649 to 1660.

Navigation Act Parliamentary act of 1651 requiring overseas goods destined for England to be carried in English ships or ships of English colonies.

and religious toleration. The debates and the conflicts unleashed during the civil war and revolution would shape the future of the English-speaking world.

15-5 Christian Reform, Religious Wars, and the Jews

» **How did Europe's Jews define themselves as a community in the larger Christian world?**

» **How were the Jews in Poland affected by the war that broke out there in 1648?**

» **What explains the rise and fall of Sabbatai Sevi?**

The expulsion of Jews from Spain and Portugal destroyed Europe's largest Jewish community. In the early sixteenth century, Italy alone in western Europe had a significant Jewish population. In eastern Europe, Poland also admitted large numbers of Jews. Then, after 1550, Jews returned to western Europe when the Dutch Republic, Bohemia, France, and England once again admitted them. But the rising religious passions of the Christian reformations led to an upsurge of anti-Jewish attacks, including devastating massacres in eastern Poland. Like some Christians, Jews believed that the troubles they experienced were signs of the world's end. In 1665, thousands of them looked to a young Jew from Smyrna in Ottoman Turkey, Sabbatai Sevi, who proclaimed that he was the long-awaited Jewish Messiah.

15-5a Jews in Poland and Western Europe

Following their expulsion from England and France in the late Middle Ages, western European Jews were permitted to settle in Poland-Lithuania, where the Black Death had reduced the number of people on the agricultural estates of the king and the nobility. Soon Jews were working the land as peasants, supplying local needs as craftsmen, and serving as estate managers. Jews prospered with the growth of grain and timber exports to the West, acting as agents in organizing this trade. They also played an important role as moneylenders. By the end of the seventeenth century, Polish Jews numbered some 450,000, or about 4.5 percent of Poland's population and 75 percent of Jews worldwide.

Whether they lived in towns or the countryside, Jews were governed by local councils made up of prominent community members, who often dressed and acted like non-Jews. Like the Christian population, Jewish communities were hierarchically organized. At the top were a few rich and socially prominent people as well as rabbis and Talmudic scholars. Below them were craftsmen, peddlers, and shopkeepers. Lower still were the poor.

Most Polish Jews were separated from the larger Christian population not only by religion but also by culture. Like the Arabic-speaking Moriscos of Spain, they spoke their own distinctive language, Yiddish. Aware of their minority position, the Jews worked hard to maintain a strong sense of community solidarity that fostered a distinctive Jewish identity. At times, however, internal tensions threatened to fracture the community, as when rich Jews adopted non-Jewish ways or well-to-do moneylenders seized land and other collateral from fellow Jews who defaulted on loans.

Beginning in the mid-sixteenth century, Jews started to return to western Europe. The largest Jewish community in the West, Rome excepted, was in Bohemia, where the Habsburgs encouraged Jewish settlement and used Jews as bankers and moneylenders. Bohemian nobles also courted Jews, who served as estate managers like their counterparts in Poland. Even Emperor Ferdinand II welcomed them, despite his determination to eliminate dissident Protestants. In his eyes, heretics were a greater danger to the Christian community than unbelievers. Throughout the Thirty Years' War, both the Habsburgs and the Swedes turned to the Bohemian Jews for the funds they needed to continue fighting.

The Dutch Republic also welcomed Jews. Both Ashkenazim, from Poland and Germany, and Sephardim, from Spain and Portugal, congregated in Amsterdam. Overall, some 18,000 Jews settled in the Dutch Republic. Although this community was smaller than the ones in Poland and Bohemia, it played a crucial role in the booming Dutch economy. Its original members were Sephardim who had economic ties to merchants in the Iberian Peninsula, the Spanish Empire, and Brazil. The Dutch West India Company exploited these contacts to develop trade with Spain and to push into the profitable trade with the New World. Some 4,000 Portuguese Jews eventually settled in the Dutch colonies.

France and England also permitted new Jewish settlements. French kings permitted expelled Portuguese Jews to settle in some cities as part of their struggle with Habsburg Spain. In England, Oliver Cromwell fostered a growing Jewish community in London. Like many Protestants, Cromwell believed that the conversion of the Jews to Christianity, along with the destruction of the Antichrist (that is, the pope), would usher in the Second Coming of Christ. He, therefore, welcomed the visit of an Amsterdam rabbi who came to London seeking formal recognition of a Jewish community there.

The rabbi also had a religious agenda; for him, Jews had to settle in all parts of the world as a prelude to the coming of the Jewish Messiah. Although formal recognition of an English Jewish community was not forthcoming, as merchants and clergy resisted, Jews were allowed unofficially to settle in London and engage in trade.

15-5b War in Poland

In 1648, the year of the Peace of Westphalia, war broke out in Poland-Lithuania when **Cossacks**, warriors protecting lands bordering on Muslim territory, rebelled in Ukraine. The rebellion was provoked in part by a decision to reduce the number of Cossacks in the Polish army and in part by religious clashes—the Polish Cossacks were Russian Orthodox, and the kings of Poland were Roman Catholics. Catholic-Orthodox tensions were particularly high in the seventeenth century after the **Union of Brest-Litovsk**, which united Orthodox bishops in Polish Ukraine with the Roman Catholic Church, despite Orthodox Christian opposition.

The Cossack revolt of 1648 inaugurated nineteen years of warfare. Like the Thirty Years' War, it started as a local dispute but was soon internationalized when both Sweden and Russia joined in. In 1655, Sweden, fresh from territorial gains during the Thirty Years' War, hoped to amass more lands on the Baltic's southern shore. The Russian tsar also used the war for territorial gain. The Swedes withdrew in 1660 after receiving territory from the king of Denmark, with whom they were also at war. The Russians signed a peace treaty in 1667 that gave them the eastern half of Ukraine.

The devastation caused by two decades of warfare was immense. The Polish economy was disrupted, and food shortages occurred, followed by periods of famine. Predictably, armies of all sides spread disease, and epidemics ravaged a population already weakened by disruptions in the food supply. At the beginning of the war, the Cossacks slaughtered Catholics, Jews, and signers of the Union of Brest-Litovsk indiscriminately. These atrocities matched the worst incidents during the French Wars of Religion. Like the French slaughters, those in Poland were intended to ritually degrade the bodies of a socially polluting enemy. Eventually, all warring sides committed atrocities, and all Poles were victims of them, but Polish Jews suffered disproportionately. The lucky ones fled to Jewish communities in western Europe. Others fled south into Muslim lands, where they were enslaved and then sold in Constantinople. In all, some forty to fifty thousand Jews, a quarter of Poland's Jewish population, perished in the war. Faced with this calamity, many Jews looked for a decisive divine intervention on behalf of the Chosen People of Israel.

Cossacks Warriors organized locally to protect frontier lands bordering on Muslim territory; also used by Polish kings and Russian tsars as fighting forces.

Union of Brest-Litovsk Agreement in 1596 uniting Orthodox bishops in Polish Ukraine with the Roman Catholic Church.

Sabbatai Sevi (1626–1670) Jew from Smyrna of Sephardic ancestry who proclaimed he was the Messiah.

Lurianic kabbalah, an intensely mystical and ecstatic form of kabbalah taught in the sixteenth century by Isaac Luria (1534–1572).

CONNECTIONS: For a discussion of the conditions of Jewish life in the West during the Middle Ages, see Section 11-5d Jews Under Christian and Ottoman Rule.

15-5c Sabbatai Sevi

In some Jewish circles, 1648 was widely held to be the year in which the Jewish Messiah would appear to gather the exiled children of the Covenant, lead them into the land of Israel, and rebuild the Temple in Jerusalem. The greeting "Next year in Jerusalem!" gave voice to this longing for restoration, which grew more intense after the expulsions from Spain and Portugal and the slaughters in Poland. But the Messiah did not appear. Then, in 1665, a twenty-nine-year-old Jew, **Sabbatai Sevi** (SA-bah-tie SAY-vee), proclaimed that he was the Messiah.

Sevi grew up in Smyrna (Izmir), a commercial center on the western coast of Turkey. From an early age, he excelled in Jewish religious studies. Before Sevi claimed to be the Messiah, he had wandered around the Ottoman Empire from Greece to Egypt. He experienced dramatic shifts in his mental state, ranging from deep depression to frenzied exaltation. He also fell into religious ecstasies that some believed revealed his Messianic status. Although it has been speculated that Sevi suffered from bipolar disorder, there were also historical reasons for his intense spiritual experiences, since they were at the heart of the Jewish mystical tradition centered on the kabbalah that Spanish Jews had developed during the late Middle Ages. In Sevi's case, the version of kabbalah he embraced was a particularly emotion-laden and ecstatic one. Known as **Lurianic kabbalah**, it had been taught by Isaac Luria, a Jew living in the Galilee region of the present-day state of Israel. Its mystical emphasis on union with the Divine influenced a number of movements in early modern Judaism.

In 1665, after his return to Smyrna, Sevi openly proclaimed that he was the Messiah and started to gather followers. He dressed in royal robes and ordered changes in Jewish worship, turning fast days into feasts and altering synagogue services as signs of the dawning End Time of Jewish restoration. In the past, other men had claimed to be the Messiah, but none attracted the following that Sevi gained. News of him spread quickly along trade routes. Soon Jews in the Ottoman Empire and Europe were performing the penitential acts prescribed for the time of the Messiah's arrival and saying prayers for Sevi in their worship. People said that Sevi was about to seize the sultan's crown or that he performed miraculous cures. In their own way, these proclamations were like contemporary Christians' belief in the Second Coming. Both Jews and Christians shared a hope for a decisive divine event that would right all wrongs and usher in a golden age of peace and prosperity. The economic hard times after 1550, along with a seemingly endless cycle of war, slaughter, and religious conflict, heightened these expectations in both

Culture Club / Contributor/Getty Images

communities. In the Jewish world, Sevi's messianic claims raised a fever pitch of excitement; nothing quite like it had happened for many centuries.

Sabbatai Sevi Portrayed as Messiah

In the upper part of this engraving, Sabbatai Sevi is enthroned as the Messiah. The Hebrew inscription above his head reads "The Crown of Sabbatai." Below him is an inscription from the prophet Jeremiah, "I will cause to sprout for David the root of righteousness." In the bottom panel the tribes of Israel study Torah under the Messiah's guidance.

In 1666, Sevi set out for Constantinople. Before he arrived, the Turks arrested him for disturbing the peace and jailed him. His followers were allowed to visit, and he continued to act as the Messiah and even signed his letters, "I am your God Sabbatai Sevi." In September, Sevi was brought before the sultan and threatened with execution. He then converted to Islam, and the sultan named him Mehmet Efendi, gave him a pension, and appointed him a doorkeeper in the sultan's palace. He died ten years later.

As news of Sevi's apostasy spread, shocked congregations throughout the Ottoman Empire and Europe erased his name from their records. From the beginning, many Jews had doubted Sevi's claims and had been appalled at his self-deification. A few, however, continued to believe that Sevi was the Messiah. His conversion was part of his Messianic strategy, they thought, by which he burrowed like a worm into Islam with the aim of destroying it from the inside out. Some of his followers also converted to Islam and established communities that lasted into the twentieth century.

The furor over Sabbatai Sevi marked a turning point in Jewish history. Following his apostasy, any claim of Messiahship was severely scrutinized. Forms of Judaism that emphasized present faithfulness to the law and focused less on the mystery of the Messiah's future appearance gained ground. Nevertheless, the traditions of Lurianic kabbalah that had inspired Sevi continued to serve as a rich matrix for future mystical movements in Judaism.

CHAPTER Review

Summary

» After 1550, the European economy turned downward. A price revolution aggravated an economic crisis brought on by overpopulation.

» Hard times produced widespread anxiety, which in turn led to social unrest, fears that the world was coming to an end, and panic about witches.

» For the next century, religious strife tore Europe apart.

» In Spain, Philip II undertook aggressive campaigns against Muslims and Protestants. He defeated his Morisco subjects in Spain and fought the Turks at sea. He also opposed the Protestant movement in

England and fought his own Protestant subjects in the Netherlands.

» When Philip II died in 1598, Protestantism had survived, and Spain's military might was in decline.

» The Netherlands were split in half, and the economically prosperous Protestant provinces of the north were virtually independent from Spanish rule.

» England under Elizabeth I was Protestant and prepared to challenge Spain on the seas and in the New World.

» Henry IV of France had granted religious toleration, along with a good deal of political autonomy, to the Huguenots, but he had also strengthened the French monarchy.

» Warfare continued throughout the first half of the seventeenth century.

» Europeans believed that religious unity was essential for the well-being of the community, but renewed warfare failed to reestablish the unity lost in the sixteenth century.

» Louis XIII defeated the Huguenots and stripped them of their political autonomy, although they still had the right to worship.

» In Germany, the Thirty Years' War failed to curb Protestantism in the Holy Roman Empire, and the emperor's power was greatly weakened.

» When the war ended, German princes now had a third religious option for their states: Calvinism, Lutheranism, and Catholicism.

» In England, Anglicans and Puritans fought each other in a civil war that ended in the execution of Charles I, the dismantling of the Anglican Church, and the establishment of a commonwealth.

» In 1660, monarchy and Anglicanism were restored.

» All English Protestants agreed that the Catholic Irish must be conquered.

» The creation of the Ulster colony and Cromwell's campaign in Ireland established England's dominance of the island. By 1660, it was clear that the religious unity of western and central Europe was shattered.

» Europe's Jews were allowed once again to settle in the West, where some benefited from the global trading networks established in the sixteenth century. But Jews were still often despised and sometimes suffered catastrophic losses, like the ones occurring in Poland after the Cossack rebellion of 1648.

» Many Jews, like many Christians, hoped for divine deliverance from the troubled times, and some turned to the self-proclaimed Messiah, Sabbatai Sevi.

Chronology

1540s	Spain's silver mines in the Americas open [Americas]
1555	Peace of Augsburg allows Lutheranism [Europe]
1556	Philip II becomes king of Spain [Europe] Ferdinand I becomes Holy Roman emperor [Europe]
1558	Elizabeth I becomes queen of England [Europe]
1559	Francis II becomes king of France [Europe]
1562	French Wars of Religion begin [Europe]
1564	Maximilian II becomes Holy Roman emperor [Europe] Scotland makes witchcraft a crime punishable by death [Europe]
1566	Calvinists rebel in the Netherlands [Europe]
1571	Spain defeats Turkish navy at Battle of Lepanto [Europe, Middle East]
1572	French Catholics attack Protestants in Saint Bartholomew's Day Massacre [Europe]
1588	Spanish Armada attacks England [Europe]
1589	Henry IV becomes king of France [Europe]
1598	Edict of Nantes grants religious toleration to Huguenots [Europe]

1603	James VI of Scotland becomes James I of England and Ireland [Europe]
	Beginning of the Tokugawa Shogunate in Japan (1603–1867) [Asia]
1610	Louis XIII becomes king of France [Europe]
1618	Thirty Years' War begins [Europe]
1625	Charles I becomes king of Scotland, England, and Ireland [Europe]
1629	Peace of Alès ends French Wars of Religion [Europe]
1642	English civil war begins [Europe]
1643	Louis XIV becomes king of France [Europe]
1644	Beginning of the Manchu (Qing) Dynasty of Emperors in China (through 1799) [Asia]
1648	Peace of Westphalia ends Thirty Years' War [Europe]
1649	England becomes a republic [Europe]
1659	France and Spain sign Treaty of the Pyrenees [Europe]
1660	Monarchy is restored in the British Isles [Europe]
1667	War ends in Poland [Europe]

Critical Thinking Questions

Take a moment to pull together all the important information from the chapter by answering the following questions:

Europe's Economy and Society

» What effects did the rise in the silver supply have in the sixteenth-century European economy?

» What caused Europe's witchcraft hunt, and why did it eventually decline?

The Fate of Spain and the Flourishing of the Netherlands

» What train of events led to the disappearance of the cultural and religious pluralism that had characterized the Iberian Peninsula in the Middle Ages?

» What made the Dutch trading network truly global?

Political Contests and More Religious Wars

» What made the Thirty Years' War the most devastating conflict of the seventeenth century?

» Compare and contrast the motivations for European warfare before and after the signing of the Peace of Westphalia.

Reformation and Revolution in the British Isles

» What were the constitutional issues dividing the king and Parliament during the reigns of James I and Charles I?

» What were the lasting legacies of the English civil war, the execution of the king, and the establishment of the Commonwealth?

Christian Reform, Religious Wars, and the Jews

» How did Jews in Poland-Lithuania foster a sense of a distinctive Jewish community and a distinctive Jewish identity?

» Where were Jews found in the Dutch Republic's overseas empire, and what role did they play in it?

MindTap® is a fully online personalized learning experience built upon Cengage Learning content. MindTap® combines student learning tools—readings, multimedia, activities, and assessments—into a singular Learning Path that guides students through the course and helps students develop the critical thinking, analysis, and communication skills that are essential to academic and professional success.

State-Building and the European State System, 1648–1789

Chapter Outline

As you read, consider the following questions:

❭ How did governments try to establish good working relations with the people?

❭ What effect did state-building have on the various religious communities of Europe?

❭ What factors worked to develop or retard a collective sense of national identity?

View of the Chateau and Gardens of Versailles
This modern-day photograph of Versailles shows the enduring attraction for visitors of the palace and its grounds. Louis XIV would have loved it.   Photononstop / Photononstop / Superstock

Louis XIV was one of the most successful rulers in the years after the Peace of Westphalia and the very embodiment of absolutism—a style of monarchy that spread across Europe in the seventeenth and eighteenth centuries. Royal absolutism was a way to build the power and effectiveness of the central state. A century of religious warfare had taught Louis and other absolutist rulers that only a strong central government, coupled with a policy of either tolerating or crushing religious dissent, could bring political stability. Rulers promoted absolutist agendas with laws enforced in state courts and also with images that proclaimed the power of the centralized state embodied in the monarch. Louis XIV of France's palace at Versailles, shown here, is a famous example of how landscaping and architecture could also be recruited to announce the grandeur of the central state embodied in the person of the king.

Although wars continued to be fought after 1648, religiously motivated warfare declined. Increasingly, the roots of conflict focused on issues of territorial expansion, power, and prestige. By the mid-eighteenth century, European warfare had also taken on global dimensions as states fought each other for control of overseas empires.

To meet the challenges of European and global warfare, rulers increased the size of their armies and brought them under tight state control. Absolute monarchs saw war as a means to enlarge their territories and, simultaneously, to deny the territorial ambitions of other states. In their eyes, Europe, and then the world, was like a chessboard on which each state's diplomatic and military moves were met with countermoves from other states.

But war and territorial gains were expensive, and throughout the century after the Peace of Westphalia, states increased taxes, tried to collect them more efficiently, and sought to improve their economies to increase their tax base.

All over Europe, the needs of almost continual warfare drove expansion in state administration and improvements in financial and judicial bureaucracies. State authority aimed to direct economies and to reach more aspects of people's lives. Key to these expansions was the creation of officials accountable to the Crown. In western Europe, loyal middle-class people were recruited into these bureaucracies, while in eastern Europe monarchs drew their officials from the ranks of the lesser nobility.

The goodwill of the public in general was also essential, as was the allegiance of the nobles in particular because they constituted the political and social elite. Some states also tried to increase services to their subjects, such as infrastructure improvement and better policing of town and country.

On the European continent, states tended to develop along the absolutist model pioneered by Louis XIV in France. In Britain, however, the rebellion and revolution of the mid-seventeenth century ended the absolutist ambitions of the early Stuart kings. After 1660, their successors ruled with Parliament in a constitutionally limited monarchy. The joint rule of king and Parliament ensured a high degree of political stability and proved important to Britain's success in empire building, trade, and manufacturing.

In some parts of Europe, warfare and state-building fostered a strong sense of national identity as people embraced the policy perspectives of their rulers and defined themselves as the opposite of their enemies. In other European states, however, the religious and ethnic roots of collective identity were so strong that a common sense of community centered on the state failed to emerge.

16-1 Absolutism in France, 1648–1740

» **What were the characteristic features of French royal absolutism?**

» **What were the outcomes of the French monarchy's attempts to strengthen the state?**

Louis XIV of France dominated Europe in the second half of the seventeenth century. After assuming personal rule (see Profiles in Change: Louis XIV Decides to Rule France on His Own), he launched wars that added to France's territory. He also continued the policy of stamping out Protestantism in his kingdom,

Louis XIV (r. 1638–1715) King of France and the most powerful ruler in Europe during the second half of the seventeenth century.

tarnishing his image in Protestant Europe. Eventually, continual warfare drained his treasury and forced him to reorganize the French state. His successor built on Louis's successes, expanding state activity in several new directions (see Map 16.1). But France was also rocked by a new religious crisis, which pitted the state against a dissident Catholic movement.

16-1a The Sun King at Versailles

Since 1500, Europe's royal courts had grown in size. In the 1520s, the French court had just over five hundred members. **Louis XIV**'s court had 10,000, half of them nobles. For the nobles, closeness to the king brought honor, appointments in the royal army, and pensions. Since nobles had a prickly sense of self-worth, a tradition of military service, and extravagant lifestyles that strained their purses, Louis's attentions were highly prized. Thus, nobles flocked to the king's court, and, as he established a working relationship with this

Map 16.1) Europe in 1715 In 1715, when Louis XIV died, France was still the dominant power in Europe. But other centers of power—the Austrian Habsburg lands, Great Britain, Russia, and a small newcomer, Prussia—were prepared to challenge France.

1. Looking only at this map, try to figure out how the possible territorial ambitions of the Austrian Habsburgs, the Russians, and the Prussians, might affect the goal of maintaining a European-wide balance of power.

2. Compare the eastern boundary of Sweden and the western boundary of Russia as shown on Map 15.1 in Chapter 15 to the boundaries of these two states in 1715. Which was the gainer and which the loser? What advantages came to the winner?

3. Compare the boundary of the Austrian Habsburg lands as shown on Map 15.1 in Chapter 15 with the boundary shown on this map.

Louis XIV Decides to Rule France on His Own

On March 9, 1661, France's prime minister, Cardinal Jules Mazarin, wracked by gout, kidney stones, and fluid in his chest cavity, died. When news of Mazarin's death was announced, the royal court was abuzz with rumors about who would be next in line for the position. Within hours of Mazarin's death, King Louis XIV made his choice: himself. Standing before the highest officials in the kingdom, he announced: "Up to this moment I have been pleased to entrust the government of my affairs to the late Cardinal. It is now time that I govern them myself. [Monsieur the Chancellor], you will assist me with your counsels when I ask for them. . . . I request and order you to seal no orders except by my command. And you, . . . my secretaries of state, I order you not to sign anything, not even a passport . . . without my command."

Courtiers were astonished by Louis's announcement. The twenty-three-year-old seemed more interested in dancing the role of the god Apollo in court ballets and engaging in sexual escapades with young ladies-in-waiting than in sitting at his desk and shuffling through reports on wool weaving in this province or sheep farming in that one. Besides, Louis's announcement that he would rule by himself broke with family tradition. Both his father and grandfather had relied on strong prime ministers to help them with the affairs of state, and since 1643, Cardinal Mazarin had guided France skillfully through the last years of the Thirty Years' War. In the 1640s, France seethed with unrest as taxes rose to pay for the war and great nobles rebelled against Mazarin's policies. There was fearful talk that France—like England—would slip into a civil war. Would

monarchy be attacked in France? Would the French king be executed like Charles I? Would the French Calvinists, tolerated but no longer politically independent, rise up like the Puritans and declare a republic? Mazarin had played on these fears of chaos and bloodshed in order to keep the monarchy safe.

By 1653, calm was restored, and the fourteen-year-old Louis XIV's throne was secure. Louis believed that Mazarin had saved the monarchy, and his devotion to his prime minister knew no bounds. For the rest of his life, Mazarin continued to advise the king on policy and even chose his companions, dismissing young men he thought unfit for association with Louis. Mazarin also amassed the largest personal fortune ever known under the monarchy. On his deathbed, he gave it to the king.

Given Mazarin's role in guiding the French monarchy through tumultuous times and the seeming frivolity of the young Louis, it is no wonder that courtiers looked askance at the young king's surprising decision to rule on his own. In the end, however, Louis fooled them all. For the next fifty-four years, until his death in 1715, he refused to appoint a prime minister and directed the affairs of state himself. The discipline, endurance, and stamina this "bureaucrat king" showed in running the government became legendary. Both the successes and the failures of his very long reign rested on his determination to control all the affairs of state.

Source: Louis XIV by John B. Wolf, p. 134. Copyright © 1968 by W. W. Norton & Company, Inc. Used by permission of W. W. Norton & Company, Inc.

Louis XIV of France

This painting by Henri Testelin shows Louis XIV presiding over the opening of the French Academy of Sciences and the Observatory in Paris. Here the king, in the center of the canvas, is receiving members of the Academy while members of the royal court look on.

» *Can you identify one or two things that set the king apart from everyone else in the room?*

powerful elite, Louis was also able to keep his eye on them.

Life at Court At court, the entire day focused attention on the king. From his rising to his bedtime, great nobles attended him. At midday, Louis ate alone while courtiers stood and watched. The dinner table etiquette was so complicated that it took three men seven minutes to give the king a glass of wine. Louis believed that he ruled by **divine right** because God had decreed monarchy to be the correct form for France's government and had called Louis to the throne as the eldest legitimately born son of his father.

The elaborate court rituals proclaimed that Louis, as an absolute monarch, was the only real political player in France. He alone made policy and laid down the law. He was also the only person who unified the different regions and peoples of France because he alone ruled over them all.

Louis was also the perfect gentleman, famous for his politeness and beautiful manners. Courtiers commented that they rarely saw him lose his temper. If someone misbehaved, a simple look or short comment was enough to convey his displeasure. Like court etiquette, the king's gentlemanly behavior had a political purpose; it reinforced a new trend in noble society that emphasized polite speech and good manners as necessary qualities for the highborn and powerful. Encouraged by noblewomen in Paris, who presided over **salons** in which this conduct was required, the new emphasis on manners disciplined the often violent and crude behavior of nobles.

The setting for Louis's court was **Versailles** (ver-SAI), originally a hunting lodge for Louis XIII. Throughout his reign, the king worked to turn his father's modest building into Europe's most magnificent palace. He laid out acres of grounds decorated with lavish fountains. Louis adopted the sun god Apollo as Versailles' symbol and symbolically identified himself with Apollo as the "Sun King," spreading radiance on his lands and subjects. At Versailles, an entire town sprang up to meet the needs of courtiers and their thousands of servants. The palace itself was the centerpiece in a carefully orchestrated propaganda campaign designed to celebrate the king's *gloire* (glowhar)—that is, his glory or renown—in architecture, painting, sculpture, and other artistic media. Above all, Louis's gloire rose when he led his troops into battle and fought other kings for territory, honor, and prestige.

16-1b Forty Years of Warfare

The early years of Louis's reign were marked by peace at home and victory abroad. But after 1668, the king, increasingly worried about the weakness of France's eastern border, launched a series of wars. The greatest of these campaigns was the **Dutch War**. Resenting the "maggots" who dominated European trade and shipping, in 1672, Louis ordered his generals to invade.

Louis Versus the Dutch Faced with French invasion, the Dutch **stadholder**, **William**, broke the dikes that protected his low-lying country and flooded it, as the government had against the Spanish in 1579. The strategy obviously caused much hardship for the Dutch, but it also bogged down the French. In the end, neither side could defeat the other, and a peace was signed in 1679. The chief consequence of the war was to alienate William, who was now dedicated to the defeat of France.

To further challenge Dutch economic predominance, Louis's financial minister, **Jean-Baptiste Colbert** (JAHN-bap-TEEST colbair), developed a strategy for increasing France's national wealth. Known as **mercantilism**, it regulated economic policy for France's benefit. Consumers were encouraged to "buy French," and the state supported porcelain manufacturers capable of competing with imports from Asia. Monopolies were given to trading companies that would challenge the Dutch in overseas markets.

French Colonies To strengthen the French economy, colonies were encouraged to grow. The population of Canada, known for its exports of furs and fish, rose from

divine right Theory that kings were called by God to rule and that opposition to the king was therefore opposition to God.

salons Meetings in great Parisian homes presided over by wellborn women who set the style for discussions of literature, science, and other matters of current interest.

Versailles Louis XIV's palace near Paris begun in the 1660s and housing the king after 1683.

Dutch War France's 1672–1678 invasion of the Netherlands aimed at breaking Dutch control of international trade and shipping.

stadholder Chief executive in the Dutch Republic.

William Stadholder of the Dutch Republic (1672–1702) who later became king of England as William III (r. 1689–1702).

Jean-Baptiste Colbert (1619–1683) Louis XIV's financial minister who implemented French mercantilist policies.

mercantilism State-initiated economic policy encouraging exports, discouraging imports, and stimulating domestic industries.

3,000 to 25,000, and the French founded settlements on the Gulf of Mexico at Mobile and New Orleans. These colonies secured the French in the North American heartland watered by the Mississippi and Ohio Rivers. **Saint-Domingue** and other colonies in the Caribbean specialized in cash crops, first tobacco and then sugar. Colbert's mercantilism established a new goal for the monarchy—the development of a national economic policy.

The War of the League of Augsburg The mid-1680s brought a downturn in Louis's fortunes. In 1683, Louis refused to declare war on the Turks when they besieged Vienna. His decision was in line with France's traditional anti-Habsburg policy, but his refusal to help a Christian state attacked by Muslims scandalized many Europeans. Then, in 1689, Louis again went to war on France's eastern frontier, this time against Austria, a war that was quickly joined by the Dutch. The **War of the League of Augsburg** lasted until 1697. Louis, who had the largest army in Europe, strengthened the eastern frontier by conquering the province of Alsace and the city of Strasbourg. But his finances were exhausted. In 1693, crop failures, caused by a drop in average yearly temperatures during the Little Ice Age, led to a terrible famine in which more than a million people perished from hunger and disease.

The War of the Spanish Succession Then, an even greater political crisis loomed—the succession to the Spanish throne. Spain was ruled by Charles II, who was childless. On his death, the vast Spanish possessions would have to pass either to the Austrian Habsburgs or to the French Bourbons, and both had claims to the Crown. Although on his death in 1701, Charles had willed his lands to the Bourbons (Louis XIV's grandson, Philip), the Austrian Habsburgs disputed the will and went to war.

This **War of the Spanish Succession** was the most devastating one Louis ever fought. At war's end, Philip remained king of Spain and its empire, but the **Treaty of Utrecht** stipulated that France and Spain could not be united as a single state. The Austrians received northern and southern Italy, along with the Spanish (now the Austrian) Netherlands.

Louis's many wars had increased the size of France by 12 percent and strengthened its eastern borders, now protected with state-of-the-art fortifications. But they had left a bitter legacy. In 1713, France was virtually bankrupt and the economy in a shambles. Moreover, other European states, especially the Dutch Republic and Britain, feared that the Sun King was trying to upset the balance of power, which aimed to prevent any one state from establishing permanent military dominance in Europe.

16-1c A Unified French State

Within France, however, the wars had a unifying effect. Continuous warfare after 1688 had led Louis to search desperately for new revenue, and he sold waves of new offices. Then, in 1695, he took the unprecedented step of imposing a tax, the **capitation**, on all his subjects without exception.

The Intendants and the Parlements To supervise the collection of these taxes, Louis relied on his **intendants**, chief local royal administrators appointed on the basis of their ability and loyalty to the Crown. The intendants also gathered information about local conditions for the central government, and their reports allowed the king and his ministers to be better informed about the state of the economy. The result was better policy making.

Thus, in his later years Louis was able to transform the French state. He reduced the power of the royal courts, known as **parlements**, which were now forbidden to criticize royal edicts. But their members were guaranteed their right to hold office and encouraged to enforce the law. As royal administration became more efficient, relations between the king and his subjects improved. Well-run parlements appealed to the king's subjects, who increasingly used them instead of church or landlords' courts, believing that they offered fairer rulings.

Taxes and the Army Although taxation was still resented, the better-organized collection of taxes, along with a continuing shift to indirect taxation on items like paper and tobacco, took some of the sting out of payment. Even the royal armies were appreciated. During the religious wars earlier in the century, royal troops had been hated because of their violence and unruliness, but Louis's army, though huge, was well disciplined. His troops were now seen as protectors, welcomed by civilians and local vendors who supplied their needs. Under Louis, the French government functioned more fairly and efficiently.

Curbing the Nobles, Defending Catholicism The unity of France was important to Louis. As a child, he

---

Saint-Domingue (sant-do-MING) Sugar-producing French island colony in the Caribbean.

War of the League of Augsburg (1689–1697) First of Louis XIV's two great wars fought against Austria, England, and the Dutch Republic.

War of the Spanish Succession (1701–1713) Louis XIV's last great war, with France and Spain allied against the Austrians, Dutch, and English.

Treaty of Utrecht (YEW-trecht) Treaty signed in 1713 between France and the states fighting France that ended the War of the Spanish Succession.

capitation Royal tax imposed on all French subjects in 1695 that introduced the idea of taxation of all people in defense of the state.

intendants In the second half of Louis XIV's reign, the most important local royal administrators, appointed by the king.

parlements France's highest royal courts, which enforced the king's edicts.

had to flee Paris twice for his safety during a noble revolt against royal rule known as the **Fronde** (frond). When he assumed personal rule of France, he was determined to prevent a similar rebellion. His policy of coaxing the most powerful nobles to his court with promises of honors, careers, and money was designed to tie them closely to the fortunes of the Crown.

Louis also sought to secure religious unity in France, believing the kingdom should have "one king, one law, one faith." In Louis's mind, the French Huguenots were potentially rebellious, so in 1685, he revoked the Edict of Nantes, thereby ending the limited religious toleration Louis's grandfather had granted. Huguenots who failed to convert to Catholicism were forced to flee. Around 300,000, many of them middle-class merchants, left for the Dutch Republic, England, and America, spreading tales of the king's brutality.

The Huguenot exodus cost France dearly because it deprived the kingdom of a commercially skilled group just as the Anglo-French struggle for global commerce was beginning. Those still in France were subject to the quartering of troops in their houses, and in the mountainous south, where many Protestant peasants lived, royal troops burned hundreds of villages. In retaliation, peasants carried on a **guerrilla war** against the royal army.

In Protestant Europe, news of the army's atrocities, coupled with exiles' grim accounts, produced a new image of Louis. The glorious Sun King was now a vicious tyrant. In France, however, most Catholics supported the king's policy. Louis's campaign against the Huguenots resulted not only from a belief that France should be religiously unified but also from fear that the Huguenots were secretly republicans, a charge that bedeviled them after English Calvinists declared a commonwealth in 1649.

Louis and the Pope Louis also quarreled with the pope by supporting the French clergy's adoption of the **Four Gallican Articles**, which proclaimed that church councils were superior to the pope and that the pope could not alter the way the French church was governed. The attack on the Huguenots was designed in part to heal the rupture with the pope. Relations with the papacy were further improved when Louis supported the pope's condemnation of the **Jansenists**, austere Catholics whose notions about human sinfulness struck some Catholics as too close to the views of John Calvin.

During a famine in 1709, Louis took the unprecedented step of issuing a letter directly asking his subjects for help. This appeal went against the principles of absolutism, in which the king was the only political player, but it was well received. As a result, king and subjects bonded in an effort to meet the crisis, and a new sense of collective identity was forged. Now, people started to think of themselves as part of a unified nation facing a common task.

Summing Up the Reign Louis XIV's regulation of religious affairs, his control of the French nobility, his efficient royal administration of tax and economic policies, and his establishment of better working relations with his subjects all promoted a growing sense of national unity, exemplifying French royal absolutism in action.

Yet, in 1715, seventy-seven years old and dying, Louis reflected on his failings. He told his five-year-old great-grandson and heir, **Louis XV**, "Try to remain at peace with your neighbors. I loved war too much. Do not follow me in that or in overspending." (See Learning from a Primary Source: Louis XIV Advises His Son, to read an excerpt of his memoirs intended for his son.)

16-1d Louis XV

After 1715, France avoided prolonged warfare. Capitalizing on peaceful times and a smoothly functioning state administration, Louis XV continued his great-grandfather's absolutist policy of expanding the state's activity in new directions; one was policing.

Strengthening the Police Traditionally, cities maintained rudimentary police forces, and the army was the real maintainer of public order. Under Louis XV, the army's policing role declined, and professional police forces were created. Paris saw the first changes. Its police force, which numbered 193 in 1700, grew to 725 by 1760. In the rest of the kingdom, about 3,000 men functioned as police. These forces were spread thinly over a population of 24 million, but they represented the beginning of a modern, professional police network.

Poor Relief Another area of activity concerned poor relief. Increasingly, the state assumed care of poor children and the elderly, who were housed, clothed, and fed in urban "hospitals." Life in the hospitals was strict; attendance at morning and evening prayers was obligatory, and the able-bodied were forced to work. Some historians argue that the new state program aimed to isolate the socially undesirable from society at large, whereas others see it as the beginning of a modern state-sponsored welfare system.

The Jansenist Problem In religious policy, however, Louis XV struggled, as the problem of the Jansenists remained. While his

---

Fronde (1648–1653) Rebellion of the French nobles against Cardinal Mazarin and the regent, Queen Anne, during Louis's early years as king.

guerrilla war An undeclared, irregularly fought war.

Four Gallican Articles Decrees of 1681 proclaiming church councils superior to the pope and denying Rome's power to alter internal rules governing the French church.

Jansenists Austere Catholic reformers who were accused of holding views about human sin similar to the Protestant John Calvin and were condemned by the pope.

Louis XV (r. 1715–1774) Louis XIV's five-year-old great-grandson who became king on Louis XIV's death.

Louis XIV Advises His Son

In 1666, Louis XIV assembled a team of collaborators to help him write his memoirs, which were intended for his young son, another Louis, when he became king. Such memoirs were common in early modern Europe. Charles V had written one for Philip II, and Cardinal **Richelieu** (REECH-eh-lew) had composed one for Louis XIII. Although Louis's son died before the king and, therefore, could never follow his father's advice, the memoirs reveal the preoccupations and principles of Louis XIV some five years after he became his own prime minister.

1 What do these remarks say about Louis's understanding of his relationship with his subjects?

2 Why would Louis argue that the happiness and tranquility of France depended on the union of authority in the king?

3 Why would the king be concerned that a division of political authority would lead to the "greatest misfortunes?"

4 What do these remarks tell you about the king's personality?

1 My son, many very important considerations caused me to resolve to leave you, at the cost of much labor in the midst of my most important duties, these memoirs of my reign and principal acts. . . . I even hoped that in this way I might be the most valuable person in the world to you and consequently to my subjects. For no one with more talent and experience has ever reigned in France, and I do not hesitate to say to you that the higher one's position, the more it has qualities that no one may perceive or understand without occupying it. . . .

2 For it is generally agreed that nothing preserves the happiness and tranquility of the provinces with greater certainty than the perfect union of all authority in the person of the sovereign. **3** The slightest division of authority always produces the greatest misfortunes, and whether the alienated portion falls into the hands of individuals or groups, it cannot remain there except in a state of violence. . . .

4 As for the work of [governing], my son, . . . I imposed upon myself the rule to labor twice daily. I cannot tell you what benefit I received immediately after making this resolution. I felt elevated in spirit and courage, a changed man, discovering in myself unknown resources and joyfully reproaching myself for having ignored them for so long. . . . I now seemed to be king and born to be so. As for those who were to assist me in my work, I resolved above all else not to appoint a first minister. . . . For in order to unite in myself all sovereign authority, I resolved after I had chosen my ministers to call upon them when they least expected it, even though their duties might involve

government continued its predecessor's condemnation of the Jansenists, the Parlement of Paris, following the Four Gallican Articles, declared that the pope was illegally intruding into the French church's affairs. The conflict was intense because in 1715 the Duke of Orléans, the regent for the new child king, had once again permitted the parlements to criticize royal policy. By 1730, the Parlement of Paris was openly defying Louis on the Jansenist issue and challenging the absolutist principle that the king alone made law.

Neither side could silence the other, and it now seemed that Louis XV could no longer keep religious peace in the kingdom. Despite this failure, however, absolutism in France had brought the state into new areas of people's lives and made the state more demanding, as well as more responsive, than ever before.

CONNECTIONS: Louis XIV's and Louis XV's expansion of the power of the state and the expansion of government's role in shaping people's lives continued in the West long after their reigns had ended. (See, for example, Section 22-3 The Expanding Role of the State.)

16-2 The Austrian Habsburgs, 1648–1740

>> How was the Austrian Habsburg form of absolutist kingship similar to and different from French royal absolutism?

>> What factors delayed the implementation of state-building in the Habsburg lands before 1740?

The Habsburg emperor Leopold, a lifelong rival of Louis XIV, successfully contained France's bid for dominance in European affairs, thus maintaining the balance of power. His reign, too, was marked by warfare. Positioned between the French in the west and the Turks in the east, Leopold often had to fight both at the same time.

❺ How did Louis's concern to promote the interest of the state shape his behavior toward others?

details to which my role and dignity would not ordinarily allow me to stoop, so as to convince them that I would follow the same procedure regarding other matters at any time. The knowledge that resulted from this small step, which I took but rarely and more for diversion than because of any principle, instructed me gradually without effort regarding a thousand things that were of value in making general decisions. . . .

❺ Kings are often obliged to do things contrary to their inclinations and good nature. They should enjoy giving pleasure, but they must frequently punish and ruin persons whose good they naturally desire. The interest of the state should take precedence. One should counter one's inclinations and not place oneself in position to regret mishandling something important because some individual's interest interfered and diverted attention from the aims that one should have for the grandeur, the good, and the power of the state. . . . The mistakes that I have made and have given me infinite pain have been caused by kindness or allowing myself to be too easily guided by others' advice. Nothing is as dangerous as weakness of any kind whatsoever.

Source: From *Louis XIV* by John B. Wolf. Copyright © 1968 by W. W. Norton & Company, Inc. Used by permission of W. W. Norton & Company, Inc.

Schönbrunn Palace and gardens, 1759-61 (oil on canvas), Bellotto, Bernardo (1720-80) / Kunsthistorisches Museum, Vienna, Austria / Bridgeman Images

Schönbrunn Palace

This eighteenth-century painting of the Habsburgs' palace of Schönbrunn shows the same marriage of architecture and landscaping that had been employed in the building of Versailles.

» *Compare this image with this chapter's opening image of Versailles. What strikes you as similar and different in the two palaces?*

Unlike France, warfare in the Habsburg lands did not accelerate a drive for unity in the state, and Austria was not remodeled along absolutist lines. Its reach was simply too great and its population too diverse—particularly after the reconquest of Hungary—to permit the perfect alignment of the king and the law that had been Louis XIV's aim.

16-2a Leopold I

In 1657, on the death of his elder brother from smallpox, the seventeen-year-old **Leopold I** unexpectedly became Holy Roman emperor and head of the Austrian Habsburgs. He had been destined for a career in the church, and at first he did not play the role of monarch very well. Throughout his, life he remained deeply religious. He married three times and had sixteen sons and daughters, only five of

whom outlived him. He was also withdrawn and bookish as well as an accomplished musician who composed many pieces performed at his court in Vienna.

Like most rulers of his day, Leopold was aware of the political implications of Louis XIV's Versailles and set out to rival him by building his own palace, **Schönbrunn** (SHOWN-brun), on the outskirts of Vienna. Plans to convert the building, which like Versailles had been a hunting lodge, were drawn up during his reign. They included an imposing residence of four hundred

Leopold I (r. 1657–1705) Head of the Austrian Habsburgs, emperor, ruler in Austria, king of Bohemia, and king of Hungary, which he reconquered from the Turks.

Schönbrunn (in German, "beautiful spring") Leopold I's palace on Vienna's outskirts, built on the model of Versailles.

rooms as well as gardens and fountains in the manner of Versailles.

16-2b The Turkish Siege of Vienna and the Reconquest of Hungary

In 1683, a Turkish army, under the leadership of the Ottoman **grand vizier**, Kara Mustafa, marched up the Danube River and besieged Vienna. Once again, Europe shuddered at the threat of Muslim conquests. Leopold, forced to flee the city, tried to rally support from Christian princes. Many responded, though not Louis XIV, for whom dynastic rivalry was more important than Christian solidarity. In September, after a savage two-month siege of the city, a united force, which had received the pope's blessing, defeated the Turks, and Kara Mustafa fled south.

Reconstructing Royal Rule in Hungary These events opened the way for the Habsburgs' reconquest of Hungary. By 1687, Leopold was master of most of the kingdom and the semi-independent principality of Transylvania. But Leopold did not trust the Hungarians. Earlier in his reign, some of their great nobles had rebelled against him, and others were Protestants. Hungarians were also culturally distinct, dressing in local costumes and speaking their own language—Magyar.

Turkish occupation and the war of reconquest had devastated the Hungarian countryside, and vast stretches of farmland lay unoccupied. To restore agriculture, and also to neutralize possible Hungarian rebellions, Leopold encouraged Serb, Bohemian, and German peasants to resettle the lands, promising them limited freedom from royal taxes and the obligations of serfdom. This resettlement complicated the religious situation in Hungary, where, for a century, Hungarians had been split over religion; along with Catholics, there were Calvinists, Lutherans, Unitarians, Eastern Orthodox, and Muslims. The resettlement also reduced the proportion of Hungarians. In 1526, they had constituted 85 percent of the kingdom's population; by 1700, they made up only 40 percent.

Renewed War and Peace in Hungary Peace in Europe during the 1680s had freed Leopold to concentrate on Hungary. When the War of the League of Augsburg with France broke out in 1689, he was forced to turn west once again. Then, with Habsburg troop strength reduced in the east, the Turks attempted to retake Hungary, only to be defeated again in 1690. Finally, just as war in the west was ending, in 1697 Leopold scored another smashing victory. At **Zenta**, 30,000 Turks were slaughtered before the sultan's eyes, for this time the sultan himself had accompanied the Turkish army into Hungary. In 1699, the **Treaty of Carlowitz** confirmed the Habsburg conquests. Although the Ottomans had lost Hungary, they continued to hold the Balkans and challenged the Russians in the northern Black Sea region.

The Rákóczi Rebellion During the War of the Spanish Succession, more trouble flared up in the east, this time a rebellion led by a Transylvanian prince, **Francis II Rákóczi (RAH-ko-zi)**. Rákóczi typified the touchy Hungarian noble resentful of Leopold's preference for Germans. His father, mother, and stepfather had all led rebellions against the Habsburgs, and he was determined to guarantee Hungary's traditional rights. By 1711, however, he had been defeated, as the Habsburgs were now able to rely on the enlarged non-Hungarian population of the kingdom for support. War and plague devastated the kingdom during the rebellion; almost a half million people perished. Rákóczi eventually sought protection from the sultan and died in exile in Turkey. The **Peace of Szatmár** (ZAHT-mar) (1711) united Hungary to the Habsburg lands through a common ruler.

16-2c The Habsburg Monarchy

The Habsburgs ruled over lands that were far more socially polarized than Louis XIV's France. At the top were the **magnates**, who were often fabulously rich. Visitors to the magnate Esterházys in Hungary could travel for days before they reached the end of their lands, passing through entire towns that were under the family's exclusive control.

Magnates and Serfs Magnate families were few in number, but their cooperation with the Habsburgs was essential for the smooth functioning of the government, and they dominated Habsburg administration at the central and local levels. Unlike in France, there were few independent cities and towns in the Habsburg lands. The vast majority of people, tied to the land as serfs, lived in the countryside.

Serfdom had expanded in the sixteenth and seventeenth centuries as eastern European landlords, all of whom were noble, successfully bound peasants to the soil as a labor force producing grain and timber for the western European market. During the dislocations of the Thirty Years' War, they also bound

---

grand vizier Chief minister of the Ottoman sultan.

Zenta Battle in 1697 in which the Habsburgs defeated the Turks and reconfirmed Habsburg conquests in Hungary.

Treaty of Carlowitz Treaty of 1699 between the Austrian Habsburgs and the Ottoman Turks confirming the Habsburg reconquest of Hungary.

Francis II Rákóczi (1676–1735) Prince of Transylvania who led the last major rebellion against the Habsburgs in Hungary.

Peace of Szatmár Treaty of 1711 uniting Hungary with the other Habsburg possessions through a common ruler.

magnates Politically powerful nobles in the Habsburg lands who owned vast agricultural estates worked by serfs.

them to the soil to prevent them from fleeing to more peaceful areas.

Landlords used their serfs to work their estates without compensation. Leopold tried to reduce uncompensated work to three days a week, but his success was limited because direct control of serfs lay with the landlord class, not the Habsburgs. Thus, Leopold's policy had to accommodate noble self-interest before it could become effective.

A Limited Central Government Because Leopold's direct rule over the mass of his subjects was very limited, he never established the kind of centralized, intrusive state that Louis XIV and Louis XV created. The Habsburg state was also characterized by a high degree of ethnic and religious diversity, particularly in Hungary. Habsburg rulers manipulated these groups to their own ends, with the result of enhancing the sense of difference between communities. Unlike in France, no sense of common identity emerged that spanned all the people of the Habsburg hereditary lands.

Leopold died in 1705, leaving two sons, Joseph I (r. 1705–1711) and Charles VI (r. 1711–1740), to rule. But Joseph died during the War of the Spanish Succession.

Charles VI Charles was now the sole surviving Austrian *and* Spanish Habsburg male. He was thus poised to inherit the Austrian territories along with Spain and its lands in the Netherlands, Italy, and America, thus reconstituting Charles V's empire. This was too much for the other European states, which feared that an Austrian Habsburg succession in Spain would upset the European balance of power. They, therefore, supported the division of lands between Habsburgs and Bourbons that was written into the Treaty of Utrecht ending the War of the Spanish Succession.

Warfare did not lead Charles to reform the Habsburg state, as it did in France. Instead, during his twenty-nine-year reign, he devoted his mediocre talents to two basic policies: making sure that his brother's daughters did not succeed him and that his own daughter did. The matter was complicated. The emperor had always been male, so Charles's daughter, **Maria Theresa**, could not follow him in that office. But she could succeed him as ruler of the family's hereditary lands.

The War of the Austrian Succession To this end, Charles coaxed the magnates into recognizing Maria Theresa's succession and then sought guarantees from the other European rulers that they, too, would recognize it. When Charles died in 1740, his careful plans exploded. In the **War of the Austrian Succession**, another new ruler, **Frederick II** of Prussia, attacked Maria Theresa during the opening phase of the two world wars that convulsed Europe in the mid-eighteenth century. The new war showed just how weak the Habsburgs had become.

16-3 The Rise of Prussia, 1648–1740

» **What factors accounted for Prussia's rise in power?**

» **What role did the army play in forging a collective Prussian identity?**

North of the Habsburg lands, another state emerged out of the chaos of the Thirty Years' War—Prussia. Prussia was a poor country, lacking the human and material resources of France and the Habsburg lands. But its rulers wanted it to become a major European power. To this end, they consolidated the state's territories, strengthened the state administration, raised revenue, and above all enlarged the army. These ambitious plans meant that the state had to mobilize the country's limited resources to a unique degree (see Map 16.2).

16-3a Territorial Consolidation

In 1640, a twenty-year-old, **Frederick William von Hohenzollern**, known as the Great Elector, became ruler of Brandenburg and a string of other territories that stretched across northern Germany from the Rhineland to the Polish border. In the west, little Cleves and Mark owed him allegiance; in the center were Brandenburg and its capital, Berlin, where he ruled as margrave; to the east was the duchy of Prussia, which he held as a vassal of the king of Poland. These Hohenzollern lands were separated by territories belonging to other rulers, and each had its own jealously guarded political traditions.

Because Frederick William was one of eight German princes entitled to elect the Holy Roman emperor, he had an important place in imperial politics. But his own lands were weak. Those in the center had been devastated during the Thirty Years' War, and some were still under foreign occupation. Overall, the population of his lands had fallen by 50 percent since 1618. But the Peace of Westphalia allowed Frederick William to reestablish princely authority in his territories.

Maneuvering in War In 1655, when Sweden went to war against Poland in hopes of gaining territory on the

Maria Theresa (r. 1740–1780) Daughter of Charles VI and ruler of the Habsburgs' hereditary lands whose husband was elected Holy Roman emperor.

War of the Austrian Succession (1740–1748) Mid-eighteenth century world war, fought on land and sea in Europe, the Americas, and India.

Frederick II (r. 1740–1786) King of Prussia during the War of the Austrian Succession and the Seven Years' War.

Frederick William von Hohenzollern (r. 1640–1688) Known as the Great Elector, ruler who started to create the modern state of Prussia.

Map 16.2 **The Growth of Austria and Prussia to 1748** Both Austria and Brandenburg-Prussia were expanding in the first half of the eighteenth century. The Austrians continued adding territories in their southeast, but in the north lost Silesia to Brandenburg-Prussia. Prussian lands were still scattered.

1. Consult the map legend and trace the stages of Prussia's territorial expansion to 1748.
2. How many territories in the Prussian state were not connected geographically to one or more of the others? What effect could this situation have on state-building in Prussia?
3. Trace the stages of Austria's territorial expansion to 1748.
4. How many territories in the Austrian state were not connected geographically to one or more of the others? What effect could this situation have on state-building in Austria?
5. Drawing on your knowledge of Austrian Habsburg history, what factors explain the marked territorial expansion toward the southeast of western Eurasia?
6. By 1748, was most of Austrian territory inside the Holy Roman Empire or outside the Empire or was the amount roughly the same? Why is this an important question to answer?

southern shore of the Baltic Sea, Frederick William faced his first test since the Peace of Westphalia in the treacherous game of warfare and diplomacy that was the norm among European states. At first, he proclaimed his neutrality. When the Swedes suffered temporary losses, he allied with them on condition that they recognize the independence of Prussia from Poland.

When the Poles started to lose, he joined them, again demanding that they abandon any claim to the duchy. At war's end in 1660, he was master of an independent Prussia. Now, the Hohenzollern lands were scattered from the Rhineland to the Russian border.

16-3b Taxes to Support an Army

For the rest of his reign, the Great Elector set two policy goals: to build up his army and to reorganize his finances to pay for it. Between 1653 and 1688, the army grew from 1,800 to 30,000. As the one institution established in all territories from east to west, it became the primary unifying force in the elector's state.

Taxes and the Diets A bigger army called for more taxes, and more taxes led to a confrontation between Frederick William and his diets, local political assemblies dominated by the nobility. Like their Habsburg counterparts, the Hohenzollern diets had traditionally granted taxes to the ruler. The elector had obtained a six-year grant from the diet of Brandenburg in 1653 that he continued to collect on his own authority during the war of 1655–1660.

Also in 1653, he proposed supplementing the grant with a general **excise tax**, taking his cue from the French, who had lowered direct taxes while raising indirect ones. When the local nobility objected that the excise violated their traditional rights of tax exemption, the elector asked only towns to pay it.

Two Tax Systems This solution created two tax systems. The countryside, dominated by nobles, paid a land tax, while towns adopted the excise tax. In creating this twofold system in Brandenburg, the elector split the united opposition of urban and rural taxpayers to new taxes. When Prussia balked at taxes, Frederick William introduced the two-tiered system there with the same results. Shorn of their taxing power, the diets withered away, and, as in France, political power was increasingly consolidated in the hands of the ruler and his government.

Income from the Royal Domain Frederick William had another source of revenue from his own domain. All European rulers had these private income streams, but the Hohenzollerns were blessed by very large family landholdings, constituting about one-third of their country's agricultural land and worked by 30 percent of the country's serfs. Under the leadership of an efficient administrator, Dodo zu Knyphausen, these domain lands produced ever-larger amounts for the elector's treasury.

Stimulating Economic Growth The elector also encouraged economic growth along mercantilist lines by increasing exports and introducing new manufacturing centers. As a youth, he had spent time in the Dutch Republic and seen firsthand the thriving economic life there. After 1685, he welcomed some 20,000 exiled Huguenots. These French artisans, merchants, and manufacturers played a vital role in the economic recovery after the Thirty Years' War.

During his reign, Frederick William had united his far-flung lands into a single state, imposed his right to tax them on a regular basis, and reinvigorated the economy. His growing army made him the most important military figure in Germany after the Habsburgs. In 1688, the elector was succeeded by his son, Frederick, who ruled until 1713.

Frederick spent most of his time in Berlin, presiding over a lavish court in the style of Louis XIV. His one major accomplishment was to adopt the title of King in Prussia in 1701 after obtaining Leopold I's recognition with promises of military aid in the looming War of the Spanish Succession. The title gave Frederick the standing he thought appropriate for his state's new power.

16-3c King Frederick William I

In 1713, King Frederick was succeeded by his son, **King Frederick William I**. Although Prussia was Lutheran, Frederick William was a strict Calvinist who believed in the absolutist principle that he was responsible to God alone for his rule. His subjects were to obey him without question. The king hated all elegance and refinement and spent most of his free time with his military men, smoking and getting completely drunk. These "tobacco evenings" sometimes ended with a participant being set on fire, a great joke in the king's eyes. Frederick William also stalked the streets of Berlin, roaring at his subjects, beating them with his cane, and leaving them with broken noses and teeth. Frederick William was a strange, violent, and crude man, but he was also a very successful ruler.

Strengthening the Royal Administration; Enlarging the Army Like his grandfather, the Great Elector, Frederick William I pursued the twin policies of strengthening the royal administration while enlarging the army. The excise tax was expanded to new commodities, and the land tax was imposed directly on the nobility in East Prussia, as the old duchy was now called. Income from the royal domain was further increased through yet more efficient management. Town councils were abolished and new royal officials put in their place.

A new administrative body called the **General Directory** was created in 1723 that brought together all officials involved in collecting taxes and revenues from the royal domain and supervising the overall economy of the kingdom. The directory improved administrative centralization and efficiency.

A Personal Absolutism The king stood at the apex of this new administrative system. Unlike his predecessors, Frederick William I did not consult regularly with his top officials because he had a low opinion of the men who worked for him, criticizing them for laziness and greed and paying them poorly. Instead, he worked in private, receiving reports and then secretly making decisions that were transmitted in

excise tax Indirect tax imposed on consumer items and collected at the moment of sale.

Frederick William I (r. 1713–1740) King of Prussia who further centralized the state administration and continued to build up the army.

General Directory Prussian central administrative agency created in 1723.

Frederick II Playing the Flute

Frederick's musical ability was well-known during his lifetime and his flute concertos are still played. After his death, his musical skill became part of "Old Fritz's" legend, as this nineteenth-century painting makes clear.

>> *Can you think of other political figures who have legends surrounding them?*

writing to his officials. His was a system of personal absolutism unknown even in Louis XIV's France, where the king always consulted with a handful of trusted advisers.

The king's government produced what Frederick William I wanted above all else—an enlarged army. At his death in 1740, the Prussian army had 80,000 men, making it the fourth largest in Europe. Command of the troops was given to the Prussian nobility, who also served in the civil administration. The king thus bound the nobility to his government and created a tradition of loyal state service among his nobles that was to last into the twentieth century. He also guaranteed the nobility's economic preeminence by recognizing their rights as landlords to control the serfs on their estates.

The Prussian Military The military had always been the one institution common to all the Hohenzollern lands, and the state's financial administration was geared to its maintenance. The military budget was met with tax and domain revenues, not with borrowing, as in other states. As he enlarged the army, Frederick William drafted more and more of his own

subjects. All parts of the kingdom were required to present men, mainly peasants, for service.

To lower costs, the soldiers were quartered in civilian homes, where they paid for their food and lodging and thereby stimulated the local economy. Because the rank and file of the growing army was made up of Prussians who lived among the civilian population, historians have described eighteenth-century Prussia as a "barracks state."

Frederick II When Frederick William died in 1740, he was succeeded by his son, Frederick II. Frederick was everything his father was not—refined, an accomplished flute player and composer, and a lover of philosophical discussion. He and his father had not gotten along. Relations between ruling monarchs and their successors were often stormy because the next in line attracted those who were out of favor in the current reign. But Frederick William I's treatment of his son was particularly violent. At one point, having beaten Frederick bloody with his cane, he put him in solitary confinement and forced him to witness the beheading of his closest friend on largely falsified charges.

Frederick William I had doubled the size of his army, but he was reluctant to use it in war. Frederick II's first act as king was to attack Charles VI's successor, Maria Theresa, seizing Silesia, her richest territory, and thereby starting the War of the Austrian Succession, the first of two world wars that engulfed the major European states in the mid-eighteenth century.

16-4 Russia and Europe, 1682–1796

>> **How were the state-building efforts of Russia's rulers similar to or different from the reform programs of European rulers farther to the West?**

>> **How were Russian rulers' relations with their nobility similar to and different from relations between monarchs and nobles farther to the West?**

Beginning in 1700, Russia began to realize Tsar Ivan the Terrible's dream of turning westward to expand its territory. In addition, rulers restructured Russia's state and church, along with its economy and society, along western lines. By the end of the eighteenth century, Russia was a major player in European politics.

16-4a Peter the Great and Westernization

Following Ivan the Terrible's death in 1584, Russia sank into a thirty-year period of political instability during which aristocratic factions fought for control of the state. In 1613, stability was restored when the first **Romanov** tsar, Michael, ascended the throne. At the end of the century, another Romanov, **Peter I the Great**, transformed Russia into a major European power. Peter was six feet seven inches tall and powerfully built. His huge size had a personality to match—restless, energetic, and always on the move.

In 1697, he traveled to western Europe under an assumed name, which fooled no one. Settling in the Dutch Republic, he spent hours visiting sawmills, cloth manufacturers, botanical gardens, and museums. But, above all, he visited Dutch shipyards to learn about shipbuilding, and then, having bought his own tools, he worked alongside Dutch shipbuilders. On a visit to England, he went to Anglican Church services, attended a Quaker meeting, went to the theater, and visited Parliament, which did not impress him. And, again, he studied ships.

Cutting Off Beards and Creating Assemblies

Peter worked for the rest of his life to apply what he had learned in the West to Russia. He began with fashion. Immediately on his return to Moscow, he forbade men to grow beards, the traditional sign of manhood in this Orthodox Christian country, and personally cut them off his courtiers. Traditionalists were horrified and protested that their hairless faces made them look like Protestants, Poles, or monkeys. His court was then ordered to dress in Western clothes and to meet in "assemblies," where men and women together conversed and engaged in other polite pastimes. This mingling of men and women overturned traditions decreeing the separation of women in special quarters.

The Great Northern War

In 1700, the tsar began a two-decade struggle with Sweden, the greatest power in northeastern Europe, for control of the Baltic Sea. Since the sixteenth century, tsars had believed that Russian access to the Baltic, the central sea link between eastern and western Europe, was essential if Russia hoped to be a major European power. Peter acted on this belief in the **Great Northern War**, which marked a turning point in Russian history.

After early Russian victories on the Baltic, Peter took the examples of Louis XIV and Leopold I further by building not a palace but a city, **St. Petersburg**, founded in 1703 on swampy coastal land seized from the Swedes at the mouth of the Neva River. The new city proclaimed his success in securing a Baltic port. In 1712, Peter made St. Petersburg the new capital of Russia, and the next year the court and state administration moved there from Moscow. In 1718, well-to-do landowners were required to build a house there and spend some of the year in the city.

Reforming the Military and Raising Taxes

Peter knew that continuing military success in the war with Sweden depended on an unprecedented refashioning of Russia's fighting forces and tax structure. He therefore reorganized his army along Western lines, ordering a draft for soldiers and introducing up-to-date Western drill and weapons. By 1715, he had an army of 215,000, supplemented by 100,000 Cossacks, locally organized warrior bands used by tsars as fighting forces. Peter also built a Baltic navy from scratch.

To pay for this huge military mobilization, he imposed new taxes on everything from beehives to beards to baths. Overall, taxes skyrocketed during Peter's reign, as they had in France during the Thirty Years' War. To improve his tax base, Peter inaugurated a mercantilist stimulation of the Russian economy by encouraging exports, discouraging imports, and sponsoring new industries in metallurgy, mining, and textiles.

Poltava The decisive battle in the Great Northern War came in 1709 at **Poltava**, where Peter destroyed the Swedish army. Nine thousand Swedes lay dead on the battlefield, and 16,000 more surrendered a few days later. The Swedish king, Charles XII, who commanded the army, fled into Turkish territory. Although the war lasted another twelve years, the Swedes never recovered from the disaster at Poltava. At the end of the Great Northern War, in 1721, during a solemn ceremony in St. Petersburg, Peter was proclaimed emperor of Russia, a title taken from Rome that was to supplant the traditional one of tsar.

Restructuring Society Peter also continued to restructure Russian society. Traditionally, Russians thought of their society as a three-tiered hierarchy. At the base were the millions of serfs who toiled for their landlords. Serfs, who constituted more than half of the Russian population, were under the complete control of their landlord, needing his permission to marry or leave his estate. They also had to work for him without pay, often as many as six days a week. In their lack of freedom of choice, they resembled the African slaves laboring in the fields in the Americas more than the European peasants farther to the West.

The landlords in turn worked for the emperor. Peter intensified this traditional pattern, first by demanding more in taxes and military service from the serfs and then by requiring the landlord class to serve for life in either the

Romanovs Family that ruled Russia from 1613 to 1917.

Peter I the Great (r. 1682–1725) Greatest Romanov tsar who westernized Russia and made the country a major European power.

Great Northern War (1700–1721) War between Russia and Sweden that resulted in Russian dominance of the Baltic.

St. Petersburg City founded by Peter the Great in 1703, which became the Russian capital in 1712.

Poltava Decisive battle of the Great Northern War in 1709 in which Peter the Great defeated Charles XII of Sweden.

military or the civilian administration. Candidates for state service had to start at the bottom of their service branch and then work to the top on the basis of personal merit. Peter applied the test of merit to himself when he rose through the ranks of the army and the navy.

This system was codified in the **Table of Ranks**. Administrators received noble status as they moved up. Peter's reform of his civil and military administration was one of the first attempts in modern European history to overturn the idea that nobles had a right to govern in favor of the notion that government should be in the hands of a civil service staffed by experts whose advancement depended on their performance.

To train experts for state service, Peter established engineering, artillery, and medical schools, a school of mathematics and navigation, and a naval academy. In 1725, he established an Academy of Sciences that quickly gained an international reputation for excellence. Peter's insistence on able and expert administrators was central to his program of state-building.

"The Most Drunken Council" Peter loved alcohol, coarse language, and even coarser practical jokes. Throughout most of his reign, he presided over a "Most Drunken Council" that engaged in monumental drinking bouts while mocking Catholic, but not Orthodox, church ceremonies. His practical joking was often violent, as when he forced food down the throat of a courtier, who collapsed in a fit of coughing with blood running from his nose and mouth. Peter's violence matched that of Frederick William I of Prussia and contrasted sharply with the refined manners promoted at the court of Louis XIV and the piety of Leopold I.

Reform of the Church Peter's most radical reform was to abolish the office of patriarch in the Russian Orthodox Church. In the Orthodox world, patriarchs were bishops with great prestige and influence. The patriarch of Moscow, who had received the title in 1589, had served as a counterweight to tsars and a check on their power. By Peter's time, however, the patriarchate had been weakened by a schism in the church when the **Old Believers** rejected his authority and denounced him as the Antichrist.

The patriarch had tried to reform church practice, and although Russian church councils and the other patriarchs approved the reforms, Old Believers rejected them because they had not been used traditionally in "Holy Russia." Moreover, people unhappy about Peter's policy of cultural westernization looked to the patriarch for support of traditional ways.

Peter never openly attacked Orthodoxy, but his own theological beliefs were heavily influenced by Lutheranism. In 1721, he abolished the patriarchate and replaced it with a **Holy Synod**, which embodied his Lutheran leanings because it reduced the church to a simple department of the state.

© Joeri de Rocker/Alamy Stock Photo

The "Tsar Carpenter"

This is a copy of a sculpture by Leopold Bernshtam, which Emperor Nicholas II presented to the Russian Admiralty in St. Petersburg in 1909 to commemorate the Russian victory at Poltava. It shows Peter the Great at work as a shipbuilder in the Dutch city of Zaandam. The original was destroyed at the beginning of the Russian Revolution in 1918. This copy was presented to Zaandam in 1910. In 1996, the Dutch government gave it to Russia and once again Peter stands in front of the Admiralty. Compare this image with that of Ivan the Terrible in Chapter 13.

❯❯ *How has the image of the tsar changed from the sixteenth to the early twentieth century?*

❯❯ *What might account for the changes?*

Table of Ranks Decree by Peter the Great in 1722 that restructured civil and military administration into a system of advancement based on merit.

Old Believers Orthodox Christians who rejected the Russian patriarch's attempt to alter church ceremony.

Holy Synod Council of clergy established by Peter the Great in 1721 that made the church a department of the state.

Catherine II the Great, ca. 1765

For her portrait, Catherine II the Great is dressed in shiny splendor. On her head is the Romanov crown, and in her hands are an orb and scepter, emblems of royal and imperial rule. She gazes straight out at the viewer with a kindly expression, perhaps to convey an image of her womanly concern for her subjects.

》 *Compare this portrait of Catherine to that of Peter the Great earlier in this chapter and to Ivan the Terrible in Chapter 13.*

》 *Is Catherine's depiction more or less in line with the way rulers had been depicted before her? If less in line, why might she have chosen to deviate from the norm? If more in line, why might she have preferred this conventional approach?*

Peter's Achievements   Peter's plans for the remaking of Russia were far reaching, and many of them looked better on paper than they worked in reality. But his reforms brought a new centralization and rationality to government while demanding more from all Russians and advancing the country as a major European power. Thus, he set Russia on a new course.

16-4b Catherine the Great and Russian Expansion

From 1725 to 1762, Russia was allied with Austria against France, the traditional ally of the Poles, the Swedes, and the Turks, all enemies of Russia. The Austrian alliance implemented Peter's policy of bringing Russia directly into the European system of international politics and diplomacy. Domestically, one far-reaching change took place: in 1762, the landlord class was freed from Peter's compulsory state service obligation. From then on, landlords served voluntarily, and many did so because service brought prestige, influence, and wealth.

In 1762, Peter III, Peter I's grandson, became emperor. Peter III was violent, crude, and dimwitted. Raised in Germany, where his Romanov mother had married a duke, Peter feared Russians and loved Germans, thereby alienating many at court. In religion, he also leaned toward Lutheranism and ordered icons removed from Russian churches while demanding that Orthodox clergy dress like Lutheran pastors. No one dared to implement these decrees. Peter was married to Sophie, a princess from a minor German state. Six months after Peter's accession, Sophie plotted with powerful courtiers, one of whom was her lover, to depose Peter in a palace **coup d'état** (koo-deh-TAH). He was soon murdered, and the conspirators proclaimed Sophie his successor. For the next thirty-four years, she ruled Russia as **Catherine II the Great**.

Seizing Church Lands; Land for Her Favorites
Catherine's first major decision was to continue Peter III's seizure of all ecclesiastical lands, thereby further reducing the church's independence from the state. She then granted large tracts of state land and their peasants to her favorites. This action increased the number of serfs because state peasants were reduced to serfdom when their lands passed into private hands. Catherine also continued her predecessors' policies of exempting the landlord class from compulsory state service and freeing them from taxation while forbidding serfs on their lands from directly petitioning the empress for redress of grievances.

Partitioning Poland and Fighting the Turks   Like
Peter the Great, Catherine dramatically expanded Russia's borders. In 1772, she joined Prussia and Austria, which were also looking to expand their territories, in the first **partition of Poland**. In the 1760s, Prussia and Russia had instigated a civil war in Poland by demanding full toleration for its Protestant and Orthodox inhabitants. Claiming that they were putting an end to that civil war, Austria,

coup d'état (in French, "blow of state") Abrupt overthrow of a government by a small group of conspirators.

Catherine II the Great (r. 1762– 1796) German princess who, as Russian empress, was one of Russia's most powerful rulers.

partitions of Poland Divisions of Poland carried out by Austria, Prussia, and Russia in 1772, 1792, and 1795, leading to the end of an independent Polish state.

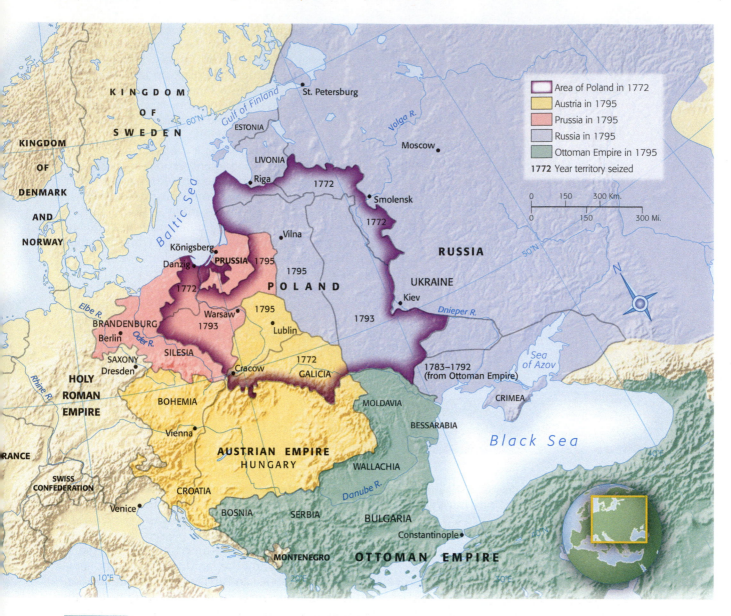

Map 16.3 **The Partition of Poland and the Expansion of Russia** Prussia, Russia, and Austria all benefited from the partitions of Poland.

1. Consult the map legend and then note the new territories the partitions of Poland added to:
    a. Prussia
    b. Austria
    c. Russia
    d. Drawing on your knowledge of these three states, how would the territories added further the state-building agendas of each state?

Prussia, and Russia proceeded to divide up sections of Poland among themselves. Two more partitions took place in 1792 and 1795, bringing an end to an independent Poland (see Map 16.3).

Catherine also fought two wars with the Turks. In 1792, when the second war ended, Russia seized the north shore of the Black Sea and the Crimean peninsula along with the northern Caucasus. These conquests, along with the partitions of Poland, rivaled Peter the Great's advances in the Baltic region and established the modern western boundaries of Russia.

Catherine encouraged colonization in the lands of the south by urging Russian landlords to move there with their serfs and sponsoring German immigrants in the region. At the end of Catherine's reign, the Russian empire contained dozens of different ethnic and religious communities, 50 percent of whom were Russian. Thus, cultural diversity in the Russian empire rivaled that of the Habsburg lands and similarly retarded the development of a common identity among the peoples ruled by the empress in St. Petersburg.

16-4c The Pugachev Rebellion and Russian Society

In 1773, during the Turkish war, a massive rebellion against the empress broke out in the south. It was led by a Cossack, **Emelian Pugachev**, who claimed to be Peter III. Popular revolts led by men pretending to be long-lost tsars were a feature of early modern Russia's political life. So were Cossack frontier rebellions. What made Pugachev's revolt distinctive was its size and its social composition. Thousands rose with him, including many serfs. In 1774, when the Turkish war ended, Catherine was free to turn her professionally trained army against the insurgents, who were no match for the imperial troops, and the revolt fell apart. Pugachev was taken to Moscow in a cage and then executed.

Russian Society in Crisis Although the revolt failed, it was a sign of a deep social crisis in Russia. The elimination of compulsory state service for the landlord class had undercut the traditional structure of the Russian community, in which landlords toiled for the state while their serfs toiled for them. When the landlords were freed of their obligations, many peasants believed they should be free as well. When they were not freed, alienation and anger exploded into revolt. Those who followed Pugachev demanded an end to serfdom, taxation, and the military draft. In 1775, Catherine clamped down. She imposed administrative centralization by reorganizing Russia into fifty provinces and putting the landlords in charge of local government, where they had enough force to control peasant protests.

Russia Becomes a European Power Under Peter I and Catherine II, Russia emerged as a first-rate European military and diplomatic power. Coercion from above was crucial in this transformation. Modernization and westernization also increased privileges for the landowning class and reduced the condition of the peasant population, which (serfs and free peasants together) constituted more than 90 percent of Russia's inhabitants. The gulf between the landowning elite and the mass of inhabitants was as great as, if not greater than, any in Europe.

16-5 The English Constitutional Monarchy, 1660–1740

» **How did religion continue to play a role in English politics?**

» **In what ways did political development in England differ from that in the absolutist regimes on the continent?**

In 1660, after eleven years of civil war, religious controversy, republican government, and Oliver Cromwell's dictatorship, monarchy was restored in the British Isles when Charles I's son, already crowned king of Scotland, was crowned king of England and Ireland. Restoration, however, did not bring either political or religious peace. For the next seventy years, the British Isles were torn apart by conflicts pitting king against Parliament. Religious divisions also persisted, as restored Anglicans refused all compromise with the Puritans.

When the Catholic king James II seemed to have established a permanent Catholic dynasty, he was overthrown, and his Protestant daughter Mary II, along with her husband, the Dutch stadholder William III, were crowned with Parliament's blessing. But Mary and then her successor, Anne, died without heirs, and Parliament again determined who would rule when it chose a German Protestant prince, George I. In this turbulent period, as Parliament made and unmade monarchs, its power grew. Political stability was achieved in the early eighteenth century, when Crown and Parliament started to cooperate in governing the country.

16-5a The Restoration of Charles II

The restoration to the throne of Charles II in 1660 sparked a repudiation of Oliver Cromwell's Calvinist moral reform of society. The king led the way. Charles was a charming, witty man with a taste for good living and an eye for women. A string of mistresses, along with packs of spaniels, shared his bed. "God will not damn a man for taking a little unregular pleasure along the way," he once quipped. In pursuit of pleasure, Charles reopened London theaters and canceled the traditional prohibition against women playing female roles. Now people could revel in worldly comedies like *Love in a Wood* or *The Gentleman Dancing-Master*.

King and Parliament Underneath the glitter of **Restoration** society, the

Emelian Pugachev (1742–1775) Cossack who claimed to be Peter III and led an unsuccessful rebellion of thousands of serfs against Catherine the Great.

Restoration Name given to the period 1660–1689 in which the restored Stuart kings Charles II and James II ruled.

long-standing political conflict between king and Parliament continued to shape events. Like his predecessors, Charles could conduct foreign policy on his own and choose his ministers. He could also call Parliament into session and dismiss it, veto its legislation, and override any parliamentary law by suspending it or dispensing people from its provisions.

For its part, Parliament could impeach royal ministers. It also controlled state finances through its right to raise taxes. In sum, both sides had formidable powers, and neither could gain a permanent advantage over the other. This situation contrasted to the absolutist monarchies on the continent, where power was increasingly concentrated in the hands of the king.

Fights over Religion   The issue that provoked the greatest political fights was religion. Although Charles II was officially Anglican, he favored some form of religious toleration in England. But the Parliament elected in 1661 was determined to promote Anglicanism alone and force conformity to the Book of Common Prayer. Therefore, it enacted the **Clarendon Code**, which required all clergymen to swear an oath supporting Anglican theology and prohibited non-Anglican Protestants from worshiping in public. About 10 percent of the clergy refused to accept it and turned their backs on Anglicanism. These clergymen and their supporters, known as **dissenters**, supported the king's more tolerant attitude.

Most Anglicans suspected that the king's policy of religious toleration was shaped by loyalty to his Catholic family—his mother, wife, and younger brother, James, Duke of York, were all Roman Catholics. These suspicions deepened when Charles allied with his cousin, Louis XIV, in the Dutch War of 1672. But Charles was always politically astute, and he postponed his conversion to Catholicism until he was on his deathbed.

The Problem of James: Tories and Whigs   The problem of Catholic members of the royal family became especially acute in the 1670s. Although Charles fathered at least seventeen illegitimate children by his many mistresses, he had no legitimate heir to succeed him, so his brother James would be the next king if the rule of strict hereditary succession was applied. The prospect of a Catholic king created a rift among the Anglican elite, which controlled Parliament and ran local government, because Anglicans hated Catholics as well as dissenters.

Soon two parties, the **Tories** and the **Whigs**, fought each other over the issue of succession. Tories supported the Duke of York's right to the Crown, even if this meant that Protestant England would have a Catholic king, because they believed that hereditary monarchy was divinely instituted and that opposition to it was a sin.

Whigs wanted a Protestant monarch at all costs. Following the argument of the English philosopher **John Locke**, they believed in the contractual theory of government. The English monarchy was based on a contract between the ruler and his subjects, represented in Parliament, which could be broken for good reason. As battles between the two parties raged, a new politically active press emerged under the relatively moderate censorship regime of the restored monarchy. Press and parties encouraged the English publicly to discuss politics and take sides on issues in ways that were inconceivable under the absolutist monarchies on the continent.

16-5b James II

In 1685, when Charles II died, the principle of hereditary succession won out, and the Duke of York became **James II**. James kept up some Anglican appearances, being crowned in public according to the Anglican rite after being crowned in private according to the Catholic one. When one of Charles II's illegitimate sons, the Protestant Duke of Monmouth, rebelled against his uncle, the duke was taken prisoner and executed. At first, many Tories and Whigs could accept James because his heirs were his two Protestant daughters, Mary and Anne, the children of his first marriage. Although James had remarried, none of the ten children by his second marriage had survived past infancy.

James and Religious Toleration   Like his brother, James promoted religious toleration of both dissenters and Catholics, granting them the right to worship in public and using his power of exempting people from the law to override a provision in the Clarendon Code forbidding non-Anglicans from serving in high civil and military office. This action infuriated the Anglicans, who saw the king's actions as a backdoor way of promoting Catholicism. When Anglican bishops objected, James resurrected King Charles I's hated church courts, and purged Anglican opponents

Clarendon Code Law of 1661 requiring clergy and officeholders to swear allegiance to the Anglican Church and banning non-Anglican Protestants' public worship.

dissenters Non-Anglican Protestants.

Tories Supporters of strict hereditary succession to the Crown.

Whigs People who believed in the necessity of a Protestant monarch, even if this meant that the rule of strict heredity would have to be violated.

John Locke (1632–1704) Political philosopher who argued that legitimate government rested on a contract between rulers and subjects.

James II (r. 1685–1689) King of England who was removed from the throne by Parliament.

from local government office, replacing them with Catholics and dissenters.

In 1688, England was rocked by news that James's wife had given birth to an eleventh child, a baby boy who would rule as James III. Outraged Protestants tried to argue that the queen had faked a pregnancy and that the baby had been smuggled into the palace in a bed-warming pan. Tories and Whigs alike were horrified at the prospect of a perpetual Catholic monarchy and furious with James's high-handed exempting of the law in favor of non-Anglicans. Joining forces, they asked the stadholder William, the husband of James's daughter Mary, to come to England in defense of Protestantism. When William landed, James panicked. Unable to sleep and suffering from endless nosebleeds, he led an army against William but failed to find him because his generals had no maps. After sending wife and baby out of the country, James fled to France.

16-5c The Glorious Revolution

When Parliament reconvened in 1689, it determined who would rule, proclaiming that in leaving the country James had abdicated and then offering the Crown to Mary, his daughter, who accepted on condition that William rule jointly with her.

The Bill of Rights Parliament then passed the **Bill of Rights**, which upheld the Whig view that monarchs ruled not by hereditary right but by right of a contract with their subjects. It overturned James II's suspension of parliamentary law, stating that "the pretended power of suspending the laws or the execution of laws by regal authority without consent of Parliament is illegal." It also undercut royal power by denying the king the right to raise an army on his own, saying that "raising and keeping a standing army within this kingdom in time of peace without the consent of Parliament [is] contrary to law."

This bill also guaranteed subjects' right to petition the government as well as to a jury trial, along with freedom from "cruel and unusual punishments," excessive bail, and excessive court fines. It did not, however, guarantee the right of all subjects to vote for members of Parliament's **House of Commons**. Voting for this lower house, made up of non-nobles, was still limited to a relatively small number of property-owning adult males. Candidates for the Commons also had to meet substantial property qualifications.

In support of Protestantism, Parliament also repealed the most oppressive portions of the Clarendon Code in the **Toleration Act** (1689), which granted religious toleration to all dissenters except Unitarians, people who did not believe in the doctrine of the Trinity. Dissenters, however, were still subject to a law that required all officeholders to take Holy Communion in an Anglican Church.

Overall, the Bill of Rights and the amendments to the Clarendon Code implemented the contract theory of government by strengthening Parliament while providing subjects of the Crown with a wide range of rights that were spelled out in detail and had the force of law.

A Government of Large-Scale Landowners Large-scale landowners controlled Parliament. After 1689, these people also enjoyed control of local government in the countryside with little interference from the king. This situation contrasted with the absolutist monarchies on the continent, where royal control of local affairs was implemented. William knew that his predecessor's dismissal of Anglican landlords from local office in favor of Catholics and dissenters had contributed to his overthrow and did not intend to provoke these powerful people again.

The Rule of Law In 1701, royal judges were given life tenure, subject only to impeachment and removal from office by Parliament. This reform, which created an independent judiciary, was intended to strengthen the **rule of law** called for in the Bill of Rights. William accepted these reforms from below and thereby acknowledged that he ruled by right of contract with his subjects.

William had come to England as part of his grand strategy to defeat Louis XIV. As king, he could take England into the War of the League of Augsburg on the Dutch side. Mary reluctantly accepted the Crown, believing that she was sinning against her father, who led a French landing in Ireland to reclaim the monarchy. When William defeated James, James fled once again to France, where he died in 1701.

A Constitutional Monarchy The changes brought about in 1689 spelled the end of royal absolutism in the British Isles and laid the foundations for a **constitutional monarchy** in which the monarch and Parliament ruled as partners following the principles of the rule of law.

Bill of Rights Parliamentary act passed in 1689 stipulating the basic rights of English subjects; based on the contract theory of government.

House of Commons Lower elected house of Parliament made up of non-noble men (commoners); nobles sit in the upper house, the House of Lords.

Toleration Act Parliamentary act of 1689 granting religious toleration to all Protestants except Unitarians, and also excepting Catholics.

rule of law Principle that law has a higher authority than rulers, governments, and officials; rulers must obey the laws.

constitutional monarchy Form of government in which the monarch and legislature rule as partners following the principles of the rule of law.

National Portrait Gallery, London/The Bridgeman Art Library

The House of Commons by Karl Anton Hickel

In this painting of the House of Commons, the Speaker of the House sits with his hat on at the center behind secretaries. The MPs (Members of Parliament) flank him on either side. The man standing is the king's first minister, William Pitt the Younger, who is addressing the House.

» *What impression does this painting give of the way Parliament conducted its business?*

» *Is it surprising or not that the king is not there?*

CONNECTIONS: Placing restraint on royal authority and protecting subjects' rights was a long, slow development in England (and other European states). For glimpses into the English process, see Section 10-3a From Weak Kings to Strong and Section 20-4 Reform in Great Britain.

Act of Union Parliamentary act of 1707 uniting Scotland and England in the one kingdom of Great Britain.

Glorious Revolution (1688–1689) Name given to the events leading to the dethronement of James II and the rule of William and Mary.

The reign of William and Mary inaugurated twenty-five years of war against France. Whigs supported William's pursuit of Louis XIV, while Tories grumbled about rising land taxes. The two parties fiercely contested elections to seats in the House of Commons. In principle, Parliament controlled taxation and the Crown controlled foreign policy. But ongoing warfare forced the two sides to work together because William had to explain his policies to Parliament if he hoped to get the money he needed.

Mary died childless in 1694, and when William died in 1702, the Crown passed to James II's younger Protestant daughter, Anne. Anne had had nineteen children, all of whom were stillborn or died in infancy. She believed this calamity was God's judgment on her father's removal from the throne. As Anne had no heirs, Parliament determined who would rule when Anne died. In 1701, fifty-seven Catholic Stuarts were passed over in favor of a Protestant granddaughter of James I, Sophia, of the German state of Hanover.

The Act of Union and the "Glorious Revolution" In 1707, Scotland, still an independent kingdom ruled by the English monarch, but suffering from an economic depression and a financial collapse, agreed to accept the **Act of Union** with England to create a united Great Britain ruled over by a Protestant monarch. In 1714, when Anne died, Sophia's son George became king. Later generations in England referred to the events of 1688 and 1689 as the **Glorious Revolution**, which kept the state Protestant while advancing the power of Parliament and repudiating absolutist and divine right theories of kingship.

16-5d The Georges from Germany

George I was already middle aged when he became king of Great Britain in 1714. He spoke no English and had to communicate with his ministers in French. He also spent half his time in Hanover. The Great Britain he presided over had emerged victorious from the wars against Louis XIV, and his right to the British throne had been recognized by the Treaty of Utrecht ending the War of the Spanish Succession in 1713. The treaty had also awarded Britain Gibraltar, Hudson's Bay, Nova Scotia, Newfoundland, and the *asiento*, which gave the British the exclusive right to import African slaves into Spanish America.

In addition to the asiento, Britain was allowed limited rights of trade with the Spanish colonies. These concessions spurred development of the British navy and the establishment of trading posts that were vital to the kingdom's growing colonial empire. The territorial grants in North America intensified the contest between France and Britain for control of Canada.

An Uprising in Scotland and the Decline of the Tories Recognition of George as king provoked James II's baby boy, now grown up, to lead an uprising in Scotland to regain the Crown. It failed, but when a number of Tories expressed sympathy for the **pretender**, the Whigs accused them of treason. This charge, coupled with George's clear preference for the Whigs, turned the Tories into a minority party for the next forty-five years.

Sir Robert Walpole The leader of the triumphant Whigs was **Sir Robert Walpole**, a rich landowner and country gentleman. Walpole, unlike his ministerial predecessors, refused the king's offer to ennoble him and give him a seat in the House of Lords, the upper house of Parliament. Walpole preferred to stay in the Commons because he believed he could be more effective there in creating majorities to support royal policies. His skill in winning over both the king and Parliament contributed to the smooth running of the central government, while his decision to remain in the Commons added to the power of that house.

Walpole also tried to calm the partisan passions that had agitated the country since 1660. He emphasized good manners in politics and signaled his willingness to accept moderate Tories into his political coalitions. Thus, in his own way, he agreed with Louis XIV that politeness had its political uses. Under Walpole, Britain enjoyed a period of political stability that contrasted sharply with the turmoil preceding George I's reign.

Britons: A New Collective Identity At the same time, a new sense of collective British identity was forming. Britons enjoyed the rights guaranteed in 1689 and were thereby freeborn, in opposition to what they thought were the "slavish" Catholic peoples of France or Spain. This new sense of identity was given voice in the poem "Rule, Britannia," set to music in 1740: "Rule, Britannia! Britannia, rule the waves/Britons never never never shall be slaves."

After their union with England, Scots could also identify with this sense of national unity, especially since they profited increasingly from British overseas and colonial trade. The Catholic Irish, however, conquered and impoverished, were excluded from the community of the freeborn.

George II: "Mixed Monarchy" When George I died in 1727, Walpole survived the change of reign and continued to serve George II. Throughout his career, he promoted a policy of peace with the rest of Europe and used this time to consolidate the religious and political gains of the Glorious Revolution. When he left office in 1742, the principle of mixed monarchy, in which a constitutionally sanctioned Protestant king ruled jointly with Parliament, had become the cornerstone of British political life. Finally, the defeat of James II in Ireland in 1689, along with the union of Scotland and England in 1707, consolidated English dominance.

16-6 Two World Wars, 1740–1763

> ❯❯ How did the competitive European state system affect the conduct of war?

> ❯❯ What were the outcomes of the two world wars for the states that fought in them?

In the middle of the eighteenth century, all the major states of Europe were drawn into two great wars. Warfare, a permanent feature of relations between states in early modern Europe, often ended in stalemate, but the midcentury wars fundamentally altered European power relations. Because they were also fought in the overseas empires of Britain, France, and Spain, they had long-lasting consequences for peoples in the Western Hemisphere and Asia.

George I (r. 1714–1727) Elector of Hanover who became king of Great Britain.

asiento Monopoly on the importation of African slaves into Spanish America granted to English merchants by Spain in 1713.

pretender Claimant to a throne.

Sir Robert Walpole (1676–1745) Leader of the Whigs and the most important minister in England from 1721 to 1742.

Table 16.1　The Eighteenth-Century World Wars and the Diplomatic Revolution

The War of the Austrian Succession, 1740–1748

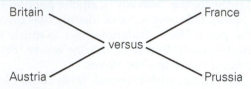

Britain versus France

Austria versus Prussia

The Seven Years' War, 1756–1763

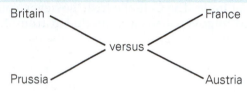

Britain versus France

Prussia versus Austria

bpk, Berlin/Art Resource, NY

Prussian Troops

In this engraving from a Prussian army manual of 1726, a drill master supervises the marching and field maneuvers for which the Prussian army was famous. Soldiers who fail to follow his commands will have to mount the donkey punishment device shown on the left.

» *What artistic devices does the engraver employ to give the viewer a sense of the precision and orderliness of the troops at drill?*

» *Compare this presentation of military orderliness and precision with the account of soldiers' behavior during the Thirty Years' War given by Johann Grimmelshausen (see Chapter 15, "Learning from A Primary Source:* Simplicius Simplicissmus *Encounters Some "Merry Cavalrymen").*

16-6a The Wars

In 1740, Frederick II of Prussia attacked Maria Theresa of Austria, beginning the War of the Austrian Succession. The rulers of Bavaria and Saxony challenged Maria Theresa's right to rule on the grounds that they were more legitimate heirs to Charles VI than she. Frederick, however, accepted the legitimacy of her succession. What he wanted was Silesia, the richest of Austria's territories. Taking advantage of challenges to Maria Theresa's right of succession, he claimed that Silesia rightfully belonged to Prussia and then seized the province.

Britain had been at war with Spain since 1739 over the trading rights conceded to it at the end of the War of the Spanish Succession. In 1740, Britain joined Austria to fight Prussia, renewing the British-Austrian alliance that had been forged in the wars against Louis XIV. The British also attacked the French in North America and India. France, in turn, stood by its traditional ally, Prussia, in order to check Austrian power. In 1748, at war's end, Prussia emerged victorious, keeping Silesia. The war between Britain and France ended indecisively.

The Seven Years' War　War broke out again in 1756 between Austria and Prussia over Silesia, this time with Russia allied with Austria against Prussia. Since 1754, France and Britain had again been at war in North America along the western frontier of the British colonies there. In 1756, they continued the fight in Europe and India during the **Seven Years' War** (see

Seven Years' War (1756–1763) World war fought in Europe, North America, and India.

diplomatic revolution Shift in alliances between European states that preceded the Seven Years' War.

Map 16.4). Because Austria had recently concluded an alliance with France, Britain also switched sides and joined with Prussia against the two in the **diplomatic revolution**. The war ended in 1763. (See Table 16.1 for a summary of the complicated alliances in these two wars).

16-6b Eighteenth-Century Warfare

The complex, ever-shifting alliances and counter-alliances that characterized the world wars of the mid-eighteenth century were typical of the culture of war in early modern Europe. War was accepted as an inevitable and ongoing feature of the relations between European states. Rulers did little to counteract this idea; the old ideal of the king as head of the warrior band was too deeply embedded in European tradition. Moreover, the growth of large professional armies in the hundred years between 1650 and 1750 reinforced the idea of the inevitability of ongoing warfare.

The Professional Standing Army　The professional standing army, pioneered by Louis XIV, became a standard feature in eighteenth-century states. The one exception was Britain, which preferred to keep its army small while offering financial aid to

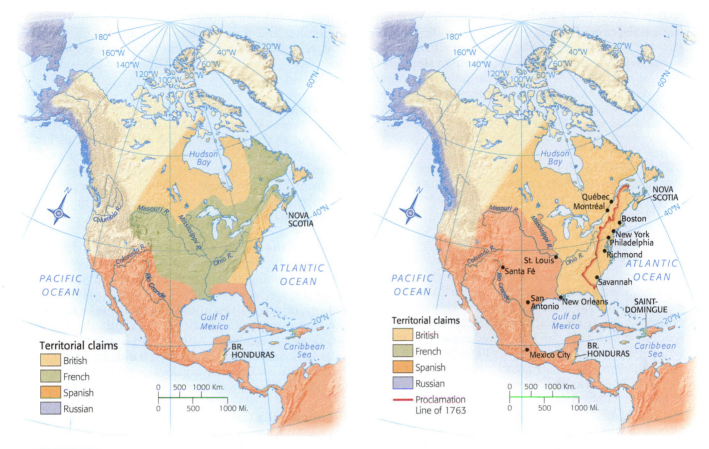

Map 16.4 **European Claims in North America before and after the Seven Years' War** In losing the Seven Years' War, France lost its continental North American empire. New France went to Britain, and Louisiana went to Spain. France retained only Newfoundland and its island colonies in the Caribbean.

1. A comparison of these two maps shows very significant territorial gains and losses for Britain, France, and Spain as a result of the world wars of the mid-eighteenth century.

2. Consult a map of North and Central America in 2000. How are North and Central America politically configured today? Did all three European states lose territory after 1756? Which lost the most, which the least?

its continental allies' forces. Armies were now better provisioned and disciplined than they had been during the period of religious warfare and were, therefore, less of a danger to the civilian population. Although troops were sometimes quartered in civilians' homes and taxes were imposed for the armies' upkeep, the fear of military pillaging lessened.

The Science of Warfare A science of warfare also emerged, taking several forms. One was an interest in military engineering. In France, Sébastien le Prestre de Vauban improved the architecture of fortresses and supervised their construction along France's northern and eastern frontiers. The idea that impregnable fortresses could protect France from its enemies was to shape French military planning into the twentieth century. Military scientists also produced new drill manuals for soldiers, specifying a series of increasingly complicated battlefield maneuvers, including the Prussian "goose step," which kept soldiers in a straight line.

Not surprisingly, Frederick William I was a pioneer in this field, earning him the nickname "the royal drill sergeant." Soon, other armies were training their troops in similar ways. Army officers, almost always drawn from the nobility, received instruction in drill and battlefield tactics in new military academies and then applied them to the common soldiers under their command.

The Balance of Power Eighteenth-century statesmen used warfare to enforce the doctrine of the balance of power, based on the assumption that Europe's international system functioned best when power was evenly distributed among states, thereby preventing any one of them from achieving dominance over the others. Thus, the coalitions against Louis XIV were explained as restoring the balance that the Sun King's aggressive military activity had threatened.

Of course, agreement on the balance rested on the agreement of all the interested players. And that was where the problems began. Because one player's "balance" was often another's "domination," European states were thrown into a never-ending defensive and offensive scramble. Adjusting alliances was a way to juggle the desire of each state to strengthen itself against the others while maintaining a rough balance of power. Religious division played a smaller role in the wars of midcentury than it had a century earlier. Now issues of territory, power, and prestige were central.

CONNECTIONS: For discussion of the flaws in the West's balance of power on the eve of World War I, see Section 25-1a An Unbalanced Balance of Power.

16-6c Winners and Losers

When war ended in 1763, there were clear winners and losers. In central Europe, Frederick II was a winner; Silesia was never returned to Austria. But the wars put huge strains on Prussia's finances and military, and at times it looked as if the kingdom would be defeated. In 1762, Frederick was saved when the pro-German emperor Peter III broke Russia's alliance with Austria and signed a peace with Prussia. This was the most consequential act of Peter's short reign.

After 1763, Prussia rested. "Old Fritz," as his subjects called the king, lost his taste for wars of conquest. Now, he preferred more peaceful means for gaining territory, such as joining with Austria and Russia in 1772 to partition Poland and finally link Prussia with Brandenburg.

Reform in Austria: The Army Austria was a loser. Before 1740, the Habsburgs had not followed Prussia and Russia in reforming state finances, strengthening the central administration, and updating the army. The shock of Silesia's loss galvanized Maria Theresa into a frenzy of state-building. She began with the army, founding a military academy, introducing advanced drill and maneuvering techniques, and expanding the government's ability to house and supply its troops. To pay for reform, she overhauled the state's tax structure.

Tax Reform Beginning in 1748, she coaxed the diets of Bohemia and Austria to grant taxes for ten years. In effect, this action made state taxation permanent, and the power of the magnates in the diets to control state finances waned, just as it had in Prussia under the Great Elector.

Joseph II (r. 1780–1790) Holy Roman emperor and head of the Austrian Habsburg lands who tried to strengthen his realm through radical reform of its social structure.

Administrative Reform To increase government efficiency, she founded a school to train state administrators. In 1761, she decreed that her state council, staffed by experts, could make policy decisions that were binding on her and the state administration. She, therefore, repudiated the king-centered decision-making that Louis XIV and Frederick William I of Prussia had developed.

Austria in the Seven Years' War In 1756, when the Seven Years' War began, Maria Theresa's reforms were put to the test and failed. With Silesia still in Frederick's hands at war's end, Austria initiated more reforms, primarily to increase revenue to pay for a better army. This time, however, Maria Theresa tackled the problem by focusing on the economic improvement of the mass of her subjects, the serfs.

Helping the Serfs Like Leopold I, she tried to reduce serfs' uncompensated work for their landlords, decreeing that the traditional minimum of three days a week would now be the maximum. Reform of serfs' lives pitted Maria Theresa against the interests of the landlord class, but she made headway, especially in Austria and Bohemia, when serfs took matters into their own hands by going on rent strikes and fomenting local rebellions against landlord demands.

Reforming the Catholic Church Maria Theresa also imposed new taxes on the Catholic Church. Although she was a pious Roman Catholic who hated heresy, she believed that the church should assume a greater part of the expenses needed to defend the state against competitors. The clergy were taxed without the pope's permission, and the church was forbidden to acquire new land that would be tax-free.

Partitioning Poland Defense of the Habsburg lands against enemies went hand in hand with attacks on weaker states, as the Polish partition of 1772 shows. Maria Theresa had moral scruples about the partition, but fear of continuing vulnerability in the competitive international system overcame her qualms. Frederick II of Prussia remarked unkindly, "The more she weeps, the more she takes."

Joseph II Maria Theresa died in 1780 and was succeeded by her son, **Joseph II**, who was also determined to strengthen Austria against Prussia. But as his foreign policy never resulted in clear victories, he pushed domestic reforms in a more radical direction. In the 1780s, he abolished serfdom. Then, in 1789, using new property tax rolls, he abolished the rents and uncompensated work obligations peasants owed their landlords, replacing them with a single cash payment. He also imposed state taxes on the ex-serfs.

Traditional procedures had denied the state direct jurisdiction over peasants; the state had to work through the noble landlord class. But Joseph's reforms asserted direct state control. Peasants were to keep 70 percent of their income, the rest going in payments to the landlord and the state. Predictably, landlords resisted his radical restructuring of political and social relations, but peasants rose up in support of the reforms. The result was widespread rebellion when Joseph died in 1790. His brother, who succeeded him as Leopold II, restored order by making concessions to the landlords. He reinstituted serfdom and landlords' control of peasants. Serfdom was not permanently abolished until 1848.

Austria's defeat in war led to radical social reforms intended to increase peasant prosperity, which in turn would allow for higher taxes and more money for the army. Thus, the dynamics of Europe's fiercely competitive international system fundamentally shaped the course of Austrian state-building over the second half of the eighteenth century.

Britain a Winner; France a Loser Although Britain and France fought each other in Europe alongside their respective allies, their real contest was overseas in North America and India. In 1763, at the end of the Seven Years' War, Britain was the undisputed winner. British victories drove the French off the North American mainland. Britain also secured its predominant place in India. But the victory in North America created problems of its own that led directly to the American Revolution and indirectly to revolution in France.

CHAPTER Review

Summary

» After 1648, Europe's rulers engaged in vigorous state-building. In France, Louis XIV pressed change from above based on the principle of royal absolutism, as did rulers in Prussia, Russia, and, eventually, Austria.

» In the British Isles, absolutism gave way to limited constitutional monarchy after the Glorious Revolution, but William III's wars against Louis XIV increased the effectiveness of the central government in Britain while strengthening Parliament's role in policy making and administration.

» In all cases, the frequent warfare fostered by the competitive European state system was the prime incentive for strengthening the state.

» Successful state-building involved establishing good working relations between rulers and elite groups.

» In France and Prussia, nobles' political independence was curbed while their social preeminence was confirmed with honors and opportunities for state service.

» In England, after the failure of royal absolutism in 1689, the monarch had to cooperate with the landowning classes who controlled Parliament as well as local government.

» In Russia, rulers after Peter the Great wooed the landlord class by canceling compulsory state service but confirming landlords' rights over the serfs on their estates.

» Failure to establish working relations with the elite could lead to rebellion, as it did in Austria when Joseph II antagonized the nobility with his attacks on serfdom.

» Joseph's abolition of serfdom was motivated in part by a desire to use state power to improve the lives of ordinary people, and the serfs responded by cooperating in the updating of property rolls and rising in support of reform when nobles resisted change.

» In France, Louis XIV's reforms also had the same effect; control of the army eased fears of violence and looting, and efficient and fair royal courts encouraged confidence.

» Louis XV's reforms of police forces and poor relief offered new services to his subjects.

» But when ordinary people's needs were overlooked by rulers, revolt could follow, as Pugachev's rebellion in Russia shows.

» After 1648, religious commitments continued to shape identity and sometimes led to conflicts.

» Although Protestants throughout Europe denounced Louis XIV's revocation of the Edict of Nantes, the French Catholic population supported it.

» In England and Scotland, attacks on Catholics had widespread popular support.

» The Old Believers in Russia refused any cooperation with the state-supported Russian Orthodox Church.

» In France, Huguenots who refused conversion to Catholicism were also brutally dealt with.

» In general, however, the trend after 1648 was toward limited toleration of religious dissenters.

» In addition, forms of collective identity shifted from religion toward the national community.

» Wars between Britain and France produced a surge of patriotism in each country.

» While religious difference contributed to the stereotyping of the enemy, more state-centered issues, such as control of colonies or prosperity in trade, also whipped up patriotic fervor.

Chronology

1640	Frederick William becomes elector of Brandenburg [Europe]
1650s	Madeleine de Scudéry presides over her salon in Paris [Europe]
1657	Leopold I becomes Holy Roman emperor [Europe]
1660	Charles II is restored as king of England, Ireland, and Scotland [Europe]
1661	Louis XIV becomes his own prime minister [Europe]
1672–1679	Dutch War between Louis XIV and the Dutch Republic [Europe]
1682	Peter I the Great becomes tsar [Europe]
1685	Louis XIV revokes Edict of Nantes [Europe]
1688–1689	Glorious Revolution dethrones James II [Europe]
1700–1721	Great Northern War between Russia and Sweden [Europe]
1701–1713	War of the Spanish Succession between Louis XIV and most of Europe [Europe]
1702	Anne becomes queen of England, Ireland, and Scotland [Europe]
1707	England and Scotland unite to form the kingdom of Great Britain [Europe]
1711	Charles VI becomes Holy Roman emperor [Europe]
1713	Pope condemns the Jansenists [Europe]
1713	Spain grants Britain the *asiento* [Europe, Americas]
1714	George I of Hanover becomes king of Great Britain [Europe]
1715	Louis XV becomes king of France [Europe]
1727	George II becomes king of Great Britain [Europe]
1740–1748	War of the Austrian Succession ends in a draw [Europe]

1756–1763	Seven Years' War leads to British and Prussian victories [Europe]
1757	Ottoman Sultan Mustafa III begins his reign [Middle East]
1761	British seize the French colony of Pondicherry on India's east coast [Europe, Asia]
1762	Catherine II the Great becomes empress of Russia [Europe]
1772	First partition of Poland [Europe]
1780	Joseph II becomes ruler of the Habsburg lands [Europe]
1780s	Joseph II abolishes serfdom in the Habsburg lands [Europe]
1790s	Leopold II reestablishes serfdom in the Habsburg lands [Europe]

Critical Thinking Questions

Take a moment to pull together all the important information from the chapter by answering the following questions:

Absolutism in France, 1648–1740

» What steps did Louis XIV take to unify the French state and to eliminate the possibility of rebellion and disorder in the kingdom?

» What motivated Louis XIV to deny religious toleration to the Huguenots, and what were the reactions to his policy at home and abroad?

The Austrian Habsburgs, 1648–1740

» How did Leopold I's involvement in the wars against Louis XIV affect his reconquest of Hungary? What were the specific stages in the reconquest?

» What was Leopold I's attitude toward the local Hungarian population, and what were his relations with them?

The Rise of Prussia, 1648–1740

» How did the Great Elector use war and diplomacy to gain full control over the duchy of Prussia?

» What techniques did the Great Elector and King Frederick William I use to strengthen the central state and make its running more efficient?

Russia and Europe, 1682–1796

» Which reforms of Peter the Great were kept by his successors, and which were modified or eliminated?

» How was Russian society organized at the beginning of Peter the Great's reign, and how did it change under his successors?

The English Constitutional Monarchy, 1660–1740

» Why was James II driven from the throne?

» What were the features of the "mixed monarchy" that emerged out of the Glorious Revolution?

Two World Wars, 1740–1763

» What steps did Maria Theresa and Joseph II take to reform Austrian society and the state, and what were the results of these efforts?

» What was the doctrine of the balance of power, and how did it influence the diplomatic revolution of 1756?

MindTap® is a fully online personalized learning experience built upon Cengage Learning content. MindTap® combines student learning tools—readings, multimedia, activities, and assessments—into a singular Learning Path that guides students through the course and helps students develop the critical thinking, analysis, and communication skills that are essential to academic and professional success.

Chapter Outline

As you read, consider the following questions:

❱ What were the basic differences between traditional Christianity and the New Science on views of God, the natural world, and the human world?

❱ How did the Enlightenment draw on and expand the method and findings of the scientific revolution?

❱ How did the principle of autonomous human reason shape the institutions and programs of the Enlightenment?

❱ How did Enlightenment debates reshape Europeans' sense of their identity and the identity of non-European peoples?

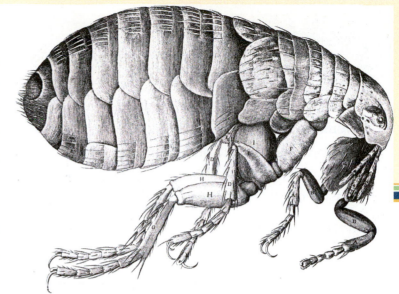

Engraving of a Flea, from Robert Hooke's *Micrographia*, 1665. akg-images / Universal Images Group

IN EUROPE DURING the seventeenth and eighteenth centuries a general shift in scientific theory and method, which had begun in the sixteenth century, gained wider and wider ground. This scientific revolution, which first occurred in astronomy, physics, and anatomy, fundamentally altered people's view of the universe. Improvements in lens making for telescopes allowed people to see the stars and planets in new detail while the use of new lenses in microscopes revealed in detail a new world of very small things, like the flea shown at the beginning of this chapter. These developments led to the articulation of a scientific method that relied more on human reason to arrive at truth and less on the authority of ancient authors and sacred scripture. Now a new intellectual figure, the scientific expert, began to challenge the views of traditional theologians and those who believed that the best human knowledge was found in the works of ancient Greeks and Romans.

The New Science also inspired attempts to apply scientific methods to other fields of inquiry in an intellectual movement known as the Enlightenment. Relying on the scientific method's use of human reason to arrive at truth, the Enlightenment created the modern social sciences. Traditional Christianity also came under scrutiny; many supporters of the Enlightenment thought religion should be based on observation of the natural world and the exercise of human reason. Some abandoned traditional Christianity altogether. As a result, the Christian worldview that had dominated European thought for more than a thousand years now competed with non-Christian and even nonreligious alternatives.

The principles of both the New Science and the Enlightenment were spread through new communication networks. Scientific societies, polite salon gatherings, coffeehouses, Masonic lodges, and debating clubs, for all their differences, created environments for discussion of the ideas and methods of both movements. Discussion also filled the pages of a growing number of books, newspapers, and pamphlets, as writers and publishers produced a wide variety of reading material for increasing numbers of literate Europeans.

As more and more people engaged in public discussion of current affairs, a new intellectual and political force arose—public opinion—that could determine an author's success or failure and even sway the policies of kings.

Debate was a central feature of both the scientific revolution and the Enlightenment. Women participated in these debates, and soon their increasing presence in European intellectual life led to a debate over issues of gender equality and the relations between men and women. Growth in commerce and the establishment of overseas colonies around the world also provoked debate about Europe's place in the larger world. By the end of the century, debate also centered on a central feature of commerce and colonization—the institution of slavery. In these debates, as in religion, Christian ideas had to compete with approaches that paid more attention to nature, climate, and biology than to traditional theology.

17-1 A Revolution in Astronomy

» **What were the central features of the new scientific method?**

» **What factors explain the rise of the New Science?**

The religious crises that shook Europe in the sixteenth and seventeenth centuries were accompanied by an intellectual crisis. Beginning as a new theory of the universe that placed the sun, not the earth, at its center, it grew into a questioning of the traditional sources of authority guiding European thought about the natural world—ancient authors, and Christian scripture. Gradually, as the new view of the universe gained acceptance, new sources of authority based on close observation of natural phenomena and the use of independent human reasoning were embraced. These changes are usually described as the scientific revolution (see Map 17.1).

17-1a Ancient and Medieval Astronomy

Following the translation of classical works in the twelfth century, Europeans' views of the universe had been shaped by two ancient Greek authorities: the philosopher Aristotle and the astronomer Ptolemy (TOHL-eh-mee). For centuries, medieval universities had synthesized their teaching with Christian theology to describe how the universe worked.

The Earth as Center of the Universe In this system, the earth was at the center, created by God to be fixed and unmoving. But in terms of worth, the earth was the lowest element in the cosmic scheme. It was the place of decay; as one philosopher put it, our world was "the worst, the lowest, most lifeless part of the universe, the bottom story of the house." It was only in this region, which stretched upward to the moon, that change took place. Here, night turned to day; plants sprouted, bloomed, and died; and human beings moved from cradle to grave.

The innate nature of objects determined some of the movement in this region. Thus, acorns grew into oaks and kittens into cats because both strove to realize their potential and reach their goal as mature organisms. The same striving toward their goals also characterized nonliving things; fire leapt upward because its proper place was in the heights, while a rock thrown in the air fell because its place was on the earth. Essentially, objects were urged along by their inner natures to come to rest in their rightful place.

Rest was the natural state of being for objects; it was only motion that had to be explained. In the case of human beings, God's decrees determined the movement of their lives; they hurtled toward death and decay because of their sinful rebellion against God until Christ redeemed them and they found their place of rest in Heaven.

The Heavens Above the moon, a radically different part of the universe reigned. In these regions, there was no change or decay. The sun and the planets, made of a uniquely pure and perfect substance, moved endlessly in circles (the noblest form of motion, as Plato had taught). Above them were the fixed stars, which also moved in a circle, propelled by the angels. As all these bodies moved, they created a wondrous music, the harmony of the spheres. Beyond the stars the universe ended, and the mysterious realm of God's Heaven began.

Map 17.1 **Europe During the Scientific Revolution and the Enlightenment** This map shows that most scientific and Enlightenment centers were in the cities of western and central Europe.

1. What factors might explain this geographical spread?
2. What factors might explain the absence of scientific and Enlightenment centers in parts of Europe?
3. Why do you think intellectual life was focused in cities?

A Plausible Picture of the Universe? This picture of the natural world seemed to work because it was confirmed in multiple ways. First, it corresponded with common sense (sun, moon, and planets *did* move across the sky). Common sense was in turn reinforced by prediction. Ptolemy had shown that it was possible to calculate the trajectories of the planets in advance, and astronomers in the centuries after him had confirmed and refined his calculations. Finally, this view

corresponded with what were taken as the revealed truths of Christian scripture.

17-1b A New View of the Universe

In the sixteenth century, a new view of the universe challenged the traditional one. As it spread, an intellectual crisis developed, rivaling the crises in faith and certainty created by the Protestant Reformation,

The Trial and Condemnation of Galileo

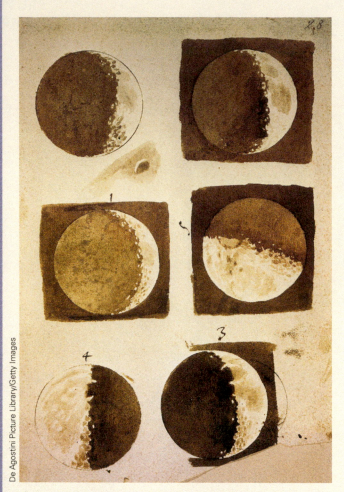

De Agostini Picture Library/Getty Images

Illustration from Galileo's *The Starry Messenger*, 1610
The surface of the moon seen through a telescope.

On June 22, 1633, Galileo Galilei, aged seventy, stood before the judges of the Roman Inquisition to hear the sentence passed on him. Galileo was found "vehemently suspect of heresy" for advocating a sun-centered theory of the universe and sentenced to house arrest for life. The judges then banned the publication of all his past works and ordered him to recant his views.

The trial of 1633 brought to a head Galileo's role in the long dispute between the defenders of the Aristotelian understanding of the universe and the supporters of Copernicus, which had been raging for more than twenty years. In 1609, when Galileo began to view the heavens through the newly invented telescope, he saw astonishing things that would turn traditional understandings of the universe upside down—mountains on the moon and moving spots on the sun. How could these phenomena be reconciled with the traditional view that the heavens were free of imperfections and unchanging? Galileo concluded that they could not, and this decision led to the train of events resulting in his condemnation in 1633. But there were many twists and turns along the way.

In 1610, Galileo published his telescopic findings in *The Starry Messenger*. His gifts as a writer made his works widely popular but also stirred up angry opponents among the traditionalists. Friendly readers carried out their own observations and confirmed what Galileo reported while enemies continued to deny the accuracy of his reports and some, it seems, simply refused to use the telescope. As the controversy widened, Galileo's sympathy with the Copernican view became more and more apparent, and in 1614 he was denounced to the Roman Inquisition. Brushing aside the advice of friends in Florence, he decided to go to Rome to defend himself in person.

the Wars of Religion, and the discovery of the New World—an entire hemisphere with previously unknown plants, animals, and human beings.

Nicholas Copernicus
(1473–1543) Polish astronomer who posited a sun-centered universe in which the earth and the other planets move around the sun.

Tycho Brahe (1546–1601)
Danish astronomer who partly confirmed Copernicus's theory of a sun-centered universe.

The Sun-Centered Universe
The challenge began with a Polish clergyman in East Prussia, **Nicholas Copernicus**. Seeking to improve Ptolemy's predictions of planetary movement by making them simpler, Copernicus started with the assumption that the earth and the planets moved about the sun. His *On the Revolutions of the Heavenly Bodies*, published in 1543, was quickly denounced by both Protestants and Catholics. Nevertheless, Copernicus caught the attention of some astronomers, who began building on his work.

Tycho Brahe and Johannes Kepler One of the first was a Dane, **Tycho Brahe** (TY-co BRA'heh), who spent years producing the best logs of planetary movement yet compiled. He also described in detail a new star that appeared in 1572 and, thereby, disturbed the traditional view that the universe above the moon was changeless. But Brahe held the traditional view that the earth was the unmoving center of the universe; for him, the planets moved around the sun, but the sun moved around the earth.

Brahe's work was continued by his pupil, **Johannes Kepler**, who used Brahe's calculations to argue that the planets moved in elliptical, not circular, orbits around the sun and that the speed of their movement

In Rome, Galileo faced the power and authority of the Catholic Church in the person of Cardinal Robert Bellarmine. Bellarmine, a Jesuit, was one of the most learned theologians of his generation, and he took the challenge of Copernicanism seriously. In the end, he arrived at a carefully crafted position on the matter. Copernicanism, he said, was best taught as a theory about the universe that was not based in fact. If, however, it could be demonstrated *conclusively* through observation that it was factual, it could be embraced with the proviso that contrary statements in Scripture were true but simply not properly understood by human beings.

In 1616, the conflict became even more intense when the Roman Inquisition condemned Copernicanism outright. Bellarmine was told to convey this judgment to Galileo and to order him to stop teaching Copernicanism. Shortly thereafter, books supporting the sun-centered view were placed in the Index.

In 1623, the climate suddenly seemed better for Galileo when a friend and fellow Florentine became pope as Urban VII. When Urban encouraged Galileo to take up the two positions and to make a careful presentation of the pros and cons of each, it seemed possible to reopen the debate.

Urban also stipulated that his own traditional views should be presented as well. The result was the *Dialogue Concerning the Two Chief World Systems*, published in 1632. Galileo employed all his wit and skill as a writer in this work, which brought together an Aristotelian, a Copernican, and a neutral commentator. In the end, the Copernican and the neutral commentator demolished the views of the Aristotelian, named Simplicio ("simpleton" in Italian). When readers finished the book, many realized that Simplicio the Simpleton was the one who proposed the pope's views. Urban was furious and Galileo taken aback because he had modeled Simplicio not on the pope but on well-known Aristotelians. The result was the trial, condemnation, and house arrest of 1633.

Beginning in the mid-eighteenth century, the Catholic Church began a slow retreat from its condemnation of Copernicanism and Galileo when it dropped the general prohibition of any book defending Copernicus. Galileo's *Dialogue*; however, along with Copernicus's work, were not formally dropped from the Index until 1835. In 2000, Pope John Paul II issued a formal apology for the trial and condemnation of Galileo.

Print Collector / Contributor/ Hulton Archive/Getty Images

Johannes Hevelius's *Selenographia*, 1647

In an engraving from Johannes Hevelius's *Selenographia* (1647), an astronomer, perhaps Hevelius himself, looks at the heavens through a telescope. After Galileo's pioneering efforts, observatories sprang up all over Europe. Hevelius's observatory, on the roof of his house in Danzig, was one of the best.

❯❯ *Why do you think the artist decided to put passing clouds in the sky?*

varied. Both points also challenged older ideas about the unchanging nature of the upper universe.

Galileo Galilei, a professor of mathematics from Florence, continued the work of Copernicus, Brahe, and Kepler. While these men had viewed the heavens with the naked eye, Galileo used the newly invented telescope. He also confirmed Copernicus's theory that the planets and the sun rotated on their own axes and posited that the earth did the same. These phenomena further undermined traditional ideas (see Profiles in Change: The Trial and Condemnation of Galileo). Galileo also conducted carefully controlled experiments on earthly bodies, rolling metal balls down slopes of varying degrees. He argued that material bodies were naturally in motion, thereby questioning the older idea that they moved only when they were displaced from their homes and rested once they arrived there.

Sir Isaac Newton Galileo's work was built on by others interested in the New Science. The greatest of them was the Englishman **Sir Isaac Newton**. In his *Mathematical Principles of Natural Philosophy* (1687), Newton brought together

Johannes Kepler (1571–1630) German student of Brahe who argued that the planets moved in elliptical orbits around the sun.

Galileo Galilei (1564–1642) Italian astronomer who first used the telescope to view the heavens and argued in favor of the Copernican system.

Sir Isaac Newton (1642–1727) English mathematician and philosopher who established the modern science of physics.

Sir Isaac Newton

Sir Isaac Newton was sixty years old when this portrait was painted by Sir Godfrey Kneller in 1702. He had published his *Mathematical Principles* some fifteen years earlier and was at the height of his fame. National Portrait Gallery, London/The Bridgeman Art Library

Sir Francis Bacon (1561–1626) English defender of the New Science who endorsed the inductive method of inquiry.

inductive method Method starting with observation of phenomena and then making general statements about them based on the observations.

René Descartes (1596–1650) French philosopher who argued for the principle of autonomous human reason as the basis for human knowledge.

deductive method The process of drawing logically coherent conclusions from self-evident first principles

the work of Copernicus, Brahe, Kepler, and Galileo to present a complete picture of the universe. Planets, rotating on their axes, traveled around the sun in elliptical orbit. Their orbits and the variations in their speed were controlled by gravity, a force of mutual attraction that kept the planets from flying off into space. Gravity also explained the behavior of bodies on the earth, as described by Galileo. Beyond the solar system, the universe stretched out infinitely. Newton presented his picture mathematically. Although only a handful of his contemporaries understood his advanced equations, his ability to knit the work of his predecessors into an all-encompassing description of the universe

proved compelling and established the modern science of physics.

17-1c Models of Scientific Knowledge

Just as important as the new view of the universe were the methods developed for proposing it. Taken together, they radically altered traditional European views of how human beings know anything.

Bacon and the Inductive Method Sir Francis Bacon, lord chancellor of England under James I, was an early advocate of an approach to knowledge grounded in careful observation and experimentation. For him, the source of authority for knowledge about the natural world was found in that world itself, not in the writings of Greeks or Romans. He was, therefore, an early defender of a purely **inductive method** of reasoning, which based general statements on observation of phenomena as the only proper way to gain knowledge.

René Descartes (reh-NAY day-CARTs) Just as influential was a French mathematician and the inventor of analytic geometry, **René Descartes**. Descartes was deeply affected by the intellectual crisis the Protestant-Catholic split had created in Western Christendom. The constant attacks of each side against the other had led to massive intellectual confusion. Some maintained that since no human opinion could ever be shown to be definitively true, one had to take a leap of faith and submit to the authority of the church and its teachings. Others embraced a thoroughgoing skepticism about the truth of any human argument. Descartes began by examining himself.

"I Think, Therefore I Am" Self-examination was something Christians had practiced for centuries, but Descartes struck off in a new direction. He decided that he would submit every statement he had heard about humans and their world to radical doubt. If there was any reason, no matter how small, to doubt it, he would treat it as worthless. Statement after statement was tossed aside until, finally, Descartes came upon something that, try as he would, he simply could not doubt: "I think." This undoubted truth became his principle of knowledge. From it he drew another equally firm conclusion: "Therefore I am." I exist as a thinker—that was the starting place for knowledge.

The Deductive Method and Autonomous Human Reason Descartes then went on to reconstruct the world, moving from previously established points to new ones that followed logically from them. This **deductive method**, modeled on geometry, lay behind his *Discourse on Method* (1637). In arriving at reliable knowledge, Descartes departed from Bacon.

Instead of looking out at the natural world, he looked inside himself and found an authoritative source for all knowledge—the principle of autonomous, or independent, human reason.

Human reason had always played an important role in traditional Christian views about the sources for human knowledge; the medieval Scholastic movement had placed a premium on logically presented argument. But in the older view, reason was also supplemented by divine revelation, which corrected or completed what human beings could think on their own. For Descartes, human reason stood alone as a reliable source for human knowledge.

The Newtonian Synthesis: The Scientific Method

Newton combined Bacon's and Descartes's methods to argue that any statement about the natural world had to pass two tests. First, it had to correspond to what was found by observation and experimentation. Second, it had to fit logically with all else that was known about the phenomenon being investigated. He thus combined inductive and deductive methods to arrive at knowledge about the world and thereby laid the foundations for the modern **scientific method**. Newton's method impressed people as much as his description of the universe. His mighty mind had swept the heaven and the earth, revealing for the first time how the universe worked. As the English poet **Alexander Pope** exclaimed:

> *Nature and Nature's laws lay hid in Night:*
> *God said, Let Newton be! and all was light.*

(Excerpted from Alexander Pope's poetry (1688–1744).)

17-1d Why Change Occurred

Many factors contributed to the new view of the universe. One stemmed from Renaissance humanists' rediscovery of ancient authors, including Plato. In the medieval West, Aristotle had reigned supreme. With the recovery of other ancient works, it became clear that Aristotle's theories had been contested in their own times and could be challenged again by new approaches to nature.

The Role of Mathematicians and Craftsmen

Another factor concerned the people engaged in the study of nature. Traditionally, philosophers pursued natural studies in a university setting. Much of the new work, however, was done by mathematicians working outside the universities. Copernicus, Kepler, and Descartes worked on their own or sought support from princely patrons.

Mathematicians' prestige rose when they were called on to help with land reclamation and canal building in places like the Dutch Republic or land surveys for taxation purposes in states trying to raise more revenue. Applying mathematics to solve specific problems was also in tune with the humanist emphasis on useful knowledge.

Usefulness also lay at the heart of another tradition contributing to the New Science, that of craftsmen. As sailors ventured out into the Atlantic, the need for precise astrolabes and quadrants to measure their positions had enhanced the work of those who produced these instruments and improved them through experimentation. Thinkers such as Galileo employed craft traditions of experimentation using metal balls, telescopes, and other devices to examine natural phenomena more precisely. They then wedded observation and experimentation to mathematics.

The Role of Alchemy

Another intellectual pursuit fostering experimentation was **alchemy**. Alchemists believed that nature contained hidden powers that influenced how the world worked and that these powers might be revealed through careful observation of and experimentation with chemical and other natural processes. Isaac Newton, for example, was an accomplished alchemist, and his experiments in a little shed outside his rooms at the University of Cambridge contributed to his endorsement of the inductive method in physics. In addition, his theory of gravity was influenced by the belief that hidden forces determined how the universe functioned.

CONNECTIONS: For developments in physics after Newton, see Section 23-4c Chemistry and the New Physics.

Vesalius and the Role of Anatomy

Developments in anatomy also fostered increased attention to observation and experimentation. **Andreas Vesalius**, a Flemish professor at the University of Padua in Italy, broke with medieval tradition by conducting his own dissections of corpses during his lectures. Previously, anatomists had lectured from ancient authorities on what dissections would reveal but left the actual cutting to surgeons, who were considered inferior to professors.

Vesalius's dissections, which students loved, revealed that Galen, the greatest ancient medical authority, was incorrect when he stated that the interior wall of the heart separating the ventricles was perforated, allowing for the

scientific method Newton's combination of the inductive and deductive methods to establish a twofold method for scientific inquiry.

Alexander Pope (1688–1744) English poet and literary critic who championed Newtonian physics and the Enlightenment's emphasis on the study of human beings.

alchemy Discipline practiced in the Middle Ages that searched for the hidden relations between natural phenomena.

Andreas Vesalius (1514–1564) Flemish physician who dissected human corpses and corrected some ancient statements about human anatomy.

circulation of the blood. That the heart wall was solid now required a whole new theory of blood circulation. An English student at Padua, **William Harvey**, worked one out in 1628 after examining animals slaughtered for their meat. Harvey combined Vesalius's insistence on direct observation with the craft traditions of butchers to develop his theory and thereby laid the foundation for modern physiology.

The Old Science and the New Defenders of the New Science argued that it stood in sharp opposition to the rigid, unalterable medieval version. In fact, however, the relationship was more complex. For example, both the old and new science insisted on the importance of a logical presentation of an argument. Medieval science had also raised issues like the nature of the terrestrial and celestial realms that preoccupied the New Scientists, and medieval terminology continued in use.

But as the **scientific revolution** progressed, the criteria for making arguments shifted. Scientists who relied more on mathematics, craft traditions, and careful experimentation were developing a new view of the universe as a place full of motion, with much still to be discovered, a view in stark contrast to the unchanging and unchangeable world of Aristotle, Ptolemy, or the Bible.

17-2 The Impact of the New Science

» **Who participated in the scientific revolution and how did the participants characterize themselves?**

» **What was the impact of the New Science on theology and political theory?**

William Harvey (1578–1657) English physician who described the circulation of blood in the human body.

scientific revolution Name given to the new views of the natural world and the new methods for obtaining them that began in the sixteenth century.

Royal Society One of the earliest scientific academies, founded in London in 1660.

Robert Boyle (1627–1691) Founder of the Royal Society who advanced understanding of air pressure and chemistry.

Those practicing the New Science were from many regions of Europe. Their findings were spread by means of a new institution, the scientific society, made up of well-to-do men who thought of themselves as a new type of educated person, the modern man of science. The societies developed procedures for presenting and verifying scientific experiments. They also provided guidelines for reproducing them and published new information for the interested public. As new views of the universe spread, along with the new scientific method and the principle of autonomous human reason,

traditional European religious and political thought expanded in new ways.

17-2a Scientific Networks

The first scientific societies developed in princely courts. In Prague, the emperor Rudolf II (r. 1576–1612) established one of the first. Rudolph was a moody, reclusive man who fought with his brother for control of the Habsburg empire, but he was also interested in artistic and scientific developments and joined with the king of Denmark to support Tycho Brahe's work. In Florence, Cosimo II not only patronized artists such as the French printmaker Jacques Callot but also supported Galileo and encouraged scientific discussion. In England, Bacon called for a research institute whose members would be royal employees collecting information to enhance state power. In fact, no such institute was created. Scientists' connections with the state were therefore looser than Bacon had hoped. Although Charles II of England and Louis XIV of France granted charters to the **Royal Society** of London and the French Royal Academy of Sciences, respectively, scientists generally worked free of direct royal control.

Membership Membership in scientific organizations was overwhelmingly male. That men interested in science had to have a formal education further limited membership to the economically well-off. Members met to discuss issues of method and to learn what experiments others in the organization had performed. Some societies followed the lead of the English Royal Society and published reports of scientific findings.

Demonstrating Physical Phenomena Demonstrations of observable physical phenomena played an important role in scientific meetings. The correctness and accuracy of observations could be confirmed when many members agreed on them. During meetings, orderly procedures and polite behavior were insisted on. In addition, gentlemanly codes of honor and honesty helped to guarantee that the experimenters could be taken at their word. In printed presentations of experiments, detailed descriptions of equipment, procedures, and results were given so that readers could feel that they, too, had been present when the experiment took place. Detailed description also made possible the reproduction of the experiment.

"Priests of Nature" Members of scientific societies believed they were a new class of people called to interpret the book of nature. **Robert Boyle**, a founder of the Royal Society of London who made important contributions to the study of air pressure and chemistry, called its members "priests of nature" because they revealed God's work through experimentation and observation. Boyle was a deeply religious man.

He believed that men performing experiments must be modest and unassuming, in contrast to university debates, which had traditionally been conducted in public with lots of verbal fireworks. Personal ambition, prejudice, and passion had no place in proper scientific work. From these ideas emerged the modern concept of scientific objectivity.

17-2b Science and Religion

Newton's theory bound the earth to the heavens, describing both as operating under laws that made motion as natural as rest. In his view, the universe seemed to function like a machine or a huge self-regulating clock. After being wound up, clocks ticked away in orderly fashion, following the laws governing their construction. The universe, he proposed, operated in the same way.

In addition, Descartes and others argued that everything in the universe was made up of tiny particles that moved mechanically by universal laws of attraction and repulsion. Rocks, plants, animals, and human beings were like the planets—matter in motion. So it now seemed that there was a man-machine as well as a universe machine. If all this was true, where did God fit in? For a few, the answer was clear: he didn't. For the great majority, however, there was definitely a place for God in the new order.

The Argument from Design Clocks required a clockmaker, and, by analogy, the universe required a universe maker. This widely held belief was reinforced by the **argument from design**. Newton's wonderfully regulated universe could not have come into being without a designer. The microscope, perfected by the Dutch lens maker Anton van Leeuwenhoek, was also important in this regard because it revealed previously unknown worlds, small in size but intricate in detail, that also pointed to a divine designer.

Innate Ideas Descartes's view that all bodies, including human ones, were simply matter in motion struck many as **atheistic**. But Descartes, a Catholic, believed in the Christian God. He argued that humans were unique. Not only did they have bodies made of matter, which were governed by the laws of attraction and repulsion; but they also had minds, which were nonmaterial.

God endowed human minds with the ability to reason, and Descartes reasoned his way to God's existence. For example, he argued that humans were finite beings who yet had a clear and distinct idea of God as an infinite being. Since the idea of an infinite being cannot be conceived by a finite one, it must be an **innate idea** given to humans by God himself. Arguments like these were meant to preserve the basic features of traditional Christian theology while relying solely on the principle of autonomous human reason for arriving at them.

A "Dwarf-God?" If the universe was like a huge clock, did God wind it up at the beginning and then allow it to run on its own? Some of Descartes's arguments seemed to imply this belief, while others made room for ongoing divine intervention. Newton also insisted on God's regular activity in keeping the universe running and denounced the idea of a "dwarf-god" who did nothing more than set the world machine in motion.

The Book of Nature For the New Scientists of the seventeenth century, the universe was not only a great machine, but it was also the book of nature. Like the book of scripture, it could be consulted for knowledge of the Christian God. Protestants argued that the book of nature could be enlisted in the battle against Catholic error. A universe operating in a regular way under natural laws had no place for Catholics' superstitious beliefs in miracles performed by saints. The Catholic Galileo argued that knowledge of nature led to a proper interpretation of scripture. Biblical references to the sun's motion around the earth should not be taken literally; they were simply God's concession to "the shallow minds of the common people."

Blaise Pascal One mathematician and scientist, **Blaise Pascal**, took issue with the heavy reliance on observation and reason as the best guides for religious thought. Pascal was a devout Jansenist who worried that Descartes's emphasis on autonomous human reason and innate ideas improperly downplayed the traditional Christian emphasis on revelation as a source of religious knowledge. Pascal gave reason and observation their proper place in the construction of human knowledge: Although humans were mere specks in an infinite universe, and frail as reeds tossed about in the wind, they were thinking reeds. But Pascal introduced another source of knowledge: "heart." Heart drew on intuition, allowing a deeper view into the human condition than either reason or observation.

"Heart has its reasons that Reason does not know," Pascal explained. For him, the human condition was characterized by both wretchedness and grandeur. Human wretchedness manifested itself in people's selfish, passion-driven, sin-filled lives as they hurtled toward the abyss of death. Grandeur

argument from design Widely held belief in the seventeenth century that the complex and beautiful design of nature was proof of a divine designer's existence.

atheism Belief that there is no God.

innate ideas Ideas about God, the human mind, or anything else that seem to be a primary part of human mental equipment.

Blaise Pascal (blaiz pas-KAL) (1623–1662) Scientist and defender of traditional Christianity who stated that "heart" could lead one to the deepest religious truths.

manifested itself in the deep self-awareness of that wretchedness that "heart" opened up. Life as it is, is not life as God originally meant it to be. Pascal died before he could present his ideas in a defense of traditional Christianity, but his notes have survived in his *Pensées* (*Thoughts*), one of the great philosophical and religious statements of the seventeenth century and published in various editions since 1670.

Pascal was one of many seventeenth-century scientists whose beliefs were shot through with traditional Christian values and concerns. Bacon believed that the accumulation of natural knowledge would prepare for Christ's return to the earth, and Newton believed that human mastery of nature was a step in restoring the human race to Paradise, where Adam was master of the world before he fell into sin.

17-2c Science and the State

On April 2, 1662, Jacques-Bénigne Bossuet (zhahk-beyneenyeh BOS-ou-way), a bishop in the Catholic Church, preached a sermon "On the Duties of Kings" before Louis XIV in which he celebrated the theory of absolute monarchy. "You are gods," he said to Louis. "You are all sons of the Most High." These flattering words came from Psalm 82. Bossuet then went on to describe how the king ruled without any human check on his power. Each point was justified by an appropriate quotation from Christian scripture.

Basing politics on the Bible had been practiced since the days of the first Christian emperors of fourth-century Rome. Bossuet was, therefore, the heir to centuries of European political thought. At the same time, however, justifications for absolutism based on the New Science were also being proposed. Descartes's endorsement of the sun-centered universe, for example, was adopted as a model for Louis XIV's monarchy. Just as the planets orbited around the sun, so French subjects should be obedient to the Sun King.

Thomas Hobbes The Englishman **Thomas Hobbes** also drew on scientific thought to argue for absolutism. Hobbes had lived through the turmoil of the English civil war and Commonwealth and had accepted Descartes's idea that human beings were matter in motion. Combining his experience of political instability and violence with his mechanical view of human beings, he argued in *Leviathan* (1651) that people, if left to themselves, would simply attack each other. The pre-political, or natural, state was "every man against every man" because each human piece of matter in motion would try to fulfill its desires at the expense of the others. "Man is a wolf to his fellow man," he concluded, and all life is "nasty, brutish, and short."

Thomas Hobbes (1588–1679) English political theorist who tried to defend absolutism on scientific grounds.

The solution was to submit to an ironclad authority, a "mortal God," who would rule over everyone and force obedience to laws that restrained the aggressive impulses in people.

Hobbes's defense of absolutism differed from traditional ones by not being based on the ruler's divine right to rule. He believed that the people created the absolute ruler (who might be a king or a parliament) to end the self-defeating violence of pre-political society. Absolutism was, therefore, based on a contract between ruler and ruled, not on God's will.

John Locke Another Englishman, John Locke, also argued that government rested on a contract between ruler and ruled. But he drew quite different conclusions from this premise. Locke was an opponent of absolutism and had fled to Holland when James II became king in 1685. Returning to England with William and Mary, he published *Two Treatises on Government* (1690), in which he justified the Glorious Revolution. Locke had a more optimistic view of human nature than Hobbes. He believed that people could curb their aggressive impulses without coercion from an absolutist government. People entered into a political contract voluntarily and could withdraw from it when it no longer suited their purposes. The chief purpose of government was to protect private property rights. Locke's notions of contractual government and rights of private property supported the overthrow of James II, the repudiation of absolutism, and landowners' control of Parliament under a constitutional monarchy. His thought also had an impact on the American revolutionaries of the eighteenth century.

Although Hobbes and Locke had different views of human nature and endorsed different kinds of states, both tried to construct their politics on the basis of experience and reason rather than tradition and scripture. Their work represents some of the first attempts to construct a "political science."

17-2d The Nature of History

Growing enthusiasm for the New Science also provoked a sharp argument over the nature of human history. Traditional seventeenth-century understandings of history were pessimistic. Some stated that history was the sad story of decline and decay from an original high point, sometimes identified as the Garden of Eden and sometimes as Greek and Roman culture. In either case, humanity's passage through time was simply a slide downhill from an earlier golden age.

A less dismal view presented history in cyclical terms. Humanity passed through high stages and then slid into decay until, once again, it started to ascend to a high point that, in turn, would provoke another period of decline. Thus, in a Protestant version of the cyclical theory, the high point of Christianity's first days was followed by a decline as Catholicism spread, until Martin Luther's or John Calvin's day, when Protestantism returned Christianity to its original purity and a high point was once again reached.

Traditionalists sometimes argued that the natural world was subject to decay as well; plants and animals, along with people, had degenerated over time. People who held these traditional views of natural and human history were called Ancients.

The "Moderns" Beginning in the late seventeenth century, a new view of history gained ground, held by people dubbed Moderns. Inspired by the New Science, the Moderns argued against a decay over time of the natural world, citing the timeless, universal laws that Newton had discovered. Moderns also optimistically argued that human history was the story of intellectual progress. Although ancient Greek and Roman poets and playwrights were as good as contemporary ones, ancient scientists had been surpassed. Progress pointed to the overall superiority of Moderns. The battle between Ancients and Moderns continued on into the eighteenth century.

17-3 The Enlightenment

> » How did the Enlightenment employ the methods of the New Science?

> » What were the major items on the Enlightenment's agenda for reform?

Isaac Newton was the inspiration for a new European intellectual movement that emerged in the last years of the seventeenth century. People who joined it described themselves as enlightened because they had embraced Newton's view of the universe along with his scientific method. Historians have adopted the term for the movement itself. The Enlightenment was the most energetic current in European thought during the eighteenth century.

17-3a The Early Enlightenment

England, the home of Isaac Newton, was one center for the early **Enlightenment**. The power of Newton's scientific method inspired his fellow countryman, John Locke, to apply it to a new field of study, the human mind. In 1690, Locke published *An Essay Concerning Human Understanding*, in which he took issue with Descartes's belief that God had planted some innate ideas in the mind. Instead, Locke argued, our minds at birth are like "white paper, void of all characters, without any ideas." Ideas arise only through experience of the world around us. And that experience comes through our senses of sight, hearing, taste, touch, and smell.

A Science of the Mind Locke's *Essay* was one of the foundational documents of the Enlightenment. It showed how Newton's scientific method could be used to establish a new science, that of the human mind, and thereby laid the foundations for the modern discipline of psychology. At the same time, it ratified a central tenet of the scientific method—reasoning on the basis of experience and observation. The *Essay* also had one profound implication. Sense knowledge can come only from the physical, material world because it alone is capable of registering on the senses. That meant that human beings could not directly know the immaterial or supernatural world, even if it exists.

An Unknowable Supernatural World? Thus, the *Essay*, repudiating the notion of innate ideas and limiting human knowledge to sense impressions, cast serious doubt on the reality of divine revelation as an authority for guiding people's lives. Messages from the supernatural beyond seemed less and less likely in Locke's world.

"The Proper Study of Mankind Is Man" Locke's interest in the mind testifies to a central concern of the Enlightenment: the study of human beings. In the sixteenth century, when the Western Christian world split into two warring camps—Catholic and Protestant—the problem of God was a central intellectual issue. The scientific revolution brought the study of nature to the fore. In the Enlightenment, attention shifted once again. As Alexander Pope put it:

Know then thyself, presume not God to scan;
The Proper study of Mankind is Man.

(Excerpted from Alexander Pope's poetry (1688–1744).)

The Baron de Montesquieu Another center of the Enlightenment was France, where the **Baron de Montesquieu** (MON-tes-qew) took the study of humans in a different direction. A nobleman and a lawyer, Montesquieu sat in the French Parlement of Bordeaux. He made his literary debut in 1721 with *The Persian Letters*, a witty critique of French society supposedly written by Persian tourists.

In 1748, he published one of the great works of the Enlightenment, *The Spirit of the Laws*. Unlike Locke, who had studied the individual human mind, Montesquieu focused on human beings as a group. Assuming that there was a universal human nature, he then sought the causes for the great variety of human political arrangements—monarchies, republics, despotic states—and found them in environmental factors. A comparative analysis led him to argue that climate and geography played an important role in shaping the features of any given society. He concluded that a society's traditions concerning religion,

> **Enlightenment** European intellectual movement of the eighteenth century using the scientific method of the New Science.

> **Baron de Montesquieu** (1689–1755) One of the founders of the modern discipline of sociology and author of *The Spirit of the Laws*.

government, and economic activity also contributed to its distinctive shape, or "spirit."

Government in France Montesquieu argued that good government in France depended on the nobility, seated in institutions like the parlements, which put restraints on both the monarchy and the common people. He also greatly admired the constitutional monarchy of Britain. Montesquieu's interest in the role of natural and historical factors in shaping a society laid the foundations for the modern discipline of sociology.

17-3b Voltaire

If any person embodied the Enlightenment, it was the French philosopher and author **Voltaire**. The son of a middle-class Parisian lawyer, Voltaire attended the prestigious Jesuit school of Louis-le-Grand. He then defied his father, who wanted him to enter the law, by deciding to make his living as a writer. In 1718, his first play, *Oedipus*, which recounted the Greek legend of the king who killed his father and slept with his mother, ran on the Paris stage for an unprecedented forty-five nights. This success established the young man as France's foremost author of tragedies. A few years later, he published an epic poem on the reign of Henry IV of France, the *Henriade*, his most popular work.

The Philosophical Letters on the English In late 1725, a quarrel with a descendant of one of France's greatest noble families landed Voltaire in the **Bastille (bas-TEEL)**, a notorious royal prison. He was released in 1726, on the condition that he go into exile in England. He did, and his exile set him on the path that made him France's greatest *philosophe*, the name French supporters of Enlightenment gave themselves.

Voltaire stayed in England until 1729, becoming familiar with Newton's and Locke's writings and learning about the English form of monarchical and parliamentary government. In 1733, he published *Philosophical Letters on the English*, a seemingly innocent account of English politics, religion, and society that was, in fact, a scathing denunciation of contemporary France. The issues Voltaire raised in the *Letters* formed the basis for his subsequent career as a reformer.

The subversive tone of the book was not lost on the

Voltaire

In this contemporary portrait, Voltaire is fashionably dressed and wears a wig. His eyes have moved slightly to his right so he can look directly at the viewer. Mary Evans Picture Library/The Image Works

》 *Why might the painter have chosen this way to depict Voltaire?*

》 *Compare this portrait to that of Newton earlier in this chapter. How are they similar? And different?*

French authorities, who ordered it burned in public by the royal executioner and issued a warrant for Voltaire's arrest. Fleeing Paris with his new mistress, **Emilie du Châtelet**, he took up residence near the French border in case a quick getaway was needed. Mme. du Châtelet, an accomplished physicist and mathematician, helped Voltaire deepen his understanding of Newton. In 1738, he published *Elements of Newton's Philosophy*, which helped to establish Newton's reputation in France.

The Calas Affair Voltaire was also interested in the improvement of French society. He sought reform of the criminal justice system, especially an end to the use of torture. In 1761, he heard of the perfect case to make his points. In the southern French town of Toulouse, a young Huguenot, Marc-Antoine Calas, was found hanged in his father's shop. It was rumored that Calas was about to convert to Catholicism. Although his family claimed that Calas had committed suicide, the Parlement of Toulouse, dominated by Catholics, charged his father, Jean, with

Voltaire (1694–1778) Social critic, attacker of Christianity, defender of the principle of autonomous human reason, and author of *Candide.*

Bastille Medieval fortress in Paris serving as a royal prison.

philosophes (in French, "philosophers") Name French supporters of Enlightenment ideas gave themselves.

Emilie du Châtelet (1706–1749) Voltaire's mistress and intellectual companion who was an expert in Newtonian physics and mathematics.

murdering him to prevent his conversion. The elder Calas was found guilty and then subjected to excruciating torture to get him to confess to his crime before his execution. The elder Calas refused, even when his bones were broken, and he was finally strangled to death.

Was the father guilty or not? If he was, for Voltaire he demonstrated Protestant fanaticism; if not, the court demonstrated Catholic fanaticism. Either way, the case demonstrated the barbarity of judicially sanctioned torture. Voltaire turned the **Calas affair** into a European scandal that widely discredited the use of torture in criminal proceedings.

The Attack on Christianity The affair also gave Voltaire the opportunity to attack traditional Christianity, whether Protestant or Catholic. For years he had rejected Christian teaching. Now, he openly subjected Christianity to withering ridicule and began closing his letters with the phrase "Stamp out the infamous thing," by which he meant the churches, their ministers and priests, and their teachings. The Jesuits, in particular, came under heavy attack, perhaps because, as Voltaire told Alexander Pope, they had sexually molested him while he was a student at Louis-le-Grand. Although most supporters of the Enlightenment remained Christians, Voltaire's public, passionate attack on Christianity marked a turning point in the religious history of Europe.

Candide Voltaire's campaign to improve human society was waged despite his sense of the limits of reform. When a huge earthquake destroyed the city of Lisbon in Portugal, he published his most famous work, *Candide, or Optimism*, which ridiculed the German philosopher Gottfried Wilhelm Leibnitz and the English poet Alexander Pope, who argued that we live in the best of all possible worlds. Nevertheless, Voltaire endorsed a limited optimism. As Candide says at the end of the novel, "We must cultivate our gardens," by which Voltaire meant that despite calamities like the Lisbon earthquake, which are beyond any human control, some things can and should be changed.

Voltaire also carried on a huge correspondence, exchanging letters with his fellow philosophes, and also with Catherine II of Russia and Frederick II of Prussia, who invited him to his court outside Berlin. No European writer since Erasmus in the sixteenth century was as well connected as Voltaire.

In early 1778, Voltaire, now eighty-three, returned in triumph to Paris. The city's most prestigious theatrical company, the Comédie-Française, performed his tragedy *Irene* and placed his statue in their theater, the only living author to be so honored. At his death, in May of that year, he was arguably the most famous man in Europe. The modern edition of his works fills more than 135 volumes.

17-3c The Enlightenment and Religion

Although Voltaire declared war on Christianity, he was no atheist. He embraced **deism**, a rational religion based solely on the observation of nature. Deism drew on Locke's sense-based psychology, the argument from design, and Newton's clock-like universe. As a religious movement, it denied the Christian doctrines of the Trinity, the divinity of Jesus, and the divine authority of the Bible. Most deists also rejected Newton's notion that God intervenes in the universe to keep it going. Deists emphasized the need for humane treatment of human beings, supporting the campaign against judicial torture.

The Fight for Religious Toleration For Voltaire and other deists, like Benjamin Franklin and Thomas Jefferson, deism and religious toleration went hand in hand. Since traditional religion, whether Jewish or Christian, was based on fraud and foolishness, it could never be legitimately defended by attacking those who rejected it. Even acceptable religious belief, like deism, was a matter of individual conscience over which no state or church authority ought to have jurisdiction.

Voltaire's pursuit of these points in the Calas affair met with growing sympathy, and, in 1787, on the eve of revolution in France, Louis XVI signed an edict granting limited religious toleration to the Huguenots. Deist-inspired calls for religious toleration also spread in Britain's North American colonies. After gaining independence, the new United States proclaimed religious toleration in its own Bill of Rights (1791).

Atheism: La Mettrie In addition to battling traditional Christians, Voltaire also denounced atheists. On this score, however, he was fighting a losing battle. By the mid-eighteenth century, more and more philosophes believed that the existence of God could never be proved by an argument from design or demonstrated as necessary for explaining the world and human beings. The **materialism** of Descartes, stripped of its Christian beliefs, could account for everything. The universe simply was, and humans were wholly material beings without souls or immaterial minds. At death, they ceased to exist.

Calas affair Trial, torture, and execution of Jean Calas, who was accused of killing his Huguenot son to prevent his conversion to Catholicism.

deism Religious belief that rejected traditional Christian teachings and tried to base its theology on scientific method.

materialism Argument that material things alone exist, therefore denying the existence of a soul or of an immaterial world.

Enlightenment Attitudes About Tradition

THE TWO SOURCES THAT FOLLOW BELOW WERE BOTH WRITTEN IN THE EIGHTEENTH CENTURY, ONE BY A JAPANESE PHYSICIAN AND ONE BY A FRENCH *PHILOSOPHE*. Despite their composition at roughly the same time, at first glance they seem to have little in common. Upon closer examination, some common threads emerge.

As you read, think about the two men's audiences, about their attitude to tradition, and their assumptions about the nature of human thought and observation. In what ways do they each reflect Enlightenment and scientific revolution ideas?

❶ In his account does Sugita Gempaku have his eye primarily on Japan? Or Europe? Or both?

❷ Were the roles of butchers in anatomical studies the same in Europe and Japan?

❸ Compare the reactions of these Japanese physicians to their established anatomical authorities to those of the European anatomists discussed in this chapter.

❹ What might lie behind this conjecture? How does it relate to some Europeans' thought about non-Europeans?

A Dutch Lesson in Anatomy, Sugita Gempaku

Sugita Gempaku (su-ghee-ta Ghem-pah-koo) (1733–1817) was a Japanese scholar and a pioneer in Dutch studies, a field that allowed Japanese scholars to gain information about the West. Trained as a physician and surgeon, Sugita Gempaku was present at a dissection of a cadaver in 1771. Here is his account of the events that led up to the dissection and his reactions to it:

❶ Somehow, miraculously I obtained a [Dutch] book on anatomy. [Then] I received a letter from . . . the Town Commissioner: "A post-mortem examination of the body of a condemned criminal by a resident physician will be held tomorrow. . . . You are welcome to witness it if you so desire."

The next day, when we arrived at the location . . . Ryotaku reached under his kimono to produce a Dutch book and showed it to us. "This is a Dutch book of anatomy called *Tabulae Anatomicae*. I bought this a few years ago when I went to Nagasaki, and kept it." As I examined it, it was the same book I had and was of the same edition. We held each other's hands and exclaimed: "What a coincidence!" Ryotaku continued by saying, "When I went to Nagasaki, I learned and heard," and opened this book. "These are called *long* in Dutch, they are the lungs," he taught us. "This is *hart*, or the heart." . . . However, they did not look like the heart given in the Chinese medical books, and none of us were sure until we could actually see the dissection.

Thereafter we went together to the place that was especially set aside [for] us to observe the dissection. . . . That day, the butcher pointed to this and that organ. After the heart, liver, gall bladder and stomach were identified, he pointed to other parts for which there were no names. **❷** "I don't know their names. But I have dissected quite a few bodies from my youthful days. . . . Every time I had a dissection, I pointed out to those physicians many of these parts, but not a single one of them questioned 'What was this,' or 'What was that?'" We compared the body as dissected against the charts both Ryotaku and I had, and could not find a single variance from the charts. The Chinese *Book of Medicine* says that the lungs are like the eight petals of the lotus flower, with three petals hanging in front, three in back, and two petals forming like two ears. . . . There were no such divisions, and the position and shapes of intestines and gastric organs were all different from those taught by the old theories. The official physicians . . . had witnessed dissection seven or eight times. Whenever they witnessed the dissection, they found that the old theories contradicted reality. **❸** Each time they were perplexed and could not resolve their doubts. Every time they wrote down what they thought was strange. They wrote in their books, "The more we think of it, there must be fundamental differences in the bodies of Chinese and of the eastern barbarians [i.e. Japanese]." I could see why they wrote this way. . . . **❹**

We decided that we should also examine the shape of the skeletons left exposed on the execution ground. We collected the bones, and examined a number of them. Again, we were struck by the fact that they all differed from the old theories while conforming to the Dutch charts. . . .

Source: *Japan: A Documentary History*, ed. David J. Lu (Armonk, NY: M. E. Sharpe, 1997), pp. 264–267. Used with permission of M. E. Sharpe, Inc.

1 How does Voltaire turn the technical theological terms he uses here against the doctrine of the Trinity?

2 Why would Voltaire choose to mock the Jesuits in this little dialogue? (Hint: See Chapter 14.)

3 Why would Voltaire introduce the Chinese Emperor in this dialogue? (Hint: See Chapter 14.)

4 How does Voltaire develop this story for comic effect?

5 In this dialogue does Voltaire have his eye primarily on Europe? Or China? Or both?

Voltaire Attacks Christianity

Voltaire wanted to present the ideas of the Enlightenment to a large reading public. He therefore polished a literary style that sparkled with wit and was laced with biting satire and moral outrage. The two pieces presented below illustrate Voltaire's attack on traditional Christianity, "the infamous thing." They were published anonymously, without the approval of the French royal censors, and represent the Enlightenment attack on Christianity in its most radical form, but they expressed views that many people repeated in the years to come.

On the Trinity

Here is an incomprehensible question which for over sixteen hundred years has exercised curiosity, sophistical subtlety, bitterness, the spirit of cabal, the rage to dominate, the rage to persecute, blind and bloodthirsty fanaticism, barbaric credulity, and which has produced more horrors than the ambition of princes, which indeed has produced enough.

1 Is Jesus Word? If he is Word, did he emanate from God, is he co-eternal and consubstantial with him, or is he of a similar substance? Is he distinct from him or not? Is he created or engendered? Can he engender in turn? Has he paternity, or productive virtue without paternity? Is the holy ghost created or engendered or produced? Does he proceed from the father, or from the son, or from both? Can he engender, can he produce? Is his hypostasis consubstantial with the hypostasis of the father and the son? And why, having precisely the same nature, the same essence as the father and the son, can he not do the same things as these two persons who are himself?

I certainly do not understand any of this; nobody has ever understood any of this, and this is the reason for which people have slaughtered one another.

The Story of the Banishing of the Jesuits from China

2 *Brother Rigolet:* Our God was born in a stable, seventeen hundred and twenty-three years ago, between an ox and an ass…. [His mother] was not a woman, but a girl. It is true that she was married, and that she had two other children, named James as the old gospels say, but she was a virgin none the less.

3 *The Emperor:* What! She was a virgin and she had children!

Brother Rigolet: To be sure. This is the nub of the story: it was God who gave this girl a child.

The Emperor: I don't understand you. You have just told me that she was the mother of God. So God slept with his mother in order to be born of her?

Brother Rigolet: You've got it Your Sacred Majesty; grace was already in operation. **4** You've got it I say; God changed himself into a pigeon to give a child to a carpenter's wife, and that child was God himself.

The Emperor: But then we have two Gods to take into account: a carpenter and a pigeon.

Brother Rigolet: Without a doubt, Sire; but there is also a third, who is the father of these two, and whom we always paint with a majestic beard: it was this God who ordered the pigeon to give a child to the carpenter's wife, from whom the God-carpenter was born; but at the bottom these three make only one. The father had engendered the son before he was in the world, the son was then engendered by the pigeon, and the pigeon proceeds from the father and the son. Now you see that the pigeon who proceeds, the carpenter who is born of the pigeon, and the father who has engendered the son of the pigeon, can only be a single God; and that a man who doesn't believe this story should be burned in this world and the other. **5**

The Emperor: That is as clear as day.

Source: Extract from Peter Gay, *Voltaire's Politics: The Poet as Realist* (New Haven, CT: Yale University Press, 1959), pp. 246–247. Reprinted by Yale University Press.

In 1746, a French physician, **Julien Offroy de La Mettrie**, argued these points in *Man the Machine*. His work caused a scandal in conservative circles, but, undaunted, he followed it up in 1749 with *Man the Plant*. La Mettrie also preached a gospel of pure physical pleasure, which made him doubly scandalous. In 1751, when he died after gorging himself on pheasant pâté, his enemies said the punishment fitted the crime.

CONNECTIONS: For a discussion of materialism in the ancient world, see Section 4-4c The Intellectual Approach to Identity.

The Methodists In 1738, **John Wesley**, a priest in the Church of England, wrote in his diary that on the evening of May 24, while listening to a reading from Martin Luther, "I felt my heart strangely warmed, I felt I did trust in Christ, Christ alone, for salvation." This experience of intense spiritual conviction shaped his life for the next fifty-three years. Up to that May evening Wesley had served as a cleric in England and then in the new English colony of Georgia, where he divided his time between preaching to the Native Americans and serving in the colony's church in Savannah. After nearly two years in Georgia, Wesley returned to England, after becoming embroiled in a legal dispute over his strict conduct as priest in the Savannah church. That was in December 1737. Then, the following May, he experienced the evening that changed his life.

Wesley's conviction of salvation in Christ led him to dedicate his full energy to preaching the good news of redemption to as many souls as he could reach. He preached from the pulpits of Anglican churches, and when no pulpit was available he took to "preaching in the fields," that is in the open air, to any group that would listen. This was a controversial move; the Church of England had rules governing the preaching of its priests. They had to be licensed and had to respect the jurisdiction of the parish in which they found themselves. Wesley broke with these regulations, following the example of another priest and close friend, George Whitefield. Preaching out of doors meant that many who would not ordinarily go into an Anglican church, and worship there in the forms set down in the Book of Common Prayer, would be able to hear the Christian message. And for Wesley and Whitefield, proclaiming this message was their overriding concern.

Over the years Wesley travelled throughout England and Ireland, preaching wherever and whenever he could. His message was clear: Christ's saving grace was available to all who chose to accept it. As he proclaimed this message he challenged those hearing it to decide how they would act. The choice was stark and the stakes were high—Christ or Satan, salvation or sin.

As Wesley and Whitefield's movement grew, and new preachers joined them, they came to be called the **Methodists** because of their distinctive method of preaching. Since preaching was the overriding imperative in the Methodist movement, Wesley accepted new preachers who had not been properly licensed by the Church of England. This created a deeper division between him and the church establishment. Wesley himself was deeply committed to the theology and worship of the Anglican Church, and was reluctant to make a formal break with it. But in the face of growing criticism over his unorthodox ways, a breach finally came. When Wesley started ordaining clergy on his own it was clear that the Methodists had becomes a separate Christian community in Britain.

Wesley's intensely heartfelt Christian preaching with its emphasis on sin and salvation was far removed from the religious world of Voltaire and the deists and even more far removed from the materialism of men like the Baron d'Holbach. But Methodists shared some common ground with those whose religious beliefs were very different from their own. Like many caught up in the Enlightenment movement, they joined a number of humanitarian causes. They called for the reform of squalid conditions in Britain's prisons and joined the fight against slavery even as they embraced their fervent and emotion-drenched form of Protestant Christianity.

The Enlightenment and the Jews After the self-proclaimed Jewish Messiah, Sabbatai Sevi, converted to Islam in 1666, his movement began to fall apart. Although a few "Sabbateans" continued to cling to parts of Sevi's discredited proclamation, in subsequent years Judaism in western and eastern Europe took shape around three other movements: Hasidic Judaism, traditional Rabbinic Judaism, and the Jewish Enlightenment.

CONNECTIONS: For more on Sabbatai Sevi's life, see Section 15-5c Sabbatai Sevi.

Hasidic Judaism In the 1730s, an emotion-drenched, mystically oriented form of Judaism inspirited in part by the kabbalah emerged in eastern Europe and spread through Poland and Lithuania. Its founder

Culture Club / Contributor/Getty Images

Sevi as Messiah

Julien Offroy de La Mettrie (1709–1751) French author of the materialist and atheistic works *Man the Machine* and *Man the Plant*.

John Wesley (1703-1791) Priest in the Church of England who preached salvation in Christ to many who were not regular churchgoers.

Methodists Name given to the movement stared by John Wesley and George Whitefield.

was known as the **Baal Shem Tov** (the "Master of the Good name [of God]"), an orphan who came from southwestern Ukraine and had received no formal schooling in the rabbinic traditions of Judaism. Eventually, the Baal Shem Tov, or Besht for short, became a charismatic travelling preacher and faith healer. The heart of his teaching was found in his understanding of prayer. Prayer started with the words in the Jewish prayer books but then moved down into the letters making up the words of the prayer. When the letters of the words were repeated with a concentrated intensity, they slowly disappeared, revealing the mysterious divine world they pointed to. Hasidic prayer was often an enthusiastic and noisy affair as its followers shouted the words and letters while swaying and dancing to them, and sometimes, smoking, drinking, and turning cartwheels. This intense, ecstatic form of prayer was at the heart of Hasidic understandings of what it meant to be a Jew. At times, it seemed to overshadow the idea that Jewishness was tied to a faithful following of God's commandments enshrined in the Law reveled on Mt. Sinai. To emphasize the distinctiveness of their movement, Hasidic Jews did not join other Jews in synagogue services conducted by rabbis but met in their own separate prayer halls.

The Besht also revived the concept of the *tzadik* (the righteous one), an extraordinary figure with heavenly powers who could guide Hasidic Jews as they entered into the mystery of prayer and union with the Divine. Eventually, the concept of the tzadik would shape the movement's understanding of the *rebbe*, the leader of later Hasidic communities. Hasidism was a popular movement formed at first outside the boundaries of the scholarly world of the rabbis and appealing to ordinary men and women. Its emotion laden practice of prayer and its appeal to ordinary people bore a general resemblance to John Wesley's Methodist movement in England.

Rabbinic Judaism From the beginning the Hasidic movement faced opposition. One of its earliest critics was **Elijah of Vilnius** in Lithuania, known to his admirers as "the Genius (*gaon*) of Vilnius." Elijah of Vilnius was a scholarly prodigy, delivering a commentary on the Jewish Law in the Vilnius synagogue at age six. He was also a prodigious Biblical scholar who allowed himself only two hours of sleep in any twenty-four hour period. To keep his mind focused on the study of Scripture he refused to heat his study in winter and kept his feet in cold water. Although he consistently refused the title of rabbi, he embodied the religiously inspired scholarly traditions of rabbinic Judaism with its concentrated study of the divinely given Law and the classical commentaries on it that stretched back to Antiquity and even, as the rabbis said, to Moses himself who had received the Law from God. For Elijah of Vilnius faithful observance and love of the Law was at the heart of what

it meant to be a Jew. As the Book of Psalms put it, "I shall acclaim You with an honest heart as I learn Your righteous laws . . . I opened my mouth wide and panted, for Your commands I craved (*Psalm 119: 7,131*)." Much of Elijah of Vilnius's effort was therefore spent on a mastery of Hebrew grammar that allowed him to correct errors in Scripture and the classical rabbinic texts that had crept in through scribal miscopying and threatened to obscure the divine precepts embodied in the Law.

The Hasidic movement horrified Elijah of Vilnius. The agitated, ecstatic praying of its followers was meaningless, along with the faith healing of the Besht. The movement's idea of the tzadic as a heaven-sent guide was blasphemous and smacked of Sabbatai Sevi's teaching. So he urged his fellow Jews to shun members of the movement and exclude them from their communities. But still, the movement grew and grew.

The Jewish Enlightenment Alongside Hasidic Jews and the rabbinical traditionalists another group emerged over the eighteenth century, "the enlightened ones (*maskilim*)." Like a number of their non-Jewish contemporaries, they were caught up in the debates over revealed versus natural religion and atheism. One of the best known of the enlightened ones was the German Jew **Moses Mendelssohn**. Mendelssohn argued for a Judaism stripped of miracles and other supernatural phenomena. Its basic truths could be proved by reason. Thus, at heart, Judaism was a code of enlightened human conduct that any reasonable person could arrive at and accept. This meant that no religious community, including the Jewish one, could claim to have a monopoly on religious truth. Throughout his life, Mendelssohn remained an observant Jew, following the Law and studying the Scriptures because these were the specific ways in which Jews entered into a relationship with God. Non-Jews entered into their own relationship with the divine using their God-given reason to guide them.

Although Mendelssohn denied that the Jews had a monopoly on religious truth, he had no trouble in arguing that in the larger European world they were an oppressed people and he worked tirelessly to end discriminatory legislation against them. He also urged

Baal Shem Tov (Besht). Israel ben Eliezer (1700–1760): the founding figure of Hasidic Judaism.

Hasidic From the Hebrew word "hasid (pious)."

Elijah of Vilnius (1720–1797) "The Genius (*gaon*) of Vilnius." Defender of traditional rabbinic Judaism and an opponent of Hasidism.

Moses Mendelssohn (1729–1786) German Jew who said that Judaism's basic beliefs were rationally provable and who worked to end discrimination against Jews.

Jews to be more open to the larger European culture. They should stop using Yiddish as a literary language and follow his example of writing in German. Mendelssohn shocked many Jewish traditionalists, but his views appealed to others and gained considerable acceptance, especially in western Europe.

The differences between the Hasidic movement, the rabbinical traditionalists like Elijah of Vilnius, and the "enlightened ones" like Mendelssohn were deep and real. But it would be wrong to think that they shared no common ground: Elijah of Vilnius, for all his criticism of the Hasidic enthusiasts, knew the traditions of the kabbalah and had no fundamental quarrel with them. And while he concentrated most of his efforts on expounding the divine Law given to Moses, he appreciated aspects of the secular learning of his time, urging his pupils to study them, and even wrote a textbook on mathematics. In turn, members of the Jewish Enlightenment appreciated and praised his careful editing and correcting of classical Jewish texts. All three of these types of Judaism continued to influence the life and thought of European Jewry from the eighteenth century on.

17-3d Diderot and the *Encyclopédie*

While Voltaire was crusading against Christians and atheists, some of his fellow philosophes were embarking on a highly successful publishing venture. In 1751, the first volume of the **Encyclopédie** appeared. Under the editorial leadership of **Denis Diderot (DEE-der-oh)**, sixteen more volumes followed over the next twenty-one years. The *Encyclopédie* was a huge commercial success, making millions for its publishers.

A Work to Present All Knowledge Diderot wished to present current knowledge on all subjects in a single multivolume reference work. He also wanted to show how all knowledge was interconnected and that the key to it rested on observation, experiment, and autonomous reason. Throughout the *Encyclopédie*, Diderot drew on the works of Bacon, Descartes, Locke, and Newton. He also got major Enlightenment writers, such as Montesquieu and Voltaire, to contribute articles.

In addition to standard articles on religious, philosophical, scientific, and artistic subjects, the *Encyclopédie* also had

Encyclopédie Multivolume work with contributions from philosophes throughout Europe that summed up the philosophy of the Enlightenment.

Denis Diderot (1713–1784) French writer and editor of the *Encyclopédie*.

Jean-Jacques Rousseau (1712–1778) Genevan Swiss social critic, philosophe, and novelist who pioneered modern democratic theory in his *Social Contract*.

groundbreaking contributions on craft and manufacturing processes such as brass making, printing, tapestry weaving, and fishing with nets. Inclusion of these articles testified to the importance that craft traditions had played in the emergence of the scientific revolution. They also met Diderot's insistence that the *Encyclopédie* should be useful. Usefulness also lay behind articles like "Asparagus," which not only described the plant and its cultivation but also gave five recipes as well.

Evading Censorship Diderot had to work under conditions of government press censorship, which was always on the lookout for unorthodox political or religious ideas and often forced him to make controversial points in subtle ways. One device he and his associates perfected for sneaking in inflammatory material was a system of clever cross-referencing. For example, in the article on "France," when Louis XIV's revocation of the Edict of Nantes was described, a cross-reference to "Toleration" was given. If Voltaire was the one man who best embodied the ideals of Enlightenment, the *Encyclopédie* was the one work that summed them up.

17-3e The Late Enlightenment

As editor of the *Encyclopédie*, Diderot had to be discreet in voicing his own opinions, but his works make clear that he, too, had embraced materialism and atheism. The leading philosophe of the late Enlightenment, however, did not. He was **Jean-Jacques Rousseau**, the son of a Genevan watchmaker. Rousseau was a Calvinist who converted to Catholicism and then embraced deism. His *Profession of Faith of a Savoyard Vicar*, an emotional defense of deism, won Voltaire's praise.

Rousseau's Attack on Civilization Rousseau was touchy, paranoid, and blunt. In the 1750s, he attacked the refined world of the philosophes and their aristocratic patrons. Rejecting the Christian idea of original sin, Rousseau believed that human beings were good by nature but that civilization had corrupted them because it encouraged injustice and inequality. His attacks alienated Voltaire, Diderot, and others who believed that civilization was a sign of human progress, not degeneration. Voltaire said he thought Rousseau wanted him to walk around on all fours. In fact, however, Rousseau did not want to abolish civilization; he wanted to reform it.

The Social Contract In 1762 Rousseau published *The Social Contract*, which advocated a democratic society and pioneered modern democratic theory. This work set him apart from other philosophes. For all their radicalism, Voltaire and Diderot were part

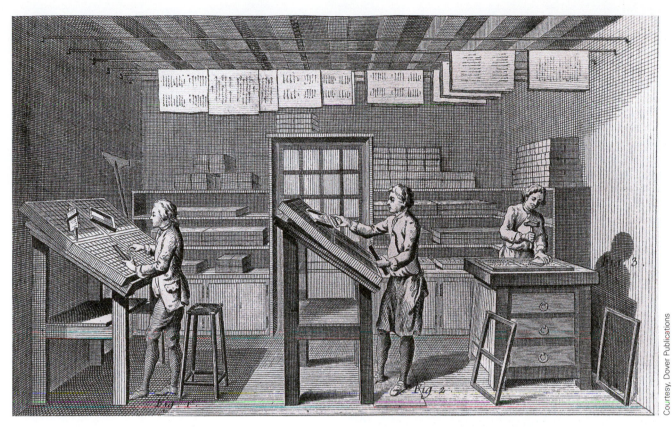

Courtesy, Dover Publications

A Printing Shop

This engraving of a craft process from Diderot's *Encyclopédie* shows a printer's shop. From left to right, men set type for a page, arrange lines, and lock the type in place. The type will print four pages at once. Previously printed pages are drying on lines above workmen's heads; when dry, they will be folded to arrange the pages in proper sequence. Diderot's emphasis on craft and manufacturing processes reminded readers of their importance and gave them a new dignity.

of the eighteenth-century literary establishment. Like the gentlemen who gathered in the scientific societies of the seventeenth century, they criticized society but did not want to overturn it.

In contrast, Rousseau wanted fundamental change. He argued that the good society is one in which all members voluntarily give up their individual rights and submit to what he called the general will. Usually, the general will amounted to the will of the community's majority, although Rousseau was careful to say that sometimes it did not. This point has confused some of his readers. What Rousseau really wanted was a community in which people participated in politics and acted openly for the true good of all the community's members. This ideal has served as a benchmark for democratic societies ever since.

The Confessions Rousseau's hunger for openness in human relations prompted him to write his *Confessions*. Published in 1781, three years after his death, the *Confessions* recounted in detail many of the most private facts of his life, among them acts

of theft, sex with a sailor, and the abandonment of a child he had fathered. While some were shocked by these revelations, Rousseau's real intent was to demonstrate that he was a man who hid nothing but presented himself fully to other human beings. If all people were as open, society could be fundamentally transformed.

Pamphlet Wars Rousseau's radicalism and rejection of refined aristocratic society was also endorsed by a host of pamphleteers and writers for hire who never made it into Voltaire's or Diderot's elite publishing circles. These people produced political criticism that mixed opposition to government policies with pornographic accounts of the degenerate lives of kings, queens, and nobility. Although these works had roots in earlier traditions of satire and slander, their volume and intensity increased in the late eighteenth century, especially in France after its defeat in the Seven Years' War. Overall, they undermined the legitimacy of traditional government as much as Rousseau's democratic criticisms did.

17-4 Society and the Enlightenment

>> **What impact did developments in publishing and reading habits have on European intellectual life?**

>> **What additional trends promoted the Enlightenment?**

Just as scientific societies helped to spread Newtonian physics, so new institutions served to popularize the Enlightenment. Publishers expanded the types of books they produced from religious works to new literary forms like the novel. Newspapers also became increasingly available to readers. This wider array of reading materials, which encouraged readers to digest the news of the day or enter into the world of the novel, offered new ways of thinking about human experience. The Enlightenment's insistence on rational discussion of topics spread through society as new opportunities opened for comment on current affairs in coffeehouses, salons, and Masonic lodges. Critical discussion of issues also spilled over into the political realm as ordinary people commented on rulers' policies and required rulers to justify their actions before a new political force, public opinion.

17-4a The New World of Reading

The invention of the printing press in the mid-fifteenth century, along with the Protestant Reformation and Catholic reforms of the sixteenth, ushered in a new era in the history of European book reading. Both Protestants and Catholics used print to attack their opponents and to present their coreligionists with catechisms and prayer books. Most of this popular literature was written in the languages spoken by the people rather than Latin, which was still the official language of learning. In Protestant countries, translations of the Bible also multiplied.

Prayer books, catechisms, and Bibles were read reverently and reread many times; Bible study required returning to passages over and over again, while prayers for the morning and evening were repeated daily. Habits of devout, repetitive reading, a reading style intimately linked to Christian belief, were predominant among literate people in the sixteenth and seventeenth centuries as religious publications multiplied.

New Types of Literature and New Styles of Reading
In the eighteenth century, both the types of literature available to people and styles of reading changed. Throughout the century, religious publications declined dramatically, and **novels**, a new literary type, rose to first place. Novels were particularly popular with women, who were now more likely to read than they had been earlier. Women like the

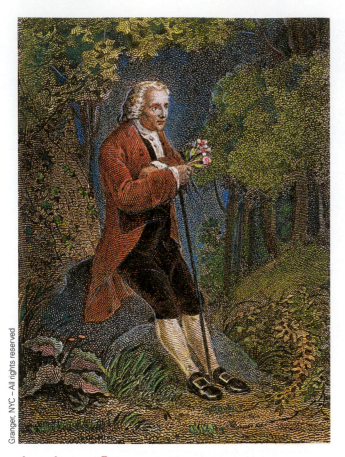

Jean-Jacques Rousseau

In this etching Jean-Jacques Rousseau is depicted as a "man of nature" who rejected the refined world of the salons. Leaning against a tree and holding a bunch of wildflowers, he contemplates the beauty of the natural world, which his deist God had created.

>> *Compare this etching with the portrait of Voltaire in this chapter. What do you think Voltaire would make of the differences?*

Immanuel Kant Other parts of Europe were less receptive to the radicalism that swept over France after 1750. In Prussia, **Immanuel Kant** summed up the philosophes' program in *What Is Enlightenment?* (1784): "Dare to know…. Have the courage to use your own understanding is … the motto of enlightenment." Kant, however, never advocated democracy or any real social or political reform. People were free to use their minds to seek the truth but, according to Kant, should submit to the current political, social, and economic orders in which they found themselves.

Immanuel Kant (1724–1804) Leading German philosophe of the late Enlightenment.

novel Literary form of prose fiction that was popular in the eighteenth century and sometimes used to promote social criticism and programs for reform.

Pierre-Antoine Baudoin's
Reading

In Pierre-Antoine Baudoin's *Reading*, the woman reads in private. Note how the screen behind her would prevent anyone coming through the door to see directly into the room.

❯❯ *Her book is a novel. What has become of it?*

❯❯ *And what does her posture and facial expression tell the viewer about her reading experience?*

Englishwoman **Aphra Behn** also figured prominently as authors of novels.

Although some people seemed to have read and reread novels many times, and thereby used the same technique for reading them as for Bibles or prayer books, most readers read the latest bestseller only once, then turned to something else.

Newspapers   In addition to novels, newspapers and political pamphlets became increasingly available in the eighteenth century, especially in Britain and the Dutch Republic where censorship laws were relaxed or abolished. Reading newspapers had often been a collective activity in which one person read aloud to a group, but increasingly newspapers were read privately and silently, like novels, and passed along until the next day's newspaper was available. As the variety of reading material expanded, it is likely that Europeans received more information about the world and, often lost in the contents of the page in front of them, had a wider range of imaginative reading experiences than people had ever had before.

Lending Libraries   One of the clearest signs of Europeans' expanding reading habits was the spread of **lending libraries**, which allowed anyone who joined to check books out to read where they wished and thus eliminated the cost of purchasing them.

Changes in Writing and Publishing   The nature of writing and publishing changed with new reading habits. Formerly, writers had either worked as

Aphra Behn (1640–1689) English novelist who pioneered the form and made a financial success of writing.

lending libraries Institutions allowing readers to borrow books from their shelves and then return them, thus avoiding the need to buy them.

London Coffeehouse

In this London coffeehouse, as the elegantly dressed owner looks on, a waiter pours coffee for the well-to-do men sitting at tables.

>> *How many different activities are they engaged in? (Note the coffee pots being kept warm in front of the fire.)*

economically self-sufficient gentlemen or had sought commissions from wealthy patrons. In the eighteenth century, some thought that the profession of author was beneath the wellborn, but others, like Voltaire and Diderot, were eager to make a living from writing. Few became as rich or famous as they, but many managed to survive on wages paid for their work.

Those wages came from publishers. Publishing became big business in the eighteenth century. Publishing houses often specialized in certain types of literature. Some produced cheap editions of fairy tales or almanacs, which peddlers carried in their packs throughout the town and countryside. Others, especially in the Dutch Republic, concentrated on controversial works that might be censored in other countries; Diderot, for example, used a publisher in the Netherlands for the *Encyclopédie*. Many of these works were then smuggled into places like France, where censors were sometimes bribed to look the other way when the books went on sale. Authors also tried to evade censors when they wrote something particularly scandalous; Voltaire was fond of blaming his literary rivals for his anti-Christian works.

Meeting and Shaping Readers' Demands
Publishers stayed in business by both meeting and shaping readers' demands and tastes. When a particular type of novel sold, they urged other writers to produce similar works. This worked well for Rousseau, whose *The New Heloise*, a runaway bestseller in 1761, fed a growing late-eighteenth-century taste for novels describing domestic settings that were full of romance, heartbreak, and feeling. His *Emile* (1762), a novel that advocated a "natural" course for children's education based on direct observation and experience at the various stages of a child's

development, also sold well. In fact, during his life, Rousseau was better known for these novels than for *The Social Contract*.

Increasing numbers of Europeans could afford books and newspapers, or lending library fees, in part because their disposable incomes rose as Europe entered a new period of prosperity in the early eighteenth century. Moreover, printed material was viewed less as an avenue to God or a source for spiritual improvement than as a means to worldly information and pleasure.

The new world of reading, writing, and publishing constituted a major shift in the intellectual activities of Europeans that the philosophes put to good use for popularizing their ideas and advocating programs of reform. Reading still remained, however, a practice that only a minority of Europeans engaged in, and the ideas of the philosophes were embraced by only a part of this reading public.

17-4b Enlightenment Sociability

Along with new types of literature and changing styles of reading, new institutions sprang up in which people could discuss what they read and put into practice the central method of the Enlightenment—thought based on autonomous human reason.

Coffeehouses and Teahouses Chief among them were coffeehouses and teahouses. Europeans' consumption of coffee and tea rose significantly during the eighteenth century as a result of expanded colonial trade and an improving European economy. While both beverages were drunk at home, many people, especially men, liked to take them in cafés where there were newspapers and pamphlets to read, opportunities to buy and sell stocks in joint-stock companies, and people to talk to.

The coffeehouse phenomenon had begun in Restoration London when Whigs took tea or coffee and discussed politics at Old Slaughter's, while the Tories gathered at the Cocoa Tree. Coffeehouses then sprouted up in Paris, Vienna, and other major European cities. The atmosphere in them was informal; one dropped in and left at will.

Originally patronized by the rich and fashionable, coffeehouses became more socially inclusive over the century. Men of different backgrounds who would normally be separated on more formal occasions mixed easily with one another in the coffeehouse atmosphere. And always, politics and other current events were discussed. Because coffee is a stimulant, animated discussion was the rule. Unlike taverns, however, where drinking often led to brawling, coffeehouse conversation was supposed to be orderly and polite, even if heated.

Salons Conversation was also the rule in salons. Invented in Paris during the seventeenth century, the salon became a central Enlightenment institution for the educated and wellborn. Women like Madame du Deffand, the wife of a rich Parisian financier, presided over salons that met in their homes on specified days and discussed topics that the hostess announced. The hostess also set rules for conversation that prohibited shouting, swearing, and name-calling. Guests were to converse politely, intelligently, and amusingly about the scientific, artistic, or political matters assigned for discussion. Anyone able to do this would be admitted. Thus, men and women, nobles and commoners, joined in. Although the hostess was usually rich and often noble, salons, like coffeehouses, were relatively informal institutions in which an ability to converse well counted more than wealth or social background. Even religious differences were overlooked in salons, especially in Berlin, where Jewish hostesses brought together Jews and Christians.

Masonic Lodges Masonic lodges also offered a new form of social interaction in which religious or class differences played a minor role. Guilds of masons who laid brick or stone had existed since the Middle Ages, but modern **Freemasonry** began in London in 1717, when a group of middle-class men formed a club in which Newton's science and other issues of current interest were discussed. By the 1720s, 75 percent of the London lodge members also belonged to the Royal Society.

Although Masonic lodges modified old rituals from the medieval guilds when they initiated new members, their main purpose was to create an environment like that of the salons, in which polite conversation on issues could occur. Masonic lodges spread throughout Europe in both Catholic and Protestant countries, despite the pope's condemnation of the movement in 1738 on the grounds that it advocated anti-Catholic ideas.

Like the salons, the lodges downplayed the social and economic differences of their membership. Brotherhood in the lodge made all members equal. These Masonic ideals were articulated in one of the century's great operas, *The Magic Flute*, written by **Wolfgang Amadeus Mozart** and performed in the last year of the composer's life. Mozart made a point of stressing Masonic ideals of human equality. At one point, when a priest exclaims that the hero is a prince, the high priest corrects him: "More than that! He is a man!"

17-4c The Enlightenment and Politics

The rational discussion taking place in new social settings also extended to politics, taking different forms in eastern and western Europe. In Scandinavia, Germany, and Russia, Enlightenment rationalism melded with an older political tradition, **cameralism**.

Cameralism Developing in the seventeenth century, cameralism aimed at increasing a state's wealth through direct management of people and resources. Government should intervene in people's lives to make them better fed, better housed, and better behaved so that they could become more productive. Cameralism also emphasized the need for a rational assessment of a state's strengths, weaknesses, and needs as the basis for good government policy. The state itself was compared to a machine. When properly managed, it could regulate society in the interests of increasing its wealth.

Cameralism was taught in eastern European universities to candidates for posts in the state bureaucracy. At the head of the bureaucracy was the ruler, whose job was to see that the machine of government ran smoothly and produced good results. Thus, kings were viewed more as supreme political managers than God-appointed rulers endowed with the sacred authority to govern. Many of the policies of Frederick William I and Frederick II of Prussia, as well as Peter the Great of Russia, were inspired by cameralist principles. Cameralism's emphasis on rational assessment of political needs, along with its conception of government as a well-run machine improving people's lives, fitted into many Enlightenment principles.

Freemasonry Social and intellectual movement that originated in England during the eighteenth century and spread across Europe.

Wolfgang Amadeus Mozart (1756–1791) Composer of symphonies, operas, and many other works who perfected the classical style in music.

cameralism Eastern European tradition of political thought emphasizing rational government policy making that melded with Enlightenment principles.

Politics in Britain In western Europe, greater discussion of politics by ordinary people gave rise to increased popular participation in politics. In Britain, the political turmoil of the seventeenth century, which led to constitutional monarchy and a permanent role for Parliament in shaping government policy, fostered ordinary people's discussion of political affairs.

Elections to the House of Commons also stimulated political debate, and, occasionally, commoners with widespread popular support could force the king to accept them as government ministers. In 1757, George II thus accepted **William Pitt the Elder**, though he despised Pitt's insistence that Britain's imperial interests were more important than Hanover's, the German principality from which the king and his father had come. It was Pitt who later masterminded the British victories in the Seven Years' War.

Parliament and the Public For its part, Parliament tried to shield its debates from the public by forbidding publication of its proceedings. But intense interest in the kingdom's politics, along with the growth of the press, forced Parliament to back down in the early 1770s. With parliamentary proceedings now publicly distributed, popular discussion of politics intensified.

Politics in France Similar developments also occurred in France. There the monarchy still clung to its absolutist principles, which proclaimed that there was only one political player in the realm, the king. Everyone else was supposed to be a mere spectator watching royal politics from the sidelines. While court etiquette at Versailles and official press accounts of the king's daily activities reinforced this view, it proved increasingly difficult to maintain.

Absolutism Under Siege Prolonged conflicts between the French king and the parlements over Jansenism, during which the parlements published their grievances, made it clear that others beside the king claimed a political role. The growth of the newspaper press and the rise of rational discussion in new social settings also encouraged the king's subjects to become actively engaged in discussion of policies and events.

Public Opinion In both England and France, therefore, public opinion played a growing role in politics. Its advent constituted a major shift in European political life. Monarchs who had previously argued that they ruled by divine grace and operated in a political world, whose rules could not be understood by the mass of their subjects, now had to contend with a growing chorus of voices commenting on and even criticizing what they did.

Although criticism of rulers could lead to charges of treason, it also forced governments to become more open in explaining and justifying their policies. As states made increasing demands on their subjects, rulers were increasingly expected to account for their actions.

17-5 Enlightenment Debates

>> **How did ideas about Europe's place in the world change during the Enlightenment?**

>> **How did Enlightenment thinkers confront ideas about difference among human beings?**

Discussion and debate were at the heart of Enlightenment intellectual life. Debating clubs, where men and women could hear opposing views on subjects of current concern, often addressed the degree of likeness and difference in the human community. The philosophes believed in universal natural laws and a universal human nature.

At the same time, they lived in a world where difference separated some people from others and thereby challenged universalism. Debates on human likeness and difference, which raged throughout the eighteenth century, focused especially on three issues: the relation between Europeans and non-Europeans; the institution of slavery; and the relation between men and women.

17-5a Europeans and Non-Europeans

As early as the 1540s, the debate over the humanity of non-European people had pitted Bartolomé de Las Casas against Juan Guinés de Sepúlveda. Las Casas argued that New World Indians were fully human, whereas Sepúlveda said they were not. In the sixteenth century, Europeans thought of their culture primarily in religious terms; they lived in Christendom, while others were either infidels (Jews and Muslims) or pagans (everyone else).

During the Enlightenment, as the debate continued, the terms in which it was conducted started to change. Under the influence of the New Science, natural factors like geology and climate, rather than the traditional religious categories of Christian and non-Christian, were used increasingly to explain diversity in the human community and to shape separate collective identities.

A Degenerate New World? Debate centered on two sets of people: those in the New World and those in the South Pacific. In 1770, a French priest and

William Pitt the Elder
(1708–1778) British minister during the Seven Years' War.

philosophe, the **Abbé (a-bey) Raynal**, published *The Philosophical History of the Two Indies*, which quickly became a runaway bestseller. Raynal argued, like Sepúlveda, that the Indian natives of the Western Hemisphere were inferior human beings. But Raynal went further, arguing that the natural world in America was as degenerate as the human one.

America, he wrote, had been formed later than Europe, rising from the sea in the recent past. This explained why the climate was damp and cold, making New England, which was on the same latitude as Spain, so snowy in winter. This chilly, watery New World produced plants and animals that were puny compared to their counterparts in Europe. Going even further, Raynal stated that Europeans who migrated to North America soon degenerated. Thus, America's geological history produced a climate that was inhospitable to all forms of life.

Jefferson and Franklin Strike Back

Raynal's attack provoked a sharp response from the North Americans. In 1781, **Thomas Jefferson** published his *Notes on the State of Virginia*, a spirited refutation of Raynal's work. Was Raynal correct when he wrote that Virginia's Indian men were less manly than Europeans because they had no facial hair? No. The Indians simply chose to pluck out their beards, and such warlike men could not be considered unmanly.

Did the New World produce puny animals? No. Look at the newly discovered bones of a huge American elephant, the **mammoth**. Were Americans of European origin degenerate descendants of their ancestors across the ocean? No. Look at **Benjamin Franklin**.

Franklin was Raynal's cleverest opponent. When the Continental Congress sent him to France in 1776 to seek French aid for the American Revolution, he made a point of refuting Raynal at every turn. Franklin's earlier experiments with electricity made him the ideal man of science, someone who, like Newton, revealed the workings of nature. His invention of the lightning rod made him the philosophe who worked for the betterment of humanity.

At Versailles, Franklin shunned the silks and lace fashionable men favored and dressed in plain brown, presenting himself as a simple American who was, nevertheless, the intellectual equal of any European. The French court was charmed. Franklin was a natural but noble man who showed no trace of deformity.

One evening, he and other Americans found themselves at a dinner party with Raynal. When the theory of American degeneracy came up, Franklin asked all the Americans at the table to stand, and then all the Frenchmen. The Americans towered over the French, and especially over Raynal, whom Franklin dismissed as a "mere shrimp." Soon afterward, Raynal retracted his unflattering picture of America. Franklin triumphed again in 1777, when France signed an alliance with the Americans in their war for independence from Britain.

The People of the South Pacific

Debate about non-Europeans also focused on the peoples of the South Pacific. In the 1770s, an Englishman, **James Cook**, and a Frenchman, **Louis-Antoine de Bougainville (LEW-ee-AN-twon deh BOO-gan-veel)**, led scientific voyages through the region and published accounts of their expeditions, feeding French and British thirst for travel literature.

The South Pacific was a new frontier for Europeans, and these accounts sparked interest in the local peoples. Diderot wrote a fictional *Supplement to the Voyage of Bougainville* (1772) in which he used Bougainville's account of Tahitians' free and open sexual activity to attack traditional Christian sexual morality as cruel and unnatural.

Raynal's denunciation of a degenerate America and Diderot's titillating account of the Tahitians' erotic freedom were part of a sustained discussion of European civilization and Europe's proper place in the larger world. One central issue was the nature of civilization itself.

Eurocentrism

Many Europeans continued to think in Eurocentric terms and to assert the superiority of their way of life, and most philosophes encouraged this view. Kant declared that the spread of Enlightenment and of reliance on autonomous human reason was a sign that Europeans, after centuries of immaturity, had finally reached adulthood.

Voltaire celebrated the refined world of salon conversation, seeing it as a sign of a truly civilized world. But Rousseau attacked civilization as a corrupter of humanity's original goodness and purity. Pointing to the tea and coffee drunk in Enlightenment salons, he claimed that overseas trade and colonies promoted an improper love of luxury and harmed other peoples.

Raynal also had his doubts. His depiction of America as an alien and hostile place that Europeans should have avoided arose in part from his belief that colonization had harmed

Abbé Raynal (1713–1796) French priest (*abbé*) and philosophe who argued that the natural world of the Americas was as inferior as its Indian inhabitants.

Thomas Jefferson (1743–1826) American revolutionary and author of the Declaration of Independence who refuted charges of the New World's inferiority to Europe.

mammoths Extinct American elephants of great size whose bones were found in the eighteenth century.

Benjamin Franklin (1706–1790) American revolutionary, diplomat, and scientist who refuted Raynal's claims of American inferiority.

James Cook (1728–1779) Head of three British Royal Society—financed expeditions into the South Pacific.

Louis-Antoine de Bougainville (1729–1811) French explorer in the South Pacific who gave his name to the bougainvillea, a flowering vine he discovered there.

UCLA Charles E. Young Research Library, Department of Special Collections. © Regents of the University of California, UCLA Library

New Zealand Warrior

This painting of a New Zealand warrior was made by Sydney Parkinson who accompanied James Cook on his first voyage to the South Pacific. It would seem both familiar and odd to Europeans. Their warriors often wore plumes on their hats, but a cape of fluffy flax and dog skins would never be seen on Europe's battlefields.

≫ *Why do you think this painting was included in Parkinson's account of his voyage?*

indigenous people Original inhabitants of a region, or "natives."

Declaration of Independence Document justifying separation of American colonies from Britain in 1776 and defending the theory of self-government.

human rights Rights given to all human beings by God or the natural order and that neither the state nor society may take away.

New Ways of Explaining Human Difference As philosophes like Rousseau, Raynal, and Diderot debated the nature of non-European peoples and the worth of commerce and colonies, they increasingly sought nonreligious explanations for differences among human beings and tried to articulate a sense of European identity in non-Eurocentric terms. Europe was simply one human community among many others in the world and could make no valid claims for superiority on religious, cultural, or commercial grounds.

17-5b Slavery

"We hold these truths to be self-evident: That all men are created equal; that they are endowed by their Creator with certain inalienable rights; that among these are life, liberty, and the pursuit of happiness." These words in one of the Enlightenment's most famous documents, the **Declaration of Independence** (1776), were written by Thomas Jefferson and proclaimed the philosophes' belief in universal **human rights**. But Jefferson was a Virginia plantation owner who never freed his slaves. This contradiction lay at the heart of Enlightenment debates over slavery.

The Slave Trade By the eighteenth century, trade in slaves from sub-Saharan Africa had gone on for more than a thousand years. During the Middle Ages, Arab traders had brought millions of them into the Islamic world. Beginning in the fourteenth century, the Portuguese brought African slaves to the Atlantic islands. Later Spanish, English, French, and Dutch traders transported Africans to Europe's colonies in the Western Hemisphere, where they worked the plantations that produced the coffee that Europeans drank in their coffeehouses and the sugar that sweetened their tea.

By the end of the eighteenth century, 11 million slaves had been forcibly taken to the Americas to labor for the 2 million Europeans who had migrated there. As demand for slave-produced commodities rose, the slave trade rose also, justified again and again with traditional arguments about biblical passages accepting the practice and the subhuman nature of Africans.

The Philosophes and Slavery The philosophes' attitude toward slavery was mixed. Both Hobbes and Locke endorsed the practice. Although Voltaire had attacked slavery in *Candide*, he came, reluctantly, to accept it as a fact of human life. Montesquieu argued against it, claiming that it undermined a society's moral well-being by oppressing the slaves while giving slave owners too much power. On the other hand, supporters of slavery could point to Montesquieu's argument that the hot, humid climate of the tropics had conditioned the people who lived there to resist work unless forced to do it.

indigenous people, as indeed it had. Following their first encounters with Europeans, the native populations of the Americas declined by 90 percent, largely as the result of epidemic diseases that swept through their communities, a demographic catastrophe unparalleled in human history.

Diderot's Tahitians also suffered from European intrusion into their world. In the *Supplement*, a Tahitian complains to Bougainville that "the idea of crime and the fear of disease entered among us only with you." Diderot rejected Rousseau's attack on all civilization but agreed that European colonization had introduced corruption and inequality to other peoples.

Growing Opposition to Slavery Moral objections had been raised against slavery since the late seventeenth century. In England, several Protestant groups called for its abolition. For example, **Quakers**, who believed that God's "inner light" shone in every human being's heart, argued that the taking of slaves was simply kidnapping and should be stopped, and Quakers in America who owned slaves were urged to free them. Some Anglicans also condemned the trade, arguing that slavery was incompatible with Jesus' gospel of love, despite scriptural passages that sanctioned it. Thus, both Christian and Enlightenment arguments could be made for or against slavery. Over the course of the eighteenth century, however, the balance tipped toward the antislavery position.

Aphra Behn Novelists, poets, and playwrights played a crucial role in this development. Writers of fiction took the lead in arousing sympathy for slaves and an imaginative understanding of the conditions in which they lived. One of the first was Aphra Behn. Her novel *Oroonoko*, published in 1688, described the enslavement of an African prince and his beautiful love, Imoinda. Prince Oroonoko is a physically handsome and morally upright man with an unquenchable love for freedom, and Imoinda displays all the womanly virtues.

Showing her readers that Oroonoko and Imoinda possessed the physical traits and moral qualities that Europeans admired, Behn wanted to evoke admiration for them and outrage over their enslavement. Her novel was eventually turned into a play, and its themes were repeated in a growing body of antislavery literature.

Works like *Oroonoko* and later narratives by slaves who escaped to tell their story drew readers into a world in which slaves were upright and blameless human beings who had suffered terrible cruelty and injustice. The effect was to cut through centuries of dehumanizing stereotypes and indifferent or hostile theological traditions.

By the late 1780s, both the London Committee for the Abolition of the Slave Trade and the French Society of the Friends of the Blacks were campaigning tirelessly for an end to the slave trade and the abolition of slavery. Although both the trade and slavery itself ended only gradually, the antislavery momentum would not, from this point, be reversed.

17-5c Men and Women

The problem of difference and likeness in human beings, which shaped the debate on slavery, was also addressed in debates over the nature and roles of men and women.

Women participated actively in the Enlightenment. Those who, like Madame du Deffand, presided over Europe's salons were arbiters of intellectual

Self-portrait, Vigee-Lebrun, Elisabeth Louise (1755–1842) / Ickworth House, Suffolk, UK / National Trust Photographic Library / Bridgeman Images

Elisabeth Vigée-Lebrun, *Self-Portrait*, 1790
Following a fashion made popular by Marie-Antoinette, the artist is dressed in fairly simple clothing with her hair in a natural style. She gazes at the viewer while her right hand paints the portrait.

❯❯ *Do you notice anything odd in this? Should her gaze be elsewhere? If so, why isn't it?*

discussion. Those who, like Aphra Behn, joined men as professional writers became respectable public figures. Women also wrote some of the pamphlets that increasingly shaped public opinion, and others, like Mme. du Châtelet, contributed to the spread of Newtonian science. In the arts, France's most sought-after society painter was a woman, **Elisabeth Vigée-Lebrun** (vee-zhay le-brun). Women's new social, intellectual, and professional activities raised the issue of similarity and difference between men and women and the proper relations between them.

Men and Women as Intellectual Equals To Descartes and Locke, it seemed self-evident that men and women not only possessed a common human nature but also were intellectual equals. Descartes had coupled his arguments about the power of autonomous human reason with a discussion of the mind's relation to

Quakers An English Protestant sect that rejected ceremony and an ordained ministry, relying instead on a mystical "inner light" to guide conscience.

Elisabeth Vigée-Lebrun (1755–1842) French society painter.

the body. He argued that the two were radically different; humans' bodies were wholly material and were subject to the laws of matter in motion. The mind, however, was nonmaterial. This **Cartesian dualism** made one thing perfectly clear: mind was not shaped by the body it went with, whether male or female. It floated free in a nonmaterial and, therefore, sexless world.

Locke's picture of the human mind pointed to similar conclusions. If the mind was like a blank sheet of paper, there seemed no good reason to argue for different male and female minds because both were subject to the same stimulus from sense experience.

Many philosophes accepted the implications of Locke's and Descartes's arguments. Diderot did not think that men and women were all that different and agreed with Montesquieu that a woman's sexually based role as a mother was only one part of her life, not its defining characteristic. Voltaire rejected the idea of distinct male and female minds; men and women were intellectual equals, as his collaborator, Mme. du Châtelet, demonstrated.

Acceptance of intellectual equality between men and women, however, did not prevent many philosophes from assigning them separate social roles. Rejecting the traditional idea that men had to rule women because women were prone to irrational and unruly behavior, the philosophes now argued that women should enforce the rules of civilization in society and thereby tame *men's* unruly behavior. The salon hostess performed this task and did so in women's traditional sphere, the household, while other women performed it as mothers who educated their children in proper behavior.

Rousseau on Men and Women Some philosophes rejected outright the idea of gender equality. Chief among them was Rousseau. Resurrecting old ideas about women's inferiority, Rousseau argued that women were irrational. Above all, they should play no public role in society as salon hostesses or commentators in the realm of public opinion. Their actual roles in this regard were simply another symptom of civilization's corrupting effect.

Women belonged at home, breast-feeding their children and obeying their husbands. As creatures of feeling, they played a central role in training children. Men alone, however, should carry on rational discussion and engage in politics.

A growing body of medical literature seemed to support Rousseau's denial of women's equality to men and their banishment from public life. Works by physicians, such as Pierre Roussel's *The Physical and Moral Makeup of Women* (1775), offered a new view of male and female differences that in good Enlightenment fashion claimed to be based on scientific observation.

Rejecting the traditional view that women were simply incomplete men, Roussel and others argued that women were completely different from them. For example, their nervous system, which included smaller brains, made it impossible for them to develop men's rational capacities. Their job was to nurture their babies and their husbands.

Mary Wollstonecraft Rousseau and the medical men found their opponent in **Mary Wollstonecraft**, the author of *A Vindication of the Rights of Woman* (1792) and the ablest defender of women's equality. Wollstonecraft pointed out the basic paradox of their views on women. These men attacked the despotism of kings and rejected the institution of slavery but endorsed the subordination of some human beings to others on the basis of gender.

Wollstonecraft believed with Rousseau that women as mothers should take charge of the moral and emotional education of their children, but she denied that they were inferior to men. If defects existed, she pointed out, they came from the inadequate education women received in a world where the best teaching was available only to men. Wollstonecraft argued that if women were educated with men on an equal basis, their seeming deficiencies would disappear.

A New Way of Discussing Men and Women In the Enlightenment, ideas about a universal human nature and gender-neutral minds mixed ambiguously with older ideas about women's inferiority and their proper place in the private, domestic sphere. But the debate among people like Rousseau, Roussel, and Wollstonecraft was conducted in increasingly nonreligious terms. Despite their differences, all sides looked less to Christian scripture and traditional church teaching on gender issues and turned instead to biology, psychology, and an examination of social conventions to demonstrate their respective positions.

Cartesian dualism Descartes's idea of the radical difference between material human bodies and nonmaterial human minds.

Mary Wollstonecraft (1759–1797) English writer and feminist who rejected the idea that women were physically and mentally inferior to men.

CHAPTER REVIEW

Summary

» The scientific revolution changed European views of the earth in fundamental ways. No longer were humans at the center of things; now they spun around the sun in an infinite universe. "These vast spaces terrify me," Pascal lamented in his *Pensées* (*Thoughts*).

» Many others, however, were excited by the new understanding of the universe. It rested on a scientific method that relied on autonomous human reason and careful observation to demonstrate that it was true, thereby advancing knowledge far beyond anything achieved in the ancient world.

» So great was the prestige of the New Science that its method was quickly applied to other fields of learning in hopes of turning them into sciences as well.

» The application of the scientific method to an ever-expanding set of problems was at the heart of the intellectual movement known as the Enlightenment.

» The philosophes employed autonomous human reason and careful observation to establish the modern disciplines of political science, psychology, and sociology.

» At the same time, they subjected traditional Christian views on politics, human beings, and human society to systematic criticism. Above all, traditional Christian theology was scrutinized and often rejected, wholly or in part.

» The Enlightenment promoted the principle of rational discussion in a variety of ways. Discussion and debate were put into practice firsthand in salons, coffeehouses, Masonic lodges, and debating clubs. There people met as equal intellectual partners regardless of their social backgrounds. As more and more people gathered in these new institutions, the habit of collective discussion of and participation in matters of current interest spread.

» The growing numbers of books, newspapers, and pamphlets also aided this sense of participation in current affairs as readers learned of debate and discussion going on in other parts of Europe.

» Although gossip and misinformation jostled uncomfortably with accurate information in this new world of talk and print, participation gradually turned people into a public whose opinions mattered.

» The growing activity of an engaged public would soon manifest itself in demands for more popular participation in political life, a fact that states recognized when they began appealing to public opinion for support of their policies.

» Although rational discussion was central to both the New Science and the Enlightenment, it did not always resolve problems to everyone's satisfaction.

» Ongoing debates over Europe's place in the world, the nature of non-European peoples, the acceptability of slavery, and issues of gender equality demonstrated disagreement as well as agreement. That these debates were conducted in increasingly nonreligious terms indicates a profound shift in western culture and an erosion of Christianity's dominance in Europe's intellectual life.

Chronology

1543	Copernicus publishes *On the Revolution of the Heavenly Bodies* [Europe]
1637	Descartes publishes *The Discourse on Method* [Europe]
1651	Hobbes publishes *Leviathans* [Europe]

1653	The Taj Mahal completed in India [Asia]
1687	Newton publishes *Mathematical Principles of Natural Philosophy* [Europe]
1688	Behn publishes *Oroonoko* [Europe]
1690	Locke publishes *An Essay Concerning Human Understanding* and *Two Treatises on Government* [Europe]
1717	First Masonic lodge opens in London [Europe]
1718	Lady Mary Wortley Montagu introduces smallpox inoculation in England [Europe]
1733	Voltaire publishes *Philosophical Letters on the English* [Europe]
1746	La Mettrie publishes *Man the Machine* [Europe]
1748	Montesquieu publishes *The Spirit of the Laws* [Europe]
1751	First volume of Diderot's *Encyclopédie* is published [Europe]
1761	Voltaire takes up the case of Jean Calas [Europe] Rousseau publishes *The New Heloise* [Europe]
1762	Rousseau publishes *The Social Contract and Emile* [Europe]
1770	Raynal publishes *The Philosophical History of the Two Indies* [Europe]
1772	Diderot publishes *The Supplement to the Voyage of Bougainville* [Europe]
1775	Pierre Roussel publishes *The Physical and Moral Makeup of Women* [Europe]
1776	Declaration of Independence states independence of American colonies from England [Americas]
1778	Voltaire returns in triumph to Paris [Europe]
1781	Thomas Jefferson publishes *Notes on the State of Virginia* [Americas]
1784	Immanuel Kant publishes *What Is Enlightenment?* [Europe]
1789	Olaudah Equiano publishes his *Life* [Global]
1791	Mozart's opera *The Magic Flute* is performed in Vienna [Europe] *The Dream of the Red Chamber* is published in a print edition in China [Asia]

Critical Thinking Questions

Take a moment to pull together all the important information from the chapter by answering the following questions:

A Revolution in Astronomy

» Compare and contrast the medieval and Copernican theory of the universe.

» How did Sir Isaac Newton draw on the work of his predecessors, and what was original to his theory of the universe? What were the component parts of his scientific method?

The Impact of the New Science

» What did religious thought based on the conclusions of the New Science have in common with traditional Christian theology, and where did it differ from that theology?

» What characterized the people drawn to scientific societies in the sixteenth and seventeenth centuries?

The Enlightenment

» How did John Locke's sense-based psychology influence the Enlightenment movement?

» What were the various positions on religion put forward by people caught up in the Enlightenment movement?

Society and the Enlightenment

» What kinds of social relations did coffeehouses and teahouses, salons, and Masonic lodges promote?

» What accounts for the rise in public opinion since the eighteenth century, and what effect did it have on politics?

Enlightenment Debates

» What were the similarities and differences in Europeans' understandings of non-European peoples and their understandings of men and women?

» What techniques did novelists use to argue against the institution of slavery?

MindTap® is a fully online personalized learning experience built upon Cengage Learning content. MindTap® combines student learning tools—readings, multimedia, activities, and assessments—into a singular Learning Path that guides students through the course and helps students develop the critical thinking, analysis, and communication skills that are essential to academic and professional success.

CHAPTER 18

Trade and Empire, 1700–1800

Chapter Outline

As you read, consider the following questions:

❭ How did changes in overseas empires and trading networks contribute to Europe's economic development in the eighteenth century?

❭ How did Enlightenment thinking influence Europe's economic and social development?

❭ What new forms of individual and collective identity emerged?

❭ How did the Industrial Revolution change the production of goods, and why did it occur in Britain?

By the eighteenth century a bustling transatlantic economy was fueling Europe's economic growth. In addition, Europe once again experienced population growth, which in turn stimulated economic production and a rise in consumption of goods and services at all levels of society. People bought

Chained African Slaves in the Cargo Hold of Slave Ship
African slaves by the millions were carried across the Atlantic in ships' holds to work in the plantation and mining economies of the Western Hemisphere. From The New York Public Library

more clothing, household items, and food. Increased economic activity led European thinkers to explore the reasons for economic growth and to lay the foundations for the modern discipline of economics. These new economists viewed people primarily as rational beings who exercised individual choice as consumers of the goods available in the marketplace.

The Atlantic economy also reshaped the European empires that had been formed in the Western Hemisphere beginning in the sixteenth century (see Map 18.1). Portugal, founder of the first overseas empire, relied more and more on the riches of Brazil for its continuing prosperity. The Spanish and French empires declined as the British Empire rose, outstripping all others in vitality and prosperity and making London the commercial center of Europe. Britain's leading role in the Atlantic economy stimulated manufacturing and early forms of industrialization, thus laying the foundations for the modern economic world. But for the British as for every other New World empire, commerce and wealth depended on the labor of enslaved Africans, transported to the Americas in ships like the one shown at the beginning of this chapter.

Prosperity in Europe was accompanied by changes in upper- and middle-class behavior, as the well-to-do, influenced by Enlightenment ideas, began to expect greater privacy and comfort in the home and indulged in more spontaneous displays of affection among family members. The poor continued to live more tradition-bound lives, and the social and cultural gap between them and the rich widened. Government officials developed new theories about the causes of poverty and new institutions to eliminate them, while the poor took action by rioting. Food shortages and unacceptable working conditions could provoke popular rioting. So could long-simmering religious hatred. Europeans also began to rethink the basic nature of society, rejecting traditional ideas that emphasized group membership more than individual autonomy. Some people argued that wealth, not birth, was the proper basis for social ranking, whereas others maintained that society was made up of individual citizens bound together in a unified nation.

18-1 Economic Recovery

>> **What new ideas about economic development and the value of work accompanied Europe's economic recovery?**

>> **What effects did the consumer revolution have on the daily lives of Europeans?**

After 1700, Europe's population began to grow once again. Unlike the sixteenth-century demographic expansion, the eighteenth-century growth did not produce a crisis of overpopulation and economic hard times. Instead, it produced prosperity. But economic growth also caused people to question older ideas about how wealth was generated and to search for the laws that made the economic world function. Europeans also began to consume a greater variety of products than ever before, thus further stimulating the economy.

18-1a The Expanding Population of Europe

Europe's sixteenth-century overpopulation crisis was followed in the seventeenth century by a stagnating or declining population in many places. Then, in the early eighteenth century, population again began to grow, increasing from 95 million in 1700 to 146 million in 1800—an increase of more than 50 percent. Growth was greatest in England and France; in general, western Europe experienced more growth than eastern Europe (see Map 18.2).

Population Growth: Disease and Hygiene Historians have identified several factors contributing to population increase. The first was the disappearance of bubonic plague. The likely cause for the plague's decline is found in Europe's shifting rodent population as large brown rats, carrying fleas that stayed on them, overtook the earlier black rat population, which hosted fleas that jumped onto human beings. The fleas carried the plague bacillus. This change in the rat population coincided with better government quarantines of infected areas, which reduced the spread of disease.

Other killers, like smallpox, dysentery, and typhoid fever, periodically exploded into epidemics, but their effects were moderated by a growing interest in community and personal hygiene. Recognizing that filth bred disease, urban governments launched campaigns to clear out the garbage and human waste in the cities.

In the eighteenth century, Europeans also began to bathe regularly. Bathing had been common in the Middle Ages, at least in towns with communal baths. After the Black Death, however, many cities closed their baths, thinking that they spread the disease. Later, Protestant and Catholic reformers campaigned to shut them down, arguing that baths promoted lewdness and sexual license. As a result, Europeans became dirtier and smellier than their medieval ancestors. By the eighteenth century, doctors had started to prescribe cold baths to build up the body, and the resumption of bathing improved hygiene and reduced disease.

Warfare and Population Growth Changing patterns of European warfare also encouraged population growth. The religious wars of the sixteenth and seventeenth centuries devastated the civilian population where they were fought. Armies were huge breeding grounds for disease, which spread beyond their own quarters. Battle also disrupted agriculture and brought on food shortages in a population already straining Europe's agricultural resources. Shortages, in turn, weakened people's resistance to disease. In the eighteenth century, Europe fought some of its wars elsewhere—in the Western Hemisphere and in Asia—and those fought in Europe were shorter and therefore less disruptive than earlier wars. Moreover, troops were better fed, better supplied, and better disciplined than they had been, making their presence less dangerous to the surrounding civilian population.

Population Growth and Diet Finally, improvements in Europeans' diets encouraged population growth. Better climatological conditions gradually

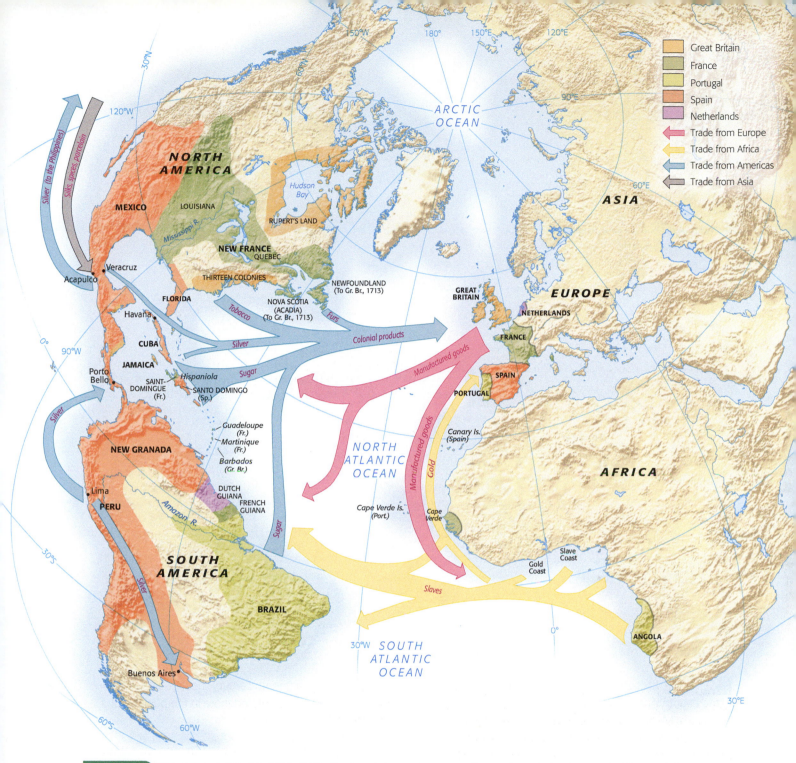

Map 18.1 **The Atlantic World, 1700–1789** By the eighteenth century, Europe's trade had expanded beyond the routes from an earlier time between northern and southern Europe and eastern and western Europe. It now refocused on a cross-Atlantic trade that united Europe, Africa, and the Americas in new trading patterns.

1. Trace the trade routes shown on this map.
2. What role did each of the following play in this Atlantic economy?
   a. Agricultural products
   b. Metals
   c. Manufactured goods

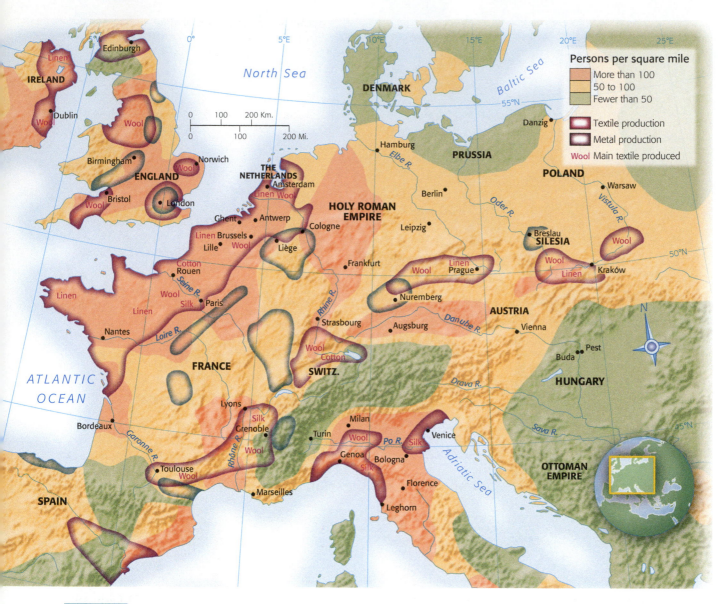

Map 18.2 **Industry and Population in Eighteenth-Century Europe** In the eighteenth century most people lived in the countryside and many manufacturing processes, like textile weaving, were concentrated there in the putting-out system. Metal production, especially iron and copper, was also located in the countryside.

1. Identify the areas of population density from densest to least dense.
2. Now identify the areas of textile and metal production.
3. Overall, is there a significant correlation between population density and textile production? Or is the correlation hard to make?
4. Is there a significant correlation between population density and metal production? Or is the correlation hard to make?

agricultural revolution
Improvements in agricultural method and livestock breeding in the sixteenth to the eighteenth centuries that greatly increased crop yields.

set in after 1700 as the Little Ice Age ended and harvests improved. In addition, some farmers kept up with rising demand by changing the agricultural practices in what has been described as an **agricultural revolution**.

The changes developed first in the Rhineland and the Netherlands and then spread to England in the seventeenth and eighteenth centuries.

The Agricultural Revolution Traditionally, farmers had let fields lie fallow, or uncultivated, to restore their fertility. Beginning in the sixteenth century, farmers discovered that instead of taking fields out of production, they could plant clover or turnips, which not only replenished the soil but could also be used as fodder for livestock.

Larger Herds and More Manure Now larger herds could be developed for milk, hides, and meat, so people began breeding livestock to improve quality. In England, local cows were bred with Dutch cattle to increase milk yield, and sheep were bred with specimens that were bigger than normal or that had fine wool coats. Growing herds meant nitrogen-rich manure that could be spread on fields to further increase their productivity. With fallowing eliminated and more manure available as fertilizer, land could be kept in continual production, thus greatly increasing the yield.

The End of the Open-Field System Increased yields created surpluses; so did a reorganization of farmland for agricultural production that ended the open-field system. In the past, cropland was usually divided into individually owned plots that were small but had no barriers between them. Sometimes people owned plots separated from each other by other owners' land. This exposed and fragmented pattern of landholding worked as long as the farming community operated as a single unit, planting and harvesting crops in the same sequence and at the same time. Village councils or the local landlord usually regulated planting and harvesting. After harvest, the community's livestock was allowed to range freely over the fields, grazing on what was left in them. This system discouraged experimentation with new crops and agricultural techniques.

Enclosure Beginning in the middle of the eighteenth century, Britain's Parliament encouraged more efficient and productive use of farmland by passing laws permitting **enclosure** in a given area. Single strips were bought or traded to create large, consolidated blocs of land that were fenced off. Enclosure allowed for economies of scale in agricultural production and made experimentation with different crops and crop rotations possible.

Improving the Soil New land was also brought under cultivation and improved with new techniques. Underground drainage systems were installed in waterlogged fields, and heavy clays were lightened by working in crushed limestone. Improvements in crops, land organization, and soil quality also greatly increased yields. During the eighteenth century, improvements in agriculture spared Europeans from the devastating famines of earlier centuries.

Enclosure increased agricultural productivity, but it came at a social cost. Small-scale owners and poor squatters were forced off their plots, and traditional rights to common grazing after harvest were eclipsed. As the rural poor lost even the chance to maintain livestock, many became landless wageworkers on enclosed farms.

Declining Mortality Rates, Rising Marriage Rates Nevertheless, the decline in epidemic diseases, coupled with improvements in military behavior, people's diet, and agricultural production, reduced mortality rates. During the eighteenth century, more people could count on their children surviving infancy and then living longer, healthier lives. In addition, people had more children because they were marrying earlier than before. In previous centuries, death had been the great social equalizer because rich and poor were equally defenseless in the face of disease. Now, the rich began to live longer than the poor because they were better fed and lived in the cleanest, healthiest environments.

18-1b The World of Work

For many Europeans, patterns of work remained as they had been in previous centuries. Despite innovations in agriculture, most peasants toiled in the countryside using age-old techniques for planting and harvesting crops. In cities, guild members continued to think of themselves as the elite of the working world and jealously guarded their privileges. Alongside this traditional world, however, other types of work began to engage growing numbers of people.

The Putting-Out System During the economic slump of the seventeenth century, Europe's peasants and urban working poor, especially in the west, supplemented their incomes by making things at home. Many women spun wool into yarn and sold the surplus—the yarns they did not use themselves. Most likely, they would put their children to work cleaning and carding (combing) the wool, while husbands would weave on hand looms. Eventually, merchants delivered raw wool to the household and paid cash for finished cloth. This arrangement, known as the **putting-out system**, was Europe's first means of manufacturing.

Merchants got involved because they could pay low and sell high. They might buy raw wool in large volume from sheep farmers, put it out to many different households, and pick up spun yarn or even woven cloth for a pittance—so much for a certain amount, or by the piece. Linen cloth—both coarse and

enclosure Process of consolidating agricultural land and enclosing it with hedges or fences.

putting-out system System whereby workers manufactured consumer goods for a merchant who supplied them with raw material.

fine—and nails were also produced in the putting-out system.

Workers accepted the arrangement because the entire family could be put to work. But the spread of the system, in which household workers only occasionally saw the merchant who bought their **piecework**, created a personal and physical distance between workers and merchants that did not exist in the older owner-operated workshop of the guild system.

The Pros and Cons of the Putting-Out System

When Europe's population once again began to grow in the early eighteenth century, demand for manufactured products rose, offering people further employment. Because prices for food and other basic products tended to rise faster than workers' incomes, there were always people willing to do piecework.

But the putting-out system also carried risks. Merchants would pay for products as long as demand was high, but an unpredictable decline in demand, often in a distant market, would lead to drastically fewer pieces bought and a sharp decline in income for workers. Overall, however, the putting-out system dynamically increased Europe's manufacturing capacity. For example, English linen exports jumped from 180,000 yards in 1730 to 9.6 million yards in 1760.

New Types of Urban Work

Other new types of work were urban based. Europe's cities were growing in the eighteenth century, offering work for architects, engineers, bricklayers, stonemasons, street repairers, plumbers, and those who catered to them. In Paris, a kind of "take-out" developed, as people bought prepared food for their meals.

Women found work as dressmakers, seamstresses, linen workers, and clothes washers. Paris had 2,000 washerwomen scrubbing along the banks of the Seine River. Women also operated stalls in outdoor markets. As in the past, women's wages lagged noticeably behind men's.

Servants

All over Europe, migrants from the countryside to the city often ended up as servants. Servants regularly made up a city's largest single group of workers, and Paris may have had more than 90,000 of them. Usually, servants constituted about 10 percent of the total urban population. Servants benefited from some job security because their employment was continuous and they were given room and board and sometimes clothing. But work in an employer's house also could be dangerous. Angry masters might accuse their servants of theft, and women could be seduced or raped by their employer or fellow servants and then abandoned.

Skilled and Unskilled Servants

The servant world was divided into the skilled few and the mass of the unskilled. The skilled worked as butlers, cooks, and personal attendants. They often served the same employer for many years and then retired into the middle class. Most servants, however, worked as footmen, stable boys, or chamber and kitchen maids. These lower servants usually calculated employment opportunities carefully, regularly leaving one employer for another if the new job promised a better wage, a new set of clothes, or better food and lodging.

Male servants viewed their work as a temporary measure until something better came along. Many women worked to save a dowry and then marry a prosperous peasant or artisan in their home village or in the city where they worked.

The Underemployed

At the bottom of the urban world were the underemployed. These were men and women who passed in and out of work. Men looked for odd jobs, hauling water or carrying messages across town. Women washed clothes, or took up prostitution when nothing else was available. All of them eked out a life through begging, petty thievery, and occasional work, depending on what seemed the best opportunity from day to day. With Europe's population rising, their numbers probably grew over the century.

18-1c Changing Notions of Wealth

As work diversified and patterns of work changed during the eighteenth century, Europeans debated the nature of the economic world. Gradually, new ways of thinking about work and the economy emerged.

Mercantilism

During the seventeenth century, states had adopted mercantilism as an economic policy. Mercantilists believed that the world's wealth was limited and that a state needed to increase its overall share at the expense of others. This belief led to programs for stimulating domestic prosperity and establishing favorable trade balances. Mercantilism emphasized the needs of states and their rulers above all else; economic policy was a means of strengthening states locked in the competitive struggle for dominance in Europe. Europe's colonies were absorbed into this mercantilist agenda; their purpose was to provide the things that the mother country needed to secure a greater share of the world's wealth and to increase its competitive advantage at home and abroad.

piecework Work paid for by the number of pieces produced.

The Physiocrats In the eighteenth century, economists started to argue that economic activity did not simply shift wealth from one state to another. Economies were capable of growing, and new wealth could be generated if states stopped interfering in economic life. In France, the **Physiocrats** argued that the government's traditional regulation of the grain trade harmed agricultural productivity and that the economy would work best if the government left it alone. *"Laissez faire, laissez aller!"* ("Leave it alone, let it go!"), they cried. Thus, the term **laissez-faire** (laiz-ay fayr) came to stand for a government policy of noninterference in the economy.

The Physiocrats also thought of the economy as a complex mechanism, each part of which depended on the others. In this way, it was like the natural world. And, like the natural world, the economy was governed by laws. Just as Isaac Newton had discovered the laws of physics, the Physiocrats proposed to discover the laws of economic activity and to construct a science of economics.

Adam Smith When **Adam Smith**, professor of moral philosophy at the University of Glasgow, visited with the Physiocrats on a trip to France, he became interested in this new science. His *Inquiry into the Nature and Causes of the Wealth of Nations*, published in 1776, quickly became a foundational text for modern economic thought based on the Physiocrats' idea that economies could grow.

Smith adopted the laissez-faire principles of the Physiocrats. Governments, he argued, should regulate economic activity as little as possible, restricting themselves to defending the community against foreign attackers, establishing a judicial system to police people's behavior, and supporting improvements in transportation, such as roads and canals, that would facilitate commerce.

Human Beings as Consumers: The "Invisible Hand" Smith believed that human beings wanted to acquire material goods to make their lives more comfortable. They were consumers by nature. Their economic activity was driven by their own needs and those of their immediate families, not by any concern for the public good. Nevertheless, as individuals pursued their private and often selfish economic interests, the larger economy benefited. An "invisible hand" linked all these private pursuits into an overall economic dynamic that brought prosperity to the whole community.

So, when tea drinkers satisfied their desire for tea by buying tea leaves, a teapot, and teacups, they enriched the merchant who had brought the tea from Asia and the workers in porcelain who had made the pot and cups. These people then used their profits to satisfy their own desires, thereby enriching yet another group of merchants and manufacturers.

The Division of Labor Smith knew that satisfying consumers' desires meant that production of goods had to keep up with them, and he argued that production could grow with the **division of labor**. Each stage in the production of a commodity—Smith used the example of pins—should be done by specialists. Division and specialization would result in a greater volume of production than when one person made one pin, start to finish.

This division of labor was already happening in the putting-out system, as merchants brought raw wool to spinners, picked up yarn and took it to weavers, and then picked up woven cloth to sell on the market. In their writings, Smith and the Physiocrats analyzed economic behavior on its own terms, and, like the philosophes, they formulated the laws underlying it.

Manual Labor Attitudes toward manual work were also changing during the eighteenth century. Traditionally, manual labor was held in contempt because it involved working with material things like dirt, wood, or animal skins. The material world was thought to be lower than the spiritual world, and, following the story of Adam in Genesis, manual labor was believed to be punishment for sin.

When the philosophes rejected traditional Christian ideas about human beings' inherent wickedness, they also cast aside the idea of work as punishment. No one did this more forcefully than Denis Diderot. His *Encyclopédie* extolled the social usefulness of crafts that depended on working with one's hands and presented readers with detailed articles, accompanied by engravings, of manufacturing processes.

Thus, Smith's idea that people could increase their productivity through division of labor was coupled with Diderot's celebration of the workers who produced goods for consumption. Throughout the eighteenth century, a surge in consumer demand across all economic groups created new employment opportunities in a wide range of firms manufacturing consumer products. New attitudes help to explain why the manufacturing sector of the European economy grew so dynamically during the eighteenth century.

Physiocrats French economists who argued against mercantilist regulation of the economy.

laissez-faire (in French, "leave it alone") Economic principle that economies develop best when free of government interference.

Adam Smith (ca. 1723–1790) Scottish philosopher and economist whose *Wealth of Nations* (1776) became a foundational text for modern economic theory and economic liberalism.

division of labor Manufacturing arrangement whereby each stage in production is done by specialists, thus increasing volume of production.

18-1d The Consumer Revolution

Smith's and Diderot's interest in the production of goods was connected to an important shift in many Europeans' economic behavior that has been described as the **consumer revolution**. As more goods became available, people bought more than ever before, stimulating the production of even more, and more varied, kinds of things to buy.

The Consumer Revolution and the Rich Consumer demand rose over most of Europe, but especially in the states of the northwest—Britain, the Netherlands, western Germany, and France. Imported goods made the array of items to purchase even more enticing. The rich purchased wallpaper, paintings, mirrors, and elaborate clocks, as well as expensive furniture. Fine porcelain began to replace pottery on dining tables and was used for such things as candlesticks that earlier had been made from wood or metal. Cotton clothing, made from fiber imported from India and Europe's American colonies, became increasingly popular, replacing wool and rivaling linen and silk as the fabric of fashion. Snuffboxes for men, elegant scarves for women, and bejeweled walking sticks for both came increasingly into fashion.

The Consumer Revolution and the Middle Classes The rich had always spent heavily on decorative and luxury commodities, and their spending habits in the eighteenth century represented a quantitative but not a qualitative increase in conspicuous consumption. The real change over the century occurred among the middle and lower economic groups in European society; now, for the first time, they bought many of the same items, copying the tastes of the rich. The change is reflected in wills and lists from estate sales.

Now a merchant would have a set of razors for shaving, along with porcelain shaving mugs and washbowls, all of which sat on a wooden stand made of fine wood in the latest fashion. His wife would have several changes of clothes, hung in a new wooden clothes closet set against a wall. Chamber pots placed in toilet chairs became a common feature of their well-appointed bedroom. By the end of the century, some people were installing indoor plumbing and flush toilets that connected to improved sewer systems.

consumer revolution Term used for the eighteenth-century rise in consumer demand that stimulated the economy, especially in northwestern Europe.

pawnshops Institutions that lend money to persons who deposit goods there as security against the loan.

The Consumer Revolution and the Working Poor Even the working poor furnished and decorated their rented rooms. Inexpensive prints hung on their walls, and pieces of pretty porcelain were brought out for special occasions. They bought more bed frames and mattresses than ever before and started to put their children in their own beds instead of adding them to the parental bed, as they had in the past. They also accumulated several changes of clothes, buying from secondhand dealers who sold the used clothes of the rich.

The Pawnshop Several factors lay behind working people's accumulation of possessions. Increasingly, workers were paid in cash rather than kind. The growth of a cash economy offered new forms of investment. Extra clothing and nonessential household items served as a hedge against catastrophic poverty during hard economic times.

If demand for textiles in the putting-out system declined, workers could take their new possessions, purchased when work and incomes were good, and pawn them for cash in the growing number of **pawnshops** that emerged during the eighteenth century. When good economic times returned, the pawned items were redeemed, enjoyed once again, and held in reserve for the inevitable bad times.

A New Sense of Empowerment Moreover, as people became consumers of a variety of products, they developed a sense of empowerment. They saw their choices in the marketplace as reflecting their taste, and they sought to cultivate their taste through knowledge of goods and markets. As they made personal choices about what they wanted to buy, they increased their role as individual actors in the marketplace. Adam Smith's picture of an economy based on private individuals' pursuit of their own interests was embodied in the consumer revolution.

Coffee, Tea, Chocolate, Sugar In addition to buying more clothes, accessories, and household items, Europeans also added new foodstuffs to their daily diets. Four items, in particular, stand out: coffee, tea, and chocolate, all of which were drunk, and cane sugar, which started to replace honey as a sweetener. All four depended on the growth in overseas trade and the establishment of colonies. Tea was imported from East Asia, and coffee came from either the Middle East or the Western Hemisphere. Chocolate was raised in tropical colonies. Above all, sugar was produced in ever-larger quantities in the plantations of the Caribbean and Brazil. By century's end, sugar had become a standard item on the tables of both the rich and the poor.

New Foodstuffs and New Manufacturing The introduction of these new foodstuffs often stimulated European manufacturing. For example, as the consumption of tea increased, so did demand for teapots and teacups. A well-to-do hostess, preparing for

Oloff Fridsberg, Ulla Tessin in her Study © Photo: Nationalmuseum, Stockholm

Ulla Tessin in Her Study

Olof Fridsberg's painting of *Ulla Tessin in Her Study* shows a rich Swedish woman caught up in the consumer revolution. Her study contains many luxury goods— an oriental rug, two desks, a clock, figurines, a Chinese vase, and a Chinese lacquered cabinet on a shelf.

❯❯ *Can you identify other consumer items this lady has crammed into her room?*

❯❯ *In all, how many pieces can you find?*

a tea party, would also have purchased many other new goods—canisters to store the tea, special clippers to cut sugar from the cones in which it came, a tea table, a porcelain pitcher for cream, a sugar basket and tongs for the cut sugar, and teaspoons for stirring.

18-2 The Atlantic World

❯❯ **How did the Atlantic trade link Europe, Africa, and the Americas in an integrated economy?**

❯❯ **What explains Britain's leading role in this trade?**

During the eighteenth century, trading networks across the Atlantic, which had formed during the sixteenth century, reached their fullest development. Northern Europe's trade with the Mediterranean and East Asia flourished, but the dynamic center shifted decisively to the Atlantic Ocean. The older empires of Spain and Portugal continued to send products to Europe, but they were being overtaken by the French and the British. In the end, it was the British who occupied the central place in an Atlantic trade system. This system was based on the seizure and transport of, ultimately, millions of Africans to the Western Hemisphere, where they labored as slaves to produce agricultural commodities, especially sugar, to satisfy rising consumer demand in Europe. In return, Europeans manufactured shoes and cheap clothing for slaves and a variety of household items, tools, and luxuries for colonists.

18-2a The Atlantic Economy

Samuel Gamble's triangular voyage (see Profiles in Change: Samuel Gamble Sets Out from London on a Slaving Voyage) was commonplace in the eighteenth century. British, French, Dutch, and Portuguese slavers sailing from Europe headed to

Samuel Gamble Sets Out from London on a Slaving Voyage

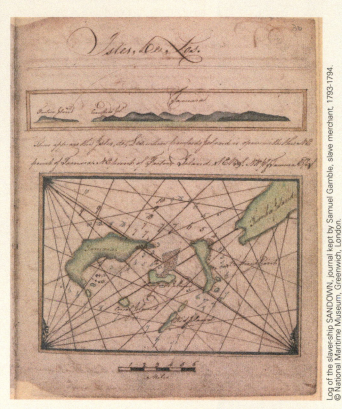

Log of the slave-ship SANDOWN, journal kept by Samuel Gamble, slave merchant, 1793-1794.
© National Maritime Museum, Greenwich, London.

Gamble's Log This is the first page of the ship's log for the *Sundown* on its 1793 voyage to Africa and the West Indies under Samuel Gamble's command. Subsequent pages document the problems Gamble faced in this ultimately unsuccessful slaving voyage across the Atlantic.

On April 7, 1793, Samuel Gamble weighed anchor and eased his ship, the *Sandown*, along the Thames River to the North Sea. Gamble had contracted with a group of British investors in January to gather a cargo of slaves in Africa for sale in the British colony of Jamaica. He had been in the slave trade for years, but this time business conditions were dangerous. France and Britain were once again at war, and the French were attacking British ships on the high seas. The Royal Navy was seizing ships' crews for its men-of-war, and Gamble had replaced twelve seized sailors only days before he set sail. Despite the dangers, Gamble and his backers were willing to put down money for the voyage. High risk meant high yield if the venture was successful.

The *Sandown* was provisioned for long sailing because a round-trip could last for a year or more. For weeks, supplies had been taken on board: beef, pork, pigs, tripe, potatoes, butter, and beer to feed the captain and crew; lead bars, gunpowder, earthenware dishes, and brandy to trade for slaves; and "big Iron Handcuffs, Neck chains & collars" to bind the slave cargo on the voyage to the West Indies. After leaving the Thames estuary, Gamble sailed along the southern coast of England in a convoy of merchant ships protected by the Royal Navy. Then they headed southwest into the Atlantic. On May 16, some of the ships veered off for the West Indies, while Gamble sailed south for the west coast of Africa. After stopping in Portugal's Cape Verde Islands, where he picked up cotton cloth to trade in Africa, Gamble arrived in what is today Sierra Leone on June 12, prepared to trade his cargo for slaves.

From then on, things went badly. June was the beginning of the rainy season in West Africa, and wet ground brought swarms of disease-carrying mosquitoes. Already, yellow fever was ravaging the coastal areas. This disease often killed within a week, as victims, vomiting blackish blood, fell into a coma while their liver deteriorated, causing them to turn yellow from jaundice. Gamble's stop in Africa had to be short if profits were to be made. He had contracted to carry 250 slaves to Jamaica in time for the beginning of sugarcane cutting in December, when market demand for new slaves would be high. But yellow fever had disrupted the African trading networks, and Gamble had to wait nine and a half months before he could collect 234 slaves, 16 short of his contract. They were listed in his journal simply by age, sex, and an assigned number.

As Gamble tried to fill his ship with slaves, and he himself began to shake with fever, some of his sailors fell ill or died. The crew as a whole became, he wrote in his journal, "quite Peevish, fraxious, ill natur'd and Childish." In mid-January 1794, a slave uprising broke out on board, and eight Africans drowned, most likely as they tried to swim to freedom. Troubles continued after the *Sandown* set sail across the Atlantic in March—yellow fever, fights between sailors and slaves, more deaths. The ship's water kegs were leaking, and the *Sandown* had to make an unplanned stop in Barbados to take on more. There, sixteen crew members abandoned ship and hired lawyers to get their back wages from Gamble. With the lawyers demanding the removal of *Sandown*'s sails and rudder to prevent it from leaving, Gamble sneaked out of port before daybreak and limped into Kingston, Jamaica, with a crew of five.

Yellow fever awaited him there. It had swirled across the Atlantic on other ships, disrupting the Jamaican slave markets and leaving Kingston's harbor crowded with earlier arrivals from Africa. In any case, Gamble had arrived too late to take advantage of high prices at the beginning of the cane-cutting season. "Slaves complaining of pains in their Bowels," he wrote glumly in his journal on May 25. The next day's entry read, "Slaves as before, they go off very slow (Market glutted)." After taking on provisions and a new cargo, probably of sugar and rum, the *Sandown* joined an armed convoy for the return trip to London, arriving there on October 11, 1794, a year and a half after the outbound voyage.

Gamble and his backers were disappointed in their profits. In a trade economy that pitted high gain against high risk, they had lost.

Source: Excerpts from Samuel Gamble's journal (c. 1793). Included in Bruce L. Mouser (ed.), *A Slaving Voyage to Africa and Jamaica: The Log of the Sandown*, 1793–1794.

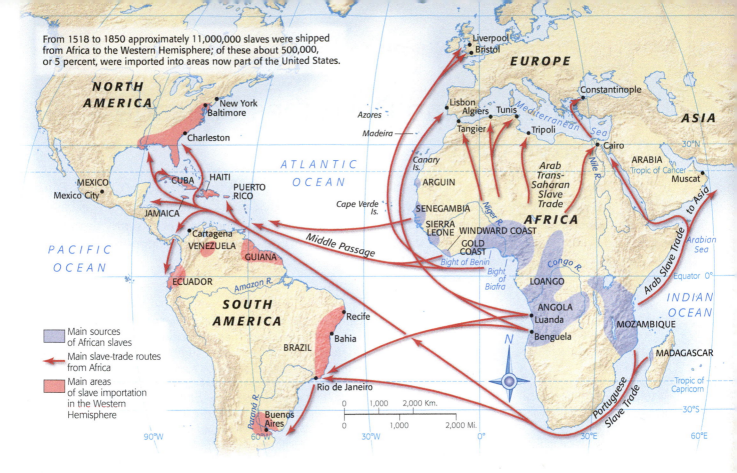

From 1518 to 1850 approximately 11,000,000 slaves were shipped from Africa to the Western Hemisphere; of these about 500,000, or 5 percent, were imported into areas now part of the United States.

Main sources of African slaves

Main slave-trade routes from Africa

Main areas of slave importation in the Western Hemisphere

Map 18.3 **The Worldwide Slave Trade** In the eighteenth century, slave trading out of Africa went in many directions. Africans from central Africa were taken north to Muslim ports on the Mediterranean, while the Arab-controlled slave trade east from Mozambique to Asia also flourished. Most slaves bound for the New World were taken from Mozambique and from the central and southern west African coast.

1. How many destinations globally for African slaves can you count on this map? Does the number surprise you?
2. What besides slaves entered the four trading networks shown in this map?

the West African coast. There they turned to resident Europeans with links to local African rulers, who supplied the slaves. Guns and gunpowder, alcohol, cloth, tobacco, and iron bars were traded for the human cargo (see Map 18.3).

The Middle Passage Once slaves were collected, the voyage across the Atlantic, the dreaded **Middle Passage**, began. For weeks, the ship sailed west, following the trade wind patterns of the North Atlantic. Death stalked the slave ships. On average 10 to 20 percent of the Africans died before reaching the Caribbean, along with 20 to 25 percent of the ship's crew, from diseases contracted in Africa or on board. The Portuguese called these slave ships hearses. Death rates were even higher for Europeans who manned the outposts on the African coast because of malaria and other diseases. (See Learning from a Primary Source: Olaudah Equiano Describes Passage on a Slave Ship.)

The Impact of the Slave Trade on West Africa The European colonies' import of slaves reshaped the communities of West Africa. Slaves were sometimes captives taken in warfare, and others were simply kidnapped. Some rulers, anxious to take advantage of European demand, extended their power and created centralized kingdoms where the capture and sale of slaves was a central feature of the local economy.

The rich soils of West Africa assured a good food supply, especially after manioc, a nutritious root vegetable, was imported from America. In turn, the food supply encouraged growth of the local population, which slavers could seize for the transatlantic trade. Overall, some 11 million slaves were taken across the Atlantic to toil in American plantations, mainly in the Caribbean and Brazil.

Why Were So Many Slaves Imported to America? The colonies' importation of slaves resulted from an insatiable demand for labor and slaves' high mortality rate; perhaps one-third died within a few years of arriving in the Western Hemisphere. An imbalanced sex ratio also worked against a stabilization of the slave population. Male slaves, considered more desirable for plantation labor because

Middle Passage Slave ships' weeks-long voyage across the Atlantic from West Africa to the Caribbean.

Olaudah Equiano Describes Passage on a Slave Ship

In 1789, Olaudah Equiano, a freed slave, published *The Interesting Narrative of the Life of Olaudah Equiano (OH-lau-dah AIY-qwee-ahn-oh), or Gustavus Vassa, the African*. He claimed that his account was based on his own memories as an African boy of ten taken aboard a slave ship. The claim is currently disputed, but there is no doubt that Equiano's narrative, whether fact or fiction, helped to gain support in England for the abolition of the slave trade.

1 How does Equiano manage to convey these experiences from the point of view of a ten-year-old child?

2 Why would Equiano be flogged for not eating?

3 Why does Equiano make these remarks?

4 Does this act of kindness lessen or sharpen the horrors of Equiano's account?

1 The first object which saluted my eyes when I arrived on the coast was the sea, and a slave ship . . . waiting for its cargo. These filled me with astonishment, which was soon converted into terror. . . . When I was carried on board I was immediately handled, and tossed up, to see if I were sound by some of the crew, and I was now persuaded that I had gotten into a world of bad spirits and that they were going to kill me. Their complexions too differing so much from ours, their long hair, and the language they spoke, which was very different from any I ever heard, united to confirm me in this belief. . . . When I looked round the ship too, and saw a large furnace or copper boiling and a multitude of black people of every description chained together, every one of their countenances expressing dejection and sorrow, I no longer doubted of my fate; and, quite overpowered with horror and anguish, I fell motionless on the deck and fainted. . . . I became so sick and low that I was not able to eat, nor had I the least desire to taste anything. **2** I now wished for the last friend, Death, to relieve me; but soon, to my grief, two of the white men offered me eatables, and, on my refusing to eat, one of them held me fast by the hands and laid me across, I think, the windlass, and tied my feet, while the other flogged me severely. . . . **3** I had never seen among my people such instances of brutal cruelty; and this not only shewn towards us blacks, but also to some of the whites themselves. One white man in particular I saw, when we were permitted [Sic] to be on deck, flogged so unmercifully that he died in consequence of it; and they tossed him over the side as they would have done to a brute. . . .

The stench of the hold while we were on the coast was . . . intolerably loathsome. . . . The closeness of the place, and the heat of the climate, added to the number in the ship, which was so crowded that each had scarcely room to turn himself, almost suffocated us. This produced copious perspirations, so that the air soon became unfit for respiration, from a variety of loathsome smells, and brought on a sickness among the slaves, of which many died, thus falling victims to the improvident avarice, as I may call it, of their purchasers. This wretched situation was again aggravated by the galling of the chains, now become insupportable; and the filth of the necessary tubs, into which the children often fell, and were almost suffocated. The shrieks of the women and the groans of the dying, rendered the whole a scene of horror almost inconceivable. **4** Happily perhaps for myself I was soon reduced so low here that it was thought necessary to keep me on deck; and from my extreme youth I was not put in fetters.

Source: From Olaudah Equiano, *The Interesting Narrative of the Life of Olaudah Equiano, or Gustavus Vassa, the African* (London, 1793), pp. 31–33, 45–49, 51–53.

Olaudah Equiano

This engraving of Olaudah Equiano appeared in his autobiography, which was published in 1789. National Portrait Gallery, Smithsonian Institution/Art Resource, NY

》 *The engraver has given prominence to Equiano's face. What strikes you about it? How might an eighteenth-century viewer react to it?*

》 *Given eighteenth-century ideas about slaves and Africans, what impression might Equiano's European dress have made on the reader of his book?*

of their strength, outnumbered females, and adults were enslaved more frequently than children.

Slavers returned to their home ports loaded with New World products: coffee, chocolate, cocoa, and sugar from the tropics as well as fish, tobacco, and furs from farther north. Above all, it was Europe's demand for sugar that fueled plantation owners' demand for slaves.

Sugar Raising and Refining Sugar raising and refining was a highly complex process that required hundreds of workers laboring in lockstep. When the cane was ripe, it had to be quickly cut and crushed between giant rollers before it dried out and the sap deteriorated. Huge vats heated by roaring fires reduced the sap to a syrup that could be further refined into cones and loaves. Slaves' frenzied cutting and crushing of cane, along with the unbearable heat of the fires beneath the vats, led one Portuguese priest in Brazil to write that "a sugar mill is hell, and all the masters of them are damned."

Clothing and Feeding the Slave Population The need to clothe the huge slave populations of the Americas stimulated the shoe and textile manufacturers of Europe. Food for slave populations was produced in the tropics where they worked, but dried fish was also shipped in from New England. Thus, all the lands that bordered the Atlantic—Africa, the Americas, and Europe—were linked in a complex trading system that depended on the forced labor of African slaves.

18-2b The Spanish and Portuguese Empires

After a decline in production during the mid-seventeenth century, Spain's colonial silver mines boomed and produced half of the world's silver in the 1700s. The silver and other trades were organized as they had been in the sixteenth century; the Manila galleon sailed once a year to the west coast of Mexico, from which its goods were transferred to the Caribbean and then shipped with New World silver to Spain in a convoy of merchant ships guarded by men-of-war.

Problems in the Spanish Empire This highly centralized system no longer worked well. By 1700, some 2 million Spaniards had migrated to the Spanish colonies, and their demand for European goods could not be met by the annual trips to and from Spain. Although Spanish law forbade trade with foreigners, smuggling flourished in the empire's ports, where French and British traders brought needed goods from Europe or other parts of the Western Hemisphere and returned to their ports with emeralds, pearls, and cocoa.

The British benefited most from Spain's inadequate trading network. In 1709, during the War of the Spanish Succession, when Britain was fighting both France and Spain, merchants in the western port of Bristol financed a privateer to capture the Manila galleon. The venture was successful, and the galleon's cargo brought a profit of £786,000 to the overjoyed investors. The ship itself was sailed to London, where it became a tourist attraction. In 1713, at the end of the war, the Spanish granted the British the *asiento*, permission to sell slaves in Spanish colonies. In addition, the right to sail into Spanish ports enhanced the possibility for trade in other goods.

Brazil: The Heart of the Portuguese Empire In the fifteenth and sixteenth centuries, Portugal had created an empire that stretched westward from India to outposts in Africa and then across the Atlantic to Brazil. In the seventeenth century, Brazil had produced most of the sugar for Europe. By the 1680s, however, competition from French and British colonies in the Caribbean had led to a decline in prices for Brazilian sugar, and the industry slumped.

Mary Evans Picture Library/The Image Works

Sugar Mill

Sugar was processed on Caribbean plantations where it was grown. In this painting, sugar cane stalks are on the left. In the right rear some slaves crush the stalks for their juice, and in the foreground others tend the vats in which the juice is boiled down until the sugar crystallizes.

> *What might have moved the painter to make the sugar cane stalks on the left almost as large as the palm trees in the background?*

> *Is there anything of the "hell" of sugar cane processing that some people commented on? If not, why not?*

Soon afterward, gold was discovered. During the first half of the eighteenth century, gold became the main export, and Brazil was Portugal's most profitable colony. Each new find sparked a fevered gold rush as people from Portugal and the Atlantic islands joined local people in the hunt for treasure.

Gold Reshapes Brazil The influx of these fortune seekers greatly increased the European population in the colony. The slave population also increased because Africans were brought in to work the mines. The largest gold strikes were in Brazil's interior, so, for the first time, Europeans started to move away from the coast, where the sugar plantations were located. The push inland also brought increasing contact between whites and the local Indian population, which declined, like Indians in the Spanish Empire, as the result of disease and exploitation. Historians estimate that the Indian population of Brazil fell by 75 percent during the Brazilian colonial period. Unlike the Spanish, who studied Indian culture even as they exploited the local peoples, the Portuguese showed hardly any interest in the Brazilian Indians except as a labor force.

The Treaty of Madrid Portuguese occupation of the Brazilian interior was capped off by the **Treaty of Madrid**, signed in 1750, which adjusted the boundary between Spanish and Portuguese America, set by the Treaty of Tordesillas, in Portugal's favor. The territory assigned to Portugal west of the old line of demarcation created a colony that covered roughly the same territory as modern Brazil.

Treaty of Madrid Treaty between Spain and Portugal in 1750 that revised the boundaries of Brazil by adding more land in the west to the colony.

By the time the treaty was signed, gold mining was in decline, but the sugar industry was on the upswing as demand and prices rose. Diamonds were also found and sent to Europe in such numbers that their price fell by 75 percent. Sugar, gold, and diamonds ended up making Brazil far richer in resources and income from trade than its mother country.

18-2c The French and British Empires

In theory, the French New World Empire was vast, stretching from Quebec in eastern Canada to the Great Lakes and down the Mississippi River to Louisiana and the Gulf of Mexico. It also included the Caribbean islands of Saint-Domingue, Guadeloupe, and Martinique. In fact, however, these lands were sparsely inhabited by European colonists.

Canada In the mid-eighteenth century, Canada contained 60,000 Frenchmen as compared to the 1.8 million European inhabitants of the British mainland colonies. Canada's main export to Europe was furs, especially beaver pelts, which were used for making hats because their tight nap allowed them to shed water easily. French traders paid local trappers and Indians with guns and woolen clothes manufactured in the mother country.

The French Caribbean The Canadians also supplied the sugar islands with grain, timber, and leather goods. The sugar produced there was shipped back to France for refining, along with locally grown coffee. Seventy-five percent of the sugar and 80 percent of the coffee were then reexported to markets in northern and eastern Europe.

The slave population in the French Caribbean, which far outnumbered the white colonists, stimulated French manufacturing because textiles were shipped overseas to clothe the African workforce. The sugar island of Saint-Domingue was the single most productive colony of any European empire in the eighteenth century. Despite its profitability, the French, like the Spanish and Portuguese, lost ground to the British. Smaller European populations in the French colonies meant a less dynamic transatlantic economy.

The French in India The French also established trading posts in India, supplanting the Portuguese and Dutch and rivaling the English, who were also expanding their trade on the subcontinent. The main French post was at **Pondicherry**, on the southeast coast, from which silk and pepper were exported to France. In addition to these traditional commodities, printed cotton cloth was exported to supply the growing demand for cotton clothing in Europe.

Britain and the Atlantic Trade Britain benefited most from the Atlantic trade. Its success rested on two things: A slave-worked plantation economy in the Caribbean and the southern half of the mainland colonies combined with a thriving colonial demand for the products of the mother country. In addition, the needs of the mainland colonies' many coastal cities provided other trading opportunities across the Atlantic world.

Beginning in 1651, a series of Navigation Acts passed by Parliament excluded foreigners from the trade between British colonies and the mother country, decreed that all shipping must be in British or colonial vessels, and prohibited American manufacturers from sending their products to Britain if the products would compete there with locally made products.

British Exports to the Colonies London and the ports on Britain's west coast prospered from the trade goods they shipped to all parts of the Atlantic world. In addition to those sent to West Africa for slaves, merchant vessels carried textiles, tools, metal utensils, and a variety of household items to West Indian and North American consumers. Cheap cloth was in demand to provide clothing for the thousands of slaves, and household items like desks, chairs, wallpaper, curtains, china, carriages, and silverware were bought by the white population, who were caught up in Europe's consumer revolution.

Growing Colonial Population Colonial demand also increased because of a rising population. Not only did Britons continue to migrate to the American colonies; birthrates there were exceptionally high and large families the rule. The relatively easy availability of land for agriculture resulted in a high standard of living, perhaps the highest in the world at the time, that allowed colonials to buy nonessential items that pleased them or made their lives more comfortable. British manufacturers responded to this overseas demand by producing more and more for the overseas market.

Colonial Exports to Britain Colonials also produced products that were shipped either to the mother country for consumption or reexport, or to other parts of the empire. In addition to the sugar, coffee, and chocolate that went from the Caribbean colonies to Britain, rice grown in South Carolina and Georgia on slave-labor plantations was shipped to markets in Portugal, Spain, and Mediterranean ports, where it was a staple in local diets. Indigo from the two colonies was also a highly prized blue dye for textiles. Beaver pelts were also shipped—80,000 of them by midcentury. Tobacco grown on slave-labor plantations in Maryland and Virginia was sent to Europe as demand rose. Europeans had imported 9 million pounds of New World tobacco in the 1660s; in 1775, they imported 220 million pounds.

New England No region in British North America prospered more from Britain's Atlantic trade than New England. Despite their cool climate and rocky soil, the New England colonies played a vital role in imperial commerce as the American center for the **carrying trade**. The abundant timber in the region gave rise to a local shipbuilding industry as well as supplying tall fir trees as masts for ships built in Britain. Corn and salt fish were shipped to the sugar plantations of the West Indies in return for tropical fruits, spices, and slaves taken to the mainland colonies.

Molasses, Rum, and Slaves Barrels made from local wood were also sent to the West Indies and filled there with molasses, which New Englanders turned into rum. The rum was then shipped to Africa as payment for slaves who were brought to the Caribbean. Newport, Rhode Island, was the capital of this molasses-rum-slaves trading triangle. Molasses were also sent to the **wine islands** off the northern coast of Africa as payment for **Madeira**, which became the drink of choice for well-heeled Americans. Thus, the New England ports of Boston and Newport rivaled British ones in the scope and complexity of their trading networks.

Merchant Networks The merchants who managed the Atlantic trading network had to master the dynamics of moving many different cargoes over long distances to multiple delivery points. None of them could personally know all the people they had to deal with, and all of them knew

Pondicherry Most important French trading post in India.

carrying trade Shipping enterprise that moved commodities from one part of the empire to another.

wine islands Portuguese islands of Madeira and Porto Santo.

Madeira Wine fortified with brandy.

that risk was high. To lessen the dangers of a failed voyage, merchants tried to establish reliable correspondence networks based on kinship, religion, or ethnic identity. Thus, merchant families often had members stationed across the world at crucial trading junctures, while Jews and Quakers relied on coreligionists and Scots tended to stick to fellow Scots. Traders also tried to establish a reputation for creditworthiness—a reputation for keeping one's word and being a sound financial risk.

18-2d World War and Britain Victorious

The British Navigation Acts had been aimed against the preeminence of Dutch shipping in the emerging global trading networks of the seventeenth century. By 1700, Dutch power was on the wane and England was the major maritime power, thanks to the growth of the Royal Navy. In 1664, the Royal Navy seized the Dutch colony of **New Amsterdam** on Manhattan Island and renamed it New York. The War of the Spanish Succession, known in British America as Queen Anne's War, gave Britain control of Hudson's Bay, Newfoundland, and Nova Scotia (Acadia) in present-day Canada.

War in North America Territorial gains in Canada, along with trade rivalries in India, set the stage for renewed warfare between Britain and France. By the mid-eighteenth century, fur traders in Britain's mainland North American colonies started to cross the Allegheny Mountains into the Ohio River valley and thereby threatened French control of the Mississippi valley. In response, the French built forts and allied with local Indians. War between the two sides broke out in 1754 when a young George Washington led Virginia troops into the Ohio River valley to block French expansion there. He was defeated, but the event was soon embroiled in a larger conflict, the Seven Years' War, known as the French and Indian War in British America.

Britain Wins, France Loses The war's decisive turning point came in 1759, when the British captured Quebec. At war's end, France was forced to cede Canada and all lands east of the Mississippi River to Britain. Louisiana—lands west of the river—was ceded to Spain in compensation for its ceding Florida to Britain. France also lost in India, where it surrendered almost all its trading posts to the British, who consolidated their rule there.

18-2e The American Revolution and Britain Subdued

The world wars of the mid-eighteenth century had put huge strains on the finances of all belligerent states. After 1763, the new king, **George III**, and Parliament decided that the American colonies should contribute to the expenses of running an enlarged British Empire. In 1765, the **Stamp Act** levied the first direct tax on the colonies, and the Americans howled in protest. It seemed to them that Parliament was acting in a high-handed, unconstitutional way, just like James II before 1688.

The American Revolution The Americans had embraced the Whig notion that government involved the consent of the governed. But Parliament had no members from the colonies. "No taxation without representation!" summed up the colonists' objections to British policy. Protests over taxes and a lack of parliamentary representation led, within a decade, to the **American Revolution** and, in 1783, to Britain's loss of thirteen very profitable North American colonies.

Crucial to the American victory was help from the French, who had been looking for an opportunity to redress the power balance that tipped in Britain's favor after 1763. The losses at the end of the Seven Years' War had reshaped French notions of what was at stake. In French eyes, the English had violently seized what rightfully belonged to France. In 1777, the French entered the war on the revolutionaries' side, but they paid dearly for their involvement. War costs imposed a crushing debt on the monarchy that led to an unraveling of French state finances and the collapse of the royal government in the late 1780s.

The British in India The British fared better in India than they did in America. After driving the French out of most of their trading posts, Britain's East India Company, which had carried on trade there since the seventeenth century, extended its control indirectly by forming alliances with Indian princes who allowed the company trading rights. Gradually, this indirect rule gave way to direct British control of the country.

CONNECTIONS: The British presence in India continued in various forms until 1947. See Section 24.3 The British Raj in India to learn more about British empire building and colonialism in India in the nineteenth century.

New Amsterdam Dutch colony on Manhattan Island seized by the English in 1664 and renamed New York.

George III (r. 1760–1820) British king during whose reign the American Revolution occurred.

Stamp Act British revenue-raising measure imposed in 1765 on the American colonies at the end of the Seven Years' War, provoking American resistance.

American Revolution Rebellion of thirteen British colonies on mainland North America leading to their independence in 1783 as the United States of America.

18-3 European Society in the Age of Enlightenment

» How did European ideas of home life change in the eighteenth century?

» What caused Europeans to rethink the nature of society?

The consumer revolution coincided with a new emphasis on privacy, comfort, and displays of affection. As population rose, governments began to rethink the problem of poverty, but the poor were not simply an object of study. They also took matters into their own hands through rioting. New ways of thinking about society challenged traditional views emphasizing group membership more than individual autonomy. At the same time, many Europeans also started to think of themselves as members of distinct nations.

18-3a Comfort and Privacy

The consumer revolution coincided with new standards of privacy and comfort that changed the lives of Europe's upper and middle classes. Traditionally, nobles and other people of high social standing believed they had to make a public display of their grandeur. They surrounded themselves with many servants dressed in **livery**. They also acted as patrons to networks of clients who joined the servants in waiting publicly on their patron.

In this world of display, privacy meant little, and the houses of the great reflected their public nature. Rooms served multiple purposes; people ate, slept, and received guests in the same space. Servants slept in the rooms of their masters, and both shared their beds with other people of similar standing. The lack of concern for privacy extended to the dining table, where people dipped their fingers into a common bowl, shared drinking cups, and used the edge of the tablecloth as a common napkin.

A New Demand for Privacy Beginning in the eighteenth century, the traditional emphasis on public display began to change. In Europe's cities, the houses of the rich were built for greater privacy. Multipurpose rooms gave way to specialized ones—bedrooms for sleeping; dining rooms for eating; and drawing rooms for conversation, card games, and music. Houses also incorporated a new architectural feature, the hallway. Hallways allowed people to pass from one part of the house to another without entering every room in between, thus increasing each room's privacy. To ensure even greater privacy, servants were no longer housed in the same space as their masters but placed in restricted servants' quarters, and their numbers were reduced to keep domestic space as free from them as possible.

Bedrooms also became more private. Now people slept one to a bed and often one to a room. Dining also became a more private affair. People no longer shared food and utensils. Each person at the table had separate silverware, glasses, and dishes. Food was served onto plates with specialized spoons and forks so that no person's silverware went into prepared food that everyone was eating.

A New Demand for Comfort The growing demand for privacy among Europe's upper and middle classes was accompanied by a demand for comfortable domestic spaces. The older display society had emphasized grandeur, even if that meant that people had to live in uncomfortable surroundings. Although the rich and wellborn still put elegance above comfort in dress on formal occasions, they now preferred a more relaxed pattern at home.

Men wore dressing gowns in their private rooms, and women favored looser clothes when they read or visited with friends. Little tea or supper tables covered with simple cloths were placed in front of soft upholstered chairs. Rooms were smaller than before, and thus fires could keep them warmer. Dinner parties also tended to become more informal.

Family Life The emphasis on domestic privacy and comfort also affected family life. Families, now enclosed in the cocoon of the home, often welcomed more openly spontaneous displays of affection and intimacy. Mothers increasingly breast-fed their babies instead of sending them away to **wet nurses** in the country. Parents had always loved their children and shown concern for their futures, but traditional child-rearing practices had stressed discipline: Parents punished children's failures and mistakes to prepare them for the rough-and-tumble of the adult world.

During the eighteenth century, however, aristocratic and middle-class parents began to express love more openly, and they praised their children more frequently than before. One reason for Jean-Jacques Rousseau's popularity was his endorsement of these displays of feeling.

Why Did Change Occur? Historians have debated the causes for the rise in domestic privacy, comfort, and displays of familial

livery Clothing with distinctive colors worn by servants of an important person.

wet nurses Women who nursed other women's babies for a fee.

Michel Barthélemy Olliver's *Supper at the Prince of Conti's Residence in the Temple*, 1766
Michel Barthélemy Olliver's *Supper at the Prince of Conti's Residence in the Temple* shows the prince and his guests enjoying supper in an informal atmosphere. Conti belonged to a junior branch of the French royal family. © RMN-Grand Palais / Art Resource, NY

» *How does the artist convey a sense of the relaxed nature of this party?*

affection. In part, they resulted from examples given at the highest levels of society, at royal courts. Louis XV of France toned down the public court ritual of his great-grandfather Louis XIV and spent much time in his private apartments with a few close friends. Stiff and silent at formal court events, Louis XV was relaxed and chatty in his private rooms, where he sat with cats on his lap.

No one promoted a comfortable lifestyle more than the French queen Marie Antoinette, wife of Louis XVI. Turning her back on the marble and gilt of Versailles, she built a play village, Le Hameau, on the palace grounds. There she and her ladies-in-waiting dressed in country clothes and pretended to be milkmaids. Rousseau's rejection of corrupt civilization and his call for people to live closer to nature inspired Le Hameau. So did the enthusiasm for the "natural" natives of the South Pacific pictured in the travel reports of James Cook and Louis-Antoine de Bougainville. But the new standards for simpler living also shaped it.

Some historians attribute the new privacy to a growing sense of individualism fostered by the Enlightenment's emphasis on each person as an autonomous rational being. Others look to Protestant and Catholic reformers, who called for more modesty in people's daily lives. These reformers also preached that Christians should be bound together by love, thus encouraging an open affection within the family and the idea that affection should take precedence over financial considerations or social advancement when it came to marriage and children. The new emphasis on privacy, comfort, and family affection represented a profound shift in people's sense of how they should relate to others.

18-3b The Problem of the Poor

The changes in domestic life in Europe's upper and middle classes had little impact on the mass of working people, whose lives, as in the past, continued to be lived more in public view and were, therefore, shaped by community opinion and standards. Farthest removed from the world of the well-to-do were the poor. About 10 percent of Europe's population lived in permanent conditions of poverty.

The "Deserving" and the "Undeserving" Poor

As in the past, people made a distinction between the "deserving" and "undeserving" poor. Old or sick people, along with the disabled, deserved support, but able-bodied beggars and vagabonds should be forced into work. Throughout the century, these undeserving poor were treated both as a social problem and as a criminal threat. British authorities regularly rounded up beggars along with convicted felons and transported them to its overseas colonies, first to America and then to Australia. In the early eighteenth century, France adopted the same policy and shipped poor men and women to Louisiana.

Workhouses Another way of handling the able-bodied poor was to place them in publicly sponsored **workhouses**, where they were forced to be productive and were reeducated in the value of labor. After the German state of Bavaria cleared its territory of beggars and vagabonds by building a huge workhouse that confined them, other European governments ordered similar institutions.

In England, the law allowed two or more parishes to build a common workhouse for the poor. In France, Louis XV's government ordered a workhouse for each province. Their inmates either engaged in unskilled work, spinning wool and unwinding silk cocoons, or were drafted to do roadwork.

New Ways of Thinking About Poverty During the eighteenth century, the problem of poverty began to be looked at in new ways. When church reformers of the sixteenth century had called on the state to administer poverty programs, they had argued that it was the government's duty to care for the poor just as a father cared for his needy children.

By the eighteenth century, the view that the state had a fatherly obligation toward the poor was giving way to the argument that poverty relief was a *right* that human beings could demand. The idea of the rights of the poor was stimulated by the Enlightenment notion that human beings were endowed with natural rights that society had to acknowledge. People who accepted this view sometimes argued that poor relief should be supplemented by old-age and medical insurance for the needy. Although insurance programs were never implemented and policy makers concentrated solely on relief or forced work, the idea of a comprehensive state-sponsored welfare system had entered European thought about society.

The Causes of Poverty The Enlightenment also lay behind another new aspect of thought about the poor. Previously, Europeans believed that poverty was the result of human sin, which made the rich greedy and the poor lazy. Programs to eliminate poverty aimed, therefore, to reform the sinner. In the eighteenth century, a more secular approach developed. The Englishman Gregory King and the Frenchman Sébastien de Vauban signaled the change when they called for a careful count of the number of poor people. Once the magnitude of the problem had been established, the state could determine its causes and develop rational policies to deal with it.

The Enlightenment idea that people were naturally good undermined the notion that human sinfulness lay at the root of poverty. Now people looked for social and economic causes and argued that poverty resulted from such things as the rise in the cost of living, shifts in the demand for workers, and problems of overpopulation. On the European continent, the central state took direct control of poverty programs, while in England the state turned the problem over to local government and ordered parishes in the kingdom to undertake the care of the poor. Overall, government-sponsored poor relief was confined to western and central Europe. Farther east, the family or the village commune was called on to deal with its destitute members.

CONNECTIONS: For a nineteenth century analysis of poverty, see Section 21-4a Poverty in Industrial Societies.

18-3c Popular Social Protest

In times of economic crisis—when harvests failed and the food supply dropped or demand for goods produced in the putting-out system declined—the ranks of the poor could swell to almost 50 percent of the population in an affected area. During these bad times, Europeans rioted.

Grain and Food Riots A sudden rise in grain and bread prices often triggered food riots. Because many peasants did not produce enough grain to feed themselves, they had to buy it. When prices shot up, they would lie in wait for wagon convoys carrying grain and attack them—often at stream fords or during the loading of cargo onto riverboats.

In cities, the working poor attacked bakeries. Although the attacks sometimes involved looting, many people, after seizing bread, paid what they thought was a fair price. Records testify to people returning to bakeries following a riot to put their money down on the counter, saying that they had forgotten to pay in the heat of the moment.

Rioters did not think of themselves as thieves and maintained their honor by paying what they could. In times of need, honor was often the only thing poor people possessed, and it was, therefore, carefully protected. Women always played a prominent role in food riots. As the family's food providers, it was their duty to take the lead in putting bread on the table.

The Labor Riot Laborers also rioted to obtain higher wages or better working conditions. Secretly forming organizations with ominous names like "The Conquering and Bold Defiance,"

workhouses State-run prison-like institutions housing vagabonds and beggars.

Guildhall Library, City of London/The Bridgeman Art Library

Rioters at Newgate Prison

In 1780, anti-Catholic sentiment in London exploded in a week of violence known as the Gordon Riots. Rioters destroyed Catholic establishments and homes. In this engraving, they set fire to London's notorious Newgate Prison after freeing the inmates. Attacks on public buildings, including prisons, were common in eighteenth-century riots.

>> *How does the artist convey a sense of turbulence and danger in this scene?*

weavers destroyed their employers' looms or cut the threads in them. Coal miners also destroyed machinery, throwing it down mine shafts while trying to set fire to the coal.

Antilabor Legislation Employers regularly denounced these riots as the work of wild mobs, and governments looked unfavorably on any form of labor organization. In 1791, the French revolutionary legislature passed the **Le Chapelier (cha-pel-ee-ay) Law** outlawing labor unions, and the British **Combination Act** of 1799 made unions unlawful conspiracies. Workers themselves, however, viewed riots and unions as necessary negotiating tactics in a world where they had no legal rights to **collective bargaining**.

Government Authorities and Rioters Government authorities held complicated views about riots. Generally, they took a dim view of popular disturbance in any form and severely punished those they caught. At times, however, they had some sympathy for rioters who seemed to be truly hard-pressed by food shortages or deteriorating working conditions and would soften the punishments.

Authorities also held women less accountable than men because of widespread beliefs that women by nature were emotional and disorderly. Male protesters took advantage of this view by occasionally disguising their faces with charcoal dust and then putting on women's clothes to protect themselves by symbolically assuming female disorderliness.

18-3d The Social Order

Throughout the eighteenth century, theories about how European society should be organized jostled with one another. Traditionalists argued that people were born into their proper social group: Children of peasants were peasants, children of nobles were nobles. Others argued that levels of wealth, and not the accident of birth, should determine who fell into the upper, middle, and lower groups.

A Society of Orders and Estates In the eighteenth century, most Europeans lived in a society made up of **orders**, also sometimes called **estates**. These were social groupings based largely on hereditary principles. Thus, one was born into the estate of nobles or the estate of commoners. Some orders were entered through recruitment; clergy, for example entered their order through the rite of ordination.

Le Chapelier Law (1791) and **Combination Act** (1799) French and British legislation, respectively, that outlawed labor unions.

collective bargaining Negotiations over working conditions between an employer and an organized group of workers.

orders/estates Form of social organization in which people's identity was largely defined by the groups to which the law assigned them.

Orders could include the family, the official residents of a certain city, and professional or occupational groups like lawyers or members of guilds. People in a society of estates and orders could belong to many of them simultaneously. For example, a French duke living in Paris would be a member of his ducal family, the order of the nobility, and an official resident of Paris. To a large degree, people's sense of self, along with other people's recognition of their place in the community, was defined by their participation in these groups. As a consequence, individuality was less noticed or regarded than group membership.

To enforce this point, European governments defined the orders legally and issued laws stating who were proper members of them. Thus, illegitimate children were not legally family members, and vagabonds or the floating population of underemployed poor people were not legally recognized as residents of cities.

Privileges Each order and estate had certain rights that belonged exclusively to it. For example, in France the male head of family had the legal right to request the imprisonment of a disobedient son or daughter, and in eastern Europe the nobility alone had the right to own land. The distinctive legal rights belonging to an order were known as **privileges**. Privilege was something one had a right to that others did not have because it belonged only to one's order. Thus, the clergy of France had the right to be exempt from state taxation, but nobles and commoners were taxed in varying degrees.

In a society of orders, one's right to enjoy one's privileges was as strong as other people's right to enjoy theirs, but the privileges varied from order to order. As the conservative English political philosopher **Edmund Burke** put it, "Everyone has equal rights, but not to equal things."

A Hierarchical View of Society A society of orders and estates was also hierarchical. Orders were not only unequal in privileges, they were also unequal in social status. Thus, the **Prussian General Code of 1791** assigned the top position to the nobility, while the middle classes were placed below nobles, and the mass of peasant serfs made up the lowest social order. The law codes of France, the largest society of orders in western Europe, did the same. Societies organized this way recognized that the orders occupied the same general space, such as the kingdom of Prussia or the kingdom of France, but within that space they were walled off from each other by their legally defined privileges and ranked hierarchically. The only thing they had in common was obedience to the king, who presided over all the orders and held them together as a unit—a principle of royal absolutism.

The view of society as comprising orders encouraged people to signal their position in the social hierarchy by surrounding themselves with liveried servants or insisting on their right to wear distinctive kinds of clothing—swords, lace, and bright clothing for nobles; dark-colored, simply cut clothes for commoners. Supporters of the society of orders argued that it was the divinely established form of social organization. People had a duty to live within their order and to respect the hierarchical arrangement of society.

Britain: The Social Importance of Money During the eighteenth century, the idea of society as a hierarchy of orders and estates based on privilege increasingly had to compete with other ways of thinking about the human community. In Britain, the older structure of society had been largely dismantled during the religious and political turmoil of the seventeenth century. Although a privileged nobility, the **peerage**, continued to exist, its numbers were small and its boundaries weak because the younger sons and daughters of peers were classified as commoners.

In its place, a new social structure emerged in which money largely determined people's social position. In this **plutocracy**, an aristocracy made up of peers and commoners, or **gentry**, occupied the highest social position. Membership in it depended on land ownership. Although old landed families often looked down on recent purchasers of land, the newly arrived could count on a general acceptance of their place in the aristocracy.

Britain's dominant position in the Atlantic economy led to the growth of a middle class engaging in trade, manufacturing, and banking. Aristocrats invested in their businesses, sent their younger sons to work in their firms, and welcomed their daughters into their families as well-heeled brides. At the end of the century, the British emphasis on money as a social marker shaped the novels of **Jane Austen**, which are full of discussions about the annual incomes of their heroes and heroines.

privileges Exclusive rights that belonged to members of an order or estate.

Edmund Burke (1729–1797) Political writer and member of Parliament, Britain's leading opponent of the French Revolution, and the founder of modern conservatism.

Prussian General Code (1791) State law code that defined Prussia as a society of estates.

peerage Legally recognized British titled nobility.

plutocracy Society in which wealth is the main determinant of social standing.

gentry British landowning aristocracy composed of commoners and peers.

Jane Austen (1775–1817) British novelist who depicted provincial life in classics such as *Sense and Sensibility* (1811) and *Pride and Prejudice* (1813).

Money and Social Standing in France French society was legally organized as a society of orders and estates, but money also played an increasingly important role in determining people's social standing. Wealth bought noble titles for commoners and opened the doors to the best schools for the sons and daughters of the rich, whether noble or not. The consumer revolution, with its emphasis on people as buyers of products, fostered plutocratic conceptions of society, and the increasing importance of money in determining social standing broke down traditional ideas that birth determined one's place in society. In addition, the choices the consumer revolution gave to individuals also undermined the idea that people's identity was largely determined by membership in group-based orders.

18-3e The Nation

By the middle years of the eighteenth century, yet another way of thinking about society emerged in which people now argued that a primary component of a person's identity derived from being a citizen of a distinct **nation**. The idea of the nation emerged in both the plutocratic society of Britain and the more traditional society of France. The world wars of the mid-eighteenth century between these two peoples fed a growing sense of national unity on each side.

The British Nation For the British, their common identity was rooted in the belief that they were a unique "island race" united behind a Protestant monarchy and church. The king fostered the sense of national unity by traveling throughout his realm and appearing at carefully staged events that brought rich and poor and men and women together. For many Britons, war with France was a war between antagonistic religious communities. Britons, as defenders of Protestantism, were a free, peaceful, righteous nation, whereas the French were slaves who groveled before a tyrannical monarchy and an oppressive Catholic Church.

The French Nation The French took an equally dim view of the British. They saw themselves as the defenders of enlightened civilization, while the British were addicted to a vulgar materialism that concentrated simply on trade and making money. Hadn't Adam Smith himself referred to them as a "nation of shopkeepers?" French losses in the Seven Years' War fueled the notion that Britain was bent on world domination. The conflict had not been one of king against king, or Protestant against Catholic, but of nation against nation. Thus, by midcentury, the French had forged a new sense of collective identity as they embraced the ideal of a united nation fighting a wicked foreign enemy whose culture and values were incompatible with their own.

The French monarchy, like that of the British, fostered this sense of national identity in the face of a dangerous enemy. But religious concerns were less prominent in the French concept of the nation. While the British thought that Protestantism had united the English, Welsh, and Scots into a single nation, the French thought that the nation was a purely human construction that the French people themselves had willed into existence. Its task was to resist British power and arrogance.

In both France and Britain, people thought that each individual had an active role to play in protecting the nation from enemy outsiders. This sense of individual engagement, along with the rising political importance of public opinion, contributed to a growing popular interest in politics and a desire to participate more directly in the political process.

18-4 The Beginning of Industrial Production

> » **What factors favored industrialization in Great Britain?**
>
> » **How did new manufacturing processes revolutionize the production of goods?**

As antagonism between the French and British increased over trade and empire, the beginning of industrialization in Great Britain gave the British the upper hand. At the same time, industrialization had a radical impact on Britons' everyday life. It altered the living habits and psychology of people touched by it—sometimes positively, often negatively, but always unavoidably and without any possibility of returning to an earlier, less complicated era.

18-4a Mechanization and Mass Production

Increased international trade and rising consumer demand had fueled growth in British manufacturing under the putting-out system. During the second half of the eighteenth century, continuing increases in population and trade created a need for innovations that would increase productivity, standardize quality, and lower the cost of products. These innovations altered British manufacturing.

Innovations in Cotton Cloth Weaving Cotton cloth weaving was one of the first areas to see radical changes in production. In 1733, the **flying shuttle** doubled the speed at which a weaver could work.

nation Way of thinking about society that emphasizes common citizenship in a community as a primary component of a person's identity.

flying shuttle Weaving device invented in 1733 that doubled a weaver's speed.

Universal History Archive/Getty Images

Wedgwood Manufactory

At Josiah Wedgwood's pottery manufactory in Staffordshire, kilns belching coal smoke fired thousands of pieces of china at the same time. The china was then stacked and packed in special containers for distribution around England.

›› *In early industrial enterprises, housing for workers was built in the midst of factory buildings. What might be the reasons for this?*

The quicker looms demanded more thread, leading James Hargreaves to invent the **spinning jenny** in the 1760s. Previously, spinners produced only one thread at a time; with one person operating Hargreaves's jenny, eight to eleven threads could be spun simultaneously, although the thread produced was unevenly strong. The spinning jenny was further improved by Richard Arkwright who invented the **water frame**, which produced a uniformly strong thread, thereby standardizing quality. Unlike the hand-powered spinning jenny, the water frame relied on a water mill for power.

The Factory The water frame's size and complexity required construction of a special building, the **factory**. Now spinners had to leave their cottages and report to a workplace where their work was supervised, regulated, and timed. Arkwright set up his first factory in 1771, employing nearly six hundred spinners. In 1785, Samuel Crompton patented the **spinning mule**, which combined the best qualities of the jenny and water frame and produced a thread that was both strong and fine. Weavers now could make high-priced, thin cotton cloth as well as cheaper, coarser cloth.

Mechanization Improvements in thread production, however, outstripped the ability of weavers using hand looms to convert thread into cloth, creating a bottleneck in production. In 1785, Edmund Cartwright, an Anglican clergyman, invented the steam-driven **power loom**, eliminating this bottleneck. The power loom also required weavers to leave their homes for power-driven factories. With the power loom, the **mechanization** of the cotton cloth industry was complete; machines now did work that had previously been done by hand. In 1793, the American Eli Whitney invented the **cotton gin**, which quickly separated seed from fiber in the cotton boll.

As American cotton cultivation expanded, British cotton cloth production soared. Between 1750 and 1800, alone, it increased tenfold. The British navy and the merchant marine played an important role by transporting raw cotton from the American South and India to the spinning machines and looms in Britain.

Josiah Wedgwood In addition to cotton cloth, pottery making was at the heart of what would be described as the **Industrial Revolution**. In 1759, **Josiah Wedgwood** transformed British porcelain production. Using the good clay of the English Midlands, Wedgwood opened a porcelain factory, based on Adam Smith's theory of the division of labor. Each stage in production—unloading the clay, mixing it, shaping it into pieces, dipping it in a glaze, placing it in kilns, and firing it—was carried out by specialized worker groups.

spinning jenny Hand-operated spinning device invented by James Hargreaves in 1768 that allowed multiple strands of yarn (or thread) to be spun at the same time.

water frame Water-operated spinning device invented by Richard Arkwright in 1769 that improved the spinning jenny by producing a uniformly strong thread.

factory Building or series of buildings where workers in a particular industry are gathered together to increase the speed and volume of production.

spinning mule Spinning device invented by Samuel Crompton in 1785 that combined features of the jenny and water frame.

power loom Steam-driven loom invented by Edmund Cartwright in 1785 that doubled the speed of weaving.

mechanization Manufacturing process in which machines replace hand work.

cotton gin Device invented by Eli Whitney in 1793 that allowed easy removal of seeds from raw cotton, thereby making cotton more easily processed for cloth.

Industrial Revolution Changes in manufacturing involving mechanization of production and the use of power sources other than human or animal muscle.

Josiah Wedgwood (1730–1795) English pottery manufacturer whose success came from an efficient division of labor in his manufactory.

In addition, Wedgwood bypassed the individual potter's wheel, which had been used in pottery production for millennia, and shaped his pieces using molds of standardized size. The finished pieces were therefore identical, allowing for easy stacking and storage. Wedgwood hired salesmen to crisscross the country, demonstrating his wares.

Mass Production True to Smith's prediction, division of labor ensured quality control and lowered production costs; for the first time, English porcelain could compete with Asian imports because of lower price. Eventually, Wedgwood replaced workers with steam engines to mix his clay. Division of labor, uniform products, and competitive prices were central to **mass production**, another feature of the early Industrial Revolution.

The Steam Engine The development of steam power was also vital to industrialization. The **steam engine** had been invented by Thomas Newcomen in 1702 and had found practical application in pumping water out of coal mines. But its inefficiency limited use away from coalfields. Broader use of steam power in industry had to wait for the improvements of **James Watt**.

Watt improved on Newcomen's invention, developing a steam engine that was efficient and safe enough to be used in industry. By the 1780s, Watt's engines were pumping water out of mines, driving cotton looms, and powering Wedgwood's clay mixers. The engine's steam was produced by a fire fueled with coke—coal, abundant in England, that had been heated to eliminate impurities preventing it from burning hotly and evenly.

Steam engines were made of iron, and their spreading use stimulated iron production in Britain. Steam, coal, and iron, along with mechanization and mass production, were at the heart of the early Industrial Revolution.

CONNECTIONS: For further developments in industrialization, see Section 24-1 The Second Industrial Revolution.

mass production Production technique based on the division of labor, uniform products, and competitive prices that increased both quantity and quality of production.

steam engine Engine that uses steam power to supply energy, invented in 1702 by Thomas Newcomen and perfected by James Watt.

James Watt (1736–1819) Scottish inventor who improved Newcomen's steam engine, making it safe enough to be used in industry.

capital Wealth available for investment in the production of goods for the market.

entrepreneur Person who manages economic activity by assuming the risks and enjoying the profits.

18-4b Why Britain?

Britain was the first country in the world to experience the Industrial Revolution. Six important factors made industrialization possible: High levels of agricultural productivity, available skilled workers, ease of transportation, natural resources, political stability, and **capital** for industry.

Agricultural Productivity Before industrialization can take place anywhere, that area's agriculture must be efficient enough to be able to allow some workers to leave agriculture for industry. Britain's agricultural revolution had fulfilled that condition, freeing up surplus labor in the countryside that would be absorbed into the industrial working class.

Skilled Workers Another precondition for industrialization was the availability of skilled workers. In Britain this precondition was also present. The growth of the putting-out system, stimulated by Britain's leading role in the Atlantic economy, increased the number of merchant **entrepreneurs** as well as the pool of workers who had mastered many basic processes in the production of goods. Industrialization would build on this basis by using the existing skills of both entrepreneurs and workers. Water and steam power also supplemented human and animal muscles.

Ease of Transportation Geography also helped Britain to industrialize. Because Britain was an island country with many navigable rivers and a well-developed canal system, British industry could transport both raw materials and finished products more economically than its continental competitors. Before the development of the railroad, transporting bulk materials such as coal, wool, or cotton by land was very expensive. Mass industrial production demanded that these materials either be located near the factory (as in the case of coal) or that they be transported cheaply—that is, by water.

Natural Resources Britain was also blessed by nature with a large supply of the raw material that fueled the early Industrial Revolution: Coal. The coal belt that extends across Europe from northern England to southern Poland was first exploited in Britain, particularly in such early industrial cities as Manchester, Birmingham, Glasgow, and Sheffield. Because of their endless appetite for coal, the first factories were usually built on top of or next to existing coalfields. Britain was also lucky in that the coal deposits lay relatively close to the surface, allowing easy exploitation of this fuel source.

Political Stability Political factors were no less important. Since the Glorious Revolution of 1688,

England had enjoyed peace and political stability. Unlike the continent, Britain was one unified market: no tolls or internal **duties** had to be paid to ship goods from Scotland to England or Wales. The British government also actively encouraged industrial development by such laws as the **Calico Act** of 1721, which restricted the import of cotton cloth, called calico, from India.

Capital Accumulation Britain was also ahead of other European states in the accumulation of capital, thanks to the economic growth produced by the Atlantic trade. Some of this capital came directly from profits in the slave trade, but most of it came from other sources. Although per capita income in Britain in the mid-eighteenth century was probably not significantly greater than that in France, this income was better distributed among larger groups in the population.

More important still, access to capital was easier in Britain than in any other European country, in large part because of the existence of a central national bank. The **Bank of England**, founded in 1694, remained for over a century the only central bank in any major European country. The Bank of England loaned money to smaller banks, thereby helping increase the circulation of capital by making it easier for savings to be funneled into investment. This well-developed system of banks and credit made it relatively easy for British entrepreneurs to obtain financing—venture capital—to build factories, purchase steam engines or power looms, advance credit to purchasers, and the like. The combination of accumulated capital (that is, savings) and a well-developed system of credit helped Britain to industrialize. For all these reasons—agriculture, labor supply, transportation system, natural resources, politics, and capital—Britain managed to take the industrial leap before the rest of the world.

Was the "Industrial Revolution" Revolutionary?
Some scholars have pointed out that *revolution* might be an inappropriate term for this process, which began around 1760 but only really took off during the period of the French Revolution and the Napoleonic Wars, a period of fifty-five years. The impact of industrialization was revolutionary, however, because it altered work patterns, family life, income distribution, society and culture, the availability of material goods, wealth and poverty, and the thinking of intellectuals and politicians about all these developments.

> **duties** Taxes, usually charged on products crossing a regional or national boundary.

> **Calico Act** (1721) British act that limited the importation of cotton cloth (calico) from India.

> **Bank of England** National bank established in 1694 that facilitated the circulation of capital during the Industrial Revolution.

CHAPTER Review

Summary

» Europe's eighteenth-century population growth stimulated economic growth and led to new forms of work, especially in manufacturing.

» As a result, some theorists began to argue that economies were capable of ongoing expansion, and they searched for the laws that made growth possible, founding the modern discipline of economics.

» As the consumer revolution took root, some economists began to praise all forms of work equally, repudiating the older view that the mental work of philosophers or theologians was superior to manual labor.

» Trading networks across the Atlantic, which had formed during the sixteenth century, reached their fullest development in the eighteenth century.

» The networks also fueled European economic growth, as the French and then the British Empire overtook the older Spanish and Portuguese empires.

» Because of their populous colonies in North America and their sugar islands in the Caribbean, the British developed the most far-reaching and profitable Atlantic trading networks, making London the commercial center of Europe.

» African slaves made possible the commercial exchanges of the Atlantic trading system. They were forcibly imported by the millions to labor in the plantations of the New World, where they cultivated the crops and mined the silver and gold that Europe's people and economies demanded.

» As part of the trading system, Europeans sent manufactured goods to colonies in the New World.

» Well-to-do European consumers developed new standards of domestic life during the eighteenth century.

» Older behaviors emphasizing public display as a sign of high social standing gave way to a concern for privacy and comfort.

» Enlightenment ideals, which stressed life in this world, were partly responsible for these new ways of life.

» Farther down the social scale, the poor continued to live as in the past because their lives were more in public view and were shaped by community-enforced norms.

» The Enlightenment also inspired European governments to reconceive poverty less as a consequence of sin than as the product of social, economic, and demographic conditions.

» The poor also shaped their place in society by means of the riot, the classic form of social protest in the eighteenth-century world.

» Rethinking the problem of poverty was symptomatic of a larger change in social thought, as corporate and hierarchical understandings of society now competed with ideas of status based on land and wealth.

» Some argued that each individual's primary identity was as a citizen of a nation, whose rights and values had to be defended from threatening outsiders.

» Nationalist antagonism between the French and British increased with the beginning of industrialization, which in Britain started as a mechanization of textile production and spread to other forms of manufacture.

Chronology

1713	Spain grants Britain the *asiento* [Europe, Americas]
1720	Last plague epidemic breaks out in France [Europe]
1721	Calico Act restricts the import of cotton cloth from India [Europe, Asia]
1733	Flying shuttle doubles weavers' speed [Europe]
1750	Treaty of Madrid between Spain and Portugal [Europe, Americas]
1760s	Industrial Revolution begins in Britain [Europe]
1763	France loses its empire in North America [Europe, Americas]
1768	James Hargreaves invents the spinning jenny [Europe]
1769	Richard Arkwright invents the water frame [Europe]
1771	Arkwright opens the first water-powered factory [Europe]
1776	Adam Smith publishes *The Wealth of Nations* [Europe]; American Revolution begins [Americas]
1780	Gordon Riots destroy Catholic property in London [Europe]

1780s	James Watt's improved steam engines are introduced in Britain; Prussian General Code becomes law [Europe]
1783	American independence is won [Americas]
1785	Parliament regulates pawnbrokers in the United Kingdom [Europe]
1791	Prussian General Code becomes law [Europe]
1793	Eli Whitney invents the cotton gin [Americas]

Critical Thinking Questions

Take a moment to pull together all the important information from the chapter by answering the following questions:

Economic Recovery

» What were the causes and the consequences of Europe's expanding population in the eighteenth century?

» How did the Physiocrats' and Adam Smith's notions of wealth and economic activity differ from those of the seventeenth-century mercantilists?

The Atlantic World

» What were the goods European states sent to their colonies overseas, and what goods did the colonies send back to Europe?

» How was the American Revolution linked to European colonial rivalries and the outcomes of the two world wars of the midcentury?

European Society in an Age of Enlightenment

» How did European thought about the poor change during the eighteenth century?

» What were the similarities and the differences in British and French concepts of the nation?

The Beginning of Industrial Production

» How was the steam engine employed in mining, cloth manufacturing, and pottery making?

» How did Britain's political stability, along with its banking system, promote industrialization?

Revolutionary France and Napoleonic Europe, 1775–1815

Chapter Outline

As you read, consider the following questions:

❯ From 1789 to 1815, what changed and what remained the same in French political, social, and religious life?

❯ How did revolutionaries and opponents of the Revolution in France define their collective identities and those of their enemies?

❯ What was the impact of revolutionary France and Napoleonic rule on Europe?

❯ How did the French define the nation, and what role did nationalism play in French expansion in Europe during the revolutionary and Napoleonic periods?

O N JUNE 11, 1775, in the Gothic cathedral of Rheims, a young man of twenty was crowned king of France. The coronation was an ancient ceremony in the kingdom's collective life that bound the French people to the king as his loyal subjects. At the climax of the ceremony, when the archbishop of Rheims (reems) lowered the jeweled crown of Charlemagne onto the head of the new king, Louis XVI prayed, "O Christ, may You Yourself crown this king!" Eighteen years later, in Paris, that same head was severed from its body and lifted from a bloodstained basket to be displayed triumphantly to thousands of the king's former subjects.

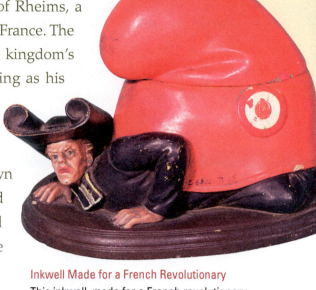

Inkwell Made for a French Revolutionary

This inkwell, made for a French revolutionary, shows a Catholic priest being crushed by a "Phrygian cap," a hat favored by the revolutionaries. Musée de la Ville de Paris/Musée Carnavalet, Paris/Giraudon/The Bridgeman Art Library

In 1775, no one could foresee the king's execution. In retrospect, however, it is clear that the new king faced a growing political crisis. Finally, in 1789, revolution broke out, and thousands of French men and women joined in the movement to reshape the French community from the bottom up. First, France's absolute monarchy was modified into a limited constitutional monarchy. Then, the monarchy was abolished and a republic proclaimed. When the conservative states of Europe sought to restrain the republic, a revolutionary dictatorship was established to crush France's foreign and domestic enemies. Then, France was a republic again. Then, Napoleon Bonaparte took control and shortly proclaimed himself emperor. During all these years, almost all of Europe was at war against France. France gained control of most of the continent, then lost it all (see Map 19.1). Napoleon was defeated and exiled. In 1814, the monarchy was back, and Louis XVI's youngest brother was proclaimed king. Then, for a hundred days, Napoleon was back, then gone, and the king returned and remained.

Beneath this dizzying change of regimes in France, fundamental change was taking place that would alter Europe forever. The French revolutionaries created Europe's first modern representative democracy, sweeping away the old world of orders and estates and creating a new world of citizens bound together in a single nation. The revolutionary regime also broke with the Catholic Church, rejecting the centuries-old ties between church and state and creating a secular political and social order. The break with the church was accompanied by attacks on the Catholic clergy like the one shown in this chapter's opening image. War led to Europe's first mass mobilization of citizens to defend the country from external enemies as well as to a harsh dictatorship that crushed opposition at home.

France's wars spread the revolution outside France, and as victorious French armies occupied foreign territory, Napoleon enforced revolutionary reform across the continent.

Written constitutions were introduced, state-sponsored religious discrimination was ended, the principle of equality before the law for all citizens was advanced, and a military draft was imposed. When Louis XVI's brother was restored as king of France, it looked as though the clock had been turned backward. But that was not the case, and Europe was never again as it had been in 1775 when Louis XVI was crowned.

19-1 From Crisis to Constitution, 1775–1789

» **What were the causes of the French Revolution?**

» **At the end of 1789, how had the political and social order in France changed?**

In 1775, the year Louis XVI was crowned king of France, American colonists began a revolution that challenged British royal authority. Many in France, which aided America's revolutionary war, embraced America's revolutionary rhetoric about fairness in taxation, the rights of citizens, and representative government. At the same time, the French monarchy, nearly bankrupt and facing challenges to its own royal authority, was poised to unravel. Its financial problems peaked in the late 1780s, just as bad harvests forced up the price of bread. An unprecedented crisis quickly escalated into revolution.

19-1a The French Monarchy in Crisis

Louis XVI intended to use his absolute political power to rule for the good of his subjects. But absolutism worked only as long as people did not question the king's exercise of that power. By the 1780s, however, many people were questioning it, accusing the king and his ministers of everything from indecisiveness to despotism.

Louis XVI (r. 1775–1792) King of France whose monarchy was abolished by the creation of the French Republic.

Parlement of Paris France's most important royal court, which resisted the king's absolute rule.

Marie Antoinette (r. 1775–1792) Austrian Habsburg princess married to Louis XVI who as queen of France was his controversial political adviser.

The Crisis in State Finances The chief problem was the king's inability to manage state finances. The cost of the world wars of the midcentury had put huge strains on the French treasury, and for naught, as France lost its overseas possessions. French involvement in the American Revolution was also expensive. The French government was forced to raise taxes, distributing the burden unequally among its subjects because nobles and clergy were traditionally exempt from some taxes. But state income still regularly fell short of state expenses, so new loans were required. As loans increased, so did interest on them, which only increased shortfalls in revenue. The result was a policy muddle indicating to many that the monarchy had lost its grip on the country's affairs.

Attempts at Reform By the mid-1780s, the king had realized that a complete overhaul of royal finances was needed to solve the problem of declining revenues and rising debt. Hoping to gain the support of the greatest nobles and churchmen, Louis appealed to them to join in a reform of the system. But these powerful people demanded to see the royal accounts before they agreed. Louis took their demand as a direct challenge to his absolute authority and turned it down.

The king then turned for support to the **Parlement of Paris**, but this royal court, too, was reluctant to help and engaged in a fierce struggle over control of policy, claiming that it alone could protect the people of France from government mismanagement. By July 1788, the conflict between Louis and the Parlement had become so severe that public order started to break down as pro-Parlement rioters and royal troops clashed in several provinces of the kingdom.

Queen Marie Antoinette Failure to resolve the financial crisis drove the king into a deep depression. He frequently burst into tears and ate and drank excessively. He also turned increasingly to his wife, Queen **Marie Antoinette**, for political advice. The queen, an Austrian princess, had never been popular; her marriage to Louis in 1770 had been intended to forge an alliance with France's long-standing Austrian Habsburg enemy. Now her extravagant personal spending on clothes and hairdos was also blamed for the financial crisis. Her enemies started calling her Madame Deficit. The queen's new political role, therefore, further enflamed people who had lost confidence in the king's ability to govern.

Map 19.1 **Europe in 1789** In 1789, France was only one of Europe's great powers.

1. Not counting the Ottoman Empire, how many separate states were there in Europe in 1789?

2. Now turn to Map 16.1 "Europe in 1715" at the beginning of Chapter 16. What changes occurred over the eighteenth century in Sweden's eastern boundary? What changes occurred in the Italian peninsula?

Map legend:
- France
- Austrian Habsburg lands
- Prussia
- Spanish Bourbon lands
- Great Britain
- Russian Empire
- Ottoman Empire
- Boundary of the Holy Roman Empire

Crop Failure and State Bankruptcy On July 13, 1788, an unexpected turn in the weather deepened the crisis. A massive hailstorm swept across much of France, with hailstones so big that they killed humans and animals alike. Much of the grain ripening in the fields was destroyed, ruining chances for a good harvest and substantial tax revenues. The losses, the worst incurred in a series of mediocre harvests from the 1760s on, also meant that bread prices would rise sharply, threatening many with starvation. Grain and bread were diet staples; ordinary people spent between a third and a half of their income on them.

Now the government's creditors, individuals and banks at home and abroad, lost confidence in France's ability to pay interest on its debts and refused to lend any more money to the king. In a desperate move to restore confidence, Louis announced that a traditional assembly of his subjects, the **Estates-General**, would convene in May 1789 to deal with the crisis. But lenders were not reassured, and on

Estates-General Kingdom-wide deliberative body convened in 1789 to deal with the Crown's financial collapse and to reform the government.

August 16, 1788, France went bankrupt, suspending payments on its loans.

19-1b The Estates-General

The Estates-General had not met in 175 years, and no one in 1788 had a clear idea of how it should be organized. In September, the Parlement of Paris resolved the question by ordering the Estates-General to convene as it had in 1614, in three orders, corresponding to the three estates of the realm. The First Estate was the clergy and religious orders, and the Second Estate was the nobility; together they stood at the top of France's society of orders and accounted for about 3 percent of France's population. The Third Estate was everyone else—the 97 percent of the French population that included merchants, lawyers, shopkeepers, urban workers, landowning peasants, and rural laborers. The estates would meet separately, and each would have one vote, though the Crown allowed the Third Estate to elect as many delegates as the First and Second Estates combined.

The End of Press Censorship At this very moment, the Crown also decided to suspend the old system of royal press censorship. Hundreds of pamphlets debated the implications of the arrangements for the Estates-General: Voting by delegates instead of by orders would give the Third Estate a voice.

What Is the Third Estate? The most widely read pamphlet was *What Is the Third Estate?* written by a Catholic clergyman, **Joseph Emmanuel Sieyès** (see-yez). Though a member of the First Estate, Sieyès argued that the clergy and nobility were parasites in French society. They contributed nothing to the wealth and skills of the kingdom but simply lived off the labor and talents of the Third Estate even as they monopolized political power. "What is the Third Estate? Everything," he exclaimed. "What has it been up to this point in the political order? Nothing." Sieyès wanted the Third Estate's political power to match its economic productivity and social usefulness.

Elections to the Estates-General In this supercharged atmosphere, France went to the polls to elect deputies to the Estates-General. The elections, which took place from January to April 1789,

Joseph Emmanuel Sieyès (1748–1836) Catholic priest who championed the political rights of the Third Estate.

cahiers Lists of grievances drawn up by voters electing deputies to the Estates-General in 1789.

patriots People who rejected absolutism and supported revolutionary reform of France.

National Assembly First French revolutionary legislature, in session from 1789 to 1791.

Table 19.1 The Revolution Unfolds in 1789

January–April	Elections to Estates-General
May	Estates-General meets
June	National Assembly formed Tennis Court Oath
July	Storming of the Bastille
July–August	Great Fear
August	Night of August 4 Declaration of the Rights of Man and the Citizen (Late August)
October	October Days

represented the greatest experiment in democratic politics that Europe had ever seen. They were also the largest public opinion poll to be carried out in Europe until the twentieth century, as voters—taxpaying men who were at least age twenty-five—were asked to state their suggestions for reform in books called **cahiers** (kai-yays).

Generally, the cahiers of all three estates called for an end to absolutism and the creation of a representative assembly of citizens that would join with the king in governing. There was also agreement that taxes needed to be restructured and that the exemptions the clergy and nobility traditionally enjoyed should end. (Table 19.1 summarizes the unfolding of the French Revolution in 1789.)

The Estates-General Meets On May 4, 1789, nearly 1,000 newly elected deputies to the Estates-General gathered at Versailles. Most looked to the king for leadership in the question of whether the estates would vote by order or by delegate, but it was not forthcoming. Well-intentioned but timid, Louis XVI feared to take the initiative. The deputies, left to figure things out on their own, could do no more than disagree. Weeks passed in stalemate, and tensions mounted dangerously. Finally, in June, the deputies of the Third Estate followed the lead of a minority of self-styled **patriots**, including Sieyès, who had been elected a deputy of the Third Estate, and declared that they were the **National Assembly**, the true representatives of the whole of the French people. Inviting the clergy and nobility to join them in a common meeting, they aimed to proceed with the business of reform.

The Revolution Begins The formation of the National Assembly was the beginning of the constitutional revolution as the deputies' action had no justification in either law or precedent. Over the

Réunion des Musées Nationaux/Art Resource, NY

The Tennis Court Oath

This painting of the Tennis Court Oath, based on an unfinished painting of Jacques-Louis David, enshrines the moment in French collective memory. Here, representatives of the revolutionary nation stretch out their hands to swear that they will not disband until they have written a constitution for France.

❯❯ *Why has the painter decided to show the curtains billowing in the fresh air and the shaft of light shining directly upon the figure in the center who is reading the oath?*

❯❯ *What do you make of those figures at the windows?*

next several days, a significant number of clergy from commoner families, along with a few members of the nobility, joined the new National Assembly. Some of these privileged defectors were influenced by Enlightenment ideas that government should be based on a contract with the governed. Others joined the patriots out of political calculation, recognizing that there was no other realistic course of action.

The Oath of the Tennis Court These events finally shook Louis XVI into action. He announced that he would address the estates in a special "royal session," but, in the meantime, he prohibited any further meetings of deputies. The problem was that no one informed the deputies of the prohibition! So, on June 21, when the National Assembly tried to reconvene in its usual meeting place, it found the doors locked and barred by royal troops. In a frenzy of excitement and anger, the deputies seized a nearby indoor tennis court and took a solemn oath—the **Tennis Court Oath**—not to disband until they had written a constitution for France.

Two days later, Louis held his royal session, which accomplished nothing, and the Assembly went on meeting. On June 27, the king faced the inevitable and ordered all members of the clergy and nobility to join the deputies of the National Assembly. Reluctantly, they did. But the king was humiliated, and at the end of the month he changed his mind again, ordering his soldiers to disband the National Assembly by force. When these troop movements were reported in Paris, fear combined with tension to explode in ways that were to have huge, if unforeseen, consequences for the emerging revolution.

> **Tennis Court Oath** Oath of the National Assembly not to disband before a written constitution had been drafted.

19-1c Trouble in Paris, Trouble in the Countryside, Trouble in Versailles

By late June 1789, Paris had become a hotbed of politics as patriot orators, fearful for the fate of the National Assembly, whipped up a feverish state of excitement. Anxiety intensified as food prices skyrocketed following the hailstorm and bad harvest of 1788. Then, on July 11, the king dismissed his latest finance minister, **Jacques Necker**, thought to be the most pro-patriot person in the government.

Paris and the Storming of the Bastille Paris panicked. Rioters, convinced that the king was about to attack the people, broke into arsenals, seizing weapons and ammunition. Soon up to a quarter million people were carrying weapons. On July 14, a huge crowd, armed with cannons, headed toward the Bastille, a medieval fortress that served as a royal prison and had long been a symbol of the king's absolute power.

At first the insurgents tried to negotiate with the prison governor for a surrender of the ammunition they sought. When this failed, they took the Bastille by force, releasing prisoners (there were only seven) and killing the governor, whose head, hacked off with a pocketknife, they paraded triumphantly about the city on the end of a pike. Frightened by the disorder, on July 15, the king recalled Necker to office and ordered the troops around Versailles and Paris to disband. Thus, the uprising in Paris saved the National Assembly at Versailles.

Jacques Necker (1732–1804) Louis XVI's financial minister whose dismissal provoked the uprising in Paris on July 14, 1789.

Great Fear Widespread peasant uprisings in July and August 1789 that abolished feudal dues to landlords.

Night of August 4 French legislative session in 1789 that abolished many traditional taxes, payments, and privileges.

Declaration of the Rights of Man and the Citizen Statement of revolutionary principles, proclaiming universal and inalienable human rights.

Revolution in the Countryside But immediately there was a new crisis, as peasant revolts erupted throughout most of the kingdom. Called the **Great Fear**, these uprisings in the countryside were sparked by the same high food prices and political excitement that had ignited Paris. The peasants believed that they were about to be attacked by people they called brigands and aristocrats.

Rising up in self-defense, they vented their fury against their landlords, looting manor houses and ransacking the offices that housed records of payments to the landlord. These payments, often cited in the peasants' cahiers, included fees for the use of the landlord's mill or bake ovens, which all peasants paid in addition to their regular land rents. Even peasants who owned their own land had to pay them. In the Great Fear, rural communities all over France spontaneously attacked these symbols of remaining feudal dues.

The Night of August 4 Faced with the peasant uprising, the National Assembly feared that all public order was about to collapse. In May, most deputies had wanted a reform of government. Now they realized that fundamental changes were needed. Therefore, on the **Night of August 4**, 1789, in an evening session of the Assembly, some deputies proposed to abolish the feudal dues that peasants were attacking. As it turned out, this limited proposal quickly turned into something extraordinary.

In a flash of enthusiasm, the deputies rushed to renounce all sorts of traditional taxes, payments, and privileges: The clergy gave up the tithe, military appointments previously reserved for nobles were opened to commoners, and the tax privileges of many towns and provinces were abolished. By dawn, when the session ended, the deputies had swept away virtually all of France's old society of orders and privilege.

The all-night meeting on August 4 dismantled the old social order of France, just as events in Versailles and Paris, culminating in the storming of the Bastille, had dismantled the old political order. But what was to replace them?

The Declaration of the Rights of Man and the Citizen Three weeks later, the National Assembly, led by Sieyès and other patriots, gave its answer when it issued the **Declaration of the Rights of Man and the Citizen**, the single most important document produced during the Revolution. In it, France's new regime was laid down in principle. The declaration drew on both Enlightenment thought and the language of the American Revolution, especially as expressed in the Declaration of Independence.

It proclaimed the "natural, inalienable, and sacred rights of man," which included the rights to "freedom, property, safety, and the right to resist oppression." It also guaranteed security from arbitrary arrest and freedom of speech and religion. France was still to have a king, but he was no longer to be absolute; rather, he was to govern according to a new written constitution.

The Revolutionary Principle of Liberty One word summed up the content of the declaration: Liberty. Human rights guaranteed by a government representing the people, limited by a constitution, and promoting the rule of law would make liberty possible. The declaration's affirmation that "all people shall have equal rights upon birth and ever after" would have a huge impact across Europe and eventually the world.

Conquering the Bastille

Claude Cholat, one of the "conquerors of the Bastille," painted this picture, thereby enshrining another moment in the collective memory of the French people. The awkward perspective indicates that Cholat was not trained in an art academy.

>> *How does the work capture the drama of the moment as Cholat remembered it?*

The October Days The National Assembly's program for a constitutional monarchy was worked out during August 1789. Now, it was up to Louis XVI to state his position on it, and, once again, the king hesitated. Then, in early October, the initiative passed to a new element of the population—the workingwomen of Paris, who were furious about the high cost of bread and believed the king should do something about it. On October 5, 6,000 women seized cannons and in pouring rain marched to Versailles to demand food. As the patriots joined them in the streets, the king capitulated. He promised flour for bread and agreed to accompany the marchers back to Paris, where he and his family were resettled in an old palace. A few days later, the National Assembly also moved to the city. These **October Days** shifted the center of power from aristocratic Versailles to turbulent Paris, where the king and the new National Assembly were under the watchful eye of the most militant revolutionaries.

Remembering 1789 By October, the events of the previous months were well on their way to becoming legends. The Tennis Court Oath came to symbolize the defiance of the French people in the face of royal despotism, and the storming of the Bastille became the symbol for the overthrow of royal oppression. The Night of August 4 stood for the destruction of the **Old Regime** and the inauguration of the new.

These events were memorialized in monumental paintings, like *The Tennis Court Oath* by **Jacques-Louis David**, and celebrated as national festivals. To this day, July 14, Bastille Day, is France's chief national holiday. The message these events conveyed was clear: In the Old Regime, politics was something done by the king and the court. In the new, politics would be done by the people. This momentous shift in the understanding of politics was at the heart of the French Revolution.

October Days Uprising of Parisian workingwomen in 1789 that brought the royal family to Paris.

Old Regime Revolutionary name for prerevolutionary France.

Jacques-Louis David (1748–1825) Important artist who celebrated the Revolution's great turning points in monumental paintings.

Parisian Women March to Versailles

In this contemporary image of the October march on Versailles, the artist shows women dragging a canon along the road to the palace.

≫ *Thinking back to what you know about the role of women in early modern Europe, why would they, and not men, take the lead in the march?*

≫ *How does the artist convey the determination and power of the marchers even on a rain soaked day?*

19-2 The Constitutional Monarchy, 1789–1792

> ≫ **What was new in the revolutionary concepts of the citizen and the nation?**

> ≫ **What were the causes and effects of the Revolution's break with the Catholic Church?**

From the fall of 1789 to the summer of 1792, France was a constitutional monarchy, with rule by the king and the National Assembly, the new national legislature. Writing a constitution, the Assembly scrapped the old haphazard administrative system, replacing it with uniform institutions and procedures. It also redefined French collective identity, reshaping France as a new nation made up of a community of citizens and defining the nature of citizenship. Many of these changes remain in place today. At the same time, however, new conflicts arose that were equally long lasting. One centered on the

Jacobin Club Most important French revolutionary political club, whose members were called Jacobins.

rights of women in the new regime. Another raised the problem of slavery in a reformed France. A crucial conflict was the rupture between the Revolution and the Roman Catholic Church. These issues increased the hostility between the revolutionaries and Louis XVI, who never really accepted his new constitutional role. Other European rulers, frightened by revolutionary radicalism, turned against France's new regime. After war broke out between revolutionary France and conservative Europe, France's monarchy fell.

19-2a The New Constitution

By November 1789, fear of hunger began to subside following a good harvest that reduced grain prices. Political excitement nevertheless remained high. Dozens of newspapers appeared, with names like *The Daily Thermometer* and *The National Whip*. New political clubs sprang up in Paris, where deputies and their supporters passionately debated legislative proposals.

The Jacobin Club The most famous club was the Society of the Friends of the Constitution, nicknamed the **Jacobin Club** for the building in which it met, once owned by Jacobin Dominican friars. The

Réunion des Musées Nationaux/Art Resource, NY

Jacobins were mainly middle class and often well-to-do. They supported the democratization of politics, but they also defended the rights of private property and favored an economy free from government regulation. The Jacobin leader **Maximilien Robespierre** (rohbs-pee-ayr), a prim provincial lawyer called "the Incorruptible" because of his dedication to the revolutionary agenda, praised the street violence that had led to the storming of the Bastille and the October march on Versailles.

The Constitution of 1791 By late 1789, the old political and social structures of France had been swept away. Now the National Assembly, following Article 3 of the Declaration of the Rights of Man and the Citizen, which stated that "the principle of all sovereignty resides in the Nation," began to write a constitution for the new regime. The **Constitution of 1791** reinvented French society and politics and redefined what it meant to be French.

The Constitution discarded the old estates and orders, declaring France to be a single nation, uniting all people who resided permanently on French soil. **Sovereignty** now resided in the nation, no longer in the king. The goal of the constitution was to create a community in which each person was equal, with equal natural rights. Ability, not birth, proclaimed the deputies, should determine success and status. Thus, the National Assembly abolished all titles of nobility.

The Departments and the Metric System As French society was pushed to be uniform and unified, the administration of government was made uniform and unified too. The Assembly swept away the overlapping muddle of administrative districts and replaced it with **departments**. Departments were to be alike in size and organized into standardized subdivisions. The departments reflected the revolutionaries' goal of creating efficient administrative districts and implemented the Enlightenment ideal that good government should be based on rational principles (see Map 19.2). Rationality also lay behind the introduction of the **metric system**, based on the meter, calculated as one ten-millionth of the quarter meridian. From now on, length was to be measured naturally, with a uniform unit based on the size of Earth itself.

Citizenship The National Assembly also addressed the issue of citizenship. The idea of citizenship had been discussed during the Enlightenment and was associated with self-government in the tradition of ancient Rome. It had been put into practice during the American Revolution. When it came to implementing citizenship in France, the Assembly, on the advice of Sieyès, backtracked on its principles of unity and uniformity by decreeing that people in the one nation were to be divided into two categories, **active and passive citizens**.

Active Citizens Only men who owned or otherwise controlled a certain amount of property could be active citizens, and only active citizens could vote and hold public office. The deputies believed that property ownership gave men a stake in society that would make them a band of citizen brothers who would act responsibly when making political decisions.

Passive Citizens Women and non property-holding men were to be passive citizens. Despite these restrictions, these formulations secured France a level of participatory democracy that would not be reached elsewhere in Europe for many decades. About two-thirds of adult French males met the qualifications for active citizens, and Protestants and Jews, who had been discriminated against during the Old Regime, were now admitted to full rights of citizenship.

Women and Citizenship The restructuring of France as a nation composed of equal (male) citizens was summed up in a new revolutionary slogan: "Liberty, Equality, Fraternity." Although women like Olympe de Gouges (see Profiles in Change: Olympe de Gouges Becomes a Revolutionary), with the support of a few deputies in the Assembly, protested their

departments Local French administrative districts, uniform in size.

metric system Standardized system of weights and measurements based on the unit of ten, introduced following the French Revolution.

active and passive citizens Two categories of citizenship in which only property-owning men (active citizens) were allowed to vote and hold public office.

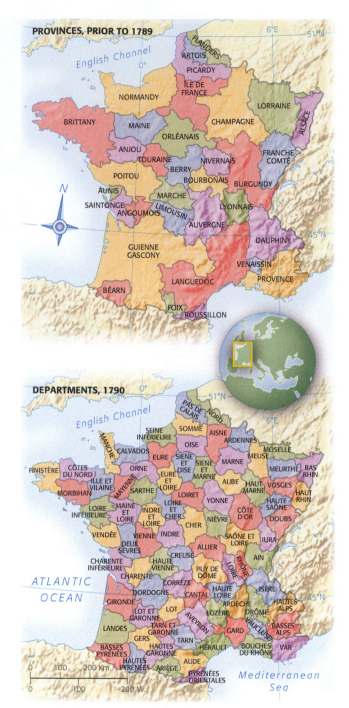

Map 19.2 **The Rationalization of French Administration, 1789 and 1790** These maps show the revolutionary reorganization of French territory. The map on top shows the traditional provinces of the monarchy as they were in 1789. The map on the bottom shows the new departments created in 1790.

1. Note that the French provinces were very unequal in size. Which was the largest and which was the smallest?

2. How does the map on the bottom illustrate Enlightenment and revolutionary principles of rationality and efficiency?

Olympe de Gouges Becomes a Revolutionary

Olympe de Gouges
An aquatint portrait of the revolutionary feminist, from 1784.

INTERFOTO / Alamy

In 1768, a twenty-year-old widow left her hometown in southern France and headed for Paris to make her fortune. For the next twenty years, Olympe de Gouges (oh-lamp de goo-jeh) struggled to live independently and to establish herself as a playwright in a world dominated by male privilege and aristocratic intrigue. When the French Revolution broke out, she sided with the revolutionaries, calling for a new political and social order based on equality—including equality between men and women.

As a single woman alone in Paris, Madame de Gouges found few respectable options open to her; she could either remarry or work. Vowing not to marry again, she relied on her beauty and wit to get ahead and offered love to men of means, who gave her financial help in return. For ten years, she lived a life of pleasure while quietly amassing enough money to obtain what she truly desired—economic independence. Then, at the age of thirty, she announced she would devote the rest of her life to philosophy by writing plays that praised the ideals of the Enlightenment.

The theatrical world Gouges threw herself into was lively, but not open to new talent. The Crown had granted a monopoly on theatrical performances in Paris to a handful of privileged theaters, which used their power ruthlessly to promote the work of favorites while denying access to others. As a woman without powerful connections, time and again Gouges had the theater doors slammed in her face. She therefore took to publishing her work, often at her own expense, in hopes of building support for the performance of her plays.

In 1789, she wrote *The Slavery of the Blacks*, a controversial play in which the hero, a black, murdered a white man to prevent him from raping the hero's mistress. Finally, this play made it to the stage when the Comédie-Française, the most prestigious theater in Paris, performed it. But after just three performances, it closed. Perhaps the plot was too controversial, or perhaps, as Gouges claimed, the theater management had sabotaged the play to avoid paying her.

By this time, France was in the midst of revolution, and Gouges turned to applying Enlightenment ideals to the crisis at hand. To solve the monarchy's bankruptcy, she called for a voluntary tax to be paid equally by all. She called for a state system of social security and government employment to care for the poor. She denounced the filthy conditions in the maternity wards of hospitals and called for local community ownership of agricultural land to help poor peasants. Above all, she demanded complete political and social equality for men and women. In 1791, she published *The Rights of Woman*, one of the most important feminist statements of the French Revolution. "Woman," she wrote, "is born free and remains equal to man in rights." This single sentence summed up her years of struggle against the injustices she had experienced and seen around her.

Olympe de Gouges promoted the ideals of France's Revolution, but she never joined revolutionary clubs and refused to take part in the street violence that erupted periodically in Paris. She also never gave up her belief in the French monarchy. She did her best to save the king, even offering to defend him in the trial that led to his execution. For this, she herself was executed. Olympe de Gouges's life was caught up in many of the forces that shaped revolutionary France—resentment at aristocratic privilege, anger at social injustice, excitement over the possibility of fundamental change, and anxiety over the violence that so often accompanied revolutionary action. Most of all, her defense of women's rights raised issues that remained at the center of political debate long after her death.

exclusion from active citizenship, they were not able to change the categories. Most male revolutionaries, influenced by philosophes such as Jean-Jacques Rousseau, considered women too emotional and illogical to participate in political life. Their place was in the home, where they could serve as wives to their patriot husbands and raise children to serve the nation.

For working-class women, Gouges's agenda had little appeal. Food for their families and wages in their traditional occupations were much more important. When these were threatened, workingwomen could be roused to public action that often had profound political consequences, as the October Days had proved.

Although the deputies denied women the vote and the right to hold public office, the legislature eventually endorsed other elements of Gouges's program by expanding women's rights in the important areas of domestic relations and inheritance law. In 1792, divorce, advocated by Gouges but forbidden by the Catholic Church, was legalized. Both women and men were allowed to file for divorce by mutual consent or on account of "incompatibility of temperament." Many women used the new law to separate from their husbands.

Another law benefiting women ordered the equal division of estates among all heirs, male and female. These new divorce and property laws reflected the emphasis on individual rights and the freedom to act even in opposition to Catholic Church teaching or traditional family values.

Citizenship and Slavery Debates over the nation and its citizens sparked a reconsideration of slavery. France had long been considered "free land," but slavery was practiced in French colonies in the Caribbean. There the Declaration of the Rights of Man and the Citizen was a bombshell; white colonials denied that it applied to slaves, while the slaves considered it a signal for revolt. Trouble continued into the spring of 1791, when the Assembly cautiously granted citizenship to a small number of free blacks on Saint-Domingue, France's most important remaining colony, where 57,000 whites and free blacks ruled more than 465,000 African slaves.

In August, there followed a massive uprising led by **François Dominique Toussaint** (too-sant) **L'Ouverture** (loo-ver-ture), a former slave inspired by Enlightenment thought. Many plantation owners were slain, while others fled to the new United States. The uprising, which ended French control of the island and France's Atlantic trade, was the first successful slave revolt in history. In early 1794, France became the first European country to abolish slavery and to grant full rights of citizenship to ex-slaves. Because citizenship touched on so many aspects of reform, both at home and overseas, it became the central issue in defining the new regime.

CONNECTIONS: The debates over the Constitution of 1791 opened a forum for proposing fundamental changes in the French political, social, and economic world. A century and a half earlier in England a similar rethinking of society had occurred. In both cases, issues were raised that would have a long future ahead of them. (See Section 15-4c Civil War, Revolution, and the Commonwealth.)

19-2b The Break with the Catholic Church

The French church had been involved in the new regime from the beginning. Clergy like Sieyès continued to sit in the new National Assembly. Many welcomed the reordering of society into a nation of equal citizens as a fulfillment of the "gentle fraternity" of Jesus, which incorporated everyone equally. The clergymen who were deputies, therefore, accepted the Assembly's increasingly radical restructuring of the church.

The Civil Constitution of the Clergy After abolishing the tithe on the Night of August 4, the Assembly decided to confiscate church property, which constituted about 10 percent of French land, and to use it to back new government bonds and restore confidence in the state's finances. It also withdrew state enforcement of monks' and nuns' religious vows and forbade all future vows. Then, in 1790, the Assembly took even more drastic action, decreeing the **Civil Constitution of the Clergy**. Dioceses were adjusted to conform to new departments, clergy were put on state salary, and parish priests were to be elected by active citizens, including Protestants and Jews.

Should the Church Be Consulted? The Assembly issued the Civil Constitution of the Clergy without formal consultation with the church, and while the clergy generally were grudgingly prepared to accept it, they were not prepared to have it imposed on them. In the Old Regime, the king had always consulted with the First Estate over religious affairs. The Assembly argued that since the estates were abolished, consultation was no longer possible.

The issue of consultation was solved, temporarily, by turning to the pope. He was a power outside the nation, but a positive word from him could be taken as final.

François Dominique Toussaint L'Ouverture (1743–1803) Former slave who led the first successful slave revolt in history in the French colony of Saint-Domingue.

Civil Constitution of the Clergy Legislative decree of 1790 radically reforming the Catholic Church in France.

Toussaint l'Ouverture, engraved by Francois Seraphin Delpech (1778-1825) 1838 (hand-coloured litho), Maurin, Nicholas Eustache (1799-1850) (after) / Private Collection / Courtesy of Swann Auction Galleries / Bridgeman Images

TOUSSAINT L'OUVERTURE.

Toussaint L'Ouverture

This portrait of L'Ouverture shows him in profile. Although published some years after his death, it probably best captures his distinctive features.

» *How do the artist's choices about his hat, hair, and coat proclaim him as both French and a revolutionary?*

The Oath to the Civil Constitution of the Clergy

When the Assembly ordered all French clergy to take a solemn oath in favor of the Civil Constitution, only 7 out of 160 bishops complied, though half of the lower clergy stepped forward to take it. Then in May 1791, Pope Pius VI publicly condemned the Civil Constitution.

The Split in the French Church

Instantly, the French church was split between those who had taken the oath and those who had rejected it. Because the oath had been phrased to demand loyalty to the Revolution as a whole, clergy who refused it, called **nonjurors**, were quickly branded counterrevolutionaries. Thus, the failure to consult the church led to a rupture between the church and the new

regime. This was a fateful development. There had been opposition to the Revolution from the beginning, but it was never widespread. Now it increased and solidified.

Traditionally minded Catholics who opposed the Civil Constitution harassed the "constitutional clergy" who supported it, jeering at them in the streets, shooting at their houses, or throwing dead animals onto their doorsteps. The police force representing the new regime attacked these protesters, identifying them as enemies of the nation, and arresting and imprisoning them. As these conflicts widened, opposition

nonjurors Clergy refusing to take an oath supporting the Civil Constitution of the Clergy.

Thomas Paine Defends the French Revolution and Attacks Edmund Burke

The following excerpts from Thomas Paine's *The Rights of Man* (1791–1792) reveal the qualities that made him such a successful polemicist: The clarity of his arguments and the artfulness with which he made them.

❶ Why would Paine specify the number of Burke's "errors" at the *beginning* of his refutation?

❷ Why would Paine make the point about the differences between the revolts in England and France with specific references to Charles I and James II?

❸ How does this argument relate to the point made in the second excerpt above? Where is the artfulness in it?

❹ Why is this the concluding point in Paine's argument?

"We have seen," says Mr. Burke, "the French rebel against a mild and lawful monarch, with more fury, outrage, and insult, than any people has been known to rise against the most illegal usurper, or the most sanguinary tyrant." This is one among a thousand other instances, in which Mr. Burke shows that he is ignorant of the springs and principles of the French Revolution. **❶**

It was not against Louis XVI but against the despotic principles of the Government, that the nation revolted. These principles had not their origin in him, but in the original establishment, many centuries back: and they were become too deeply rooted to be removed, . . . by anything short of a complete and universal Revolution.

In the case of Charles I and James II of England, the revolt was against the personal despotism of the men; whereas in France, it was against the hereditary despotism of the established Government. **❷**

When despotism has established itself for ages in a country, as in France, it is not in the person of the king only that it resides. It has the appearance of being so in show, and in nominal authority; but it is not so in practice and in fact. It has its standard everywhere. Every office and department has its despotism, founded upon custom and usage. Every place has its Bastille, and every Bastille its despot. The original hereditary despotism resident in the person of the king, divides and sub-divides itself into a thousand shapes and forms, till at last the whole of it is acted by deputation. This was the case in France; and against this species of despotism, proceeding on through an endless labyrinth of office till the source of it is scarcely perceptible, there is no mode of redress. **❸** It strengthens itself by assuming the appearance of duty, and tyrannies under the pretence of obeying. **❹**

A constitution is not a thing in name only, but in fact. It has not an ideal, but a real existence; and wherever it cannot be produced in a visible form, there is none. A constitution is a thing antecedent to a government, and a government is only the

to the course of events in the capital mounted, especially in western France, where support for the nonjurors was strongest.

19-2c Foreign Intervention

On June 20, 1791, Louis XVI and his family, shocked by the rupture between the new regime and the Catholic Church and fearing for their personal safety, attempted to flee France. The next day, they were caught east of Paris, in the town of Varennes. People had recognized the king along the way, but it was the postmaster at Varennes who claimed public credit for the identification after he compared the face of the man before him to the one on a banknote in his pocket.

Louis and his family were immediately returned to Paris under armed guard. With the king back in the capital, the deputies made the best of the situation by claiming that Louis had been "kidnapped." Nobody really believed this accusation because the king had written a letter condemning the new regime in harsh terms. The fiction of kidnapping, however, allowed the deputies to proceed with their constitution making.

5 In 1791, was there an earlier constitution meeting these criteria that Paine could point to?

6 Could Edmund Burke point to an English constitution in 1791 or 1792 that met Paine's criteria?

7 In light of what Paine had already argued, why would he write this paragraph? Clarification? Overkill? Mockery? You decide.

creature of a constitution. The constitution of a country is not the act of its government, but of the people constituting its government. It is the body of elements, to which you can refer, and quote article by article; and which contains the principles on which the government shall be established, the manner in which it shall be organised, the powers it shall have, the mode of elections, the duration of Parliaments, or by what other name such bodies may be called; the powers which the executive part of the government shall have; and in fine, everything that relates to the complete organisation of a civil government, and the principles on which it shall act, and by which it shall be bound. **5** A constitution, therefore, is to a government what the laws made afterwards by that government are to a court of judicature. The court of judicature does not make the laws, neither can it alter them; it only acts in conformity to the laws made: and the government is in like manner governed by the constitution. Can, then, Mr. Burke produce the English Constitution? If he cannot, we may fairly conclude that though it has been so much talked about, no such thing as a constitution exists, or ever did exist, and consequently that the people have yet a constitution to form. **6**

I will here finally close this subject. I began it by remarking that Mr. Burke had voluntarily declined going into a comparison of the English and French Constitutions. He apologises (in page 241) for not doing it, by saying that he had not time. Mr. Burke's book was upwards of eight months in hand, and is extended to a volume of three hundred and sixty-six pages. As his omission does injury to his cause, his apology makes it worse; and men on the English side of the water will begin to consider, whether there is not some radical defect in what is called the English constitution, that made it necessary for Mr. Burke to suppress the comparison, to avoid bringing it into view. **7**

Source: Text < Thomas Paine - The Rights of Man (1791-1792) < 1786-1800...
www.let.rug.nl/.../documents/.../thomas-paine...rights-of-man/text.php
Text - The Rights of Man (1791-1792).

The Émigrés Those who shared the king's doubts, however, now thought it best to get out of France. These **émigrés** (em-ee-grayz) had first started to leave the country in the summer of 1789. In all, about 150,000 people, out of a total population of 28 million, fled France during the 1790s. Thus, another kind of opponent of the Revolution, unhappy with the revolutionaries' treatment of the king, emerged alongside those unhappy with their treatment of the Catholic Church. These two opposition movements soon joined forces to oppose the Revolution both at home and abroad.

Reactions to the French Revolution Public opinion outside France was sharply divided over the merits of France's revolution. The newly independent Americans fiercely debated the meaning of events in France and formed pro- and anti-French political parties. In Britain, Edmund Burke, a political theorist and member of Parliament, denounced the Revolution's headlong rush to change. "Liberty without wisdom," he argued in his *Reflections on the Revolution in France* (1790), "is folly, vice, and madness." Burke, in turn, was quickly attacked by **Thomas Paine**, an Englishman who had defended the American Revolution in his *Common Sense*, the most widely read pamphlet in the American revolutionary period. Now Paine defended the French against Burke in *The Rights of Man*. "From what we now see," Paine wrote, "nothing of reform in the political world ought to be held improbable. It is an age of Revolutions, in which everything may be looked for" (see Learning from a Primary Source: Thomas Paine Defends the French Revolution and Attacks Edmund Burke).

émigrés Counterrevolutionaries who fled France during the Revolution.

Thomas Paine (1737–1809) Englishman who defended both the American and French Revolutions.

The English poet **William Wordsworth**, twenty-one years old and visiting France, also championed the Revolution's assertion of reason and rights: "Bliss was it at that dawn to be alive," he later wrote, "but to be young was very Heaven!" Mary Wollstonecraft not only attacked Burke's views in *A Vindication of the Rights of Man* (1790) but went further in her *Vindication of the Rights of Woman* (1792) to argue, like Olympe de Gouges, for women's full participation in public life.

Heading for War While politicians and intellectuals debated France's Revolution, Europe's governments, based on traditions of royal rule over societies of estates and orders, became increasingly alarmed by the implications of universal human rights and the example of France's democratic government. Monarchs began to suppress local pro-French ferment. For example, the Austrian emperor Joseph II, Marie Antoinette's brother, ordered the state police to arrest revolutionary sympathizers in Vienna. The king of Prussia, Frederick William II, also considered crushing the Revolution and restoring Louis XVI's authority.

Indeed, Louis hoped for just such an invasion, and war between the conservative European states and the Revolution began to seem inevitable. In France, most revolutionaries thought that a war against Austria would end agitation by the émigrés, consolidate the Revolution, and unmask any plotting by the king. In April 1792, in a preemptive strike, France declared war on Austria and its ally Prussia.

The French Monarchy in Peril As it turned out, the war set the stage for the fall of the French monarchy. Austrian troops quickly crossed into France and moved on Paris, with the announced intention of rescuing Louis XVI. Just then, a poor harvest once again sent food prices skyrocketing. Faced with these crises, radical deputies in the legislature, convinced that the king was at the heart of all their problems, started to plan the overthrow of the monarchy. For their muscle, they turned to the old militants of July 1789, now nicknamed the **sans-culottes** (literally, "without knee breeches") because they advertised their democratic principles by wearing long laborers' trousers rather than the shorter breeches with hose favored by the well-to-do.

The Sans-Culottes The sans-culottes were a cross section of Parisian society. Many were artisans and day laborers, but the movement's leaders were often well educated and economically well-off. They championed "equality" over the "liberty" celebrated in the Declaration of the Rights of Man and the Citizen. Before 1792, many sans-culottes had fallen into the category of passive citizens. Now they demanded full political participation in the Revolution and the right to advance themselves economically and socially. They denounced the "idle" rich, demanding government regulation of private property rights and state-sponsored welfare programs that would provide them with basic necessities like food and jobs. They also called for government controls on the price of bread.

Jacobins and Sans-Culottes The sans-culottes' advocacy of government regulation of the economy put them at odds with the Jacobins and most deputies in the revolutionary legislatures, who favored the laissez-faire principles of the Physiocrats and Adam Smith. To achieve their ends, the sans-culottes advocated the direct use of violence. For the next two years, they played a major role in Paris politics, mobilizing mass street demonstrations and marching on the legislature to demand more and more equality.

The Fall of the French Monarchy On August 10, 1792, the sans-culottes invaded the palace where the king and his family were held. Palace guards put up a bloody fight, but in the end Louis XVI was imprisoned and the Constitution of 1791, in effect for less than a year, was scrapped. New elections took place for yet another legislature, the **National Convention**. In these elections, property and occupational qualifications for voters were abolished. All adult males could go to the polls. This arrangement responded to sans-culotte demands for a more thoroughly democratic regime.

19-3 The Republic and the Reign of Terror, 1792–1795

>> **What measures did France's new republican government take to secure the Revolution?**

>> **By 1795, how far had the Revolution traveled since the Estates-General was called to initiate tax reform?**

The National Convention, which met in Paris in September 1792, served as France's government until October 1795. These years saw the proclamation of a republic and the execution of Louis XVI. At the same time, revolutionary France faced both the ongoing foreign war and a new civil war that broke out in 1793. In the end, the republic triumphed, but

---

William Wordsworth (1770–1850) English poet famous for his nature poetry and his defense of the French Revolution.

sans-culottes (in French, "without knee breeches") Parisian militants who overthrew the French monarchy in 1792.

National Convention First republican legislature in France, governing from 1792 to 1795.

at a terrible cost, when the Convention created a revolutionary dictatorship that ruthlessly pursued its enemies by means of state-controlled terror. The dictatorship's repression set in motion the forces of its own destruction.

19-3a The End of Monarchy and Monarchs

Following the imprisonment of the king and queen, as enemy troops moved closer to Paris, panic swept through the city. A fiery orator from the Jacobin Club, **Georges Danton**, proclaiming that the Revolution needed "boldness, boldness, boldness forever," persuaded the outgoing Assembly to create a special tribunal to try people who continued to support the monarchy. Those found guilty of opposition to the new regime were beheaded high on a platform in a public square by a new execution device—the **guillotine**, invented by a French doctor who argued that the fast fall of its heavy blade resulted in a painless and efficient means of execution.

The September Massacres   By early September 1792, the Paris prisons were full of people accused of counterrevolutionary activity. Fearful that they were still plotting in their jail cells, the sans-culottes invaded the prisons and slaughtered 1,300 inmates, sometimes mutilating the corpses. These **September Massacres** were publicly defended by Danton and Robespierre as the will of the people, but some who had thus far supported the Revolution were secretly alarmed, seeing in them a chilling example of brutal popular violence. When news of the massacres spread, people throughout Europe and America turned against the Revolution in horror.

The Trial of the King   On September 22, the National Convention proclaimed France a republic. Now the problem was what to do with the king. In December, Louis was put on trial before the Convention, where he mounted a dignified defense. But the deputies overwhelmingly found him guilty of "conspiracy against the general security of the state." Now debate turned to the king's punishment.

The **Mountain and the Girondins** Deputies who argued for execution were known as the **Mountain** because they occupied a steeply rising set of seats in the Convention's meeting hall. The Mountain was also the dominant faction in the Jacobin Club. Robespierre took the lead in pressing the Mountain's case for execution, declaring that the king's conviction required it.

Some deputies, however, wanted a punishment that fell short of execution—perhaps banishment to the United States, as Paine, now a deputy in the Convention, argued. The opponents of execution were known as **Girondins** (jir-ohn-dins), because their leaders were from the department of the Gironde.

They argued that Louis's execution would energize the Revolution's enemies at home and abroad, thereby increasing the dangers France faced.

Both the Mountain and the Girondins were committed to the new republic, but their power bases were different. The Mountain relied increasingly on the radical Parisian sans-culottes, who had overthrown the king on August 10, whereas the Girondins looked to revolutionary moderates in the provinces. By a narrow vote, including that of Sieyès, the Convention sided with the Mountain and ordered the king's execution. On January 21, 1793, Louis XVI went to the guillotine. His last words to his subjects were deliberately drowned out by a drumroll from the execution squad.

19-3b Foreign War and Civil War

The execution of the king caught the attention of Europe's royalty, who now condemned the revolutionaries as "king killers." Shortly after Louis's death, Great Britain and Spain joined the war against France. Austria and Prussia regrouped with a coalition that now included the Dutch Republic and the Italian kingdom of Sardinia.

The Committee of Public Safety   Facing enemies on every border, the National Convention formed the **Committee of Public Safety**, made up of twelve deputies, led first by Danton and then by Robespierre, who were given dictatorial powers to deal with the wartime emergency. The committee ordered a mass mobilization of French citizens to defend the Revolution: Unmarried men were drafted to fight in the army, married men were to make weapons, women were to sew clothes and nurse the wounded, while children and the elderly were to make bandages. Never before had a European government tried to harness the energy of a whole people in the service of the state.

In ordering this mass mobilization, the National Convention appealed to the revolutionary principle of fraternity. Now the revolutionaries identified

---

Georges Danton (1759–1794) Radical Jacobin revolutionary who rose to prominence after the overthrow of the monarchy.

guillotine Execution device used by the French revolutionaries for beheading, invented by a doctor as a humane way of executing people.

September Massacres Slaughter of 1,300 prisoners by the sans-culottes in Paris in 1792 that alienated many early supporters of the Revolution.

Mountain and Girondins Two revolutionary factions vying for control of the National Convention in late 1792 and early 1793.

Committee of Public Safety Committee of the National Convention created in 1793 and granted dictatorial powers to implement the Terror.

The Art Archive at Art Resource, NY

Execution of Louis XVI

In this engraving of Louis XVI's execution, the executioner displays the king's head to the soldiers and citizens witnessing the event. The king's body still lies on the plank of the guillotine. A basket beside it will receive the head and the body after a priest prays for Louis's soul.

» *Compare this rendering of Louis's execution to that of Charles I in Chapter 15. What are the similarities and differences?*

themselves as a "Nation, one and indivisible" and put this slogan on their flags, their stationery, and even their dinner plates.

The Reorganization of the French Army The most important effect of the mass mobilization of 1793 was the reorganization of the French army. Conscription greatly increased the number of men under arms. They were badly needed because the old royal army, which numbered about 165,000 in 1789, had fallen to approximately 130,000 in 1793, owing to deaths, desertions, and the resignations of noble officers who opposed the Revolution.

The new recruits brought the numbers up to 750,000—the largest army Europe had ever seen. It was also Europe's first citizen army, in which volunteers or draftees replaced the professional soldiers of the Old Regime. The new army also offered career advancement on the basis of talent, not birth or wealth, fulfilling one of the principles of 1789. After 1793, many of France's best generals rose up from the rank and file on the basis of ability.

Victory on the Battlefield Many soldiers were fired up with revolutionary patriotism. As one put it, "The war which we are fighting is not a war between king and king or nation and nation. It is the war of liberty against despotism. There can

be no doubt that we shall be victorious. A nation that is just and free is invincible." Over the next two years, this new revolutionary army launched mass assaults that crushed opponents and drove enemy troops from French soil, thus ending the foreign threat, and then carried the war outside of France by invading the Dutch Republic and northern Italy.

Insurrection in the Vendée If the reorganization of the army saved the Revolution in the long run, it also created dangerous short-term problems. In March 1793, when the draft was imposed on peasant communities in western France, the **Vendée** (vahn-day) burst into open insurrection against the National Convention. In 1789, peasants throughout France had supported the Revolution, but after the Great Fear ended feudal payments to their landlords, many turned conservative and resisted further change. In the Vendée, the execution of the king and the break with the Catholic Church were especially unpopular.

The Vendée was one example of a gulf opening up between parts of provincial France and Paris, where militant revolutionaries continued to push for ever-more radical change.

Rebellion in Lyon Another hotbed of discontent was the southeastern city of Lyon, the second largest in France, where opposition to the Convention's emergency measures sparked a rebellion against the central government. With the Vendée and Lyon in rebellion, the National Convention found itself fighting both a civil war and a foreign war.

Vendée Part of western France in open rebellion against the National Convention in early 1793 following the break with the Catholic Church and the execution of the king.

The Fall of the Girondins In early 1793, the Mountain blamed the Girondins for both the foreign war and the civil war. Robespierre, Danton, and other members of the Mountain accused the Girondins of being secret counterrevolutionaries. This accusation outraged the Girondins' supporters, who denounced Robespierre as an "insect wallowing in the filth of corruption." Finally, in May 1793, the Mountain purged the Girondins from the Convention with sans-culotte support. In return, the sans-culottes expected the Mountain to enact yet more economic controls and measures against those accused of counterrevolutionary activity.

19-3c The Republic of Virtue

Maximilien Robespierre had been active in the Revolution from the beginning, first as a deputy to the Estates-General and then as a fiery orator in the Jacobin Club and a deputy in the National Convention. Now "the Incorruptible" became the Revolution's leader. Elected to the Committee of Public Safety in July 1793, Robespierre and the other committee members moved to crush opposition to the Revolution at home, just as the republic's reorganized armies were crushing France's foreign enemies.

The Reign of Terror In early September, the Convention declared that "terror is the order of the day": enemies of the Revolution would be ruthlessly suppressed by force. Robespierre saw terror as necessary for the establishment of a truly virtuous republican regime: "If the mainspring of popular government in time of peace is virtue, the mainspring of popular government in time of revolution is both *virtue and terror*. Terror is nothing but justice, prompt, severe, and inflexible; it is therefore an emanation of virtue."

In practice, the **Reign of Terror** meant government control of the economy and the execution of those deemed counterrevolutionaries. New laws greatly expanded offenses against the Revolution. Now people that the committee identified as high-profile counterrevolutionaries were tried and guillotined, including the imprisoned Girondins, Marie Antoinette, and Olympe de Gouges. Their public beheadings attracted huge crowds.

Crushing Rebellion in the Provinces In the provinces, the Committee moved against the rebels in the Vendée, where the army crushed opposition, as self-styled revolutionary "columns from hell" burned, looted, and killed indiscriminately. Tens of thousands of people, mostly peasants, died. The army also besieged Lyon, and when the city surrendered, more executions followed. "Lyon no longer exists," wrote the triumphant agent of the Committee. What remained of the city after the siege was renamed Freed City.

The Politicization of Everyday Life A crisis mentality seized the revolutionaries as they moved to defeat their enemies at home and abroad, and everything took on political meaning. Now revolutionaries scrutinized how people dressed, looking to see if they wore the sans-culottes' long trousers and no longer powdered their hair as men of means had done before 1789.

They listened to how people spoke, making sure they treated each other as equals, using "Citizen," instead of "Monsieur" and "Madame," and addressing each other with *tu*, the familiar French form for "you," instead of the more formal *vous*. They looked to see if people ate and drank from plates and cups with revolutionary slogans on them. They formed processions and marched to the singing of revolutionary songs like the **Marseillaise**—to this day the national anthem of France.

This politicization of all facets of everyday life was one of the most striking features of the Reign of Terror, and one of the most threatening because it narrowed choices down to two—those who were united with the revolutionaries 100 percent and those who were not. The revolutionary ideal of fraternity had now taken on a grimly exclusive meaning.

The New Revolutionary Calendar The most ambitious attempt to ensure that the new republic broke with the monarchical and aristocratic past was the creation of a new calendar. No longer were years to be counted from the birth of Christ. Now they began with the birth of the republic. Thus, September 22, 1792, the day the republic was proclaimed, became the First Day of the Year One. Months were renamed after the seasons of the year, and weeks were lengthened from the biblical seven days to ten to accord with the metric system. Thus, time and the seasons were reconfigured in a new republican way.

De-Christianization In the prerevolutionary past, Catholicism had been the official religion of France. It, too, was radically repudiated in a movement known as **de-Christianization**. Unlike earlier attacks on the nonjurors, the de-Christianizers made no distinction between supporters and opponents of the Civil Constitution of the Clergy. All priests and their congregations were roughed up and their churches pillaged. As a result, Catholics were driven underground in much of France. Protestants fared no better; their pastors were assaulted and their meeting places vandalized.

Reign of Terror Government's systematic coercion to defeat the Revolution's enemies, implemented in 1793 and 1794.

Marseillaise Revolutionary battle song favored by the sans-culottes, now the national anthem of France.

de-Christianization Attack on all forms of Christianity initiated by the sans-culottes in 1793.

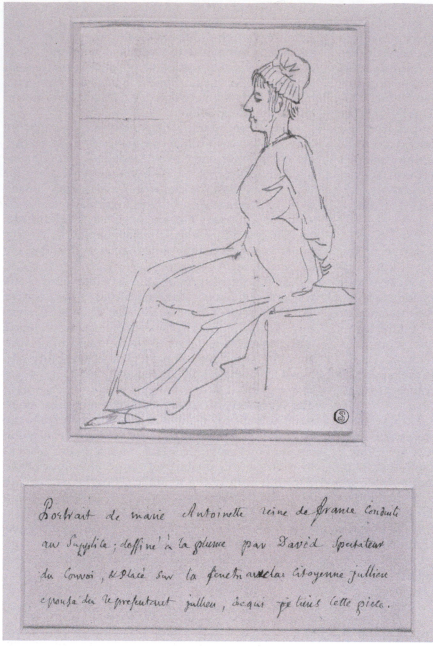

Réunion des Musées Nationaux/Art Resource, NY

Marie Antoinette

Jacques-Louis David drew this sketch of Marie Antoinette as she passed by his window on her way to execution in 1793. She sits tall, but her face is drawn. Her hands are tied behind her back so she can easily be positioned on the guillotine's plank, and her hair has been cut to give the blade access to her neck. David knew how royalty had been depicted before he sketched the queen, and you have seen some of those depictions in this book.

» *With those depictions in mind, what do you think David was trying to communicate in this drawing?*

Revolutionary Religion As an alternative to Christianity, the Committee of Public Safety sponsored new republican religious observances that celebrated the deist divinity of the philosophes. In Paris, a singer from the Paris Opera, dressed as Liberty, presided over a celebration in the former Cathedral of Notre Dame, renamed the Temple of Reason. Robespierre himself presided over a Festival of the Supreme Being. This new religion aimed to cement the unity of all true revolutionaries and provide the republic with its base of virtue.

Great Terror Culminating phase of the Reign of Terror in 1794, when more than thirteen hundred people were convicted and executed in Paris.

The Great Terror By early 1794, the crises France had faced during the previous year had subsided. Yet state terror increased as the Committee of Public Safety began to root out fellow revolutionaries accused of deviating from correct republican principles. Thus, the Revolution was now devouring its own. Then in June 1794, at Robespierre's urging, the Convention passed a law that denied accused persons any right of self-defense in court, inaugurating the **Great Terror** in Paris. During the next month, more than thirteen hundred people were convicted and executed. The guillotine had to be moved to the edge of the city following complaints about the amount of blood in the streets and the stench from rotting corpses.

The Fall of the Committee of Public Safety Faced with the end of rebellion at home and improved conditions abroad, many deputies believed that the Terror, instituted to meet the crises of civil and foreign war, was no longer needed. They supported yet another uprising in Paris in the revolutionary month of Thermidor (July), during which some members of the Committee of Public Safety, including Robespierre, were arrested and executed. The fall of Robespierre inaugurated a wave of reaction against the Terror, known as the **Thermidorian reaction**. The Convention released political prisoners and closed the Jacobin Club, which was identified with Robespierre. It also dismantled the price and wage controls of the previous year, restoring free-market conditions.

Why Did the Reign of Terror Occur? The Reign of Terror of 1793–1794 was the product of two factors. The first was the pressure of foreign and civil war, to which the Committee of Public Safety responded with realistic, if bloody, repression. But this is not the whole story. The second factor contributing to the Terror had more to do with revolutionary politics than with outside pressures.

Since 1789, the identity of the revolutionary nation had rested on its oneness and indivisibility. The nation could not be divided against itself. If opposition arose, it therefore had to come from somewhere outside the nation and from people who were opposed to the republic. These people, condemned as counterrevolutionaries, were to be stamped out. It was this kind of thinking that led the Committee of Public Safety to execute fellow revolutionaries who questioned its policies and made Robespierre inaugurate the Great Terror in June.

By the end of the Revolution, some 17,000 people had been officially executed. Another 10,000 to 12,000 were lynched or assassinated for political reasons, and between 6,000 and 11,000 died in prison awaiting trial for political crimes. In all, some 35,000 to 40,000 people perished out of a population of 28 million.

CONNECTIONS: Historians have debated the similarities and differences between the French revolutionaries' attempt to create a new society, the Republic of Virtue, and programs to remake the human community in the early twentieth century. (See Sections 27-2b Stalin's Totalitarian State and 27-3a Hitler's Consolidation of Power.)

19-4 The Rise of Napoleon, 1794–1804

>> How did the Revolution make possible the rise of Napoleon?

>> Which parts of the revolutionary heritage did Napoleon Bonaparte accept, and which ones did he repudiate?

The revolutionary republic survived for five years following the overthrow of the Committee of Public Safety. France's citizen armies continued to win on the battlefield until, in 1797, all the continental states warring against France made peace with the republic. Only England remained to fight at sea. In 1799, continental war broke out again when Austria and Russia attacked France. That same year, France's leading general, Napoleon Bonaparte, seized power. The early years of Napoleon's rule were marked by significant achievements. He reorganized the French state, brought an end to the war, healed the break with the Catholic Church, and instituted a new law code. In these years, there was widespread support for Bonaparte's regime. Some émigrés even returned to France.

19-4a French Expansion

The restoration of free-market conditions following the collapse of the Committee of Public Safety had dire consequences for many sans-culottes. The fall harvest of 1794 proved one of the worst of the decade, creating economic hard times in the capital as the price of bread once again soared. By spring 1795, hardship had provoked two sans-culotte uprisings, which were put down by the army. From then on, a new Ministry of Police kept a sharp eye on sans-culotte leaders and periodically rounded them up for "preventive detention" in the city's prisons. Both the Terror and the Thermidorian reaction used coercion to control political enemies, and both whittled away at the human rights proclaimed in the Declaration of the Rights of Man and the Citizen.

The Directory In October 1795, the National Convention installed a new regime, which consisted of a two-house legislature and a five-man executive committee, the **Directory**. In another retreat from the Revolution, only men owning property could vote and hold public office. The Directory skillfully alternated in supporting republicans and royalists, who reemerged after the dismantling of the Terror. The Directory tried to keep either from dominating, but the result was permanent political instability and increasing cynicism about a government that stifled dissent.

Yet during this time, the French achieved significant gains in the foreign war. In 1795, Prussia, preoccupied once again with Poland, dropped out of the coalition, as did an exhausted Spain. For France, the next four years saw spectacular military victories and territorial expansion, as the Directory pursued a high-minded desire to create a ring of republics around France and a hard-headed aim to make France the leading power in western Europe.

Napoleon Bonaparte French generals, eager for increased military and political power, also drove

Thermidorian reaction Period in 1794–1795 during which the Terror was dismantled.

Directory Executive committee that ruled France from 1795 to 1799.

the conquests. The most ambitious was **Napoleon Bonaparte**. Bonaparte was born to a minor noble family on the island of Corsica, which France had annexed in 1768. Sent to a French military school at age ten, he was a good student but a loner, hazed by his classmates because of his odd name and modest origins. In 1789, the year the Revolution began, Napoleon was twenty and a lieutenant in the royal army. The Revolution gave him his great chance when it opened careers to talent. Bonaparte sided with the revolutionaries, and by 1793, he had risen to the rank of general.

In 1795, Bonaparte's role in putting down a royalist uprising in Paris led to his appointment as commander of the Army of Italy. In that same year, he married Josephine de Beauharnais, the widow of a French nobleman who had been executed during the Terror. Napoleon was deeply in love with Josephine and devastated when he learned of her love affairs with other men after their marriage. From then on, he shut himself off from close relations with people and concentrated on advancing his career.

Victory in Italy In 1797, Bonaparte drove Austria out of northern Italy and negotiated a treaty, thus bringing peace to the European continent for the first time since 1792. Britain alone remained to fight. Bonaparte's Italian victories displayed his qualities as a military commander. He planned carefully, struck fast, and was not afraid to take risks. He also knew how to gain maximum military and political advantage from a win.

The Sister Republics Following the invasion of northern Italy, Bonaparte reorganized his conquered territory into a new state, the Cisalpine Republic, staffed by pro-French locals under his control. In this, he followed the pattern established in 1795, when the French had invaded the Dutch Republic and set up the Batavian Republic. In 1797, Napoleon would also establish another republic in Switzerland. The old society of estates and orders was abolished in these **sister republics**, replaced by the French model of a nation composed of citizens.

The sister republics were required to pay France for its war costs, to provide supplies to French troops in their territory, and to maintain their own armies at local expense. In Italy, Bonaparte also organized wholesale looting of churches and palaces, seizing statues and paintings that were shipped to Paris for display in the new **Louvre Museum**, where many can still be seen today.

Bonaparte in Egypt When land fighting ended in late 1797, Bonaparte feared his career would falter, so he began angling for a new command. In early 1798, he and the Directory decided on a campaign in Egypt. If the French had access to the Red Sea, they could threaten the British in India. The French force set off by sea in May, landed near Alexandria, and soon occupied Cairo. Then, disaster struck. On August 1, the British navy under Horatio Nelson destroyed the French fleet off Alexandria. With his line of supplies now cut, Bonaparte was bottled up in Egypt. To make matters worse, the Austrians and Russians, alarmed at France's creation of sister republics and a French presence in the Middle East, declared war on France in early 1799.

The Fall of the Directory Now the French were put on the defensive, just as they had been in 1792. The military crisis galvanized a group of politicians disgusted by the failure of the Directory to establish domestic stability. One was a new member of the Directory, Joseph Emmanuel Sieyès, whose pamphlet had touched off the furious debate over the Estates-General exactly ten years before. Sieyès did not have the power or popularity to lead a plot against the government, so he turned to someone who did: Napoleon Bonaparte.

Bonaparte in Charge Leaving his army in Egypt, Napoleon had slipped through the British naval blockade off the coast and arrived back in France. In November 1799, after the conspirators overthrew the Directory in a coup d'état, Napoleon quickly assumed unchallenged leadership of the government. Now all of Napoleon's talents came to the fore—his charm and intelligence, his ability to awe people and inspire their loyalty, and his sense of his own exceptional abilities and destiny.

19-4b Order and Administration

The new constitution of December 1799 made Napoleon **First Consul** in a three-man consulate. In fact, however, he was the only one with real power. Members of the new legislature had little say in government; Napoleon, assisted by a council of experts, made all the important decisions. The new constitution did not include the Declaration of the Rights of Man and the Citizen. Opposition to the new government was silenced when a rigid press censorship was instituted. All these changes signaled a repudiation of the Revolution's participatory politics. Yet, the repudiation was ambiguous because Napoleon kept up appearances by submitting the new constitution to a carefully controlled popular vote of adult males.

Napoleon Bonaparte (1769–1821) French general who seized power in 1799 and ruled France until 1814.

sister republics French satellite states formed from territories conquered between 1795 and 1799.

Louvre Museum Paris museum of art founded in 1793 and housed in a former royal palace, one of the great museums of the world.

First Consul Title taken by Napoleon Bonaparte when he seized power in 1799.

The Prefects In early 1800, Bonaparte reorganized administration throughout France. **Prefects**, put in charge of the departments, were under the strict control of the minister of the interior in Paris, who was second only to Napoleon himself. The prefects were chosen on the basis of administrative experience and political leanings. The First Consul was deliberately upholding the revolutionary ideal of careers open to talent, from which he himself had benefited, while trying to win over all factions except die-hard royalists and radical republicans.

Influenced by Enlightenment thought, Napoleon also believed that governing was a science based on reason and careful observation, which allowed administrators to act logically by objectively analyzing problems and finding rational solutions to them. With this system in place, far less stood between the state and the citizen in 1801 than had stood between the Crown and its subjects in 1789.

Reform of State Finances One of Napoleon's biggest problems was the continuing crisis in state finances, which had been the immediate cause of the Revolution in the first place. Each revolutionary regime since 1789 had assumed the debts of the old monarchy, but by the late 1790s, these debts had become intolerable. To stabilize the state's finances, Napoleon instituted a standardized system of taxation that fell on all citizens in accordance with the revolutionary principle of equality. Remembering what had happened to the monarchy in 1788, he refused to put his government at the mercy of financiers who could indirectly dictate policy by their lending strategies.

Bonaparte and the Catholic Church In 1801 and 1802, peace returned to Europe as Napoleon signed treaties with the Austrians and the British, confirming France's territorial gains and acknowledging the sister republics. Another peace, which proved more lasting than the others, was signed with the Catholic Church in the form of a new concordat between Napoleon and Pius VII, elected pope in 1800. The Concordat of 1801 established French Catholics' right to worship publicly, but it did not renew the ancient connection between church and state. Catholicism was simply recognized as the "religion of the majority of the French," and the state remained separate from the church.

Napoleon himself was a nominal Catholic who thought of religion as a tool for maintaining social and political order. He believed that religious toleration for Catholics was a way to end the political headache caused by the Civil Constitution of the Clergy and de-Christianization. But the concordat also gave the state tight control over church activities, including the regulation of seminaries. A new national catechism for religious instruction secured church endorsement of the regime. Many French people returned to Catholic worship with fervor, especially in the countryside, where women led the revival, demanding the return of priests and urging neighbors to join once again in communal worship.

Protestants and Jews Protestants also benefited from Napoleon's religious policies; they, too, were allowed to worship openly without harassment. The fate of the Jews, however, was somewhat different. Like the revolutionaries, Napoleon wanted to integrate Jews into society. But he also wanted to place them under state supervision. Although Jews were granted freedom of worship, laws put limits on their economic activities and increased their military obligations. The government assumed control of Jewish moneylending, forbade foreign Jews from settling in France, and ordered Jewish men serving in the army to obey all military rules and regulations, even if these conflicted with Jewish religious observance.

The Reinstitution of Slavery French Jews received limited benefits from Napoleon's regime, but another group saw its condition worsen catastrophically. These were the ex-slaves in the Caribbean. In 1801, Toussaint L'Ouverture, who had led black resistance to French rule a decade earlier, conquered the Spanish half of Santo Domingo and proclaimed himself president of the united island. Initially, L'Ouverture had French support, but in 1802, Napoleon turned against him and sent an army to Santo Domingo. It captured and executed L'Ouverture yet was unable to reassert French control over the former colony, now called Haiti.

In the course of the campaign against L'Ouverture, Napoleon restored slavery in Martinique and Guadeloupe, France's other Caribbean possessions. Thus, France, which had been the first European state to abolish slavery in 1794, reinstituted it in 1802. It was not finally abolished until 1848. This act was Napoleon's clearest repudiation of the revolutionary heritage. In 1803, he sold Louisiana, which France had received back from a defeated Spain, to the United States. His failure to retake Haiti convinced him that there was no hope for reestablishing a French empire on the North American continent.

19-4c The Napoleonic Code

Napoleon's most lasting achievement was a reform of French law codes. Faced with a confusing and contradictory tangle of laws developed over centuries under the old monarchy, the revolutionary governments of the 1790s had declared in principle that French law needed to be rationalized and standardized as part of the great reorganization of the country into a single, undivided nation. Napoleon carried the principle into practice.

prefects Napoleon's local government administrators in France.

Réunion des Musées Nationaux/Art Resource, NY

Coronation of Napoleon

Jacques-Louis David painted this official representation of Napoleon's coronation as emperor. Having crowned himself, Napoleon now crowns his wife Josephine. Pope Pius VII, seated, is simply one of the spectators. The painting emphasizes two of Napoleon's governing principles: The separation of church and state and the subordination of women to men.

》 *Compare this painting with David's sketch of Marie Antoinette on her way to the guillotine. Does the sketch also show David as a propagandist for revolutionary principles?*

The Reform of Civil Law The most important new code was the Civil Code of 1804, later renamed the **Napoleonic Code**. In it, the revolutionary principles of equality before the law and security of persons from arbitrary arrest were reaffirmed. Private property rights were guaranteed, as well as the principle of a free-market economy in which individual economic initiative was encouraged. Workers' rights to form unions or other associations were again prohibited as a form of interference with market forces.

Women in Bonaparte's France The code reversed many of the gains women had made during the 1790s. Laws relating to families upheld patriarchal authority; the male head of the household stood over all other family members and controlled their property. The revolutionary equality between spouses in filing for divorce was revoked, giving men more grounds for divorce than women. Many of these provisions remained a part of French law until 1965. They reflected Napoleon's view that women belonged in the private sphere, where, he said, men would protect them and make them happy.

The End of Democratic Politics Overall, Napoleon's reworking of the revolutionary legacy, culminating in the Civil Code, promoted what he called "order." In 1789, the rallying cry of revolutionaries had been "liberty." In 1793, the sans-culottes had called for "equality," and the Committee of Public Safety had promoted "fraternity" to unite citizens against internal and external enemies. Now liberty, equality, and fraternity were condemned as excuses for **anarchy**. Under Napoleon, democratic politics ceased. Freedom of speech was silenced by censorship and police surveillance.

Society was dominated by the **notables**, a class of landowners created by Napoleon from the middle

Napoleonic Code Code of civil law implemented in 1804, applied first to France and then to French-occupied territories in Europe.

anarchy Absence of government, marked by disorder and lawlessness.

notables Elite group of large-scale landowners created by Napoleon.

classes and the old nobility. Along with civilian administrators and army generals, they were the real powers in France. Once again, French national identity was based on the Old Regime model of a pyramid with a small and powerful elite at the top.

Emperor Napoleon I In 1802, at the height of his popularity, Napoleon modified the constitution to make himself consul for life. In 1803, after a peace that had lasted a mere fourteen months, France and England went to war again. Britain wanted more access to continental markets for its manufactured goods, and France feared English preeminence at sea.

Soon afterward, Napoleon moved closer toward hereditary rule. In December 1804, he summoned Pius VII from Rome to preside over a coronation ceremony in Paris in which he became Emperor Napoleon I. When it was time to place the new imperial crown on his head, Napoleon crowned himself, asserting the separation of the state from the church. He then whispered to his brother, "If only our father could see us now!"

The new emperor modeled his court on the old one at Versailles and started referring to Louis XVI as "my uncle." In 1808, he created a new imperial nobility. Thus, the republican state was eroded, but never completely destroyed: The Napoleonic Code was still in place; legislatures met, even though they had little to do; a written constitution still existed; and changes in the regime were carefully submitted to popular ratification in special elections.

CONNECTIONS: The codification of French law in the Napoleonic Code was a major event in French and European history. But it was not the first time rulers tried to rationalize the laws of their lands. For other examples, see Section 1-2d The Code of Hammurabi, Section 8-1c The Codification of Roman Law, and Chapter 13 Learning from a Primary Source: Isabella of Castile Writes Her Last Will and Testament.

19-5 The Napoleonic Empire, 1804–1815

» **What did Napoleon demand from the men who administered his empire and its satellite states?**

» **What impact did Napoleon's rule have on Europeans outside of France?**

From 1803 until 1815, France was again at war with the rest of Europe. Beginning in 1805, France won spectacular victories on the continent, crushing Austria, Prussia, and Russia and occupying most of Germany. Conquered territories were added to the ever-expanding French Empire. In 1807, when he controlled Europe from the Atlantic to Russia, Napoleon attempted the economic ruin of his sole remaining enemy, Great Britain. But his policy of closing this vast territory to British manufactured goods stirred up resistance. In 1812, Napoleon invaded Russia, a disaster from which he never recovered. In 1814, a renewed coalition defeated Napoleon and drove him from his throne. Napoleon's empire was short lived, but it had a lasting impact.

19-5a Renewed War on the Continent

In 1805, continental war broke out again when Austria and Russia joined Great Britain, at war with France since 1803. Austria was soon defeated for the third time, and the Holy Roman Empire formally came to an end when Napoleon decreed its demise. But the British navy defeated the French navy in the Battle of **Trafalgar** (trah-FAL-ger) off the Spanish coast. Admiral Nelson, who had destroyed Napoleon's fleet in Egypt, destroyed it once again in this battle, losing his life in the process. From now on, Britain enjoyed unchallenged control of the high seas and imposed a blockade on Napoleon's ports to stop France's international trade. On the continent, Napoleon fared better; Prussia, which joined the Allies in 1806, was quickly defeated, and in 1807 Russia, too, succumbed.

Redrawing the Map of Europe Emperor Napoleon, now at the height of his power, redrew the map of much of Europe. All the states in the old Holy Roman Empire, except Prussia and Austria, were made French allies and consolidated in the **Confederation of the Rhine**, a prelude to German unification in the nineteenth century. An independent Poland reemerged as the **Grand Duchy of Warsaw**.

To organize his vast territory, Napoleon used the techniques of the Directory: The creation of satellite states, now called kingdoms instead of republics, and annexation to France. Napoleon made his numerous brothers and sisters the heads of the satellite kingdoms or relied on close confidants to rule them— Joseph Bonaparte went to Spain, Louis to the kingdom of Holland, and Jerome to the new kingdom of Westphalia. Napoleon expected unquestioning obedience from them.

A French Model for the Satellite Kingdoms Rulers were to remake their kingdoms using France as a model. Written constitutions formed

Trafalgar Naval battle fought 1805 in which the British destroyed the French navy and gained unchallenged control of the high seas.

Confederation of the Rhine Napoleon's union of all German states except Prussia and Austria.

Grand Duchy of Warsaw Napoleon's restored independent Poland.

the basis of government. The Napoleonic Code was imposed, sweeping away the society of estates and orders and establishing the principle of equality before the law, careers open to talent, and trial by jury. Local legislatures usually controlled taxation rates, which were lower than those in France. Religious discrimination ended, and Jews were admitted to full citizenship. This last reform was particularly important in Holland and Germany, where there were large Jewish populations. Except in Russia, serfdom was abolished.

Government administration was to be based on the scientific principles employed in France. Military conscription was imposed everywhere, and local people were required to pay the costs of French troops stationed in their territory. Napoleon discouraged concessions to local customs because he thought the French model of government was universally applicable. Many of these reforms outlasted the Napoleonic period, particularly in Holland, Germany, and northern Italy. Even Prussia and Austria adopted some of them, in hopes of combating the French challenge by strengthening their states.

Military Conscription in France Napoleon's stunning victories between 1805 and 1807 were the result of his skill as a general and his ability to raise huge armies by means of conscription. In 1793, France had relied on the mass mobilization of the nation to build up the army to 750,000 men. By 1797, however, the army had fallen to about half this number because of death and desertion. The Directory, therefore, resorted to annual conscription. Napoleon continued the new practice. Some two million French men were conscripted between 1799 and 1814.

At first, the draft was fiercely resisted. Married men were exempt, and potential draftees rushed to marry, sometimes taking wives as old as eighty. If marriage was not an option, men cut off their trigger fingers or hacked away at their shins and testicles to induce debilitating infections. Slowly, however, through persistence and power, the state made its policy stick. By 1806, when the war against Prussia began, the battle against the draft was over; from then on the French submitted to this permanent new intrusion into their lives. Overall, in both the revolutionary and Napoleonic wars, about 916,000 men were lost to the French army, half from death and half from desertion.

The Continental System In late 1806, Napoleon undertook economic warfare against Great Britain. This program, the **Continental System**, closed European ports in French-dominated areas to British merchant shipping. Napoleon reasoned

that Britain's economy would slump and its government revenues decline when its traditional continental markets were taken away. As a bonus, French manufacturers would benefit from a market now closed to British competition. But the system's success depended on the closure of *all* ports, and here the problems began.

France itself could be brought into compliance, but in the satellite states merchants who had profited from trade with Britain protested. Even Napoleon's siblings, under pressure from their subjects, complained. The emperor's response was to annex more territory to France: The kingdom of Holland was absorbed in 1810, as was the north German coast. When Pope Pius VII refused to join the system and excommunicated Napoleon, the pope was put under house arrest and then deported to France, where he lived as Napoleon's prisoner. Italy as far south as Rome was annexed (see Map 19.3). Pius's imprisonment shocked European Catholics and produced a great wave of sympathy for the suffering pope.

Britain Fights Back, France Responds Britain responded to the Continental System by tightening its blockade on French-controlled ports. The French responded by authorizing privateers to slip through the blockade and harass British merchant shipping. The new United States, a self-declared neutral in the war, was hurt by the blockades and saw its trade with both France and Britain decline. Eventually, in 1812, the United States declared war on Britain in an effort to assert its economic independence.

The "Spanish Ulcer" As military intervention and annexation became the means of enforcing the Continental System, Spain entered a period of crisis. Ever since it had withdrawn from the war against France in 1795, the country had been unstable. In 1808, a French army of occupation was sent to close Spain's ports to the British, and Napoleon put his brother Joseph on the Spanish throne. But a riot in Madrid quickly spread into open rebellion across the country, and cries for Spanish national unity in the face of the French occupier grew ever more insistent. More and more French troops were required to keep order. Napoleon denounced the "Spanish ulcer," but the British saw it as an opportunity to reopen the land war against France and sent an expeditionary force to aid the rebels.

Was the Continental System a Success? Despite the problems in Spain, the Continental System was a considerable success. Although British overseas trade never collapsed, it was badly damaged. At the worst of the crisis, Britain survived only by developing new markets in Spain's American colonies, where regulations against foreign traders crumbled in the face of government paralysis at home. On the continent, French traders also opened new markets. French goods now moved east across Europe instead of west to France's Caribbean colonies, as they had before 1789.

Continental System Closure of all French-controlled ports to British merchant shipping initiated by Napoleon in 1807 as a form of economic warfare.

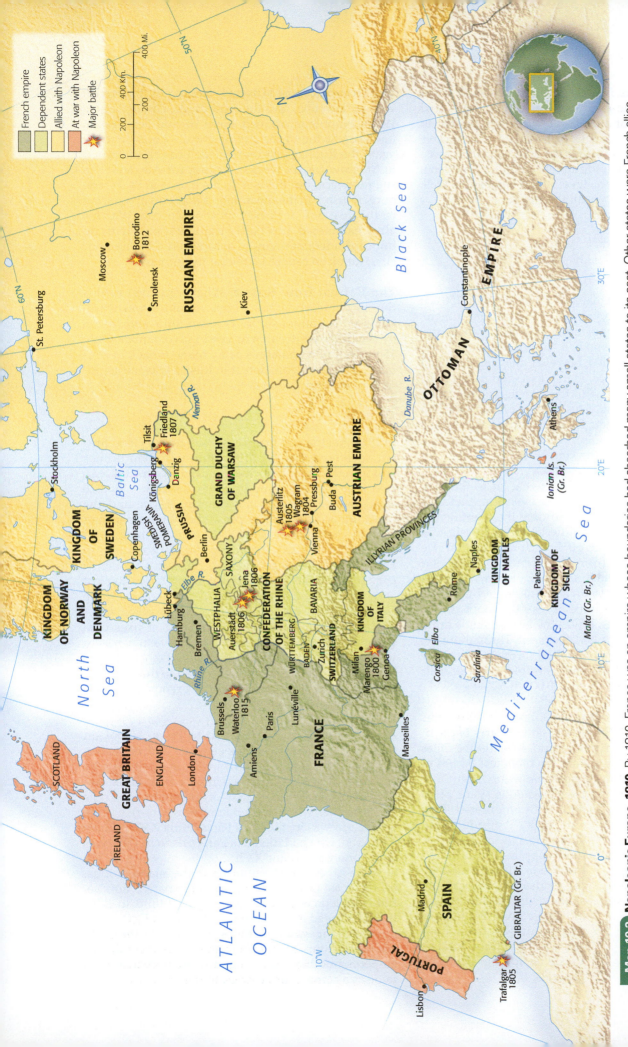

Map 19.3 Napoleonic Europe, 1810 By 1810, France was an empire whose boundaries had absorbed many small states to its east. Other states were French allies or dependencies. Napoleon's domination of Europe rivaled Charlemagne's empire and the empire of ancient Rome.

1. Compare the boundaries of France in 1810 to those of 1789 as shown in the first map in this chapter.
2. Remembering how many separate states there were in 1789 (see Map 19.1 earlier in this chapter), count the number of separate states in 1810. What is the difference? What do you think were the consequences of this difference?
3. Some states were neither at war with France nor part of Napoleon's empire and system of alliances. What are they?
4. Why was Portugal one of the states at war with Napoleon in 1810?

Legend:
- French empire
- Dependent states
- Allied with Napoleon
- At war with Napoleon
- ★ Major battle

Map labels:

ATLANTIC OCEAN

North Sea

Baltic Sea

Black Sea

Mediterranean Sea

SCOTLAND
IRELAND
GREAT BRITAIN
ENGLAND
London

KINGDOM OF NORWAY AND DENMARK
Stockholm
Copenhagen
KINGDOM OF SWEDEN
St. Petersburg

RUSSIAN EMPIRE
Moscow
Borodino 1812
Smolensk
Kiev

PRUSSIA
SWEDISH POMERANIA
Königsberg
Danzig
Tilsit
Friedland 1807
Neman R.
Berlin
Lübeck
Hamburg
Bremen

GRAND DUCHY OF WARSAW

WESTPHALIA
SAXONY
Auerstädt 1806
Jena 1806
CONFEDERATION OF THE RHINE
Elbe R.
Rhine R.

Austerlitz 1805
Wagram 1804
Pressburg
Buda
Pest
Vienna
AUSTRIAN EMPIRE
Danube R.

BAVARIA
WÜRTTEMBERG
BADEN
Zurich
SWITZERLAND
Lunéville
FRANCE
Paris
Amiens
Brussels
Waterloo 1815

Marengo 1800
Milan
Genoa
KINGDOM OF ITALY
Marseilles

ILLYRIAN PROVINCES

Rome
Naples
KINGDOM OF NAPLES
Palermo
KINGDOM OF SICILY

Corsica
Sardinia
Elba
Malta (Gr. Br.)

Ionian Is. (Gr. Br.)
Athens

OTTOMAN EMPIRE
Constantinople

SPAIN
Madrid

PORTUGAL
Lisbon
Trafalgar 1805
GIBRALTAR (Gr. Br.)

Manufacturers in Belgium and central Europe benefited from the exclusion of British goods and the development of a unified continental market. In Poland, however, the loss of British grain markets caused an economic crisis for landlords and their peasants. Overall, French trade advanced under Napoleon, but it never reached the level it had enjoyed in 1789. That would not return until the 1830s.

19-5b The Austrian War of Liberation and the French Invasion of Russia

In late 1808, Napoleon marched into Spain with 150,000 men to take direct command of French forces there. Austria seized the opportunity to attack France, urging all Germans to rise up in a "war of liberation." Few German states responded, however, and Napoleon had time to return to France, march east, and defeat Austria for the fourth time. Shortly after signing the peace treaty, Napoleon divorced his wife, Josephine, who had failed to give him an heir. He then married an Austrian archduchess, Marie-Louise, who soon gave birth to a little Napoleon, named the king of Rome.

The Invasion of Russia In Russia, far to the east, Tsar **Alexander I** watched these events and laid his plans. Though required to enforce the Continental System on his coasts, he now believed Russia was strong enough to shake off French domination. He therefore withdrew from the French alliance and resumed trade with the British. Napoleon was furious and began preparing to invade Russia. In June 1812, he moved east with a force of 650,000 troops drawn from twenty countries. It was the largest single army in the field that Europe had ever seen. Throughout the summer, French troops marched farther and farther into Russia, as the Russians withdrew because their army numbered only about 200,000.

Smolensk and Borodino In August, the Russians fought Napoleon at Smolensk, and in early September, they fought again at Borodino, seventy-five miles west of Moscow. These were the bloodiest battles of the revolutionary and Napoleonic wars. After Smolensk, wagons were piled high with amputated arms and legs. Wounded and survivors alike crumpled as food supplies ran out, and hundreds of men died by the roadside from exposure as they slipped into vodka-induced comas. Battle dead and wounded from both sides at Borodino stood at 75,000, including 47 French generals.

Alexander I (r. 1801–1825) Russian emperor defeated by Napoleon who then broke with the French, provoking the Russian campaign of 1812.

Louis XVIII (r. 1814–1824) Younger brother of Louis XVI of France who became king after Napoleon's defeat.

The Occupation of Moscow Technically, the French won at Borodino, and the road to Moscow lay open. When Napoleon arrived there in mid-September, however, he found the city practically deserted; once again the Russians had retreated. The French stayed in Moscow for six weeks, waiting for Alexander to sue for peace. But the tsar, in his palace in St. Petersburg, refused. In the meantime, a fire, perhaps started by the Russians, destroyed most of Moscow. With his army exhausted and badly depleted, and with no hope of adequate winter quarters in a burned-out city, Napoleon ordered a retreat to Germany.

The Retreat from Russia What happened next is the stuff of legends: the Troops stumbled westward, harassed continuously by Russian units and frozen by the bitter winter that arrived in November. Only 15 percent of Napoleon's army made it back to Germany. For Napoleon, defeat in Russia was the beginning of the end.

19-5c Europe's Defeat of Napoleon

In 1813, Austria and Prussia, subsidized by Great Britain, reentered the war after reforming their armies and introducing a French-style draft. Napoleon realized that the next campaign was the one he had to win. The conscription machine in France and the other imperial territories pressed down harder than ever; by the summer of 1813, the emperor had raised an army of 400,000, including 100,000 rounded-up French draft evaders and deserters. In October, it engaged the Allies in eastern Germany. Napoleon lost and began to retreat westward. As he drew back, the Germans finally rose up in an anti-French revolt, rallying behind their traditional rulers. Years of taxes, conscription, and the hardships of the Continental System were taking their toll. In addition, the French ideal of a united nation of citizens had spread to the occupied peoples. Now they countered the French with their own nationalist fervor.

Abdication After he returned to Paris, Napoleon tried once again to rally his generals and ministers, but they refused to fight on. Finally, in April 1814, he abdicated. The Allies marched into Paris, with Alexander I of Russia at their head. Not far behind was Louis XVI's brother, who had fled France twenty-five years earlier. He was installed as King **Louis XVIII**. Louis XVI's son, who had died in a Paris prison in 1795, was thus honored as Louis XVII.

The Allies exiled Napoleon to the island of Elba, off the coast of Italy not far from his native Corsica. But Napoleon outwitted them one last time. In 1799, he had slipped away from his enemies in Egypt, and now he did it again, secretly setting sail for the south of France. Louis XVIII sent troops to intercept the ex-emperor, but they joined him instead; once again, his fame as a commander carried the day.

The Hundred Days Louis XVIII promptly fled to Belgium, and Napoleon triumphantly reentered Paris, where he was to rule again for a **Hundred Days**. He quickly reorganized the government and prepared yet again for battle. Miraculously, the conscription machine pulled up 100,000 men. On June 18, 1815, Napoleon engaged his old enemies at **Waterloo** in present-day Belgium, where he was defeated for the last time by an English general, the Duke of Wellington, leading a coalition of Prussians, Austrians, and Russians. Once again Napoleon abdicated, Louis XVIII entered Paris, and Napoleon was sent into exile. This time, however, the Allies shipped him into the far South Atlantic, to the island of St. Helena, where he died in 1821 at the age of fifty-two.

The Restored French Monarchy Throughout his years in exile in Allied lands, Louis XVIII had promised a full restoration of the prerevolutionary monarchy if he returned to France as king. But that proved to be impossible; too much had changed since 1789. He therefore issued a Constitutional Charter, which bore a marked resemblance to the Constitution of 1791, as the basis for his rule. The one thing from the past that Louis wanted was a coronation like the one held in 1775 for his brother. But it never took place. The king was old, Rheims was far away, and the revolutionaries had destroyed most of the sacred implements used in the ceremony.

> **Hundred Days** Period in 1815 of Napoleon's briefly restored rule in France between his return from exile on Elba and his permanent exile on St. Helena.

> **Waterloo** Napoleon's last battle, fought in Belgium in 1815 against an international coalition headed by the British Duke of Wellington.

CHAPTER Review

Summary

» At one level, the era of the French Revolution and Napoleon was characterized by political instability as regimes came and went in a matter of years. From 1775 to 1815, France moved from an absolute monarchy to a constitutional one, and then to a republic, an empire, and back to a restored monarchy.

» Beginning in 1792, the wars between France and conservative Europe deeply influenced the policies of these shifting regimes. A similar instability affected the territories France occupied, as lands became sister republics and then kingdoms, or were annexed outright.

» On another level, however, it was clear by 1815 that despite political instability, the revolutionary and Napoleonic years had brought about fundamental changes in three areas of European life.

» The democratic experiments of the 1790s, despite their limitations and failures, introduced a new model for political life that was lasting. Frenchmen, endowed with inalienable human rights, became citizens of the state and participants in government.

» Even Napoleon, who detested this democratic world, could not quite stamp it out. Both at home and in the occupied lands, Napoleon relied on written constitutions to give legitimacy to his regime, recognizing the necessity of legislatures and popular voting.

» Although women did not achieve the same level of political participation that men did, demands for their inclusion, first made by revolutionaries like Olympe de Gouges, were to remain central to political debate in the years after 1815.

» The old society of orders and estates based on privilege, abolished first in France and then in Napoleonic Europe, never really returned. The inhabitants of a country were constituted as citizens of a nation. Even Napoleon's reintroduction of nobility did little to alter this new form of society. The notables ignored the old distinctions between commoners and nobles, and the revolutionary ideal of careers open to talent, which had so benefited Napoleon himself in the 1790s, persisted.

» In the end, the occupied peoples adopted the nationalist ideals of France and then turned them against the French.

» Finally, the state's power had grown enormously. The abolition of orders and estates had swept away institutions like the Parlement of Paris that had stood between the state and its subjects. The state had also freed itself from its attachment to the Catholic Church.

» The process of centralized state control, begun by the Committee of Public Safety, was continued after 1799.

» Both at home and abroad, Napoleon used the reorganization of France into standardized units to extend the state's reach into ordinary people's lives. The chief sign of the state's expanded power was conscription.

» The ideals of the Revolution—broad political participation, the end of privilege and the beginning of merit-based advancement, and the increased power of the state—have had repercussions throughout the world.

Chronology

1775	Louis XVI is crowned king of France [Europe]
1776	American Revolution begins [Americas]
1788	Parlement summons Estates-General [Europe] France declares bankruptcy [Europe]
1789	Estates-General meets [Europe] National Assembly is formed [Europe]
1790	National Assembly decrees the Civil Constitution of the Clergy [Europe]
1791	Slaves revolt in Saint-Domingue [Americas] Olympe de Gouges publishes The Rights of Woman and the Female Citizen [Europe]
1792	France becomes a republic [Europe] France declares war on Austria and Prussia [Europe]
1793	Louis XVI is executed [Europe] Reign of Terror begins [Europe]
1794	France abolishes slavery [Europe] Reign of Terror ends [Europe]
1795	Directory is created [Europe]
1799	Napoleon seizes power [Europe]
1800	Napoleon reorganizes French administration [Europe]
1801	Napoleon and Pius VII sign Concordat [Europe]
1802	Napoleon makes himself consul for life [Europe] Slavery is reestablished in French colonies [Global]
1804	Napoleonic Code reforms French law [Europe] Napoleon becomes emperor [Europe]

1806	Continental System closes French ports to British shipping [Europe]
1812	Napoleon invades Russia [Europe]
1814	Napoleon is defeated by European allies, abdicates [Europe] Louis XVIII becomes king of France [Europe] Congress of Vienna opens [Europe]
1815	Napoleon is finally defeated at Waterloo [Europe]

Critical Thinking Questions

Take a moment to pull together all the important information from the chapter by answering the following questions.

From Crisis to Constitution, 1775–1789

» How did the crisis in French royal finances lead to the collapse of the monarchy?

» What impact did (a) the events in Paris on July 14, 1789, and (b) the Great Fear have on the National Assembly meeting in Versailles?

The Constitutional Monarchy, 1789–1792

» What were the underlying principles guiding the drafters of the Constitution of 1791? To what degree were these principles realized or violated in the specific provisions of revolutionary reform?

» Why wasn't the French clergy consulted during the drafting of the Civil Constitution of the Clergy, and what were the consequences of the failure to consult?

The Republic and the Reign of Terror, 1792–1795

» What actions did the Committee of Safety take to defend the Revolution from enemies at home and abroad?

» Were the democratic principles of 1789 advanced or compromised by the actions of the Committee of Public Safety?

The Rise of Napoleon, 1794–1804

» How were the French sister republics created, and what were their relations with France?

» Which of the revolutionary programs and policies of the 1790s did Napoleon Bonaparte benefit from, repudiate, or maintain?

The Napoleonic Empire, 1804–1815

» What did Austria and Prussia do to defend themselves against France and the Napoleonic empire?

» Why did the peoples of the Napoleonic empire rise up against the French at the end, and what did they want as an alternative?

MINDTAP
From Cengage

MindTap® is a fully online personalized learning experience built upon Cengage Learning content. MindTap® combines student learning tools—readings, multimedia, activities, and assessments—into a singular Learning Path that guides students through the course and helps students develop the critical thinking, analysis, and communication skills that are essential to academic and professional success.

CHAPTER 20

Restoration and Reform: Conservative and Liberal Europe, 1814–1847

Chapter Outline

As you read, consider the following questions:

❯ How did the Congress of Vienna attempt to create a stable Europe after the Napoleonic Wars?

❯ What were the main tenets of Romanticism and the new political movements of conservatism, liberalism, and nationalism?

❯ Why did nationalism have different impacts in Poland, Belgium, the Balkans, and Germany?

❯ Why did political reform take place first in France and Great Britain, then in the rest of Europe?

In the decades after Napoleon's final defeat, Europeans lived in the shadow of the French Revolution and its political legacy. In 1815, it appeared that the French Revolution had failed. Monarchs held fast to power throughout Europe, from London to St. Petersburg and even in Paris, where a successor to the Bourbons occupied the throne. The peace conference ending the Napoleonic Wars, held in Vienna, established a conservative political system aimed specifically at preventing the spread of liberal and revolutionary ideas.

Wartburg Festival, 1817

German students celebrate the 300th anniversary of Martin Luther's famous theses that sparked the Reformation. The students carry a flag symbolizing German unity — though this national flag would only be adopted by a united Germany over fifty years later. These students exemplify early nationalism that was liberal and democratic in its aspirations.   Students with black-red-gold flags march to the Wartburg Festival, to which the first student fraternity Jena (German fraternity) has invited all German students, 1817 (colour litho), German School, (19th century) / © SZ Photo / Sammlung Megele / Bridgeman Images

However, appearances were deceiving, as the French Revolution had changed European politics forever. The revolutionary ideals of "Liberty, Equality, Fraternity" continued to inspire active political participation. These ideas dominated the development of political ideologies during these decades.

These ideologies were conservatism, liberalism, and nationalism. Conservatives aimed to retain the power of monarchs, despite the fact that few still believed in the divine right of kings. Liberals called for parliaments, constitutionalism, civil rights, the rule of law, and a withdrawal of the state from economic matters. Nationalists denounced kings and princes, naming the nation—that is, the entire people—as the ultimate authority in politics. Until 1848, liberals and nationalists often joined forces; most liberals were nationalists. Nationalist movements in the Balkan Peninsula attempted to gain independence from Ottoman rule, and the Greeks succeeded. In central Europe, German and Italian nationalists sought to bring together existing small states into large, unified nation-states. Young liberal nationalists, like the German students shown in the image here, participated in marches, speeches, and even the burning of reactionary books to press for political change. Later in the century they would succeed.

Paralleling and crisscrossing these national movements was a literary and artistic movement known as Romanticism, which championed the individual human spirit.

The Romantics rejected the cold rationality of the Enlightenment and looked back in longing to the preindustrial, deeply religious world of the Middle Ages. They celebrated the strong and dynamic individual who—like Napoleon—could change the world. Romantic thinkers and artists also challenged social conventions of the day, openly calling for more freedom in love and sexuality, even as they experimented with new forms of artistic and poetic expression. The Romantics' mystical brand of Christianity clashed with conventional religious institutions and dogmas.

Although most governments of this period were conservative, the ideas of the French Revolution continued to influence politics and culture. A series of uprisings in 1830 realized some national and constitutional ambitions, and in Great Britain political reform was achieved through a series of parliamentary acts. Even in conservative-dominated central Europe, liberal and nationalist ideas were spreading and gaining in strength. In 1848, these new ideologies would burst forth in a wave of revolutionary uprisings across the European continent.

20-1 The Old Order and New Challenges

» **What were the main aims and outcomes of the Congress of Vienna?**

» **How did Romantic poets and artists challenge the existing social order?**

A quarter century of revolution and war was brought to a close by the defeat of Napoleon at Waterloo in June 1815. But even before Napoleon's defeat, monarchs and diplomats from all over Europe were meeting in the Austrian capital to hammer out a peace settlement. Presided over by the Austrian Prime Minister Prince Clemens von Metternich, this would be a conservative peace.

The Congress of Vienna restored prerevolutionary rulers and drew borders that lasted into the twentieth century. Metternich wanted to restore the preindustrial, absolutist social and political order of the eighteenth century, but he was realistic enough to recognize that he could not set the political clock back to 1788. Instead, he aimed to prevent revolutionary outbreaks and to suppress the new ideologies of liberalism and nationalism by strengthening traditional rulers and the landowning nobility. Even as he did this, however, the new cultural and artistic movement called Romanticism was challenging the social and spiritual norms of this conservative world.

Congress of Vienna (1814–1815) International meeting that redrew the European map and restored order after the Napoleonic Wars.

Clemens von Metternich (1773–1859) Austrian statesman, architect of the Congress of Vienna and the Congress System, foreign minister and then prime minister of Austria, 1809–1848.

20-1a The Congress of Vienna

Napoleon's campaign against Russia in 1812 spelled his doom as a leader. In 1814, he was ejected from power when allied troops marched into Paris. The allied powers generously granted Napoleon the island of Elba off the Italian coast. How to fill the power vacuum in Europe with a neutralized France? The **Congress of Vienna**, called by the Austrian Prime Minister **Clemens von Metternich** (MET-er-nikh) in mid-1814, aimed to answer that question. Metternich was a brilliant and cynical man who combined wit and charm with cold calculation. When the congress disbanded in 1815, a new conservative, post-Napoleonic Europe had been established (see Map 20.1). In many ways that order would survive until the First World War.

Besides Metternich, two other statesmen played important roles in the congress's work: the foreign minister of Great Britain, Robert Castlereagh (CASsel-ray), and Tsar Alexander I of Russia. Prussia's king Frederick William III seemed reluctant to press his

Legend

- France
- Kingdom of Prussia
- Austrian Empire
- Spain
- United Kingdom
- Russian Empire
- Ottoman Empire
- Boundary of the German Confederation

Map labels:

ATLANTIC OCEAN

North Sea

Baltic Sea

KINGDOM OF SWEDEN AND NORWAY — Oslo, Stockholm, Helsinki, St. Petersburg

RUSSIAN EMPIRE — Moscow, Riga, Kiev

DENMARK — Copenhagen, SCHLESWIG, HOLSTEIN, HANOVER

UNITED KINGDOM OF GREAT BRITAIN AND IRELAND — SCOTLAND, IRELAND, Dublin, Manchester, WALES, ENGLAND, London

KINGDOM OF THE NETHERLANDS — Amsterdam, Antwerp, Waterloo

KINGDOM OF PRUSSIA — Danzig, Berlin, Göttingen, Cologne, Frankfurt, SAXONY, Elbe R., Rhine R.

KINGDOM OF POLAND (Russia) — Warsaw, Vistula R.

FRANCE — Paris, Luxembourg, LORRAINE, ALSACE, BADEN, Seine R., Loire R., Garonne R., Rhône R.

GALICIA, Cracow, UKRAINE, Dniester R., Dnieper R.

AUSTRIAN EMPIRE — Prague, BOHEMIA, Vienna, Munich, BAVARIA, Buda, Pest, HUNGARY, CROATIA

SWITZERLAND

LOMBARDY, PIEDMONT, Milan, Po R., Venice, PARMA, MODENA, LUCCA, TUSCANY, PAPAL STATES, Rome, Elba, Corsica (Fr.), NAPLES

KINGDOM OF PIEDMONT-SARDINIA

KINGDOM OF THE TWO SICILIES, Sardinia, Sicily

PORTUGAL, SPAIN, Madrid, Ebro R., GILBRALTAR (Gr. Br.)

Marseilles

BESSARABIA, MOLDAVIA, WALLACHIA, SERBIA, Belgrade, BOSNIA, BULGARIA, Danube R.

OTTOMAN EMPIRE, Istanbul, ALBANIA, GREECE, Athens

Black Sea

Adriatic Sea

Mediterranean Sea

MOROCCO, ALGIERS, TUNIS, Malta (Gr. Br.)

Scale: 0 — 150 — 300 Km. / 0 — 150 — 300 Mi.

Map 20.1 **Europe After the Congress of Vienna, 1815** The Congress of Vienna redrew the map of Europe in order to strengthen conservative governments. In Eastern Europe multinational empires and not nation-states dominate this map.

1. Compare this map with Europe before the Napoleonic Wars (Map 19.3) and in 1918 (Map 26.1). What has changed? What new countries appear in the second map?

2. Western European countries tend to conform more with the concept of "nation-state" than do countries in central and eastern Europe. Why do you suppose that is so, and what exceptions to that general rule can you see?

3. Looking at this map, why would rulers of states in central and eastern Europe feel threatened by nationalism? Which countries were most threatened?

The Congress of Vienna

The Congress of Vienna brought together the crowned heads of most of Europe. It was quipped that "The Congress does not work, but it dances" (which sounds better in French). In this image, we see the gorgeous clothing and rich jewels of the aristocrats who still governed most of Europe. They appear confident that their world would continue undisturbed, despite the interval of the French Revolution.

» *Looking at this image, how can you tell that this is a gathering of the rich?*

» *What elements of fashion help you date this painting?*

concerns, perhaps remembering his military humiliation at the hands of Napoleon and salvation with Russian help. Even defeated France sent a representative, the cunning but utterly cynical survivor Charles Maurice de Talleyrand, once memorably described as "a piece of dung in a silk stocking." Talleyrand cleverly exploited divisions among the Allies, particularly the widespread fear of growing Russian power, to gain better conditions for France. Castlereagh expressed no interest in territorial gain but aimed to restore a European balance of power in which no European state would ever again be able to dominate the continent. Tsar Alexander I hoped to extend Russian influence in Europe, and Metternich aimed to neutralize it. Talleyrand attempted to convince all sides that only a strong France could ensure each ally's goals.

Frictions over Poland

Competing interests came to a head over the issue of Poland. Alexander felt that the partitions of Poland of the late eighteenth century had been immoral and wished to resurrect Poland in some way. More practically, he knew that a reconstituted Poland connected to Russia would considerably enhance Russian influence in central Europe. Understandably, Prussia

and Austria opposed this extension of Russian power, though they agreed that Russia should be compensated for its important role in defeating Napoleon. This dispute almost split the congress apart, but in the end a compromise was reached. The kingdom of Poland (or **Congress Poland**) was established as an **autonomous** kingdom, with Alexander as king and Warsaw as its capital (see Map 20.2). Russia gained the largest amount of Polish territory, but millions of Poles continued to live in Prussia and Austria.

CONNECTIONS: Poland has the geographical misfortune of being located between strong Russian and German states. Since the eighteenth century, Poland's neighbors have often interfered in Polish affairs, most notoriously in the partitions of Poland when Russia, Prussia, and Austria divided up the country among themselves. At the Congress of Vienna, a new Poland was set up—but with the Russian tsar as its king. In the twentieth century, Nazi Germany and the USSR would again divide up Poland (see Section 27-3 The Third Reich), and after 1945 Poland came under communist rule, despite Poles' general loathing of that political system. (see Section 28-3 The Restructuring of Eastern Europe).

Restoration of Conservative Power in France and German States

Talleyrand succeeded in keeping France from being punished. The Bourbon dynasty, in the person of Louis XVIII, was restored to France's throne, though not to absolute rule. The king was subject to a constitution and had to share power with a legislature. France was obliged to give up lands occupied after 1795 and to pay a war **indemnity** but remained intact, an important player in European politics.

Congress Poland Polish kingdom under the Russian tsar created at the Congress of Vienna (1815), enjoying until 1831 its own constitution, legislature, army, and bureaucracy.

autonomous Self-governing but not entirely independent, usually in a certain region or for a certain ethnic/national group.

indemnity Money or goods paid by the losing side after a war to compensate for the cost and damage of military action.

Map 20.2 **Kingdom of Poland, 1815** The Kingdom of Poland was created at the Congress of Vienna and attached to the Russian empire; the Russian tsar was also the king of Poland. The kingdom was ruled by a viceroy and a parliament in the capital, Warsaw. Although most Poles lived in this so-called Congress Kingdom, millions continued to live under Austrian and Prussian rule.

1. Why would both Poles and Russians be dissatisfied with this compromise solution of the Polish question?
2. Which present-day Polish cities were located in the kingdom of Poland? Which were outside it?

The German states and principalities that had fought against Napoleon were restored to their rulers, but their total number was reduced from around three hundred to thirty-nine. These ranged in size and importance from Prussia and Austria (the Habsburg empire contained, of course, much non-German territory as well) to tiny Liechtenstein with only 5,000 residents. This was a step toward a more unified Germany, but far from enough

for patriots such as the German students at the Wartburg Festival.

These German states were loosely connected in a confederation but remained independent. Prussia gained the territory west of the Rhine River that Napoleon had incorporated into France. The Netherlands regained independence and acquired the southern provinces that had belonged to Spain and then to Austria. The Spanish Bourbons were restored to power in the person of King Ferdinand VII, who at first promised to work together with liberals, then turned on them and ruled as an absolute monarch. The congress restored the Papal States, including the city of Rome and covering much of central Italy, to the Pope.

Besides the territorial changes set down at the Congress of Vienna, the powers also agreed to work together in concert—the so-called Concert of Europe—to prevent future military and civil disturbances. In this they were astonishingly successful: Europe would see no general war for nearly a century.

20-1b The Congress System

The four Great Powers of Prussia, Austria, Russia, and Great Britain (later joined by France) planned regular congresses, like the one at Vienna. Their **Congress System** aimed to root out revolution, even if it meant interference in the internal affairs of sovereign states. Such interference was considered less dangerous than allowing liberal and radical ideas to grow.

The Holy Alliance The guiding principle of the Congress System, urged by Tsar Alexander I, was to be the **Holy Alliance**. Alexander, very much under the influence of Christian mysticism, proposed to his fellow monarchs (not just those present in Vienna) that in the future they model their policies on principles of the Christian faith. This suggestion was greeted—at least in private—with a good deal of skepticism and even ridicule. Clearly, even Christian statesmen and monarchs considered international relations a realm distant from Christian morality. Castlereagh denounced the Holy Alliance as "nonsense," and Metternich called it "a loud-sounding nothing." Nonetheless, the diplomats were reluctant to offend the tsar and at least acted sympathetic to Alexander's proposal.

Threats to the Congress System In fact, the system's real guiding power was Metternich, who sought to limit Russian power in Europe, to expand Austrian influence, and to suppress

Congress System Conservative political system put in place at the Congress of Vienna aiming to preserve peace and prevent the spread of nationalism and liberalism.

Holy Alliance Political agreement advocated by Tsar Alexander I at the Congress of Vienna calling for international relations to be based on Christian morals.

bpk, Berlin/Hamburger Kunsthalle, Hamburg/Art Resource, NY

Wanderer Above a Sea of Fog by Caspar David Friedrich, 1818
Caspar David Friedrich's paintings exemplify the romantic sensibility. Often, as in the painting above, the lone human figures are overwhelmed by the rough and beautiful natural world.

» *Romanticism was also obsessed with death and religion. How are those themes reflected in the images you see in* Abbey Surrounded by Oak Trees *(1809) later in this chapter?*

all the ideas that had come out of the French Revolution. For Metternich, constitutionalism, civil rights, and the rule of law all came down to the same thing—revolution. For a **multinational state** like Austria, nationalism was every bit as much a threat as liberal ideas. The Congress System was a deeply conservative, even **reactionary**, set of policies that aimed mainly at preventing change.

From the start, however, serious practical problems challenged the Congress System. When the Greeks rebelled against their Ottoman rulers in 1821, setting off the Greek War of Independence, Tsar Alexander of Russia took up their cause, but Metternich and Castlereagh opposed any measures that could increase Russian power. The strain between British insular interests and the obligations of the Congress System proved too much for the already unstable Castlereagh; he took his own life in the midst of the Greek crisis. In the end, Metternich's crafty diplomacy prevented Russia from declaring war on the Ottoman Empire, and the Greeks had to wait another decade for independence.

Castlereagh's suicide revealed a fundamental contradiction between British interests and European unity in the form of the Congress System. Following more than twenty years of warfare on the continent, the British were extremely reluctant to get involved in European affairs, especially in military action. When, in 1823, France intervened against a more liberal order in Spain, Britain openly broke with the alliance. Across the Atlantic, the United States also sought to guard against European intervention. President James Monroe issued what became known as the Monroe

multinational state
Country in which more than one ethnic group ("nation") resides—for example, the Habsburg, Ottoman, and Russian Empires.

reactionary Exceedingly conservative, wishing not only to prevent change but to retreat into the past.

akg-images

Caspar David Friedrich's *Abbey Surrounded by Oak Trees*, **1809**

Doctrine, declaring that European meddling in the Western Hemisphere would not be tolerated. Alexander I died two years later, and his successor, Tsar **Nicholas I**, was much more reactionary and less interested in European affairs than his elder brother had been. From this point on, the Congress System became little more than a weapon in the hands of Metternich to suppress nationalist and revolutionary movements in central Europe and Italy.

20-1c The Age of Romanticism

In his attempts to root out nationalism, Metternich was battling a new cultural movement that was sweeping Europe and would eventually, in a political form, tear apart Austria and the multinational states he sought to preserve. Metternich embraced tradition, privilege, and the existing political order. In contrast, the artistic and literary movement **Romanticism** embraced emotion, individuality, and new forms of expression. Romanticism was everything Metternich was not: mystical, antirational, and passionate. Although often deeply religious, the Romantics opposed most existing institutions—even the church—and demanded freedom for human beings to realize their emotional, cultural, and even sexual potential. Reacting against what it saw as the cold rationality and dull universalism of the Enlightenment, Romanticism celebrated the human soul and mystical nature that connected directly with God.

Romanticism in Literature and Painting The Romantics saw God in nature, as Wordsworth conveyed in his poetry and **Caspar David Friedrich** expressed in his starkly beautiful landscapes. Wordsworth would wander lonely through England's Lake District and return to his cottage to write poems about the glories of nature—and the deeply felt sense of God's majesty in such things as daffodils, clouds, or landscapes. The German poet Friedrich von Hardenberg, better known as Novalis, portrayed man, woman, nature, and God as merged in an infinite unity. Romantic art also sought out exotic localities, tempestuous nature, and common people as its subjects. In France, Eugène Delacroix's paintings showed exotic scenes (especially in northern Africa and the Muslim world), stormy seas, and his most famous painting of all—a bare-breasted Liberty leading the people to victory over their oppressors. Common to all Romantic art is a burning desire to overcome feelings of personal loneliness and alienation, to submerge individual identity in a cosmic whole combining human, natural, and divine elements.

The Romantics—and it is not by chance that most of these were poets or painters, not accountants or college professors—rejected the Enlightenment's mechanical universe and its method of seeking the truth through the scientific

Nicholas I (r. 1825–1855) Russian tsar noted for conservatism and his hatred for the political ideals of the French Revolution.

Romanticism Literary and artistic movement of the late eighteenth and early nineteenth centuries that extolled artistic genius and opposed many traditional social conventions.

Caspar David Friedrich (1774–1840) German artist whose landscapes often featured craggy mountains, mighty forests, and Romantic ruins that overwhelmed petty human figures.

method of studied observation, experimentation, and reason. They were profoundly disturbed by the idea of a clockwork universe in which human beings were just a cog. The most important aspects of life, they contended, cannot be understood by rational scientific experimentation. Rather, the irrational—powerful emotions, the sense of beauty, the ecstasy of love—makes us human. In "The Tables Turned," Wordsworth called on a friend to "quit your books," "Our meddling intellect/Mis-shapes the beauteous forms of things—We murder to dissect." In the Romantic view, the scientific method can never fathom the mystery of life or answer fundamental moral questions such as why human beings are here, why we love, and why we suffer. The English poet John Keats, in his famous "Ode on a Grecian Urn," proclaimed: "'Beauty is truth, truth beauty,'—that is all/ Ye know on earth, and all ye need to know."

Romantics likewise rejected the restraints of middle-class respectability. They mocked hardworking, narrow-minded pillars of society. Instead, they extolled the Romantic hero, a dashing figure who often ended tragically, like **Alexander Pushkin**'s Eugene Onegin and Lord Byron's Don Juan.

The Romantics and the Sexes The German poet Friedrich Schlegel praised sexual love even outside marriage in his poem *Lucinde*. Novalis's *Hymns to the Night* were inspired by a teenaged girl, though it is clear that his feelings for her were more spiritually exalted than physical. Intellectual women figured prominently in the Romantic movement as organizers of salons where Romantic writers gathered as well as writing themselves. Women like Dorothea (Veit) Schlegel and Mary Wollstonecraft Shelley (daughter of the early feminist Mary Wollstonecraft) worked as equal partners with their writer-husbands and published works of their own.

In their art—and sometimes in their personal lives—the Romantics created a world where man and woman interacted in full equality, the female and the male principles supplementing and inspiring each other. The German writer Johann Wolfgang von Goethe, who had exerted a great influence on the Romantics, had concluded his epic poem, *Faust*: "The eternally feminine leads us forward." At the same time, the Romantics' conception of "artistic genius" took for granted that most people would not be able to understand or appreciate him—or her! The image of the starving and alienated artist so familiar to us today took on modern form with the Romantics. (See also Profiles in Change: The Grimm Brothers Begin Work on Their *German Dictionary* and Learning from a Primary

Alexander Pushkin (1799–1837) Russian nobleman and poet considered Russia's greatest writer.

utopian (from Greek, "no place") Consisting of unrealistic attempts at reforming human life.

Alexander Pushkin

Active during the reign of Tsar Nicholas I, Russian poet Alexander Pushkin reflects the romantic temperament of the age. Both in his poetry and his life – he died after a duel with a Frenchman who had been too openly courting his wife – Pushkin was a romantic hero. In this engraving, he sits at his desk creating his historical poem "The Bronze Horseman" (1833) in which the famous statue of Peter the Great comes to life and pursues the poem's hero through the gloomy streets of St. Petersburg.

❯❯ *How would the figure of a lone man who dares to defy Tsar Peter the Great reflect romantic sentiments?*

Source: Jacob Grimm Writes a Foreword to the *German Dictionary* for more on the German literary tradition.)

Romanticism in Philosophy and Politics Romanticism was an all-embracing philosophy of life that emphasized unity, organic growth, inspiration, and creative genius. While Romantics often combined their mystical longings for the unity of all nature and humanity with religious sentiments, they were rarely Christians in any conventional sense. Furthermore, their emphasis on creative genius bordered on blasphemy: Geniuses became in their own way gods, creating new worlds. The established churches could hardly embrace such ideas, even from individuals who opposed the anticlerical Enlightenment. The Romantics were fundamentally **utopian**—visionaries who believed perfectibility was possible in human relationships and societies. But they lacked the detachment and willingness to compromise that are essential to achieving reform in the political arena. Even those Romantic figures like Friedrich Schlegel who wrote on political subjects were not successful in influencing contemporary politics.

CONNECTIONS: Peter the Great, celebrated by Pushkin as well as by the tsars, changed Russian history. And his image has been variously interpreted by later Russians. In the nineteenth century, the Slavophiles—like Fedor Dostoevsky—rejected Peter's reforms and argued that the great tsar had betrayed Russia's true nature and religion by Europeanizing the country (see Section 23-3 Art and Industrial Society). And during the Soviet period, the tsar was called "Peter I," never "Peter the Great," because of the great suffering he inflicted on the peoples of the Russian Empire. And yet in the twenty-first century, Peter is once again "great," pictured on the Russian currency, and praised by the country's current strong man, Vladimir Putin.

Despite its fundamentally utopian nature, Romanticism had an important impact on future politics through its influence of nationalism. Nationalists, embracing the Romantic spirit, rejected universalism and glorified the individual—in this case, the individual language, culture, and nation. Like the Romantics, nationalists in the early nineteenth century rejected existing institutions and looked forward to a golden age in which not just French and German but also languages like Czech, Lithuanian, and Serbian would be cultivated and respected. The Romantics themselves welcomed the French Revolution in its early stages—a nation coming to power—though the bloodshed soon disillusioned them. For many, Napoleon Bonaparte resembled the ideal Romantic hero who swept away old institutions and ideas and brought the ideals of liberty, equality, and brotherhood to the lands he "liberated" (not "conquered").

Romanticism in Eastern Europe In different forms, Romanticism spread across the European continent. The homeland of Romanticism is arguably either Germany or England, but Poles also participated with their national poet, **Adam Mickiewicz (mits-KYE-vich)**, or the patriotic composer and pianist **Frederic Chopin (sho-PAN)** as archetypical Romantics. Mickiewicz's poetic masterpiece, *Pan Tadeusz*, evokes a lost homeland and a world that no longer exists. Even today it is a rare Pole who cannot recite the poem's first lines: "Lithuania [for Mickiewicz, a province of Poland], my homeland! You are like health; only he who has lost you can appreciate your true worth." Chopin was born in Warsaw but, like Mickiewicz, spent most of his life in France. His most famous works used traditional Polish folk melodies and musical forms. Both Chopin and Mickiewicz exemplify a fusing of Romanticism and nationalism.

Among Russian writers, Pushkin exhibits Romantic strains, and even more typically Romantic are Mikhail Lermontov's rousing stories and poems of dashing young soldiers, beautiful maidens, unrequited love, and exotic locales along the Black Sea and in the Caucasus Mountains.

20-2 The Beginnings of Modern Ideology

» **What were the most important differences between liberals and conservatives in this period?**

» **How has the meaning of the term "liberal" changed from then until now?**

» **Why did conservatives in the early nineteenth century oppose nationalism?**

The nineteenth century has been called the century of "isms." Besides the literary and artistic movement of Romanticism, the most important among these are conservatism, liberalism, nationalism, and socialism. All these modern political ideologies trace their origins back to the French Revolution. Conservatives opposed the Revolution and favored traditional authority and a slow rate of change, carefully directed from above. Liberals generally supported the Revolution's ideals of "Liberty, Equality, Fraternity," though they rejected the violent excesses of the Reign of Terror and Napoleonic period. Nationalists latched onto the Revolution's idea of the "great French nation" in which all citizens were equal in rights and responsibilities. In central and eastern Europe, nationalists— almost always political liberals or radicals—called for democratic nation-states to replace the old multinational states. Conservatives like Metternich, on the other hand, rejected nationalist arguments as destructive for existing state structures.

20-2a
Conservatism

Conservatism is often understood as the political ideology that opposes change. In fact, conservatives recognize that some degree of change in human society is inevitable. In these years, They did, however, oppose the rapid and thoroughgoing change advocated by the French Revolution. Most conservatives were not so much ideological as practical: they saw that change threatened their own position. Metternich is a good example. He believed that "the people" were not capable of choosing their

Adam Mickiewicz (1798–1855) Polish writer, mainly of lyric and patriotic poetry, born in Polish Lithuania but spent most of his life in exile.

Frederic Chopin (1810–1849) Polish composer and pianist, best known for his expressive Romantic piano works and his dances, especially polonaises, that celebrated Polish nationalism.

conservatism Political ideology emphasizing tradition, slow change from above, and respect for existing institutions.

The Grimm Brothers Begin Work on Their *German Dictionary*

Portrait of brothers Jacob and Wilhelm Grimm, 1855 (oil on canvas), Jerichau-Baumann, Elisabeth Maria Anna (1819-1881) / Alte Nationalgalerie, Berlin, Germany / De Agostini Picture Library / Bridgeman Images

The Grimm Brothers

The Grimm Brothers spent their entire lives working together to create a modern and scholarly understanding of the German language. As patriotic Germans, they also worked for a liberal and democratic Germany. Here, the elderly brothers seem to communicate without words.

» *Why do you suppose that the painter chose to portray the brothers in this pose, with one holding a quill pen?*

In 1838, the middle-aged professors Jacob and Wilhelm Grimm were expelled from their university for their liberal and patriotic ideas. They were well known in academic circles for their many pathbreaking studies in the field of linguistics and German philology, the study of words and texts. Individually and together they had published dozens of studies, including a book on German mythology, a grammar of the German language, and collections of German stories, fairy tales, and myths. And linguists speak of "Grimm's Law" to describe a regular shift in consonant sounds (*p : v : f*) in the development of European languages; for example, *pater* in Latin became *vater* in German and "father" in English. The Grimms' analysis revealed connections among languages derived from Indo-European roots that showed a linguistic relationship between nearly all European languages and even languages as far away as Persia and India.

The Grimms' collection of German fairy tales was first published in 1812—just as Napoleon was on his way to Moscow. They oversaw the collection of hundreds of stories, often venturing into villages to hear the tales that had been passed down orally from generation to generation. By writing down these narratives for the first time, the Grimm brothers saw themselves as carrying out a patriotic duty to preserve German folk traditions. By the end of the century, these stories would be published in hundreds of editions and dozens of languages.

The Grimms' work aimed to elevate the prestige of German culture and language. They wanted to prove that German culture was every bit as rich as the cultures of unified nations such as England and France. Throughout the century, Russian, Hungarian, Irish, and Slavic folklorists would carry out similar research with the same patriotic purpose. In a similar way, the American Noah Webster published his *American*

---

government or governing themselves. Only royalty or the nobility were **legitimate** rulers, and they would direct change from above, based on existing traditions and institutions. For conservatives, religion and the Catholic Church played a fundamental role in maintaining respect for established rules of conduct and obedience to authority. The people themselves were incapable of governing themselves because of their ignorance. Conservatives have a pessimistic view of human nature and believe the people must be held in check and told how to behave.

legitimacy Conservative view of the political and social order that assumes the right of kings and the nobility to rule.

Edmund Burke: Moderate Conservative Perhaps the greatest ideological conservative was the Irish philosopher, political theorist, and member of Parliament Edmund Burke. When the French Revolution broke out, he was almost sixty, and his most famous book, *Reflections on the Revolution in France*, was published in 1790. Burke argued that the French Revolution was doomed to descend into violence and anarchy because it was based on abstract principles instead of firmly rooted institutions. Having swept away the king's legitimacy, Burke warned, the revolutionaries had nothing to put in its place except the abstraction of popular rule that would mean a despotism far worse than Louis XVI's bumbling. Burke did not reject change out of hand but insisted that it must be "organic"—that is, growing naturally out of existing ideas, institutions, and individuals. This metaphor of organic change was to become very common among conservatives.

Dictionary of the English Language in 1828 to emphasize the legitimacy of American English. All these early nationalists believed that the development of individual national cultures contributed directly to the enrichment of world culture.

The Grimm brothers' political views combined liberalism and nationalism. When, in 1837, the new king of Hannover (the German kingdom where their university, Georg-August-Universität, was located) cast aside the constitution in effect since 1833, the Grimm brothers, along with five other Göttingen (GÖT-in-ghen) professors, protested. The "Göttingen Seven," as they came to be known, refused to swear an oath to the despotic new king. For daring to stand up for their political principles, they were expelled from the university. Their fame as scholars was now enhanced by admiration for them as political martyrs, and a public collection helped fund their continuing research.

In the same year as their expulsion, the Grimm brothers embarked on their most ambitious project of all: a German dictionary that would "contain the endless richness of our fatherland's language from Luther to Goethe." The Grimms wanted to do more than simply to compile definitions of German words: they aimed to document the history of the German language and the changing usage of words from late medieval times to the present day. Their *Deutsches Wörterbuch* (*German Dictionary*) was a monumental undertaking. The work went forward slowly, and the first volume (A to Biermolke) was published after sixteen years of work. Wilhelm died in 1859, a year before the second volume appeared. The third volume (E to Forsche) appeared in 1862, one year before Jacob's death. The massive project started by the Grimm brothers was continued by their students and was not completed until the early 1970s. In the twenty-first century, this enormous historical dictionary remains one of the marvels of nineteenth-century philology and is a valuable research tool for specialists in German language and literature.

Burke certainly did not admire absolutism. After all, he had defended the American colonists in their revolt against the British monarch. He valued highly the rights enjoyed by British men of his class, talents, and education. He did reject, however, the idea that all men should be treated as equal and should participate on an equal footing in politics. This, he argued, was a recipe for disaster and the worst kind of tyranny. Describing the National Assembly in Paris, Burke wrote, "Their liberty is not liberal. Their science is presumptuous ignorance. Their humanity is savage and brutal." Burke did not reject the ideal of political liberty but insisted that most men—ignorant, lazy, and undisciplined—were not yet ready to appreciate this lofty sentiment. By eliminating the political and moral institutions that helped keep the masses of humanity in line, the French Revolution threatened to unleash a flood of destructive brutality and anarchy.

Pessimistic Conservative: Joseph de Maistre

Burke, like Thomas Hobbes before him, thought pessimistically that unfettered liberty would inevitably lead to lawlessness. The terrible events of the Reign of Terror and Napoleonic Wars only served to confirm this pessimism. Perhaps the most extreme political conservative of the post-Napoleonic period was **Joseph de Maistre (MAY-ster)**. This nobleman from Savoy, on the border between France and Italy, fled his homeland when in 1792 it was invaded by French armies led by Napoleon. For the rest of his life, much of which was spent in St. Petersburg, Maistre wrote against the ideals of the French Revolution and liberalism.

Like Burke, Maistre based his political ideology on authority, religion, and tradition. Unlike Burke, Maistre emphasized the pope and the Catholic Church as central to legitimate authority. Maistre argued directly against certain central tenets of the Enlightenment, and in particular despised Jean Jacques Rousseau's famous line "Man was born free, and everywhere he is in chains." Maistre rejected the idea of natural freedom put forth by Rousseau; for him, men were brutish and violent in a state of nature and, without Christianity, were no better than slaves. Only accepting and obeying existing authorities, first among them the pope, prevented the "natural bondage" of humanity from reasserting itself. In other words, mankind's sinful nature required the strict control of church and legitimate rulers. Like Burke, Maistre stressed the importance of history and tradition, rejecting written constitutions as harmful abstractions: "Man cannot make a constitution, and no legitimate constitution can be written." In other words, political legitimacy comes only through the slow evolution of traditional authority, never from abstract principles.

Russian Conservatism: The Slavophiles

A unique kind of European conservatism in this period arose in Russia, the most conservative of Europe's Great Powers, under Tsar Nicholas I. In the Russian context, **Slavophilism** called for a return to pure Russian Orthodox religious values and a rejection of foreign—specifically Western—influences. The Slavophiles demanded the abolition of Tsar Peter the Great's Europeanizing reforms in order to restore Russia's inner harmony and religious purity.

The Slavophiles rejected representative government, institutionalized democracy, and industrial development, arguing in a Romantic vein that such rational Western institutions were alien to the Russian soul. At the same time, they argued for the abolition of serfdom, but

Joseph de Maistre (1753–1821) Conservative theorist whose pessimistic outlook on human nature led him to advocate severe limits on human freedom.

Slavophilism ("love of Slavs") Russian social philosophy of the 1830s and 1840s, calling for a return to religious values and a rejection of Tsar Peter the Great's reforms.

from a uniquely conservative point of view. By ending serfdom, the tsar could reestablish the mystical unity that had existed between the Russian people (that is, the peasantry) and himself. Like the Romantics in other parts of Europe, the Slavophiles yearned for mystical unity while championing the uniqueness of their own Russian historical and religious experience. Slavophilism had little influence in Russian governmental policy, but the Slavophiles demonstrated that one could oppose the Russian status quo not only from a left-wing, radical perspective but also out of conservative conviction and religious belief.

The era 1815–1847 was in most respects a conservative, even reactionary one. It is remarkable that this conservatism owed very little to the thinkers discussed here and much more to Metternich's practical politics. These thinkers did, however, share with Metternich many fundamental attitudes. All rejected the legitimacy of written constitutions, representative government, and political change based on abstract rights and reasoning. In this way, conservatism both in theory and in practice lined itself up directly against the most important traditions of the Enlightenment.

20-2b Liberalism

Where conservatism rejected the Enlightenment, **liberalism** embraced it wholeheartedly. Liberalism enthusiastically took up the Enlightenment's call to "dare to know," to transform knowledge into practical measures that improve the world. Classical liberalism, like the Enlightenment, put the individual at the center of its political ideology.

Unlike conservatism (and socialism), liberalism emphasized above all constitutionalism and individual rights, including the right to own property, express one's opinions freely, and profess any religion—or no religion at all. The abstractions of law and constitutions so despised by the conservatives formed the very center of liberal politics. Only through the impersonal rule of law could true liberty be guaranteed for all citizens. Standing above all individuals—rich or poor, noble or peasant—law would regulate the relations of the individual citizen and society as a whole. In this way, the liberals argued, the rule of law assured true equality of rights. Laws also restrict the individual's actions, of course, but liberal theorists recognized that some individual freedoms must be sacrificed for the good of society

as a whole. Liberals also stressed the importance of private property for a free society. Owning property gave an individual a stake in the existing order and transformed the abstractions of law into concrete rights and duties.

Unlike conservatives, liberals were fundamentally optimistic about human nature and the possibility for transforming the world for the better. The liberals were middle-class men (and, increasingly after the midcentury, women) whose political ideology may be termed the politics of the industrial **bourgeoisie (bur-zhwa-ZEE)** and educated middle class. Liberals opposed traditional forms of authority like royal absolutism or the pope. On the economy, they differed fundamentally from what present-day Americans understand as liberal, as they firmly opposed government interference in the economy and everyday life. In principle, liberals were in favor of the equality and fraternity of all humanity, though in practice they remained wary of granting full political rights to poorer and less-educated elements in the population. Similarly, very few liberals thought that women were truly equal to men. Rather like the Enlightenment thinkers themselves, they argued that "in time" even these groups would be ready for full political rights—when they were educated. With its insistent call for constitutionalism, civil rights, protection of private property, and the rule of law, liberalism was for this period a markedly progressive political ideology.

Liberalism in Great Britain Great Britain was the homeland of classical liberalism. Classical economic liberal thought is epitomized by Adam Smith's renowned work *The Wealth of Nations* (1776). Smith argued that nations enrich themselves not by amassing precious metals and restricting their exports, a central tenet of mercantilism, but by allowing the greatest possible freedom for market forces, in other words, **free trade**. Government should stay out of economic matters, avoid high taxes and tariffs, and let markets set prices. Smith spoke of the "invisible hand" of the market mechanism that through the **law of supply and demand** would maximize economic efficiency. Smith did concede that government could not stay out of the economy entirely because of the need for infrastructure, such as roads and harbors, which the profit motive would not create. On the whole, however, Smith thought that by limiting government expenditures, keeping taxes low, and encouraging free markets, a country would prosper. Economic liberals demanded a laissez-faire economic policy from the state, calling on government to keep out of the economy and let it develop naturally according to market forces.

Political liberalism grew out of Jeremy Bentham's *Introduction to the Principles of Morals and Legislation* (1789), which contained the now famous statement that the aim of legislation should be the greatest happiness for the greatest number of citizens. Bentham, like Adam Smith, believed that enlightened self-interest was the best guide for reforming institutions and politics. Not abstract principles but practical applications should be the reformer's primary

liberalism Political ideology emphasizing constitutionalism, civil rights, private property, and the rule of law.

bourgeoisie The middle class, especially capitalists, well-to-do investors, factory owners, and educated professionals.

free trade Unrestricted trade between different countries, not hindered by high tariffs or taxes.

law of supply and demand Economic law according to which prices increase when supply is low and demand high.

goal. Because of his emphasis on practical reforms, Bentham's thought has been called **utilitarianism**. His influence may be seen clearly in the political demands of liberals like James Mill and also more radical thinkers. Like Smith, Bentham held a basically optimistic outlook: if human beings followed their own interests in an enlightened way, a better society would result.

James Mill developed these ideas further, emphasizing that proper education would enable individuals to recognize their own true self-interest. Mill argued that the greatest happiness for the greatest numbers may not necessarily require **universal suffrage**, in which everyone had the right to vote, but it certainly did demand a political system in which the participation of educated and propertied individuals was guaranteed. Mill took his own ideas on education seriously enough to apply them to his son, **John Stuart Mill**, perhaps the most famous liberal of all. The younger Mill began to study Greek at the age of three, Latin at eight, and by twelve had read through most of the ancient classics, as well as studying mathematics, history, and philosophy. While morality was a central aspect of this education, religion and poetry were specifically excluded from it.

Not surprisingly, given his father's intense educational regime, as a young man John Stuart Mill underwent a shattering spiritual crisis from which he only gradually recovered. Mill's most famous work, *On Liberty* (1859), forcefully made the case for individual liberty, justice, and toleration. Unlike his father, John Stuart Mill was greatly troubled by the possibility that the spread of democracy could strengthen a tyrannical majority that would limit and crush individual freedoms. Mill defended the right to minority views, which he feared majority rule could threaten.

Liberalism and the Woman Question: John Stuart Mill Mill also believed that women must be recognized as intellectual and political equals—if not superiors—of men, a radical view that he expounded in his *Subjection of Women* (1869). As a philosopher, moralist, and political thinker, Mill was the epitome of liberalism. At the same time, his works reflected the progress of industrialization, mass society, and even socialism that challenged the fundamental beliefs of liberalism: individualism, the rule of law, and private property.

Mill's life was intimately related to that of the woman he described in his autobiography as "the most admirable person I had ever known," Harriet Taylor (later Harriet Taylor Mill). Taylor herself published relatively little, but her impact on John Stuart Mill's works was enormous. Mill himself wrote in a highly Romantic vein that when two persons are so close in spirit and mind and spend so much time together conversing on topics of interest to both, then "it is of little consequence in respect to the question of originality, which of them holds the pen." Mill dedicated *On Liberty* to her, calling it "our joint production."

20-2c Nationalism

Like liberalism, **nationalism** underwent profound changes as a political philosophy in the course of the nineteenth century. Before 1848, nationalism was generally associated with liberalism and democracy. In the second half of the century, nationalism became more and more closely aligned with conservative forces. The realignment of nationalism after 1848 reflects its success, and our present-day acceptance of the **nation-state** (in principle, at least) as the political norm is part of this triumph.

Key Terms: Nation and State To understand the political ideology that nationalists propagated, two often-confusing terms need to be distinguished: *nation* and *state*. In English, as in French, these words are often used as synonyms. In most of Europe, however, they are entirely different concepts. Indeed, in most European languages it is impossible to confuse the two: German, for example, distinguishes *Staat* ("state") and *Volk* ("nation").

The state is easiest to define: It is a political entity that levies taxes; finances an army and a state bureaucracy; issues passports; and demands certain obligations of its citizens such as military service, payment of taxes, and obedience to laws. In the classic phrase of the German sociologist Max Weber, the state "holds the monopoly on legitimate violence." Examples of present-day states include Japan, Germany, the Russian Federation, Zambia, Israel, and the United States. It is an example of the linguistic confusion in English mentioned above that the so-called United Nations is in fact an organization of independent *states*.

While states are political units, the term *nations* refers to groups of people bound together by common language, culture, religion, history, ancestry—or some combination of these factors. The Romantics glorified the distinctive qualities of each nation, rejecting the idea that any one nation had the right to consider its language or culture better than any other. In the nineteenth century, one of the most important markers for claiming nationhood was ethnic and

---

utilitarianism Practical philosophy, usually associated with Jeremy Bentham (1748–1832), whose goal was the greatest happiness for the greatest number of people.

universal suffrage Right to vote for everyone.

John Stuart Mill (1806–1873) Liberal philosopher who supported universal suffrage, including for women; son of James Mill and author of *On Liberty and Utilitarianism*.

nationalism Political ideology arising in the late eighteenth century that demanded that the nation (a group of people) have control of its own state.

nation-state Independent political unit, usually dominated by one culture or ethnicity, in which the ultimate political legitimacy rests with the people (the nation).

linguistic. Thus, Germans—like the Grimm brothers—championed their own language as the element that made them a single national group, despite the fact that they lived in dozens of separate states. German nationalists in Vienna, Munich, Hamburg, or Berlin all demanded a united Germany. Similarly, Italian nationalists in Rome, Palermo, Venice, and Turin wanted to bring all Italians together in one political unit: Italy.

Nationalism in Eastern Europe In central and eastern Europe there were nations that lacked states altogether. Congress Poland was not truly independent of Russia, and Poles lived elsewhere outside of the Kingdom of Poland, in Russia, Austria, and Prussia. Polish nationalists demanded that all Poles live together in a single independent Polish state. At least Poles had the historical memory of a strong Polish state; many nations, such as Latvians, Ukrainians, and Romanians, lacked even that.

On a practical level, it was often difficult to decide just where a given nation's boundaries lay, and nations did not usually live in compact, easily defined regions. The people now known as Belarusians and Ukrainians were considered by the Russian government to be branches of the Russian nation. There was considerable debate on whether they could, or should, be considered separate nations, as they are today. It was also debated whether Croats were a nation or should join an "Illyrian" or **Yugoslav** nation with Serbs, who spoke the same language but followed a different religion. Hence, nationalism pulled in opposite directions. Even as it called for members of a nation to live together in one state, it threatened the territorial integrity of such multinational states as the Russian, Habsburg, and Ottoman Empires.

Nationalists also faced difficulties created by class. In this period, some nationalities consisted almost exclusively of peasants, with the upper classes belonging to a different national group. Such was the case for Latvians, whose landlords were German. And there remained the problem of where to put the Jews, who in the context of east-central Europe, at least, certainly fit the criteria of a separate nation with their distinct language (Yiddish), religion, culture, and forms of everyday life. Where—and even whether—Jews would fit in the emerging nation-states of Europe would be known in the late nineteenth century as the Jewish question. Before 1848, however, these practical difficulties were rarely considered. Nationalists overwhelmingly felt that national

liberation would lead to cooperation among different ethnic groups. Like the liberals (and most nationalists were liberals), nationalists were optimistic about human nature, predicting that education and economic development would help put an end to strife and wars.

Before 1848, nationalism often did not always take a specifically political form. At this point, nationalists emphasized the need to develop the nation's culture and language and worked to expand national consciousness—that is, the feeling of belonging to a nation. In the early nineteenth century, most Europeans, aside from a thin (though growing) stratum of educated people, lacked strong national consciousness: Their identity was based rather on belonging to a religion and social group (peasant, noble, artisan, and so on) and having origins in a certain village or town. They often did not think much about the language they spoke, as they had no experience with foreigners. The concept that a peasant speaking some form of German in, say, Bavaria, belonged to the same nation as the king of Prussia would have been completely incomprehensible to these people. Nationalists set out to change this mind-set.

Jacob and Wilhelm Grimm were liberal nationalists. So was **Johann Gottfried von Herder**, a German who spent much of his life in Riga on the Baltic. Herder wrote widely on the philosophy of history, language, and literature and insisted that all cultures and languages have something to add to world culture and world history. All ethnic groups, Herder insisted, should develop their own culture, enrich their own language, and create their own literature. In this way, Herder argued, Latvians and Estonians could develop a linguistic culture every bit as valuable as that of the English or French.

Just as Herder demanded that the German language be treated on an equal footing with French or English, later in the nineteenth century, young Lithuanians would refuse to use Polish, Czechs would reject German, and Jews would insist on using Yiddish or, even more radically, Hebrew in daily life. In his own way, Herder was an individualist Romantic challenging the universalist assumptions of the Enlightenment. He was both a nationalist and a democrat, arguing for equal rights and respect not just for individuals, but for entire cultures.

Nationalism contained in its very essence a strong democratic element. For nationalists, political legitimacy arose out of the unity of the state with the nation. The term *nation-state* describes this unity. For this reason, politics must be influenced by the sentiments of the nation as a whole. Obviously, very few of those in power in the early nineteenth century could accept such an ideology. Kings might claim to rule for the good of their people, but they rarely welcomed the people's influence in making policies. Nationalists and liberals thus shared an interest in breaking down the royal status quo. Conversely, kings and conservatives like Metternich saw in nationalism one of their greatest enemies.

Yugoslav (literally, "south Slav") Group of related languages and ethnicities, including Slovenes, Croats, Serbs, and sometimes Macedonians and Bulgarians.

Jacob and Wilhelm Grimm (1785–1863, 1786–1859) German linguists famous for their collections of fairy tales and monumental dictionary of the German language.

Johann Gottfried von Herder (1744–1803) German critic and historian who urged small nations to develop their language and culture.

Jacob Grimm Writes a Foreword to the *German Dictionary*

Before the mid-nineteenth century, the German language suffered from an inferiority complex. Even the celebrated Prussian king Frederick the Great had preferred speaking French over his native German. Most educated Europeans knew little about German literature and culture. And even Germans themselves were not always certain about the correct usage and pronunciation of their language—indeed, often there was no single standard language to guide them, only dozens of dialects.

The Grimm brothers set out to change this situation. They worked to establish a standardized form of German that everyone could accept as "correct." Part of this enterprise was the publishing of a mammoth dictionary. The dictionary would have two main purposes: to demonstrate the richness of the German tongue and to standardize usage and spelling of German words. This text is taken from the foreword to the Grimm brothers' *German Dictionary*.

❶ Grimm uses words like *treasure, shrine, sublime monument*. Why do you suppose language is so precious for him as a German? Do you think someone from France or England would find language so important at this time? Why or why not?

❷ Grimm calls language a "mystery" and speaks of the "common folk." How do these two concepts fit into the ideas of Romanticism and nationalism?

❸ Why does Grimm claim that the "endurance of your nation" depends on holding fast to the German language? What does he mean by "nation?" What other European ethnic groups might place similar emphasis on the development of their language?

❹ Look at Map 20.1 at the beginning of the chapter. How do the geographical limits of the German nation mentioned by Grimm differ from the area where German is spoken today? What happened to bring about this change?

What is the purpose of a dictionary?

❶ It should establish a shrine to the language, preserve its treasure intact, open up the language to everyone. The written word, like the honeycomb, grows and becomes a sublime monument for the folk whose past and present are tied up with it.

❷ Language is known by everyone and is at the same time a mystery. Just as language powerfully attracts the scholar, so too do common folk feel an affinity and interest toward it. "What is that word I can't think of right now?" "There must be better ways of expressing this—let's look it up."

Beloved German compatriots, no matter what your religion or country, come together in the open halls of your ancient ancestral tongue! **❸** Sanctify it and hold fast to language; the strength and endurance of your nation depends on it. **❹** The German language still reaches beyond the Rhine to Alsace and Lorraine, north to Schleswig-Holstein, on the Baltic to Riga and Reval (Tallinn), beyond the Carpathians to Transylvania. And for you, too, German émigrés beyond the salty sea, this book will bring wistful yet pleasant thoughts of your homeland's language.

Source: From the preface to Grimms' *Wörterbuch* (published in 1838).

20-3 Political Pressures on the Continent

>> **How did nationalist ideology affect politics during this era?**

>> **Where, and why, did liberal ideas succeed in this era? Where, and why, were they suppressed?**

These new political ideologies of conservatism, liberalism, and nationalism had a direct impact on politics in continental Europe. Conservatism was the driving principle at the Congress of Vienna, but even where monarchs were restored, concessions were made to liberalism in the form of constitutions and elected legislatures. In France, the restored Bourbon king, Charles X, was overthrown by a middle-class revolt in 1830. In Russia, Tsar Nicholas I's conservative regime refused to allow any kind of political reform. But even there and in the Ottoman Empire, nationalist movements challenged the authority of the tsar and sultan by demanding political and cultural rights for specific nations. Across the continent, the growing influence of liberal and nationalist ideas caused kings and emperors to sit uncomfortably on their thrones.

20-3a Restoration and Liberal Revolt in France

The French Revolution and the guillotining of Louis XVI changed French politics forever. Even conservatives like Metternich and Talleyrand at the Congress of Vienna recognized this fact. Thus, they did not attempt to restore the absolutist monarchy of 1788. Instead, they put in place a system that kept most power in royal hands but also allowed some political participation for the wealthiest (and, they hoped, most conservative) elements of French society.

Charles X (r. 1824–1830) French king renowned for his refusal to compromise with modern political ideas, swept from power by the July Revolution of 1830.

Louis Philippe (r. 1830–1848) French constitutional monarch, known as the "bourgeois king" for his unpretentious lifestyle and political connections with the bourgeoisie.

Restoring Monarchy: Louis XVIII The new French king was Louis XVIII, younger brother of the ill-fated Louis XVI. Louis XVIII did not rule as an absolute monarch: he had to share power with a legislature. Louis was a narrow-minded and selfish person whose obesity and atrocious table manners made a horrible impression on Parisian society. He was also a terrible politician. In a few months, he had so alienated the political elite that when Napoleon reappeared on the scene, having escaped from Elba in March 1815, the entire Bourbon court fled. No one was willing to take up arms in defense of Louis XVIII.

Luckily for Louis, Napoleon was soon defeated by the Allies at Waterloo, and Louis returned to Paris. For the next decade and a half, French politics was dominated by conservative royalist policies under Louis and his successor, Charles X. Under pressure from Britain and Russia, whose troops were occupying Paris at the time, Louis allowed more moderates into the legislature. In 1818, France paid off its war indemnity, foreign troops left Paris. Thus, only a few years after Napoleon's defeat, for all practical purposes France was once again accepted as a fully legitimate Great Power in the Concert of Europe.

The following decade was a period of calm and growing prosperity. The royalists aimed to restore the Catholic Church to dominance in French society, roll back the revolutionary changes of the previous decades, and combat the specter of "democracy" (at this point the word nearly always had a negative connotation, suggesting mob rule). The French liberals were hindered by a lack of effective leadership and by the vivid memories of chaos and bloodshed during the revolutionary period.

Reaction and Discontent: Charles X In 1824, Louis XVIII died. The new king was his younger but already elderly brother, **Charles X**, who was intent on restoring royal absolutism. His coronation at Rheims was a medieval extravaganza; more seriously threatening to the interests of the middle class were his plans to give financial compensation to émigrés who had lost property during the revolutionary years. Other laws considerably tightened censorship and threatened those guilty of sacrilege with severe punishments, even death.

Tensions between Charles X and the Parliament came to a head in 1830, when elections failed to secure a majority for Charles's supporters. Instead of compromise, Charles chose the path of direct confrontation—in effect, a royal coup d'état. He dissolved the legislature and prepared a new electoral law that would deprive even the wealthy bourgeoisie of the vote. This was too much. Led by the brilliant journalist Adolphe Thiers, the liberals demanded a truly constitutional monarchy and the replacement of Charles X by his cousin, the Duke of Orléans. Faced with barricades, street fighting, and a clear lack of broad support, Charles X abdicated in favor of his grandson and left France to spend the last half-dozen years of his life in Prague. Thus began the reign of the "bourgeois king" **Louis Philippe**—so-called for modest habits and reliance on middle-class political support—which would last for almost twenty years.

20-3b Nationalist Movements in Belgium, Italy, and Germany

In France, nationalism played very little role in politics. After all, the French nation and the French state were closely identified with each other, with non-French ethnic groups such as Basques, Bretons, and Catalans living far from the capital and not politically organized. In other parts of Europe, however, nationalism was often the single greatest rallying cry for change of the political status quo.

Nationalism Creates Belgium Just to the north of France, nationalism provided the driving force for a revolution in Belgium in 1830. At the Congress of Vienna, the Belgian provinces had been united with the Netherlands. Both economically and religiously, however, these southern provinces differed significantly from Holland. The Belgian provinces were rich in coal, and the textile industry in this region had always been closely linked with England. By 1830, this region was, after England, the most industrialized area in Europe. The Belgian provinces were also predominantly Catholic—unlike the much more Calvinist north—and in great part did not use the Dutch (or Flemish) language, but French.

Discontent with rule from Amsterdam broke into open insurrection in Brussels in late August 1830. When the Dutch king William I was unable to restore order, the Congress System went into action, and the Great Powers called an international conference to decide the fate of the Belgian provinces. The British and French decided to support Belgian independence. The international agreement of 1831 made Belgium a constitutional monarchy, with Leopold of Saxe-Coburg (related not only to German royalty but also to the British ruling house) as its first king. The Great Powers also decreed that Belgium would always remain neutral in international disputes. The creation of Belgium was a triumph for liberal nationalist forces.

Italian Nationalism: Aspirations for Unity Elsewhere liberal nationalists fared less well. In Italy, underground nationalist organizations like the radical *carbonari* opposed clericalism and the conservative order. In 1832, **Giuseppe (jew-SEP-ee) Mazzini** called for all Italians to unite and create a liberal nation-state. In a famous appeal, he urged liberal Italians to form Young Italy—"a brotherhood of Italians who believe in a law of *progress* and *duty*, and are convinced that Italy is destined to become one nation." His writings inspired the **Risorgimento (ri-sor-jih-MEN-toh)**, a movement calling for a renewal of Italian culture and nationalism. Mazzini organized Young Italy throughout the Italian peninsula, often in dangerous circumstances, and gathered funds for the cause from wealthy supporters. Though Mazzini's supporters often had to operate in secret to avoid arrest, even in the 1830s the membership of Young Italy was estimated at more than 50,000 people.

One of those inspired by Mazzini's Young Italy was **Giuseppe Garibaldi**. Garibaldi and Mazzini shared more than a first name. They were both born in northern Italy, barely two years apart. Both dedicated their lives to the Italian nation and were key figures in the unification of Italy. But there were also significant differences between them. Mazzini had middle-class origins (his father had been a physician and professor at the University of Genoa); Garibaldi came from a poor fisherman's family. Mazzini was a writer, thinker, and organizer. Garibaldi was an enthusiast, a revolutionary, and a military man. Indeed, few men so resembled the Romantic hero—passionate, handsome, dedicated to a cause—as Garibaldi did. During the 1830s and 1840s, Garibaldi worked as a sailor, fighting for republican liberties in Italy and South America. Only in 1848 would he return from Uruguay to Europe in hopes of overthrowing the conservative order set down at the Congress of Vienna. Garibaldi and Mazzini helped pave the way for future upheavals, but during the 1830s and up to 1848, politics in the Italian principalities remained firmly in the hands of conservatives and clericals.

German Nationalism: Challenging Metternich and Conservatism Like supporters of Mazzini and Garibaldi in Italy, young educated Germans opposed the existing political order, calling for a liberal united Germany. German universities were hotbeds of nationalist thought and agitation. There young men (no women would enter German universities until the twentieth century) gathered together in fraternities to discuss politics over beer. After the patriotic fervor of the Napoleonic Wars—in German known as the Wars of Liberation (from Napoleonic rule)—they found the conservative and antinationalist Congress System intolerable.

Liberal nationalists called the first all-German gathering in October 1817 at the Wartburg, the castle where Luther had translated the New Testament into German. At this

carbonari Members of secret societies existing throughout Europe, but especially in Italy, aiming to fight political reaction and work for liberal political reform.

Giuseppe Mazzini (1805–1872) Italian political thinker and revolutionary who advocated bringing together all Italians under a single republican government.

Risorgimento (from Italian, "to rise again") Era of political and cultural nationalism in early nineteenth-century Italy calling for Italian unification and political liberalization.

Giuseppe Garibaldi (1807–1882) Italian political leader who worked to translate Mazzini's nationalist ideas of Italian unification into reality.

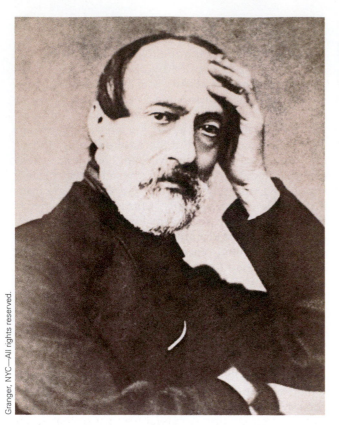

The Liberal Italian Nationalist Giuseppe Mazzini (left) and Radical Giuseppe Garibaldi (right)

Giuseppe Mazzini and Giuseppe Garibaldi both dedicated their lives to the cause of Italian nationalism. Mazzini was the thinker and writer, Garibaldi the fighter and revolutionary.

» *How does their dress in these images reflect their different roles in promoting Italian nationalism?*

» *Judging from these images, which one do you find more trustworthy? More exciting?*

Wartburg Festival, they celebrated German history, life, and culture—Luther's challenge to the pope in 1517, the German victory over Napoleon at Leipzig in 1814, and the beauty of the German language. Speeches called on Germans to transcend the political boundaries that divided them. But transforming speeches into political reality proved difficult.

When the mentally ill young patriot Karl Sand assassinated the reactionary poet August von Kotzebue in 1819, the German authorities moved to restrict the activities of the nationalists. The Carlsbad Decrees of 1819 put severe restrictions on freedom of expression in the press and especially in the universities, which were known for their strong support of nationalist and liberal ideals.

Yet they would not be suppressed. In 1832, at the ruins of a medieval castle in southwest Germany, some twenty to thirty thousand young people gathered and marched, carrying the black-red-gold national banner. At the Hambach Festival, named after the castle where they gathered, German patriotic youth called for national liberation: Both from foreign influences—from French culture—but even more importantly from the conservative policies of Metternich. As in Italy, these young radicals organized themselves into a group loosely called Young Germany. And as in the Italian case, Metternich worried about the appeal of these liberal nationalist groups and set his police to work gathering information about their subversive actions. It was in this repressive atmosphere that the Grimm brothers, who shared many of the ideals of Young Germany, were harassed and ultimately dismissed from their jobs.

20-3c National Liberation Movements in the Balkans

The Ottoman sultan officially still ruled over most of the **Balkan Peninsula**, from the Adriatic Sea to the borders of Austria-Hungary, but local elites held most of the power. These elites were more often

Wartburg Festival Patriotic meeting at Wartburg castle in central Germany in 1817 promoting German national and liberal ideals.

Balkan Peninsula Region between the Black and Adriatic Seas where present-day Bulgaria, Serbia, and Greece are located.

Greek than Turkish in culture, though, in some areas, Slavic-speaking Muslims held local control. By the 1790s, many were unhappy with Ottoman rule, with its high taxes, general lawlessness, and the arbitrary behavior of troops and local officials.

Complicating the political situation was competition among the extremely diverse ethnic and religious groups who made their home in the Balkans. Greeks, Romanians, "Turks" (as all Muslims tended to be called), Germans, Hungarians, and many groups of Slavic peoples lived in close proximity. By faith, the population was Roman Catholic, Orthodox Christian, Muslim, and Jewish, with religion playing a central role in national identity. For example, Croats and Serbs spoke the same language: It was their religion (Catholic or Orthodox, respectively) that divided them. The Muslims of the Balkan Peninsula—who numbered in the hundreds of thousands—were often mistrusted by the nationalists and in many cases fled as nationalists gained power. Though small in numbers, Jews in the Balkans were significant in the region's commerce and trade. Most Balkan Jews traced their roots to the expulsion of Jews from Spain in 1492 and continued to speak Ladino, a version of Spanish written in Hebrew letters.

Nationalism not only presented a huge challenge for the Ottoman overlords; it also threatened to destabilize traditional life entirely. As throughout eastern Europe, nationalists formed a quite small group of educated, relatively privileged individuals who dedicated their lives to the struggle for rights on behalf of the entire Serbian, Romanian, or Greek nations. These first nationalists were fervently concerned with developing their own culture, and especially their language.

In the early nineteenth century, the languages spoken in the Balkan Peninsula were mainly peasant tongues, lacking many words and expressions necessary to express abstract concepts and to carry out modern scientific research. More crucial still, these languages were seldom written and were not standardized. Each tongue had many local dialects, and speakers of different dialects often had great difficulty understanding one another. Hence the early Balkan nationalists were obliged to develop their program on at least two fronts: the cultural (to develop a modern standardized written language and literature) and the political (to gain their own state or autonomy).

Nationalists' programs also had a social component. Elites often differed in ethnicity and religion from the peasant majority. In many regions, such as the future Yugoslavia and Bulgaria, Muslim landlords and officials ruled over Christian peasants. Thus nationalists combined demands for political independence, cultural rights, and social development of the impoverished masses.

Serbia Nationalist aspirations first came to a head in the Pashalik ("district") of Belgrade, where discontent with Ottoman rule among Serbs ran high. Decades of struggle against Ottoman rule dominated by two Serbian families, the Karadjordević and Obrenović, culminated in the latter family gaining in 1815 the title of supreme prince of Serbia from the sultan. Although Serbia officially remained under Ottoman rule, for most practical purposes, local affairs in the Pashalik of Belgrade were now in the hands of Serbs. Official independence came in 1833, along with an expansion of the borders of Serbia and the establishment of the Obrenović dynasty on the Serbian throne. For the next century, descendants of the two original Serbian rebels, Karadjordje and Miloš Obrenović, would occupy the Serbian (and later Yugoslav) thrones.

Romania To the east of Belgrade, in the Danubian provinces of Walachia and Moldavia (now in Romania), an impoverished peasantry was ruled by a corrupt Greek upper class. The Greek middle class joined Romanian landlords and peasants in an 1821 revolt that was based on a general call for justice and an end to oppression—and not on specific Greek or Romania ethnic demands. The rebels hoped for Russian assistance, but Tsar Nicholas I was too much of a traditional conservative to support the nationalist cause. The weakness of the Romanian national movement enabled the Ottoman army to crush the rebellion. Although the revolt did not bring independence to the provinces, it did strengthen the position of local (Romanian) nobles, who replaced Greeks in high church and administrative offices. Full autonomy was attained in 1829, and in February 1862 the modern state of Romania was created, officially still under Ottoman control but in practical terms an independent constitutional monarchy. The choice of the name Romania underscored the new state's connection to classical civilization and the European mainstream.

Greece Nationalist sentiments also gained ground in the Greek provinces of the Ottoman Empire. Greek nationalists took pride in the heritage of classical Greece, though the language of Plato and Aristotle had splintered into a bewildering array of mutually incomprehensible dialects, their speakers divided by mountainous terrain. The question of what form of Greek to adopt as the official, standard tongue continued to plague Greeks long after political independence had been won. Further complicating matters was the fact that Greek merchants lived all around the Black Sea, including in territory ruled by the Russian tsar.

The Greek War of Independence broke out in April 1821. Greek independence fighters attacked both Ottoman authorities and local Muslims.

Christian atrocities were matched by Ottoman reprisals, including the slaughter of thousands of Greeks on the island of Chios and the hanging of the Greek Orthodox patriarch. Reports in the European press of Ottoman atrocities (Christian atrocities against Muslims were generally ignored) forced the Concert of Europe to intervene in support of the Greeks.

England's Romantic poet Lord Byron and other idealists set off for Greece to fight for Greek independence, often—like Byron—sacrificing their lives. The rebellion ended with a treaty signed in London that created an autonomous (but not independent) Greek state. The new state proved unworkable, and in 1830—in another Concert of Europe action—France and Russia established Greek independence. Greece, like Belgium, was to be a constitutional monarchy, and Prince Otto of Bavaria became its first king. The new Greek state was small, impoverished, and lacked a common language, administration, or educational system. The Greek nationalists had their state; they now had to create the Greek nation.

Erich Lessing/Art Resource, NY

Eugène Delacroix's *Liberty Leading the People*, 1830
Possibly the most famous image of "Marianne," the embodiment of the French revolution or, indeed, of the French nation itself. Notice her headgear, which resembles the Phyrgian Cap (from the French Revolution) and her "apparel dysfunction" as she enthusiastically leads rebels forward. Compare the dress of people in this painting with those in the painting of the Congress of Vienna that appears earlier in this chapter.

❯❯ *How is social class reflected in apparel in both cases?*

❯❯ *Would you say that this painting glorifies revolution? Why or why not?*

20-3d Autocracy in Russia

While liberal and nationalist ideologies grew in strength throughout much of Europe, Russia's rulers did what they could to insulate their empire from such ideas. After Napoleon's invasion of Russia, Tsar Alexander I became mystical and suspicious of change. Meanwhile, Russian society—at least at the educated upper levels—did not stagnate. Young Russian officers who had participated in the campaign against Napoleon returned home from Paris with new liberal ideas. They desired greater influence in the politics of their native land. Some even spoke of constitutions and legislatures, though censorship prevented open discussion of such revolutionary ideas.

The Decembrist Revolt
When Alexander I died in 1825, these dissatisfied Russian liberals decided it was time to act, especially as the question of who should replace Alexander on the throne was confusing. He had left no male heirs, and by law his eldest brother, Constantine, should have succeeded him. But Constantine had given up his right to be tsar when he married a woman not of royal blood, though curiously his renunciation of the throne had never been made public. Most Russians were unaware that the younger brother Nicholas was in line to be tsar.

In this confused situation, conspirators aimed to seize power in the name of Constantine and demand a constitution for Russia. But Nicholas was well informed of their plans. These liberal revolutionaries, who have gone down in history as the **Decembrists**, called on the army not to swear allegiance to Nicholas. The Decembrist-led rebels were surrounded by troops loyal to Nicholas on the banks of the Neva River in St. Petersburg. After several hours of fruitless negotiations, Nicholas gave the order to open fire, and the revolt disintegrated on the spot.

The conspirators were soon arrested, tried, and exiled to Siberia or executed. The Decembrists quickly entered into Russian liberal and radical

Decembrists Supporters of liberal reforms in Russia whose plot was crushed by Nicholas I in December 1825.

mythology as the "first Russian revolutionaries," but the practical effect of their revolt was negative. Nicholas had always been suspicious of liberalism, and indeed of any abstract political ideologies, and now his worst fears were confirmed. His rule would be marked by a complete rejection of compromise with these new ideologies. Nicholas insisted that the Russian empire would remain an **autocracy** and that the tsar alone would decide the country's political future.

Russia's Polish Question Nowhere was the contrast between liberal nationalism and the forces of conservatism so stark as in Russian Poland. It was perhaps inevitable that the Russian autocracy would clash with the Polish elite in the autonomous Congress Poland ruled by Nicholas I, where many Poles believed that the new tsar was violating their constitutional rights. A rebellion against Russian rule broke out in Warsaw in November 1830, but the rebels, counting on French help for their independence struggle, miscalculated badly. The French were unwilling to provide more than verbal support, and, after initial Polish successes, the Russian army crushed the rebellion. Most Polish peasants refused to support the rebels, seeing in them not national kin but hated landlords. Nicholas abolished the Polish legislature and army and incorporated the Polish provinces more closely into the Russian empire. But the Polish national spirit remained unvanquished, celebrated in the poetry of Mickiewicz and the music of Chopin. Polish patriots continued to sing the now forbidden Polish national anthem, dating from the Napoleonic period, in secret: "Poland is not yet lost/ As long as we are alive."

Tsar Nicholas I: The Apogee of Autocracy The Polish uprising confirmed Nicholas's hatred for political abstractions and strengthened his determination to base his rule on tradition and the army. He was never so happy as when inspecting his troops, and woe to any soldier found with a button unshined or a medal out of place. At one such review, it was said, the tsar was considerably vexed because while the soldiers were lined up in exact rows, their continued breathing upset perfect symmetry. Nicholas wanted the entire country to be just as orderly as his army on the parade grounds.

To prevent the spread of liberal or revolutionary ideas (Nicholas made little distinction between the two), the tsar created a secret police force—the Third Section of the Tsar's Chancellery. Censorship was tightened, reaching truly paranoid levels in the late 1840s, when the phrase "free air" in a cookbook was struck as possibly subversive and censors examined musical scores for signs of secret revolutionary codes.

Yet foreign influence and change could not be kept out of Russia. It was during Nicholas's reign that there occurred what one historian has called a "parting of ways" between Russian educated society and the Russian government. The Russian **intelligentsia** emerged, a social group whose identity derived not from birth (unlike the nobility or peasantry) but from education and a desire to work for the good of Russia and the Russian people. Such aspirations brought these reformers into direct conflict with the inefficient but all-powerful Russian state—and Nicholas's secret police.

After the midcentury, the Russian intelligentsia would split into liberals who wished to reform Russia and revolutionaries who saw the present system as completely rotten and worked for its complete destruction. Nicholas was successful in driving dissent underground during his reign. In the long run, however, his refusal to accommodate new ideas or to share power even on a limited level alienated most educated Russians from their rulers and helped pave the way for a far more destructive revolution.

20-4 Reform in Great Britain

» **Why did the British establishment agree to political reform?**

» **What specific liberal reforms allowed Britain to avoid revolutionary outbreaks?**

While Russia staunchly opposed any change in the first half of the nineteenth century, the course of political reform in Great Britain presents a strong contrast. The British middle classes—stronger here in numbers and wealth than anywhere else in Europe—gained significant political rights. These wealthy merchants and industrialists demanded and gained a voice in British politics. In triumphs for political and economic liberalism, the parliamentary system was reformed, suffrage considerably broadened, and restrictions on religious minorities reduced.

Even in Britain, many groups remained outside the political system. Reform barely touched the lives of Britain's peasants and factory workers, an impoverished class that expanded rapidly as Britain industrialized. Living and laboring in dangerous conditions, workers sought to organize to improve their lives, but

autocracy Form of government headed by a ruler whose power is not limited by constitutional or other political restraints, as in Russia before 1917.

intelligentsia Social class of educated, progressive individuals wanting liberal reforms in Russia; later also applied to Russian revolutionaries.

their efforts were opposed by a government committed to a free-market economy. Still, in Great Britain, the existing order was able to bend and modify itself to accommodate new ideologies and social classes, and in the second half of the century most worker demands would be realized. By agreeing to timely reforms, Great Britain avoided the social and political turmoil that took place in other parts of Europe.

20-4a Conservative Domination and Reform

At the beginning of the nineteenth century, political participation in Great Britain was limited to an extremely small group of men (women would continue to be shut out for another century). Both political parties—the conservative Tories and the more liberal Whigs—were dominated by the aristocracy, but the Whigs were more sympathetic to including wealthy middle-class men in the political system. King George III was still on the throne, though his off-and-on insanity meant that his son, crowned **George IV** in 1820, often carried out his father's duties. Ruling in his own right, George IV discredited the Crown (and thereby played into the hands of political reformers) by his immoral behavior, including his notorious attempt to divorce his estranged wife, Caroline, and his unwillingness to allow her to be crowned queen.

George IV (r. 1820–1830) King of Great Britain and Ireland, hated for his sexual immorality; most notorious for his failed attempt to divorce his wife, Caroline, in 1820.

Corn Laws Series of laws passed in 1815 that prevented the import of grain ("corn") until prices reached a certain (high) level; kept grain and bread prices high; repealed in 1846.

Peterloo massacre Repression of workers' gathering at St. Peter's Fields outside Manchester in 1819, leaving eleven killed and hundreds injured.

Catholic Emancipation Act Act of 1829 allowing Catholics to be elected to Parliament and to serve in most public offices in Great Britain.

CONNECTIONS: From ancient times to the present day, political figures have come under scrutiny due to perceived or real sexual excesses. George IV gained notoriety by his endless flirtations with numerous women, both married and unmarried. In the first years of the Roman Republic, Julius Caesar divorced his wife just on the possibility that she may have been complicit in the affections of a political rival, Clodius (see Section 5-4b Late Republican Politics for more on the rise of Julius Caesar). One wouldn't have to look far to find recent examples in the United States. Could it be that sexual morality has declined over the ages or that such private behavior is almost impossible to hide in the modern world? One thing is certain: the mixing of sex and politics has a long history—and quite likely, a long future ahead.

The first decade after 1815 was dominated by the Tories, who set a very conservative course by passing the **Corn Laws**. These laws, which made the import of cheap grain ("corn" in British English) into Great Britain almost impossible, were designed to reduce British dependence on foreign foodstuffs, but they had a disastrous effect on the poor. By keeping the price of grain—and thus bread—high, they impoverished working people, who had to spend most of their minimal wages on food. The high cost of bread also led to protests and violence. In Manchester, which tripled in size between 1801 and 1831 (to a population of 238,000) as peasants from the countryside took jobs in new textile factories, a series of public meetings culminated in 1819 with the notorious **Peterloo massacre**. A cavalry charge dispersing the more than 60,000 people gathered to petition Parliament for political representation and repeal of the Corn Laws ended with eleven dead and hundreds injured. The government's answer to the public uproar after Peterloo was to restrict civil liberties and free speech. In 1824, however, Parliament repealed the Combination Acts, which had forbidden workers from forming unions. Strikes were still illegal, but the important right of labor to organize had been won.

Broadening Politics: Including Catholics, Dissenters, and Jews The Tory administration also moved toward fulfilling the liberal principle that religion should not bar an individual from full participation in political and social life. In 1829, with the **Catholic Emancipation Act**, Catholics and dissenters (non-Anglican Christians) gained the right to participate in Parliament and to occupy all public offices in the realm, with the exception of lord chancellor of England and lord lieutenant of Ireland. The practical effect of this measure was not immediately great—very few Catholics in England and Ireland were wealthy enough to qualify for the vote—but the measure was significant as a further broadening of religious toleration in Britain.

English Jews also gained rights in this period. The first bill for Jewish emancipation (that is, equal rights with Christians) passed the House of Commons in 1833 but was defeated in the House of Lords. However, individual Jews were knighted (Moses Montefiore, in 1837), admitted to the bar, and elevated into the hereditary nobility (Isaac Goldsmid, in 1841). The process of Jewish emancipation was completed in 1858 when Lionel de Rothschild was—after more than a decade of debate—allowed to take the oath on a Hebrew Bible and take his seat in the House of Commons.

20-4b The Reform Bill of 1832 and the Abolition Act of 1833

King George IV died in 1830 and was succeeded by his son William IV. In the parliamentary elections that, by tradition, accompanied the ascension of a new king, the position of the more liberal Whigs and their middle-class supporters was strengthened by the example of France, where the conservative Bourbon dynasty had been ousted, replaced by a new political order under the "bourgeois king" Louis Philippe. Britain's captains of industry likewise wanted to exert political influence, arguing for a government that would support the interests of manufacturing and trade rather than representing only landowners and landowning interests.

To accommodate the wealthy manufacturers, parliamentary districts, unchanged since the seventeenth century, had to be modernized. Since that time, the huge shifts in population that accompanied industrialization had created entire districts controlled by a few large landowners (**pocket boroughs**) and depopulated districts where only a few dozen people lived (**rotten boroughs**), while large industrial cities like Manchester and Birmingham had no representatives in Parliament at all.

Once in power, the Whigs pushed the **Reform Bill of 1832** through Parliament. Though suffrage was still tied to property ownership, the new law increased the number of voters by 50 percent and significantly redistributed parliamentary representation to benefit the heavily populated new industrial cities. In short, the Reform Bill of 1832 was a triumph for English liberalism, the first step in a gradual expansion of the political system set in motion by an enlightened class of relatively privileged individuals. Men espousing the liberal ideals of constitutional rule, free trade, and a gradually expanding electorate now increasingly took seats in Parliament. Still, only one in five Englishmen (and, of course, no women at all) could vote. Reform bills in 1867 and 1884 further extended the franchise, but not until the twentieth century was universal suffrage—first for men, then for all men and women—achieved.

A Liberal Triumph: Abolition of Slavery Liberals had long demanded the abolition of slavery. British law did not recognize slavery within England, Scotland, Ireland, and Wales, and in 1807 Parliament had forbidden British vessels and captains from engaging in the slave trade. But in demanding the complete abolition of slavery, liberals found themselves in a perplexing ideological position. The demand for human liberty was, of course, central to liberalism. But so was the protection of private property, and slaves were, besides being human beings, also a form of property. In 1833, this contradiction was overcome when Parliament passed the Slavery Abolition Act, which abolished slavery throughout the British Empire. At the same time, the enormous amount of £20 million was appropriated by Parliament to pay slave owners for their freed "property." In this way, British liberals succeeded in extending basic human liberty to slaves while compensating their former owners.

20-4c The Repeal of the Corn Laws

The expanded Parliament now included middle-class industrialists who opposed the Corn Laws both out of general commitment to free trade and because the higher cost of bread put pressure on the wages they had to pay workers. Two outspoken opponents to the Corn Laws elected to Parliament in the 1840s were John Bright, son of a cotton manufacturer in Lancashire, and **Richard Cobden**, a calico printer from Manchester. Both proponents of laissez-faire economics, they had founded the Anti-Corn Law League in 1838, an effective and well-financed pressure group that rapidly came to exert influence even on the Tory prime minister, Sir Robert Peel. The league was also extremely successful in appealing to the working class with slogans such as "Give Us This Day Our Daily Bread," taken from scripture. The actual repeal of the Corn Laws came, however, as a direct result of one of the most tragic events of the nineteenth century—the **Irish potato famine**.

The Irish Potato Famine Ireland was, at the time, an impoverished and backward colony of England. The landed gentry was almost entirely Protestant, often living far from their property in Dublin or London, while the Catholic peasantry eked out a miserable existence on shrinking plots of land, living entirely on potatoes, a New World vegetable adopted by Irish peasants because it produced more calories per planted acre than any other crop. By 1840, it was clear that the land and people were stretched to their utmost limits and malnutrion was widespread. Then fungus struck the Irish potato crop, wiping out sustenance for

---

pocket boroughs and **rotten boroughs** Electoral districts in Britain that were controlled by a single landowner or where few people lived, respectively, abolished by the 1832 Reform Bill.

Reform Bill of 1832 British reform increasing suffrage and redistributing electoral districts to reflect actual population, thereby giving more representation to industrial cities.

Richard Cobden (1804–1865) English liberal who in 1838 formed the Anti–Corn Law League to fight for free trade in grain.

Irish potato famine Demographic catastrophe in the mid- to late 1840s caused by a fungus infection, or blight, of the Irish peasantry's staple food, the potato.

View of the Great Chartist Meeting on Kennington Common, 1848 (daguerreotype), Kilburn, William Edward (fl.1846–62) / Royal Collection Trust © Her Majesty Queen Elizabeth II, 2017 / Bridgeman Images

View of the Great Chartist Meeting on Kennington Common, 1848

The Chartists pushed for democratic change through legal, non-violent methods in Great Britain. Here we see a huge public meeting of the Chartists, coming together to press for more political rights for the common man.

» *Why might meetings of this kind disturb conservatives?*

» *Judging from the people you see in this image, what social class did most of these individuals belong to?*

millions. The Protestant landowners and English Parliament seemed indifferent to the famine, and from 1845 to the end of the decade, millions in Ireland either starved or left their homes for England or the United States. Around one-third of the Irish population perished or emigrated. To this day, the population of Ireland remains lower than it was two hundred years ago—a fact unparalleled in European demographic history.

In the public mind, the Corn Laws had been a decisive factor in causing the famine by preventing grain imports from abroad. The tragedy thus dealt the Corn Laws a decisive blow, and they were abolished in 1846. This triumph for free trade could not, unfortunately, help the victims of the famine. While grain prices did drop after the abolition of the Corn Laws, not Irish peasants but factory workers in Britain were able to take advantage of cheaper bread.

From 1846 until the First World War, free trade and liberalism dominated British economic policy. Presided over by **Queen Victoria**, the Victorian Age represented the pinnacle of British prosperity and prestige. As the first fully industrialized country,

Queen Victoria (r. 1837–1901) English queen whose reign was a period of British prominence in world politics, the world economy, science, trade, and culture.

Chartism Workers' political movement in Britain, 1838–1848, that demanded a People's Charter guaranteeing universal male suffrage and other reforms.

Great Britain had a significant economic advantage, while other countries—such as the United States, Germany, and Russia—erected trade barriers to protect their own fledgling industries from a flood of cheap British imports. Not until the end of the nineteenth century did the United States and Germany catch up with Britain's industrial head start. The Victorian Age was also the pinnacle of British imperialism. With colonies and dominions in Asia, Africa, and North America, the British were proud to claim that "the sun never sets on the British Empire."

20-4d The Chartist Movement and the Factory Acts

Yet not all of Victoria's subjects were content. The middle classes could point to solid gains in political and economic aspects of their lives, but most industrial workers continued in dangerous jobs for little pay. **Chartism**, a workingmen's reform movement that agitated for increased political rights, translated worker dissatisfaction into political action. The movement took its name from the People's Charter, a document published in 1838 that announced six demands: annual Parliaments, universal male suffrage, voting by secret ballot, the elimination of property requirements for members of Parliament, salaries for members of Parliament, and equal electoral districts.

Using modern techniques of political agitation such as mass meetings, pamphlets, and a popular newspaper, the *Northern Star*, the Chartists took their case to Parliament in the form of a petition with several hundred thousand signatures. Parliament rejected the petition overwhelmingly, and when some of the more radical Chartists spoke of armed resistance, the movement's leadership was arrested and jailed. Thus ended the first Chartist movement. Two more petitions were brought to Parliament—and rejected—in the 1840s; afterward, the movement fell apart.

The Factory Acts Though Chartists appeared to have failed in their efforts to improve the political situation of workers, by the early twentieth century five of their six demands had been met. Perhaps even more important for workers' everyday lives, the government continued to intervene—despite laissez-faire liberalism—to improve conditions in mines and factories, which were revealed in a series of government investigations and reports to be appalling.

A series of **Factory Acts** passed in the first decades of the nineteenth century had intended to restrict child labor but lacked enforcement. In 1833, a new Factory Act ruled that children under nine years of age were not to be employed in textile works and set maximum work hours for workers under eighteen. Most important, these laws were enforced by a newly created factory inspectorate. An 1842 law prohibited women from underground work in the mines. Most pathbreaking of all, an 1847 act forbade women and children from working more than ten hours a day. Government responsibility for regulating the conditions of labor was now firmly established, as the interests of public order and safety triumphed over the interests of the manufacturers. Thus, in England parliamentary rule proved capable of reform and of responding to the needs of the people in time to prevent either the middle-class revolt that changed French politics or the working-class revolution that in the next century would convulse Russia.

> **Factory Acts** British laws of 1833, 1842, and 1847 that limited the number of hours manufacturers could require children and women to work.

CHAPTER Review

Summary

» The period 1814–1847 lacked major upheavals or revolution. We can characterize it as a "breathing space" or rest between the French Revolution/ Napoleonic Era and the 1848 Revolution.

» The major political ideologies of conservatism, liberalism, and nationalism all derived from the French Revolution and were developed further in this period.

» Liberalism opposed rule by monarchs and nobles, advocating instead constitutional rule, parliamentary democracy, and the rule of law.

» Nationalism stressed the need for each nation to have its own state, an inherently democratic ideal. Before 1848, liberalism and nationalism went hand in hand.

» In this period, conservatives like Austria's Metternich and Russia's Tsar Nicholas I continued to hold most political power. In Great Britain, however, gradual reforms pushed by middle-class liberals spread parliamentary representation to large segments of the population.

Chronology

1814–1815	Congress of Vienna restores prerevolutionary rulers [Europe]
1815	Napoleon is defeated at Waterloo [Europe] British Parliament passes Corn Laws [Europe]
1817	Wartburg Festival [Europe]
1818	Mary Wollstonecraft Shelley publishes *Frankenstein* [Europe]
1819	Peterloo massacre in Manchester kills eleven, wounds hundreds [Europe]
1821	Greek War of Independence begins [Europe]
1823	United States issues Monroe Doctrine [Americas]
1825	Nicholas I becomes tsar [Europe]
1828	Noah Webster publishes his *American Dictionary of the English Language* [Americas]
1829	Catholic Emancipation Act furthers religious tolerance in Britain [Europe]
1830	Greece achieves independence [Europe] Revolutions break out in Paris and Brussels [Europe] Death of Simón Bolívar, hero of South American Independence struggle [Americas]
1831	Independent Belgium is established [Europe]
1832	Reform Bill in Britain expands suffrage [Europe] Giuseppe Mazzini forms Young Italy [Europe] Egypt declares independence from the Ottoman Empire [Middle East]
1833	Slavery Abolition Act initiates emancipation of slaves in British Empire [Global] Serbia wins independence [Europe]
1837	Victoria becomes queen of England [Europe]
1838	Grimm brothers begin work on their *German Dictionary* [Europe]
1838	Richard Cobden forms Anti-Corn Law League in Manchester [Europe]
1844	Maori rebellion in New Zealand [Oceania]
1845–1849	Potato famine sweeps Ireland [Europe]
1846	Corn Laws are abolished [Europe]
1847	Factory Act in Britain reduces working hours for women and children [Europe]
1848	Revolutions topple governments from Paris to Budapest [Europe]

Critical Thinking Questions

Take time to pull together all the important information from the chapter by answering the following questions:

The Old Order and New Challenges

» In what ways did the Congress of Vienna stabilize European politics after the Napoleonic period?

» How did the worldview of Romanticism differ from that of the Enlightenment?

The Beginnings of Modern Ideology

» What did Edmund Burke, Joseph de Maistre, and the Russian Slavophiles have in common? How did they differ?

» What similarities in political outlook were shared by liberalism and nationalism in this period?

Political Pressures on the Continent

» Where was nationalism most important in this period? Where least? Why?

» Compare this period in France and Russia. What were some of the major differences between these two states?

Reform in Great Britain

» Why could both conservatives and liberals point to the British system as a political model? What appealed to each?

» How did the repeal of the Corn Laws and the Factory Acts reflect Britain's relatively advanced level of industrialization?

MindTap® is a fully online personalized learning experience built upon Cengage Learning content. MindTap® combines student learning tools—readings, multimedia, activities, and assessments—into a singular Learning Path that guides students through the course and helps students develop the critical thinking, analysis, and communication skills that are essential to academic and professional success.

CHAPTER

21

Industrialization and Society, 1800–1850

Chapter Outline

As you read, consider the following questions:

❯ Why did industrialization first occur in Great Britain?

❯ What were the changes that industrialization caused in economics, everyday life, the environment, society, and politics?

❯ What is the definition of the term "class"? Which groups in society belonged to the working and middle classes?

❯ What were the most important socialist critiques of capitalism and industrialization?

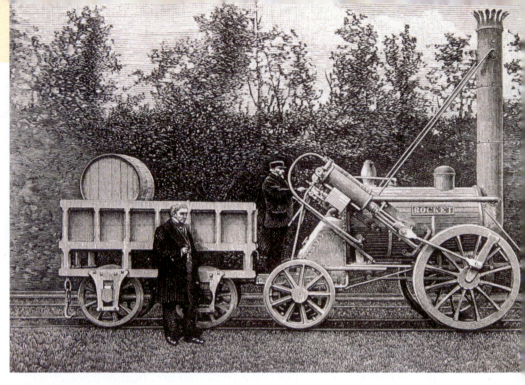

Stephenson's Rocket

Early locomotives resembled steam engines on wheels which, after all, was exactly what they were. One of the earliest, Stephenson's Rocket, built in 1829, was designed to climb hills while towing impressive amounts of freight. At this point, few even conceived the idea of passengers using railroads as transportation.   Danita Delimont/Getty Images

INDUSTRIALIZATION **T**RANSFORMED **E**UROPEAN SOCIETY and everyday life in the course of the nineteenth century. Starting first in Great Britain, industrialization soon took the continent by storm, affecting all segments of society, transforming every aspect of life. Skilled artisans and craftsmen found their jobs threatened by mass production in factories, where dozens and even hundreds of workers labored side by side, doing repetitive and monotonous tasks in dangerous conditions. At the same time, the economic power of the middle classes, from factory owners to professional people, grew rapidly, increasing their political power.

One of the most noticeable changes came from a revolution in transport. Take the "Rocket," illustrated here. One of the first railroad steam engines, when it went into service on the Liverpool and Manchester Railway in 1830, it was considered a technical marvel. The Rocket's design would influence railway locomotives for many decades. With the launch of the Rocket and the railroad between two of England's most important industrial cities, Liverpool and Manchester, the age of rail was born. A locomotive was in essence a steam engine mounted on wheels. The steam engine was key to the industrial revolution, consuming enormous quantities of coal but allowing coal mines to reach deeper into the earth. Besides railroad locomotives, steam power ships made possible much more rapid trips with passengers and freight across the seas.

The Industrial Revolution transformed Europe on various levels. On a physical level, the coal mines, coal-burning factories, and railroad tracks and trestles altered the European landscape. Soot and pollution literally blanketed industrial cities and their outskirts. Other effects were more subtle. Factory owners and other middle-class people came to think of themselves as "self-made"—that is, they perceived their identity as derived from their work, accomplishments, or training. The thousands of men and women congregated in factories also began to perceive themselves differently: as members of a new and potentially powerful working class. In both cases, this class consciousness meant that identity was derived not from birth but primarily from one's position within the economy.

Industrialization revolutionized production, efficiently mass-producing huge numbers of items far more cheaply than could be done by hand. But the wealth produced by industrialization was uneven, and the gap between wealthy industrialists and their workers grew. Reformers fought against terrible working conditions, poverty, and exploitation of the workers by the capitalist system. Other reformers thought that justice for workers could be attained by government intervention, cooperation, and reforms. The Factory Acts in Britain in the 1830s seemed to remedy the worst conditions, and eventually workers' pay also rose. But the socialist Karl Marx argued forcefully that only revolution would end exploitation of the working class and create a truly just and humane society.

In many ways the world we know—running by the clock, fast paced, full of mass-produced consumer goods, accepting constant change as normal—is a direct outcome of the Industrial Revolution, which began in the late eighteenth century and continued throughout the nineteenth century. Industrialization rearranged economies, altered the rhythm of daily life, and changed attitudes, first in Europe and North America, then around the world.

21-1 The Spread of Industrialization

> » How did the process of industrialization differ in Britain and in continental Europe?

> » How did industrialization create class identities?

In Britain, the Industrial Revolution took place over several decades in the late eighteenth century and was fueled by technological innovation and private capital. In other parts of Europe, industrialization came later but often developed even more quickly, pushed along by government investment and subsidies. Technology continued to develop rapidly, and new means of transportation—especially the railroad and steamships—shrank distance and time, encouraging intercontinental trade and migration (see Map 21.1). The revolution in transport also opened the way for worldwide trade, even in fairly inexpensive products, and would help the European powers to establish control over a great deal of the world in the new imperialism.

The initial effects of industrialization were usually horrible—pollution, crowded and unsanitary cities, and the disruption of family life. Peasants had lived by the natural rhythms of the seasons, sunrise, and sunset, but the clock and precisely measured time ruled over the industrial world. By the mid-nineteenth century, some benefits of industrialization were evident—an increase in affordable consumer goods, the growth of middle-class prosperity, and, in some cases, even higher wages for industrial workers. Thus, in just half a century, industrialization altered both lifestyles and attitudes, sometimes positively, often negatively, but always permanently.

21-1a Industrialization on the European Continent

In the late eighteenth century, as Britain's manufactured goods began to enter continental European markets in increasing numbers, European states became alarmed. Believing that a strong economy was the basis of political power, France restricted British imports until the **Eden Treaty** of 1786, after which British cloth swamped the French market.

Eden Treaty Treaty between France and Great Britain in 1786 permitting the import of British manufactured goods into France.

ATLANTIC
OCEAN

North
Sea

KINGDOM OF
SWEDEN AND
NORWAY

Oslo

Stockholm

St. Petersburg

Moscow

Riga

RUSSIAN
EMPIRE

DENMARK · Copenhagen

Baltic
Sea

UNITED KINGDOM
OF GREAT BRITAIN
AND IRELAND

Newcastle

Dublin
IRELAND

Liverpool
Manchester

Leeds

Birmingham

London

Amsterdam

Antwerp

KINGDOM OF THE
NETHERLANDS

Elbe R.

Danzig

Essen
Liège
Cologne

KINGDOM OF PRUSSIA

Berlin

Warsaw

Kiev

Dnieper R.

Göttingen

SAXONY

Luxembourg
Paris

LORRAINE

Seine R.

Frankfurt

Prague

Cracow

Dniester R.

Loire R.

Mulhouse
Le Creusot

FRANCE

ALSACE

Zurich

SWITZERLAND

Munich

Vienna

AUSTRIAN EMPIRE

Buda Pest

Belgrade

Danube R.

Black
Sea

Lyons

Garonne R.

Rhône R.

Turin

Milan
Po R.

Venice

Adriatic Sea

OTTOMAN EMPIRE

Marseilles

KINGDOM OF
PIEDMONT-
SARDINIA

TUSCANY PAPAL
STATES

Istanbul

PORTUGAL

Ebro R.

Madrid

SPAIN

Elba
Corsica
(Fr.)

Rome

Sardinia

KINGDOM
OF THE
TWO SICILIES

Athens

GIBRALTAR
(Gr. Br.)

Mediterranean Sea

Sicily

Malta
(Gr. Br.)

Railroad
Coal field
Industrial area
Scattered ironworks
Textile production
City with population over 500,000

0   200   400 Km.
0   200   400 Mi.

Map 21.1 **Railroads and Industrial Development in Europe in 1850** By 1850 industrialization had spread from western to central Europe, and railroad construction expanded outward from major cities from Moscow to Manchester.

1. Where was industry most developed?
2. What logic lay behind the routes taken by railroad lines? Where was the railroad network most dense and why?
3. Where could you go by railroad in 1850? What regions had the fewest railroads?
4. Which regions in central Europe were most industrialized?

Some French manufacturers responded to the competition by introducing spinning jennies and water frames in local production. Others blamed the failure of French manufacturers to compete on Britain's passion for world economic domination, which French nationalists had always denounced.

Reasons for the Delay of Industrialization on the European Continent

Continental European states soon found that developing their own industries would be more complicated than just copying Britain's model. First, Britain jealously guarded its artisans and inventors, even forbidding them from leaving the country. Furthermore, on the European continent, water transport was less widely available and more expensive than in Britain. Coal was also in short supply. European guilds were stronger, and their members often actively opposed industrialization as a threat to their livelihood. Finally, much of Europe was simply too poor to provide a market for mass-produced industrial goods. In France, where wealth and educational standards rivaled those in Britain, different taxation systems in various provinces and the innumerable tolls that had to be paid when shipping goods across the kingdom severely handicapped commerce. And just as Britain was making its **industrial take-off** in the 1780s and 1790s (see Map 21.2), France exploded in revolution.

On the European continent, industrialization had to wait for the end of the Napoleonic wars in 1815. Even then, few regions had the capital, skilled laborers, and resources required for industrializing. From the 1820s, Belgium, northern France, and western Germany began to experience the economic and social transformations of industrialization. By 1850 industry had spread to central Europe, and in 1851 a railroad connected the two largest Russian cities, St. Petersburg and Moscow. Railroads were built, coal mined, and factories and corporations founded. Despite these developments, most of Europe—in particular, the continent's southern and eastern regions—remained mainly agricultural and without significant industry in 1850. British industry was the most advanced in Europe, and this is reflected in Britain's high degree of urbanization: in 1851 more than half of the English population lived in cities. But by 1850, Britain no longer monopolized European industrial textile production, coal mining, or railroad building.

Industrialization in Belgium

Belgium was the first region on the continent to industrialize. Just across the English Channel, it had long had close commercial ties with Britain, and since the late eighteenth century, British manufactured goods destined for the continent often passed through Belgium. The country also possessed the building blocks of industrialization: good communications by water (to bring raw materials to factories and finished goods to market); raw materials like coal, lumber, and iron ore; a well-trained population with many artisans; and, from 1831, a government favorable to the development of industry. By 1850, Belgium could boast a degree of industrialization unrivaled by any other continental country. At first, Belgian industry concentrated on textiles, but by midcentury a boom in railway building spurred growth in mining and iron production.

Industrialization in France

Industrialization in France followed a different road. As a large and diverse country, quite unlike Belgium, and with its historical suspicion of Britain, France could hardly be expected to follow the British example closely. France did possess the prerequisites for industrialization, such as agricultural efficiency, natural resources including coal and iron, and sophisticated scientists and artisans. For example, French gunsmith Honoré Le Blanc had pioneered the use of **interchangeable parts** in the mid-eighteenth century, and in 1801 inventor **Joseph Marie Jacquard** invented a power loom that could be programmed to produce different patterns of cloth. On the other hand, most French peasants continued to live on their own small farms and were not interested in becoming industrial workers, whereas in England large numbers of landless peasants had little alternative. The French government, again unlike the British, did little to encourage a "pro-industrialization climate"; Le Blanc's innovation of interchangeable parts was not taken up in France and had to wait for the initiative of another inventor, the American Eli Whitney, to be introduced into manufacturing. The size of France and the lack of economical transport delayed industrialization in many regions until the coming of the railroads.

Traditionally, French manufacturing had concentrated on high-quality luxury items like silk, fine carpets, and exquisite furniture. Entrepreneurs and skilled workers in these traditional manufactures were hostile to the idea of mass production, which, they claimed, was capable of producing only cheap and shoddy articles. Angry weavers attacked and destroyed Jacquard's looms. Despite the resistance of skilled artisans, industrialization did advance in France. In the Paris region, modern textile factories were established, and the long-standing silk industry

---

industrial take-off The point at which industrialization continues to grow on its own—that is, becomes self-perpetuating.

interchangeable parts Precision manufacture of identical parts so that if the original part breaks or wears out, it can be replaced.

Joseph Marie Jacquard (1752–1834) French inventor and businessman who used punch cards to "program" complicated weaving styles on the power looms called by his name.

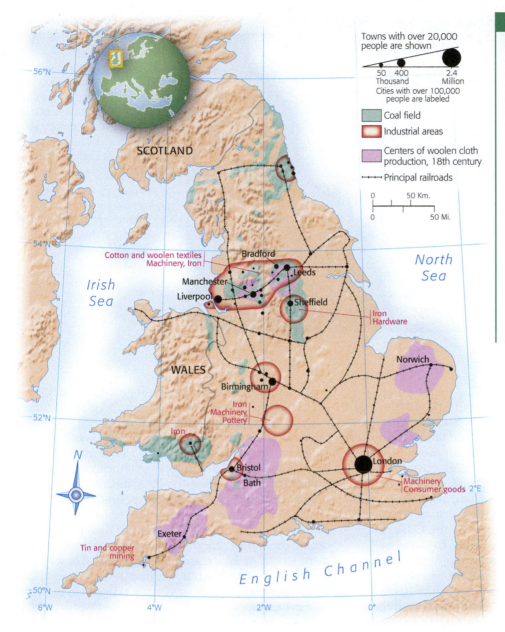

Map 21.2 **Industrialization in England, ca. 1859** By the middle of the nineteenth century, England was heavily industrialized. Most industrial regions were close to the sea or other waterways and near coalfields. In England and throughout Europe, major industrial areas almost always arose on top of major coal reserves.

1. Locate Manchester on the map. What about its location made it a prime industrial site?

2. What does the location of railroads tell us about industrialization here?

in France's second-largest city, Lyon, began to use modern industrial techniques, such as the Jacquard loom. On the whole, however, most French manufacturers continued to produce small amounts of high-quality luxury items rather than the cheap, mass-produced articles of the industrial age.

French industrialization before 1850 was concentrated in **Alsace-Lorraine**, in the northeast, and in the northern part of the country, where coal and iron reserves were located. In the 1830s the first French railroads were built, and in 1842 the government set down a master plan for railroad construction. Private firms built the lines, but with significant government aid and, later, profit guarantees. This cooperation between government and private business would become typical for the construction of railroads from

France to Russia. By 1850, one could go by rail from Paris to Brussels, Frankfurt, Bordeaux, and Marseilles via Lyon. Even greater railroad expansion would come in the second half of the nineteenth century.

Industrialization in the German Lands In the German lands, industry grew on top of coalfields in the **Ruhr** (Roor) and **Saxony** regions, and entrepreneurs built small factories in the

Alsace-Lorraine Region of northeastern France in which French industrialization was concentrated before 1850.

Ruhr Region in western Germany that became a center of industrial production and metal industry.

Saxony Region in southeastern Germany, formerly an independent kingdom, important in German industrialization.

Bradley Coal Mine, near Bilston, England, from 'Cyclopaedia of Useful Arts and Manufactures' by Charles Tomlinson (engraving). English School, (19th century) / Private Collection / Photo © Ken Welsh / Bridgeman Images

Workers Mining Coal

The conditions for coal miners were — and often still are — quite appalling. As we see here, human beings and animals worked together to dislodge coal and bring it to the surface of the mine where it would quickly be used in various steam engines, including those used to pump water out of the damp mines.

❯❯ *Note the rails used to transport the coal out of the mine. What differences can you notice between this early locomotive and later coal-powered locomotives?*

Prussian capital, Berlin. In 1837, August Borsig set up a machine shop there that would become one of the largest locomotive factories in Europe. Ten years later, **Werner Siemens** established a company in Berlin to manufacture telegraph equipment; Siemens remains a major manufacturer of electronic goods in the twenty-first century. Despite the fact that industrialization had come to many German regions in the 1840s, most Germans continued to live in the countryside and earn their livelihood from the soil. In Prussia, less than 10 percent of the population lived in cities larger than 20,000, even in 1849, and only two Prussian cities boasted populations above 100,000.

At the same time, the German Customs Union (**Zollverein** (TSOHL-fer-ayn)), established in 1834, helped push German industrialization forward by enabling industrialists to sell their products freely across a large area. While the Zollverein did not include all German states, it laid the groundwork for an economically and politically united Germany. Economically, it created a market of 26 million potential customers. Railroads followed rapidly. The first German line ran from Nuremberg to Fürth in Bavaria—a distance of only a few kilometers—in 1835, but by 1850, Germany could boast of nearly six thousand kilometers of railroad lines, nearly double that of France. As in France, in central Europe governments promoted railroad building. Often the Prussian, Saxon, or Austrian governments would guarantee profits for a certain stretch of track to the company willing to undertake its construction. Private investors would then provide the capital for railroad building, confident that their investment would make a reasonable return. In this way, the construction of railroads in Germany, Austria, and Russia involved much more state support than had been the case in Britain.

Comparing with British Industrialization Industrialization on the continent always looked to the example of Britain. For many, like **Friedrich Engels**, this example was negative. Industrialization in Britain had caused misery for thousands of workers, who crowded into the new industrial towns and lived in unhealthy and expensive slums. From the start, continental governments feared the revolutionary potential of impoverished industrial workers, or the **proletariat**, a word that rapidly appeared in many European languages. And they took action in a way that Britain, devoted to laissez-faire economics, did not. Not only did continental governments promote railroads, they restricted the use of child labor and more closely regulated the conditions of industrial work than in Britain, hoping to reduce working-class discontent. In short, governments on the continent always took a much more active role in regulating

Werner Siemens (1816–1892) German inventor and businessman who established his first factory in Berlin in 1847 and was a major figure in the manufacture of electrical goods.

Zollverein German Customs Union, or free-trade area, dominated by Prussia and important in Prussian unification of Germany in 1871.

Friedrich Engels (1820–1895) Karl Marx's closest collaborator, son of a German industrialist who spent most of his life in England.

proletariat Industrial workers or, more generally, people who own absolutely nothing except their own labor.

relations between **capitalists** and industrial workers. They also protected their new industries through high **tariffs** that discouraged the consumption of imported goods by increasing their price. Many argued that Britain's great head start in industrialization made it necessary to shield developing industry from a flood of cheap British manufactured goods. Britain, in contrast, had long been a promoter of free trade—that is, British trade.

CONNECTIONS: A major issue in the early twenty-first century is free trade between nations (see Section 30-3 Europe and Globalization). Classical nineteenth-century liberals embraced free trade and protection of property as the very cornerstone of their ideology. Later totalitarian governments such as fascist Italy, communist USSR, and Nazi Germany considerably restricted international trade, arguing that the role of the state was to protect domestic workers. After the end of communism in 1989, it seemed that free trade had won the day with western industrial goods pouring into formerly communist countries and trade barriers falling among most countries. And yet, the early twenty-first century is witnessing new demands to limit free trade. Perhaps history really does repeat itself.

21-1b The Revolution in Transportation

New industries required the transport of both raw materials and manufactured goods. At first, rivers and canals were sufficient, but they were rapidly supplanted by railroads. Railroads originated in the coal mines of Britain, where the problem of how to more efficiently bring the heavy, bulky coal to the surface called forth a simple but ingenious solution: coal wagons on metal rails.

The Railroad Soon the principle was transferred outside the mines. At first, horses pulled these wagons on metal tracks, but it was only logical that animal power would be replaced by steam. The culmination of this process occurred in 1829, when **George Stephenson**'s locomotive, the *Rocket*, won a competition for the new Manchester-Liverpool line by traveling at a top speed of twenty-nine miles per hour over thirty-five miles. The railroad age had begun.

In the next two decades, more than six thousand miles of track were laid in Britain. On the European continent, railroad construction was also impressive: by 1850, Berlin, Paris, Vienna, Frankfurt, and other major cities were linked by rail. The first railroad entrepreneurs envisioned these new "iron roads" mainly as a means of bringing bulky raw materials like coal or iron ore to factories and manufactured products to market (such as textiles from Manchester to the port of Liverpool). Very soon, however, railroads were transporting not just freight but also large numbers of people. Railroads made it easier for people to migrate from the countryside to the city in search of work, thereby increasing the labor pool for further industrialization.

Steamships Steam engines proved easier to use in locomotives than in ships. Harnessing steam to propel watercraft was plagued by two separate difficulties. First, a high degree of efficiency was required because of a boat's limited ability to carry coal. Second, for an onboard steam engine, safety was extremely important, as an explosion could well mean the destruction of the entire ship, possibly far out at sea. By the late 1830s, however, these problems were effectively solved, and by midcentury steamships were replacing even the swift-sailing clippers on the open seas. Steamships were innovative not only in their use of steam propulsion but also in their construction, being made of iron instead of wood. The use of iron in shipbuilding allowed ships to be larger, more durable, and economically more efficient. In 1838, two iron steamships, the *Great Western* and the *Sirius*, raced across the Atlantic to New York, making the journey in a record-breaking fifteen days. Rapidly, wooden sailing vessels were retired, no longer able to compete.

Road Building Industrialization spurred improvements in roads and overland transport as well. At the beginning of the century, roads in most parts of Europe were worse than they had been during the Roman Empire eighteen centuries earlier. But by 1850, significant improvements had been made, partly in connection with the creation of a European-wide postal system. Post roads with stations where horses could be changed were established along major trade routes from England to Russia. In Britain, by 1830 more than a thousand private "turnpike trusts" had built roads and then charged tolls to recover their investment. **John McAdam**, a surveyor for the Bristol Turnpike Trust, developed a method of road construction that improved foundations and drainage. His method, using gravel and broken rock, formed a hard surface that was more durable and less muddy than dirt roads. Soon similar roads were being built throughout Europe, called in many different languages "macadam."

capitalists Individuals whose income comes from capital—wealth in money rather than land—invested in factories and commerce for profit.

tariffs Taxes charged on imported goods that raise consumer costs and add to government revenues.

George Stephenson (1781–1848) English railroad pioneer, inventor, and engineer who designed some of Britain's earliest locomotives and rail lines in the 1820s and 1830s.

John McAdam (1756–1836) Scottish engineer who developed a technique for a harder, less muddy road surface known as "macadam" in various languages.

NRM/Pictorial Collection/SSPL/The Image Works

Railroad Cutting through Countryside

The railroad sliced through the countryside, serving as a constant reminder to rural people of the great industrial changes taking place elsewhere. The rural landscape was transformed by the "iron road" itself, with its bridges and viaducts. Rushing through quiet agricultural lands, the loud, sooty, and dangerous trains must have seemed like monsters from another world. And these monsters also enticed farmer youth with the promise of a more exciting life in the cities.

❯❯ *In what ways did industrialization change everyday life, even in the countryside?*

urbanization Process by which cities grow as population shifts from rural to urban areas; a major effect of industrialization.

New Lanark Cotton mill town on the Clyde River in Scotland where Robert Owen combined profitmaking with efforts to improve workers' lives.

Robert Owen (1771–1858) Scottish industrialist and utopian socialist who attempted to incorporate cooperative principles in his factories.

Canals Water transport continued to be vital for transporting raw materials and manufactured goods. Though the Bridgewater Canal, built in 1761 to carry coal by barge to Manchester, was hard-pressed by competition from the Liverpool and Manchester Railroad, the canal's success in generating an entire network of canals around Manchester inspired the Erie Canal in New York State. This canal's completion in 1825, connecting the Hudson River and Lake Erie, opened the American interior to overseas commerce. Even backward Russia improved its canal system, in 1808 rebuilding the Moscow-Petersburg canal first constructed by Peter the Great, and linking the Vistula,

Bug, and Dnieper Rivers by canal in 1841 to allow the passage of goods by water from the Baltic to the Black Sea. Many smaller canals throughout Europe connected industry with raw materials and markets, increasingly working together with railroads.

21-1c The Social Impacts of Industrialization

The most noticeable—even shocking—impact of industrialization was **urbanization**, the rapid growth of cities. In the first half of the nineteenth century, hundreds of thousands of individuals both in Britain and on the continent left the countryside for work in cities. Factory owners needed large numbers of workers, and served as a magnet for the influx of thousands into urban areas. New factories built in the countryside to take advantage of waterpower, such as the mills established at the falls of the Clyde in Scotland, soon drew so many workers that mills became towns—in this case **New Lanark, Robert Owen**'s model factory town. Workers required food, clothing, medical care,

From The New York Public Library

Manchester in 1851

This etching of the industrial city of Manchester in 1851 graphically depicts the enormous impact of industrialization with the dozens of smokestacks pouring pollution into the air, rendering the city's air foul and difficult to breathe. The stunted trees in the foreground suggest the impact of industrialization on nature.

» *Looking at this image, how do you perceive the impact of industrialization?*

» *Comparing the depiction of nature in this painting and those of Caspar David Friedrich (see Section 20-1c The Age of Romanticism), what differences can you point out?*

and housing, so more people migrated to the industrialized towns to provide these services. Factory owners and managers in their large houses required servants, who added to the population. For all these reasons, industrial cities grew at breathtaking rates, so fast that available housing was overwhelmed. As thousands of strangers were forced to live and work together in small, cramped spaces, disease and crime were the inevitable result.

Manchester, City of Industry The English city of **Manchester** offers a spectacular example of population growth. Located some thirty miles from the English port of Liverpool, Manchester had long been a center of wool cloth production, powered mainly by human muscle. Directly under and surrounding the city were huge coal deposits that would fuel the transition to steam power, and the opening of the Bridgewater Canal made coal transport cheap. These three factors—a nearby port, large reserves of coal, and the availability of skilled laborers—made Manchester the birthplace of industrialization. In 1750, the

city's population was 20,000. In the next twenty-five years, the population doubled, but that was before the industrial take-off. By 1831, the population had soared to more than 250,000, and by 1850, it was 400,000.

This rapid growth came at an enormous price: overcrowding, industrial pollution, and filth in the streets that made the stench of Manchester notorious. The air was full of soot and exhaust gases from the coal-powered engines in the factories. A French visitor in midcentury, the journalist Hippolyte Taine, described the "dreary streets," full of "masses of livid children, dirty and flabby of flesh. Even to walk in the rich quarter of town is depressing." A medical doctor described this poverty in 1833: "Too often the dwelling of the factory family is no home; it sometimes is a cellar, which includes no cooking, no washing, no making, no mending, no decencies of life." But as the liberal French writer Alexis de Tocqueville observed, "From this filthy sewer pure gold flows."

> **Manchester** Textile manufacturing city in northern England.

Friedrich Engels Denounces Capitalist Exploitation

Portrait of Friedrich Engels / © SZ Photo / Bridgeman Images

Friedrich Engels Friedrich Engels, with his more famous partner, Karl Marx, helped create the socialist movement that revolutionized European politics in the late nineteenth and twentieth centuries. Depicted here in an early photograph, Engels resembles the middle-class industrial manager (which he also was) more than our conceptions of a revolutionary.

Friedrich Engels was just twenty-two when his father sent him away from home to keep him out of trouble. Home was Barmen (now Wuppertal), Germany, where the family owned textile mills. The "trouble" was Friedrich's interest in philosophy, which caused him to reject his father's stern brand of Christianity. Hoping to distract his son from such irreligious studies, the elder Engels sent young Friedrich to manage a textile mill outside Manchester, England, in which the family had an interest.

Once in Manchester, young Engels was appalled by what he saw: overcrowded housing; entire districts lacking sewers and clean drinking water; families competing for foul, half-rotten food. The horrifying conditions in which the working people of Manchester lived changed Engels's life, causing him to dedicate his life to exposing the misery caused by industrial capitalism and to helping workers organize to improve their lives. Engels decided to write a book. Though he represented his father's interests at the mill during the day, at night he roamed the slums of Manchester, gathering material for what would be published as *The Condition of the Working Class in England in 1844*.

Engels documented entire families living in a single room, sleeping together in a single bed that was alive with lice and vermin. He recorded the physical effects of grueling work, poor nutrition, and lack of hygiene. These terrible living conditions meant that the majority of industrial workers died before they reached the age of twenty. Even as he gathered his data, Engels was asking himself more fundamental questions: What factors cause such poverty? How could factories that were so efficient at increasing production make the lives of their workers so miserable? In short, Engels wanted to understand the workings of industrial capitalism.

tenements Cheaply built, crowded, and often squalid multistory dwellings, often constructed by factory owners to house workers.

tuberculosis Infectious disease that affects the lungs and if untreated often leads to death; a common killer in the nineteenth century, now treatable with antibiotics.

Negative Effects of Industrialization Unscrupulous landlords threw up cheap, unventilated, and crowded **tenements** in which several families lived in a single room. Water had to be fetched from outdoor wells, often contaminated by outdoor privies. Food was expensive, in part because Britain's 1815 Corn Laws forbade the import of grain. The lack of clean water and the overcrowding made epidemics of diseases like cholera and typhoid common. The polluted air caused respiratory problems that often developed into diseases such as asthma and **tuberculosis**. By the 1830s, British reformers had realized that only government intervention could help solve the problems associated with industrialization. (See also Profiles in Change: Friedrich Engels Denounces Capitalist Exploitation.)

The pollution and environmental degradation was, literally, breathtaking. Industrial cities were black with soot; light-colored clothing would be filthy by the end of the day. One early solution to the problems of air pollution in Manchester and other industrial towns was to build factory chimneys ever higher so that winds would carry the fumes far away

In 1844, Engels returned home to Germany, stopping on the way in Paris to meet Karl Marx. Within two years, the two young men (Marx was only two years older than Engels) would be calling themselves communists and calling for an overthrow of the existing economic and political order. But for now Engels went home to write his book. It was published the next year in German, but its dedication was in English: "To the Working Classes of Great-Britain." Engels praised English workers, dedicated his book to them, and urged them to fight for their rights against "the middle classes intend to enrich themselves by your labour."

This was more than a documented report; it was a political manifesto, and Engels called on England's workers to take control of their own destiny. Scholars at the time and later complained that Engels exaggerated the misery wrought by industrialization, provided a one-sided picture of life in Manchester, and based his sweeping accusations against the middle class on his own narrow experience in Barmen and Manchester. These criticisms are reasonable, but on another level they miss the point. Engels was not writing a scholarly analysis; he was trying to change the world. His conclusion was a warning: "The war of the poor against the rich will be the most bloodthirsty the world has ever seen." This war would be a revolution, he claimed, that would usher in a world of justice and dignity for all.

In 1848, only three years after the book's publication, revolutions did sweep the European continent, including Germany. In the same year, Marx and Engels published the famous *Communist Manifesto*, in which they argued that a workers' revolution would soon put an end to capitalism. The workers' revolution did not come in 1848. For political reasons, both Marx and Engels had to flee their native Germany and live in permanent exile in England. There they maintained a fruitful partnership and friendship that lasted until Marx's death in 1883.

Although Engels's *Conditions of the Working Class in England* made him famous among German radicals, it was not published in England until 1891. Still, the book's impact was enormous. For some young Russian socialists, Engels's descriptions of the degradations of industrial capitalism made them hope to avoid industrialism altogether—an aim that Marx and Engels firmly rejected as impossible and undesirable. Instead, Engels argued, radicals needed to harness industrialization's wealth-generating power for the good of all workers and all society. In a sense, Engels did this himself as an individual: he worked all his life as a businessman and manufacturer, devoting much of his income to radical causes and supporting the ever-impoverished Marx family. Ironically, industrial capitalism made Engels a radical and also financed his quest to destroy it.

from the city. But this method simply spread pollution farther from the factories themselves. Mining ripped up the face of the earth and brought to the surface toxic substances that were simply dumped aside unless they had commercial value. Rainwater ran through these slag heaps, spreading the poison into rivers. In the absence of municipal water treatment plants—no industrial city of the time had any—people were obliged to drink this foul, polluted water. Little wonder that in industrial towns, infant mortality was high and life expectancy low.

Space, Time, and Industrialization Industrialization changed the human sense of space and time. With railroads, cities were hours apart instead of days. But railroads and factories also demanded a more precise keeping of time and spurred on another industry—the manufacture of clocks and watches—as well as standardized time. Railways not only linked major cities but cut through less-developed agricultural regions, ending their isolation. The physical presence of rails traversing the countryside reminded rural people that the excitement and economic promise of the big city lay mere hours away.

The conservative Duke of Wellington worried that railways "would encourage the lower classes to move about," and they did. Inexpensive fares in third-class carriages made possible travel on a scale hitherto unheard of: 27.7 million railroad journeys were taken in Britain in 1844. Cheap fares encouraged the migration of impoverished rural people into the growing industrial cities, further accelerating their growth. By midcentury, more-distant journeys to America and Australia usually began with a train ride to the port, where emigrants boarded a steamship. Thus the transportation revolution wrought by industrialization had a major impact not just in Europe but also around the world.

The Creation of Class One of the most far-reaching effects of the Industrial Revolution was the creation of social categories based on economic, not legal, status. Until industrialization, most people identified themselves by the social category of their birth: peasant, noble, artisan, merchant. These were legal, not merely economic, categories. It was quite possible for nobles to be poor and even (though more rarely) for peasants to be wealthy. Industrial societies, however, are ordered along class lines. One's class derives primarily from one's economic position in society, or as **Karl Marx** would later describe it, one's relation to the **means of production** (see also Learning from a

Primary Source: Marx and Engels Set Down the Political Program of the Communists in The Communist Manifesto (1848)). The factory owner controlled the means of production (the factory) and derived profit from it; the workers were an element in the means of production, much like the machines they tended.

The idea of class also implies a feeling of belonging together, or **class consciousness**. This consciousness was new in the early Industrial Revolution. Nobles had long distinguished themselves from commoners by dress, manners, and luxurious lifestyle. Now the growing middle classes, or bourgeoisie, differentiated themselves from nobles by their emphasis on the dignity of work and self-improvement, and from the working class by the way they spoke and dressed. Workers, crammed together on factory floors and tenement houses, began to recognize their shared interests too. With the coming of industrialization, society was no longer divided into three estates—the nobles, clergy, and peasants of France—or the lords and commoners of England. Now it was divided into capitalists, who had wealth available to invest in the means of production, and workers (the proletariat), who had no source of income other than their labor.

Social Mobility Industrialization also enhanced the possibility for social mobility. An intelligent, hard-working peasant boy could go to work in the city and hope to rise into the lower middle class or, if not he, then at least his children. To be sure, most of those born poor died that way—and died much earlier than their middle- and upper-class contemporaries. But the possibility of becoming a "self-made man" and rising above the class of one's birth was an aspiration—and a reality—for many in this era.

21-2 The Middle Classes

>> **Who belonged to the middle classes?**

>> **What moral and political values characterized the middle classes?**

In the classic formulation, the middle class was, of course, in the middle—between the nobility on one hand and the peasants on the other. In the nineteenth century, the middle classes distinguished themselves from the working classes too. This group grew rapidly as industrialization progressed, and as they prospered, their political importance and influence grew as well. Speaking of "middle classes" in the plural suggests the great variety of occupations

class consciousness Identification with other members of one's economic class—for example, industrial workers or middle-class professionals.

and mentalities that this category embraced. But all middle-class people defined themselves not by their birth but also by what they did—their occupation and, increasingly, their education. Their shared interests included pride in their respectability, sobriety, and hard work, often contrasting these "middle-class virtues" with the drunken and wasteful behavior of both workers and those born into great wealth. The middle-class home reflected this proud, sober, and somewhat smug attitude, with a wife who devoted herself entirely to her family, not needing to earn money outside the home. To be sure, reality reflected this ideal only partially.

21-2a A Variety of Middle Classes

Europe had had a strong and growing class of merchants since the Middle Ages, and as commerce grew, so did banking, investing, and shipping. In the eighteenth century, lawyers, doctors, professors, and other educated professionals might have felt that their income and lifestyle gave them something in common with those who had grown rich from trade. And in the nineteenth century, these middle classes expanded rapidly. The spread of industrialism demanded and created capitalists with the liquid wealth, or capital, to invest in new factories. Complex machinery, production methods, and business arrangements created an increased need for engineers, skilled technicians, foremen, and managers as well as distributors and salesmen. All those who filled such positions were members of the middle classes.

Early Industrialists Some of those who established new enterprises were aristocrats, such as the Duke of Bridgewater, who sank his fortune into the Bridgewater Canal. The canal returned an even greater fortune and also brought great earnings to the duke's engineer, James Brindley, a craftsman's son with little education. Brindley was a self-made man who achieved success through his own effort; in fact, biographers attributed his early death to diabetes and overwork. He is representative of a new class of men whose fame and fortune derived directly from industrialization.

Richard Arkwright, a barber whose water frame made him rich, and James Watt, whose improvements on the steam engine made him wealthy, are others. So are Richard Cobden, son of a farmer who gained wealth as a calico printer and prominence as a member of Parliament from Stockport, near Manchester. His close associate in the Anti—Corn Law League, John Bright, was the grandson of a farmer. For these men, social status and identity derived not from birth but from accomplishment. The middle classes were varied and fluid enough to be open to newcomers. Industrialization increased social mobility.

The "Petty Bourgeoisie" Differences within the middle classes were enormous. The richest industrialists, for example, married their daughters into aristocratic families; thus their grandchildren would be "upper class" and frequently embarrassed by the grandfather's coarse speech and unrefined manners. On the other hand, impoverished clerks, owners of small shops, teachers, governesses—the so-called petty bourgeoisie—were in constant peril of sinking down into the "lower depths" of society. The greater possibility for social mobility brought about by industrialization thus cut both ways, enabling the strong, intelligent, and lucky to rise but also making it easy to fall from respected middle-class status into poverty and social disgrace.

21-2b Middle-Class Culture

Although some of the self-made men in the new middle classes had limited schooling themselves, they all believed firmly in the value of learning, and they made certain that their sons—and, increasingly, their daughters—had good educations. A secondary or university education almost guaranteed middle-class status, and university enrollments grew steadily throughout the nineteenth century.

New Universities New universities were founded, often specifically to fulfill the requirements of the new, industrializing society, such as University College London, which provided practical educational opportunities to middle-class men and women. In Berlin, a *Bauakademie (BOW-ah-kah-deh-mee)*—academy of architecture and engineering—was founded by the Prussian state in 1799 and was joined in 1821 by a *Gewerbeakademie (geh-VERB-uh-ah-ka-deh-mee)*, or business or trade school. These institutions were merged in 1879 to form the Royal Technical Higher School of Berlin, the forerunner of today's Technical University of Berlin. Significantly, these university-level institutions to train engineers and businessmen in Berlin were founded by the government, whereas University College London arose from private initiative.

In central Europe, the emerging class of the *Bildungsbürgertum (BILD-ungs-bur-ger-tum)*, the educated bourgeoisie, testifies to the importance of education for middle-class status. Despite **Wilhelm von Humboldt**'s revitalization of German universities in the first years of the nineteenth century, entrepreneurs, technicians, and engineers seldom attended university. Instead, individuals wishing to pursue such practical studies enrolled in institutions like the business or engineering academies in Berlin. In the decades between 1830 and 1860,

Third-Class and First-Class Passengers

Accommodations in railroad coaches reflected social class divisions. Aristocrats and the rich traveled in first-class coaches, "respectable" middle-class people in second, and everyone else in third. Although passengers in third (above) and first (below) classes traveled in very different style, the railroad aided social leveling by the simple fact that everyone left and arrived at the same time.

›› *Compare the passengers shown in first and third class. Judging from their attire, what sort of professions do you suppose these people pursued?*

Wilhelm von Humboldt
(1767–1835) German philosopher, linguist, and statesman, after whom Berlin's main university is named.

(top): Mary Evans Picture Library/The Image Works

Roger Viollet/Contributor/Getty Images

the most popular subjects at German universities were theology and law (around 30 percent of students each), medicine and liberal arts (15 percent each), with only 5 percent of German students majoring in science.

Education and the Middle Class

A university education secured one's middle-class status, most likely as a member of a profession such as law, medicine, or the church, but middle-class people valued hard work equally. The enterprising writer, physician, and editor **Samuel Smiles** provided a formula for success in his 1859 book *Self-Help*. Thrift, hard work, and sobriety were important, as were self-denial, good habits, and the ability to learn from mistakes. "Life will always be to a large extent what we ourselves make it," wrote Smiles. As inspiration, he also wrote biographies of self-made men, such as potter Josiah Wedgwood and engineer George Stephenson. Smiles also believed that self-improvement would contribute to the improvement of society as a whole.

Victorian Morality

In their emphasis on practical knowledge, middle-class people may be seen as the heirs of the Enlightenment, but their strict views on sobriety and sexual morality derive rather from Protestant Christian traditions. Young people were admonished to avoid the temptations not only of sexual intercourse before marriage but even of sexual thoughts or masturbation. Many manuals and self-help books warned that "self-abuse" would lead to bad eyesight, insanity, and other misfortunes, including death. Ideally, men and women were to find sexual pleasure only within the bounds of marriage.

Sexual love between members of the same sex was literally unspeakable: the word *homosexuality* was not coined until 1869. It is not by chance that later generations would use the word **Victorian**—referring to the reign of British queen Victoria—to mean preachy, sexually repressed, hypocritical, and narrow-minded. Still, this characterization is at best one-sided. Middle-class ideology in the nineteenth century did have its humorless, self-righteous aspects, but its grinding emphasis on work reflected a desire to validate middle-class identity and to assert

that individual dignity should be gauged not by birth but by service to society.

Middle-Class Respectability

As members of a largely new and growing social grouping, middle-class people felt keenly the need to establish and augment their prestige and respectability, often by spreading their values of self-improvement, education, and sobriety among the less fortunate. Smiles argued that only by adopting middle-class values and habits could workers lift themselves out of poverty. Many middle-class women, especially, engaged actively in charity work, sometimes alienating those they intended to help with their strident self-righteousness. The **temperance movement**, for example, was a middle-class reform directed mainly at the working class. Alcoholism was a problem, but the well-dressed preachy women who scolded workers about their drinking habits seldom achieved positive results.

The middle-class belief in hard work as the key to success implied that the root of poverty could be sought in personal laziness, immorality, and other weaknesses. Thus the structural causes of poverty, unleashed by industrialization, were obscured. The historian **François Guizot**, who dominated French politics in the 1840s, believed that the opportunity for riches was open to all and that failure to achieve wealth reflected an individual's own limitations and weaknesses. Rather than blaming society for their misery, Guizot argued, the poor had only themselves to blame. If they would stay sober, work hard, and live frugally, they would better their social condition. Many middle-class liberals would have agreed, pointing to their own success as proof that hard work alone brought material wealth and social status.

Religion and the Middle Classes

Middle-class respectability involved both self-control and self-righteousness—overall, an avoidance of extremes. In their churches, the middle classes avoided ostentatious ceremonies, mysticism, and overly emotional displays of devotion. The Church of England and the official Protestant churches in central Europe and Scandinavia reprimanded clergy who showed excessive "enthusiasm" or religious fervor, and pastors who pressed their middle-class parishioners too strongly about their sins might find themselves snubbed by the parish. But some Protestants found worship without ceremony and emotion sterile and devoid of profound religious meaning. A few left the Church of England for dissenting chapels, and at Oxford, a group of prominent Anglican clergymen who sought to revive certain Roman Catholic rituals drew much attention, particularly when some of them converted to Catholicism.

As Jews began to assimilate into the middle class, dressing and speaking like other members of that class, they also sought to reform their religious

Samuel Smiles (1812–1904) Scottish writer who achieved fame through books promising success through hard work, such as self-help, thrift, character, and duty.

Victorian Term referring to the reign of Queen Victoria (r. 1837–1901) and carrying a connotation of sexual restraint, humorlessness, and social conservatism.

temperance movement Movement to ban the use of alcoholic beverages, often affiliated with Christian churches and led by middle-class women.

François Guizot (1787–1874) French historian and politician who believed that the poor must improve their own economic condition through hard work without government aid.

practices. The traditional long caftan of the rabbi was exchanged for a sober outfit resembling that of a Protestant pastor. Within the synagogue, a more orderly religious service was inaugurated, sometimes even with choirs and organs, which were quite foreign to Jewish religious traditions. While generally remaining true to their religious laws, avoiding certain foods and keeping the Sabbath (Saturday) holy, these middle-class Jews attempted in all other ways to resemble their Gentile neighbors.

Their **Reform Judaism** was strongest in German areas, but even among the overwhelmingly traditional and Orthodox Polish Jews in Warsaw and Lwów, Reform synagogues were opened in the 1840s. More traditional Jews regarded these innovations as the first step toward conversion to Christianity, and in their own way, they were right. Later Reform Judaism was to significantly relax the strict requirements to eat only kosher food, to abstain from work on Saturdays, and to orient one's life around prayer, worship, and study. Moreover, many of the middle-class Jews who shed their traditional Jewish garb and habits later abandoned Judaism altogether, as did the children of the preeminent Jewish Enlightenment figure, Moses Mendelssohn. For them, as for the fathers of Karl Marx, English conservative statesman **Benjamin Disraeli**, and many others, social **assimilation** was the first step toward conversion.

21-2c The Middle-Class Home

As industrialization spread, concepts of home and work diverged from each other. In a preindustrial society, artisans lived in or near their workshops, and peasants lived near the fields they tilled, sometimes even sharing their lodgings with their domestic animals. But in industrial societies, just as "work" became associated with a "workplace"—a factory—so, for the middle classes, did the home become distinctly apart from the dirt and noise of manufacturing and the fast-paced and high-pressure world of business. The newly wealthy industrialists built large houses far from their factories, and their wives were expected to create a restful and pleasant haven for their hardworking husbands to return to after a hard day's work. To be sure, these **separate spheres** of home and work were more an ideal than a reality for all middle-class homes, but this ideal had a strong influence on middle-class identity and on ideas of a woman's "proper place." Women's legal status remained unchanged; legally, women were an extension of their fathers or husbands.

Marriage and Family Life Marriage was a vital and central institution of middle-class life; this society rejected as peculiar, and even suspicious, the idea of remaining unmarried, with a few exceptions, such as Roman Catholic priests. The first line of Jane Austen's *Pride and Prejudice* reflects this fact: "It is a truth universally acknowledged, that a single man in possession of a good fortune must be in want of a wife." Founding a family was of vital importance, but first, a middle-class man had to establish himself in business—in effect, earn his fortune. Men were typically older than the women they married and were expected to guide and train their wives as well as to love them. The husband had to earn a sufficient amount to pay for a middle-class home and servants and, of course, to allow his wife to devote herself exclusively to her family without needing to work outside the home.

Middle-Class Women

Middle-class girls were raised to see marriage as their main purpose in life. Failing to make a suitable marriage was also feared, as it might mean an unpleasant dependency on wealthier relations or a meager livelihood as a "genteel" lady's maid or governess. Once she was married, a middle-class woman's role included running the household, supervising servants, educating her children, and in some cases helping her husband in his professional or scientific endeavors. Outside the home, a middle-class woman was often active in charitable and religious organizations. Women did not have careers, though they might make their own way as teachers, seamstresses, or milliners—the latter two professions perilously near "working class."

Nineteenth-century novels often examine the dilemmas of bright and sensitive young women of marriageable age. Their authors were themselves women who were trying to make their way as writers—**Charlotte Brontë**, author of *Jane Eyre*, is one example. She and her sister **Emily** published under male names, as did **George Sand** (Amandine Aurore Lucile Dupin) in France and **George Eliot** (Mary Ann Evans) in England.

Reform Judaism Movement to modernize Jewish life, retaining the religious core of Judaism but eliminating many differences from Gentiles in everyday life.

Benjamin Disraeli (1804–1881) English writer and conservative statesman who was a favorite of Queen Victoria; the son of a converted Jew but very proud of his Jewish origins.

assimilation Process by which one ethnic or cultural group takes on the attributes of another.

separate spheres Middle-class ideal whereby home life was strictly separated from the workplace, with women running the household and men earning money outside it.

Charlotte and Emily Brontë (1816–1855, 1818–1848) English novelists and poets, authors of novels including *Jane Eyre* (Charlotte) and *Wuthering Heights* (Emily).

George Sand (1804–1876) French female author of more than eighty novels who took a man's name and dressed in male attire to protest the treatment of women.

George Eliot (1819–1880) Major English novelist, born Mary Ann Evans, whose novels portrayed social and moral problems of the lower middle class.

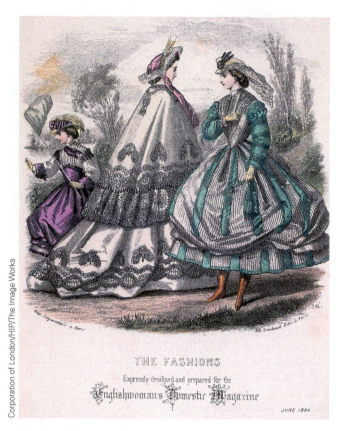

Corporation of London/HIP/The Image Works

Middle-Class Fashion

The Englishwoman's Domestic Magazine's illustrations reflected middle-class women's desire for respectability and even extravagance in fashion. Increasingly able to afford new outfits frequently, women of the middle class consulted such magazines to learn the latest style.

» *What about the fashions shown here indicate to you that this publication was aimed at middle-class women?*

By publishing under male names, these pioneering women writers aimed to force readers to take their writing more seriously, and they also sought to avoid criticism by their own middle-class families about earning money with their pen. While some women published—at times with great success—under their own (female) names, they often found that male critics considered their work a mere pastime, not real literature.

Middle-class women were not supposed to earn money—just to spend it. Although servants usually did the shopping, it was the "lady of the house" who ordered goods, checked prices, kept accounts, and made sure that neither servants nor merchants were cheating her. Even when she had a housekeeper to perform most of these duties, she was expected by her husband to make sure that the household ran smoothly and efficiently. The middle-class woman also had to purchase clothes for herself and her family and to furnish her home tastefully. To help homemakers make choices in their selection of furnishings and clothing, entrepreneurs began to publish books and

periodicals devoted to proper, respectable fashions, such as *The Englishwoman's Domestic Magazine*, which began appearing in 1852.

Middle-Class Children Children in middle-class families were trained to be obedient, clean, respectful, and orderly. Physical punishment of children was considered normal, indeed inevitable, though usually the task of the man: respectable French fathers had a small whip for that purpose. At the same time, the ideas of Jean Jacques Rousseau on education and allowing children free time for play and physical development were spreading. Middle-class children were usually educated at home by governesses and tutors, as there was not yet a well-developed state-run school system. Looking back at their childhood later in the century, many middle-class people recalled the great freedom they had enjoyed compared with later youths, who would be obliged to spend more regimented days in schoolrooms. Because of improved nutrition and sanitation, middle-class families were likely to have many children; it was not unusual for a woman to become pregnant ten or more times during her lifetime. As the century progressed, infant mortality decreased, and the size of middle-class families grew.

CONNECTIONS: Who's middle class? For most of known history, the vast majority of humanity has toiled simply to survive. Only with industrialization did a significantly large part of society start to regard itself as "middle class," that is, earning its own keep but not working the land. In early ages such people—scribes, traders, doctors, teachers, artisans, artists—made up a tiny proportion of the total population. And in present-day America, only some 2 to 3 percent of citizens work to produce the food we eat: and most of them consider themselves middle class! Without industrialization, none of this could have happened. Still, it is important to remember that even today the "middle class" represents a distinct minority among the world population.

21-3 Working Classes

» **How did industrialization and urbanization change everyday and family life?**

» **How did industrial workers attempt to improve their work situations?**

Industrialization created the working class—or classes. This large group included miners, industrial workers, servants, and artisans, who worked and lived in conditions that were often appalling. Industrialization and urbanization disrupted working-class family life. Increasingly, mothers, fathers, and children went to different workplaces, carrying out separate tasks. The crowded conditions, combined with the city's many

Vasily Perov, *Tea Drinking at Mytishchi near Moscow*, 1862

Realist artist Vasily Perov portrays the misery of the Russian peasants and the indifference of a respectable Russian Orthodox clergyman in this bitter painting.

» *How does the artist make you feel sympathy for the beggars?*

» *What about the portrayal of the priest renders him unsympathetic to the viewer?*

Tretjakov Gallery, Moscow/akg-images

temptations, made the proper upbringing and discipline of children all the more difficult. But workers did not simply accept their lot passively. Working-class people banded together to protect themselves from the worst aspects of early industrialization, organizing labor unions, demanding better working and living conditions, and insisting on their own dignity in the face of what they saw as middle-class indifference.

21-3a Diversity Within the Working Class

Manchester exemplifies the triumphs and contradictions of early industrialization better than any other city. Here huge amounts of money were made by a few, but for the workers, life was harsh, brutish, and often short. The workday was long—sometimes stretching to fourteen and sixteen hours, six and even seven days a week. Workers who arrived late were beaten and fined or their pay was docked.

Dangers of the Industrial City Slippery factory floors, complex systems of gears and transmission belts, and the constant presence of fumes endangered life and limb. If injured, workers could expect to be fired instantly. Workers' health also suffered from damp and dank workplaces, sometimes overheated, sometimes chilled by open windows. The air was always filled with acrid smells, fibers, and particles

of cloth. Tuberculosis and cholera were common. The reformer and Manchester native **Edwin Chadwick** pointed out in 1842 that smoke in Manchester was killing vegetation. In the same report he described workers' housing in another industrial city, Leeds: "walls unwhitewashed for years, black with the smoke of foul chimneys, without water, and sacking for bedclothes, with floors unwashed from year to year."

Artisans As industrialization proceeded, artisans often found themselves out of work, replaced by machines. In the early years, artisans' skills had been essential to factory design and operations. But soon mass production deprived many tailors, clockmakers, and shoemakers of their livelihood and way of life. Even more directly threatened were weavers and others engaged in textile production. Those who found new employment in mechanized, power-driven textile factories often perceived the change from artisan to industrial worker as painful and humiliating. They resented the constant surveillance of foremen and felt dehumanized by the need to adapt their skills and their personal rhythms to the tempo of the machine. The life of a hand-loom weaver had not been easy, but at least he (weavers were usually men) worked his own hours and earned a living wage. As artisans were driven out of work and forced to accept factory jobs, they no longer had these satisfactions.

Servants The working classes also included servants. The majority of servants were women, often young girls who came from the countryside to seek employment in the growing number of middle-class households. Hannah Cullwick of Shropshire, for example, lost her parents as a teenager, moved to London, and took a job in the house of a middle-class beer merchant. Remembering her experiences, Hannah described the great gulf between her drudgery as a servant and the life of a "real lady," who "couldn't wash a plate or a saucepan or peal a tato." But the servant class was itself divided into classes. At the very bottom was the harried "girl of all work" who scrubbed, fetched water, washed dishes, and generally carried out any tasks the housekeeper or cook ordered her to do. The cook and chambermaid were her superiors, and they enjoyed a bit more respect. At the very top of the servant class were the housekeeper and butler, who not only dressed and spoke (or attempted to) like the master and mistress but also supervised their fellow servants.

Peasants In the new economy-based social divisions, peasants can be considered working class as well. In Britain, while thousands of peasants left the countryside for work in the cities, some farmers who

Edwin Chadwick (1800–1890) English social reformer who worked to improve conditions for the poor through better hygiene and government programs.

remained on the land enjoyed increasing prosperity. But peasants in Ireland lived in extreme poverty and suffered from malnutrition and catastrophic famine in the 1840s. French peasants, on the whole, lived more comfortably than peasants elsewhere, a condition that explains in part their reluctance to leave their farms and migrate to cities to work in industry.

Conditions for peasants were worst in eastern Europe, where serfdom still prevailed. Serfs were not only impoverished but could not even leave their village without their landlord's permission. In Russia, the Habsburg empire, and the Balkan Peninsula, serfdom was not abolished until 1848 or later. Legal serfdom, combined with the extreme poverty of these countries, constituted a severe hindrance to industrial development.

Employment for the working classes was fluid. Some young men sought temporary work in the cities before returning to the village to establish a family. Peasant girls often spent several years "in service" before returning home to marry. Servants might take factory jobs, which paid better and gave them more personal freedom. Generally, however, the flow of country people to the city was one way: after living in the city, few young people wished to return to the strict supervision of elders (and neighbors) in the boring village. Despite the crowded and unhygienic conditions of early industrial cities, for many workers, life there brought a degree of personal freedom unknown in the countryside.

21-3b Working Families

On farms and in farming villages, families worked together; in artisan shops, families were often productive units. Early factories transferred this pattern to a new location. Men, women, and children continued to work side by side. The heavier physical work, such as operating looms, was usually carried out by men. Women predominated among spinners and in other tasks that required less heavy work, as they were assumed to have more manual dexterity than men. And children worked at a variety of light jobs, handling small spools of thread and reaching into places where adult hands could not fit. Even as industry developed, parents often chose to bring their children along with them to work rather than leave them unattended at home.

Women and Children of the Working Classes Long before the factory system, women had worked alongside their menfolk in the putting-out system. Spinning wool (later, cotton) into yarn was an almost exclusively female occupation. Factory owners also liked to hire entire families as a means of reducing individual wages. Sometimes men and women would work in the same factory but in different workshops. Men always predominated in metalworking and mining. Children also worked in coal mines, where boys and girls as young as age eight pushed carts laden with coal up from narrow shafts.

Children's labor brought in much-needed income for their families, but increasingly the working family was separated by work. It no longer functioned as an economic unit. From 1802 onward, the British Parliament passed laws limiting child labor, but it was only after 1833 that these laws were really enforced. Eventually child labor was banned altogether, as reformers argued that childhood should be spent in school or at play—not in mines or textile mills. But few children actually went to school at this point. Instead, they were excluded from factory work largely because of the increasing complexity of machines and industrial processes.

In Prussia, the employment of children under nine in factories was forbidden in 1839. In France, the Child Labor Law of 1841 forbade the employment of children under eight years of age and set down that children under age twelve could not work more than eight hours daily. King Leopold of Belgium proclaimed a similar law limiting child labor in 1842. But such laws were very hard to enforce because governments seldom wanted to pay for inspectors who would actually check factories for violations.

The employment of women was a different matter. Factory owners often preferred to hire women over men because they could pay women lower wages. Women were also less likely to cause trouble, being much less inclined to alcoholism, insubordination, and union activity. But as industrialization developed, women's work in industry was limited to certain occupational categories, especially in textiles, and was the subject of considerable debate.

Middle-class women were almost entirely shut out of paid labor. But some commentators—usually middle-class men—denounced work outside the home as endangering healthy family life for the working class as well. Others argued that women needed to be protected from the bad effects of factory work on the delicate female body and possible harm to their ability to produce healthy children. Midwives did, in fact, note that the babies of factory women were often delicate and prone to illness, and in 1847 Parliament limited the working day of women and children in textiles to ten hours. Nevertheless, women continued to work, as their wages were often necessary for the family's survival and, if single, they enjoyed the independence wage work gave them.

Everyday Life Working families' domestic life was vastly different from life in middle-class homes. Working women did their own housework, washing and cooking in dwellings that were cramped and at times even squalid. Young babies had to be "farmed out" to wet nurses so that the mother could continue working. Frequently these babies died in their first months of life, and estimates of child mortality up to the age of five reach as high as 50 percent in the early to mid-nineteenth century.

One common practice for keeping infants still was to give them drugs such as **laudanum** or a highly alcoholic "cordial." Malnutrition and the conditions of early factory work had a negative impact on children's health. One doctor wrote that children working in the Manchester cotton mills were "almost universally ill-looking, small, sickly, barefoot and ill-clad . . . a degenerate race." Military leaders also complained that young men who had grown up in working-class families were smaller in stature, thinner, and less hearty than peasant lads. More generally, parents came to recognize that children—despite the pennies they might earn working in a factory—were a drain on the family's resources. As industrialization and urbanization progressed, birthrates almost always declined.

Taverns and Drinking Culture Workingmen sought refuge from the conditions of factory and tenement in the taverns, which were generally off-limits for respectable women. Drinking was more than an attempt to forget one's misery in an alcoholic haze; visiting the pub was an integral part of male working-class camaraderie. A workingman who never visited the tavern would be considered abnormal—asocial and probably thinking too highly of himself. But the money spent on drink meant that much less remained for the family's support. Not by chance women spearheaded the temperance movement, calling on men to abandon the bottle and spend more time with and money on their families.

Criminality, Amusements, and Methodism Many working families barely earned a living, and the lures of the criminal world described in nineteenth-century novels were all too real. Like Fagin's band of boy thieves in **Charles Dickens**'s *Oliver Twist*, orphans in London's slums engaged in pickpocketing and other petty crime. Like Sonya Marmeladov in **Fyodor Dostoevsky**'s *Crime and Punishment*, young women turned to prostitution to support their families. Gin, opium, gambling, cockfights, bearbaiting: a variety of unsavory and illegal pastimes were available in industrial cities, enriching some but impoverishing many. Yet the industrial cities held opportunities that peasant life could not offer: taverns, theaters, coffeehouses, music halls, and the dream of advancement—the chance, however unlikely, of making one's fortune.

Moreover, family life was not entirely dismal. Parents and children celebrated holidays and played games together. Religion provided comfort and companionship. Working-class people in Britain were often attracted to **Methodism**, a religious movement founded by John Wesley in the eighteenth century that preached self-control, hard work, and self-respect. Methodism gave working-class people a sense of mission, dignity, and community.

Methodist preachers (often themselves from the working class) emphasized that working people were separate from, but in no way inferior to, members of the middle and upper classes. Methodism stressed the fundamental Christian beliefs that honored the meek and humble over the rich and powerful, specifically identifying working people with Christ's teaching that the "poor in spirit" would inherit the "kingdom of heaven" and the "meek" would "inherit the earth." On a practical level, Methodist preachers often set up Sunday schools to teach workers and their children how to read and write. Methodist worship services were emotional occasions during which preachers and congregation would shout, groan, leap up, faint, and sing praises. Methodist revival meetings, often held in the open air, attracted thousands of enthusiastic worshipers in the early decades of the nineteenth century.

21-3c Working-Class Consciousness and Trade Unionism

Industrialization brought workers together in densely packed spaces. Few enjoyed their work. Their lives were constricted by factory rules and hours, and whatever independence they might have formerly enjoyed as farmers or artisans was gone. So was pride in their craft and in the products they made: many early mass-produced goods were less durable and attractive than items produced by skilled artisans. Moreover, in the factory no one worker made something from start to finish. In a textile factory, for example, spinners spun the thread and weavers wove it into cloth. In a garment factory, one worker cut the cloth, another stitched only sleeves, another finished buttonholes. This division of labor was efficient, but it made work repetitive and monotonous. Workers often felt like they were cogs in a machine. Without any control over their work, they sensed they had lost a part of their humanity. Karl Marx would later attribute this sense to what he described as factory workers' **alienation** from the product of their labor.

laudanum Opium dissolved in alcohol, a popular though habit-forming sleep aid in the nineteenth century.

Charles Dickens (1812–1870) Famous English novelist, author of *Oliver Twist*, *A Tale of Two Cities*, and *A Christmas Carol*, among many others.

Fyodor Dostoevsky (1821–1881) Russian writer, author of *Crime and Punishment*, *The Brothers Karamazov*, and other novels.

Methodism Religious movement in nineteenth-century Britain that preached self-control, frugality, and hard work, appealing primarily to working-class people.

alienation Marx's concept of the breakdown, under capitalism, of workers' pride in and identification with the product of their labor.

Marx and Engels Set Down the Political Program of the Communists in *The Communist Manifesto* (1848)

In the 1840s, Karl Marx and Friedrich Engels both reacted against the terrible conditions created by early industrialization. Engels's book, *The Condition of the Working Class in England* (1845) described the unsanitary living conditions, poor wages, and exploitation of child labor that existed in Manchester and other English cities at that time. Marx and Engels began collaborating around this time, writing political works and organizing workers in Brussels, where both lived for a time. When revolution swept Europe in 1848, Marx and Engels thought it was high time to explain for a mass audience their own radical views, which they were convinced would take the world by storm. The result was *The Communist Manifesto*, published in 1848. While this short book hardly had any effect on the revolutions in 1848, it became a kind of "short course" for radicals in the later nineteenth and twentieth centuries. Its rousing language, sarcasm, and clear program made it easy to read, remember, and pass along.

❶ Why do Marx and Engels start off on a sarcastic note, speaking of a "specter"? Drawing on what you know about the political context in Europe at this time, why would they mention pope, tsar, Metternich, and German police spies?

❷ Why do Marx and Engels stress the opposition to communism? Why do you think they chose to stress (even exaggerate) this factor?

❸ Do these points really "result" from what has been said here? How do Marx and Engels justify their plan to publish this manifesto?

Beginning of the Communist Manifesto

❶ A specter is haunting Europe — the specter of communism. All the powers of old Europe have entered into a holy alliance to exorcise this specter: Pope and Tsar, Metternich and Guizot, French Radicals and German police-spies.

❷ Where is the party in opposition that has not been decried as communistic by its opponents in power? Where is the opposition that has not hurled back the branding reproach of communism, against the more advanced opposition parties, as well as against its reactionary adversaries?

❸ Two things result from this fact:

I. Communism is already acknowledged by all European powers to be itself a power.

II. It is high time that Communists should openly, in the face of the whole world, publish their views, their aims, their tendencies, and meet this nursery tale of the Specter of Communism with a manifesto of the party itself.

Working-Class Resistance Increasingly, working people recognized their common interests and joined together to press for political changes to improve their lives. The workers of Manchester who gathered at St. Peter's Field in 1819 were protesting the Corn Laws that kept the price of grain artificially high. Chartist protests of the 1830s and 1840s were democratic, aiming to gain political rights for workingmen, though women also participated. **William Cobbett**, the most famous working-class radical, argued tirelessly against child labor and the unfairness of a society in which some enjoyed great wealth while many could not provide for their most basic needs. "No society," he proclaimed, "ought to exist where the labourers live in a hog-like sort of way." Cobbett's protests help bring about Britain's 1832

William Cobbett (1763–1835) English political reformer who advocated radical working-class politics, elected to Parliament after the Reform Act of 1832.

4 Why do Marx and Engels stress the need for workers to take capital and property away from the bourgeoisie and transfer it to the state? Why do they stress that the state equals "the proletariat organized as the ruling class"?

5 Why do they insist on "despotic inroads on the rights of property"? How would liberals feel about this? Utopian socialists?

6 Looking at these nine points (point 4 about "emigrants and rebels" was specific to 1848 so not pertinent for later socialists), which seem reasonable goals in the twenty-first century? Which of these goals were reached, in whole or part, in the twentieth century in the United States? In the USSR? In Sweden? In China?

From Chapter 2 of Communist Manifesto

4 The proletariat will use its political supremacy to wrest, by degree, all capital from the bourgeoisie, to centralize all instruments of production in the hands of the State, i.e., of the proletariat organized as the ruling class; and to increase the total productive forces as rapidly as possible.

5 Of course, in the beginning, this cannot be effected except by means of despotic inroads on the rights of property, and on the conditions of bourgeois production; by means of measures, therefore, which appear economically insufficient and untenable, but which, in the course of the movement, outstrip themselves, necessitate further inroads upon the old social order, and are unavoidable as a means of entirely revolutionizing the mode of production.

[... Marx and Engels set down general goals.] **6**

1. Abolition of property in land and application of all rents of land to public purposes.
2. A heavy progressive or graduated income tax.
3. Abolition of all rights of inheritance.
4. [...]
5. Centralization of credit in the hands of the state, by means of a national bank with State capital and an exclusive monopoly.
6. Centralization of the means of communication and transport in the hands of the State.
7. Extension of factories and instruments of production owned by the State; the bringing into cultivation of waste-lands, and the improvement of the soil generally in accordance with a common plan.
8. Equal liability of all to work. Establishment of industrial armies, especially for agriculture.
9. Combination of agriculture with manufacturing industries; gradual abolition of all the distinction between town and country by a more equable distribution of the populace over the country.
10. Free education for all children in public schools. Abolition of children's factory labor in its present form. Combination of education with industrial production, &c, &c.

Source: Marx and Engels, *The Communist Manifesto* (1848).

Reform Act, but for many political change was too slow and not enough.

Some workers resorted to violence. In the second decade of the nineteenth century, textile workers in Britain's industrial cities occasionally destroyed their machines. They claimed to be followers of "General Ludd," a mythical figure, and for this reason they came to be known as **Luddites**. In France, artisans attacked the hated symbol of industrialization, the Jacquard loom. In the city of Lyon, the weavers' guild staged a public execution for the Jacquard loom in 1806, smashing it to bits, then setting the fragments ablaze. A generation later, worker dissatisfaction boiled over in a series of bloody riots and insurrections. The largest uprising occurred in 1831, again in Lyon, where thousands of workers, most from the silk industry, took to the streets. Government repression of these outbreaks took hundreds of lives. On a more personal level, workers avenged themselves on hated foremen by waylaying them after work, sometimes stuffing them headfirst into a sack, then thoroughly beating it.

Other forms of worker resistance took less violent forms. Common was the practice of "blue Monday," in which workers—often hung over from overindulgence on their one day of rest—failed to show up for work. Workers also engaged in petty theft or purposely worked at a slow pace. But all these methods had one great disadvantage: the employer could at any moment, without giving any reason, fire workers. Thus any kind of protest, absence, or work

Luddites Workers and artisans who destroyed the machines depriving them of a livelihood during early stages of industrialization; now anyone who opposes technological change.

slowdown could bring unemployment—a word that is itself a product of industrialization.

Working-Class Organizing: Trade Unions

Machine breaking and other forms of resistance were random and unorganized, and so were many strikes, when workers just illegally walked off the job. But coordinated efforts increasingly testified to a strengthening working-class consciousness. In Britain, the Combination Acts of 1799 and 1800 severely limited workers' ability to "combine"— that is, to organize for better wages and working conditions. This law made it necessary to disguise workers' organizations as self-help societies that collected money from members to provide support in case of injury, illness, or family emergencies — a kind of insurance scheme for workers. In Russia, even these organizations were illegal, and in most of Europe, **trade unions**, worker organizations that demanded higher wages and better working conditions, were suppressed until after 1850.

Britain, however, repealed the Combination Acts in 1824, allowing workers to organize openly. The repeal also permitted strikes in certain cases, but while the number of strikes did increase after 1824, most often factory owners found it easy to intimidate or simply fire union organizers and other troublemakers. Furthermore, Parliament also took action, passing Conspiracy Laws in 1825 that again restricted the right to strike.

British unions concentrated on trying to restrict work hours. The 1847 act that limited the workday for women and children to ten hours was an early success, though somewhat ironic, as women were excluded from union membership. Trade unionists claimed that working women depressed workingmen's wages, preferring instead to press for a "family wage," sufficient for a husband to allow his wife to stay home and raise a family. Most trade unions combined social and educational activities like schools and clubs with larger appeals for international working-class solidarity. So did the working-class newspapers that began to appear in France in the 1830s and 1840s, though their readership was limited.

Before 1850, working-class organizations were weak and largely ineffective. In most European countries, such as Russia and Germany, workers had no right to organize whatsoever. In Britain and France, laws restricted the ability of workers to organize and strike. Governments tended to side with factory owners against the workers, seeing investors and capitalists as necessary for economic development of the state. Improvements for workers would not come until their organizations were stronger and their perspective put forward in a coherent ideology.

trade unions Organizations that aim to protect workers' rights, improve working conditions, and enhance workers' prosperity.

21-4 Critics of Industrialization

» How did society's view of poverty change with industrialization?

» What were the main differences between utopian socialism and Marx's scientific socialism?

Industrialization created enormous wealth and great poverty at the same time, and the inequality between capitalist entrepreneurs and wageworkers struck many thinking people as outrageous. These critics of industrialization called for a more equal sharing of profits and even created complex schemes for perfect societies. These first socialists later were themselves criticized by Karl Marx, who insisted that their cooperative, nonviolent methods were doomed to failure. Only by organization and violent revolution, Marx argued, could the injustices of industrialization be righted.

21-4a Poverty in Industrial Societies

Poverty has existed as long as human society, but the poverty created by industrialization was both more noticeable and more frightening than rural poverty because it was concentrated in cities, close to the institutions of government and to the ruler's residence. Early concepts of the deserving (hardworking, but unlucky) and undeserving (lazy, drunken, unruly) poor were difficult to apply to the situation in industrial cities.

Workers had much more money than peasants; but they also had to pay for everything, at prices that were very high, whereas peasants usually paid little or nothing for their hut or humble housing and often grew at least some of their own food. Peasant poverty fluctuated with crop yield, but there was always a social safety net, as relatives, neighbors, and even the landlord would usually help out in cases of need. In the anonymous industrial city, no such safety net existed. Unlike the noble landlord, the factory owner rarely even knew his workers and did not consider himself responsible for them.

Worker poverty also fluctuated with the success or failure of industrial enterprises and economies increasingly subject to boom-and-bust cycles. Because of the difficulty of obtaining loans on a regular basis, businesses often went bankrupt, throwing all their employees out of work. Sometimes, as in the U.S. Panic of 1819, overproduction caused a general depression throughout the economy as one factory after another was forced to close down. But one very great difference between poverty before and after the Industrial Revolution must be noted. Previously, poverty meant being on the edge of starvation, and the periodic famines that swept Europe killed thousands. After industrialization, such famines no longer occurred. England and Ireland offer an example; both experienced bad harvests in the early 1840s, but industrialized England did not experience famine, whereas agricultural Ireland, also beset by the potato blight, did. The criticisms of industrialization focused less on absolute poverty than on the sharp difference in living conditions between factory owners and their workers. These critics pointed out the inequitable distribution of wealth in a capitalist system, though they did not generally use that word. **Capitalism** is an economic system in which the means of production are privately owned and operated by individuals for a profit and in which the market plays a dominant role. Modern capitalism developed alongside industrialization, increasing the efficiency of production, extending markets around the world, but also bringing with it new social problems.

21-4b Early Socialists

The liberal response to the poverty caused by industrialization was to promote a free market that would, liberals believed, increase prosperity for all in the long run. Middle-class liberals extolled individual rights, property, and rule by the most competent. They were inherently **elitist** in their insistence that wealthier and better-educated segments of society dominate in politics but at the same time potentially **egalitarian** in their emphasis on self-help, education, and hard work as the means for improving one's own economic and social condition. Other political thinkers held that the economic and political system itself made it impossible for workers to improve their lives. The discrepancy between the egalitarian ideals of middle-class liberalism and its elitism in practice fueled political **radicalism**, in particular in the form of **socialism**. Many early socialist writers and leaders were themselves from middle-class backgrounds, most famous among them Karl Marx and Friedrich Engels.

Socialism vs. Liberalism Liberalism defended the individual's right to property, whereas socialism put the primary emphasis on the welfare of society as a whole. Socialists disagreed on the status and morality of private property, but all agreed that the rich should share their wealth, for both moral and practical reasons. Such a social sharing was moral because every human being had a right to minimal standards of decent food and housing. It was practical because by lessening the misery of the working masses, the more privileged classes would defuse anger and hostility that could otherwise explode into violence.

Like liberalism and nationalism, modern concepts of socialism derive from the French Revolution, which proclaimed "fraternity," or solidarity among all citizens, whether rich or poor. During the French Revolution, socialist ideas were championed by the radical **François Babeuf**. Shocked by the continued existence of poor and rich, Babeuf demanded not just legal equality for all citizens but "real equality"—that is, an elimination of differences in wealth and social status. Real equality could be achieved, Babeuf argued, only by a total elimination of private property and by state control of goods and even state-sponsored employment programs. While Babeuf made little impact at the time—he was executed in 1797—his ideas of a state in which all material goods would be shared formed a cornerstone of socialist thought.

Utopian Socialists Babeuf's ideas influenced the so-called **utopian socialists** of the early nineteenth century. The term itself was coined by Karl Marx, who described these thinkers as "utopian"—that is, naive, unrealistic, and impractical—to distinguish them from his own thought, which Marx termed "scientific." Like Babeuf, the utopians looked forward to a harmonious society in which material differences would be minimized. They did not, however, advocate the total abolition of private property, nor did they call for a violent revolution that would overturn capitalism. In the details of the social transformation they proposed, the three main utopian socialists—**Claude Henri de Saint-Simon**, **Charles Fourier**, and Robert Owen—differed significantly. What united them was a desire to harness industrialization to improve life for all classes, to avoid social conflicts, and in the end to create a just, attractive, and humane society.

capitalism Economic system characterized by private property and a market economy developed by industrialization in the nineteenth and twentieth centuries.

elitist Belief that a small and superior group of individuals (the elite) has the moral right and responsibility to make important social and political decisions.

egalitarianism (from French, "equal") Belief that all people should have the same social, political, and—in its most radical version—economic rights.

radicalism Political ideologies that strive for thoroughgoing political and social changes.

socialism Political movement of the nineteenth and twentieth centuries that aimed to end industrial poverty by spreading profits throughout society.

François Babeuf (fran-SWAH bah-BÖF) (1760–1797) French revolutionary who demanded not only legal but also economic equality among all citizens.

utopian socialists Early socialists such as Saint-Simon, Fourier, and Owen who believed that the profits of industrialization should be used to improve living conditions throughout society.

Claude Henri de Saint-Simon (1760–1825) Early socialist of noble birth whose ideal society was led by an elite of technocrats.

Charles Fourier (1768–1830) French thinker who envisioned socialist communities (phalanges) having a division of labor based on passions and abilities.

Saint-Simon Claude Henri de Saint-Simon, born in 1760 to a noble family, was already an adult during the French Revolution and as an aristocrat came close to meeting his end at the guillotine. He fought on the American side during the Revolutionary War, made a fortune as a speculator during the 1790s, went bankrupt, and spent time in an insane asylum. Despite his aristocratic background, Saint-Simon detested kings, bishops, and aristocrats. He admired British society, seeing it as a system that rewarded merit and hard work. Like the British liberals, Saint-Simon admired intelligence and the entrepreneurial spirit. But in contrast to the liberal belief that competition in a free market would benefit all, Saint-Simon emphasized social cooperation and planning, led by a dedicated, well-educated elite.

Saint-Simon's last major work, *The New Christianity* (incomplete at the time of his death in 1825), attempted to place his ideas on economic justice and a new society in a Christian framework. Surveying the history of Catholicism and Protestantism, he criticized both for failing to take on the problem of poverty. His New Christianity, he claimed, would rejuvenate Christianity's fundamental rejection of violence and call for compassion. He charged rulers to: "Hearken to the voice of God that speaks through me. Return to the path of Christianity. Remember that Christianity commands you to use all your powers to increase as rapidly as possible the welfare of the poor." These ideas gained considerable prominence among businessmen, intellectuals, and politicians in France, but Saint-Simon's most significant contribution was his linking of industrial growth to general social improvement rather than simply to individual enrichment.

Fourier Charles Fourier, the most visionary of the utopians, demanded a far more thorough transformation of society than Saint-Simon. Fourier was an eccentric and difficult man. He came from a family of cloth merchants and earned his living in trade. At the same time, he spent his free moments concocting a utopian scheme of grandiose proportions that, Fourier thought, would solve the economic, social, and even spiritual problems of society. Human beings are motivated, he proposed, by twelve main passions, ranging from friendship and ambition to love of intrigue and the five senses (taste, smell, touch, sight, and hearing). While all of these passions are present in every human being, the proportion of each differs greatly. Using complex and quite incomprehensible mathematical principles (Fourier left behind several notebooks containing nothing but equations and mathematical notations), he arrived at the idea of the *phalange*.

Each phalange would include 1,620 individuals, carefully selected to include a variety of "passionate types." These small communities would live and work together, each carrying out the tasks best suited to his or her (Fourier firmly believed in women's equality) passions and abilities. For example, children, who love muck and filth, would carry out trash and clean sewers. While the division of labor would be retained, it would be based on the most fundamental drives and desires of human beings and would thus enhance, not suppress, their humanity.

While inequalities in income and wealth would continue to exist in the phalange, these differences would not cause social discontent because all individuals would freely choose their own jobs and income. Children would be brought up and educated communally within the phalange, total equality would exist between women and men, and restrictions on sexual relations would disappear. Best of all, because the phalange would put human passions to their best use in a just and cooperative community, the need for coercive government, police, armies, and prisons would disappear. Fourier believed fervently that if only one phalange could be set up, its success would rapidly transform the world into a community of phalanges.

Fourier's scheme seems eccentric, but it addressed real social problems and proposed serious methods of combating them. Industrialization had condemned millions to boring, repetitive, and meaningless work in which the workers themselves became like machines. It had destroyed social networks that protected the poor. It had also had a devastating effect on the natural environment. Fourier's scheme attempted to give people back their humanity, to end exploitation, and to create a social order consistent with fundamental human psychology (Fourier's "passions"). Although no phalange was ever set up, Fourier's ideas in various forms certainly influenced actual egalitarian communal settlements, such as Brook Farm and the Oneida community in the United States as well as the Israeli **kibbutzim**.

Owen Robert Owen, like Fourier, believed in the fundamental goodness of human nature, but Owen attempted to build practical cooperative communities. He was himself a successful industrialist who used his cotton mill at New Lanark to try out his principles. Owen believed that cooperation rather than competition would enable him to make a profit while spreading industry-generated wealth among the workers. Under his management, New Lanark became a model community in which workers enjoyed high living standards in the apartments he built for them, pleasant and hygienic surroundings, and free education for their children.

Owen tried to interest his fellow industrialists in his cooperative principles, but with little success. The community he set up in New Harmony, Indiana, failed after only a few years. In his later years, Owen was active in the trade union movement and encouraged

kibbutzim Collective agricultural settlements set up by Jewish settlers in what is now Israel in the late nineteenth century and continuing to the present.

View of a French Phalanstery (litho), Daubigny, Charles Francois (1817-78) (after) / Bibliotheque Nationale, Paris, France / Bridgeman Images

Fourier's Phalange

The utopian socialist Fourier was convinced that if he could only get financing to build one phalange — such as the one depicted here — its success would lead to his brand of socialism sweeping the world. Unfortunately his own eccentricities and those of his political ideas prevented any actual phalanges from being constructed.

》 *Looking at this picture, what kind of an institution does this appear to be?*

》 *Would you be interested in living here? Why or why not?*

the establishment of **consumer cooperatives** for workers, but he died a disillusioned man. Despite his failure to persuade contemporary businessmen to adopt the system of factory-paid housing and schools, his ideas influenced later industrial-residential complexes from the Soviet Union to Fiat's factory city of Turin, Italy.

The importance of the utopian socialists lies not so much in the communities that applied their ideas but in their ideas themselves, which later socialists would build on and develop. For example, Fourier's idea that a unified economic system would create a more efficient and humane society was taken up by Karl Marx and later in the Soviet Union. Fourier was also one of the first to advocate total equality between the sexes and to denounce bourgeois marriage as a form of prostitution, ideas that would be taken up and further developed by Friedrich Engels and later socialist and feminist thinkers. Saint-Simon's ideas were extremely influential in mid-nineteenth-century France (many cabinet ministers and businessmen considered themselves "Saint-Simonists"), and he can be seen as an early advocate of "technocracy," or rule by technologically trained elites. Owen's ideas have found practical application in various cooperative communities.

21-4c Karl Marx

Like most socialist thinkers, Karl Marx came from the middle class. His father was a lawyer of Jewish origin who converted to Christianity when Karl was a young boy, growing up in western Germany. Marx attended university in Bonn and Berlin, where he studied philosophy under **G.W.F. Hegel**, whose systematic thought

consumer cooperatives
Organizations of consumers who band together to obtain better prices from producers and share any profits derived from sales.

G.W.F. Hegel (1770–1831)
Important philosopher of the nineteenth century whose philosophy of historical progress was crucial for Marx.

would prove an important source for Marx's own ideas. Marx's passionate personality, which gained him many friends and many bitter enemies, developed early. As a university student, he believed that philosophy was the best method for understanding the world. Soon, however, Marx was ready to go beyond philosophy: "Philosophers have only interpreted the world in various ways," he stated. "The point, however, is to change it." Marx's quest to change the world would make him one of the most admired and despised figures in the late nineteenth and twentieth centuries.

Threatened with arrest by the Prussian authorities in the 1840s because of his radical views, Marx left his homeland. After the publication of *The Communist Manifesto* in 1848, he always lived abroad. During this decade he also married, started a family, and began his famous collaboration with Friedrich Engels. Meeting first in Paris in 1844, the two men quickly formed one of the most productive friendships in history. Engels's *Condition of the Working Class in England* (1845) showed that he was far more familiar with the actual conditions of industrial workers than Marx was, but Marx possessed the greater analytical mind. Engels was less of an original thinker than Marx but far more practical and easygoing—and much more successful in business. Few days in the next four decades went by without letters between the "Moor" (Marx) and the "General" (Engels), as they jokingly referred to each other.

The Communist Manifesto Marx's most famous early work, coauthored with Engels, *The Communist Manifesto*, appeared during the revolutions of 1848. In a few dozen pages, the *Manifesto* denounced bourgeois society as hypocritical, exploitative, and doomed to destruction: "A specter is haunting Europe—the specter of Communism." Marx used the term **communism** to distinguish his more radical thinking—based on class struggle and an inevitable violent revolution—from the less confrontational schemes of earlier socialists. *The Communist Manifesto* set down in stirring language both an ideological justification and a practical program for a thoroughgoing revolution: "Workers of the world unite!"

Marx, Hegel, and the Dialectic of History Marx based his ideology on the philosophy of Hegel, who had argued that history progresses in a **dialectical** way.

That is, in history, an idea that becomes prominent is inevitably challenged by its opposite, and the resolution of these two opposing principles produces a higher idea. Marx's philosophical innovation was to apply this principle to the material world and to argue that this struggle over ideas would produce revolutionary change in the economic, political, and social structure of society.

For Marx, history could be understood as class struggle: slaves versus slave owners, serfs versus lords, and now the proletariat versus the capitalists. Marx allowed that the capitalists had previously played a progressive and even revolutionary role in history by challenging the old economic order based on landed wealth and replacing it with industrial capitalism. Now, however, the leading position had to shift away from the capitalists—the bourgeois middle class to the industrial workers, the proletariat. In the end, Marx insisted, the working masses would rise in revolt, strip the bourgeoisie of their wealth and power, and create a just, egalitarian society.

Marx and Revolution Marx's practical program was violent revolution, which he saw as the natural outcome of inevitable class struggle. It would be naive, he wrote scornfully, to imagine that the bourgeoisie would give up their wealth and power without a fight. Here Marx differed significantly from the utopian socialists, who stressed cooperation over violence, and he termed his program "scientific" to distinguish it from theirs. The utopian socialists, Marx claimed, had a superficial understanding of history, economics, and society. The utopians' idea that persuasion and cooperative efforts could do away with the proletariat's misery, Marx argued, was both absurd and reactionary. Rather, workers had to organize and seize power themselves to achieve a just society. The contours of this future society may be seen by the specific goals mentioned in *The Communist Manifesto*: free education for all children, the abolition of inheritance and landed property, state control of credit and transportation, a **progressive income tax**, and an end to the distinction between urban and rural areas by spreading cultural and educational institutions outside of cities.

The impact of Marx's writing on the revolutions of 1848 was minimal. But Marx put forth his ideas about class struggle and the need for revolution at this time and then spent the rest of his life gathering and analyzing data to support his thesis. In the second half of the nineteenth century, the influence of his and Engels's ideas would grow. By the end of the century, self-proclaimed Marxist parties existed in most European countries. Even more important, liberals and even conservatives came to recognize that to avoid "communist revolution," they needed to respond to worker demands for improved working conditions and increased pay.

communism Radical political philosophy proposed by Karl Marx, advocating the abolition of private property and an inevitable violent workers' revolution.

dialectical Process of thought that achieves a higher synthesis by reconciling two contradictory ideas ("thesis" and "antithesis").

progressive income tax Tax on money earned, with high earners paying a greater percentage of income than individuals earning less.

CONNECTIONS: Industrialization brought with it pollution, bad working conditions, unemployment, and social disruption. The careful, beautiful work of artisans was swept away by crude machine-produced items. Not just in Europe, but around the world industrialization was often denounced. In India, the politician and thinker Mohandas Gandhi rejected this development, speaking of "The Curse of Industrialization" in harsh tones: "God forbid that India should ever take to industrialism after the manner of the West. If an entire nation of 300 million took to similar economic exploitation, it would strip of the world bare like locusts." (See Section 24-3 The British Raj in India.)

CHAPTER Review

Summary

» Industrialization began first in Great Britain in the late eighteenth century.

» By 1850, industrialization had spread to Belgium and parts of France, the German lands, and elsewhere in continental Europe.

» Industrialization made cities grow, often causing terrible living conditions.

» Industrialization helped create the socioeconomic category of class, a consciousness based on one's place in the economy.

» Middle-class people viewed themselves as "self-made" and respected education, sobriety, and hard work.

» Working-class people, despite the appalling conditions of work, also strove for respectability with such movements as Methodism.

» Working-class organizations strove for better working conditions, shorter hours, and to exclude children from the industrial workforce.

» Utopian socialists like Saint-Simon, Fourier, and Owen tried to solve the problems of industrialization through cooperation.

» Karl Marx, who termed his own thinking "scientific socialism," argued that only violent revolution would bring justice to the working class.

Chronology

1799–1800	English Combination Acts prohibit strikes and unions [Europe]
1801	Joseph Marie Jacquard invents the automated loom [Europe]
1810s	Luddites revolt in England [Europe]
1815	British Parliament passes Corn Laws [Europe]
1815	End of Napoleonic Wars [Europe]
1820s	Industrialization begins in Belgium, northern France [Europe]

1824	Repeal of Combination Acts permits labor unions [Europe]
1829	First steam locomotive, the *Rocket,* travels from Liverpool to Manchester in test race [Europe]
1830s	Chartists protest British Corn Laws [Europe]
1831	Belgium's independence encourages industry [Europe]
1831	Workers in Lyon destroy Jacquard loom to protest industrialization [Europe]
1833	Factory Act in Britain restricts child labor [Europe]
1833–1836	Tenpō famine in Japan kills hundreds of thousands [Asia]
1834	Zollverein (German Customs Union) established to promote trade [Europe]
1835	First German railroad opens [Europe]
1838	Iron steamships compete in race across the Atlantic to New York [Americas]
1839	Prussia forbids the employment of children under nine in factories [Europe]
1840s	Beginnings of industrialization in central Europe [Europe]
1845–1847	Mexican-American War, ending with U.S. annexation of nearly half of Mexico [Americas]
1847	British Factory Act limits the number of hours women and children can work in textile factories [Western Europe]
1848	Revolutions sweep Europe [Europe] Marx and Engels publish *The Communist Manifesto* [Europe]
1851	First major Russian railway opens, linking Moscow and St. Petersburg [Europe] Half of English population lives in cities [Europe]
1859	Samuel Smiles publishes *Self-Help* [Europe]

Critical Thinking Questions

Take time to pull together all the important information from the chapter by answering the following questions:

The Spread of Industrialization

» Where did industrialization begin on the European continent? What countries lagged behind?

» How did new forms of transportation created by industrialization change everyday life?

The Middle Classes

» How were the middle classes set off from "upper" and "lower" classes?

» What were some of the characteristics of "middle-class respectability"?

Working Classes

» Who made up the "working classes"?

» How did industrialization affect family life and gender relations?

Critics of Industrialization

» On what grounds did socialists criticize liberalism?

» How did individual "utopian socialists" plan to reform capitalism to create a better, more just society?

MindTap® is a fully online personalized learning experience built upon Cengage Learning content. MindTap® combines student learning tools—readings, multimedia, activities, and assessments—into a singular Learning Path that guides students through the course and helps students develop the critical thinking, analysis, and communication skills that are essential to academic and professional success.

The Triumph of the Nation-State, 1848–1900

Chapter Outline

As you read, consider the following questions:

❯ What was the importance of the revolutions of 1848?

❯ How did the ideologies of liberalism and nationalism affect the revolutions of 1848?

❯ What were the main events and individuals that led to the unification of Germany and Italy?

❯ How and why did nationalism shift from a liberal to a conservative ideology after 1848?

❯ Where and under what circumstances did democratic institutions like constitutions and parliaments spread throughout Europe in the decades after 1848?

❯ What were some of the different ways state (government) power grew in this period?

THE WORLD AS WE KNOW it—politically, economically, socially—took shape in the second half of the nineteenth century. While political "isms" like nationalism, liberalism, and socialism can be traced back to the French Revolution and even earlier, from the 1850s onward these ideologies fundamentally altered political and social life. It was precisely during this period that many Europeans identified with and demanded rights

for their nations. Similarly, although the Industrial Revolution had started in Britain in the late eighteenth century, only during the second half of the nineteenth century did large-scale industrialization begin to change the lives of people all over Europe and elsewhere in the world. The growth of technology and industrialization came together with new forms of politics to create a new and more democratic Europe after 1848. In that year, liberal democratic institutions existed in few European countries, and constitutionalism as a practical political program was almost unknown. By 1906, even conservative states like the German and Russian empires had adopted some aspects of constitutional government.

Perhaps the single most powerful political force of this period was nationalism. Increasingly, people identified themselves with a national group instead of with their village, occupation, or religion. Europeans came to accept the nationalist principle that all members of one nation should live together politically as citizens of a single state. At the same time, the definition of who belonged in a certain nation was contested, and many conservative multinational states opposed nationalism as a dangerous, even revolutionary, idea.

Political leaders, recognizing the force of nationalism, began to define their actions in terms of the "national will." The spread of nationalist rhetoric meant that even kings and emperors found it necessary to wrap themselves in the national banner. Before 1848, nationalism and liberalism tended to be aligned, both opposing the prevailing conservative and monarchist order symbolized by Clemens von Metternich in Vienna. After 1848, it was the conservatives who used nationalist ideology for their own political aims.

By the end of the nineteenth century, nationalism had gained broad acceptance, especially in western and central Europe, but also in many parts of the world, from Latin America to Japan to colonialized nations. Even so, nationalism was not without its opponents. The growing socialist movement argued against the aggressive demands and divisions of nationalism, calling for workers of all nations to unite against the capitalists. Socialists emphasized class identity over nationality. The Catholic Church also opposed nationalism, particularly after the formation of the secular and implicitly anticlerical Italian state in the 1860s. The rulers of conservative multinational empires in central and eastern Europe understood that nationalism threatened their empires' very existence. In different and often contradictory ways, Habsburg, Ottoman, and Romanov rulers attempted to neutralize the growing power of nationalist ideology. In the end, however, not nationalism but these empires were swept away.

22-1 The Revolutions of 1848

> » **What were the main demands of the revolutionaries in 1848?**

> » **What were the short- and long-term outcomes of the uprisings in 1848?**

In 1848, revolutions across Europe ended the conservative, antiliberal, and antinational period initiated at the Congress of Vienna and symbolized by the Austrian Prime Minister Clemens von Metternich. While different circumstances in each capital city and region sparked the uprisings, all demanded a broadening of political rights and recognition of nationalist concerns. In the short run, all were unsuccessful. The Prussian king and Austrian emperor were threatened but remained on their thrones. In France, the newly elected president, Louis Napoleon, declared himself Emperor Napoleon III and crushed political opposition. Still, the failure of 1848 helped pave the way for the triumph of national ideas—though not of liberalism—some twenty years later, when the nation-states of Italy and Germany were created. Similarly, while the constitutions granted in 1848 were not always respected, the precedent of constitutional rule had been established; its political authority would steadily increase in subsequent decades.

revolutions of 1848 Series of upheavals that shook Europe from Sicily to Paris to Berlin to Vienna, bringing first liberal change, then generally conservative reaction.

22-1a The Tide of Revolution

The **revolutions of 1848** swept through nearly every European country (see Map 22.1). Only those on the periphery—Great Britain, Scandinavia, Russia, the Ottoman Empire—were spared. But even in these undisturbed regions, rulers and privileged classes were shocked and terrified. In Russia, for example, the government increased censorship and arrested radical thinkers. In Britain, increased police surveillance following the Chartist agitation prevented revolution, but Queen Victoria regarded the events on the continent with worry.

The first uprising began in January 1848 in southern Europe, in Sicily. Street demonstrations in Palermo and Naples forced the reactionary ruler of the Kingdom of the Two Sicilies, as the southern Italian state was known, to form a liberal government and issue a constitution. These liberal concessions in one of the most conservative regions of Europe electrified rulers and liberals alike.

Map 22.1 **Revolutions of 1848** In 1848 revolutions swept many European countries.

1. Where did revolutions occur in 1848?
2. Which regions were not touched by revolutions, and why?

1848 in France Then, in February 1848, Louis Philippe, France's "bourgeois king," was forced to **abdicate**. Since his coronation in 1830 as "King of the French," Louis Philippe had attempted to steer a compromise course between the demands of royalist aristocrats and the new, wealthy bourgeoisie. Most Frenchmen, even of the middle class, continued to be shut out of the political process.

In the mid-1840s, middle-class protesters began to join with broader peasant and working-class movements demanding relief in the face of bad harvests and unemployment. Because political meetings were illegal, in 1847 a banquet campaign was launched. The king could hardly forbid Frenchmen from eating! As everyone understood, the main purpose of these banquets was not cuisine but politics; banquet speakers called for an extension of the vote, even universal male suffrage. When the government tried to prevent a "monster banquet" in February 1848, clashes with police and would-be banqueters and students escalated into major street battles. Seeing no way out of the situation, Louis Philippe abdicated and fled to London.

France was declared a republic, and the revolutionaries began the task of creating a new government.

CONNECTIONS: Eating is linked to many ceremonies, taboos, and festivals around the world. Thus, many times in history "banquet campaigns" have led to political change. In France in 1848, large banquets featuring speeches as well as delicacies led to the overthrow of the government. A half-century later in Russia, reformers and radicals got together for meals to discuss how to bring down—or at least reform—the tsarist government. These banquets were among the causes of the Revolution of 1905 in Petersburg and Moscow (see also Section 25-4 Russia in Revolution for more on the toppling of the tsarist regime). And toward the end of the twentieth century, liberals and others who opposed the dictatorship of General Pinochet (pee-no-SHAY) in Chile gathered for meals that were more feasts of words than calories. These "banquets" helped bring about Pinochet's ouster in the late 1980s.

abdicate To give up one's position as ruler, usually said of kings.

With the monarchy swept away, political strains began to appear between the liberals and radicals. When the **national workshops**, set up in March 1848 to provide relief and work for the jobless, could not keep pace with growing unemployment, moderate liberals began to grumble about supporting the lazy at the taxpayers' expense. Business leaders, too, denounced the national workshops as unfair competition and an outrageous tax burden. Yet thousands of impoverished men continued to stream into Paris, and many liberals feared the collapse of public order.

Elections in April revealed another growing divide—between Paris and the provinces. Voters in the provinces overwhelmingly supported moderate or even conservative candidates, whereas in Paris radicals managed—barely—to send radical and socialist delegates such as **Louis Blanc** to the National Assembly. Meanwhile the turmoil on the streets of Paris intensified. On May 15, large crowds declared the parliament dissolved and attempted to set up their own radical government. This attempt ended in failure and arrests, but tensions continued.

spring at Saint Paul's Church in Frankfurt. Among the more than four hundred elected representatives who gathered to write a constitution, with political rights for all, were lawyers, government officials, and professors, including the Grimm brothers, now at work on their German dictionary. Although there were also four artisans, thirty-four landowners, and one peasant, this **Frankfurt Assembly**, in which 90 percent of the representatives were educated, was indeed a "parliament of scholars," or at least of educated middle-class men.

The nationalism reflected in the Frankfurt Assembly's demand for a unified Germany was also at work in Hungary. The Hungarian elite, especially, resented the power of the central government in Vienna. In March, led by the fiery speaker **Louis (Lájos) (LA-yosh) Kossuth (KOH-shoot)**, they demanded an end to imperial rule and the establishment of a Hungarian parliament. The Austrian Habsburgs were at first conciliatory, but when the newly elected Hungarian parliament voted to create its own army and currency, the emperor sent in troops, and a regular war ensued between Austrian (imperial) and Hungarian forces.

national workshops Paris institutions set up in 1848 to give work to the unemployed at government expense.

Louis Blanc (1811–1882) French socialist who advocated the right to work and the abolition of competition.

Frederick William IV King of Prussia (r. 1840–1861) who issued a constitution during the Berlin revolution of 1848.

constituent assembly Meeting to draw up a constitution or to agree on basic fundamentals of a governing system.

Frankfurt Assembly Representatives elected throughout German states who met in Frankfurt (1848–1849) to draft a liberal constitution for a united German Empire.

Louis (Lájos) Kossuth (1802–1894) Hungarian statesman who led his people in revolt against the Habsburg (Austrian) empire during 1848 and 1849.

1848 in Central Europe

As Metternich once remarked, "When Paris sneezes, Europe catches cold." News of the Paris upheavals quickly reached Berlin, Vienna, and other central European cities, where liberals soon demanded similar political concessions from their rulers. In the Habsburg lands, street fighting in May forced the imperial family to abandon Vienna for a more easily guarded country estate. Metternich resigned and fled the city alone, abandoned by the Habsburg rulers whom he had worked to keep in power. In Berlin, clashes between the army and local citizens left many dead. The outrage over the killings was so great that Prussian king **Frederick William IV** felt himself compelled to issue a constitution and salute as heroes the bodies of those shot by his own troops.

Liberal Germans, declaring themselves the representatives of the German nation, demanded a unified Germany and organized elections for a **constituent assembly**, which met in late

1848 in Italy In the Italian states, revolution also seemed to triumph in the spring of 1848. The insurrections spread from Naples to Milan (then belonging to the Habsburg empire), Venice (where a republic was declared), and Rome (still under Papal rule). In Rome, the rebels took over the city as traditional authorities fled—and the pope sought refuge outside of town in the fortress of Gaeta. Giuseppe Mazzini and Giuseppe Garibaldi worked together to build a "Rome of the People," establishing freedom of the press, setting up secular schools, and handing over some church property to the poor.

22-1b The Restoration of Authority

If in spring the revolutionaries seemed to have the upper hand, by early summer the forces of traditional authority had gained strength, and by fall the revolutions had been stamped out nearly everywhere. In Paris, tensions between moderates and radicals led to a bloody clash set off by the moderates' abolition of the national workshops in late June. These might have been dismantled without bloodshed had the government moved slowly. Instead, the overnight action sparked an armed workers' uprising, in which more than 1,500 people, including the archbishop of Paris, were killed. After suppressing the uprising, government forces massacred more than 3,000 workers. The violence, known as the June Days, demonstrated that liberal governments, like monarchies and conservative regimes, were quite willing to use violence against political opponents. After June 1848, the forces of moderation and order were firmly in control in Paris.

In December 1848, French voters overwhelmingly chose Louis Napoleon, a nephew of the great Napoleon, as president of the French Republic. Their longing for order after a year of revolution would help pave

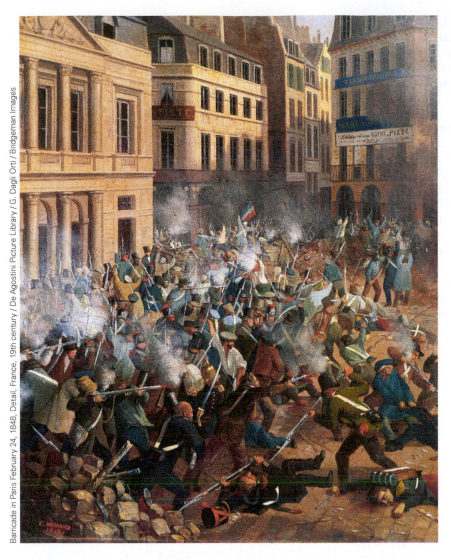

Barricade in Paris February 24, 1848, Detail, France, 19th century / De Agostini Picture Library / G. Dagli Orti / Bridgeman Images

Barricades in Paris, 1848

As the revolution developed in 1848, patriotic and liberal forces set up barricades in city streets to protect themselves from troops sent by conservative governments. Barricades were set up not only in Paris (as here), but also in Frankfurt, Vienna, and elsewhere.

≫ *What patriotic symbols do you see in this image?*

≫ *Judging from people's dress, what social classes are represented here?*

the way for his dictatorship as Emperor **Napoleon III**, beginning in 1852. Thus, the immediate outcome in France of the 1848 revolution was not a liberal republic but the Second Empire, which lasted until 1870.

Nationalism and Authority in the Habsburg Lands The situation in the Habsburg empire was complicated by its numerous nationalities and the strife between them. When the Hungarians declared their independence from Vienna, the Hungarian dependency of Croatia sided with the Habsburg emperor. Similarly, German liberals in Prague were taken aback when the eminent Czech historian František Palacký refused to participate in elections to the Frankfurt Assembly. Palacký pointed out that he was not a German but a Czech who was loyal to the Habsburg empire. Believing that cultural and political rights of small nations like his were better assured in a large multinational empire than in a nation-state like the one the representatives at Frankfurt envisioned, Palacký declared, "If Austria did not exist it would be necessary to invent her."

Unlike the Germans and Hungarians, smaller national groups in the Habsburg empire did not aspire to political independence but hoped only to be allowed to use their own language in schools, publishing, and perhaps in government offices. The **Slavic Congress**, held in Prague in June 1848, asserted its loyalty to the Habsburg empire while demanding recognition for Slavic languages (Czech, Slovak, Croatian) as equals of German. It also called for closer relations between the Slavic peoples of the Habsburg empire and Slavs in the Russian and Ottoman empires. The congress was dissolved at gunpoint by forces loyal to the new Habsburg emperor, **Francis Joseph**.

By late 1848, the emperor was back in a now subdued Vienna. The imperial army had established order in northern Italy and in the Czech lands and was preparing for battle with the Hungarians. But the Hungarians

Napoleon III (r. 1852–1870) Louis Napoleon, nephew of Napoleon Bonaparte, who was elected president of France in 1848 and declared himself emperor in 1852.

Slavic Congress Assembly of Slavic nations—Poles, Balkan peoples, Czechs, Ukrainians, and one Russian—in Prague in 1848 that called for cultural recognition for Slavs.

Francis Joseph (r. 1848–1916) Habsburg emperor of Austria from 1848 and king of Hungary from 1867.

proved hard to defeat, surrendering only after Russian units had come to the aid of the Austrians. Francis Joseph repudiated the constitution he had accepted in 1848 and vowed to rule as an absolute ruler. As in France, in the Habsburg lands it appeared that the upheavals had all been for nothing.

Liberals Defeated in the German Lands In the German Confederation, the revolution ended less violently. Except in Berlin, German states had generally avoided clashes with their citizens. Most German princes retained power after 1848, though mainly after promising liberal political reforms. Since May, the Frankfurt Assembly had been debating plans to unify Germany: Should Germans unite under Habsburg rule, the so-called *grossdeutsch*, or "big German," solution, or should a new German Empire be formed with the Prussian king at its head, the *kleindeutsch (KLINE-doich)*, or "small German," solution? At first, most delegates favored the *grossdeutsch* solution. But Francis Joseph could not agree to rule as the head of a German national state when over half of his subjects in the Austrian and Hungarian lands were non-Germans. After this refusal, the Frankfurt Assembly offered the crown of the future German Empire to King Frederick William IV of Prussia. Frederick William indignantly refused, calling the offer "from the gutter" and the crown a "diadem molded out of the dirt and dregs of revolution, disloyalty and treason."

Rebutted by Austrian emperor and Prussian king, the Frankfurt Assembly found itself in an impossible position. Lacking the will or ability to revolt violently against existing German princes, it was attacked as too conservative by radicals and workers. Ironically, the assembly was rescued by Prussian troops, and the "scholars" were unceremoniously dismissed and sent home. Sporadic attempts at revolution were countered throughout the German lands by military action.

By the end of 1849, the revolutions were over. In Paris, a moderate liberal government had demonstrated brutality toward its opponents. In the Italian lands, most of the same rulers were in place, despite a flurry of granted constitutions and promised political rights. In Berlin, the Prussian king was in control, and thousands of liberals and radicals were under arrest, in hiding, or already in exile. Friedrich Engels and Karl Marx would live the rest of their lives in England, but many "Forty-Eighters" fled to the United States. In Vienna, the Habsburg emperor was once again firmly in power. Despite the apparent calm, however, few of the political, national, or social demands of the revolutionaries had been dealt with, and the issues would be raised again. In retrospect, 1848 was a watershed.

22-1c 1848 as a Watershed Year

The role of ideology in the revolutions of 1848 is complex. There is no doubt about the importance of liberal ideals such as constitutionalism, civil rights, and the rule of law to those who tried to overthrow regimes in Sicily, Paris, Vienna, and Berlin. But when moderate liberals were confronted with radical and socialist demands and the destruction of private property, they joined with conservatives in calling for order. In central Europe, nationalist revolutionaries promoted liberal ideas, only to find themselves opposed by other liberal nationalists who remained loyal to traditional authority. In central Europe, nationalist slogans combined with liberal ideas and proposals. Socialist ideas were also discussed, though the actual influence of socialism in 1848 was small.

Liberalism, Socialism, and Nationalism Liberalism was certainly the most important political ideology in 1848. The revolutionaries called for constitutions, popular representation, and an end to censorship. In Paris, liberalism momentarily triumphed, then was challenged from the left. In central Europe, middle-class liberals learned that the masses of workers and peasants were not always willing to follow their lead, especially if liberal policies did not also promote low bread prices, decent wages, and employment opportunities.

Marx and Engels's *The Communist Manifesto*, published in 1848, had been written before the revolutionary outbreaks, and its immediate influence was minimal, in part because it was available only in German. Socialist ideas such as the abolition of inheritance and landed property, state control of credit and transportation, and free education had not yet gained broad support. Only in Paris did avowed socialists like Louis Blanc, father of the national workshops, play a significant part in the revolutions. On the whole, rebelling workers and peasants in 1848 knew nothing about socialism. Their demands were more basic: lower taxes, cheaper food, jobs. Only later in the nineteenth century would Marx's pamphlet become basic reading for a mass audience.

Nationalism played a very visible role in 1848, though it scored few victories. Neither Germany nor Italy was united, the Hungarian attempt to secure autonomy and national rights was crushed by Vienna, and the Slavic Congress in Prague was dissolved. In most parts of Europe, most people did not yet think in national terms. People spoke local dialects that were often far from standard written forms of, say, the German language that the Grimm brothers were working so hard to define. People identified themselves more often as inhabitants of a village, as Catholics, or as Jews than as Hungarians or Czechs or Germans. But nationalist movements in 1848 helped popularize the idea that languages spoken by nonelites like Czech, Ukrainian, Romanian, Slovak, and Croatian deserved respect—and rights. Crucially, the central idea of nationalism—that a state must defend the values of a nation—was expressed by revolutionaries from Paris to Berlin, from Palermo to Budapest. Although the revolutions of 1848 did not establish nation-states in central Europe, they helped spread the ideals of nationalism. (See Map 22.2 to learn more about the changing political boundaries that resulted from the rise of nationalism.)

Changes in Political Ideology After 1848 After 1848, the political center shifted significantly to the left. Few thinking Europeans continued to defend

Map 22.2 **Political Europe in 1900** The force of nationalism can be seen in the changing boundaries of European states between 1815 and 1900. Observe the political boundaries on this map from 1900, then compare it with the map of Europe after the Congress of Vienna (Map 20.1).

1. What are the most significant changes between these maps?
2. What new countries were created over that time?
3. Where did nationalism play the most important role in determining political boundaries?
4. Which countries can be termed *nation-states* and which cannot?

divine-right monarchy, and increasing numbers of educated middle-class people embraced political liberalism or even socialism as solutions to society's problems. The liberals are particularly interesting in this context. Before 1848, they constituted a small minority in the politics of every European country aside from Britain. After midcentury, liberal ideas and liberal figures took on new importance not only in Britain, France, and other western European countries, but even in Russia, the Habsburg lands (after 1867, Austria-Hungary), and southern Europe. Thus, the liberals who were defeated in 1848 had by 1900 become an important—in some cases, a predominant—part of the political landscape. And by this time, they recognized that the greatest challenge to liberalism came not from conservatives but from the growing socialist movement.

Yet conservatism was not dead. The peasant unrest of 1848 convinced rulers to abolish the last vestiges of serfdom in Europe, except in Russia. After 1848, the peasantry in western and central Europe became the mainstay of conservative and religious forces. The Catholic Church, badly shaken by the year's events, which had temporarily forced Pope **Pius IX** to flee from Rome, turned its back on any kind of liberal reform. Until nearly the end of the century, the Catholic Church would be a solid bulwark of traditional authority, condemning constitutions, nationalism, and popular representation in government.

Many of the rejected national demands of 1848 were resurrected a generation or so later. Italian unification took place in the 1860s, partly through Garibaldi's continued efforts. The Hungarian demands to Vienna in 1848 were granted two decades later in the **Compromise of 1867**, which gave the Hungarians domestic autonomy in the empire. The Slavic Congress of 1848 can be seen as a precursor of the Pan-Slav movement of the 1870s that aimed to unite all Slavic peoples from the Adriatic to the Pacific under the Romanov dynasty. Thus, immediate failures of 1848 masked future triumphs.

22-2 New Nation-States and Nationalist Tensions

» **How, in politics and personalities, were the processes of German and Italian unification similar?**

» **How did nationality identity differ in Poland, Bulgaria, and Norway? How do you explain these differences?**

Pius IX (r. 1846–1878) Pope who became a staunch conservative, refusing to acknowledge Italian unification and condemning all forms of modernity.

Compromise of 1867 Agreement between Austria and Hungary dividing the country into two autonomous parts, linked by a common budget, military, and foreign policy.

Camille Cavour (1810–1861) Prime minister and adviser to the King of Sardinia, Victor Emmanuel II, who in 1861 became the first king of united Italy.

In the second half of the nineteenth century, nationalists translated their ideology into political realities. The greatest triumph of the national principle was the creation of two large, unified states in the middle of Europe: Italy and Germany. Both had conservative constitutions under powerful monarchs (the Prussian king took on the title of Kaiser [emperor]), to the disappointment of liberal nationalists. Norway and Bulgaria also became independent states in this era. Nations lacking states, such as the Poles, stressed ethnic unity and linguistic solidarity. Throughout Europe, nationalism became exclusionary. Across the Atlantic, the United States experienced a mass immigration of European peoples.

22-2a The Unification of Italy

Since the 1830s, the idea of the Italian nation had been promoted by Giuseppe Mazzini, who exemplified the enthusiasm and almost mystical quality of early liberal nationalism. His impassioned writings reminded Italians of their glorious Roman past and called for national unity, democracy, and equal rights for all. Mazzini inspired thousands of his countrymen to think beyond the boundaries of their local town or community and aspire to be "Italians." He demanded "a sacred devotion to the fatherland" and was also a proponent of gender equality, urging Italian men to "cancel from your minds every idea of superiority over Women." Mazzini's importance lies in his writings and the enthusiasm for the Italian idea he spread.

First Steps Toward Unification The idea of a united Italy had significant obstacles to overcome, as following the revolutions of 1848 Italy was still divided into numerous sovereign political units (see Map 22.3). In the northwest, centered on the city of Turin, was the small but stable kingdom of Piedmont-Sardinia, ruled by the House of Savoy. Southern Italy was dominated by the Kingdom of the Two Sicilies, which stretched from the island of Sicily to Naples. In between were the Papal States, including Rome and Bologna, an area in which the pope not only was the spiritual head but also ruled as a secular lord, much like the dukes of Milan or Modena. In the northeast, the provinces of Veneto and Lombardy remained under Habsburg (Austrian) rule. As Metternich had famously put it, Italy was no more than a "geographical expression."

In 1859, Napoleon III, who supported the idea of an Italian state in the hopes of strengthening French influence in the region, agreed to help Piedmont drive Austria out of northern Italy. The prime minister of Piedmont, **Camille Cavour (ka-VOOR)**, saw the alliance with France as a means to position his state as the nucleus of a future united Italy. In his own personal beliefs, Cavour reflected the changes in nationalism before and after 1848. In that year, he had urged the king to issue a constitution, had sponsored some liberal policies, and had worked to end Austrian rule in northern Italy. Ten years later, Cavour continued to pursue the goal of expelling the Austrians from Milan and Veneto, but now specifically with the aim of enhancing the power of his king, Victor Emmanuel II.

Crowning the King of Italy, 1861 First Lombardy (with its capital of Milan), in 1859, and then Veneto, in 1866, were ceded by Austria to the kingdom of Piedmont-Sardinia. In the south the unification movement was spearheaded by Garibaldi, backed up by his famous Red Shirts. This informal—though

Map 22.3 **Unification of Italy** In the decade between 1860 and 1870, Italy was united. This process brought together regions of great economic and social diversity under the rule of Rome, which officially became the capital of the newly united Italy in 1871.

1. In what part of Italy did this process of unification begin, and which areas of Italy remained outside the unified state until 1870?

2. Compare the northern borders of Italy in this map to a present day map. What has changed?

effective—army fought its way across Sicily, defeating the kingdom of the Two Sicilies. In 1860, this vast region joined Piedmont, as did the central Italian states of Tuscany and Parma. Thus by 1860, the entire Italian peninsula except for Veneto in the north and the Papal States around Rome were under the rule of Victor Emmanuel II, who would be crowned king of Italy in 1861. These last two areas would become part of the new kingdom of Italy by 1870, though the pope refused to reconcile himself to the new political situation. Surrounded by Italian territory that he refused to recognize, Pope Pius IX remained in self-imposed imprisonment in the **Vatican** for the rest of his life.

Liberal Nationalists' Disappointment with United Italy Italian unity had been achieved, but the resulting constitutional monarchy was very far from the democratic ideal envisioned by Mazzini and Garibaldi. Mazzini died in 1872, bitterly disappointed by the form in which his dream had been realized by the less idealistic—but more realistic—Cavour. The new Italy was a constitutional monarchy with universal male suffrage, but the king and his ministers held much more

power than the parliament. The problems of illiteracy and poverty, especially in the southern half of the country, were an enormous challenge to the new rulers and would continue to be so well into the twentieth century. In 1870, most subjects of King Victor Emmanuel spoke not standard Italian but dialects, and retained strong regional identities. As one statesman remarked, "We have made Italy; now we must make Italians."

22-2b The Unification of Germany

"Germany" immediately after 1848 was like Italy: No more than a geographical or cultural expression. Dozens of German states existed, from powerful Prussia to the tiny city-state of Hamburg (see Map 22.4). When the 1848 revolutionaries offered the crown of a united German Empire to the king of Prussia, he rejected it. His brother would accept it in 1871 as William I, but under vastly changed circumstances. As in Italy, conservatives gained most

Vatican Seat of the Catholic Church and the pope's residence, in central Rome on the Tiber River.

from German unification. In particular, one man was responsible for Prussia's rapid rise to dominate a unified Germany. This was the Prussian Chancellor **Otto von Bismarck**.

Otto von Bismarck and German Unification Bismarck combined great energy, determination, and loyalty to the Prussian ruling house with political cynicism and cold calculation. He resembled Metternich in intelligence and ruthlessness, though Bismarck lacked Metternich's elegance and refined manners. Born into a moderately wealthy landowning family, Bismarck had been shocked by the revolutions of 1848 and appalled by the king's concessions to the liberals. A staunch conservative who had served in the Prussian Landtag (parliament) and as ambassador to Russia and France, Bismarck rose to power by chance. In 1862, King William I became entangled in a dispute with the Landtag over the state budget, in particular the funding for the Prussian army. In despair, the king appointed Bismarck chancellor, hoping that he would be able to find a compromise. Instead, Bismarck directly defied the Landtag, acting as if it did not exist. Bismarck's brash behavior revealed the weakness of Prussia's parliament in the face of a strong and ruthless statesman.

Bismarck declared that the biggest mistake made by the 1848 liberals was their attempt to unite Germany through "speeches and majority resolutions" rather than "blood and iron." By this he meant military might and warfare. In the next decade, Bismarck waged three wars that would realize the primary goal of the liberals in the Frankfurt Assembly—a united Germany. The first war came as Denmark attempted to take over the province of Schleswig, previously an independent duchy. Prussian and Austrian troops invaded Schleswig early in 1864, forcing the king of Denmark to relinquish his claims. Austria and Prussia were to administer the territory together, an arrangement Bismarck knew would soon lead to conflict. After various frictions and provocations, Austria and Prussia went to war in mid-1866.

The Prussians humiliated the Austrians at a single decisive battle. The peace terms Bismarck offered were mild: Austria lost no territory and paid no war indemnity, but henceforth, Austria would be excluded from the North German Confederation carved by Prussia from the old Austrian-dominated German Confederation set up at the Congress of Vienna. Now the North German Confederation, dominated by Prussia, stretched from the Dutch border in the west to the Russian empire in the east; to the south Austria remained isolated.

The Franco-Prussian War Bismarck had eliminated his chief rival in the German lands. Now he looked to eliminate his chief rival on the continent—France—which felt threatened by the rise of a unified, aggressive German state. Again Bismarck skillfully manipulated events—the candidacy of a Hohenzollern prince for the throne of Spain—to push strained Franco-Prussian relations over the brink. In a brilliant, though dishonest, media maneuver, Bismarck took a telegram—the Ems Dispatch—he had received from King William I on this matter, doctored it in a way aimed to provoke the French, and leaked the insulting document to the press. Napoleon III foolishly took Bismarck's bait and declared war on Prussia.

The **Franco-Prussian War** (1870–1871) was a disaster for France and for Napoleon III personally. The French badly underestimated the training and equipment of the Prussian forces and were further hampered by poor military leadership. At the Battle of Sedan in early September 1870, the Germans encircled a large French force, capturing more than a 100,000 men, including Emperor Napoleon III himself. The French declared their emperor deposed and formed a provisional government, which sued for peace.

The Paris Commune Radical Paris, though surrounded by German troops, was outraged and disgusted by the actions of the provisional government. Rather than surrender, the adult male citizens of Paris voted in March 1871 to declare the **Paris Commune**. The Commune passed legislation granting free education, moderating rents, reducing church power, and generally supporting the working class.

Two months later, the provisional government, which had temporarily withdrawn to Versailles, sent troops to storm Paris and crush the Commune. More than 20,000 people were killed, more than during the entire Reign of Terror of the French Revolution. This slaughter of mainly working-class people by the liberal middle-class government would long be recalled and memorialized by socialists, as would the myth of the Commune as the first workers' state. Writing immediately after the crushing of the Commune, Marx exclaimed, "Within sight of the Prussian army that had annexed to Germany two French provinces, the Commune annexed to France the working people all over the world."

In January 1871, before the Commune and even before a peace treaty could be negotiated, King William I had himself crowned "Emperor of the Germans"—symbolically—in Louis XIV's magnificent Hall of Mirrors in the Palace of Versailles. Bismarck had achieved his goal—a united German Empire. In the peace settlement, Germany took from France two mainly German-speaking provinces along the

---

Otto von Bismarck (1815–1898) Prominent conservative Prussian statesman, chancellor (prime minister), and architect of German unification in 1871.

Franco-Prussian War (1870–1871) Conflict provoked by Bismarck, resulting in the defeat of France and end of Napoleon III's reign; also led to German unification.

Paris Commune Radical regime in Paris after Franco-Prussian War, brutally put down by the French government in May 1871.

North Sea

Baltic Sea

SWEDEN

DENMARK

SCHLESWIG
HOLSTEIN
Kiel
Lübeck
Hamburg
MECKLENBURG
OLDENBURG
Bremen
HANOVER
Hanover

• Königsberg
• Danzig
EAST PRUSSIA
POMERANIA
WEST PRUSSIA

RUSSIAN EMPIRE

• Amsterdam
NETHERLANDS
WESTPHALIA
Essen
• Antwerp
BELGIUM
Cologne
Bonn
RHINE PROVINCE
Frankfurt

BRANDENBURG
• Berlin
POSEN
• Warsaw

Leipzig
Weimar
Dresden
SAXONY

SILESIA
POLAND
Sadowa 1866
Prague
BOHEMIA
• Kraków

Sedan 1870
Verdun
LORRAINE
Karlsruhe
Nancy
Strasbourg
ALSACE
BADEN

Luxembourg
Nuremberg
BAVARIA
Stuttgart
WÜRTTEMBERG
Munich

Olmütz
MORAVIA

Vienna
AUSTRIAN EMPIRE

FRANCE
SWITZERLAND

Innsbruck

Buda
Pest

ITALY

Rivers: Elbe R., Ruhr R., Moselle R., Mulde R., Oder R., Warta R., Vistula R., Main R., Rhine R., Neckar R., Inn R., Vltava R., Danube R., Morava R.

Legend:
- Prussia before 1866
- Conquered by Prussia in Austro-Prussian War, 1866
- Austrian territories excluded from North German Confederation, 1867
- Joined with Prussia to form North German Confederation, 1867
- South German states joining with Prussia to form German Empire, 1871
- Won by Prussia in Franco-Prussian War, 1871

⭐ Major battle
— German Confederation boundary, 1815–1866
— Bismarck's German Empire, 1871

Scale: 0 50 100 Km. / 0 50 100 Mi.

Map 22.4 **Unification of Germany, 1871** Germany was unified in great part through the efforts of Prussian Chancellor Otto von Bismarck.

1. Where did German speakers remain outside unified Germany?
2. Why did France and Russia feel threatened by German unification?

Rhine River—Alsace and Lorraine—and received from France an indemnity of $2 billion. Germany was united, but the French swore revenge.

The American president, Ulysses S. Grant, congratulated the new German government on forming a federal union like the United States and expressed the hope that Germans would soon enjoy the benefits of democracy. In fact, the German constitution did grant universal male suffrage (to those aged twenty-five and older) in elections to the **Reichstag**, or federal parliament, but German states retained considerable autonomy. The Reichstag's power was balanced by that of the Bundesrat, or federal council, in which Prussia exercised great influence. Most of all, the

emperor—or Kaiser—held enormous power, dictating foreign policy, acting as commander-in-chief of all armies, and having the right to declare **martial law**, close down parliament, and interpret the constitution. In short, while German states such as Bavaria, Baden, and Saxony could maintain their own armies and issue their own postage stamps, Prussia and its Kaiser dominated

Reichstag German federal parliament for united Germany that met in Berlin starting in 1871 and was elected by universal male suffrage.

martial law Temporary strengthening of government powers, including the suspension of certain civil rights, during public disturbances or other emergencies.

Bettmann/Contributor/Getty Images

J. Keppler

Bismarck's Dismissal by Kaiser William II, 1890

With his bald pate and bushy mustache, German Chancellor Otto von Bismarck was a favorite of caricaturists, as in this cartoon from the early 1890s. Bismarck is shown getting ready to leave (he was forced to resign by the new Kaiser) and looking in disgust at the new Kaiser William II, who gazes lovingly at a newborn labeled "socialism" while reclining on a throne bristling with weaponry. The goddess of Germania looks on in consternation.

» *How accurate is this image's depiction of Bismarck and Kaiser William II? What biases do you detect here?*

German politics. The authoritarianism and militarism traditional to Prussia would often—quite unfairly—be perceived by outsiders as "typically German."

Bismarck as German Chancellor Having engineered unification, Bismarck was secure in his position as—now—*federal* chancellor, though Kaiser William sometimes grumbled that Bismarck wielded more power than he. But Bismarck had to contend with a Reichstag considerably more diverse and demanding than the Prussian Landtag. Representatives from the Catholic south of Germany and the organization of the Catholic **Center Party** inspired worries of undue influence from the Vatican, so Bismarck embarked on an anti-Catholic campaign, the **Kulturkampf**. New laws removed priests from the state bureaucracy (most were teachers), closed down Catholic schools, outlawed Jesuit institutions, and instituted **civil marriage**. German Catholics in the south and the millions of Polish subjects of the Kaiser in the east saw these measures as a direct attack on their religion and culture. The Vatican supported their resistance with an 1875 declaration threatening to excommunicate anyone who complied with these laws. At this point, Bismarck sought a compromise with Catholic leaders, but Catholic Germans continued to view rule from Berlin with suspicion.

After the failure of the Kulturkampf, Bismarck sought to suppress what he perceived an even greater threat to the German Empire—the socialists. He had long mistrusted working-class organizations, and after two unsuccessful attempts on the life of Kaiser William I in 1878, Bismarck pushed the Reichstag to forbid German socialists to organize, meet, and publish their programs. Despite this law, which remained in force until 1890, German socialists steadily gained votes in Reichstag elections, from just over 300,000 in 1881 to almost 1.5 million in 1890. Cleverly, Bismarck implemented some of the socialists' demands, including state-sponsored unemployment insurance, health care, and retirement benefits, to undercut their appeal and ensure workers' loyalty to the state. Germany's social welfare programs were the first, but in the twentieth century nearly every European state would adopt similar policies, advancing government responsibility for aiding sick and poor citizens.

22-2c Nations Seeking States

By 1871, Italy and Germany were unified nation-states in which conservative nationalism had triumphed. Hungary, too, had achieved a degree of independence.

Center Party Catholic political party in Germany, organized in 1870.

Kulturkampf (in German, "struggle for culture") Bismarck's attack on Catholic schools, institutions, and political influence in the 1870s.

civil marriage Legal bond between two persons, usually man and wife, recognized by the state but not necessarily by religious authorities.

age fotostock / age fotostock / Superstock

Basilica of Sacré-Coeur, Paris

The Basilica of Sacré-Coeur (sak-ray-COOR) was built in a working-class area of northern Paris to commemorate the lives lost in the Franco-Prussian War and ensuing Paris Commune. Despite its official aim to reconcile all victims of 1870–1871, it quickly became a symbol of conservative Catholicism in France.

» *Why would working-class Parisians view this huge church in their midst as an alien and unwelcome intrusion?*

» *What role did the Catholic Church play in French society at this time?*

After its defeat by Prussia, Austria conceded to the Hungarians essentially what they had demanded in 1848. In the Compromise of 1867, Hungarians gained almost complete autonomy, a fact reflected in the country's new name: Austria-Hungary. Hungarians handled domestic affairs independently. They had their own parliament, used their own language without restriction throughout their part of the empire, and obliged non-Hungarians to use that language in schools and government offices. Only in matters of foreign policy, state defense, and the overall budget did Hungary have to compromise with Austria. Austria and Hungary also shared the same ruler.

Nations Without States: National Minorities But many, even most, nationalities in eastern and southeastern Europe lacked political autonomy. They lived as **national minorities** in the multinational empires of Russia, Austria-Hungary, and the Ottomans. As groups such as Ukrainians, Estonians, Romanians (in Hungary), Croatians, and Slovaks pressed their demands for autonomy, the multinational states were forced to give increasing attention to their **minorities question**—how does a state deal with a minority that refuses assimilation, insisting on using its own language and maintaining its own separate national culture instead of blending in with the majority? Newly independent states like Romania also wrestled with this problem—in Romania, particularly with regard to its Jewish and **Roma** ("gypsy") citizens. Despite pressure from the Western powers, Romania refused to grant full citizenship to members of these ethnic groups, treating them like foreigners.

Poles: An Exceptional Stateless Nation Poles were a unique national minority in nineteenth-century Europe. They looked back to a large and powerful Polish state in the medieval and early modern period, before it was partitioned by Russia, Austria, and Prussia in the late eighteenth century. Polish written culture was well developed, and a Polish nobility

continued to exist, despite the disappearance of the Polish state. While the Polish peasantry did not always identify with the "Polish nation" in midcentury, the existence of a Polish nation—without a state—could not be questioned, even by hostile Russians and Prussians like Bismarck. The Polish case stood in marked contrast to that of neighboring Slovaks, Belarusians, and Ukrainians, who did not have a long tradition of statehood or written culture.

The majority of Poles lived under Russian rule in the so-called kingdom of Poland, but after the Polish insurrection of 1830, little remained of its autonomy. A second insurrection in 1863 failed disastrously. In its aftermath, thousands of Poles were arrested, had their property confiscated, and were exiled to Siberia or fled abroad. Government schools used Russian as the language of instruction, Poles were excluded from most government jobs, and strict censorship was applied to the Polish press. The next generation of Polish intellectuals, known as the Warsaw positivists after the French intellectual movement of that name, emphasized economic and cultural development over national unity. They recognized that developing a strong, literate, and prosperous Polish nation was under present circumstances more important than fighting for independence.

From the 1890s onward, however, the cautious approach of the positivists did not satisfy the more impatient socialist and nationalist Polish youth. They argued for direct action against the repressive Russian empire, even for revolution. The

national minority Ethnic/national group not making up the majority of a state's population—for example, in the Russian empire, Jews, Poles, Ukrainians, and Latvians.

minorities question Problem of what cultural and political rights to give to national minorities.

Roma Nomadic people living especially in eastern Europe who trace their origins back to India, sometimes incorrectly referred to as "Gypsies."

Polish Socialist Party was both nationalist in its political ideas (demanding an independent Polish state) and socialist in its economic ideas (demanding state ownership of factories and means of communication).

At the end of the 1890s, it was challenged by the **National Democratic Party**, which emphasized nationalism and rejected socialism. Led by **Roman Dmowski**, the National Democrats were aggressive and exclusivist in their approach, refusing to accept non-Poles, and especially Jews, as a part of the Polish nation. Dmowski argued that the large Jewish minority living among the Poles had taken over middle-class occupations, pushing out Poles. Thus, for a healthy Polish nation to develop, Dmowski's argument continued, the Jews must either assimilate totally—shedding Jewish culture and identity—or leave Poland. Dmowski's appeals exemplified the beginnings of mass politics in Poland. On the one hand, he and his National Democrats helped organize Poles against Russian and Prussian cultural and political oppression; on the other, he rallied Poles to reject their Jewish neighbors and to embrace an aggressive, almost biological, form of nationalism.

Bulgaria Breaks Away from the Ottoman Empire While the Poles would have to wait until the twentieth century for independence, Bulgarian religious and national leaders wrested their own state from the Ottoman Empire by manipulating international tensions. The Ottomans tolerated Bulgarian Orthodox Christianity, but the ruling class in the region was made up primarily of Muslims. By the late nineteenth century, growing numbers of middle-class Bulgarians, most educated in missionary or church schools, came to resent their subordination to Muslim Ottoman authorities. They turned to Russia, which shared its religious traditions, spoke a similar language, and also used the Cyrillic alphabet. Russia had long seen itself as the protector of Orthodox Christians in the Ottoman Empire.

Launching an uprising in the spring of 1875, Bulgarian nationalist leaders drew all Europe's attention to their oppression, especially after violent reprisals by Ottoman forces took the lives of many

Polish Socialist Party
Political party founded in 1892 that combined socialist ideology with the demand for an independent Polish state.

National Democratic Party
Nationalist and Anti-Semitic Polish party formed in 1897 that advocated limiting the number of non-Poles—especially Jews—in a future Polish state.

Roman Dmowski (duh-MOFF-skee) (1864–1939) Polish politician and leader of the nationalist and Anti-Semitic National Democratic Party.

William Gladstone (1809–1898) British politician and prime minister; important figure in the Liberal Party.

Russo-Turkish War (1877–1878) Major war in the Balkans with Serbia and Russia fighting against the Ottoman Empire.

St. Cyril and St. Methodius National Library, Sofia, Bulgaria Photo: Visual Connection Archive

Bulgarian Patriotic Poster

Patriotic images like this one inspired Bulgarians to fight for their independence from the Ottoman Empire in the late 1870s. In this poster, as in many others, the nation was depicted as a woman surrounded by symbols of state. Here we see the Bulgarian flag and the two-headed eagle that represented Bulgaria's link to the Russian empire.

» *How does this image present a heroic vision of Bulgarian patriotism?*

» *How might Turks or Serbs respond to this image and its ideals?*

thousands of Christian Bulgarians. Britain's former Prime Minister **William Gladstone** produced an overwrought account of the massacre, *The Bulgarian Horrors and the Question of the East*. When, in 1876, another Balkan Slavic people in the mountainous province of Bosnia-Herzegovina rose up against Ottoman rule, Russia intervened, in defense of Orthodox Christian Serbs and Montenegrans. In the **Russo-Turkish War**, Russian troops crossed neutral Romania, invaded Bulgaria in the spring of 1877, and the following year defeated the Ottoman army.

The terms Russia imposed on the Ottomans included a large independent Bulgaria stretching from the Black Sea to the Aegean. This prospect alarmed Europe's Great Powers, which feared Russia would now gain undue influence in the Balkans and upset the balance of power. At the Congress of Berlin called by Bismarck in 1878, Germany, Austria-Hungary, Great Britain, and France forced Russia to accept a much smaller Bulgaria with a German prince, Alexander of Battenberg, as its king. The Bulgarians had received their state, not because of popular agitation or nationalist revolution but through the military and diplomatic intervention of Russia. At the same time, the Ottoman province of Bosnia-Herzegovina was placed under Austrian administration.

Norway Splits from Sweden Norway gained its independence in an entirely different way. Assigned to the Swedish Crown in 1815 at the Congress of Vienna, Norwegians cherished a separate identity derived from their rugged terrain, folk culture, and historical traditions linked to Denmark. The language used by educated Norwegians differed little from Danish, while the folk dialect was closer to Swedish. As subjects of the Swedish king, Norwegians enjoyed political and civil rights found in few other European countries. Still, Norwegian nationalists insisted on an independent Norway. After some negotiation, the Swedes agreed to a "divorce," and Norway became independent in 1905. This achievement of statehood by peaceful means stands out as a historical rarity.

22-3 The Expanding Role of the State

» In what ways did the role of the state in the life of their citizens expand? What role did nationalism play in this growth of state power?

» How did education aim to incorporate citizens into the national culture of the state?

After 1848, political participation increased throughout Europe. By the end of the century, almost all males in Britain and France could vote, as they also could in newly united Italy and Germany. Among the stateless nations in the Ottoman and Habsburg empires, agitation for political rights strengthened. Everywhere leaders used education as a means of influencing citizens to identify with the state, its culture, and its interests. States also intruded into the economy to encourage domestic industry and keep out foreign competition. Across Europe, the role of the state in citizen's lives expanded.

22-3a Mass Politics and Nation Building

The term **nation building** cannot be separated from the concept of nation-state. It describes the process by which the political unit (state) attempts to transform its population into a "nation." Nation building was also connected with new legislative assemblies and the expansion of political participation after 1848. As individuals voted in elections, held office, debated political issues, read newspapers, and traveled (often seeking employment) throughout their countries, they gained a sense of national identity that transcended local and religious ties.

The Nation-State in Great Britain In Britain, the nation-state was firmly established by the nineteenth century, and parliamentary traditions were strong. In 1832, in a triumph of British liberalism, the Reform Acts had granted the vote to middle-class men. The Reform Acts of 1867 and 1884 extended suffrage to male heads of households; further extensions brought almost universal male suffrage by the early twentieth century. Regional identities remained strong, but they did not challenge the dominance of a British identity fostered by London.

Throughout this period, Great Britain was plagued by the Irish question—what to do with the poverty-stricken Irish Catholic peasants in a mainly Protestant and industrialized British nation. The horrific famine of the mid-1840s had reduced the population of Ireland by over one-third and poisoned relations between Irish Catholics and their Protestant landlords. One proposed solution to the Irish question was home rule—autonomy for the Irish provinces with their own parliament in Dublin. Irish demands for home rule became ever louder at the end of the nineteenth century.

Changes in French Politics France also enjoyed a strong national tradition, prestigious culture, and prosperity. The centrality of Paris and the strength of the central state apparatus and of French culture overshadowed the linguistic and cultural diversity (Basque, Breton, Provençal) existing within France's borders. The extensive rebuilding of Paris in the decades before 1870 added to its glamour and attraction as the center of the French nation. To be French meant to be part of the "great nation" that included all citizens of the French Republic. Local identities hardly had a chance to take shape as separatist or national movements. After the French Revolution, being French had nothing to do with religion. French identity was political: One could "become" French by accepting the responsibilities of being a loyal citizen.

The expansion of the electorate in France followed a more abrupt path than in Britain. Following the 1848 revolution, universal male suffrage was established, but under Emperor Napoleon III, starting in 1851, democracy ended in France for two decades. The disastrous Franco-Prussian war ushered in the **Third Republic**, and from 1871 onward, French democracy would be strong.

nation building Creation of a strong nation-state, with institutions to educate the population in obedience and patriotism.

Third Republic (1870–1940) Longest continuous republic in French history, beginning with the defeat in the Franco-Prussian war and ending with military defeat by Hitler.

Theodor Herzl Creates Modern Zionism

Theodor Herzl in Basel, 1897 The First Zionist Congress was held in Basel, Switzerland. Here, we see Theodor Herzl looking pensively over the horizon during a break in the meetings. Later he was to exclaim, "At Basel I founded the Jewish state," though in fact the state of Israel gaind its independence only in 1948, a half century later.

» Why do you think that Herzl chose Basel for this important meeting?

» How would you describe Herzl's expression and appearance?

In 1895, journalist Theodor Herzl was in Paris covering the trial of Captain Alfred Dreyfus, who had been accused of spying for the Germans. Like Herzl himself, Dreyfus was an assimilated, Europeanized Jew. The trial was held more than a century after the French Revolution had promised equal rights to Jewish citizens. But the trial was unfair: Dreyfus's Jewish background was held against him. In the streets crowds shouted "Death to the Jews!" Herzl was shocked, and he wrote in his diary, "I recognized the emptiness and futility of trying to 'combat' anti-Semitism." He concluded that Jews would always be outsiders in the European countries where they lived. They would be exiles—as Hebrew teachings phrased it—until they had their own Jewish state. Jews were not just a religious group; they were a nation.

Herzl had experienced anti-Semitism. As a student at the University of Vienna in the early 1880s, he had been denied admission into a prestigious fraternity because of his Jewish origins. He had been furious, for he felt himself Austrian by culture, upbringing, and language, and more patriotic than most. Being Jewish was just a personal religious matter. But the young Herzl learned a hard lesson: For a Jew, no matter how assimilated, wealthy, and intelligent, some avenues were closed. Herzl graduated and became a well-known playwright and journalist in Vienna, indistinguishable from other middle-class Viennese, with an unhappy marriage, a lifestyle that exceeded his income, and a love for wit and culture.

Vienna was a thriving center for German Jewish culture, with such distinguished writers as Stefan Zweig and Arthur Schnitzler, composers like Alban Berg and Arnold Schoenberg, and of course the renowned psychiatrist Sigmund

---

Elsewhere in Europe political rights also increased. In newly unified Italy and Germany, all men could vote. Even in backward Russia, most men could vote in **Duma** elections after 1906, though the votes of the wealthy counted far more than those of peasants and workers. Universal male suffrage came to Austria (though not to Hungary) in 1907. In Finland, still an autonomous principality within the Russian empire, women were granted the vote in 1906. Women could also vote in local elections in some western states in the United States. Democracy was far from universal even in the early twentieth century, but great strides had been made in that direction since 1848.

Duma Russian legislature, granted by Tsar Nicholas II in 1906 and lasting until the Revolution of 1917.

Technology and Nation Building Technology played a role in nation building. Steam presses and advances in papermaking technology made newspapers cheap and abundant after the 1860s, and increased literacy meant that more people read them. Newspaper reading helped establish and spread a standard form of the language and thus weakened local dialects. Industrial development also strengthened national feelings. Railroads encouraged mobility between town and countryside and reduced differences between peasants and town dwellers, reinforcing the idea that "we are all Frenchmen" (or Germans, or Russians, or Italians). The telegraph, invented in 1844, twenty years later spanned the European and American continents, helping bring citizens in closer contact and aiding governments in administering their territories.

Freud. In this environment, surrounded by other Jews like him—German speaking, cultured, successful—Herzl tried to believe that Jews could retain their religion and still live in harmony with their Christian neighbors. But that was before he was sent as a journalist to cover what became known as the Dreyfus affair.

Despite the absurdity of the accusation and the flimsy evidence against him, Dreyfus was court-martialed and exiled to Devil's Island off the coast of South America. It was later discovered that the army had manipulated and forged evidence against him. By that time, Herzl was already a Jewish nationalist, a Zionist. In 1896, he published a small book entitled *The Jewish State*, which proposed a political solution to what Europeans called the Jewish question—the proper relation between Jews and the states where they lived. Once Jews had their own state, Herzl argued, the other nations of the world would respect them. Other central and eastern European Jewish thinkers had reached similar conclusions before Herzl—in part, in reaction to the shock of the 1881 wave of anti-Jewish violence in the Russian empire—but he apparently did not know any of them. Even the term *Zionism* had been used before Herzl, but he gave the movement new political force and vigor.

In 1897, Herzl summoned a "symbolic parliament" of European Jews to the Swiss city of Basel. At this First Zionist Congress, he issued a call for all Jews to unite to create a Jewish state. Though he did not specify where that state would be founded, the obvious place was Palestine—for Jews, Eretz Israel ("land of Israel"), an Ottoman province between Egypt and Syria. After all, Jews prayed every year at Passover to meet again "next year in Jerusalem." Most Jews in western Europe were not interested in Herzl's call. Feeling secure and patriotic in France, Britain, and Germany, they firmly rejected the idea of a Jewish nation and feared that Zionism could worsen anti-Jewish sentiment. But in eastern Europe, particularly in the Russian empire, Herzl's call was received with joy. Visiting Russia in 1903, Herzl was lauded as "king of the Jews" in towns throughout the Pale of Settlement, where Russian Jews were forced to reside.

Herzl did not live to see his ideal realized. When he died in 1904, very few people believed that Zionism could succeed—the political, economic, and religious obstacles seemed too great. But, as Herzl once remarked, "If you will it, it is not a dream." Forty-four years after Herzl's death, two thousand years after the Jewish people were sent into exile, the state of Israel declared its independence. The Jewish people had their own state.

Building of the Hôtel-Dieu, Paris, c.1866 (b/w photo), French Photographer, (19th century) / Private Collection / Bridgeman Images

Building of the Hôtel-Dieu, Paris, c.1866

The extensive rebuilding of Paris under Georges-Eugène Haussmann created the beautiful city we now know. This rebuilding required the destruction of huge swatches of medieval Paris to push through broad boulevards and squares. Here we see the vast space opened up for the building of one large building. After this reconstruction, Paris was much more healthy and easy to navigate, but also more expensive for residents.

» *Why would the government undertake such an extensive rebuilding of the capital?*

» *Who gained from this measure and who lost out?*

The impact of this expanding political participation was enormous. With mass political participation came the need for governments to respond to public opinion. Some governments used secret subsidies to influence the opinions newspapers expressed. For example, it was an open secret that the Russian government paid large sums to the Belgian daily *Le Nord*, which then gave favorable coverage of Russian affairs. Governments also paid editors to print favorable news and suppress embarrassing information. Most governments attempted to limit the information reaching their citizens through censorship, but as the amount of information freely available to citizens grew, politics could no longer remain confined to a small elite.

New Political Parties The new political power of peasant and working-class men changed the agendas of political parties. Conservative parties attempted to gain peasant support by appealing to Christian (often Catholic) values and denouncing "godless" urban socialists and, in some cases, the Jews. Liberal parties increasingly modified their laissez-faire attitudes to support restricting the employment of children and the length of the working day and provision of assistance to ill or injured workers. Nationalist politicians often used anti-Semitic slogans, blaming Jews as being responsible for higher prices.

Working-class political organizations grew steadily. In England, the **Labour Party**, founded in 1900, rapidly challenged both the Tories and the Liberals, whose party had developed from the Whigs. In other countries, socialist parties sought to represent labor, though they were often harassed or disbanded by governments. The **Social Democratic Party of Germany** was powerful enough to win more votes than any other party in the 1913 elections, but it was still kept out of the government. In France, when a socialist, Alexandre Millerand, accepted a cabinet post in 1899, other socialists vehemently criticized him for participating in a bourgeois government. Russian socialists, on the other hand, were

forced to operate underground. These illegal groupings were split between the peasant-based **Socialist Revolutionaries**, who embraced terrorist methods, and the Marxist Social Democrats, who themselves split into **Bolshevik** and **Menshevik** factions in 1903 over questions of party strategy. Everywhere, socialists believed that as the numbers of working-class people grew, their triumph over capitalism was increasingly certain.

Mass politics assumed varied and even contradictory forms. When the British Prime Minister William Gladstone, a Liberal, toured the country by rail in the 1870s to influence voters, he was participating in mass politics. When, in the 1890s, the Polish political leader Roman Dmowski and the National Democrats published the newspaper *Kurier Wszechpolski* in Austrian Galicia, in part so it could be smuggled into the Russian empire, they were also participating in mass politics. Mass-circulation newspapers attempted to influence public opinion with their coverage of events and exposés of political corruption. French writer **Émile Zola**'s article denouncing the French army's attempt to frame Captain Alfred Dreyfus, "J'Accuse!" ("I Accuse"), is a famous example of such an exposé.

22-3b Education and the Nation-State

Before 1848, few European states required their citizens to attend school. By 1914, universal schooling was accepted as a goal—though it was not yet a reality—throughout Europe and increasingly around the world. Literacy and access to education were coming to be seen as a primary responsibility of governments. In most countries of western, northern, and central Europe, parents were obliged to send their children to school. States recognized the importance of education to form the population into well-trained workers and patriotic citizens.

Spreading Education Everywhere, literacy improved, though at unequal rates. At midcentury, more than 70 percent of the population in Scandinavia, Germany, Scotland, and the United States was literate; by 1913, the figure was over 90 percent, not only in those countries but also in Great Britain (including Ireland), Australia, New Zealand, Austria, and France. Even in backward Russia, nearly half of the population was literate by 1914. Literacy rates were almost always higher in urban than rural areas, among men than women, and in Protestant countries than in Catholic countries, probably because of Protestantism's emphasis on Bible reading.

The spread of mandatory elementary education, though gradual, was steady. From the late eighteenth century onward, Prussia obliged parents to send their children to school. In France, a law promising free, compulsory, and universal elementary education was

---

Labour Party British political party founded in 1900 with the help of trade unions to represent the interests of the urban working class.

Social Democratic Party of Germany Europe's most powerful and popular socialist party in the late nineteenth and early twentieth centuries.

Socialist Revolutionaries Russian underground political party, founded in 1901, that carried out terrorist acts against the tsarist government.

Bolsheviks and **Mensheviks** Two branches of the underground Russian Social Democratic Party, the more radical of which was the Bolsheviks.

Émile Zola (1840–1902) French writer, author of "J'Accuse," an article accusing the French army of trying to frame Dreyfus.

passed in the wake of the 1848 revolution, though it took several decades to be implemented. Great Britain instituted universal primary education in 1871, and this system grew rapidly in the next few decades. Even in Russia, where the spread of literacy was hampered by poverty and the government's distrust of teachers, who were suspected of revolutionary sympathies, the numbers of primary schools increased significantly in the decades up to 1914, and plans were in place to introduce free and universal primary education.

Technical Education The nature and philosophy of education also changed radically, with its practical—rather than moral or religious—side getting more attention. In Prussia, traditional classical high schools, or *Gymnasien*, that emphasized Latin and Greek were supplemented by more practical secondary schools teaching mathematics and science to prepare workers for a new industrial economy. New institutions of higher learning—in particular the technological universities—concentrated on producing well-trained chemists, engineers, and other specialists vital to Germany's growing industries. In other countries, too, science and technology gained a larger place in the curriculum, and technological institutes were set up in St. Petersburg, Warsaw, and Boston, where the Massachusetts Institute of Technology was founded in 1861.

In many parts of Europe, the state sought to reduce the influence of the church on education. The secular French state instituted state-run primary schools with state-employed teachers, the *instituteurs*, who saw themselves as opposing the forces of backwardness and reaction they perceived as embodied in the Catholic Church and the local priest. In Germany, one goal of Bismarck's Kulturkampf was to eject the Catholic priest from the classroom. In other European countries, the tension between state education and religious authority was less open, but everywhere conservatives and traditional religious leaders felt uneasy about mass education, worrying that it could promote radical thinking and atheism.

Education and Patriotism Mass education also aimed to strengthen patriotism. Italian schools insisted that the pupils use standard Italian, a language that children in many regions could barely understand. Ukrainian and Belarusian children were taught—if at all—in Russian because the government claimed that their languages were only dialects of Russian. But the patriotic lessons taught in schools went beyond mere language. In Italian schools, children learned to see themselves as heirs to the glories of ancient Rome. Russian pupils were taught that the tsar was a kindly father looking out for all his subjects in their broad motherland, which covered one-fifth of the Earth's surface. British children learned pride in their democratic traditions and love for the queen and the British

Empire, on which "the sun never sets." In Prussia, the values of order and discipline were stressed.

Education and Class Even while opening up opportunity for a few gifted individuals, mass education also reinforced existing class lines. While more peasants and workers now sent their children to school, few could afford secondary or higher education. The British public school system prepared the sons of the gentry and upper middle class to enter Oxford and Cambridge and after graduation to occupy positions of power in government and industry. University students came overwhelmingly from the middle class and upper levels of society, and higher education was far from common. In 1900, there were fewer than 30,000 university students in France and fewer than 50,000 in Germany—less than 1 percent of the population in both cases. At the same time, less privileged people were getting more and more education that allowed hundreds of thousands to take up jobs as bank clerks, government bureaucrats, teachers, and telegraph operators. Mass education thus helped expand the middle class, which in turn increased demands for broader political rights.

22-3c The Growing Power of the State

Nation building aims to convince citizens that they have a stake and a voice in the nation-state. The nation-state's political legitimacy derives in the end from the nation—that is, all citizens taken as a whole. At the same time, the state also demands that citizens fulfill various obligations: Paying taxes, serving in the military, obeying the law. Now citizens were asked to fulfill these obligations as part of a social contract between themselves and the nation-state. In response, citizens increasingly expected the state to protect them not only from domestic or foreign enemies but also from the devastation of sickness, poverty, and old age. In the second half of the nineteenth century, state power expanded in the form of increased government intervention in everyday life and in return the state promised order, more protection for weaker segments of society, and international prestige.

Increasing State Intervention in the Economy Classical liberalism argued that the state should interfere as little as possible in economic matters, holding that legal equality would give all citizens equal access to fame and fortune. By the last decades of the nineteenth century, even liberals allowed that the state had a role to play in the economy. The failed example of France's national workshops of 1848 began to seem like an admirable idea during periods of high unemployment. Most state intervention in the economy, however, aimed to assure investors' profits. In the building of railroads in Russia and Austria, for example, where investors put forth capital, the state guaranteed a certain percentage return, at least for a specific period. The state also sought to assure decent working conditions. From Britain to Russia, government factory inspectors examined working conditions with the power to fine or even shut down workplaces that were dangerous. For some factory owners, such measures seemed an outrageous example of government interference in their businesses.

The technology of war also contributed to nation building and the growth of state power. By the 1870s, nearly every European country, with the exception of Britain, required military service of its male citizens. Serving in the Russian or French or Italian army helped young peasant lads to see themselves as part of a larger group—the nation. Before 1917, more Russian boys were taught to read in the army than in schools. Similarly, bringing together young men from different parts of France and Italy helped encourage use of the standard language rather than local dialects and impressed on the soldiers that they served not only their family, village, or region but the entire nation. And the existence of a strong national army was a matter of pride and international prestige: Few Europeans could imagine a self-respecting nation-state without a well-trained army in flashy and distinctive uniforms. Throughout Europe, the cost of these armies made up the largest item on the state budget.

Rising Taxes To intervene in industrial development, educate citizens, and build strong armies, states required revenue, that is, taxes. With the exception of Great Britain, which introduced an income tax—levied only on those with higher incomes—in 1842, European states collected revenue from tariffs and **indirect taxes**, such as taxes on salt, kerosene, and matches. In Austria-Hungary, the state had a monopoly on the sale of tobacco products, and in Russia the state budget was covered in large part by taxation on vodka. Tariffs and indirect taxes pushed up prices and fell disproportionately on the poor. Throughout Europe, taxes rose in the course of the nineteenth century.

CONNECTIONS: As the idiom goes, nothing can be said to be certain except death and taxes. But before the twentieth century, direct taxes–such as income tax–were rarely paid by more than a tiny percentage of the population. As state power grew in the decades before the World War I, taxes increased. Many conservatives, then as now, saw government interference in the economy (such as forbidding children from working in mines and industry) and growing tax rates as a threat to personal freedom.

indirect taxes Taxes levied on products of common use, like salt, alcoholic beverages, or tobacco, as opposed to direct taxes, such as income tax.

On the other hand, more and more people considered it the role of the state to protect the weak in society, for example, guaranteeing basic health care and education. For that, of course, tax revenues were necessary. In the early twenty-first century, it seems, the argument over whether to pay taxes or die early from lack of health care has not disappeared.

22-4 Nationalism and Its Opponents

>> **What links developed in the later nineteenth century between nationalism and racism?**

>> **Why did anarchists, socialists, and the Catholic Church oppose nationalism? In each case, what aspects of nationalism did they dislike?**

Despite its growing influence, nationalism was not without opponents in this period. Some objected to its increasingly aggressive, even racist, aspects, which pitted nation against nation in contests that defined some as inferior, others as superior. Both conservatives and radicals, for different reasons, saw nationalism as a destructive, even evil, movement. The conservative multinational empires in central and eastern Europe opposed nationalism as a threat to their continued political survival. The Catholic Church condemned both the democratic politics of some nationalists and the racism of others. Socialists denounced nationalism as a tool of the ruling classes to distract ordinary people from real social and economic issues, to disguise exploitation with nationalist slogans, and to increase profits through the sale of armaments.

22-4a Integral Nationalism, Racism, Anti-Semitism, and Zionism

After 1848, conservatives took up the nationalist ideas and slogans that had been the hallmarks of liberalism before the uprisings. After 1860, nationalists began to preach a more exclusionary and aggressive creed, stressing struggle and dominance rather than cooperation and mutual assistance. At the same time, conservatives recognized the utility of nationalism as a tool for rallying the masses. By painting radicals and socialists as internationalists, the conservatives suggested that leftists would support foreign interests over domestic patriotism. Most important, now everyone was expected to identify with one nation, not with a local village or religious faith. This growth in national self-consciousness was encouraged by government schools, public celebrations, mass publications such as newspapers and calendars, and political parties.

Nationalism Learns to Hate: Integral Nationalism Toward the end of the nineteenth century, nationalism took on increasingly narrow and aggressive forms. This phenomenon has been termed **integral nationalism**, to stress its all-encompassing character and distinguish it from earlier liberal nationalism. These nonliberal nationalists stressed struggle between nations and domination of other nations. Dmowski in Poland, for example, argued that only a struggle between Poles and Ukrainians would determine whether the Ukrainians would survive as a nation.

Another key ingredient of integral nationalism was a narrow definition of the nation, focusing in particular on who *did not* belong and usually seeing a nation as a community of birth, not an identity that one could choose. German nationalists came to insist that birth determined German identity. Although France and the United States theoretically defined their nations as open to anyone accepting their political ideals, discrimination belied this open, liberal attitude.

Racism Narrow and exclusionary definitions of the nation coalesced with the rise of racialist thought. As Europeans engaged in a new wave of colonizing in Africa and Asia, the idea of race emerged as a biological reality and object of study. Though race is now understood as lacking a scientific basis and the diversity of humankind as being unclassifiable in such terms, certain scientists and philosophers in late-nineteenth-century Europe developed a racial system of human classification based on a strict hierarchy, with white Europeans on top. This **scientific racism** claimed that humanity was divided into three races with different physical, mental, and sexual capacities.

Anti-Semitism Racism and integral nationalism fused most notoriously in **anti-Semitism**. The word itself was first used by the obscure German writer **Wilhelm Marr** in 1879 in his pamphlet *Victory of the Jews over the Germans* to describe a new phenomenon. While religious hatred and discrimination against Jews had long existed in Christian Europe, anti-Semitism attacked not the Jewish religion but all those of Jewish birth ("race"), no matter what their religious beliefs, as enemies of all Europeans and their society (the term **Aryan** was often used in this context to mean non-Jews). Anti-Semites insisted that Jews by their birth and very nature could not be part of European nations, Such beliefs infuriated middle-class Jews, who, believing in assimilation, considered their religion no obstacle to their strongly felt identity as patriotic Frenchmen, Germans, or Poles.

Anti-Semites held that Jews unfairly monopolized commerce and banking; were dishonest in their dealings with non-Jews; and exercised a corrupting moral influence through their activities as journalists, lawyers, and doctors. Jews were identified with modern capitalist society—disrespectful of social traditions while energetically and unscrupulously accumulating wealth and power. Anti-Semitic political parties, such as Dmowski's National Democrats in Poland, appealed to workers and lower-middle-class voters whose economic and social position was threatened by industrialization and large-scale capitalist commerce.

Anti-Semitism, the Dreyfus Affair, and Zionism Anti-Semitism gained significant popular support in the 1870s and 1880s in places with a large Jewish population, for example Austria-Hungary and Russian Poland, and where Jews were noticeable in society, despite their small numbers, because of their achievements in business or the free professions, as in Germany. But anti-Semitism within European society was so general that when the Austrian journalist **Theodor Herzl**, covering the **Dreyfus affair** in Paris, witnessed public demonstrations of hatred toward all Jews, he concluded that no Jew was safe, not even in enlightened, republican France (see Profiles in Change: Theodor Herzl Creates Modern Zionism and Learning from a Primary Source: Theodor Herzl Declares the Jews a Nation). Arguing that Jews constituted a nation, not just a religious community, Herzl initiated a movement, known as **Zionism**, that called for the establishment of a Jewish state in the historical home of the Hebrews in Palestine.

The final decades of the nineteenth century were traumatic for Europe's Jews. In 1881, in the wake of the

---

integral nationalism Form of nationalism common in the later nineteenth century, characterized by an aggressive stance toward other ethnic groups.

scientific racism Nineteenth-century pseudoscientific biological theory that claimed humanity is divided into three races with different physical, mental, and sexual capacities.

anti-Semitism Anti-Jewish political movement arising in Germany in the 1870s and spreading to many countries, in particular in eastern Europe.

Wilhelm Marr (1819–1904) German writer who coined the word anti-Semitism, arguing that Jews posed a major threat to European peoples and culture.

Aryan Designation for non-Jews, implying that Jews belonged in a specific "Semitic" race, whereas other white Europeans belonged to the "Aryan" race.

Theodor Herzl (1860–1904) Viennese journalist who founded modern Zionism.

Dreyfus affair Series of trials between 1894 and 1906 involving the false accusation of Captain Alfred Dreyfus, a Jewish officer on the French general staff, of spying for the Germans.

Zionism View that Jews are not merely a religious community, but a nation; also a movement advocating the formation of a modern Jewish state in Palestine.

Theodor Herzl Declares the Jews a Nation

Theodor Herzl was typical of a certain class of central-European Jews: Educated, acculturated, and successful. His experiences as a journalist covering the Dreyfus affair in Paris, however, convinced him that Jews could only be free once they had their own independent country. He set down these ideas in his short book, *The Jewish State (Der Judenstaat)*, first published in 1896 and now considered one of the most important texts of political Zionism. In the following passage at the beginning of this book, Herzl tries to explain why he decided that the Jewish question remains important and requires a political solution.

❶ Why do you suppose Herzl starts by stressing the technological advances of the nineteenth century?

❷ Why is it important for Herzl to argue that "the misery of the Jews is an anachronism"? Why does he mention the Enlightenment in this context?

❸ Why does Herzl mention the Middle Ages here? What events in France is he referring to in this passage?

❹ Herzl mentions five different "elements" of Anti-Semitic prejudice. Give specific examples of what he means here. Do you think that prejudice against other groups (non-Jews) also has the same elements?

❺ What does Herzl mean by calling the Jewish question a "national question" and a "political world-question"?

❻ Why does Herzl insist that the Jews are a nation (the German word he uses is *Volk*)? And why *one* nation (Herzl's emphasis)?

This century has given the world a wonderful renaissance by means of its technical achievements; but at the same time its miraculous improvements have not been employed in the service of humanity. Distance has ceased to be an obstacle, yet we complain of insufficient space. Our great steamships carry us swiftly and surely over hitherto unvisited seas. Our railways carry us safely into a mountain-world hitherto tremblingly scaled on foot. **❶** Events occurring in countries undiscovered when Europe confined the Jews in Ghettos are known to us in the course of an hour. Hence the misery of the Jews is an anachronism—not because there was a period of enlightenment one hundred years ago, for that enlightenment reached in reality only the choicest spirits. **❷**

. . .

The Jewish question still exists. It would be foolish to deny it. It is a remnant of the Middle Ages, which civilized nations do not: Even yet seem able to shake off, try as they will. They certainly showed a generous desire to do so when they emancipated us. . . . We naturally move to those places where we are not persecuted, and there our presence produces persecution. This is the case in every country, and will remain so, even in those highly civilized—for instance, France—until the Jewish question finds a solution on a political basis. **❸**

I believe that I understand Anti semitism, which is really a highly complex movement. I consider it from a Jewish standpoint, yet without fear or hatred. I believe that I can see what elements there are in it of vulgar sport, of common trade jealousy, of inherited prejudice, of religious intolerance, and also of pretended self-defense. **❹** I think the Jewish question is no more a social than a religious one, notwithstanding that it sometimes takes these and other forms. It is a national question, which can only be solved by making it a political world-question to be discussed and settled by the civilized nations of the world in council. **❺**

We are a nation—*one* nation. **❻**

UN DINER EN FAMILLE

— Surtout ! ne parlons pas de l'affaire Dreyfus !

Ils en ont parlé

French Caricatures on the Dreyfus Affair

A pair of French cartoons illustrates the bitter controversy caused by the Dreyfus affair within French society—and even within individual families. The first cartoon reads "Above all let's not talk about the Dreyfus Affair"; the second—"They talked about it."

» *Why did the Dreyfus affair cause such strong feelings? Who was Dreyfus, and what was he accused of?*

assassination of Tsar Alexander II in St. Petersburg, a wave of **pogroms**, or organized attacks on Jewish life and property, swept the southwestern provinces of the Russian empire (today's Ukraine). Despite the small number of deaths in the pogroms, their moral impact was devastating. Most Jews—and Russian liberals—concluded that the Russian government itself was behind the attacks (a view now rejected by historians), and by the end of the 1880s, tens of thousands of Jews were leaving Russia every year, mainly for the United States.

CONNECTIONS: Ethnic consciousness and a pride in one's own ethnic, cultural, and religious group seem to be a constant in world history. Indeed, many "ethnonyms" (names of ethnic groups) such as Deutsch (German) or Franc (French) originally simply mean "human being." Human beings naturally divide the world into "ours" and "theirs" and, as anthropologist and historian Jarod Diamond points out, nothing is more astonishing in the modern world than the simple fact that hundreds and thousands of people mill together in modern cities, airports, or shopping malls without attacking or murdering each other. Modern nationalism aimed to bring together—at least in people's consciousness—all members of an individual nation. But at the same time this "defining in" of all Germans, Japanese, or Americans led to the "defining out" of elements—Jews, Koreans, immigrants, or even African Americans—who did not fit the narrow definition of these nations. Perhaps prejudice is inherent in human nature? Or are nationalism and racism the byproduct of ignorance and nastiness that further education and human development will eradicate? The jury is still out.

22-4b Strains in the Multinational Empires

Nationalism also threatened the conservative multinational empires of eastern and central Europe. The Ottoman Empire, Austria-Hungary, and Russia were all defined by dynastic loyalties and contained within their borders a wide diversity of peoples increasingly conscious of their national and ethnic identities. Their demands for cultural and political rights threatened the stability of these empires.

pogrom In Russia in 1881 and later, organized attacks on Jews and Jewish property.

Armenians Christian ethnic group living in the Russian and Ottoman empires, subject to violent attacks under Sultan Abdülhamid II.

Crimean War (1854–1856) War fought on the Crimean peninsula in which Russia's defeat by France and Britain led to Tsar Alexander II's Great Reforms.

Great Reforms (1861–1876) Series of Russian reforms that included emancipation of the serfs, lessening of censorship, and reform of the military and judicial systems.

The Ottoman Empire The Ottoman Empire was a kaleidoscope of ethnic diversity, including, at midcentury, Slavs, Albanians, Arabs, and others—it was not a "Turkish" state. Sultan Abdül Hamid II himself was born to an **Armenian** mother, and among his wives were women of various ethnic groups. In the Ottoman Empire, religion was much more important than nationality. Religious toleration was practiced, though Islam held a privileged position and was considered the most perfect religion. In practice, business and commerce were dominated by Christians and Jews, and the population of Istanbul—the former Constantinople—was more Christian than Muslim in 1900. National and ethnic strife was not entirely absent, however, in the Ottoman state. When Armenians, for example, were suspected of disloyalty to the sultan, they were subjected to violent attacks.

In the course of the nineteenth century, Greeks, Romanians, Serbs, and Bulgarians gained their independence from the Ottoman Empire, while Bosnia-Herzegovina was transferred to Austria. These territorial losses were just one sign of Ottoman weakness. Though the sultan exercised absolute power in principle, in reality the empire's unwieldy size and inefficient bureaucracy meant that he could never be sure his orders would be carried out in distant provinces. Local elites from the Balkans to northern Africa often took control into their own hands. By the later nineteenth century, the economic problems of the Ottoman state had become so acute that in effect the empire was bankrupt, and state budgets had to be approved by the empire's European creditors.

The Russian Empire The Russian Empire was even larger and more diverse than the Ottoman Empire. Stretching from Finland to the Pacific Ocean, it covered one-fifth of the Earth's dry land. Like the Ottoman Empire, Russia was not a nation-state. The census of 1897 indicates that not quite half of Nicholas's subjects were ethnically Russian. The empire encompassed Ukrainians, Catholic Lithuanians and Poles, Jews, Georgians, pagan Udmurts, and Muslim Tartars, Uzbeks, and Tajiks. Germans predominated among Russia's diplomats, and German names—Benckendorff, Totleben, Kaufmann—were common among the highest officials and generals of the empire. The Finns enjoyed broad autonomy, having their own coinage, postal system, and legislature. The legal status of most non-Russians in the empire was, however, far less favorable.

Russia had been counted among the major European powers only since the Napoleonic Wars, and this status was severely shaken by its defeat in the **Crimean War** (1854–1856). Tsar Nicholas I died a broken man in the midst of the war, admonishing his son Alexander II to learn from his mistakes. While no liberal, Tsar Alexander II recognized that only sweeping reforms could save Russia's Great Power status. In 1861, he emancipated the serfs in the first of a series of **Great Reforms** that ended

Visual Connection Archive

Mountain Peoples of the Caucasus

The ethnic diversity of the Russian empire is reflected in this 1900 poster showing representatives of a half-dozen peoples (including a Georgian, Chechen, Armenian, and Lezgin) all in native dress. These peoples lived in the Caucasus Mountains that separated Russia from the Ottoman Empire, a region conquered by the Russian Empire in the nineteenth century.

» *How is cultural difference depicted in this image? What other ways of showing ethnic diversity could have been used?*

in 1876 with universal military service. Censorship was also lightened, but Alexander refused to create an elected legislature, even of an advisory nature.

Even before the Great Reforms, religious toleration had been practiced in the Russian Empire, but the Russian Orthodox Church was officially the "reigning religion," its primacy taken for granted. Catholics were regarded as untrustworthy, and Russian officials closely monitored the movements and actions of Catholic priests and bishops. The Jews were worst off: their residence, with few exceptions, was restricted to the western part of the empire, the so-called **Pale of Settlement**; they were discriminated against in government jobs and secondary and higher education. The empire's large Muslim population lived mainly far from the imperial capitals of Moscow and Petersburg, in Central Asia and to the southeast. Like other non-Christians, they were subject to certain disabilities but on the whole the tsars distrusted their Catholic and Jewish subjects far more than the Muslims.

Russia differed from the Ottoman or Habsburg empires, however, in the predominance of one religion and one language. While the tsar's subjects were generally free to speak their native tongues at home, Russian was the usual language in government offices and schools, courts, and universities. The Russian tsar had to be Russian Orthodox in religion, but in the nineteenth century, every tsar married a foreign princess, though they all converted to Orthodoxy as a condition

of marriage. The last tsar, Nicholas II, married a German princess, Alix—or Aleksandra Fyodorovna, as she was known after her conversion—who had been brought up in England at the court of Queen Victoria. At home, the imperial family usually spoke English, though sometimes German and French, as well as Russian.

In the second half of the nineteenth century, the tsar attempted to introduce a more centralized administration using Russian. This process, usually described as **russification**, did not aim to make Finns, Poles, Jews, and others into Russians, but rather to create a more unified empire where Russian could serve as the means of communication among all of the empire's inhabitants. Nevertheless, russification caused great resentment and anger among non-Russian elites who, like Dmowski, would form the nucleus of nationalist movements throughout the empire. By 1900, nationalism was a powerful antigovernment force, in particular in the empire's western borderlands. At the same time, Russian nationalism was also growing, often exhibiting an aggressive anti-Polish and anti-Jewish attitude. Among the

Pale of Settlement Area in the southwestern Russian empire—roughly equivalent to present-day Belarus, Lithuania, and western Ukraine—where Jews were allowed to reside.

russification Effort to culturally assimilate minority national groups in the Russian empire, in particular in the second half of the nineteenth century.

many problems facing the Russian empire in the early twentieth century, nationalism was one of the most threatening.

Austria-Hungary Whereas the Russian empire adopted a policy of russification and repression, Austria-Hungary attempted reconciliation. After the Compromise of 1867 divided the empire into two separate halves, Austria and Hungary ran their own domestic affairs separately, sharing military and diplomatic affairs. They also shared, of course, a ruler: Francis Joseph was emperor (Kaiser) in Vienna, but king (*király*) in Budapest. The rights of all national-linguistic groups were assured by law throughout Austria-Hungary, but in practice the Hungarians tried to impose their language on the Slovaks and Romanians who lived in Hungary. Anyone wishing to gain an education and rise socially would have to master the difficult Magyar language. Rather like in Russia, this harsh policy had the opposite effect of what Budapest hoped for. Slovak and Romanian peasants were easily propagandized by nationalists, who pointed out that they would enjoy better economic, cultural, and educational opportunities in their own national states.

In Austria, the national issue was a source of constant political complications. Among the larger non-German groups were Czechs, Poles, and Ukrainians (Ruthenians). Poles were given broad autonomy in the eastern region of Galicia, where they lived in large numbers. Somewhat later, the Ukrainians of eastern Galicia were granted special language rights. Little by little, Czechs also made significant gains, such as being able to use their language in schools and state offices. The 1882 split of Prague University into German and Czech institutions was also a major achievement for the Czechs. These concessions served to embolden rather than satisfy the nationalists. At the same time, German nationalism was on the rise, and in Vienna it was difficult to piece together a lasting government coalition from the various battling parties. By the early twentieth century, some were already predicting that the Habsburg empire would not survive the death of its elderly ruler, Francis Joseph, who had been on the throne since 1848.

Syllabus of Errors Document issued by Pope Pius IX in 1864 condemning many modern beliefs, including rationalism, socialism, communism, and liberalism.

Leo XIII (r. 1878–1903) Successor of Pius IX, pope who attempted to find ways of reconciling Catholic faith and the modern world.

De rerum novarum (*About Modern Things*) Document issued by Pope Leo XIII in 1891 condemning socialism and the exploitation of workers and calling for cooperation between classes.

Second Socialist International (1889–1914) Loose organization of working-class political parties dominated by Marxists.

22-4c Universalism in the Roman Catholic Church

The Roman Catholic Church had no reason to favor nationalism. When Rome was incorporated into Italy in 1870, Pope Pius IX refused to acknowledge the Italian state. At the time, he was pushing the Vatican Council to adopt the doctrine of papal infallibility, which holds that all Catholics must accept papal pronouncements on matters of faith and dogma. With this new doctrine, Pius aimed to strengthen the church's position against all forms of modernism, from nationalism and socialism to progress, liberalism, and lay (nonreligious) education. Pius's negative opinion of nearly all aspects of modernity may be seen in his *Syllabus of Errors* of late 1864. Here he condemned, among other things, rationalism, socialism, liberalism, and attempts to reconcile religious dogma with scientific discoveries. Pius's total rejection of constitutionalism and modern politics cut the ground out from under moderate Catholics who wished to live both as modern citizens and as good Catholics.

Pope Leo XIII's *De Rerum Novarum* In 1878, Pius IX died and was succeeded by a far more conciliatory pope, **Leo XIII**. He was no less an enemy of nationalism, socialism, and rationalism than his predecessor, but he recognized that the church needed to find a compromise that would allow Catholics both to participate in modern life, including politics, and to remain faithful to their religion. Pope Leo's social views were set down in his encyclical **De rerum novarum** of 1891. Here he took a moderate position, though he condemned socialism and the liberal principle of absolute property ownership rights. True Catholics, he set down, must neither support socialist movements nor exploit others economically. Capitalist exploitation was, Leo stressed, every bit as sinful as socialism. The pope called on the Catholic faithful to support those parties that best exemplified Christian values—for example the Center Party in Germany. Nonetheless, the church continued to emphasize its international, indeed universal, role in human affairs.

22-4d Internationalism in Politics

Socialists opposed nationalism even more vociferously than the Catholic Church. In 1864, socialists set up the "International," bringing together socialists from different countries. In particular, the **Second Socialist International**, organized in 1889 after Marx's death, worked to strengthen ties between socialists of various nationalities in different countries. Socialists pledged themselves to international solidarity and solemnly declared that they would never go to war. Practically speaking, however, they admitted that

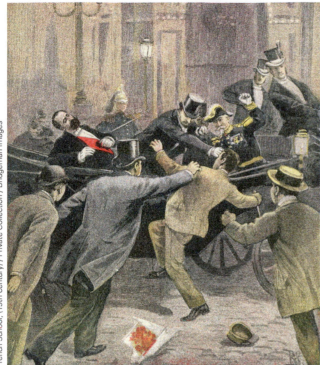

Assassination of Carnot, 1894

While visiting the city of Lyon, French president Sadi Carnot was assassinated by an anarchist. This attack was widely publicized as in the lithograph shown here. Around the turn of the century, a number of political leaders, from the Empress of Austria to US president William McKinley were killed in political attacks. The assassins claimed to represent liberty and justice against an unfair, self-satisfied bourgeois order.

≫ *What technological advances allowed such assassinations?*

≫ *Why was this wave of terrorism called "anarchism"?*

socialist organizations would need to be created on a national level. Sometimes national and socialist agendas were pursued simultaneously. The Polish Socialist Party, for example, aimed to overthrow the existing political order and establish an independent—and socialist—Polish republic.

Anarchism Some who sought to overthrow the political order called themselves **anarchists**. Like the socialists, anarchists looked forward to a world of shared prosperity, diffusion of political power, and the destruction of the powerful centralized state. But while socialists in this period mainly accepted the Marxist program of industrial development and a worldwide revolution, anarchists used more flexible tactics, from education and propaganda to **terrorism** and assassination. Some anarchists thought that killing a powerful political leader would strike a blow against state repression. The most famous anarchist, **Mikhail (mi-kha-EEL) Bakunin**, once famously declared, "The urge to destroy is also a creative urge!" Among the victims of anarchist attacks were Tsar

Alexander II (1881), President Sadi Carnot of France (1894), Spanish premier Antonio Canovas de Castillo (1897), Empress Elisabeth of Austria (1898), and U.S. President William McKinley (1901). At the turn of the twentieth century few would have understood the word "terrorism," but everyone knew about the "anarchist threat."

Pacifism Where the anarchists used violent means to achieve—in the end—peaceful ends, **pacifists** rejected war and violence at all costs. As technology and militarism advanced, the prospect of war became ever more horrific. Why not, the pacifists argued, take the millions spent on armies and weapons and use it for better housing, sanitation, cultural facilities, and education? Perhaps the most famous pacifist of this period was the **Baroness Bertha von Suttner**. Daughter of an Austrian field marshal, Suttner became a worldwide celebrity in 1889 with the publication of her bestselling novel *Lay Down Your Arms!* Suttner dedicated the remainder of her life to encouraging pacifism and working to prevent war.

One of her greatest achievements was to persuade the Swedish industrialist and inventor of dynamite, **Alfred Nobel**, to fund an annual prize for those promoting the cause of peace. The Nobel Peace Prize, along with prizes for chemistry, medicine, and literature, was first awarded in 1901. Appropriately, Suttner herself was awarded the Nobel Peace Prize in 1905. The pacifist movement could point to several successes during this period, including the establishment of international treaties on the conduct of war known collectively as the Geneva Conventions. These rules that attempted to mitigate the horrors of war were the result of meetings called by Tsar Nicholas II in 1899 and the Hague conferences and tribunals (1899–1907), which used arbitration as one method of settling diplomatic disputes.

anarchists Political radicals of the late nineteenth century who distrusted central government authority and advocated violent means to overthrow the existing political order.

terrorism Use of violence to intimidate individuals, ruling groups, or entire nations to achieve an individual's or group's political-ideological goals.

Mikhail Bakunin (1814–1876) Russian anarchist and revolutionary who espoused a political ideology opposed to all forms of state authority.

pacifists Individuals who oppose war and violence on principle and seek peaceful solutions to state conflicts.

Baroness Bertha von Suttner (1843–1914) Austrian writer and pacifist organizer whose novel *Lay Down Your Arms!* (1889) won her an international reputation.

Alfred Nobel (1833–1896) Swedish industrialist who funded the Nobel prizes, which he hoped would encourage world peace and the development of culture.

CHAPTER Review

Summary

» The revolutions of 1848 were a major watershed in European history.

» After 1848, nationalism tended to be adopted as a political tool by conservatives, as in the unification of Italy and Germany.

» After 1848, nationalism and the ideal of the nation-state became broadly accepted as a political norm, despite the continued existence of multinational states like the Russian empire and Austria-Hungary.

» In the late nineteenth century, nationalism became increasingly aggressive, even racist, and often allied with anti-Semitism.

» The increased acceptance of nationalism was challenged and criticized by socialists, pacifists, and the Catholic Church—each for different reasons.

Chronology

1848	Marx and Engels publish *The Communist Manifesto* [Europe]
1848–1849	Political uprisings sweep Europe [Europe]
1852	Louis Napoleon declares himself Emperor Napoleon III [Europe]
1854–1856	France and Britain defeat Russia in Crimean War [Europe]
1859	Napoleon III and Piedmont defeat Austria in northern Italy [Europe] Italian unification begins [Europe]
1861	Victor Emmanuel II is crowned king of Italy [Europe] Tsar Alexander II emancipates Russian serfs [Europe]
1861–1865	America fights Civil War [Americas]
1863	Polish rebellion against Russian rule fails [Europe]
1863	French troops take Mexico City [Americas]
1866	Prussia defeats Austria, opening the way for German unification [Europe]
1867	Austria grants Hungary semiautonomy [Europe]
1870–1871	Franco-Prussian War ends with French defeat [Europe]
1871	Prussian king William I becomes emperor of Germany [Europe] Paris Commune is crushed by French government [Europe]

1875	Ottomans crush Bulgarian uprising [Europe, Middle East]
1877–1878	Russians defeat Turks in Russo-Turkish War [Europe, Middle East]
1878	Bulgaria wins autonomy from Ottoman Empire [Europe, Middle East]
1893	New Zealand becomes first country to grant women the vote [Oceania]
1894	Dreyfus is convicted of espionage [Europe]
1896	Herzl publishes *The Jewish State* [Europe]
1897	First Zionist Congress is held in Basel, Switzerland [Europe]
1900	Spanish-American War [Americas, Oceania]
1901	First Nobel prizes (for peace, chemistry, medicine, and literature) are awarded [Europe]
1901	Queen Victoria dies; end of Victorian age [Europe]

Critical Thinking Questions

Take time to pull together all the important information from the chapter by answering the following questions:

The Revolutions of 1848

» What were the short- and long-term causes of the revolutions of 1848? What role did ideologies play?

» How did the demands and outcomes of the revolutions of 1848 differ in western and east-central Europe?

New Nation-States and Nationalist Tensions

» Nationalism can serve as both a unifying and a divisive ideology. Give examples of both.

» Why were liberal nationalists disappointed in the way that Germany and Italy were united?

The Expanding Role of the State

» What are some ways in which technology helped in the process of nation building?

» What are some of the pros and cons of the development toward increasingly powerful states in the later nineteenth century?

Nationalism and Its Opponents

» What aspects of modernity did anti-Semites detest and blame on the Jews?

» How did multinational empires attempt to maintain stability in this period? Which of the three empires considered here was most (and least) successful in this?

 **MINDTAP** From Cengage

MindTap® is a fully online personalized learning experience built upon Cengage Learning content. MindTap® combines student learning tools—readings, multimedia, activities, and assessments—into a singular Learning Path that guides students through the course and helps students develop the critical thinking, analysis, and communication skills that are essential to academic and professional success.

Chapter Outline

As you read, consider the following questions:

❯ What was the second Industrial Revolution? How did it differ from earlier industrialization?

❯ How did the second Industrial Revolution affect everyday life, society, and culture in different parts of Europe?

❯ What is meant by the concept of "mass society?" Why was this concept increasingly important from the late nineteenth century on?

❯ What were some of the most important advances in natural sciences (physics, chemistry) and social sciences in this period?

❯ What caused the conflict between religion and the new science? How did scientists and religious believers attempt to reconcile these differences?

INDUSTRIALIZATION GENERATED profound shifts in social, political, and cultural life. Technological advances from the telegraph to the bicycle radically created new rhythms of everyday life. No less radical were new intellectual movements that rejected religion and attempted to apply the scientific method to all realms of human experience, from social relations to the body and sex. Artists and musicians challenged accepted modes of expression, creating works of art that shocked and enraged conservative critics. Women sought a more visible place in society, even demanding political rights. The clash between traditional social and cultural expectations and new ways of experiencing the world led some to fear that the old and the new could never be reconciled.

New technology and the spread of industrial production had a broad impact on the population, helping to create what we know as mass society. Great population growth brought together people in growing cities, most arriving by railroad. The divide between "city" and "countryside" became far more easily traversed. Significant numbers of workers and peasants came to enjoy certain levels of political freedom, comfort, and leisure time. Tourism, just one example of the new forms of leisure, was a significant part of the culture and economy of England. Advertisements offered everything from seaside jaunts to—as seen here—round-the-world adventures. Despite economic differences and class prejudices, more and more people came to expect that their children would be better educated, healthier, and better off materially than they had been. The idea of progress gained broad support. Yet not everyone enjoyed social advancement, political participation, and cultural development, especially those in southern and eastern Europe. And not everyone welcomed the leveling effect on culture that the growth of mass society brought with it. Some denounced it as soulless, shallow, and mediocre.

Art and science also changed radically. Realism in art, which tried to reproduce images found in nature, gave way to abstraction, which aimed to express the artist's individual perceptions of the world. Scientific research in new fields, such as work on physics and radioactivity, compelled scientists to completely reexamine previous understandings of the physical world. The theories of Charles Darwin and Sigmund Freud sparked great controversies.

This was a period of contrasts and contradictions. Economic and industrial developments utterly transformed some regions while others—in particular, the Balkan and Iberian Peninsulas, southern Italy, and much of the Russian Empire—changed relatively little. The growth of mass culture clashed with individualistic ideologies. Atheistic materialism gained

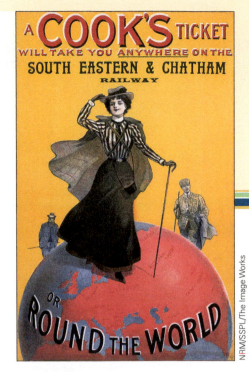

NRM/SSPL/The Image Works

A Poster Advertising Cook's Travel Services
Thomas Cook was one of the pioneers of tourism, beginning with rail trips to London to see the Great Exhibition of 1851 and, by century's end, offering round-the-world adventures.

many adherents, but the majority of Europeans retained their religious faith. Changes in economies, in technology, and in science, society, and everyday life were rapid and overwhelming, and yet, looking back after 1918, many who lived through these decades wistfully recalled the stability of the era. For many Europeans, this was a time of prosperity, peace, and cultural richness.

23-1 The Second Industrial Revolution

> » What technological advances were made during the second Industrial Revolution?

> » How did technological advances alter work and leisure?

In the second half of the nineteenth century, in particular after 1870, industrial and technological changes so profoundly altered European life that the era is called the second Industrial Revolution. These innovations included the widespread use of steel and electricity in industry, major breakthroughs in chemistry, the increasing use of petroleum to supplement coal and other energy sources, and a variety of new inventions that revolutionized transportation and communications. All these new industries created new categories of jobs and required corporate organization on a scale previously unknown. Industrial advances increased pay and decreased working hours, allowing Europeans to consume more material goods and enjoy more leisure than ever before.

The prosperity of the period gave new possibilities to artists and writers, whose works were viewed and purchased by large numbers of people. Science played a dual role in these changes, both enabling new, more efficient industrial techniques and calling into question long-held views about humanity's place in the world. For some, the discoveries and claims of science threatened traditional religious beliefs. This was an optimistic era, believing in progress and eagerly anticipating new advances. At the same time, some worried darkly that cold scientific rationality and mediocre mass society could destroy the very foundations of moral life and society.

Siemens-Martin (open-hearth) process
Technological advance that allowed economical mass production of steel.

23-1a New Materials, New Industries, New Technologies

Early industrialization in Britain and on the continent had been driven by the mass production of textiles in factories using first water power and then coal-driven steam engines. The railroad was a second driving factor in the economic upsurge that spread to the continent following the Napoleonic Wars (see Map 23.1). In the second half of the nineteenth century, however, while textiles and iron continued to be vital to the industrial economy, new materials and processes—steel, chemicals, petroleum—revolutionized industrial production.

Mass-Produced Steel The most important of these was mass-produced steel. Steel combines the advantages of pig iron (being hard and durable) and wrought iron (being flexible and resistant to cracking). The advantages of steel had long been known, but before the mid-nineteenth century, there had been no economical method of mass-producing steel. Then, in the 1850s and 1860s, the **Siemens-Martin (open-hearth) process** revolutionized steel production. In 1861, before these innovations had begun to spread throughout Europe, the total steel output in Britain, France, Germany, and Belgium was around 125,000 tons. By 1871, production had more than tripled and in 1913 exceeded 30 million tons—over eighty times the amount made in 1871. This massive output went into rails, railroad engines and cars, steamships, and increasingly sophisticated weaponry.

Steel also allowed new forms in architecture: its strength and flexibility meant that buildings could expand upward to an unprecedented degree. The skyscraper—an American invention—was the result. The ten-story Home Insurance Building in Chicago was erected in 1885, but expansion skyward was limited by the need to climb stairs. In 1887, this problem was solved with the invention of the high-speed elevator, and by the early twentieth century New York City had a number of skyscrapers, including the

Map 23.1 **Industrialization and the Railroads, 1870–1914** Industrialization and railroads went hand in hand. By 1870, nearly all major European cities were connected by rail, and railroads linked up even most provincial towns.

1. Locate on this map areas that industrialized after 1850, and compare them with Map 21.1 in Chapter 21.
2. Where were most of the post-1870 railroads built?

Modern Chemistry Creates New Products Rapid advances in textile production during the first half of the nineteenth century created a need for dyes, which scientists in Britain, France, and Germany figured out how to synthesize from coal tar. The first artificial dye of purple hue was given the French name *mauve.* Soon red ("magenta"), brown, and other colors were synthesized. These cheap new dyes meant that inexpensive, brightly colored clothing now could be manufactured for a mass market.

By the late nineteenth century the German chemical industry was far ahead of all competitors, producing some 90 percent of the world output of synthetic dyes as well as new medicines (most famous of all was aspirin), artificial materials such as Bakelite (an early plastic, 1907), and cellophane (1912). Artificial fertilizers began to be produced in the 1840s,

beautiful Flatiron Building with twenty-one stories, completed in 1902.

The Flatiron Building

When the Flatiron Building in New York City was built, it was the tallest building in the world. Here, we see it shortly after its completion in 1902. "Skyscrapers" became a symbol of American dynamism, but steel also revolutionized construction in other parts of the world.

❯❯ *What was the connection between mass production of steel and new possibilities for very tall buildings?*

❯❯ *Looking at this image, what elements of the Flatiron Building seem modern? What seems old-fashioned, compared with later skyscrapers?*

Henry Ford and his Son in the "Model F"

Like many automotive pioneers, Henry Ford grew up fascinated by machines of all types. Here we see him with his son in his Model F, a relatively luxurious automobile first produced in 1904. But the real breakthrough came in 1908 with the Model T, the first affordable car produced by mass-production assembly lines. Ford's innovations in production helped make the United States the world's first society in which automobiles were no longer luxuries, but everyday transportation.

❯❯ *What differences do you see between this car and the Model T?*

and chemists found new uses for poisons—such as the insecticide DDT, discovered in 1874, though not used until much later. The poisonous gas ammonia that formed an important part of many fertilizers was also used in the development of explosives. In 1867, Swedish businessman Alfred Nobel took out a patent for dynamite, which allowed highly explosive liquid nitroglycerine to be used more safely by combining it with a fine powder and packaging the mixture in tubes. The German firms founded in this era—such as BASF, Bayer, and Hoechst—continue today to be among the largest multinational chemical firms in the world.

Another innovation in chemistry was the process that produced paper inexpensively from wood pulp, which fostered the growth of mass-circulation newspapers and journals. The use of this inexpensive paper and mechanized printing, using steam-powered presses, made possible cheap newspapers such as *La Presse* in Paris (founded 1836) and the *Daily Telegraph* in London (founded 1855). The telegraph allowed fast-breaking stories from around the world to be reported almost instantly, and newspapers often printed special editions to cover major events. The invention of the linotype machine in 1886, which mechanized typesetting, allowed newspapers to get stories into print faster. Advances in printing allowed for more illustrations in newspapers and magazines. And the use of **lithography** from the 1830s onward allowed artists to create drawings, etchings, and other artworks in multiple copies, making artwork more affordable for a mass audience.

New Forms of Energy The original Industrial Revolution was fueled mainly by coal, but coal was difficult to mine and expensive to transport, especially for countries that lacked natural deposits, so industrialists sought new forms of energy. Coal gas came to be used for streetlights in all major cities early in the nineteenth century. Later it was replaced by natural gas, often discovered when drilling for

lithography Printing method used widely from the 1830s that produced text and color images used in posters and illustrated magazines.

oil. Petroleum products, from kerosene to gasoline, were increasingly used on an everyday basis by consumers.

Kerosene was widely used in lamps, where it produced greater light with less danger of fire than candles. Petroleum was also adopted for use aboard steamships, where the liquid fuel eliminated the need for stokers, and the reduction in labor costs helped offset the higher cost of the fuel itself. Two other distillations of petroleum, gasoline and diesel fuel, were used to propel the first automobiles; the diesel engine was patented in 1892, and the Ford Motor Company's Model T—the first mass-produced automobile—rolled off the assembly line in 1908. By 1900, the petroleum industry was growing enormously, especially in Russia and the United States, making **John D. Rockefeller** one of the world's richest men.

In the first decade of the twentieth century, the triumph of gasoline-powered automobiles was not yet clear. Many early vehicles were powered by steam and electricity, and many people complained of the dangerous and stinking gasoline engines. The greater comfort and reliability of electric cars is shown by the creation of taxi companies in Paris, Berlin, New York, and elsewhere using electric vehicles. Difficulties with the very heavy batteries (very hard on tires), which needed to be charged every hundred miles or less, ended up dooming the electric car by the 1920s. Despite the disapproval of traditionalists—Princeton University president Woodrow Wilson in 1906 groused that "Nothing has spread Socialistic feeling in this country more than the use of automobiles." But for many young men—and a few women—not necessarily only the rich and privileged, the speed and convenience of an automobile proved that technology could serve ordinary people. By 1916, there were more than two million motorized vehicles in the United States—more than the rest of the world put together.

Electricity is not so much a source of energy as a novel means of transmitting power over distance. Knowledge of electricity was not new, but the innovation of the late nineteenth century was to harness electricity for practical use and to perfect methods of generating and supplying it over long distances. The harnessing of electricity meant that industrial plants could be located away from coalfields or other sources of energy, such as water power. Unlike bulky steam engines, small electric motors could be transported from one location to another.

Within the factory, the use of electricity eliminated many of the dangerous belts and pulleys that had connected the steam engine to machinery. As cables and insulation to carry electricity became more efficient, electric power—including hydroelectric power produced by water flowing through turbines—could be generated and used over a broad area. The spread of electric light, using

Thomas Edison's invention of the light bulb (1879), proceeded in tandem with the establishment of public power stations. The first of these was set up in England by the **Siemens brothers** in 1881, and by 1914, electricity for offices, industry, and households was available in all major cities of Europe, though only the wealthiest and most up-to-date families had electricity in the home.

23-1b Communications and Transportation Networks

Perhaps no invention symbolized the compression of time and space during this period better than the telegraph, invented in the United States in the late 1830s. By the late 1860s, telegraph lines ran from one end of Europe to the other and were even connected by transatlantic cable to the United States. By the end of the century, all continents were connected by underwater cable, meaning that a message could go from London to Cape Town to Calcutta to Wellington to Vancouver in a matter of minutes.

Telegrams and Telephones Telegrams were sent using **Morse code**, a system of dots and dashes representing letters invented for this purpose, and flew through wires as electrical impulses. The telegraph required skilled operators who could translate the dots and dashes into words, offices where individuals could send messages, and messenger boys (in this period, nearly always male) to bring telegrams—often with bad news—to offices and residences. The impact on government, industry, and private life was enormous. At the beginning of the nineteenth century, news could travel no faster than horses or pigeons. By 1900, news traveled at the speed of light from one corner of the globe to the other. On a practical level, the telegraph enabled, for example, the tsar in St. Petersburg to check up on governors in distant Kamchatka or Tashkent, generals to issue orders to troops hundreds of miles away, businessmen to keep in touch with offices abroad, and ordinary people to contact loved ones, though usually only in emergencies because of the high cost.

John D. Rockefeller (1839–1937) Founder of the Standard Oil Company, which dominated the American petroleum market.

Thomas Edison (1847–1931) American inventor of the microphone, record player, and the first commercially practical light bulb.

Siemens brothers German brothers (Werner, Wilhelm, and Carl Heinrich) who, starting in 1847, established branches of their electrical firm in England, Germany, and Russia.

Morse code System combining dots and dashes representing letters, invented by the American Samuel Morse for sending messages over the electrical telegraph.

CONNECTIONS: Until the nineteenth century, with some exceptions, information traveled only as quickly as a horse, pigeon, or man. It is difficult to exaggerate the revolution in information caused by the telegraph. Suddenly it became possible to send specific and nuanced messages in an instant. Business and government recognized the importance of this new technology and quickly invested millions in it. By the early twentieth century, a young Irish-Italian nobleman, Guglielmo Marconi, successfully demonstrated that the Morse Code ("dot" and "dash") could be sent wirelessly from one (enormous) transmitting station to another (huge) antenna, even across the Atlantic Ocean. Wireless telegraphy opened new vistas, in particular in communications between Europe and the Americas, as well as Asian and African colonies (see Section 24-1 Motives and Methods of the New Imperialism for more on communication advances in the service of imperial administration). And the technology of wireless transmission would lead, with many bumps and false starts, to an entirely new phenomenon: radio broadcasts. By 1930, for the first time in world history, millions of people possessed in their own homes a device that entertained, educated, and allowed government propaganda to reach them.

In 1876, the American Alexander Graham Bell perfected a device that carried not just electrical impulses but actual sounds over a wire: the telephone. Unlike the telegraph, the telephone provided a direct link from person to person, though few working-class people could afford the new invention at first and some traditional aristocrats, such as Emperor Francis Joseph of Austria-Hungary, refused to speak on the telephone at all. Still, many in business and government quickly recognized the advantages of the telephone, and by 1900 telephone exchanges had been set up throughout Europe and North America, from London to Moscow, Berlin to Los Angeles. In Germany, the Siemens and Halske Company enjoyed a near monopoly in building telephone networks. In 1912, among the ten cities with the most telephones per capita, five were in the United States, three in Scandinavia, and two in Germany. The invention was also used to transmit other forms of sound, such as musical performances and news. By the 1890s, the *théâtrophone* in Paris allowed subscribers to hear the latest operas and concerts, and in Budapest thousands subscribed to a service providing news, musical performances, plays, stock market reports, and lectures by telephone.

The "Wireless" Radio Another invention of the 1890s, the wireless or radio, would eventually—in the 1920s—make telephonic concert and news services obsolete. In this period, however, radio broadcasts had not yet been conceived. In the years before World War I, the practical use of wireless signals was to send telegraph messages without wires. Perfected for practical purposes by the Italian **Guglielmo Marconi**, wireless telegraphy, as it was then called, allowed Morse Code signals to be sent thousands of miles through the atmosphere. One practical application for this new technology was to enable ships at sea to communicate with land and with each other. Navies of all countries spent large sums to develop and implement wireless communications. In 1899, the first distress signal from a ship at sea was sent. When the state-of-the-art ocean liner the *Titanic* went down on its first voyage on the night of April 14, 1912, it sent out distress signals; unfortunately the telegraph operator on the nearest ship was not on duty. A ship three times as far away did receive the signals, but when it arrived some two hours later, most of the *Titanic* passengers were already dead in the frigid waters of the North Atlantic. Nonetheless, the "Marconi operator" on the *Titanic* became a hero and celebrity; Marconi himself was praised as the author of this lifesaving technology. Wireless and telegraph communications meant that by the following morning, people all over the world could read in their local newspapers that the ship had struck an iceberg and had sunk rapidly with the loss of more than 1,500 lives.

Canals and Steamships The world was connected not only by telegraph wires and cables but also increasingly by steamship service and railroads during these decades. For the British, the steamship was vital in linking the homeland with India, though in the 1850s the one-way trip took around a month. The opening of the **Suez Canal** in 1869 cut travel between the Mediterranean Sea and the Indian Ocean in half and speeded up mail service between Britain and its colony India.

Steamship travel between Europe and the Americas became increasingly rapid, cheap, and—for those traveling first- and second-class—comfortable. By the 1890s, a steamship ticket from Italy to Argentina had become so inexpensive that many Italians traveled to Argentina to work as agricultural workers there during spring and summer, then returned to do the same in Italy, taking advantage of the reversed seasons in the Northern and Southern Hemispheres. Travel from northern Europe to New York took less than two weeks, and millions of immigrants made that journey in search of economic and political freedom.

Guglielmo Marconi
(1874–1937) Italian-Irish entrepreneur best known for perfection of "wireless telegraphy"; awarded the Nobel Prize in Physics in 1909.

Suez Canal An artificial waterway connecting the Red Sea and the Mediterranean, constructed by the British and French and opened in 1869.

The **Panama Canal**, which opened in 1914, connected the Atlantic and Pacific Oceans. Cutting through mountainous terrain, it was a marvel of engineering.

Railroads Connect East and West By the 1870s, railroads linked all the European capitals (Istanbul, or Constantinople, the name used by nineteenth-century Europeans for the city, followed in 1883). European capital and engineers also extended railroads through South America and Russia, as well as many places in Africa and Asia. The **Trans-Siberian Railroad**, begun in 1891, helped Russia transport hundreds of thousands of soldiers to Manchuria to fight the Japanese in the Russo-Japanese War a little more than a decade later. Military planners recognized the key role that efficient railroad transportation would play in warfare. The fact that Germany had the most developed railroad network in Europe was perceived as a direct threat by the French and Russian general staffs.

The increased traffic on rail and road required new bridges. In 1849, Buda and Pest were finally linked by a permanent bridge over the Danube, a first step to the unification of the two cities. The Royal Albert Bridge, designed by engineer and railroad innovator Isambard Kingdom Brunel, opened in 1859, stretching 455 feet over the river Tamar in southern England. Most famous of all was the Brooklyn Bridge, completed in 1883 after a decade of construction. Spanning almost 1,600 feet, it connected Manhattan with what was then a still mainly rural Brooklyn. Building bridges involved the use of new materials like dynamite and steel; similar techniques and materials were used by Gustave Eiffel in the tower named for him in Paris, completed in 1889.

New forms of transportation also took to the air. Germany became a leader in the production of dirigibles or blimps, flying an airship called a zeppelin (named for the German Count Zeppelin) for the first time in 1900. An even more startling development was the Wright brothers' successful flight in 1903, opening the skies to heavier-than-air flying machines. Although few people would travel by air until the second half of the twentieth century, thousands watched in awe as dirigibles and primitive airplanes, whose impact on warfare, the economy, and culture in the new century would be profound, took to the skies.

23-1c New Places and Patterns of Work

As Europe industrialized, it also urbanized as hundreds of thousands of people left farms and villages for better wages and a more exciting life in the cities. In 1800 there was only one city—London—with a population of over 1 million; only twenty-three cities had more than 100,000 inhabitants. By 1900, London's population had grown to over 4 million and five more European cities had over 1 million inhabitants

(Paris, Berlin, Moscow, St. Petersburg, and Vienna); 135 cities had populations over 100,000. Manchester had by then topped 600,000, almost exactly the same population as contemporary Warsaw.

The population of Berlin increased from around 500,000 at midcentury to over 2 million sixty years later. The Polish textile town of Łódź (not by chance known as the Polish Manchester) exploded in population, from a mere 519 inhabitants in 1809 to more than 300,000 at the end of the century. Throughout Europe, cities such as Budapest, Munich, Madrid, and Milan grew impressively (see Map 23.2).

Living Conditions in Cities Most of the newcomers to cities lived in wretched and expensive lodgings and tenements. In some cases, overcrowding was so severe that beds were rented out in two or more "sleeping shifts" on a twenty-four-hour basis. Hygiene and health suffered greatly in such places, and tuberculosis was rampant, claiming thousands of lives yearly. But running water and central heat were increasingly available, even for the less well-off, and electric tramways and—in Paris and London—subways made it possible for workers to live in less crowded, leafy suburbs and commute to work.

London's "underground" was the first to open, in the 1860s, and the Paris "metro" dates from the first decade of the twentieth century. By that time, even smaller cities such as Warsaw and Stockholm had streetcars and trams connecting the city's outskirts with its downtown. Public transportation allowed workers to live farther from the factories, and cities became increasingly differentiated by social class. In Berlin's West End (the name taken from a similarly affluent London district), the bourgeoisie built villas, while workers lived across town in tenements.

New Professions, Shorter Working Hours Many of the people riding the streetcars or metro to work were employed in new **white-collar** positions. As prosperity increased, so did the places to spend or save that money. Department stores, such as the **Bon Marché** (bone marchay) in Paris and KdW (Kaufhaus des Westens) in Berlin, also opened in Budapest, Milan, and elsewhere. Not just consumption, but

Panama Canal An artificial waterway connecting the Atlantic and Pacific Oceans, built from 1904 to 1914 by American military engineers.

Trans-Siberian Railroad Russia's ambitious railway project connecting Moscow with the Pacific Ocean, begun in 1891 and completed in 1916, which caused friction with Japan.

white collar Employment that does not involve physical labor, such as that of professionals (lawyers, doctors, teachers) and office workers.

Bon Marché First department store, opened in Paris in 1852 and catered primarily to middle-class people.

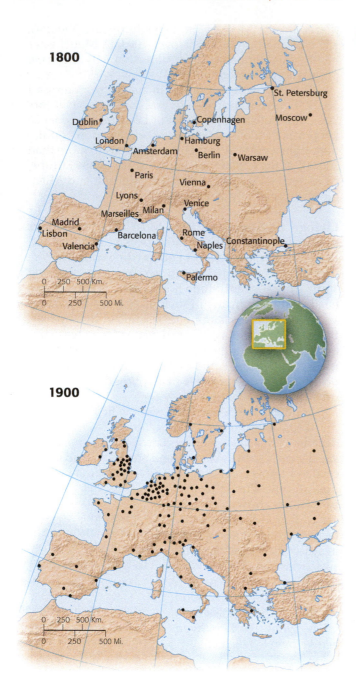

1800

1900

Map 23.2 **European Cities with Populations over 100,000, 1800 and 1900** The rapid growth of population combined with migration from rural to urban areas in Europe is reflected in the significant increase in large cities during the course of the nineteenth century, as shown in these maps.

1. Which of these cities are located in regions that industrialized before 1850 ("first" industrialization)?

2. Which regions and countries show the greatest density of urban centers? How does this correlate with their rate of industrialization?

find employment in banks, department stores, and professional offices. They were, however, expected to quit work upon marrying.

By the late nineteenth century the average workday had shrunk in western and central Europe, partly under pressure from organized labor and partly because of technological innovations. As fewer workers, both in offices and in factories, lived adjacent to their places of work and workdays shrank to ten and even eight hours, the routine of transport/work/transport became common. Through all layers of society in the industrialized countries, one fact was constant: the entire day was no longer taken up by work, freeing up precious hours for **leisure**.

23-1d The New Concept of Leisure

As the predominant form of work became employment with a fixed number of hours per day, contracted to an employer, employees also found they had "free time," time after work that they could spend as they chose. The concept of leisure was new, and it was much enjoyed in the second half of the nineteenth century, especially as the workday shrank to about ten hours and the idea of a work-free weekend took hold. Most Europeans had both more time and more money for leisure activities than had their grandparents' generation. Gas, and then electric lighting meant that dance halls and nightclubs could stay open well into and even through the night. Alcohol consumption increased considerably, worrying religious authorities and middle-class moralists who had chosen for themselves more "high-brow" entertainment such as concerts, operas, and plays.

Popular Amusements Nearly everyone in large cities spent time in cafés and dance halls. There one could eat and drink, listen to music, experience light comic and dramatic performances, and, of course, dance. Some cafés catered to a select middle-class audience, but for commercial reasons, most desired

also saving money was a middle-class concern; the number of banks increased and, with them, the number of clerks. Similarly, the number of lawyers, physicians, and dentists went up markedly, and these professionals employed even larger numbers as receptionists and assistants. Government bureaucracies also burgeoned as the state's role in the economy and everyday life grew. Most of these new positions were filled by young men, but women were able to

leisure Time for relaxation or recreation, new in the later nineteenth century owing to industrial and social advances.

the largest possible number of patrons and served anyone who enjoyed drinking, dancing, listening to music, and watching clown shows and comedy acts. By the 1890s, the Spanish flamenco and Argentine tango competed with more traditional popular music and dance for public attention.

Magic lantern slide shows were increasingly popular, allowing mass audiences to experience—at least visually—travels to exotic destinations around the world. Around 1900, the moving picture became technically and commercially viable, and cinema houses sprang up in all major European cities. In the United States, by far the leader in this new technology, millions went to the "picture show" every week. The early picture shows were often long on sensation and short on memorable artistic value, but the new medium of film opened up vast possibilities for artists in the new century.

CONNECTIONS: With major technological advances come painful social and cultural changes. When the printing press appeared in the fifteenth century, some traditional elites complained that the crude black ink of the printed books was far less pleasing than illustrated manuscripts (see Section 12-3c Printing, a New Medium). Similarly, when motion pictures appeared in the late nineteenth century, many traditionalists worried that the stage art of Shakespeare and Goethe would be swept away and replaced by semipornographic skits. In the early twentieth century, those who had been born a half-century earlier sometimes felt astonished and bewildered by the increasing pace of life, whether on land, over oceans, or through the "aether" in the form of wireless communications. In 1970, Alvin Toffler published a book which quickly become a kind of "cult classic": *Future Shock*, in which he argued that the increasing pace of technological change would soon overwhelm and "shock" the human race. Are we experiencing that in the twenty-first century?

Photography The new technology of photography, perfected in the late nineteenth century, allowed amateurs to create images with their own cameras. The word *Kodak*, specially created by American businessman George Eastman in 1888 to market his small cameras, passed into several languages. Photographic technology, which produced an image as exact as the best sketch or painting, had an important impact on artists, who no longer needed to copy the world but could instead portray their own inner impressions of light, color, and shadow. Photography also facilitated the spread of another popular diversion: pornography.

Railroads and Tourism Railroads made travel for pleasure possible for the masses. When the Great Exhibition of the Works of Industry of All Nations, better known as the **Crystal Palace Exhibition**, was

The Football players, 1908 (oil on canvas), Rousseau, Henri J.F. (Le Douanier) (1844-1910) / Solomon R. Guggenheim Museum, New York, USA / Bridgeman Images

Henri Rousseau, *The Football Players*

This 1908 painting reflects a growing interest in sports and other leisure-time activities among middle- and even working-class Europeans. Not only the football itself was mass-produced; so were the outfits worn by the players. One or two generations earlier, before the second Industrial Revolution, games were much less standardized. Rousseau's artistic treatment of these men is obviously stylized, but what elements of modern football-soccer do you see depicted here? Looking at the image, name at least two objects that would not have been present (or only in very different form) before the industrial revolution. Like industrialization itself, most modern forms of leisure, tourism, and sport began in England and spread to the rest of Europe in the second half of the nineteenth century. English words themselves invaded other languages, so that Russians and Germans speak of "sport," Swedes enjoy "fotboll," Italians engage in "turismo," and Poles refer to a bicycle as a "rower" after one British company (Rover) that manufactured them.

opened in London in 1851, about one-fifth of the people of England visited, in part on package tours from the travel entrepreneur Thomas Cook. Many of the visitors had never been away from their hometown or village. After the St. Petersburg–Warsaw railroad opened in 1862, travelers could embark from

magic lantern Early form of the modern slide projector that projected images painted on glass plates onto a screen.

Crystal Palace Exhibition Great Exhibition of the Works of Industry of All Nations, opened in London's Crystal Palace in 1851.

Moscow in a sleeping car and emerge in Paris a few days later. From 1883 onward, they could take the Orient Express from Paris through six countries, ending up in the exotic Ottoman capital, Istanbul. Russian aristocrats could now spend their summers on the French Riviera.

Wealthy Europeans traveled by railroad—the richest had their own personal train coaches—to spas such as Baden-Baden and Karlsbad (now Karlovy Vary in the Czech Republic), where they "took the waters," relaxed, played cards, flirted, and engaged in other diversions. Christian pilgrims numbering in the hundreds of thousands annually took the train to Lourdes, where the peasant girl Bernadette Soubirous (soo-bee-roos) claimed to have seen a vision of the Virgin Mary in 1858. And even workers of modest means could take suburban railroads for day trips to the countryside. The rich could travel in comfort, riding in first class or even hitching their own private railcars onto trains. They stayed in new and magnificent luxury hotels such as the Hotel Adlon in Berlin, where the Kaiser put up his own guests.

Sports Workers also enjoyed sports, both as active participants and as spectators. First in Britain, then throughout Europe, football in the forms of soccer and rugby brought together enthusiasts in increasing numbers. By the early twentieth century, it is estimated, some half million British men regularly played. Golf, spreading outside Scotland, became the sport of choice for the well-to-do. After the chain-driven bicycle was perfected in the early 1890s, cycling swept western Europe. Social conservatives were outraged by the mobility and personal freedom that bicycles gave women, as well as by the new fashions that allowed them to ride astride these new iron horses. Tennis in its modern form was invented in the 1870s and rapidly gained popularity, not least of all because it was the rare sport—golf was another—that upper- and middle-class men and women could play together.

Leisure created new industries. Originally, blown-up pig bladders were used as soccer balls, but their irregular shape made the game unpredictable. In 1855, the American inventor Charles Goodyear applied the process of vulcanizing rubber that he had invented a decade earlier to the manufacture of soccer balls. This first "modern" soccer ball did not yet have today's familiar white-and-black pattern but had a regular spherical shape. Soon others adopted Goodyear's technique, and a new industry was born. The same desire for a more regular, predictable game led to the mass production of baseballs, bicycles, tennis rackets, and sports outfits.

mass society Modern society characterized by universal legal rights, education, a large middle class, and a high level of equality among classes.

23-2 Mass Society

» **How did economic changes alter society and family life?**

» **What impact did science have on society?**

In the second half of the nineteenth century mass production in industry and mass consumption in department stores influenced the social order. High levels of literacy, political participation, and (relatively speaking) material affluence in western Europe reduced differences between social classes and expanded opportunities for social advancement. Measured by these criteria, mass society appeared first in Britain (excluding Ireland), Scandinavia, France, Belgium, and the Netherlands. Central and southern Europe, Russia, and the Balkans lagged behind.

By the early twentieth century, access to education and to some level of political participation had come to be expected, increasingly by women as well as men. Greater numbers of people were now able to enjoy better food, brighter clothes, and a longer life. Advances in the biological sciences produced new medicines and vaccines. The new opportunities for employment and consumption also influenced women's place in the home and in society, opening the way for a new movement, feminism.

23-2a Mass Consumption

The benefits of technological innovation came first to the wealthy, but in the second half of the nineteenth century, they had a positive impact on everyday life for the urban poor and peasants out in the countryside. Mass production created a **mass society** in which prosperity spread among different classes. This heightened affluence and widespread education meant that obvious external differences between "high" and "low," such as clothes and speech, were reduced. Factory-produced textiles and manufacture of garments made clothing so cheap and colorful—reflecting the availability of cheap synthetic dyes—that few peasants even in less-developed countries like Russia continued to make their own clothes. In fact, peasants could now afford several changes of clothes, including undergarments—a novelty at the beginning of the century, but taken for granted by 1900.

Consumption as Leisure: The Department Store
Cheap newspapers and magazines, distributed widely by the thickening rail networks, meant that even people in remote regions could see and seek to imitate the latest fashions from Paris or St. Petersburg. And mass production brought prices down so that more and more middle- and even working-class people could

afford to dress fashionably. The famous department store Bon Marché was ironically hailed as "a cathedral of commerce for a congregation of consumers" by the French writer Émile Zola.

The name Bon Marché means both "good market" and "inexpensive" in French—and the idea of a store for the masses was the creation of a self-made man, **Aristide Boucicaut** (boo-see-koe), and his wife, Marguerite. Their first store, opened just after the 1848 revolutions, introduced the novelty of clearly marked prices and welcomed people—mainly women—to come and look over the merchandise with no obligation to purchase. The revolutionary concept of allowing potential customers to look without necessarily buying amounted to the invention of shopping as a pastime—and was wildly successful.

In 1869, Boucicaut resolved to build a large new store using the most modern architecture. When the palatial structure opened in 1887, it delighted customers with its sumptuous decorations, sweeping marble staircases, and electric elevators. Shoppers are still delighted by the Bon Marché, a palace in which to shop and be seen shopping. Boucicaut was a masterful businessman, offering such novel services as a catalogue of merchandise, free delivery, a money-back guarantee, and various sales like the "white month" in January. Zola wrote a novel about the department store—*The Ladies' Paradise* (1883)—and a metro station was given Boucicaut's name.

Thousands of attractive young women were hired as department store clerks, though previously selling had been regarded as unseemly for women. Women also joined the growing lower middle class as teachers, nurses, postal clerks, typists, and telephone operators. Although large numbers of young women continued to work as servants into the twentieth century, the higher pay, broader personal autonomy, and social prestige of these new occupations attracted many. Although the salaries were low, the job allowed—indeed required—women to dress and behave like members of a more privileged class. Conservatives found this blurring of social distinctions outrageous and complained that it was becoming impossible to distinguish "people of good family" from servants by dress, and increasingly even by speech and manners.

23-2b Public Health

The population of Europe more than doubled between 1800 and 1900 (from around 200 million to 430 million), despite the departure of millions of emigrants for the Americas. This population explosion can be explained partly by better nutrition and the lack of massive epidemics or major wars after 1815, but improvements in medical knowledge and treatment were also a factor.

Microorganisms, Germs, and Disease Medical research paralleled work in physics: both were searching for invisible causes for specific mysterious phenomena. In physics, these were gamma rays, X-rays, and radiation; in medical science, the invisible cause was the germ, which was discovered in the 1880s. But long before that, scientists knew that *something* spread diseases, and they devised practical programs to prevent disease transmission. In the eighteenth century, it had been discovered that using matter from cowpox pustules created an effective vaccine against smallpox. Similarly, the connection between dirty water, rotting waste, and disease had long been made—but most continued to think that disease was spread by foul smells.

Around 1820 cholera, a disease spread by unclean water, spread from India and Central Asia to Russia and western Europe. Crowded towns with minimal hygiene and limited access to clean water were an ideal breeding ground for cholera, which caused epidemics in a number of cities. In London, a major outbreak in 1854 allowed the physician **John Snow** to promote his theory that the disease spread not through the air but by bad water. Snow's data showing that all the cholera victims in a certain London district had drunk water from a single source, the Broad Street pump, convinced even his critics. Snow was also one of the first physicians to use chloroform and ether to deaden pain. His most famous patient was Queen Victoria, who was grateful for his treatments during childbirth.

Around the same time in France, **Louis Pasteur** was demonstrating that heating wine to 55 degrees Celsius killed the disease-causing microorganisms in it. His technique, called pasteurization, was later applied to beer and milk. Pasteur also pioneered methods for vaccinating against a number of diseases, including rabies and anthrax. Perhaps most important for medical practice, Pasteur demonstrated methods of sterilization that reduced the risk of infection in surgery and hospitals. Pasteur's suggestion that tiny particles of organic matter floating through the air could contaminate matter and cause fermentation was seized on by the English surgeon Joseph Lister, who showed that treating wounds with carbolic acid significantly reduced infections. Lister's antiseptic technique cut in half the number of deaths from infection following surgery and was later immortalized in the mouthwash Listerine.

Germs and Hygiene: From the Laboratory to the Hospital Pasteur's pathbreaking work in microbiology

John Snow (1813–1858) English physician who proved that cholera is spread by drinking water and who pioneered the use of chloroform to deaden pain.

Louis Pasteur (1822–1895) French scientist who developed a process for heating liquids to kill disease-causing organisms, now known as pasteurization.

was continued by **Robert Koch** in Germany. Up to this point, scientists had suspected the existence of microorganisms too small to be seen under the microscope; Koch proved their existence by isolating the cholera bacillus in 1883. He showed that each disease had its own microbiological cause and devised treatments and vaccines for these diseases. During the last part of his life, Koch devoted himself to the cause and treatment of the infectious lung disease tuberculosis that plagued factory workers and city dwellers. In 1905, Koch was awarded the Nobel Prize in Medicine in recognition of his achievements. Until the mid-nineteenth century, a sick person was *more* likely to die if admitted to a hospital, where unhygienic conditions often led to infections and death, than if treated at home. **Florence Nightingale**, who helped organize military hospitals in Istanbul during the Crimean War, returned to Britain to improve hospital care there. She virtually invented the profession of nursing, which from the start was an almost exclusively female occupation—and in Catholic countries often carried out by nuns. Building on the discoveries of Snow, Pasteur, and Lister, Nightingale worked throughout her long life to create modern, antiseptic, but welcoming hospitals. By the early twentieth century, the chances of dying after surgery, during childbirth, or in a hospital had been much reduced.

Robert Koch (1843–1910) German bacteriologist who established that many diseases such as anthrax, tuberculosis, and cholera were caused by bacterial infections.

Florence Nightingale (1820–1910) English reformer and creator of nursing as a profession who was instrumental in creating hygienic, well-organized hospitals.

Rosa Luxemburg (1871–1919) Polish-Jewish socialist who criticized V. I. Lenin and was murdered in 1919 by right-wing nationalists after a communist uprising in Berlin.

Marie Curie (1867–1934) Polish-born chemist and physicist who studied radioactivity and radium; the first person to win two Nobel prizes.

23-2c Families and Feminism

The technological and economic changes wrought by industrialization pervaded all aspects of public and private life. In the industrial cities, families no longer functioned as production units, and children came to be recognized as more of an economic burden than a benefit. Medical advances reduced infant mortality rates, so a woman who gave birth to, say, a dozen children could reasonably assume (at least in western and central Europe) that ten would survive to adulthood. But these children would be expensive to raise and educate, especially as the number of years required for a good education increased. In these decades, family planning in the form of contraception and medical abortions

became widespread. Nearly everywhere, both were illegal, but laws could not prevent women from using natural methods to limit the number of their offspring.

Women, Falling Birthrates, and Education Throughout Europe, birthrates went down, but unevenly. French politicians, not coincidentally all male, expressed grave concern at France's falling birthrate, the lowest among the Great Powers. The German birthrate, though relatively high, declined steadily in this period. Birthrates remained high in the least developed areas, such as Russia, southern Italy, Spain, and the Balkan Peninsula.

Among the middle classes, having fewer children meant that women had more time for other activities. Before 1848, universities rarely admitted women, but during the second half of the nineteenth century these barriers began to break down. Women seeking higher education often went to Switzerland to receive training as doctors, lawyers, or economists, such as the famous Polish-Jewish socialist **Rosa Luxemburg**. Other exceptional women, like **Marie Curie**, studied in Paris, though not all professors—or male students—accepted women students as colleagues and intellectual equals (see Profiles in Change: Marie Skłodowska Curie Chooses to Study Physics and Learning from a Primary Source: Marie Skłodowska Curie Recalls Her Youth in Russian Poland later in this chapter). Although few women succeeded in surmounting the great economic and social obstacles and completing the university course, these first successful pioneers demonstrated that women were in no way intellectually inferior to men.

Women's Rights Yet women's educational opportunities, especially in secondary and higher education, remained limited, and it was often difficult for an educated woman to earn her own living. The laws of most European countries did not recognize women as adults. Very often a woman could not even open a bank account, sign a contract, or purchase property without her husband's (or, if single, her father's) permission.

Women also had little protection against abusive husbands. Despite the passage of the Matrimonial Causes Act in Britain in 1857, which considerably facilitated divorce (previously any divorce needed to be approved by Parliament as a specific, separate act), few women could afford the expense—and social scandal—of a divorce trial. Similarly, in France, divorce was made legal from 1884 onward, but the procedure was so complicated and expensive that few actually used it. In many countries, like Russia, divorce was not a possibility, and men who grew tired of family life often simply disappeared, abandoning wife and children. Because of the gross imbalance of power between men and women, socialists like Friedrich Engels and Clara Zetkin mocked the morality of middle-class sexuality and family life, calling it little more than a legalized form of enslavement and prostitution.

Demanding Legal Equality: Feminism Despite their legal disabilities, more and more women were literate and active in society. Whether raising children or working in factories, hospitals, or offices, women were increasingly well informed on contemporary cultural and scientific subjects. Some, like Florence Nightingale, chose to forgo marriage to devote themselves to other causes. Others, like the middle-class feminist **Emmeline Pankhurst**, dedicated themselves to achieving equal rights and opportunities for women, including the vote. Pankhurst, whose daughters Christabel and Sylvia also became notable feminists, embraced radical tactics such as arson, vandalism (like dumping jam into mailboxes), and public protests. For these activities Pankhurst was arrested several times, going on hunger strikes in jail and being force-fed. Such activities were controversial, but they attracted attention to women's unequal status before the law and in the economy. Feminists in other European countries and in the United States did not always agree with these tactics, but they recognized that such radical actions forced the male establishment to take notice of the woman question.

Feminism—use of the word to refer to the struggle for women's rights dates from this period—was mainly a middle-class phenomenon, for women workers and peasants were usually more concerned with better wages and work conditions than specific gender-based demands. Socialists denounced feminism as a bourgeois diversion, arguing that true equal rights for women would come only with socialist revolution. But the idea that women should have the same professional and political rights as men was gaining ground.

23-3 Art and Industrial Society

» **What impact did the economic and social changes of the late nineteenth century have on the visions and techniques of artists and writers?**

» **How did mass production and mass society influence art and literature?**

Industrialization so deeply permeated all aspects of life in the late nineteenth century that art was profoundly altered as well. Art reflected the new industrial mass society both in its subjects and, even more strongly, in its techniques and artistic vision. Photography and the mass production of images through lithography and other techniques called into question the need for realistic art. Artists also worried that the mass production of cheap images would degrade people's ability to appreciate the beautiful. Yet though artists experimented with new techniques, most people continued to prefer traditional realism and bought mass-produced images in the thousands and millions. Increasingly, artists found themselves out of tune with mass society.

23-3a From Realism to Abstraction in Art

The scientific and technological advances of the mid-nineteenth century made artists look at the world in a new way, leading to a new artistic movement known as **Realism**. Realists rejected conventions demanding that the proper subjects for painting should be lofty—scenes from classical Greece, for example, or the Bible. Instead, they took their subjects from among working people, the peasantry, and events of everyday life. Among the most famous Realists was **Jean-François Millet**, whose paintings often depicted peasants at work, their faces grim and resigned. Realist painters were often political radicals who wanted to convey social and political opinions in their works. The caricatures of **Honoré Daumier** (**oh-no-ray dow-mee-yay**), for example, acidly criticized the existing social order. In Russia, the paintings of **Ilya Repin** laid bare the stark misery of the Russian lower classes and the pervasive injustices existing in that society.

From Realism to Impressionism The paintings of **Edouard Manet** (**ed-oo-ar man-AY**) also laid open society's more sordid side. He shocked his contemporaries by making a well-known prostitute the subject of his painting *Olympia*. In the same year, 1863, Manet

Emmeline Pankhurst (1858–1928) English activist for women's suffrage who was often arrested for her radical activities.

feminism Movement for equal rights for women, including legal equality and the right to vote.

Realism Movement in literature and painting that aimed at the objective reproduction of reality without idealization.

Jean-François Millet (1814–1875) French painter concerned with depicting social problems in a realistic style.

Honoré Daumier (1808–1879) French artist best known for his bitingly sarcastic caricatures of contemporary political figures and bourgeois society.

Ilya Repin (1844–1930) Russian Realist artist who specialized in painting enormous scenes from Russian past and contemporary life.

Edouard Manet (1832–1883) French painter who chose scandalous subjects and influenced the later Impressionists.

Marie Skłodowska Curie Recalls Her Youth in Russian Poland

In an autobiographical memoir that appeared in 1930, Marie Curie described the major events and milestones of her life. This memoir was published together with autobiographical sketches by American activist Jane Addams, Japanese feminist Sugimoto Etsu Inagaki, and other women. The editor of this volume, Helen Ferris, aimed to provide young women with evidence that women could make their mark on society as well as positive role models. In this passage, Marie Curie recalls teaching Polish children under repressive Russian rule in the 1880s.

❶ Why did the Russian government oppose education for these Polish children? Why might the Russian government see education as dangerous?

❷ How important do you think the example of other successful women was for inspiring Marie to try to find a way to study abroad? What do you think motivated Madame Curie to write this short memoir?

❶ Since my duties with my pupils did not take up all my time, I organized a small class for the children of the village who could not be educated under the Russian government. . . . We taught the little children and the girls who wished to come how to read and write, and we put in circulation Polish books which were appreciated, too, by the parents. Even this innocent work presented danger, as all initiative of this kind was forbidden by the government and might bring imprisonment or deportation to Siberia. My evenings I generally devoted to study. **❷** I had heard that a few women had succeeded in following certain courses in Petrograd or in foreign countries, and I was determined to prepare myself by preliminary work to follow their example. . . . **❸** My solitary study was beset with difficulties. The scientific education I had received at the lyceum [high school] was very incomplete; it was well under the bachelorship program [high school curriculum] of a French lyceum; I tried to add to it

The Gleaners, 1857 (oil on canvas), Millet, Jean-Francois (1814–75) / Musee d'Orsay, Paris, France / Giraudon / The Bridgeman Art Library

Jean-François Millet's *The Gleaners,* 1857

This painting depicts women's backbreaking work of gleaning fields after harvest. Like many other realist works by Millet, this painting shows a scene from the everyday life of poor peasants.

» *In what ways can this image be seen as an example of Realist art?*

» *At first glance, industrialization appears not to have reached this area—but what objects can you see that could be products of industrial mass production?*

3 What were the advantages and drawbacks of solitary study for Curie?

4 What does this passage reveal about family responsibilities in this period? How do they differ from family obligations today?

5 How does this belief in study as a moral force compare with the teachings of Comte and the positivists?

6 Why could Polish young people in the 1880s think of study as a patriotic activity? Could students in the twenty-first century have the same attitude, and, if so, where and why?

in my own way, with the help of books picked up at random. This method could not be greatly productive, yet it was not without results. I acquired the habit of independent work, and learned a few things which were to be used later on.

4 I had to modify my plans for the future when my eldest sister decided to go to Paris to study medicine. We had promised each other mutual aid, but our means did not permit our leaving together. So I kept my position for three and a half years, and, having finished my work with my pupils, I returned to Warsaw, where a position, similar to the one I had left, was awaiting me. . . .

5 Another means of instruction came to me through my being one of an enthusiastic group of young men and women of Warsaw, who united in a common desire to study, and whose activities were at the same time social and patriotic. It was one of those groups of Polish youths who believed that the hope of their country lay in a great effort to develop the intellectual and moral strength of the nation, and that such an effort would lead to a better national situation. . . . **6** We agreed among ourselves to give evening courses, each one teaching what he knew best. There is no need to say that this was a secret organization, which made everything extremely difficult.

Source: Helen Ferris, ed., *When I Was a Girl: The Stories of Five Famous Women as Told by Themselves* (New York: MacMillan, 1930).

again outraged critics by painting together a pair of fully dressed gentlemen and an unabashedly naked woman in *The Luncheon on the Grass*, pointing to the hypocrisy existing in relations between men and women. Manet's technique remained Realist in his careful and objective attention to detail, but his subjects were deemed scandalous.

Midcentury French art had two main centers, both in Paris: the Academy of Painting and Sculpture, where young artists learned realistic techniques and painted exalted scenes; and the **Salon de Paris**, which exhibited new paintings sponsored by the academy every other year. Having one's work accepted for display at the Salon was the ambition of every young artist, as it meant professional success and often wealth. But the works of Manet and others who did not accept the Academy's narrow view of art had no chance of being accepted to the Salon. Angry at this conservatism, beginning in 1863 the rejected artists organized their own Salon des Refusés—an exhibition of refused paintings.

In the 1870s, artists began to experiment with new ways of depicting reality. Instead of striving for photographic realism, artists like **Claude Monet** sought to capture the artist's perception of light and shadows—a technique labeled **Impressionism** by a hostile critic. The label stuck but soon lost its negative connotation. The Impressionists sought to convey not an image of an object but rather the impression that image made on artists and their technique for depicting color, light, and shadow. Monet's paintings of haystacks at different times of day showed how the play of light created entirely different colors and images. Impressionists such as Edgar Degas (day-GAH), Auguste Renoir (ren-wahr), and Georges Seurat painted the new amusements of the day—dance halls, boating trips, and cafés. The great graphic artist **Henri de Toulouse-Lautrec** (toh-LOOS loh-TREK), who was close to the Impressionists, raised the poster to an artistic form, thereby blurring the distinction between art and advertising. Toulouse-Lautrec's posters advertising the Chat Noir (Black Cat) nightclub, the singer Jean Avril, and Le Moulin Rouge (Red Mill) dance hall became classics.

Salon de Paris Exhibition of paintings sponsored every other year by the Academy of Painting and Sculpture.

Claude Monet (1840–1926) French Impressionist painter best known for his studies of the effect of light on landscapes, such as haystacks and the Rouen Cathedral.

Impressionism Artistic movement in France beginning in the 1870s that aimed to reproduce the painter's impression of light on a scene.

Henri de Toulouse-Lautrec (1864–1901) French artist who created bright and compelling posters advertising nightclub singers and dance halls.

State Russian Museum, St. Petersburg, Russia/ Giraudon/The Bridgeman Art Library

Ilya Repin, *Volga Barge-Haulers*, 1870–1873

Ilya Repin's works exemplify the Realist style in Russian art and often portray the poorest Russians, as in this painting. Like other Realists, Repin did not intend merely to depict a scene from Russian life: he wanted to shock viewers and remind them of the grinding poverty and social injustice present in their country.

❯❯ *Compare this image with Millet's* The Gleaners *(see previous image).*

❯❯ *What similarities and differences do you see in subject matter and style?*

Going Beyond Impressionism During the last decades of the nineteenth century, Paris became the center of the entire art world. American painters like James McNeill Whistler and Mary Cassatt came to live and paint there; Cassatt stayed to live out her life in France. The Spaniard **Pablo Picasso** arrived in Paris in 1899 and also spent most of his life there. With its academic traditions, large numbers of young artists rebelling against those traditions, government support for the arts, and a large, wealthy and sophisticated society of art lovers, Paris attracted thousands of artists from everywhere in Europe and throughout the world.

The Impressionists emphasized the artist's perception over any single objective vision of reality, but at the beginning of the twentieth century new movements progressed even further from visual realism. The Viennese painter **Gustav Klimt** combined realistic and abstract elements in such works as *The Kiss* (1907–1908), in which the kissing faces of a couple are surrounded by colorful geometric patterns. Increasingly, artists aimed to go beyond surface reality. Picasso's influential and shocking *Demoiselles d'Avignon* of 1907 portrays the "Young Ladies of Avignon" as flat expanses of pink paint with exaggerated eyes and noses. Picasso

and other so-called **Cubists** depicted the same object as seen simultaneously from various angles, resulting in a multifaceted, fractured image that appealed to the mind more than to the eye.

The movement away from Realism in art culminated in **abstract art**. In abstract works, such as those of the Russian Wassily Kandinsky and the Swiss Paul Klee, swirling shapes and colors do not represent any specific "real" objects but depict instead the artist's emotions and perceptions of the world. The **Futurists**, who published their "Manifesto" in 1909, took these new artistic techniques and added a political twist, provocatively calling for the destruction of past artistic and literary works to blaze a trail for the new. In *Nude Descending a Staircase* (1912), the Futurist Marcel Duchamp used Cubist techniques to portray his subject—movement. These new trends in nonrepresentational art would have a great influence on the art of the twentieth century but failed to find broad acceptance or understanding in their own time.

23-3b Realism and Naturalism in Literature

Realism was not limited to the visual arts. Writers such as Charles Dickens in England, Ivan Turgenev in Russia, and Gustave Flaubert in France all wrote Realist fiction, aiming to describe life objectively and with an eye toward social criticism. Dickens's heroes such as the orphans Oliver in *Oliver Twist* (1838) and Pip in *Great Expectations* (1861) struggle to improve their social position, eventually succeeding in being accepted in middle-class society. Turgenev's most famous novel, *Fathers and Sons* (1862), highlights the generational conflict between the liberal gentry "fathers" and the radical younger generation during the Great Reform period in Russia. In Flaubert's *Madame Bovary* (1856), a woman locked in a loveless marriage to a boring and narrow-minded man seeks

Pablo Picasso (1881–1973) Spanish painter, founder of the Cubist school, and lifelong experimenter with abstract techniques.

Gustav Klimt (1862–1918) Viennese painter whose portraits integrated rich abstract patterns with realistic and expressive human faces.

Cubists Painters who challenged traditional realism by breaking up three-dimensional figures into different "cubes."

abstract art Art depicting the artist's view of the world through free use of color and shapes.

Futurists Artistic movement beginning in 1909 with a "Manifesto" that stressed energy, movement, even violence in visual and literary art.

Österreichische Galerie Belvedere, Vienna/The Bridgeman Art Library

Klimt, *The Kiss,* 1907–1908

Klimt was simultaneously an extremely popular portraitist and a controversial and innovative artist in turn-of-the-century Vienna. This painting, one of his most famous, incorporates abstract, ornamental surfaces and sinuous human figures locked in a passionate embrace.

>> *Does this image appeal to you? Why or why not?*

>> *How do the abstract shapes in the painting (especially on the figures' "garments") symbolize masculine and feminine?*

>> *Why do you think Klimt chose to stray from strictly realistic portraiture to this more abstract style?*

joy by taking a lover and is ultimately destroyed by her choice. Flaubert's sympathetic description of an adulteress led in 1857 to a court case against the novel for obscenity, but the writer was acquitted.

Turgenev's contemporary Fyodor Dostoevsky also wrote novels in the Realist style. But Dostoevsky, who despised Turgenev as a weak liberal overly fond of western European culture, combined psychological depth with political and religious passion. As a young man in the 1840s, Dostoevsky had been condemned to death for his involvement in a radical reading circle. The death sentence was called off at the very last moment, after the first among the condemned had already been bound to a post to be shot. Dostoevsky was exiled to Siberia, where he embraced conservative political ideals and rediscovered his Christian faith. In his best-known novel, *Crime and Punishment* (1866), an impoverished university dropout, seeing himself as a would-be great man like Napoleon, plans the perfect crime—the killing of a vile moneylender. After carrying out the murder, his guilt proves that no man is above God's law. In another work, *The Possessed* (or, translated more accurately, *The Devils*, 1871–1872), Dostoevsky delves into the psychology of Russian radical terrorists of the late 1860s.

Going beyond literary Realism, Émile Zola described his own approach as "naturalist," and he exposed—in extensive scientific detail—the unhealthy aspects of modern society. In a series of very popular novels, he depicted several generations of two families beset by poverty, alcohol, prostitution, and other social ills, implying that their ills are inherited and inevitable. His characters are miners, café owners, prostitutes, and their clients, whose lives are described clinically, without moralizing. Zola dismissed criticism that his novels were rough, inelegantly written, and full of the sordid. "I am little concerned with beauty of perfection," he wrote. "All I care about is life, struggle, intensity. I am at ease in my generation."

Literature was also mass-produced. All the works mentioned here were bestsellers both in their original language and in translation. Inexpensively produced books were readily available, and bookshops in railroad stations provided reading material for travelers. Nearly all novels were first published in newspapers in serial form, helping boost circulation. Unfortunately for authors, it was very difficult to earn a living from writing, as effective international **copyright** protection dates only from 1887.

copyright Legal protection for authors and artists, giving them specific rights to profit from the works they create.

23-3c Art for the Masses

Advances in technology—especially lithography and photography—were both welcomed and denounced by artists. On the one hand, lithography allowed a work of art such as Toulouse-Lautrec's posters to be printed by the thousands. On the other, artists were angered when their images were poorly copied and distributed in distorted, cheapened form. Some purists also attacked Toulouse-Lautrec and the Czech poster artist Alphonse Mucha for "prostituting" their art in posters that advertised cigarettes, bicycles, singers, and dance halls. For others, the brightly colored posters were a form of art available for the enjoyment of those who could never afford an original painting. Posters bridged the gap between "high" and "low"— a single, dynamic, brightly colored figure presented in a style unconventional enough to catch the attention. The success of these poster artists is apparent in the continued popularity of their images a century later.

Technology and Art for the Masses Lithography and photography also made possible a great proliferation of illustrations in books, periodicals, and as prints. In Russia, hardly a peasant home was without the *lubok*: a cheap lithographed print sold by peddlers. These prints were mass-produced on zinc plates and then often brightly colored by hand. Favorite subjects for the lubok were popular heroes, images from Russian history or mythology, and religious scenes. Similar mass-produced prints brightened the homes of the poor throughout Europe, though middle-class critics complained of their low artistic value, crude workmanship, and garish colors.

But it would be wrong to distinguish too sharply between "popular art" for the masses and works by "great artists" such as the Impressionists and Cubists. In Paris, tens of thousands flocked to the Salon, especially on days when admission was free. Poster art was broadly exhibited and accepted, and even the paintings of great artists were quickly available in prints and popular magazine illustrations.

Some artists seized on mass production to argue that it should aim to produce beautiful things. William Morris, founder of the **Arts and Crafts movement** in Britain, designed books, tapestries, and even wallpaper, applying medieval designs to modern uses. His burning desire to see artistic beauty incorporated into everyday life came together with his commitment to equality as a socialist who worked with Karl Marx's daughter, Eleanor. Morris aimed to merge the useful and the

lubok Brightly colored print, often of a religious or historical scene, mass-produced and sold by peddlers to Russian peasants.

Arts and Crafts movement Effort led by English artist and designer William Morris to combine beautiful design and workmanship with industrial techniques.

Vasily Perov, *Fyodor Dostoevsky*, 1872

Perov's famous portrait of the novelist Fyodor Dostoevsky shows the writer's intense gaze and haggard expression. Subject to epileptic seizures and plagued by an addiction to gambling that never allowed him to achieve material prosperity, in certain ways Dostoevsky resembled one of his own tortured characters.

❯❯ *What elements of composition and style in this painting convey a brooding, intense personality?*

Portrait of Fyodor Dostoyevsky (1821-81) 1872 (oil on canvas). Perov, Vasili Grigorevich (1833-82) / Tretyakov Gallery, Moscow, Russia / Bridgeman Images

beautiful. "Have nothing in your house that you do not know to be useful or believe to be beautiful," he advised. But Morris and his followers failed to find a broad following. His decorations and graceful designs were simply too expensive for most peasants and working-class people.

23-4 Science and Social Science

❯❯ **How did science expand and change in the late nineteenth century?**

❯❯ **How did new scientific theories challenge religious ideas, and how did religion accommodate science?**

During the nineteenth century it appeared that the Enlightenment promise of understanding the world entirely through scientific observation was about to be fulfilled. The application of the scientific method to the study of human behavior and society created new academic disciplines—the fields of anthropology, psychology, and especially sociology. Some argued that the natural world and human society could be understood without recourse to any metaphysical basis—that is, without any belief in God. Geological discoveries that the earth was far older than traditionally taught called into question the literal interpretation of the Bible.

Even more shocking to traditional religious sensibilities was the theory of evolution advanced by Charles Darwin. By suggesting that human beings evolved from less complex animals, evolution struck at the very heart of traditional religion: the idea that humanity was created in God's image. Even time and space were no longer constants, as Albert Einstein's theories in the field of physics showed. Some religious leaders of nearly every faith furiously attacked the new science, whereas others argued for a reconciliation between science and religious faith, and pointed out that scientific observation is incapable of providing a basis for morality. The arguments that started in these decades continue to fuel controversy more than a century later.

23-4a The Science of Society

Sociology was the newest and perhaps the most ambitious of the new fields of inquiry into human existence. As its name suggests, sociology saw itself as the "science of society," arguing that human society can be studied, quantified, and understood like any other part of the natural world. Indeed, nineteenth-century sociologists called their discipline the queen of sciences, from which all other human sciences derived. Others were less sure that scientific methods could explain the inner workings of human society, and some feared that trying to do so would strip away the mysteries of human relations and impoverish life.

Auguste Comte and Positivism The beginnings of sociology may be found in the philosophy of **Auguste Comte**, a student of Claude Henri de Saint-Simon. To understand world history, Comte proposed the law of three stages, which explained history as the steady progress of humanity's understanding of the world through rational observation. The first stage of history he called the "theological," the era when people's primary means of explaining the world was through reference to God. The second stage was the "metaphysical," during which religious explanations were supplanted by a belief in ideas as reality—for example, G.W.F. Hegel's theory of history. The third and final stage, and one that Comte wanted to usher in with his own work, he named the "positive"—thus, his philosophy came to be known as **positivism**. In the positive era, the world would be explained exclusively by verifiable

scientific data and method, and all branches of human knowledge would come together in a unified scientific system. The natural and social sciences would complement each other, but both would share a common methodology based on mathematics and the scientific method.

Comte's call for a scientific study of society and the idea and method of positivism were widely influential. In the second half of the nineteenth century, the discipline we now know as sociology was created in great part along Comtian lines. Among its most famous practitioners was **Émile** (ay-MEEL) **Durkheim**, who used **empirical** methods and statistics to examine the common values that held societies together. In his *Division of Labor in Society* (1893), Durkheim argued that the division of labor—so hated by Marx—actually had positive effects on society by allowing "organic solidarity" to arise, in which the various parts of society worked together like organs in a healthy body. His classic work on suicide, first published in 1897, attributed rising suicide rates (a widespread fascination of the period) to a breakdown in commonly held values.

Comte's insights were also influential in Germany. There, two sociologists, Friedrich Tönnies and Georg Simmel, made the now classic distinction between *Gemeinschaft*, a traditional community of shared values, and *Gesellschaft* (guh-ZEL-shahft), a modern industrial society in which individuals seldom knew their neighbors and felt no strong emotional attachment to the people around them. **Max Weber** looked into the inner workings of authority and obedience. He used the term *charisma* to explain why some political leaders are successful in commanding respect and power. His short work *The Protestant Ethic and the Spirit of Capitalism* (1904–1905) aimed to explain the role that religious and moral values played in the development of modern capitalism. In their own ways, all of these early sociologists were attempting to come to terms with the social change and dislocation of this era. Their work reflected concerns also present in the works of Karl Marx, whose *Das Kapital* (*Capital*) appeared in three volumes between 1867 and the 1880s.

Auguste Comte (1798–1857) French thinker, inventor of the word sociology, and proponent of positivism.

positivism Comte's philosophy of knowledge emphasizing empirical observation and the idea that all natural and human phenomena can be explained in scientific terms.

Émile Durkheim (1858–1917) French sociologist influenced by positivism who used empirical methods and statistics to study society.

empiricism Belief that all knowledge can be derived from scientific observation.

Max Weber (1864–1920) German sociologist who considered religious belief, charisma, and bureaucracy as central influences on political and social life.

23-4b The Influence of Charles Darwin

Perhaps the greatest challenge to traditional values and outlooks on the world was presented by the thought of **Charles Darwin**. Darwin was the son of a self-made man, a physician who grew wealthy from his tireless work and financed his son's studies and, crucially, a trip around the world on the *HMS Beagle* (1831–1836), during which Darwin sketched and gathered samples of thousands of exotic species. He wrote many books on topics ranging from fossils to barnacles, orchids to carnivorous plants, worms to coral reefs, and, most famously, *On the Origin of Species* (1859) and *The Descent of Man* (1871).

Evolution and Natural Selection Darwin's key contribution to science was not the idea of **evolution**—many previous thinkers, including his own grandfather, Erasmus Darwin, had noted the possibility of evolutionary change in nature. What Darwin offered, rather, was an explanation of how evolution took place: **natural selection**. In his revolutionary *On the Origin of Species*, Darwin suggested, drawing on examples taken from his extensive career as a naturalist, that in any population of animals, certain features give individuals a greater chance for survival. For example, a bird that feeds mainly on nuts and seeds needs a strong bill to crack these open. Over time, natural selection favors these strong-billed birds, and the species evolves in that direction. For birds feeding on fruit or insects, however, other characteristics are more important.

Random mutations that enhanced survival played a key role in evolution. At the time, Darwin could not explain just how mutations arose and how these changes were transmitted to future generations. The discovery of the gene and the rediscovery in 1900 of the experiments in genetics carried out earlier by **Gregor Mendel** helped back up Darwin's theories. *The Descent of Man* put forth the even more controversial thesis that humanity had descended from less advanced primates. Darwin's theory described a state of constant struggle for survival. Thus, even the smallest genetic advantages, he argued, could favor the survival of one species over another. Darwin's notion of the gradual improvement of species over time—the less favored individuals dying out—went along with the era's belief in the progress of human society.

Social Darwinism and Eugenics Darwin's theories had a huge impact, and not only on the scientific community. His ideas were widely debated by fellow scientists, who compared him with Galileo and Isaac Newton, and in the popular press, where he was ridiculed as "the monkey-man." The greatest long-term effect of Darwinism outside of biology, however, came from those who applied the concept of natural selection to human society. So-called **social Darwinists** such as **Herbert Spencer** argued that human societies also evolved through struggle, what Spencer called "the survival of the fittest," and that a society's health depended on the strongest elements being allowed to develop themselves freely, even at the expense of the weak.

Spencer—a consistently liberal and decent man—was careful not to equate the "fittest" with the most aggressive or physically able, but others used these ideas to oppose social programs that aided the poor and weaker elements in society. Social Darwinists now used the language of science to validate the long-held opinion that the poor were to blame for their own poverty. Many social Darwinists also advanced arguments about European "racial superiority" over the peoples of Asia and Africa. Allied with such ideas was the new discipline of **eugenics**, which sought to improve society by discouraging the reproduction of "undesirable elements." Increasingly in the early twentieth century, advocates of eugenics and scientific racism argued that certain races were inferior not only because of environment but in their very genes. Some even called for the sterilization of those judged to be physically or mentally inferior.

Anthropology The new field of anthropology also sought to describe and explain human diversity, especially as Europeans encountered different societies, religions, political structures, and kinship patterns in their colonies. Russian anthropologists and ethnographers, for example, described the everyday life and beliefs of Siberian and Central Asian native peoples. In St. Petersburg, exhibitions of the dress, art, and lifestyle of these exotic peoples were organized—showing not only artifacts like clothing, carpets, and dwellings but sometimes including human individuals of these ethnic groups as well. Peasants also interested

Charles Darwin (1809–1882) English scientist who formulated the theory of natural selection and authored *On the Origin of Species* (1859).

evolution Biological theory that diverse animal and plant species developed over time through a combination of genetic mutation and environmental influence.

natural selection Darwin's theory that better-adapted species survive (and reproduce) while others are eliminated.

Gregor Mendel (1822–1884) Austrian (Czech) monk credited with the discovery of the theory of genetic heredity.

social Darwinists Theorists who applied Darwin's theory of natural selection to human society, arguing that poorer and weaker segments of society should not reproduce.

Herbert Spencer (1820–1903) English philosopher and political theorist who coined the phrase "survival of the fittest."

eugenics Pseudoscience aiming to improve humanity by encouraging those with "desirable traits" to reproduce; now discredited as inhumane and racist.

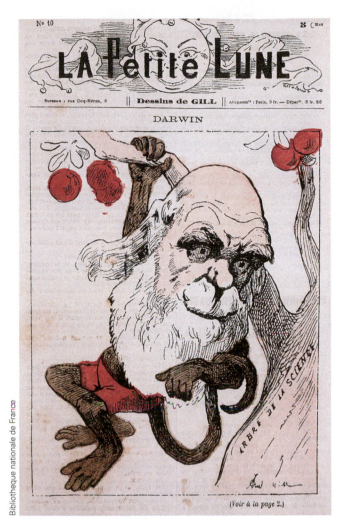

Bibliotheque nationale de France

Darwin as "Monkey Man"

Darwin's controversial theory of evolution made him a worldwide celebrity—though he had to endure many caricatures of himself as a "monkey man," as in this August 1878 issue of a French satirical journal.

» *Why did Darwin's suggestion that humanity may have evolved from other primates shock conservatives?*

anthropologists, such as **Olga Semyonova** (sim-YO-nuh-va) **Tian-Shanskaia** (tian-SHAN-ska-ya), who studied Russian peasant life. Anthropologists often saw themselves as representatives of a superior civilization, which they contrasted with the object of their research, so-called primitive or savage peoples, doomed to extinction by human progress, whose culture was put on display in museums and exhibitions.

23-4c Chemistry and the New Physics

In chemistry and physics, too, new research was fundamentally changing the understanding of the physical world. Dmitri Mendeleev's periodic table, a first version of which was published in 1869, advanced chemistry by classifying elements according to atomic weight and periodical—that is, recurring—properties. Mendeleev's arrangement of the elements allowed chemists to predict characteristics of unknown elements according to their atomic weight and place in the table, thus paving the way for later discoveries, such as Marie Curie's radium.

Up to this time, following Isaac Newton, physics had understood all phenomena and motion as the result of the action of one particle on another. But this mechanical view made it difficult to understand the action of light and other invisible rays that traveled rapidly across space and appeared to have no mass. For Newtonian physics to work, scientists had theorized that a substance called ether permeated the universe, though it had never been discovered or measured. The search for ether would lead to the discovery of many other invisible rays and forces that in the end would establish the existence of fields of force that operated over great distances. Through experimentation and rational analysis, scientists postulated a physical world more complex than previous generations had imagined.

One practical challenge was to understand the nature of electricity. The work of James Clerk Maxwell, though mainly on a theoretical level, paved the way for practical applications of electricity for use in lighting, communications, and motors. Maxwell also predicted the existence of radio waves and theorized that light itself was a form of electromagnetism. The German scientist Heinrich Hertz proved Maxwell correct by broadcasting and receiving radio waves in the late 1880s. In late 1895, Wilhelm Röntgen discovered X-rays, a form of electromagnetic radiation. This discovery spurred others—the Curies among them—to search for other forms of radiation. All of these discoveries were rapidly developed into practical inventions by other scientists and by industry: electricity was put to work in the electric light bulb, phonograph, and innumerable other inventions by Edison; Hertz's findings were translated into wireless radio communications by Marconi; Röntgen's (RENT-gun) X-rays found practical application in health care and his name became the German word for "to X-ray."

Albert Einstein The revolutionary work of **Albert Einstein** built on these scientists' research, but, in another sense, completely reformulated physicists' understanding of the universe. In 1905, the young scientist published a paper proposing the **special theory of relativity**, suggesting

Olga Semyonova Tian-Shanskaia (1863–1906) Russian ethnographer who collected folk songs and important data on the Russian peasantry.

Albert Einstein (1879–1955) German physicist most famous for his theory of relativity.

special theory of relativity Einstein's theory stating, among other things, that the speed of light is always constant while distance and time are relative to the observer.

Marie Skłodowska Curie Chooses to Study Physics

Pictorial Press Ltd / Alamy Stock Photo

Marie Curie

Marie Curie, born Maria Skłodowska in Russian-occupied Warsaw, became one of the most famous scientists of the twentieth century. She is shown here hard at work in her laboratory in Paris.

» *Why do you think she allowed such images to be taken and popularized?*

» *How does her lab differ from images of modern laboratories?*

Maria Skłodowska (skwoh-DOV-ska), better known to the world as Madame Curie, chose to dedicate her life to science. Born at a time when women scientists were rare, she left her native land, obtained a university education, and made her mark in scientific research. Her life reflects a period when dynamic women could defy social norms and succeed. Her career parallels the enormous growth in the importance of scientific discovery for the economy and everyday life.

Maria was born into an educated middle-class family in Warsaw in late 1867. Her father taught physics and mathematics at a Warsaw gymnasium. Her mother was also educated and served as the director of a local school for girls. But, as Poles, her parents could not teach in government schools, and the salaries they received in private schools were meager. Education in Russian Poland was, at the time, under severe restraints. Following the Polish insurrection of 1863, Russian authorities curtailed the use of the Polish language in schools. Almost all teachers had to be native Russians, and they treated Poles with contempt and hostility. It was in this atmosphere that Maria Skłodowska received her primary and secondary education. Then, when Maria was only nine, her mother died, leaving behind four children.

Finishing high school at age fifteen, at the top of her class, Maria was forced by family circumstances to seek employment as a governess. Many years later, she remembered these years with pleasure, recalling that she had set up secret circles to teach children literacy in Polish, an activity strictly forbidden by the Russian authorities. She also studied at the illegal "flying university" that Polish intellectuals had set up for young Poles. But even so, educational opportunities in Russian Poland were limited, so Maria vowed to continue her education abroad as soon as possible. Gathering her meager savings, she left for Paris in 1891 and two years later met Pierre Curie. The two married in July 1895.

that as particles approach the speed of light, their speed cannot be predicted by Newton's laws of motion. Two years later Einstein developed these ideas further, coming up with the now famous equation $E = mc^2$—energy is equivalent to mass multiplied by the square of the speed of light. Einstein postulated that light travels through empty space at a constant speed, thereby eliminating the need for any medium like ether. Einstein's theory of relativity also challenged concepts of absolute space and time because these were shown to depend on the relative velocity of the particle and the observer.

Within a few years, Einstein's theory was being hotly debated by scientists who attempted to verify or discredit it experimentally. As Einstein's special theory of relativity gained acceptance on both sides of the Atlantic, he followed it with the general theory of relativity in 1915, which dealt with gravity. In this theory, Einstein predicted that starlight passing near the sun would be curved by the pull of gravity. This prediction was verified in 1919 during a solar eclipse, and Einstein suddenly became an international celebrity. He was awarded the Nobel Prize in Physics in 1921.

Pierre Curie had just completed his doctorate in physics and was teaching at a Paris secondary school. The Curies' economic situation was far from enviable, but their work carried them through. Soon they had two daughters, but Marie (as she was now known) refused to give up her scientific work. With the help of a servant, she balanced her roles as mother and scientist. Pierre's teaching position and Marie's occasional tutoring brought in modest sums, and they were forced to carry out their research in their spare time and in a small laboratory that was little more than a shack outfitted with homemade equipment. Marie was interested in the study of X-rays—peculiar rays emitted by uranium salts—and, as she put it, "decided to undertake an investigation."

For several years the Curies studied the phenomenon we now call radioactivity. In 1903 they were awarded the Nobel Prize in Physics along with the French physicist Antoine Becquerel. When Pierre was killed in an automobile accident in 1906, Marie continued their work by herself. She discovered two new elements, polonium and radium, for which she was awarded the Nobel Prize in Chemistry in 1911. At this time she was named to the faculty of the prestigious Sorbonne in Paris, the first woman to be so honored. Under her leadership, research in chemistry and physics blossomed there. Her daughter Irène Joliot-Curie also became a distinguished scientist. Marie Curie died in 1934, one year before Irène and her husband Frédéric were awarded the Nobel Prize in Chemistry.

Marie Curie's discoveries advanced scientific knowledge of radioactivity, which would be expanded on later to produce both nuclear power and atomic weapons. But her choice to dedicate her life to science had other important consequences. Her dedication to science challenged conventional views of national minorities and the capabilities of women. After Marie Curie, young women could more easily envision their own place as scientists, professors, and even Nobel prizewinners.

Few scientists at the time could appreciate Einstein's relativity theories or the radical new understanding of the atom, the quantum theory, advanced by the German physicist **Max Planck** in 1900 to explain the behavior of energy within the atom. While physicists struggled with the implications of relativity and quantum theory, for many in the general public these disturbing new ideas symbolized a destruction of certainty. Just as Darwin had called into question accepted notions about the natural world and its origins, Einstein and Planck stripped away certainty from even the most fundamental elements of perception: time and space.

23-4d The Battle Between Science and Religion

Darwin's theories, especially regarding human evolution, stirred great controversy, and some of his main opponents were religious leaders who understood evolution as a direct challenge not only to the biblical story of creation but even to the majesty of God. Anglican bishop Samuel Wilberforce of Oxford decried Darwin's work as "a tendency to limit God's glory in creation," and the Catholic cardinal Henry Edward Manning denounced Darwin's ideas as "a brutal philosophy—to wit, there is no God, and the ape is our Adam." Of course, both of these statements reflect ignorance and prejudice rather than any knowledge of Darwin's arguments.

The controversy between science and religion went far deeper, representing a profound crisis of consciousness in the nineteenth century. Geological discoveries, in particular those associated with the British geologist **Sir Charles Lyell**, had already proved that the earth was vastly older than the number of generations in the Bible between Adam and Jesus Christ. In addition, the fossil remains of dinosaurs and other animals not mentioned in the Bible further eroded conventional Christian faith in literal biblical truth. Although most Europeans still professed Christianity, the content of these beliefs shifted somewhat under the weight of scientific evidence. The biblical account of creation came, for example, to be understood more and more in a symbolic rather than a literal way.

CONNECTIONS: For many Christians (and even Jews and Muslims) Darwin's theory of evolution appeared a shocking challenge to traditional beliefs. However, unless one reads these religions' holy scriptures in an absolutely literal sense, evolution and a belief in God can certainly go together, and in fact Darwin mentions the role of the Creator a number of times in later editions of *On the Origin of Species*. As we have seen, in the sixteenth century the Catholic Church rejected Copernicus's heliocentric model of the universe but today few Christians would deny that the Earth revolves around the Sun (see Section 17-1b A New View of the Universe). The rejection of Darwin by some conservative Christians probably derives in large part from the complexity of Darwin's arguments and the difficulty of integrating new concepts into an already-accepted world view. The belief in a higher being can neither be proven

Max Planck (1858–1947) German physicist and author of quantum theory who won the Nobel Prize in Physics in 1918.

Sir Charles Lyell (1797–1875) English geologist whose *Principles of Geology* (1830–1833) suggested that the world must be far older than hitherto imagined.

or disproven, but scientific truths by their nature must be upheld by repeatable experiments. This difference between these two kinds of knowledge perhaps makes frictions between the religious and the scientific spheres inevitable.

Religion, Science, and Atheism In the later nineteenth century, many Europeans came to reject religious belief as unscientific, irrelevant, or even immoral. As early as the 1840s, Marx had exclaimed that religion was the "opiate of the people." In other words, religion diverted people's attention from the real causes of their poverty and, most important, prevented them from taking action to bring about social justice. Marx and other socialists were atheists, rejecting religion, but they believed fervently in progress, science, and humanity's ability to better itself. This radical rejection of a religious worldview was also shared by the fictional hero in Turgenev's *Fathers and Sons*, Evgeny Bazarov, whose views were summed up by a friend: "He doesn't believe in principles, but he believes in frogs [to dissect]." Like Bazarov, many young radicals rejected religious authority and demanded that any principles, whether moral, political, or scientific, be proved by empirical methods. In their own way, they were simply reformulating Comte's positivism. Not religion but empirical scientific methods—in both the social and physical sciences—would bring about true progress.

Science Versus Tradition For most people, however, a world without God was unthinkable. Even scientists were not generally atheists, though they often did not accept all aspects of church dogma. Most continued at least to cherish a belief in a Supreme Being, however defined. Even though Pope Pius IX condemned materialism in the *Syllabus of Errors* of 1864, and "modernism" was denounced by the later Pope Pius X in 1907, many educated Catholics sought to reconcile their religious beliefs and elements of modern thought. In the **shtetls** (SHTET-uhls) of eastern Europe, Jewish boys were punished for daring to read "modern" authors—even in Hebrew translation. Traditional Jews claimed that the Torah, Talmud, and other religious works contained enough of human wisdom to satisfy anyone, but their attempt to shut out the modern world was in the long run doomed to failure. Some Jews discarded religious beliefs and practices entirely in their desire to become modern, rational Europeans. Others pointed out that great Jewish scholars from earlier ages had studied the natural sciences, claiming that the study of science was but another way of understanding the greatness of God's creation.

While religion could not ignore new scientific discoveries, neither could scientific materialism be entirely satisfying for most people. The scientific method could explain much, but it was mute when faced with life's most basic question: Why are we here? Even Comte conceded the existence of a Supreme Being in his positivism, and Darwin fudged: "There is a grandeur in this view of life, with its several powers, having been originally breathed by the Creator into a few forms or into one." Rationality and empirical experimentation could only explain so much of human existence.

23-4e Critiques of Reason

Toward the end of the nineteenth century, the optimism that came with prosperity, scientific advances, and the philosophy of positivism began to falter. Some thinkers saw mass production less as a triumph than a threat, burying differences and local peculiarities in sterile uniformity. Max Weber warned darkly about the "iron cage" of bureaucracy. The German philosopher **Friedrich Nietzsche** (NEE-chuh) called on gifted individuals to resist mass society, which he termed "the common herd." Austrian psychiatrist **Sigmund Freud** used scientific methodology to probe into the irrational underpinnings of human behavior. Just as artists were rejecting representations of the external world for explorations of individual perceptions, writers such as Gustave Le Bon and Henri Bergson described the limits of rationality in human experience, arguing that passion and intuition played a key role in social and individual behavior. Despite advances in science, politics, and technology, both seemed to say that human behavior remains profoundly determined by basic, even primitive, drives and passions.

Friedrich Nietzsche Nietzsche himself bore both physical and psychological scars from his service as a medical orderly in the Franco-Prussian War. Returning home, he quickly published his first book, *The Birth of Tragedy* (1872), which gained him a European-wide reputation though specialists did not accept his theses. *The Birth of Tragedy* emphasized the role of passion and ecstasy (which Nietzsche associated with the Greek god Dionysus) in the genesis of Greek tragedy, an argument that was so novel and suggestive that Nietzsche became a celebrity outside of academic circles as well.

shtetls (in Yiddish, "small cities") Towns inhabited mainly or exclusively by Jews, in particular in eastern Europe.

Friedrich Nietzsche (1844–1900) German philosopher renowned for his demand for a complete revision of human ethics and who notoriously despised mass society.

Sigmund Freud (1856–1939) Austrian psychiatrist who emphasized the role of fundamental and prerational drives, including sexual impulses, in human behavior.

In the next decade and a half, Nietzsche produced thousands of pages of books, essays, polemics, and poetry, returning time and again to the themes of personal freedom and intellectual and moral self-reliance. He despised many aspects of modern life, including mass society, and lashed out against liberal democracy, German nationalism, anti-Semitism, and traditional moral standards—in particular, the "slave morality" of Christianity. He denounced mass society, which he perceived as his era's "herd mentality" that preferred a safe, comfortable life to taking risks. Nietzsche demanded that human beings recognize their own freedom, admit that "God is dead," and then celebrate the enormous liberation that this fact implies. Nietzsche's philosophy emphasized the role of the will and passion over cool, calculated reason, and his insistence that humans discard all traditional values and create their own moral world is perhaps the most radical modern restatement of Immanuel Kant's famous dictum, "Dare to know!"

Nietzsche was never a systematic philosopher, and the sheer sparkle and wit of his writing may obscure his arguments. These qualities, combined with his meandering writing style, open his works to many different interpretations. In the twentieth century, the German National Socialists (Nazis) tried to appropriate his ideas for their cause, claiming that Nietzsche's superman—a man whose passion and will would create a new moral world—was identical to the Nazi Aryan ideal. But this interpretation is directly contradicted by Nietzsche's denunciation of Germany's anti-Semites as typical of the herd mentality. Nietzsche scorned biological explanations of human differences. On the other hand, his no less vehement attacks on such Christian values as forgiveness, charity, kindness, and mercy seem at times to parallel Nazi ruthlessness. In the light of rationality, elements of Nietzsche's thought seem contradictory, but he claimed that his philosophy operated at a higher—or deeper—level, concerning the innermost reaches of the human soul.

Sigmund Freud Nietzsche died in 1900, one year after Sigmund Freud's most famous work, *The Interpretation of Dreams*, appeared. Although the two men were utterly different in background, professional training, and temperament, both had an enormous impact on modern consciousness. Freud was born into a lower-middle-class Jewish family and lived nearly his entire life in Vienna. Like many young Jews of his generation, he studied medicine, aiming to dedicate his life to medical practice and research and discarding traditional religious belief along the way.

As early as the 1880s, Freud noticed in some of his patients—who were primarily middle-class women—symptoms that could not be explained by physical illness alone. Gradually he developed his theory of **repression**, claiming that patients repressed—that is, denied and refused to acknowledge on a conscious level—traumatic memories, usually of a sexual nature. Having diagnosed the problem, Freud began to develop a treatment. Like others before him, Freud differentiated between conscious and subconscious levels in the human psyche. On the conscious level, we may be rational, considering pros and cons and thinking through the consequences of our actions. But Freud insisted that our rational decisions were always liable to be influenced and sometimes overpowered by the subconscious. His "talking cure" (today we know it as psychoanalysis) aimed to reveal the subconscious by a steady probing of a patient's memories, reactions, behavior, and dreams. Dreams were a key component because for Freud they often revealed repressed desires that existed at a subconscious level.

To describe the human personality, Freud divided the psyche into three components: the id, ego, and superego. The id consists entirely of drives, hungers, and desires; a baby, for example, may be seen as a bundle of pure id. The ego develops as the child encounters reality and realizes that not all wants can be filled, at least not right away. The superego, the last part of the personality to develop, incorporates the moral values, taboos, and behavioral models that children internalize from their parents and society as they mature. According to Freud, all three components exist in every human being; none are inherently bad or good. Hysteria and other neuroses appear, however, when the three are out of balance. For example, in any society, individuals must control and regulate their instinctual drives. But for some neurotics the demands of the superego become so intense that they make normal life impossible.

Freud's thought combines the rationalist method of the later nineteenth century with a recognition of the limitations of rationality. In his own life, Freud was very much the model of the positivist scientist, rejecting the idea of a Supreme Being and insisting on an empirical approach in psychology. But he also recognized that in human behavior, irrational—or at least subconscious and pre-rational—elements often prevailed.

repression Freud's theory that memories and desires not acknowledged by a person's conscious thought can lead to physical and mental disorders.

CHAPTER Review

Summary

» The second Industrial Revolution, based on electricity, steel, and modern chemistry, changed the world profoundly.

» Technological advances allowed for mass production of clothing, newspapers, and many other consumer goods.

» Communications were also revolutionized with increased railroad building, steamships, and the telegraph and telephone.

» Science made considerable advances, and the fields of social sciences, such as sociology, aimed to explain human society and behavior.

» The new science, in particular Darwin's theory of evolution, presented a challenge to the traditional religious worldview.

» By the end of this period, thinkers like Friedrich Nietzsche and Sigmund Freud called into question positivism's trust in rationality, pointing out that human behavior could not be explained by reason alone.

Chronology

1851	Crystal Palace Exhibition takes place in London [Europe]
1859	Charles Darwin publishes *On the Origin of Species* [Europe]
1862	Ivan Turgenev publishes *Fathers and Sons* [Europe]
1863	Edouard Manet paints *The Luncheon on the Grass* and *Olympia* [Europe]
1867	Alfred Nobel patents dynamite [Europe]
1867	Karl Marx publishes volume 1 of *Capital* [Europe]
1869	Suez Canal opens in Egypt [Middle East]
1872	Friedrich Nietzsche publishes The Birth of Tragedy [Europe] Japan opens its first railroad, from Tokyo to Yokohama [Asia]
1876	Alexander Graham Bell invents the telephone [Americas]
1879	Thomas Edison invents the electric lightbulb [Americas]
1884	American Hiram Maxim invents the machine gun [Americas]
1885	First skyscraper, the Home Insurance Building in Chicago, is completed [Americas] Rover "safety bicycle," the first modern bicycle, first manufactured [Americas] Completion of Canadian Pacific railroad [Americas]

1888	Kodak box camera is perfected by George Eastman [Americas]
1891	Work begins on the Trans-Siberian Railroad [Europe, Asia]
1892	Rudolf Diesel patents the internal-combustion engine [Europe]
1899	Sigmund Freud publishes *The Interpretation of Dreams* [Europe]
1900	Max Planck formulates quantum theory [Europe] First flight of Zeppelin airship over Lake Constance, Germany [Europe]
1903	Wright brothers successfully fly the first airplane [Americas]
1904	Max Weber begins publication of *The Protestant Ethic and the Birth of Capitalism* [Europe]
1905	Albert Einstein publishes paper on special theory of relativity [Americas]
1907	Bakelite, the first plastic, is invented [Americas]
1908	Ford Motor Company produces first Model T [Americas]
1914	The first ship passes through the Panama Canal [Americas]

Critical Thinking Questions

Take time to pull together all the important information from the chapter by answering the following questions:

The Second Industrial Revolution

» How did the second Industrial Revolution revolutionize transport and communications?

» Why did many Europeans have more leisure time, and how did they use it?

Mass Society

» How did increased prosperity and better public health help create mass society?

» How was feminism reacting to the novelties of mass society? Where were feminists most active?

Art and Industrial Society

» In what ways can art of this period be termed part of "mass society?" How did new art forms and techniques reach out to a broader audience?

» How did Realist writers like Dickens, Dostoevsky, and Zola depict the realities of their age?

Science and Social Science

» What did Comte's "positivism" have in common with physics and chemistry?

» What common ground existed between religious critiques of science and critiques of reason presented by Freud and Nietzsche? Where did they differ?

MindTap® is a fully online personalized learning experience built upon Cengage Learning content. MindTap® combines student learning tools—readings, multimedia, activities, and assessments—into a singular Learning Path that guides students through the course and helps students develop the critical thinking, analysis, and communication skills that are essential to academic and professional success.

The Age of Imperialism, 1870–1914

Chapter Outline

As you read, consider the following questions:

❱ What is meant by the term *imperialism*? Why did European power throughout the world expand so quickly in this period?

❱ Where did the new imperialism have its greatest impact? Why?

❱ What impact did imperialism have on the Muslim world, Asia, and Africa?

❱ Why did most Europeans support imperialism? What were the arguments of Europeans who opposed it?

EUROPEAN EXPANSION AND colonialism did not start in 1870. Spain and Portugal established American colonies in the late fifteenth century, and Russian domination of Siberia in northern Asia dates from the seventeenth century. But the imperialism of the late nineteenth century was something new. Europe's industrialization and new technologies enabled it to quickly affect a huge part of the world, and more Europe countries than ever before got involved in the race for colonies. In little more than a generation, Europeans extended colonial rule over much of the globe.

Colonies provided Europeans with raw materials and markets. These were good for European economies. Imperial rule also fascinated Europeans, whose very identity became linked with their countries' role as overlords in Africa, Asia, and the Muslim world. Europeans were proud of their culture and believed it superior to any other civilization in the world. The scientific and technological advances of the nineteenth century, rising literacy rates, and the general advance in living standards convinced them that their rule over other lands benefited both Europeans and colonial peoples.

In 1870, a few European colonies and settlements already existed on the edges of Africa. Thirty years later, the entire continent had been divided up among the European powers. The largest colonial territories were held by Britain and France, but Portugal, Belgium, and Germany also ruled over thousands of square miles and hundreds of thousands of Africans. Among the colonies of the British Empire was Nigeria in West Africa, where the intricate carving of Queen Victoria seen here was produced. Only two independent states remained in Africa by 1914—Ethiopia in East Africa and Liberia on the west coast.

Yoruba Carving of Queen Victoria, Nigeria

Queen Victoria, from 1876 also "Empress of India," symbolized the age of imperialism. This carving uses local traditions of highly developed wooden sculpture to depict the empress as mighty, benevolent, dignified, and serene in her power.

Figure of Queen Victoria, Yoruba, Nigeria, c.1900 (wood), African, (20th century) / Private Collection / © Michael Graham-Stewart / The Bridgeman Art Library

Asia was also colonized by Europeans. The largest and richest colony of all was in Asia: British India. France extended colonial rule in Indochina (now Vietnam, Laos, and Cambodia), and the Dutch exerted control over the islands now known as Indonesia. Although China was never colonized directly, Western powers interfered in Chinese domestic affairs. And Japan, industrializing from the 1870s onward, became a colonial power in its own right, conquering Taiwan at the end of the century. Russia extended its rule into Central Asia, to the great consternation of the British in India. In all, around half a billion Asians and Africans fell under colonial rule.

The new imperialism extended to the Muslim world, as the Ottoman Empire, the most important Muslim state of the time, was challenged by incursions from Russia and other European powers. An even larger number of Muslims lived under imperial rule in British India and, by the end of the nineteenth century, in Russian Central Asia. Muslim intellectuals, who wondered why their culture had been unable to withstand these threats, formulated programs of reform and modernization to meet the challenge of imperialism.

Some Europeans, too, opposed and criticized imperialism, denouncing it as a highly exploitative and racist form of capitalism. These opinions would be influential into the twenty-first century.

24-1 Motives and Methods of the New Imperialism

> » What political and technological advances paved the way for the new imperialism?

> » How did Europeans attempt to justify imperialist expansion?

Many explanations have been offered for European expansion between 1870 and 1914. These include economic motivations, political and demographic factors, national rivalries, a desire to spread Christianity, and the idea that Europeans (and North Americans) had a moral responsibility to spread their culture and technology around the world (the so-called white man's burden). Governments did not follow any well-thought-out plan in expanding their colonial empires. Rather, they reacted to specific circumstances, always seeking to prevent other powers from gaining on them. The conviction of Western superiority also pushed imperialism forward. So did the new technologies of the second Industrial Revolution. All these factors help explain how, and why, millions of people around the world were brought under European and American rule.

24-1a Economic Motivations

The desire for new markets and the need for the raw materials of industry certainly fueled the **new imperialism**. Britain looked to India as a market for its textiles and other industrial products. King **Leopold II** of Belgium derived huge profits from rubber plantations in the Congo, and **Cecil Rhodes** became vastly wealthy from exploiting African labor in the gold and diamond mines of southern Africa (see Analyze and Compare: Cecil Rhodes and Lin Zexu and Profiles in Change: Cecil Rhodes Creates the Rhodes Scholarship later in the chapter). Industrial society demanded rubber for industrial uses, but also for tires on bicycles and a new invention, the automobile. Similarly, palm oil was in great demand as a machine lubricant. Fruits such as bananas and pineapples were also imported from colonized areas. These products could be obtained only in tropical regions, many of which came under European rule at this time.

And yet, the direct connection between economic motivations and the establishment of political control is not often clear. Britain enjoyed economic and political dominance of India and southern Africa *before* imperialist domination was established. For Germany, the establishment of colonies in Africa and the Pacific made no economic sense; these colonies cost German taxpayers millions. Furthermore, throughout this period, more Western European capital flowed to Russia, the United States, and South America than to territories under formal colonial rule. Thus, economic motivations alone cannot explain the late-nineteenth-century drive for colonial rule (see Map 24.1).

new imperialism Extension and strengthening of European colonial rule, mainly in Africa and Asia, from approximately 1870 to 1914.

Leopold II (r. 1865–1909) Belgian king who established personal rule over a large part of central Africa (later the Belgian Congo).

Cecil Rhodes (1853–1902) British businessman and colonial official who made a fortune in diamonds and was prime minister of Cape Colony in Africa.

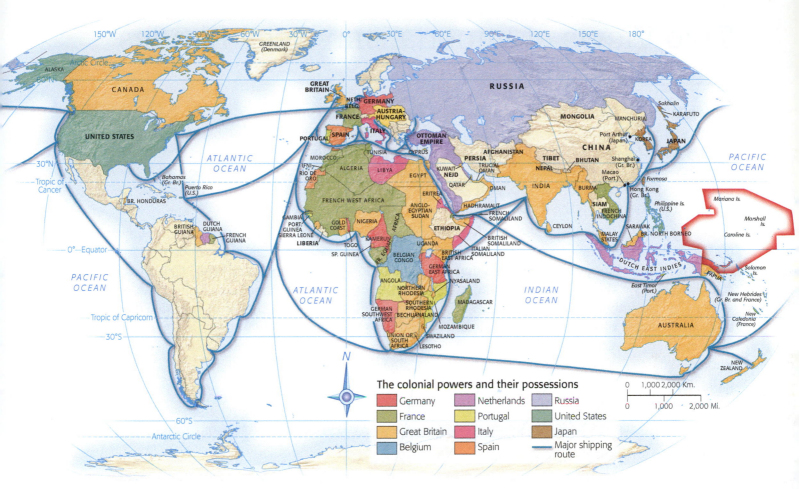

Map 24.1 **European Colonies Around the World, 1900** By 1900, European countries had established colonies on every inhabited continent. Already-existing colonies in the New World, Asia, and Oceania were joined by huge territories dominated by European powers, most notably in Africa.

1. On which continents were the majority of European colonies?
2. Which European countries had the greatest number of colonies?
3. Which parts of the world were most and least affected by the new imperialism? Why?
4. Which of these colonies had been established since 1850?

24-1b Domestic Politics and National Rivalries

A more convincing explanation of imperialism is found in the domestic politics of the major European powers. Large numbers of Britons, Frenchmen, Germans, and others came to identify their own national pride with colonial possessions.

The Popularity of Imperialism After their humiliating defeat in the Franco-Prussian War, the French, for example, were able to take pride in an expanding colonial empire in Africa and Asia. And the Germans, who had won the war, felt the need for a colonial empire too. Having failed to significantly weaken the Social Democrats even through the strategy of adopting some of their programs, Chancellor Otto von Bismarck turned to empire to enhance his political popularity. In the late nineteenth century, Europe was swept by "imperialist fever." Even sober politicians not usually concerned with popular opinion—such as Bismarck in Berlin—found it necessary, or at least useful, to beat the imperialist drum.

National rivalries contributed to imperial expansion. The establishment of one colony almost inevitably led to the perceived need to grab more territory to "protect" it. In this way, European rivalries contributed to European expansion. For example, in the early 1880s, the French government declared formal control over Tunisia in northern Africa mainly

Two Views of Imperialism: Cecil Rhodes and Lin Zexu

FROM AROUND THE MIDDLE OF THE NINETEENTH CENTURY, EUROPEAN STATES extended their control over vast stretches of the globe. In some regions, such as Africa, this was done directly by establishing colonies. Cecil Rhodes addresses this form of imperialism in his "Confession of Faith." From an early age, Cecil Rhodes had a mission—to spread British culture, values, and education. Rhodes never wavered in his belief that the world would be better off under British rule. In 1877, at age twenty-four, Rhodes set down his ideas in a "Confession of Faith" for himself. The document was never published in his lifetime.

In other places, such as China, European powers proceeded more cautiously, first by forcing unwanted trade—such as in opium—on the Chinese authorities. The Opium War of 1839–1842 can be seen as a kind of "first act" of the European imperialism that covered the globe a generation later. While China was never colonized directly, the port of Hong Kong came under British rule, and many coastal cities had districts where Chinese authority was not recognized. The Chinese official Lin Zexu (ZEH-shu) protested the forced trade in opium in his letter to Queen Victoria. This letter reveals the (politely concealed) outrage of an elite servant of the Chinese emperor when faced by British lack of respect for Chinese sovereignty. Unlike Rhodes, Lin Zexu clearly found British behavior in China outrageous and immoral.

Both men, in their own ways, represented traditional views of their own countries as the highest form of culture the world had to offer. Is there any way to reconcile their opposing views on European imperialism? Who is correct, and why? Do you find certain arguments in each document convincing? Why?

❶ What do you think Rhodes meant by "the most despicable specimens of human beings?"

❷ What would happen to these people if Rhodes's plan was realized?

❸ What kind of "extra employment" do you think Rhodes had in mind here? In what ways did imperialism increase jobs at home?

❹ What does Rhodes mean when he speaks of "race?" How does his usage differ from our present-day understanding of that word?

❺ Do you think that Rhodes's emphasis on duty was typical of the nineteenth century? Typical of someone twenty-four years old? Why or why not?

❻ Why do you suppose that Rhodes proposed a secret society to pursue his aims?

Cecil Rhodes Writes His Own "Confession of Faith"

❶ I contend that we [English] are the finest race in the world and that the more of the world we inhabit the better it is for the human race. Just fancy those parts that are at present inhabited by the most despicable specimens of human beings what an alteration there would be if they were brought under Anglo-Saxon influence, look again at the extra employment a new country added to our dominions gives. I contend that every acre added to our territory means in the future birth to some more of the English race who otherwise would not be brought into existence. Added to this the absorption of the greater portion of the world under our rule simply means the end of all wars. . . .

❷ Why should we not form a secret society with but one object the furtherance of the British Empire and the bringing of the whole uncivilised world under British rule for the recovery of the United States for the making the Anglo-Saxon race but one Empire. . . .

❸ Africa is still lying ready for us it is our duty to take it. It is our duty to seize every opportunity of acquiring more territory and we should keep this one idea steadily before our eyes that more territory simply means more of the Anglo-Saxon race more of the best, the most human, most honourable race the world possesses.

❹ To forward such a scheme what a splendid help a secret society would be a society not openly acknowledged but who would work in secret for such an object. . . . What has been the main cause of the success of the Romish [Roman Catholic] Church? The fact that every enthusiast, call it if you like every madman finds employment in it. Let us form the same kind of society a Church for the extension

7 Why does Lin mention British trade with China for almost 200 years? Do you think that Rhodes would have agreed that this trade made Britain rich?

8 Why does Lin call opium this terrible drug? Would Rhodes have agreed? Would Rhodes have supported the opium trade with China? Why?

9 Why does Lin use the language of suggesting that the opium crops be destroyed?

10 Do you think he expect this to happen? Why or why not?

11 Lin ends his letter with a call on Queen Victoria's morality—to produce good and exterminate evil? How do you think that Rhodes would have responded to this call? Rhodes supported imperialism but also considered himself moral: where in his Confession does he expound his own conceptions of morality? From your point of view, whose morality—Rhodes's or Lin's—is more convincing?

of the British Empire. A society which should have its members in every part of the British Empire working with one object and one idea. . . .

Source: From Rhodes's "Confession of Faith," an essay included in *The Last Will and Testament of Cecil John Rhodes* (1902).

Lin Zexu Protests the Importation of Opium into China

7 . . . The Celestial Empire, following its traditional policy of treating foreigners with kindness, has been doubly considerate towards the people from England. You have traded in China for almost 200 years, and as a result, your country has become wealthy and prosperous.

. . .

8 I have heard that the areas under your direct jurisdiction such as London, Scotland, and Ireland do not produce opium; it is produced instead in your Indian possessions such as Bengal, Madras, Bombay, Patna, and Malwa. In these possessions the English people not only plant opium poppies that stretch from one mountain to another but also open factories to manufacture this terrible drug.

9 As months accumulate and years pass by, the poison they have produced increases in its wicked intensity, and its repugnant odor reaches as high as the sky. Heaven is furious with anger, and all the gods are moaning with pain! **10** It is hereby suggested that you destroy and plow under all of these opium plants and grow food crops instead, while issuing an order to punish severely anyone who dares to plant opium poppies again. **11** If you adopt this policy of love so as to produce good and exterminate evil, Heaven will protect you, and gods will bring you good fortune. . . . Why do you not do it?

Source: Lin Zexu. "Letter to Queen Victoria," 1839. Andrea/Overfield, *The Human Record: Sources of Global History*, vol. 2, 3d ed., Houghton-Mifflin, pp. 331-332.

because it feared Italian expansion westward from Libya. Similarly, the British occupied Egypt in 1882 partly to deny the French any influence. At first, London did not intend to maintain permanent political control, but facing a power vacuum and fearing that hostile Egyptian groups would take over, the British stayed. Control of Egypt also allowed the British to secure the sea route to India once the Suez Canal was constructed. Protection of the canal then became an end in itself. Thus, securing access to existing colonies also served as a justification for taking new ones. All along the route to India, the British secured stopping and fueling points for ships. Aden, at the tip of the Arabian peninsula (now in Yemen), was deliberately taken for this purpose.

Competition Among Colonial Powers in Africa As Britain and France carved up Africa, other European powers demanded their place in the sun. Italy grabbed Libya from the Ottoman Empire in 1912 and established control over Eritrea and Somaliland in East Africa. Germany occupied Cameroon, German Southwest Africa (now Namibia), and German East Africa (roughly today's Tanzania). Germany also took control of a large group of Pacific islands, thereby coming into conflict with another young imperial power, the United States. None of these colonies brought wealth or significant new markets to the home country. Rather, their main purpose was to satisfy the patriotic fever of Germans and Italians who felt that without colonies their countries would be second-rate powers. In this way, domestic politics pushed imperialism, often against the wishes and advice of the imperialist powers' foreign ministers and foreign policy experts.

24-1c Christian Missions

Churches and missionaries also played a vital role in imperialist expansion. Most often, Christian missionaries had established footholds in these regions before official colonial control was declared. To be sure, missionaries sincerely desired to bring education, health care, and other benefits of European culture to Africans and Asians. They often built schools and hospitals. Missionaries seldom forced Christianity on the native peoples, hoping instead to win converts by good example. At the same time, they taught European concepts of sexual morality and gender relations and often insisted that natives dress in a "modest" European manner and discard traditional norms and taboos. All of this undermined native cultural values. When local rulers attempted to restrict or expel missionaries, even without using violence, the European powers often intervened. Thousands and eventually millions of Asians and Africans embraced Christianity, but these numbers represented a grave loss to native cultures and religions.

David Livingstone One well-known missionary was **David Livingstone**. As a small boy in Scotland, born to a working-class family in 1813, young David was influenced by stories he heard and read of Christian missionaries in China and the Muslim world. In 1840, he left England for Africa, where he was to spend the rest of his life spreading the gospel, healing the sick, and fighting European exploitation—including enslavement—of Africans.

Livingstone became famous for his expedition seeking the source of the Nile River and his discovery of Victoria Falls, now shared by Zimbabwe and Zambia. His life in the African bush and his dedication to helping Africans, even against other Europeans, made him a controversial figure. In 1871, the American reporter Henry Stanley went to Africa in search of Livingstone, famously greeting him with the words, "Dr. Livingstone, I presume?" Stanley described the elderly missionary as "a living skeleton."

David Livingstone (1813–1873) Scottish missionary, explorer of Africa, and discoverer of Victoria Falls.

Rudyard Kipling (1865–1936) English writer and poet, born in India, best known for his adventure stories, which often took place in exotic colonial locations.

white man's burden Phrase taken from a poem by Rudyard Kipling urging Americans—but implicitly all "white men"—to spread Western civilization.

Livingstone died in his tent in 1873 and was buried in London, in Westminster Abbey. At his funeral, he was praised for his efforts to spread Christian morality through good example. Livingstone's motivations for the extension of European culture contrast sharply with those of Rhodes. Clearly, imperialist motivations were highly complex.

Missionaries Helping Colonized Peoples Missionaries translated the Gospels into African languages, wrote grammars and dictionaries, and thereby helped transform tongues previously only spoken into written languages. Many—like Livingstone—stood up for native rights against European administrators. They did not always get along with European traders, but their example—the clothes they wore and houses they kept—provided Africans with incentive to purchase European manufactured goods. Thus, in spite of their own intentions, missionaries strengthened economic links between industrial Europe and underdeveloped colonies.

24-1d The "White Man's Burden"

Many Europeans, not only missionaries, saw the spread of European civilization as a precious gift to "dark peoples" of African and Asia: The figure of speech referred to alleged intellectual and cultural backwardness as much as to skin color. The English poet **Rudyard Kipling** called this impulse the **white man's burden**. Kipling was born in India, which is the setting for his well-known children's books, such as *The Jungle Book* (1894) and *Kim* (1901). In 1899, in the context of the Spanish-American War that had begun a year earlier, he addressed these lines to the United States, urging Americans to join in the imperialist enterprise:

> *Take up the White Man's burden—*
> *Send forth the best ye breed—*
> *Go bind your sons to exile*
> *To serve your captives' need;*
> *To wait in heavy harness*
> *On fluttered folk and wild—*
> *Your new-caught, sullen peoples,*
> *Half-devil and half-child.*

> Excerpt from Rudyard Kipling's poem, "The White Man's Burden."

The condescending attitude of the imperialists is evident in these lines. At the same time, Kipling argues that imperialism is not a program for exploitation and self-aggrandizement but a duty: *"to serve your captives' need." He sees imperialism as a "civilizing mission" that is self-sacrificing. The next stanza

---

*Excerpt from Rudyard Kipling's poem, "The White Man's Burden."

describes it as: "To seek another's profit, / And work another's gain." Kipling may be termed a romantic imperialist who perceived imperialism as an uplifting moral crusade that, while not always so understood by the natives ("new-caught, sullen peoples"), would in the end bring about better conditions for their lives. Of course, matters looked very different from the colonized people's perspective.

Imperialism and "Civilizing Missions" Imperialists firmly believed in Western superiority in civilization, culture, and even genetic makeup. Earlier in the nineteenth century, Americans had justified their expansion from the Atlantic to the Pacific Ocean as **manifest destiny**, claiming that God and the natural order had ordained American control over the entire continent. In a similar way, Europeans extolled the virtues of their social order, technology, and religious beliefs and assumed that non-Europeans would be grateful to be "uplifted" and assimilated into the European political and economic systems and moral values.

Pro-imperialist scholars such as the French sociologist and journalist Paul Leroy-Beaulieu argued that France had a "civilizing mission" to the world. In other words, French culture was a valuable commodity that could improve the lives of Asians and Africans. The British politician Joseph Chamberlain argued much the same for British imperialism. In a speech to Parliament in 1897 he exclaimed, "I maintain that our rule does, and has, brought security and peace and comparative prosperity to countries that never knew these blessings before." Chamberlain praised the "work of civilization" that British imperialists carried out in India, Africa, and other lands. But these attitudes contained within them a contradiction. Even as imperialists claimed that they brought civilization to colonized peoples, they frequently exploited the labor of those peoples, denying them the rights and privileges taken for granted by Europeans. The large gap between the rhetoric of imperialism and its more brutal reality meant that sooner or later imperialism would collapse.

Racism and Paternalism Racism certainly played a part in the ideology and practice of imperialism. By the second half of the nineteenth century, scientific theories of race had divided humanity into Caucasian, Negroid, and Mongoloid races, which some argued were different species and others arranged in a strict hierarchy, with Europeans (Caucasians) on top. European racial theorists believed it was self-evident that the white, or Caucasian, race had progressed further than the others. Both the categories and the argumentation revealed not scientific facts but prejudices and convenient self-justifications for European dominance. Nonetheless, these ideas about the races were widely held.

Beaulieu and Chamberlain were not overtly racist, but their assumption that European culture was superior to that of Asia or Africa was paternalistic. **Paternalism**'s greatest blind spot was its inability to respect the humanity of non-Europeans. Kipling's description of native people as "half-devil and half-child" reflects this view. Imperialists did not understand that their values were not necessarily universal and that from the colonized people's point of view, imperialist efforts to "enlighten" might well be experienced as oppression and even as the destruction of time-hallowed traditions. Hypocrisy was inherent in this system that claimed to protect and nurture native peoples while in reality privileging European economic and political interests.

24-1e The Importance of Technology

European domination over most of the world's surface would have been impossible without the technological advances of the second Industrial Revolution. Among these, advances in communications, transportation, and medicine are most important.

Telegraph and Railways in the Service of Imperialism The telegraph vastly simplified the administration of world empires by making nearly instantaneous communication possible. By the 1860s, England was connected to India by telegraph over landlines, but messages had to be sent and retransmitted many times, often by operators not entirely fluent in English. When underwater cables were laid in the late 1860s and 1870, communications between Britain and India became far faster and more reliable. By 1895, nearly 200,000 miles of underwater cables connected Europe with America, Asia, Africa, and Australia, and more than 600,000 miles of land telegraph cables sped messages to their destinations.

When, at the end of the nineteenth century, the increasingly dense telegraph system was supplemented by a growing telephone network, colonial administrators were able to be in continuous and rapid communication. At any sign of unrest, an administrator out in the countryside could telegraph the nearest military outpost with a request for troops. In this way the telegraph helped imperial administrators stifle resistance and revolt.

Developments in transportation similarly facilitated imperial administration. The imperial powers constructed railroads in the colonies, most impressively in India, which by 1900 had more than 25,000 miles of railway

manifest destiny North American ideology that saw the extension of the United States to the Pacific Ocean as fulfillment of a divine plan.

paternalism Attitude toward or control of one group (here, colonialized people) by another (here, Europeans) that resembles a father's rule over his children.

lines—more than France or Britain itself. Just as Rhodes dreamed of connecting British colonies throughout East Africa by a Cairo-to-Cape Town rail line, German imperialists dreamed of a Berlin-to-Baghdad railroad that would strengthen German influence in the Ottoman Empire. Neither line was completed, but railroads were built in many African colonies, making the extraction of raw materials and the penetration of European military control possible. Steamship lines, too, shortened distances. The trip from England to Australia, which had taken more than four months in the early nineteenth century, was down to a month by the century's end.

Tropical Illness and Modern Medicine As Europeans ventured into new climates in Africa and Asia, they encountered new microbes. In Africa, particularly, death rates among European explorers up to the mid-nineteenth century were extremely high. Among the diseases, **malaria** was probably the most devastating. Before the late nineteenth century, little was understood about germs. The disease was attributed to "bad air"—in Italian, *mal'aria*—because it was not yet understood that the disease was spread by germ-carrying mosquitoes.

By trial and error, Europeans came to recognize that regular doses of the bark of the cinchona tree were effective in staving off the worst symptoms of malaria. The bark contained quinine, which began to be commercially produced in the 1830s. Quinine became the constant companion of the imperialist in tropical areas, and the typical imperialist cocktail, a gin and tonic (containing quinine), became a pleasant way to administer a daily dose. By the end of the century, the role of germs in sickness was established, and British scientists made significant advances in studying tropical diseases. For all that, mortality continued to be high among Europeans serving in tropical regions, in particular in equatorial Africa.

Political, ideological, economic, and technological factors all contributed to the new imperialism's massive extension of European power around the globe. Imperialists saw themselves as the bearers of a superior cultural and political order. At the same time, many of them gained huge profits and prestige derived from the labor and natural resources of the colonized lands. Imperialists took for granted the superiority of European thought and culture, seeing the native populations as ignorant and backward savages who had to be "brought up" to European standards. Despite the imperialists' often sincere belief in their own "civilizing mission," their failure to appreciate the validity of other cultures led quickly to conflicts, resentment, and resistance.

24-2 The Scramble for Africa

> » How did settler colonies in Africa differ from other kinds of colonies?

> » What economic factors propelled Europeans to colonize Africa?

Africa provides the most startling example of the new imperialism. In 1870, while there were European outposts along the coasts, the African interior was almost totally unknown to Europeans. Two short generations later, in 1914, the continent was almost completely colonized. Africans resisted imperialism, but the superiority of European military and administrative organization doomed resistance to failure—at least in the short run. But competition for control led two groups of European settlers to fight against each other in the Boer War.

24-2a Settler Colonies in South and North Africa

Historians differentiate between **settler colonies**, to which colonists came in large numbers, often including entire families, and settled permanently, and colonies where only a few, usually male, administrators lived temporarily and then returned to Europe. Settler colonies were usually located in temperate regions such as Argentina, the United States, and Australia, where the majority of the current population is descended from settlers not native to that place.

South Africa and Algeria In Africa in the nineteenth century, there were only two large-scale European settler colonies. One was located at the temperate southern tip of Africa, where Dutch farmers (or Boers) had originally settled in the seventeenth century, later joined by English colonists. During the Great Trek of 1836–1846, the Boers moved north into land previously inhabited by Africans. Around 1900, perhaps 10 percent of the total population in South Africa was of European descent, but they completely dominated the economy and political system there. It was these white settlers who gained most from the establishment of the Union of South Africa in 1900.

Thousands of Indian laborers and professionals also made these colonies their home. Most numerous, of course, were the native African peoples of the region, who often saw their land and livelihoods taken over by

---

malaria Infectious parasitic disease transmitted by mosquitoes, particularly widespread in tropical areas but preventable by constant doses of quinine.

settler colonies Colonies inhabited by settlers of European origin, always located in temperate regions such as North America, Australia, and South Africa.

24-2b The Belgian Congo

One of the largest and most profitable colonies in Africa was established by the private initiative (and funds) of the king of Belgium, Leopold II. Neither the Belgian government nor the Belgian public showed much interest in an African possession when Leopold, acting on his own, established the Association Internationale du Congo in 1876 for what he called humanitarian purposes. In fact, he financed private expeditions—sending Henry Stanley, among others—throughout the Congo River basin for his own economic gain. By the late 1880s, the Congo was practically speaking Leopold's own private estate, an estate of some 900,000 square miles with millions of inhabitants. Though he set up the Congo Free State in 1885, Leopold ruled the area directly, with the help of his Force Publique, a brutal and corrupt mercenary army. Treating the Congo as his own personal financial investment, Leopold ruthlessly extracted as much rubber, ivory, and palm oil as possible with a minimum of expense, gaining vast riches in the process. African workers were forced to produce quotas of rubber. Failure to do so brought brutal punishments, including the hacking off of hands and feet. Though the king and investors grew rich, the brutality appalled Europeans, and in 1908 European pressure obliged Leopold to turn over the colony to the Belgian state, which would rule over the area as the Belgian Congo until 1960. The cruelty and inhumanity of exploitation in the Congo inspired **Joseph Conrad**'s novella *Heart of Darkness*.

Boys Mutilated by Colonial Police in the Belgian Congo

These two youths were among the many in King Leopold's Congo colony whose hands were cut off by soldiers and policemen who forced local people to produce rubber for export—or else. The printing of photographs like this one helped publicize the brutality of imperial rule in central Africa.

❯❯ *How effective do you think such images were in changing Europeans' views of imperialism?*

❯❯ *Looking at this photograph, what emotions do you think contemporary Europeans would feel?*

Courtesy, Anti-Slavery International

24-2c The Berlin Conference and German Colonies

In Germany, Chancellor Bismarck seized on tensions among Africa's colonial powers to enter Germany into the so-called "scramble for Africa." In 1884, he called the **Berlin Conference**, specifically to press Leopold to agree to free trade in the Congo. At this congress, the United States joined Great Britain, France, Russian, Austria-Hungary, and the Ottoman Empire in recognizing Leopold's authority over the Congo in exchange for the right to trade there.

Germany's African Colonies Bismarck also used the conference to

---

Europeans in this period. To fight against these injustices of colonial rule, the South African Native National Congress was established in 1912. This organization, later called simply the **African National Congress**, helped abolish white privilege and establish a more democratic order in South Africa in 1994.

In northern Africa, French Algeria was also a settler colony. By 1848, around 100,000 Europeans had settled there, and by the early twentieth century, around one million French men and women made their home along Africa's Mediterranean coast. Some 40 percent of the population was of European descent. Unlike South Africa, Algeria was from the 1840s onward considered by the French government to be an integral part of that country. However, the native Arabic-speaking Muslim population had no political rights under the French, and Europeans also dominated the economy.

African National Congress Organization established by Africans in 1912 to defend their rights that eventually brought more democratic rule to South Africa.

Joseph Conrad (1857–1924) English writer of Polish origin whose novels such as *Heart of Darkness* and *Lord Jim* often examined the morality of colonialism.

Berlin Conference Meeting in Berlin of the United States and European powers in 1884 that regulated European trade and imperial control in Africa.

declare German control over Southwest Africa, Togo, and Cameroon, to be followed by East Africa (today's Tanzania) a year later. Also during these years, 1884–1886, Germany established colonies in the South Pacific, straining relations with the United States. By establishing colonies, Bismarck was pursuing both international and domestic goals. In foreign policy, he aimed to enhance German power and prestige in the world. At home, Bismarck was responding to pressure from the **German Colonial Union**. By 1884, it appeared that if the German state did not act quickly, all chances for African colonies would be gone, the continent taken over by the British and French (see Map 24.2). So Bismarck acted swiftly and, in the short run, very successfully, as his popularity soared.

The new German colonies lacked any obvious economic or political rationale. Furthermore, Bismarck's action infuriated the British who regarded German colonies as a threat to British interests.

After attempting to administer the colonies through private chartered companies, in the 1890s, the German government took them over directly. In their effort to crush native resistance and establish control of German Southwest Africa, German colonial officials, small in number and inexperienced, carried out horrifying massacres, especially after the **Herero Revolt** of 1905–1907. This policy of **genocide** was widely criticized in Europe. On the whole, German colonies in Africa failed to bring Germany either economic or political gains. One can even argue that German imperial expansion in Africa was a major factor in worsening relations between German and Great Britain that in 1914 would explode into a world war.

this sorry tradition. While the word *genocide* would not be coined until 1944, the massacre of tens of thousands of Herero people was recognized by the German government as a genocide in 2016.

24-2d The Boer War

In South Africa, the discovery of gold and diamonds in the 1880s attracted thousands of Englishmen and other Europeans to the region. Among these new arrivals was Cecil Rhodes, whose investments in the gold and diamond mines of Kimberley made him a millionaire. The huge influx of prospectors caused the Dutch farmers, or Boers, great worries. They had earlier left their original colony near the Cape of Good Hope and trekked north to avoid English rule. Now it appeared that the English were pursuing them once again, threatening their farms and way of life. To preserve their independence, in 1899 the Boers, led by their gruff leader Paul Kruger, took a stand against the British.

The resulting **Boer War** of 1899–1902 caused great suffering and death among Africans, but the central dispute was between Europeans, in particular, the Boer's desire to retain their own autonomy and the British insistence on extending their rule to include areas of Boer settlement. The British expected to win quickly and easily, but they were wrong. Nearly 500,000 British men fought in the Boer War; around one-tenth of these lost their lives. In the end the British prevailed, however, and they granted the Boers broad autonomy and home rule. But after this expensive and bloody war between Europeans in a colonized country, many Europeans began to question whether imperialism was economically or morally defensible.

24-3 The British Raj in India

» **What was the nature of British rule in India?**

» **Why was British rule in India so important for the empire?**

British dominion over India was always unique, with its specific mystique and tradition. Even the language used to refer to this colony was unique—"the jewel in the crown" of the empire. The British presence in India dated from the seventeenth century, and domination continued in various forms until 1947. Besides the unprecedented length of British control, the huge size, large population, and complex cultures of the territory made India a colony unlike any other. The enormous diversity of religions, languages, and customs in India complicated British rule, especially as

German Colonial Union Political pressure group fo rmed in 1882 to press the German government to seek overseas colonies.

Herero Revolt Rebellion against colonial rule in German Southwest Africa followed by a German massacre of the Herero people in 1905–1907.

genocide Attempt to kill an entire people or nation.

Boer War Conflict between the British Empire and Dutch settlers (Boers) in South Africa from 1899 to 1902, ending in a costly British victory.

CONNECTIONS: Violence aimed at specific cultural groups is not a novelty in world history. In the book of Deuteronomy in the Hebrew Bible (or "Old Testament"), God commands the Hebrews to slaughter the Canaanites, sparing no individual whether old or young. And some historians have called the European treatment of Native Americans after 1492 an "American holocaust" in which Europeans systematically killed indigenous peoples with arms and with disease (see Section 13-3c The Spanish Empire). The German treatment of the Herero people of southwest Africa fits into

Map 24.2 **Partition of Africa, 1870–1914** Between 1870 and 1914 nearly all of Africa came under European colonial rule. As these maps show, British and French colonies predominated, but several other European powers also participated in "the scramble for Africa."

1. Which European countries had a presence in Africa before 1870?

2. Where were French colonies most prevalent? British colonies?

3. What African countries remained independent in 1914? Why?

the extension of British colonial power in India did not follow a well-considered plan. Rather, economic interests were gradually transformed into political dominion in reaction to threats of foreign encroachment, the perceived and real weaknesses of native Indian administrations, and resistance to British rule. More than any other colony, India influenced British home politics, national identity, and culture. The impact of British rule on Indian culture was no less significant.

Ullstein Bilderdienst/The Granger Collection, New York

African Children in Dar Es Salaam in a German School

In this missionary school in German East Africa (Dar Es Salaam, now Tanzania), African children learn to read under the gaze of the German Kaiser and his wife. As the writing on the chalkboard indicates, these children were learning to read not only in German but also in their own native African language.

24-3a Commerce and Trade

European traders had visited the Indian **subcontinent** from the sixteenth century onward. By the eighteenth century, both French and English traders were competing over Indian goods like calico cloth, spices, and luxury items.

subcontinent British India, including present-day Pakistan and Bangladesh ("sub" refers to its location on Asia's bottom edge).

Mughal Empire Muslim empire in India lasting from 1526 to 1857.

Beginnings of the Raj: The British East India Company At first, British interests in India remained strictly commercial. The British East India Company had one aim: Profit. It operated through warehouses and posts along the Indian coast, where agents traded with Indian merchants, but by the early eighteenth century the trading posts in Bombay, Madras, and Calcutta were fortified. Following Britain's victory in the Seven Years' War (1756–1763), French competition ended. Still, as the **Mughal (MOOG-hel) Empire** weakened, company officials continued to worry about their own safety and the future of trade there. In this insecure political situation, British state institutions gradually moved in (see Map 24.3).

A governor-general of India was first named in the late eighteenth century. Though supposedly merely the agent of the British Parliament and the Crown, he ruled in the absolutist style. Some regions he ruled directly; in others he ruled through subordinate Indian princes. But from the first, the ideological basis of British rule in India was contradictory. British liberals saw it as aiming to produce Indians capable of self-rule, "a class of persons Indian in colour and blood, but English in tastes, in opinions, in morals, and in intellect," explained Thomas Babington Macauley, a Whig member of

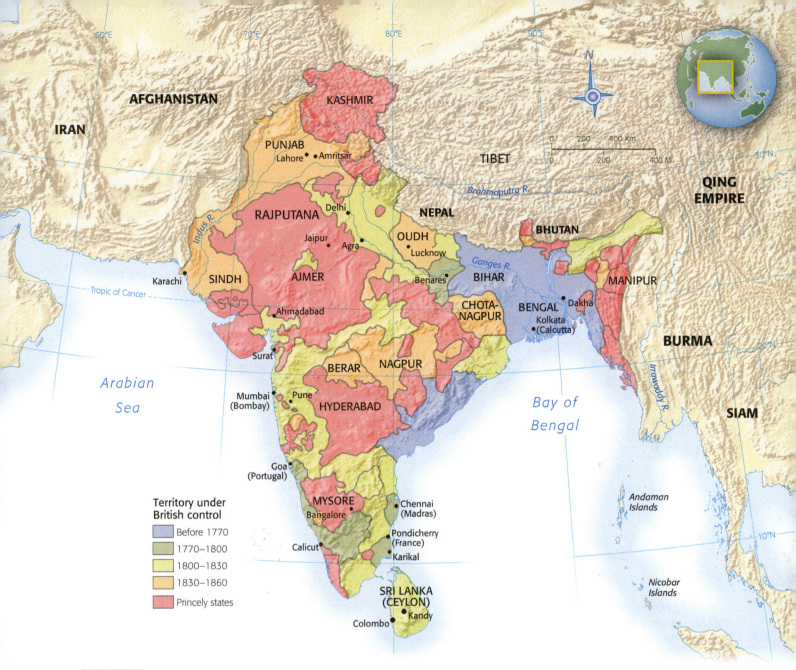

Map 24.3 **Growth of British India** India was by far the largest and most important British colony from the late eighteenth to the mid-twentieth century. As this map shows, British India—which included the present-day countries of India, Pakistan, and Bangladesh—was partly under direct British rule and partly ruled by Indian princes subordinate to the British.

1. Where was British rule in India first established?
2. How much of India was ruled indirectly, through Indian princes?

Parliament and East India Company leader. Until this class could be trained, however, India was controlled by a British administration that, wile generally honest and efficient, was conservative and on the whole quite alien, even hostile, to Indian traditions.

24-3b The Sepoy Rebellion

The **Sepoy** (she-POY) **Rebellion** of 1857 demonstrated that Indian soldiers in British service, called sepoys, had long been dissatisfied over issues of pay and rumors that the British would force them to convert to Christianity. When they were issued new cartridges greased with fat made from cows (sacred to Hindus) and pigs (forbidden to Muslims), they refused to load their weapons. The mutiny spread rapidly through northern India. British response was brutal: Thousands of Indian soldiers were massacred and entire

Sepoy Rebellion Revolt of Indian soldiers (sepoys) in northern India in 1857–1858, put down with brutality by the British.

Cecil Rhodes Creates the Rhodes Scholarship

THE RHODES COLOSSUS
STRIDING FROM CAPE TOWN TO CAIRO.

Stock Montage, Inc. / Alamy Stock Photo

Cartoon of Cecil Rhodes from *Punch*
Cecil Rhodes was one of the best-known advocates of the new imperialism of the late nineteenth century, and he reflected the mind-set of the age. A cartoon in the English humor magazine *Punch* showed Rhodes as a colossus whose mighty stride took in the entire African continent. It related specifically to Rhodes's pet project of a railroad running the length of Africa, from Cairo to the Cape of Good Hope, a project that was never realized.

❯❯ *How does this cartoon portray Rhodes as an exuberant imperialist?*

For Cecil Rhodes, as for many other young, energetic Europeans of the late nineteenth century, establishing colonies around the world was not just an adventure or means of gaining wealth but a moral duty. They wanted to spread European values and culture around the world.

Born in 1853 into a middle-class family in a country town in England, Rhodes was early singled out as an intelligent boy. His adoring and powerful mother sheltered him in his youth, and he grew up self-confident, sure of his own destiny. At the age of sixteen, he set off for Africa with his parents' blessing. In the 1870s, he divided his time between Africa and Oxford, earning his degree in 1881. Already by this time—before his thirtieth birthday—he had made a fortune in South African diamonds. His ambitions helped extend British power far to the north, into a region later named Rhodesia (today Zambia and Zimbabwe) in his honor.

As a businessman and government official, Rhodes was known for ruthlessness and an authoritarian style that created enemies among his white contacts and fear among Africans. As prime minister of Cape Colony, he authorized a military excursion that he hoped would unite South Africa as a British colony. Its failure led the House of Commons to pronounce him guilty of grave breaches of duty and he was forced to resign. Rhodes died a rich but embittered man in 1902, not even fifty years old.

But Rhodes had already made provision for funding the Rhodes Scholarships, for which he is best known today. Though a businessman and colonial official, Rhodes was also a visionary who was convinced that English culture should conquer the world. Convinced of English superiority, Rhodes maintained that the more the world came to resemble England, the better. So to preserve and spread English culture, Rhodes funded scholarships that would allow the most talented men (women could not enter most British universities at the time) to study in England—at the oldest of English universities, Oxford.

villages were destroyed. This extreme response was justified by pointing to lurid—and usually untrue—stories of sepoys committing murder and rape, specifically of "dark men" sexually abusing English women. The British insisted that they had to protect both "the white race" and "English womanhood," and this justified the mass killings.

Following the rebellion, British rule of India was fundamentally transformed. The British East India Company was disbanded and control of the colony transferred to the Crown. Large numbers British soldiers were sent to the colony. Whereas in 1857 European soldiers were outnumbered ten to one by native troops, by 1885 there were 73,000 British and 154,000 Indian soldiers. The costs of administration and the army continued to be a heavy burden for Indian taxpayers.

Religious Policy of the Raj Official British policy aimed to avoid interference in religious matters, but,

At first, Rhodes proposed thirty-six scholarships for "young colonials" from New Zealand, Australia, Canada, and South Africa. Later, scholarships were added for young men from the United States and Germany. In all cases, Rhodes's aim was the same: To produce cultured, educated English gentlemen. Rhodes had little interest in producing scholars or independent thinkers: Among the qualifications he listed for selecting scholarship winners were "manly sports," "qualities of manhood," and "moral force of character," as well as "literary and scholastic" excellence. Rhodes Scholars, he hoped, would not be mere bookworms but would carry on his own values and those of upper-class, wealthy Britons dedicated to strengthening and spreading the empire.

Rhodes set down that the scholarships would be open to all male candidates, regardless of "race or religious opinions." Rhodes did not mean race as it is understood today; he meant nationality, and by this he intended that the Dutch in South Africa—Britain's rivals for control—should be eligible. He certainly never expected Africans or Asians to apply. In practice, however, the scholarships have been awarded to individuals of diverse races and backgrounds and from many countries.

Rhodes's legacy has enabled hundreds of young men and women (the latter only since 1977) to study at Oxford. Among Rhodes Scholars are some of the most distinguished scholars, political leaders, and social activists of the twentieth century: Count Bernstorff, a German diplomat executed for conspiring against Hitler; Edwin Hubble, the astronomer after whom the Hubble Space Telescope is named; Daniel Boorstin, former librarian of Congress; David Souter, Supreme Court justice; and former U.S. President William J. Clinton. Add to this list hundreds of distinguished scholars, diplomats, and politicians from Pakistan, India, Canada, Australia, and other countries.

as the mutiny demonstrated, few British administrators understood the complexities of religious relations in India. Traditional religions involved the worship of many gods, but the large Muslim population, making up a significant proportion of native rulers, was strictly **monotheistic**. The Church of England, although not a militant missionary force, was influential through its influence on British administrators. As Christians, they found it difficult to understand and appreciate a religion not based on belief in a single God. Wishing to rationalize administration, the British encouraged the creation of a more unified Hindu religion out of thousands of separate, often local, rites, beliefs, and rituals. At the same time, Hindus perceived British rule as favoring monotheistic Muslim Indians, thereby straining relations between the diverse religious groups of the subcontinent.

24-3c The Jewel in the Crown

In the late nineteenth century, the British **Raj** (Razh) in India continued to expand. Steamships brought officials and their families back and forth between England and Calcutta (now Kolkata), the capital of British India. It became common for ambitious young men to make a career in India, amassing a fortune or pension, then returning to England to retire. Some Englishmen, however, remained in India their whole lives. Their children were known as "Anglo-Indians," the most famous of whom was probably the writer Rudyard Kipling.

Relations Between Colonizers and Colonized Even for Anglo-Indians, however, relations with Indians were seldom on an equal basis. With very few exceptions at the highest levels of society, the English in India knew native people only as servants.

An Englishwoman could not be alone with an Indian man without endangering her reputation. Racial categories and hierarchies—with the Englishman on top—dominated English colonial identity in India as well as at home. The injustice of this racially defined colonial rule helped bring about the formation of the **Indian National Congress** in 1885, an organization that would work to free India from British rule.

The allure of India also affected Englishmen who would never leave their island. Visual art, songs, and literature—like Kipling's *Jungle Book* and *Kim*—created an image of India as a place both familiar and alien, full of exotic scenes, wild animals, and exquisite dangers. British identity derived great pride in the domination and influence over this vast region, many times larger than England itself. In 1877, Queen Victoria took the title of Empress of India in well-orchestrated ceremonies both at home and in India itself. The stately processions of Indian princes, elephants, and native soldiers in exotic uniforms thrilled Englishmen in Manchester and Leeds. Their own lives might be dull and routine, but as Englishmen they, too, were part of these imperial pageants.

24-3d British Order and Indian Culture

British liberals claimed that in India their goal was an honest administration, a market economy, and individual self-development. They aimed to reduce corruption, to increase efficiency, and in the long run

monotheism Belief in the existence of only one God.

Raj (from Hindi, "rule") British Empire in India.

Indian National Congress Organization formed in 1885 demanding the end of colonial rule in India.

The Delhi Durbar, 1903

The Delhi Durbar of 1903 was an enormous celebration of British rule in India that brought together dozens of Indian princes, hundreds of British soldiers and officials, and huge crowds who watched the splendid processions and ceremonies.

» Why do you think the British orchestrated such a huge celebration at this time?

» What impression might this celebration have made on Indians?

to bring prosperity and enlightenment to the peoples of India. The British regime sought to uplift and educate, rooting out customs such as the isolation of upper-class women from men (purdah) and the suicidal burning of widows on their deceased husbands' funeral pyres (suttee). In time, the British hoped, all aspects of life, from administrative practices to religion to social roles, would be transformed by their benevolent rule.

Paternalistic Rule in India Rapidly, however, the British liberals recognized that to introduce their own cultural conceptions and standards of hygiene in India they would have to oppose the popular will. They justified these measures as "for the Indians," though not "through them." In the words of the English liberal John Stuart Mill, "Despotism is a legitimate mode of government in dealing with barbarians, provided the end be their improvement." But when Indians wished to retain traditional ways and their own cultural values, the British denigrated them as backward and ignorant. Some British administrators became disillusioned by the perceived lack of interest in the Indian community for "self-betterment."

Even those Indians who embraced British education, values, and the English language discovered that they were not accepted as equals by most Europeans. The group most receptive to British culture, the middle-class Bengali babus, was mocked as being effeminate and incapable of independent action. The word *babu*, which in Bengali denoted a respected educated figure, when used by the British meant a half-educated, slavish, and rather contemptible figure who was neither British nor Indian and neither man nor woman.

The **gendering** of British colonialism differentiated sharply between the manly "martial races" such as the Sikhs and the "effeminate" Bengalis. Predictably, imperialists equated manliness with strength, goodness, and progress, while so-called effeminate tendencies bore a negative connotation of corruption, weakness, and backwardness. The British ascribed to themselves manly virtues such as bravery, decisiveness, and energy. The Indian masses, in contrast, were denigrated as passive, backward, and unambitious.

British Cultural Influences in India British rule did have some positive aspects for Indians. It united the subcontinent as never before. The educational system, while still leaving most Indians illiterate, made significant strides in creating an educated Indian elite—the very class that would be instrumental in challenging and ending British rule in the twentieth century. By 1857 there were five universities in India, and increasing numbers of young

gendering Considering certain peoples or activities intrinsically linked with the male or female gender, generally regarding "male" as superior.

Indians entered the civil service. In 1900, Calcutta University, with 8,000 students, was the largest university in the world. Even earlier, privileged Indians had begun to attend elite British universities. In 1888, **Mohandas Karamchand Gandhi**, who would lead India's independence movement and preach nonviolent resistance to colonialism, left India to study law in London.

The English language provided a common means of communication for educated Indians, who spoke hundreds of different native languages. As this new middle class of Indians developed, they could not help contrasting the liberal British ideals of democracy and equal rights with actual British policies in India. The most talented Indians, even if trained at Oxford, could not reach the highest levels in the colonial bureaucracy or in private British firms. Nor could native Indians join exclusive British associations like the Bengal Club. The resentment and frustration of the educated Indian middle class fueled demands for an end to British colonial rule that would come in the twentieth century. Economically, British rule in India brought mixed results. One was **deindustrialization** of the subcontinent, even as railroads and telegraph lines were built. British manufacturers, particularly of cheap British cloth, put native industries out of business. On the other hand, British rule connected India to the world economy.

24-4 Imperialism and the Muslim World

» **Where did Muslims come under colonial rule in the late nineteenth century?**

» **In what ways did the Russian and Ottoman Empires confront imperialism differently?**

The Muslim world also felt the impact of the new imperialism, and not only in India. As Russia expanded its influence in southeastern Europe (the Balkans) and beyond the Caucasus Mountains on its southern border, hundreds of thousands of Muslims were affected. Nor could the Ottoman Empire, the only major Muslim state in the world at this time, remain untouched by European imperialism.

In northern Africa, southeast Europe, and elsewhere, Ottoman power was replaced by European colonial power. At the very end of the nineteenth century, a new challenge to the Muslim world arose—the Zionist movement, which called on Jews to return to their ancestral homeland, Palestine (for Jews, "Eretz Yisrael"—the land of Israel), at the time an Ottoman province. European successes called forth new movements among Muslims that strove for new forms of modern, nationalist, and democratic politics.

24-4a Russian Expansion

After the British in India, Russians had more contact with Muslims than any other Europeans. From the sixteenth century onward, the tsar had counted among his subjects Tartars and other Muslim peoples. As Russia expanded, a variety of religious and national groups came under Russian rule, including many Muslims. By 1700, Russia had extended its dominion over thinly populated Siberia all the way to the Pacific. A century and a half later, Russian control stretched across the Bering Strait, over Alaska, and down the American west coast as far south as present-day California. Amid the Great Reforms of the mid-1860s, however, Russia abandoned its American territories, selling Alaska to the United States in 1867. Russian expansion would now take place not in the New World but in the heart of the old: **Central Asia**.

Central Asia The boundary between "southern Siberia" and "Central Asia" is fluid, and Russian settlers had been moving gradually into what is now Kazakhstan at least from around 1800. In the second half of the nineteenth century, however, the Russian empire—already the largest on earth—took over vast territories in Central Asia. Like the European colonial powers in Africa, the Russians did not set out to control this region. They did not intend to settle Russians in Central Asia, only to prevent any other power from gaining a foothold there. In this respect, Russian expansion into Central Asia followed a common colonial pattern.

In 1865, Tashkent fell to the Russians, followed later in the decade by the khanates of Bukhara and Khiva. The ruling **khans** continued to rule but now formally recognized the tsar's authority. In the 1870s, Russian troops engaged in military action against the warlike nomadic Turkmen who dominated the territory to the east of the Caspian Sea, establishing Russian control there by the end of the decade. Thus, by 1887, the conquest of **Turkestan** (the prerevolutionary Russian term for Central Asia) was completed and Russian rule extended to the borders of Persia and Afghanistan.

Mohandas Karamchand Gandhi (1869–1948) Indian political and spiritual leader who fought for Indian independence and emphasized nonviolent struggle.

deindustrialization Process of reducing the level of industry in a country, generally in colonized regions, especially India.

Central Asia Geographical area including present-day states of Kazakhstan, Tajikistan, Uzbekistan, Kyrgyzstan, and Turkmenistan.

khan (in Turkic, "lord" or "ruler") Term used to describe Muslim rulers in Central Asia.

Turkestan (in Turkic, "Turkland") Central Asian region inhabited by Turkic peoples.

British Discomfort at Russian Expansion The Russian advance did not go unnoticed by other Western powers. In particular, the British were deeply concerned about the growth of Russian influence in Central Asia and how it might affect British rule over India. These fears were rather exaggerated: the Russians had neither the intention nor the means of threatening the British colony. In the end, Afghanistan remained as a buffer between Russian and British **spheres of influences**, and in the early twentieth century Persia was partitioned between a northern Russian zone and a southern British zone.

Russia's new possessions in Central Asia did little to develop the Russian economy, despite some cotton exports. The Russians did build railroads and extend telegraph lines to the new territory in the interests of more efficient administration. On the whole, however, few Russian merchants appeared in these new lands, and local economies experienced little change. The costs of administering these regions far exceeded any new tax revenues.

These territories were dominated by Muslim culture and populated by peoples speaking **Turkic** languages (as well as Tajik, which is related to Persian). Persian and Arabic remained the most powerful languages in written culture; local languages were spoken but rarely written. The Russian rulers and settlers did not make serious attempts to russify or convert local populations. Like the British in India, they tended to live apart from native peoples and to return to Russia once their service was completed.

Russian Culture and Central Asia Central Asia exerted a powerful influence on Russian artists and ethnographers, many of whom visited the newly conquered lands to study the peoples and the architectural monuments there. The popular artist **Vasily Vereshchagin**, for example, resided for a time in Tashkent and produced many drawings and paintings depicting people and places in Central Asian. The region was also hailed by Russian nationalists. "Asia will prove the outlet for our future destiny," proclaimed the conservative novelist Fyodor Dostoevsky. But well into the twentieth century, Central Asia remained impoverished, remote, and, aside from a few large cities, largely untouched by Russian or other Western influences.

Neither the Russian government nor the Orthodox church was particularly interested in converting Muslims. Few missionaries ventured out into Central Asia or Siberia. Those who did, moreover, did not attempt to convert the native populations directly. Instead, they established schools, where they taught in non-Russian languages as a first step toward "civilizing" native peoples. Only a few such schools were set up, however, and in the late 1860s the governor-general of Turkestan, Konstantin Kaufman, banned missionary activity in this huge, newly conquered Russian colony, fearing unrest among native populations. Instead of gaining converts, Russian rule in Central Asia indirectly encouraged a movement for modern Islamic education known as **Jadidism** (JAH-did-izm). As in colonized areas elsewhere in the world, the Russian presence in Central Asia ended up provoking the development of local nationalisms aimed against the imperial power.

24-4b The Ottoman Empire

In the nineteenth century, Muslims around the world looked to the Ottoman Empire as the religious and political center for their religion. The sultan held the title of Caliph, the spiritual head of all Muslims. Even more important, the holy cities of Mecca, Medina, and Jerusalem were all located in Ottoman territory. Thus, the decline of Ottoman political power and loss of Ottoman territory profoundly distressed all Muslims.

Shrinking Ottoman Power in Europe In 1800, the richest and most populous territories of the Ottoman Empire were in Europe, on the Balkan Peninsula. By midcentury, Ottoman influence over these lands had been considerably reduced, though the officially Romanian, Greek, Serbian, and Bulgarian regions remained within the empire. A key event showing the weakness of the Ottoman Empire was the Crimean War, fought ostensibly over which European power—Russia or France—had the right to protect Christians in the Ottoman Empire. Russia lost the war, but the very fact that European powers could demand—and obtain—the right to protect Christian Ottoman subjects revealed the empire's weakness. The sultan could not, of course, offer similar protection to Muslims living under colonial rule in Egypt, French Algeria, or Russian Central Asia.

During the era of new imperialism, Ottoman influence shrunk even further. The creation or expansion of Greek, Romanian, Serbian, and Bulgarian states in the Balkans was accompanied by the migration—often forced—of hundreds of thousands of Muslims to the Ottoman interior. Similarly, as Russia expanded its borders to the south, establishing control over present-day Armenia and Azerbaijan, many Muslims preferred to flee rather than live under the new Christian rulers. The Ottoman Empire was helpless to oppose the widening Russian influence or to defend Muslims (see Map 24.4).

sphere of influence Region over which a state exerts indirect political power, usually to prevent another state from extending its influence there.

Turkic Designation for a number of related languages such as Turkish, Azeri, Tartar, Uzbek, Kyrgyz, Turkmen, and Kazakh.

Vasily Vereshchagin (ver-esh-AH-ghin) (1842–1904) Russian Realist painter, best known for his paintings of exotic Central Asia scenes.

Jadidism (from Arabic, "new method") Movement attempting to reconcile Islam with modernity, especially in the Russian empire from the 1870s.

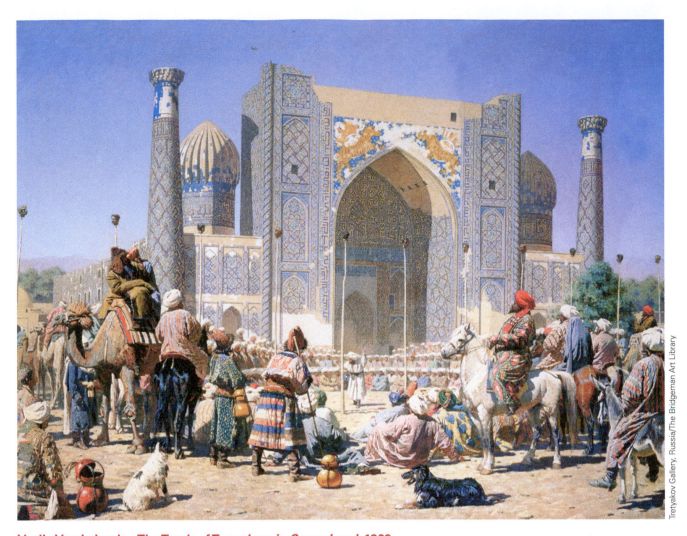

Vasily Vershchagin, *The Tomb of Tamerlane in Samarkand*, 1869

Vasily Vereshchagin's artistic works often showed scenes from regions in Central Asia that had recently been incorporated into the Russian Empire. This painting of the exquisite tomb in Samarkand of Timur or Tamerlane, the Mongol conqueror who died in 1405, combined exoticism with a deep interest and respect for Central Asian culture.

❯❯ *What elements of European exoticism can you point out in this image?*

CONNECTIONS: Xenophobia—the fear of the foreign—is a constant in world history. In the ancient world, the Greeks and Romans despised "barbarians" in part on the basis of language—they were seen as people who could not speak properly (i.e., Greek or Latin) and who simply babbled "bar-bar" (see Section 6-2 The Roman Peace). The original Russian word for "foreigner"—*nemets*: Someone who cannot speak—stems from this language difference as well. As Europeans spread their influence around the world at the end of the nineteenth century, the fear of the foreign and attraction to the exotic coexisted in a fascinating tension. During this time, racist anti-Asian statesman and educators evoked the "yellow peril" as opposition to Western civilization to justify colonization in East Asia. Today, xenophobia can be detected in political rhetoric from Warsaw to Washington that obsesses on the threat of Islamic beliefs and practices.

24-4c Muslims, Christians, and Zionists

Another challenge to the Ottoman Empire and Muslim world was the new Jewish nationalist movement, Zionism. This movement, led by Theodor Herzl, aimed at the establishment of a Jewish state in ancient Palestine, or what Jews called Eretz Israel, centered on Jerusalem. In the 1890s, this region was under Ottoman rule, and although many Jews and Christians lived there, the majority of the population was Muslim. The first Zionist settlers arrived in Palestine in the 1880s, and after that, large groups of Zionist pioneers came from Europe to establish Jewish settlements in this Ottoman province.

Initially, neither local Muslims nor the Ottoman authorities were concerned about the Zionists. After all, their numbers were small—around 20,000 by

Map 24.4 **Central Asia** The Russian Empire extended its borders southward from the 1860s to include most of Central Asia. By the late nineteenth century, the Russian Empire extended to border Afghanistan on the south, causing great concern among British officials in India.

1. In expanding into Central Asia, what countries did the Russian Empire potentially threaten?
2. Looking at this map, why would British officials be concerned about Russian expansion? How justified were these worries?

1903—and Jews had long lived in the region, even constituting the majority in Jerusalem. Still, the Ottoman sultan refused to grant the Zionist leader Herzl a charter officially sanctioning Zionist settlement, preferring to allow or forbid such activity on a case-by-case basis.

In the early twentieth century, **Arab nationalism** was beginning to take form. At first, this movement was primarily anti-Ottoman, wishing to foster an Arab identity based primarily on language and culture and only secondarily on the Muslim religion shared with the Turks. Not until the second decade of the twentieth century would Arab nationalists begin to see Zionism as a serious threat to the region and to their own identity.

Arab nationalism Movement beginning in late nineteenth century declaring that all Arabs constitute one nation and should be liberated from foreign rule.

24-5 The Far East

» **How did economic and administrative practices differ in Asia and Africa, and between different colonial powers?**

» **Why did Japan and China react differently to the threat of European imperialism?**

In East Asia or, to use an imperialist term, the Far East (far, of course, from Europe), imperialism also had a major impact. Some regions, such as Indochina and Indonesia, were controlled directly by European powers. But even in the two large East Asian countries that were not directly colonized—Japan and China—European influence had a profound effect (see Map 24.5). Western ideas as diverse as constitutionalism and Christianity entered these societies, influencing some Asians in a positive way while calling

Map 24.5 Asia in 1914 In 1914 there were both independent countries (Japan, China, Siam [Thailand]) and a number of European colonies (British, French, Dutch) in East Asia. Japan had also extended its rule over Korea to the north and Taiwan to the south. In the first years of the twentieth century, the Trans-Siberian Railroad connected Moscow with the Pacific.

1. Why did Japan see the Trans-Siberian Railroad as a threat?
2. Looking at the railroads on the map, which countries appear most developed? Most backward?

Territories held by Western powers
- Great Britain
- France
- Netherlands
- United States
- Russian Empire

- Japan and its territories
- Independent Asian states
- Ottoman Empire
- Major railroads

forth resentment and resistance from others. Both the violent and failed Boxer Rebellion in China and the peaceful reform of Japan's military and political institutions were reactions to the power of European imperialism of this period.

24-5a The French in Indochina

While the French had long held colonial outposts in Asia, including India, French expansion into Southeast Asia dated only from the 1850s. French missionaries in the region caused friction with local rulers, whose anti-Christian measures induced the French emperor Napoleon III to intervene. A treaty of 1862 forced local rulers in **Indochina** (today Vietnam, Cambodia, and Laos) to concede religious toleration for Christians. The treaty gave France a foothold in the southern part of what is now Vietnam, including the city of Saigon, and in 1867 France annexed this territory, known as Cochinchina. From there the French extended direct rule into most of present-day Cambodia and Laos to protect Catholic missions, establish naval bases, and defend French commercial interests in China. Emperor Napoleon III's foreign policy was explicitly imperialist, as he sought to increase French power and enhance French prestige in the world.

Economically, the most important product of Indochina was raw silk, but reports of rich mineral wealth in the hills of Vietnam also lured French investors and adventurers. A small group of French settlers derived large profits from plantations that produced rubber and teak wood. On the whole, however, French taxpayers paid a heavy price for France's colonial ventures. Few Frenchmen were interested in settling in the new colony, though many hundreds served there in administrative and military roles. The French also set up schools where, by the end of the century, young Vietnamese, Laotians, and Cambodians were learning to read and write French from the same textbooks used in Paris. Among the students were future leaders of Indochinese liberation movements, including **Ho Chi Minh**.

In India, higher British administrators brought their wives and raised their families, but French administrators in Indochina generally did not, instead often taking wives and mistresses from the local population. So-called native wives and their offspring did not receive equal political protection. Very often, at the end of their tour of duty, the men simply returned to Europe, abandoning their Asian wives and children.

In contrast to the British colonies, which were often ruled using already-existing political structures and local rulers, the French had a more ambitious agenda. At least initially, they hoped to assimilate their colonial subjects and to make them into genuine Frenchmen. Soon, however, the realities of colonial administration, the difficulties in financing an adequate school system, and resistance from native peoples considerably stymied this aim. Moreover, racial and nationalist prejudices made the French unwilling to allow native peoples in Indochina the same legal rights and financial advantages enjoyed by French colonists and officials.

24-5b The Dutch in Indonesia

The Dutch had been present in Southeast Asia since the sixteenth century, when Dutch explorers had opened the way for the spice trade that had been a great source of Dutch wealth. Like the British in India, the Dutch managed trading posts and spice warehouses through a trading company—the Dutch West India Company—but did not exercise direct rule over the region that is today Indonesia. In contrast to the French, the Dutch were not interested in "civilizing" the native population, whose Islamic faith had been brought to the region centuries earlier by Arab traders. The Dutch carried out little missionary activity and, on the whole, left existing native political and judicial structures and Muslim institutions in place. At no time did the Dutch attempt to influence the mainly Muslim Indonesian population to abandon their faith. Dutch schools for natives aimed primarily to train minor officials to serve in the local colonial bureaucracy.

Between 1830 and 1870, the Dutch West Indies produced huge profits for the Netherlands, but only by exploiting native labor and generating serious local discontent. After about 1870, Dutch trade with the Dutch West Indies declined. In contrast to Vietnam, where French influence may still be discerned a half century after the end of French colonial rule there, Dutch colonial control left few traces in Indonesia.

24-5c Concessions in China

China, the largest and most populous country in Asia, had long been a major cultural influence. By the mid-nineteenth century, however, under the corrupt and weak **Qing** (CHING) **dynasty**, China could not compete against the military and economic might of the European imperialists. China's defeat in the 1840s by the British during the **Opium Wars** revealed its weakness. Subsequently, the Chinese were forced to accept

Indochina Region in Southeast Asia under French colonial rule in the later nineteenth century; today Vietnam, Laos, and Cambodia.

Ho Chi Minh (1890–1969) Vietnamese national leader who in Paris helped found the French Communist Party and later led the struggle for Vietnamese independence.

Qing dynasty Ruling house of China from 1644 to 1912, also known as Manchus.

Opium Wars Conflict between Britain and China from 1839 to 1842 that ended in Chinese defeat.

'Le Voyage Autour du Monde', cover of a box for a game based on 'Around the World in 80 Days' by Jules Verne (1828-1905) (litho), French School, (19th century)/Private Collection/ Archives Charmet/The Bridgeman Art Library

massive imports of opium from British India, enriching British merchants but weakening Chinese society.

Chinese Weakness: The Unequal Treaties

Thus began the era of **unequal treaties**. Western imperialist powers negotiated concessions at treaty ports that assured them favorable trade arrangements and a minimum of Chinese interference. As part of the concessions, the Chinese agreed that the imperialist power could administer its own tax system and legal system in a specific area. The British took over Hong Kong as a colony and had a concession in the major city of Shanghai. The Germans received a concession in the port city of Qingdao (Tsingtao), establishing a beer factory that continues in operation today. The French also gained favored treatment in China. In many areas in China, foreign businessmen could trade without interference or taxation from the Chinese government. Concessions deprived the Chinese state of much-needed taxes, while Westerners—and some well-placed Chinese businessmen—reaped huge profits.

China's political weakness was also apparent in foreign policy. Defeat in the Sino-Japanese War of 1894–1895 forced China to relinquish the island of Formosa (Taiwan) to Japan. Around the same time, with Russian and Japanese power growing in northeast Asia, China lost its influence over Korea. In 1896, China gave in to Russian pressure and allowed the Russians to build a railroad across its Manchurian province to the north and to establish nearby naval bases. By the early twentieth century, foreign influence in the form of concessions, naval bases, and trade privileges had seriously compromised Chinese sovereignty.

Christian Missionaries in China

The first Christian missionaries in China were mainly Catholics such as Matteo Ricci, who died in Beijing in 1610. In the nineteenth century, however, increasing numbers of Protestant missionaries came to the "Middle Kingdom." Christian missionaries set up schools and health clinics throughout China, winning a significant number of converts. For ambitious Chinese parents, missionary schools provided some education for daughters and, for sons, a means to a higher education, usually abroad. Following this path, the future nationalist leader **Sun Yatsen** received a Christian education and then left China to attend medical school in Hawaii.

Despite the missionaries' sincere desire to educate and help the Chinese people, their teachings inevitably came into conflict with Chinese customs. For example, Christians regarded the ancestor worship so important for Chinese culture as a form of idolatry. Christian missionaries also encouraged not only education for females but an end to female infanticide and the traditional practice of binding young girls' feet so they would be the desirable tiny size in adulthood. Foreign missionaries worked with their Chinese pupils and converts to translate Western ideas into Chinese, but often without

unequal treaties Treaties favorable to Western powers (and Japan) extorted by force or threat from China during the nineteenth and early twentieth centuries.

Sun Yatsen (1866–1925) Chinese physician and political leader who aimed to transform China with patriotic, democratic, and economically progressive reforms.

much understanding of the implications of Western practices within Chinese society. Many Chinese thus feared and resented the spread of Christianity. In 1870, in Tianjin, these feelings exploded into attacks on foreigners. The so-called Tianjin Massacre did not, however, reduce missionary activity in China.

The Boxer Rebellion   By the late nineteenth century, this enormous cultural and economic influence of foreigners sparked a strong and violent reaction from Chinese patriots, the **Boxer Rebellion**. The Boxers were a group of young Chinese men who combined training in martial arts with a burning desire to free China from humiliating foreign domination. In 1900 the Boxers attacked foreign missionaries, businessmen, diplomats, Chinese converts to Christianity, and generally all forms of foreign influence. Their violence alarmed Westerners, and the imperialist powers reacted swiftly to put down the rebellion. Thousands of German, French, American, British, Japanese, and Russian troops rushed to Beijing, where they ended a siege of foreign embassies. Order was restored, but the prestige of the Qing dynasty was fatally weakened. Young Chinese intellectuals increasingly called for limitations on foreign influences and the restoration of Chinese sovereignty throughout the entire territory of China.

Boxer Rebellion Antiforeign revolt in China in 1898–1900.

Matthew Perry (1794–1858) American naval officer who in 1854 persuaded the Japanese government to allow American trade with previously closed-off Japan.

Meiji Restoration Reform of Japanese politics and economy under Emperor Meiji (r. 1867–1912).

Russo-Japanese War Conflict in 1904–1905 that began with a Japanese surprise attack on a Russian naval base and ended in Russian defeat.

Russian Revolution of 1905 Insurrection in Russia set off by military defeats in the Russo-Japanese War that forced political concessions from Tsar Nicholas II.

Tsar Nicholas II (r. 1894–1918) Russian emperor and cousin by marriage of Kaiser William II, killed by the Bolsheviks in 1918, after the Russian Revolution.

24-5d The Westernization of Japan

Japan forms an exception to many generalizations about late-nineteenth-century imperialism. The Japanese were successful in using Western models to their own advantage and, in the end, against the Western powers themselves. For the previous two centuries, foreign entry into Japan had been limited to two small trading posts. Then, in 1853, the American commodore **Matthew Perry** arrived in Tokyo harbor and, after months of negotiation, forced the Japanese to open up to foreign trade in 1854.

The Meiji Restoration   The Japanese were shocked by the foreigners' command of new and unfamiliar technology, in particular modern firearms. Noting foreign influence in neighboring China, Japanese elites vowed not to allow their own country to be cowed by Western influences. Rather than falling under foreign rule, however, the Japanese under a new emperor known as Meiji (MAY-jee) ("the enlightened one") carried out their own radical administrative, military, and economic reforms. By the end of the century, Japan was rapidly industrializing. Railroads connected the most important Japanese cities, and the Japanese army had been reconstituted along Prussian lines. The success of the **Meiji Restoration** may be seen in the Japanese defeat of China in the Sino-Japanese War.

Japanese Expansion   Japanese influence in Korea led inevitably to frictions with Russia, which was also seeking to expand its power in East Asia. Beginning in the 1890s, construction of the Trans-Siberian Railroad, linking Moscow and the Pacific Ocean, was one means by which Russia promoted its influence on the Pacific coast as well as settlement of Siberia. The railroad's terminus at Vladivostok was just a few hundred miles from Japan and even closer to Korea. Russia obtained the right to build the railroad directly across the northeastern Chinese province of Manchuria, to Japan's great consternation. The Chinese also allowed the Russians to build a naval base on Chinese territory at Port Arthur (now Lüshun), to the south of Korea, which Japan could only see as a direct threat. Fearing further Russian inroads into China and Korea, in 1904 Japan carried out a surprise attack on the Russian base at Port Arthur.

The **Russo-Japanese War** that ensued turned out to be an international and domestic disaster for Russia. To the shock of not only Russians, but all Europeans, the Japanese prevailed on the seas—destroying two separate Russian fleets—and on land. For the first time in centuries, an Asian country had defeated a European power. The success of Japan's modernization was evident in its army trained on the Prussian model and its navy of Western-style warships. American President Theodore Roosevelt helped negotiate a peace between Japan and Russia, which ended the war in 1905. The Japanese used their victory to extend their power in the region, and in 1910 they formally annexed Korea.

In Russia, the war caused a crisis, the **Russian Revolution of 1905**. When marchers who had peacefully gathered outside the Winter Palace in St. Petersburg were brutally dispersed, causing dozens of deaths, the country exploded into violent protest and strikes. **Tsar Nicholas II** seemed completely out of touch—unable to influence events and unwilling to compromise with widespread demands for political reform. General strikes that paralyzed the country in October forced him to reduce censorship,

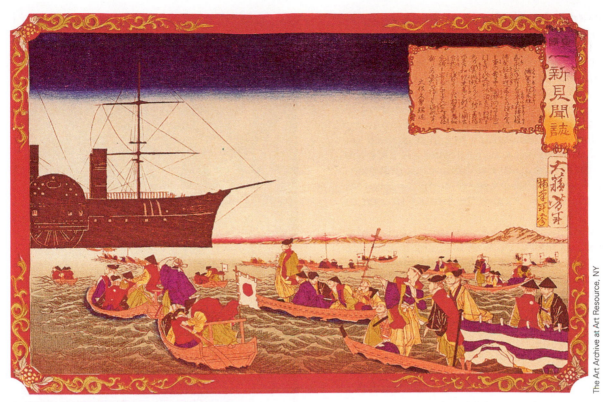

The Art Archive at Art Resource, NY

American "Black Ships" in Tokyo Harbor

In this Japanese print of the Meiji period (ca. 1860), traditionally dressed samurai set out in boats to confront Commodore Matthew Perry's looming "black ships" ("black" because of their use of coal for fuel). By signing a treaty in 1854 opening Japan to foreign trade, the Japanese reversed centuries of isolation and began a rapid process of industrialization and Westernization in their country.

≫ *How does this image contrast the Western ship and Japanese boats?*

increase religious freedom, and grant a parliament, the Duma. While limited in its powers, the Duma provided a place for political debate and, arguably, could have been the first step toward a more democratic government in Russia.

24-6 Consequences and Critics

≫ **What impact did imperialism have on the global economy and European culture?**

≫ **Who opposed imperialism in Europe and elsewhere, and why?**

Even as the new imperialism extended European influence throughout the world, it also called forth resistance and condemnation. Its benefits were greatly unequal, with Western powers profiting far more than colonized regions. Ironically, the Western ideals of liberty and democracy that the imperial powers boasted they were bringing to the unenlightened peoples of the world inspired anticolonial resistance movements among African and Asian intellectuals. But critics in Europe, too, argued that imperialism was a capitalist sham, an attempt to divert attention from injustice and inequality at home. In both negative and positive ways, imperialism had a profound effect on European politics and culture.

24-6a A Global Economy

In the late nineteenth century, European colonial empires did much to link up the world and to create a single global economy. But the linkage was uneven. Raw materials like cotton flowed from the colonies to Europe, and European goods like cloth were purchased by the colonies. British textiles were exported to Africa and India. The Indian railways used rails and locomotives that were for the most part imported from England. Textiles from Russia found a market in Central and East Asia. Because the European colonizers had little interest in developing colonial industry, the colonies became economically dependent on European industry. In some cases, most notably India, colonies deindustrialized. So as profits flowed to Europe, wages and living standards remained very low in nearly all colonial areas.

Trade Around the Globe In addition, colonial economies were reshaped to meet the needs and desires of Western imperialist powers. Tea, sugar, and chocolate had become staples in the European diet; in this era even Russian peasants began to drink tea daily. The plantations that produced these commodities expanded, and the economies of entire colonies and tropical nations were built around a single export. Bananas, which began to appear on tables in North America and Europe, are only the most prominent example. The companies that managed these commodities were Western; the laborers were native peoples. Again, the profits flowed to Europe.

Guano from Peru and nitrites from Chile enriched the fields of European farmers. Rubber for tires, belts, and gaskets, indispensable for modern machinery, had to be extracted from trees that grew only in tropical regions such as Malaya (a British colony, now Malaysia), Indochina, and the Belgian Congo. Palm oil, another tropical commodity, was used in the manufacture of soap—a product then exported back to the colonies. Cinchona trees were cultivated to provide the quinine on which the health of Europeans in tropical regions depended. Copper was imported from mines in the Belgian Congo; tin came from Malaya. Huge amounts of Indian cotton were imported to Britain, then transformed into cloth in British mills. Diamonds and gold from South African mines adorned wealthy individuals around the world.

New inventions and technological innovations facilitated global exchange. Starting in the late 1870s, for example, refrigerated steamships carried frozen meat from the United States, Argentina, and even New Zealand to the ports of Europe, pushing out less efficient meat producers. But on the whole, European economies were not challenged by colonial economies. Colonial markets were relatively small compared to European markets, and Europeans sold far more manufactured goods to each other and in the Americas than they did to their colonies. Europeans did invest in colonies, however. Global links were economic; they were only partly the result of direct colonial rule.

CONNECTIONS: At least since the sixteenth century, when precious metals mined in the Americas made their way via Europe to East Asia so that Europeans could purchase spices, silk, and other luxuries, it has been appropriate to speak of a single global "web" of interlocking economic interests. The period of imperialism further developed this web toward something we can fairly call "globalization." In the early twentieth century, many economists and cultural figures hoped that the increasing linkage between countries, both cultural and economic, would prevent war. After the catastrophies of the two world wars, global trade

THE FORMULA OF BRITISH CONQUEST

PEARS' SOAP IN THE SOUDAN.

"Even if our invasion of the Soudan has done nothing else it has at any rate left the Arab something to puzzle his fuzzy head over, for the legend **PEARS' SOAP IS THE BEST,** inscribed in hugk white characters on the rock which marks the farthest point of our advance towards Berber, will tax all the wits of the Dervishes of the Desert to translate."—Phil Robinson, War Correspondent (in the Soudan) of the Daily Telegraph in London, 1884.

Advertisement for Pears' Soap

Pears' soap advertisements like this one emphasized the "civilizing mission" of British imperialism. Bringing order, science, and hygiene to supposedly backward world regions was one of the prime justifications of imperialist rule.

》 *Why would a British company use an image like this one to sell its product?*

》 *What surprises you about this image?*

》 *What elements of this ad would we now find offensive, and why?*

helped make Germany and Japan rich and capable of withstanding communism. At the end of the twentieth century, globalization facilitated business around the world and enabled American consumers to purchase quality products at rock-bottom prices. More recently, however, the snake in this free market paradise has become more evident: Globalization also means that less efficient industries go bankrupt when confronted by low-cost rivals abroad. Open borders may also provide access for terrorists. In many countries, the early twenty-first century has witnessed a turn toward nationalism and against global trade (see Section 30-3 Europe and Globalization). The end of free trade and open societies? Stay tuned.

24-6b Indigenous Resistance

As the Sepoy Rebellion and the Boxer Rebellion indicate, colonized peoples in Asia did not simply accept European colonial domination. Similarly, in the Battle of **Omdurman**, Africans fought against European colonizers. But native troops, armed with traditional weapons, were massacred there by British troops using machine guns. European technological superiority meant that native peoples needed to seek other means of resistance.

Forms of Resistance After the establishment of European colonies, the colonized had to struggle for their rights within the existing colonial system. Some resistance assumed a heroic public form, such as Gandhi's organizing of Indian residents in South Africa to demand their rights starting in the 1890s. Other resistance was more subtle. Indigenous peoples might avoid carrying out the orders of colonial administrators, fail to pay colonial taxes, or shun European cultural and educational institutions. Some resisters insisted on wearing native clothing, despite imports from Europe, or on speaking native languages, despite schools that taught English or French.

The education that colonized peoples received at colonial schools provided them with the most effective weapon of resistance. Learning of European constitutional government and political rights, individuals like Gandhi came to challenge the racial hierarchies evident in the colonies. Pointing out the contradictions of a system that promised civilization and justice but refused equal rights to native peoples, resistance leaders exposed the hypocrisy of imperialism and demanded rights for themselves and their peoples. To the European imperialists they quoted European thinkers and ideals such as liberty, democracy, and individual rights. They pointed to the vast contrast between the luxury in which colonial officials lived and the impoverishment of natives.

Before 1914, however, resistance to imperialism was only beginning to be organized. In most African and Asian colonies, European administrators continued to dominate, at least officially. Away from cities and European settlements, however, life generally continued along traditional lines. At the same time, increasing numbers of educated Asians and Africans were formulating ways of resisting European dominance. Full-fledged independence movements would emerge after World War I.

24-6c Imperialism and European Culture

Though the dominators, not the dominated, Europeans were affected by the lands they ruled. Literature, music, visual arts, architecture, and even advertising took up themes and images of imperialism. Popular novels praised the bravery of the colonists while hinting at forbidden romantic attachments.

Exoticism in Art, Music, and Literature Painters produced scenes of entrancing foreign places, often featuring ruins, exotic vegetation, and—of course—beautiful native women. In music, the most "imperial opera," *Aïda* (ah-IEE-dah), by Giuseppe Verdi, was commissioned specifically for the opening of the Suez Canal in 1869. The story hinges on a beautiful Ethiopian slave, Aïda, and her love for an Egyptian general in the era of the pharaohs. The opera was a hit: Apparently few minded the absurdity of a made-up story about ancient Africans sung in Italian for the benefit of European audiences.

Literature of this period also reflects imperialist themes. Kipling's many stories and novels about life in British India were bestsellers of the day. The poet Alfred, Lord Tennyson celebrated the empire in verses such as "The Fleet" (1885) and "On the Jubilee of Queen Victoria" (1887). In France, **Pierre Loti** published dozens of novels that appealed to the European fascination with the peoples and customs of the colonies. Set in exotic regions, they nearly always involve a romance between a strong European man and a beautiful non-European woman. The plots are unrealistic, but Loti's novels were very popular, and in 1891 he was elected to the **French Academy**, the prestigious scholarly and literary society, at the unprecedented young age of forty-one.

International Exhibitions International exhibitions in Paris in 1867 and 1900 also reflect European fascination with the colonies. Here Parisians and visitors could "experience" an African village, listen to Tunisian musicians, or wander through a reproduction of a Cairo street. These exhibitions aimed both to educate the populace about the colonies and to promote the colonial enterprise. Ethnographic museums served similar purposes. In Paris at the Museum of the Colonies, and in museums in Moscow and St. Petersburg, colonial peoples themselves were put on display. The purpose was always to demonstrate the "savage" ways of "the uncivilized" and to reassure Europeans of their superiority.

The interests of imperialism were evident in the visual arts as well. In

---

Omdurman Battle in 1898 in present-day Sudan, in which thousands of African warriors were massacred by a British army using machine guns.

Pierre Loti (1850–1923) French writer who authored novels set in exotic climes and featuring romances between a European man and a non-European woman.

French Academy French cultural institution established in 1635 whose members make judgments on the proper use of the French language.

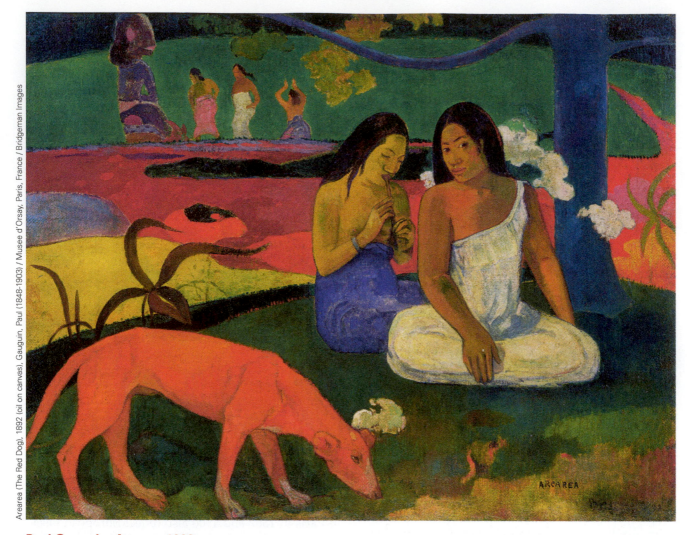

Arearea (The Red Dog), 1892 (oil on canvas), Gauguin, Paul (1848-1903) / Musée d'Orsay, Paris, France / Bridgeman Images

Paul Gauguin, *Arearea*, 1892

Many of Paul Gauguin's paintings from Tahiti, like *Arearea*, depict beautiful Tahitian women in an exotic tropical landscape. Gauguin's own biography—abandoning a respectable middle-class profession and leaving his family to pursue pleasure and painting in the South Seas—reflects the lure colonial regions had for nineteenth-century Europeans.

» *How does Gauguin convey exoticism in this image through his style and subject matter?*

Russia the painter Vereshchagin depicted the land and peoples of Russia's newly conquered territory in Central Asia. After French stockbroker **Paul Gauguin** (go-GAHN) abandoned his family and went to live in Tahiti, he painted Tahitians in their own environment. Popular postcards and prints familiarized Europeans with far-off colonies and spurred interest in the colonial endeavor. Images in advertising, too, drew on imperialist themes. In Britain, advertisements extolled Pears Soap as one of the benefits that Britons could bring to Africa and Asia.

Paul Gauguin (1848–1903) French painter who painted Tahitian life and culture.

John A. Hobson (1858–1940) English economist and influential critic of imperialism.

24-6d Capitalism and Imperialism

The heyday of imperialism lasted barely two decades, ending with the Boer War. While no crisis of European imperialism was immediately obvious in the first decade of the twentieth century, the arguments of the anti-imperialists were already being developed. The first critiques concentrated on its cruelty toward subject populations. Later, these criticisms were overshadowed by Marxist critics who portrayed imperialism as part of a decaying capitalist world order.

Hobson's Imperialism In 1902, **John A. Hobson** argued in *Imperialism: A Study* that Britain's imperial expansion was a short-term attempt to avoid social conflict. British workers at first benefited from the cheap produce and labor of the colonies, but Hobson predicted that soon their position would be undermined by this vast pool of cheap labor. As a liberal, Hobson saw a major cause for imperialism in the search for markets and investment opportunities abroad. For him, imperialism was both hypocritical and dangerous. Imperialists falsely claimed to be bringing higher culture to subject peoples, and Britain's nondemocratic rule over the colonies posed a threat to democracy at home. By placing colonial peoples at the very bottom of the social hierarchy, Hobson claimed, imperialism falsely elevated the status of England's working class.

Lenin Criticizes Imperialism Some of Hobson's arguments were developed further some years later by the Russian Marxist **Vladimir Ilyich Lenin**. Lenin's *Imperialism: The Highest Stage of Capitalism* (1916) portrayed imperialism as a symptom of a larger ill: Capitalism. Thus, when capitalism would be overthrown by socialism, imperialism would also be destroyed. Following Karl Marx, Lenin pointed out that since the early years of industrialization, profit levels had declined steadily. Capitalists were thus forced to seek new and more lucrative investment opportunities in the colonies. Although in retrospect it is evident that colonial markets and investment were of secondary importance for capitalism even in the heyday of imperialism, Lenin's exposure of imperialism as an economic, political, and moral dead end seemed convincing to many contemporary Europeans.

Vladimir Ilyich Lenin (1870–1924) Russian Marxist revolutionary and leader of the Bolsheviks.

CHAPTER Review

Summary

» In the period 1870 to 1914, Western countries, especially European ones, established colonial rule over huge parts of the globe.

» Africa was the continent most affected by this "new imperialism."

» Russia, France, and Germany established new colonial rule in Asia; Dutch and British rule continued in previously established colonies.

» Among the reasons for the new imperialism were technological advances, national prestige, and economic motives.

» The new imperialism went hand-in-hand with racism, the idea that European peoples and their descendants were biologically superior to Asian, African, and Amerindian peoples.

» The new imperialism's effects were contradictory and controversial, from the exploitation of native peoples to the spread of education and the use of European languages.

Chronology

1836–1846	Boers take Great Trek north away from English colonists in southern Africa [Africa]
1839–1842	British defeat the Chinese in the Opium Wars [Asia]
1853–1854	United States forces Japan to open to foreign trade [Asia]
1857–1858	British put down Sepoy Rebellion in India [Asia]

1865	Tashkent falls to the Russians [Asia]
1867	French annex Cochinchina (southern Indochina) [Asia] Emperor Meiji comes to the throne in Japan [Asia]
1869	Suez Canal opens in Egypt [Middle East]
1877	Queen Victoria becomes empress of India [Asia]
1882	British occupy Egypt [Middle East]
1884–1886	Germany establishes African colonies [Africa]
1885	Indian National Congress is founded [Asia] Congo Free State is established [Africa]
1887	Russia completes conquest of Turkestan (Central Asia) [Asia]
1894–1895	Japanese annex Formosa (Taiwan) [Asia]
1898	Spanish-American War begins [Americas, Asia]
1898–1946	United States rule over the Philippines [Americas, Asia]
1899–1902	British defeat Boers in the Boer War [Africa]
1900	Foreign powers crush Boxer Rebellion in China [Asia] Hawaii becomes a U.S. territory [Americas]
1902	Hobson publishes *Imperialism* [Europe]
1904	Japanese attack on Russian naval base at Port Arthur [Asia, Europe]
1905–1907	Herero Revolt takes place in German Southwest Africa [Africa]
1908	Leopold II turns over the Congo Free State to Belgium [Africa]
1910	Union of South Africa is established [Africa] Mexican Revolution begins [Americas]
1912	South African Native National Congress is established [Africa] Italy invades Libya [Africa]
1916	Lenin publishes *Imperialism, the Highest Stage of Capitalism* [Europe]

Critical Thinking Questions

Take time to pull together all the important information from the chapter by answering the following questions:

Motives and Methods of the New Imperialism

» How important were economic considerations among the causes of the new imperialism?

» What part did racism play in the new imperialism? Were all imperialists racists?

The Scramble for Africa

» What factors explain the quick penetration by European powers of the African continent in this period? Why didn't this happen earlier?

» Where were the colonial holdings of different countries (Britain, France, Belgium, Germany, Portugal) located? Which of these holdings were acquired in this period?

The British Raj in India

» How did India differ from other British colonies? Why was it called "the jewel in the crown"?

» What were the stages of British rule in India? What attitudes changed from the late eighteenth to early twentieth century?

Imperialism and the Muslim World

» Why might Muslims of the Ottoman Empire have been concerned about European expansion in this period?

» What were some of the most important effects of Russian expansion in Central Asia?

The Far East

» How did French and Dutch colonial rule differ from that of the British in India?

» In what ways was Japan "an exception to many generalizations about imperialism"?

Consequences and Critics

» How did Hobson's and Lenin's critiques of imperialism differ? How influential were their ideas at the time?

» What did Ho Chi Minh, Sun Yatsen, and Mohandas Gandhi have in common?

MINDTAP
From Cengage

MindTap® is a fully online personalized learning experience built upon Cengage Learning content. MindTap® combines student learning tools—readings, multimedia, activities, and assessments—into a singular Learning Path that guides students through the course and helps students develop the critical thinking, analysis, and communication skills that are essential to academic and professional success.

Chapter Outline

As you read, consider the following questions:

❭ What were the main causes, both long- and short-term, of World War I?

❭ Why was the actual war very different from what most Europeans expected? How did World War I changed politics, economy, and everyday life?

❭ What were the main causes of the Russian revolutions of 1917?

❭ Why did the Germans finally lose the war?

❭ Why do some historians argue that World War I ended the European era in world history? Do you agree?

USING THE TECHNOLOGIES developed during the second Industrial Revolution, World War I devoured the financial and human resources of Europe (see Map 25.1). To manage the Great War, as it was called at the time, governments harnessed civilian populations as never before. State intervention in the economy and society grew considerably during the war and had a major impact on everyday life. State propaganda ceaselessly reminded citizens why they needed to continue the fight. Throughout Europe—and the world—women took up jobs vacated by men sent to the trenches.

In August 1914, many Europeans welcomed war. For some, the chance for heroism and glory appeared attractive. Nationalists saw the war as a chance to enhance the prestige and strength of their nation-state or even to achieve a long-desired independence. Some radicals—such as V. I. Lenin—saw the war as an opportunity to overthrow the old order through socialist revolution.

Europe at war's end looked very different from anyone's expectation in 1914. The horrific and senseless massacres of trench warfare convinced many Europeans that nothing could ever justify war again. Millions and millions of soldiers and civilians had died, and an influenza epidemic killed millions more. Poverty and political unrest, as well as the Bolshevik Revolution in Russia, threatened to further destabilize the entire continent. Nothing was as it had been. The safe, secure world of aristocratic and middle-class Europeans was gone forever. But if the world was more dangerous, it also had the potential, at least, to be more democratic.

"Women of Britain Say - Go!," recruitment poster, 1915 (litho), Kealey, E.P. (20th century) / Private Collection / Photo © Bonhams, London, UK / Bridgeman Images

World War I Propaganda Poster

This poster is just one example of the propaganda that all warring powers used during World War I. Here it is suggested that any young man not going off to war would be betraying not just his fatherland but also the women in his life—mother, sisters, wife. The women here appear sad but stoic, accepting the sacrifice of their sons and brothers for the war effort.

25-1 A New Century, 1900–1914

» In the early years of the twentieth century, what factors made a general European war likely? Did Europeans expect a major war?

» How did nationalism help cause World War I?

By 1900, three generations had passed since most Europeans had personally experienced war. The balance of power set down at the Congress of Vienna, though weakened by the unification of Germany and Italy, seemed to be effective in keeping the peace. But relations between the Great Powers were strained, in particular by the huge growth of German science and industry and the aggressive style of the German Kaiser William II. Wars in the Balkan Peninsula threatened to draw Russia into local conflicts.

Advances in technology meant that any new war would be far more deadly—and far more expensive—than any previous war. Optimists hoped that the threat of the enormous killing power of modern weaponry would make states find peaceful solutions. The cost of this weaponry was another factor that made many think a future war could not last long—no state could afford it. Others pointed to the system of alliances as a factor that would prevent war: every major power knew it would be very difficult to localize a conflict, and even a small outbreak threatened a continent-wide conflagration. Surely the great danger of a murderous high-tech war would cause statesmen to step back from the brink?

25-1a An Unbalanced Balance of Power

As the twentieth century began, the balance of power established at the Congress of Vienna almost a century earlier remained shakily in place. France, Austria (since 1867 Austria-Hungary), Britain, and Russia continued to play important roles on the European continent. After 1871, however, following Germany's victory in the Franco-Prussian War, the balance was increasingly threatened by the growing economic and military might of the Prussian-dominated German Empire.

The German Threat Germany, with a population of nearly 70 million and an industrial output rivaling Great Britain's and exceeding that of France, sought to expand its economic, political, and cultural power. A latecomer to imperial ambitions, it seized colonies in Africa after the Berlin Conference

Kaiser William II
(r. 1890–1918) Prussian king and German Kaiser, noted for his impetuous and unsteady character.

in 1884. Ruled since 1890 by the neurotic and belligerent **Kaiser William II**, Germany directly threatened the European status quo. The newly independent states of Italy, Romania, Serbia, and Bulgaria also complicated the international scene. Major powers scrambled to form new alliances that would retain the balance of power under greatly changed circumstances.

The French felt most threatened by a powerful Germany. Since the end of the Thirty Years' War in 1648, France's foreign policy had aimed to keep the Habsburgs and other German states to the east divided and weak. But Otto von Bismarck had successfully isolated Austria and then united Germany under Prussian leadership. Germany's victory over France in 1871 had gained it Alsace-Lorraine and its king the title of Emperor. Avenging this national humiliation remained a burning issue in French politics. With their low birthrate, moderate industrial growth, and underdeveloped railroad network, the French could not hope to take on the German army alone: they needed an ally.

The Franco-Russian Military Alliance The obvious candidate was Russia, whose large population, enormous territory, and long border with Germany offset its technological and economic backwardness. Although relations between Russia and Germany had traditionally been friendly, Russia was disturbed by Germany's growing industrial and military power. France courted Russia, and in 1894 the two signed a military alliance in which each promised to come to the other's aid if attacked by Germany. Thus the most conservative major power in Europe, Russia, joined forces with its ideological opposite, republican France. Ideology mattered less than geopolitics and the menace of a common foe.

The Triple Alliance This agreement, however, heightened the prospect of Germany's worst strategic nightmare: a two-front war. To counter this threat, Germany sought alliances with Austria-Hungary and Italy, both second-rate military powers. Austria-Hungary was continuously embroiled in domestic crises between the Austrian and Hungarian halves of the empire, and in Austria proper there were clashes over the use of local languages, such as Czech, in schools and administration. Austria-Hungary was also concerned about the pro-Russian regimes in Serbia and Bulgaria, young states in the Balkans, and thus welcomed German military support against these Slavic nations.

The junior member in this alliance, Italy, had its own troubles trying to hold together the mainly rural and impoverished south with the wealthier and industrialized north. In 1896, eager to seize an African colony for itself, Italy had been humiliatingly defeated by Ethiopia. The military pact Germany signed with

Map 25.1 **Europe in World War I, 1914–1918** World War I divided Europe into two warring camps. Only the edges of the continent—Ireland, Scandinavia, and the Iberian Peninsula—were not directly affected.

1. What differences can you see on this map between the war's progress on the eastern and western fronts?
2. Where was the German army most successful?
3. What alliances and strategic interests caused Europe to divide up in this way?
4. Which countries did not choose sides immediately in this conflict? Why not?

Austria-Hungary and then, in 1882, with Italy was known as the **Triple Alliance**.

Great Britain's Diplomacy The wild card in international politics was Britain. Traditionally wary of continental entanglements, the British refused to join any military alliance. But the rapid growth of German industrial and military strength deeply disturbed British leaders. From the time of the Napoleonic Wars, British policy had aimed to prevent the domination of the European continent by any one power. Now

Germany seemed ready to do just that. And Britain was directly threatened by Germany's aggressive program of naval construction started in 1907.

Germany's belligerent behavior in international affairs had already alienated British public opinion as well as its Foreign Office, especially Germany's seizure of colonies in Africa. Although Britain held back from a formal alliance, it

> **Triple Alliance** Military alliance concluded in 1882 by Germany, Austria-Hungary, and Italy.

reached a friendly understanding, known as the **Entente Cordiale**, with France in 1904. It concluded a similar agreement with Russia in 1907. Now the **Triple Entente** balanced the Triple Alliance, but instead of ensuring general peace, the new alliance system seemed headed for war. In particular, the refusal of Britain to clearly commit to military intervention in case of an attack on France allowed the Germans to think that perhaps the English would remain aloof from a European war.

The Schlieffen Plan To prepare for the two-front war it feared, in the early twentieth century the German General Staff adopted the **Schlieffen (SHLEEF-en) Plan**, named for the general who developed it and spent his life tinkering with its details. In case of war, German armies were to strike quickly and decisively against the French before wheeling to the east and taking on the Russians. Thus, Germany could fight each enemy separately rather than dividing its forces between the two fronts. To knock out the French army, the Germans would march through Belgium toward the North Sea, bypassing the French border fortresses, then swing around toward Paris. For the plan to work—for hundreds of thousands of troops to move into position to threaten Paris—speed was of crucial importance. The Germans also counted on Belgium's cooperation or at least hoped that Britain would not object to a violation of Belgian neutrality, guaranteed by Britain and the other major powers at the time Belgium won independence in 1831. In 1914, this hope proved to be a fatal miscalculation.

25-1b Rivalries

The alliance system seemed to stabilize the strains in international relations caused by national pride and imperial rivalries. For the French, regaining Alsace-Lorraine—historically divided since Charlemagne between France and Germany—was a matter of pride. For Russia, there was a worry that the Ottoman weakness would allow another power to seize control over the Bosporus and Dardanelles Straits, thereby cutting off Russian access to the Mediterranean Sea. In south and east Africa,

Entente Cordiale Set of agreements signed between France and Great Britain in 1904 pledging cooperation, but not a formal military alliance.

Triple Entente Agreement signed in 1907 by Russia, France, and Great Britain pledging closer relations.

Schlieffen Plan German war plan of the early twentieth century that aimed to avoid a two-front war by a quick and massive attack first on France, then on Russia.

Pan-Slavism Movement from later nineteenth century emphasizing Russia's kinship with other Slavic and Orthodox nations, especially those under Ottoman and Habsburg rule.

German and British interests came into direct conflict. And the British had not forgotten how Kaiser William II had publicly expressed his support for the anti-British Boers of South Africa.

Empires and Nationalism National identity in Britain was connected closely with imperial prestige. In central and eastern Europe, however, nationalism was directed *against* existing empires—both Russia and Austria-Hungary. In the Russian Empire, Poles and Finns sought concessions or even independence. In particular, Poles aspired to the resurrection of Poland, which had lost its independence in the late eighteenth century. In Austria-Hungary, Romanians, Serbs, Czechs, and Italians hoped to gain broader cultural and political rights. Young nation-states in the region, such as Romania, Serbia, and Bulgaria, encouraged such nationalist agendas in Austria-Hungary. Russia considered itself the protector of the ethnically Slavic and religiously Orthodox peoples in the Balkans, including Bulgarians, Montenegrins, and Serbs. Russian public opinion strongly supported such **Pan-Slav** sentiments.

Germany Versus Russia European rivalries were not only political: they were also economic. Since 1870, both Germany and Russia had experienced very significant industrial growth, including the building of railroads that often served strategic aims. The rapid growth of German manufacturing presented French and British firms with a frighteningly efficient competitor, while modern industry in Moscow, St. Petersburg, Warsaw, and other cities of the Russian empire had the potential to threaten Germany directly. Thus, Germans felt great relief at the poor showing of the Russian army and navy in the Russo-Japanese War of 1904–1905. When the Revolution of 1905 shook the political order in Russia to its foundations, Germans mistakenly concluded that it would take Russia at least a decade to recover. Then, when the Russian economy quickly boomed again and significantly increased military spending, German leaders became alarmed.

Arms Manufacture Of Europe's many industries, arms manufacturing was among the most significant, employing thousands of workers and producing large profits. National and imperial rivalries generated an arms race that was good business for these manufacturers, which successfully lobbied their governments against any reductions in military budgets. Advancing technologies meant that a country's weaponry had to be replaced quickly. Among the military innovations of the years before 1914 were the zeppelin airship, airplanes, the machine gun, poison gas (though European powers had signed an agreement promising not to use it), and enormous artillery pieces that could destroy the most massive fortifications.

Map 25.2 **The Balkans Before World War I** The two Balkan Wars of 1912 and 1913 both weakened the Ottoman Empire and revealed hostilities among the young Balkan states. Bulgaria's territorial loss to Serbia was one reason Bulgaria sided with Germany and Austria during World War I.

1. How much of the Ottoman Empire was left in Europe in 1914? Why might this motivate the Ottoman Empire to enter the war against the Allies?

2. The map shows areas outside Serbia and Romania where many Serbs and Romanians lived. Why would this become an important factor during and after World War I?

25-1c Nationalism in the Balkans

By the end of the nineteenth century, formerly Ottoman territories on the Balkan Peninsula were now independent states: Romania, Serbia, Bulgaria, Greece, Montenegro, and Albania. Bosnia-Herzegovina, occupied by Austria-Hungary since 1878, was formally annexed to Austria in 1908 (see Map 25.2). The Russians were furious, but their army, much

weakened following defeat by Japan, was unable to help their Slavic brethren. Both Russians and Balkan Slavs—especially Serbs—were now convinced that Austria-Hungary harbored aggressive intentions. Each of the states in the Balkans had unclear frontiers with its neighbors and significant numbers of national minorities inside its borders. All were united, however, in hatred for the Ottoman Empire. Religious loyalties added to the tensions. Except for Albania, which had large numbers of Roman Catholics and Muslims, the people of the Balkans were mainly Eastern Orthodox, whereas the Ottomans were Muslims. During the First Balkan War of 1912, the Balkan League of Serbia, Montenegro, Greece, and Bulgaria attacked the Ottoman territories of Kosovo and Macedonia and nearly swept the Ottoman army from Europe. Austria-Hungary, which had significant interests in the Balkans, prepared for war until the threat of Russian intervention caused it to back down.

But the Balkan League could not hold together for long. The large territorial gains by Bulgaria excited the anger and resentment of its neighbors. In 1913, the Second Balkan War broke out when Serbia, Greece, Romania, and Montenegro banded together and attacked Bulgaria. When the Bulgarian armies had already been severely weakened, Ottoman forces crossed the border to take back some of the territory lost in 1912. The end result of the two **Balkan Wars** was a weaker Bulgaria, a stronger Serbia, and anger in Austria-Hungary over growing Serbian power, which was promoted by Russia. The 1913 peace established in the Balkans rested on shaky foundations.

25-2 The Unexpected War, 1914

» **How did the reality of war differ from expectations?**

» **Why, and how, did Europe's conflict engage the entire world?**

On June 28, 1914, a young Serbian nationalist named Gavrilo Princip shot and killed the heir to the Austro-Hungarian throne, Archduke Francis Ferdinand (see Profiles in Change: Gavrilo Princip Decides to Assassinate Archduke Francis Ferdinand). The archduke had not been popular, and at first little notice was taken of the assassination. Foreign ministers and other dignitaries continued their vacations, not anticipating a major crisis. Only some weeks later, when Austria-Hungary presented harsh demands to the Serbian

Balkan Wars Two wars, in 1912 and 1913, among countries of the Balkan Peninsula, the first ending with defeat for the Ottoman Empire, the second with defeat for Bulgaria.

Gavrilo Princip Decides to Assassinate Archduke Francis Ferdinand

Sarajevo, Assassination of Archduke Franz Ferdinand, heir to Austrian throne, and his wife, by Achille Beltrame, illustration, Illustrator Achille Beltrame (1871–1945), from La Domenica del Corriere, 5th July 1914, Beltrame, Achille (1871–1945) / De Agostini Picture Library / A. Dagli Orti / Bridgeman Images

Gavrilo Princip Assassinates the Archduke Francis Ferdinand

The June 1914 assassination of the Habsburg heir to the throne, Archduke Francis Ferdinand, shocked Europe. We see here the assassination as imagined for an illustrated magazine – the kind of image that hundreds of thousands saw weekly at this time.

❯❯ *How does the illustrator show that the assassination occurred in Sarajevo (a largely Muslim city)?*

❯❯ *What elements here appear more emotional than realistic? Why would the artist chose to depict this scene this way?*

Gavrilo Princip was born into a Bosnian Serb family in the summer of 1894. His family was of a modest peasant background, supplementing the meager harvest from their small plot of land by working at various odd jobs. For a time, Gavrilo's father, Petar, served as postman for the Grahovo Valley where the family lived. Petar was an unusual man who never swore or touched liquor. As a young man in the 1870s he had participated in the revolt against the Ottoman Empire that culminated in the occupation of Bosnia-Herzegovina by Austria. Gavrilo's mother, Nana, was a strong, uneducated woman who gave birth to nine children, six of whom died as infants. Indeed, when the baby Gavrilo was born on a hot day in July of 1894, Nana held little hope that the runty child would survive. At the Serbian Orthodox priest's insistence, the baby was christened Gavrilo, after the Archangel Gabriel.

Gavrilo was a small, quiet boy who loved reading and resembled his mother, with her light blue eyes and curly hair. His love for study sometimes led to conflicts within the family; literacy itself was rather new and by no means universal in this region. Despite his father's opposition, nine-year-old Gavrilo was sent to a nearby village school. After a difficult first year, he did well in his studies. For his hard work, he received a prize of a volume of Serbian heroic poetry, which, it was later recalled, he would read to assembled friends and relatives back home. When Gavrilo completed the four-year village school course, his brother Jovo learned that the military school in Sarajevo—at that time under Austrian occupation—was accepting healthy boys for a free course of study. So it was that in August 1907 the village lad Gavrilo found himself in the capital of Bosnia, ready to begin his studies toward a career as a Habsburg officer. His brother Jovo accompanied him, and persuaded Gavrilo that it would be wrong to be trained to serve the enemies of the Serbian people—the Habsburg Empire. So Gavrilo entered not the military school but a merchants' school in Sarajevo, where he spent three years.

government, did European leaders begin to realize the danger of the situation. By then it was already too late: within days, Europe was at war.

Imperial rivalries and military competition among European states had exacerbated international tensions to the point that any compromise seemed like fatal weakness. The complex alliance system, designed to prevent war, instead increased the likelihood that a small, regional conflict would become general. Economic interests such as those of major armament manufacturers backed up the alliance system. Individual

states hoped that war would bring territorial gains, and stateless nationalities like the Poles saw war as a chance to gain their own nation-state.

The causes of the war were multiple, but no one expected it to turn out as it did. Rather than the quick, patriotic war Europeans expected, the war became a drawn-out, murderous international conflict, the first genuine world war in which fighting took place around the globe. Both on the front and at home every element of society was called upon to serve the war effort.

It was at this time that Gavrilo began to come under the influence of Serbian (and Yugoslav) nationalism. All Serbs and other south Slavs (Yugo-Slavs), he came to believe, should live together in one state. The young and sensitive teenager, who also dreamed of becoming a famous Serbian poet, enthusiastically embraced the idea of serving his nation. Like other young Bosnian Serbs of his generation, he looked to Belgrade, the Serbian capital, as the center of his national aspirations. Early in 1912 Gavrilo was expelled from school in Sarajevo because of his participation in demonstrations against the Austrian authorities; he decided to continue his studies in Belgrade. Gavrilo spent nearly two years in Belgrade, the exciting years of the Balkan Wars in which Serbia triumphed, gaining territory that more than doubled the state in size. It was also at this point that he met other young Bosnian Serbs and decided to participate in the assassination of a high Austrian official in Sarajevo.

At first the conspirators planned to assassinate the Austrian governor in Bosnia-Herzegovina, General Oskar Potiorek. But when the conspirators discovered that the heir to the throne, Archduke Francis Ferdinand, would be visiting the Bosnian capital on Vidov Dan (St. Vitus's Day), the anniversary of the Serbian defeat at Kosovo in 1389, they chose the archduke instead as their target. All of the conspirators were young, mostly in their teens. All were committed to the ideal of a Yugoslav state.

The assassination attempt on June 28, 1914, did not, however, go as planned. The first assassin, Nedeljko Čabrinović (neh-DEL-ko cha-BRIN-oh-vich), himself the son of a police agent in the pay of the Austrians, threw a bomb that bounced off the hood of the Archduke's car and exploded, injuring several people but leaving the Archduke unscathed. Gavrilo heard the explosion and thought that the attempt had been successful, but then saw that the Archduke was unhurt. In a fury, Francis Ferdinand rushed to the Sarajevo town hall where he upbraided horrified local officials. He then gave orders to proceed to a local military hospital to visit one of the officers injured in the blast. As they passed through town, his driver took a wrong turn, then stopped to turn around—in front of the astonished Gavrilo Princip. Taking aim, Gavrilo fired several times, killing both Francis Ferdinand and his wife.

Gavrilo and his co-conspirators were found guilty of assassinating Francis Ferdinand and his wife, and several were sentenced to death. As for Gavrilo himself, under Austrian law he could not be executed because on the date of his crime he was not yet twenty years old—his twentieth birthday mere weeks away. He was sentenced to solitary confinement in the dank fortress of Theresienstadt in Bohemia, a punishment that amounted to a death sentence spread out over several years. Questioned by a prison doctor in 1916 Gavrilo explained that he did not regret his action, but felt sorry that he had killed Sophie, Francis Ferdinand's wife. Several times he repeated that he could have had no idea that a world war would result from his action. He insisted that he and his co-conspirators had acted as idealists, not as criminals. The harsh conditions in prison were too much for Gavrilo's frail health; he died on April 28, 1918, not quite twenty-four years of age. Celebrated by Serbian historians as a hero, this young man has also been denounced as a terrorist and a fanatic. As so often in history, both sides are correct.

25-2a The Slide into War

The assassination of the heir to the Habsburg throne did not immediately appear to threaten European peace. However, in the next weeks the harsh demands of Austria-Hungary—backed up by Germany—on the Serbian government made war inevitable.

Assassination, Ultimatum, and War The assassination of the Austrian Archduke Francis Ferdinand set off a fatal chain of events, tied to alliances and war plans. The shooting took place in Sarajevo, capital of Bosnia-Herzegovina, the province annexed by Austria-Hungary just six years earlier. The assassin, Gavrilo Princip, was connected with the Black Hand, a nationalist group with ties to Serbia that dreamed of a unified Slavic state.

On July 23, encouraged by its German ally, Austria presented Serbia with an **ultimatum**, a set of nonnegotiable demands so harsh that they could not be accepted by a sovereign state. For example, the Austrians demanded not only that all forms of anti-Austrian **propaganda** be stamped out, but that the investigation inside Serbia also be carried out by Austro-Hungarian officials. Recent archival work has revealed that even if Serbia had accepted every provision in the ultimatum, Austria-Hungary still planned to attack. As expected, however, the Serbians could not accept all the ultimatum's demands, and on July 28, exactly a month after the assassination, Austria-Hungary declared war on Serbia.

Europe Falls into War
Russia felt obliged to support its Serbian ally, though Tsar Nicholas II recognized that military action against Austria-Hungary would compel its ally, Germany, to declare war. Yet to abandon Serbia at this moment would have meant a humiliation for Serbia's Great Power protector, Russia, and so, on July 30, reluctantly, the tsar ordered a general **mobilization**. Now he hoped to avert

ultimatum Harsh demand requiring an immediate positive answer to avoid dire consequences.

propaganda Efforts to influence public opinion, often using dishonest or misleading means.

mobilization Calling up of military reserves and putting armies in place for battle that generally precedes a war.

a war through a personal appeal to Kaiser William, his cousin by marriage. Unfortunately, two days of frantic telegrams between "Nicky" in St. Petersburg and "Willy" in Berlin (the two communicated in English) came to nothing, and on August 1, Germany declared war on Russia. On August 3, convinced that France was about to attack from the west, Germany declared war on France and, following the Schlieffen Plan, marched into neutral Belgium. Technically in defense of Belgium, on August 4, Great Britain (whose king, George V, was also a cousin of "Nicky" and "Willy") declared war on Germany. "The lamps are going out all over Europe," observed British foreign minister Sir Edward Grey, "We shall not see them lit again in our lifetime."

Allies Versus Central Powers Europe quickly divided into two warring camps: the **Allied Powers**, led by France, Great Britain, and Russia; and the **Central Powers**, Germany and Austria-Hungary, joined by Bulgaria and the Ottoman Empire. Serbia, Romania, and Belgium sided with the Allies, and Spain, Greece, Switzerland, Holland, and the Scandinavian countries remained neutral. Italy enraged the Central Powers by refusing to honor its alliance and then, on May 23, 1915, declaring war on Austria-Hungary and thereby joining the Allies, lured by promises of territorial gain in a postwar settlement. Both the Allies and the Central Powers promised territorial gains and other enticements to bring neutral powers onto their side, a fact that would complicate postwar settlements.

25-2b War Enthusiasm

Europeans from London to Moscow greeted the outbreak of war in August 1914 with patriotic demonstrations. Huge crowds gathered in the public squares of cities. In St. Petersburg, Russians attacked and destroyed the German Embassy, and it became dangerous to be heard speaking German. In Munich, a twenty-five-year-old Austrian named Adolf Hitler cheered with the crowds on Odeonsplatz, then returned home and thanked God that he had lived to see the outbreak of war. In Paris, men rode to the front in train cars marked "To Berlin!" In Berlin, Kaiser William II told the Reichstag that he "no longer recognized parties, only Germans."

Forms of War Enthusiasm European men rushed to polling stations to enlist, and women showered them with flowers. Mothers, wives, and sweethearts dutifully sent their men off to war. Patriotism, a longing for adventure, and a desire for revenge came together in a feverish enthusiasm for war. The young soldiers expected to be home, triumphant, by Christmas. Military planners, too, expected a quick, mobile war with one or two decisive battles, like the smaller wars that had been fought since the defeat of Napoleon in 1815.

The war was initially so popular that even pacifists hesitated to oppose it publicly, for fear of attack by indignant patriots. The largest socialist party in Europe, the German Social-Democrats, betrayed their prewar antiwar stance and voted in favor of war credits. In Russia, the Social-Democrats who refused to vote to fund the war were promptly arrested. The Russian socialist **Alexandra Kollontai** (koh-lon-TAI) openly called for resistance to the war—from the safety of neutral Scandinavia. Others, following the idea of the long-time pacifist Bertha von Suttner, who had recently died, called for a "peace without victory." In the summer of 1915, an International Congress of Women in the neutral Netherlands implored all warring countries to lay down their arms. By that point, however, none of the warring countries were ready to compromise and make peace.

As the Schlieffen Plan dictated, the German army advanced rapidly through neutral Belgium, to the outrage of the world community. By September 1, 1914, the Germans threatened Paris. At this point, the French army and the British Expeditionary Force launched a counteroffensive. This **First Battle of the Marne** forced the exhausted and overextended German troops to retreat. By mid-September the opposing sides began to dig themselves in along a line stretching from the English Channel to the border of Switzerland. The stalemate of trench warfare on the western front had begun (see Map 25.3).

War in the East: Battle of Tannenberg On the eastern front, Russia mobilized more rapidly than expected. Pressed by their French allies to attack, on August 15 two Russian armies invaded East Prussia, forcing the German high command to transfer troops from France to the eastern front. Russian troops outnumbered the Germans in East Prussia, but they were poorly led and supplied. At **Tannenberg**, the Germans won a decisive victory, with some 100,000 Russian soldiers taken prisoner. Never again in this conflict would Russian troops threaten German soil. Austria was a

Allied Powers Wartime coalition of France, Great Britain, Russia, Serbia, and others, in the end a total of twenty-four countries including the United States.

Central Powers Opponents of the Allies in World War I, most importantly Germany and Austria-Hungary, later joined by the Ottoman Empire and Bulgaria.

Alexandra Kollontai (1872–1952) Russian revolutionary and diplomat, commissar for social welfare in 1918 and head of the women's section of the Communist Party.

First Battle of the Marne Crucial battle near the Marne River, just north of Paris, in early September 1914, in which the French stopped the German advance.

Tannenberg Battle in East Prussia in August 1914 in which the Germans decisively defeated the Russian army.

World History Archive / Alamy Stock Photo

Frenchmen in Paris Greet the Declaration of War, August 1914

In capitals throughout Europe, from London to St. Petersburg, the declaration of war in August 1914 was greeted with demonstrations of enthusiastic patriotism. Here we see a crowd of young Frenchmen marching to the recruitment stations. Similar images have come down to us from Berlin, London, and other cities. On the countryside, however, war enthusiasm was considerably less.

» *How are these men dressed? What does this suggest about their social class?*

different matter. Russian armies invaded the Austrian province of Galicia, remaining there until 1916. Even more embarrassing for Austria, the small Serbian army successfully defended the Serbian capital, Belgrade, until finally defeated by a much larger combined Austrian and German force in October 1914, but the Serbian army retreated and continued to oppose the Central Powers well into the following year.

It was already clear that expectations for a short, glorious war were an illusion. **Casualties** had mounted to the hundreds of thousands, and ammunition had begun to run short. Governments were forced to take drastic measures to boost arms production. On all sides, military planners and civilian authorities had known huge amounts of resources would be needed at war's outset, but no one had anticipated the need for long-term military and economic organization. The war they had expected developed in a way they did not expect.

25-2c Trench Warfare

No one had anticipated that movement on the western front would stop altogether, but by fall 1914 soldiers on both sides had dug in. Across northern France hundreds of miles of trenches were dug in which thousands of men lived, fought, and died in a sea of mud, blood, rats, and vermin. The great technological advances in weaponry produced by the armaments industry were effectively countered by primitive defenses built of earth and barbed wire. Generals continued to use old tactics of massive frontal assaults or simply attempting to weaken the opposing army by killing as many enemy soldiers as possible. Periodically, an attempt to break through to the enemies' front trench would end in slaughter and failure or, at best, the gain of a few yards of territory.

Life in the Trenches On the Allied side, a typical front trench was about six to eight feet deep, about four feet wide, and separated from the German front trench by a narrow strip of land—**no man's land**—fifty yards to a mile wide, with masses of coiled barbed wire in front of each set of trenches. A few hundred yards behind the front, or firing, trenches were parallel support and reserve trenches. All these trenches were connected by perpendicular communication trenches that enabled men to move between the rear and the front. German trenches were similar but, in general, deeper and more elaborate. British and French soldiers who saw them were impressed by their neatness and even comfort. Behind the trenches were rail lines that brought in fresh troops and supplies and evacuated the wounded and men on leave. Between the two lines of enemy trenches were the killing fields. During the day, stepping into no man's land would mean instant death, but at night this area was busy with scouting expeditions and soldiers repairing defenses.

Those who experienced trench warfare and survived recalled filth, stench, and constant noise. Imagine thousands of men living in close quarters in a muddy

casualties Deaths and injuries in battle.

no man's land Territory between the two opposing enemy lines of trenches that had to be crossed in an attack.

Map 25.3 **Western Front, 1914–1918** The western front remained mainly stable from autumn 1914 to spring 1918 with trenches stretching from the English Channel to Switzerland.

1. Why did the German military plan demand a violation of Belgian neutrality?

2. Looking at the map, why did the Germans not succeed in taking Paris in August 1914?

3. What was the logic behind the broad German sweep across Belgium? Did it have a chance of success?

hole in the ground with few opportunities for personal hygiene. Add a climate in which rainfall and dark gloomy weather are the norm. Then there was the odor of decomposing corpses fed upon by large rats. The racket of constant artillery and small-arms fire, together with flares illuminating the night sky, made sleep difficult.

The nervous strain of trench warfare produced a psychological disorder newly described as **shell shock**, which left thousands of men incapable of fighting any longer or carrying out everyday activities at home. Constant shelling pulverized farmhouses, barns and yards, roads and forests. Chemicals from thousands of explosive shells poisoned the earth itself, making it useless for agriculture. Once-familiar landscapes became eerie, lifeless moonscapes later depicted by painters like **Paul Nash**. Tense monotony alternated with solitary deaths (if, for example, one forgot to crouch down in the more shallow parts of the trench) and, periodically, the mass slaughter of an offensive.

"Going over the Top" Attempts to break through the line followed a common pattern. First, artillery shelling, often lasting days, aimed to destroy forward machine-gun placements and barbed wire defenses and force the enemy back from the front trenches. Relentless shelling also aimed to wear down and "soften" the enemy psychologically.

Then, always at dawn, came the order to advance. The nervous men were awakened and given a stiff drink to buck up their nerves. The artillery would cease its shelling, a clear signal to the opposing side of the impending attack. At the sound of a whistle, hundreds of men would "go over the top" of the front trench and run headlong into no man's land—and into machine-gun fire.

Only a few made it as far as the barbed wire barriers in front of the enemy trenches. Fewer still actually made it into the empty enemy trench, where they could do little more than sit tight, hoping for the arrival of reinforcements before enemy soldiers were able to rush back to their front trenches. Usually death arrived before reinforcements, and the stalemate was reestablished. Desperate to break this stalemate, in the spring of 1915 the Germans lobbed canisters of poison gas into enemy trenches, inflicting blindness and miserable deaths on unprepared French and British soldiers. Gas attacks and gas masks soon became standard on both sides.

The Battles of Verdun and the Somme Two battles in 1916, each lasting months, epitomize the desperation

shell shock Psychological disorder, sometimes lasting decades, caused by the extreme stress faced by men under the constant barrage of explosions during war.

Paul Nash (1889–1946) English painter whose disorienting, surreal paintings depicted the bizarre world of the trenches.

Archives Larousse, Paris/Giraudon/The Bridgeman Art Library

and gruesome absurdity of warfare on the western front. In February, the Germans launched a massive assault, aiming to capture the French fortress at **Verdun**. Calculating that the French would go to extreme lengths to defend this town, which had been fortified after defeat in the Franco-Prussian War, the German command aimed simply to kill as many French soldiers as possible. The propaganda value of the fortress far overshadowed its military importance. "They shall not pass!" declared the French general **Henri Pétain**. But the French lost more than 350,000 men, and before the battle was over, ten months later, the Germans had lost 330,000. Today Verdun is a mausoleum and a cemetery, its defenses still harboring live mines and closed to visitors.

On July 1, to take the pressure off the French at Verdun, the British launched a massive attack at the **Somme** (som) River, along a twenty-mile front, and were later joined in the battle by the French. Despite the use of a new weapon, the tank, the Allies were unable to dislodge the Germans. When the fighting finally ended in mid-November, the British and French armies had suffered one million casualties— and had advanced six miles.

25-2d War on the Seas and in the Air

The war was also fought by sailors and, for the first time in history, men in airplanes. The main importance of naval action was the bottling up of German ports by the British navy, an act decried by Germans as a violation of international law. Airplanes and Zeppelins were used in reconnaissance and to bomb enemy targets.

Gallipoli With the British army bogged down in the trenches, the British Admiralty, headed by young **Winston Churchill**, urged an assault on the Central Powers' southern ally, the Ottoman Empire. Churchill calculated that an attack on the **Gallipoli** (gah-LEE-poh-lee) peninsula would break through Turkish defenses and open the way to Istanbul, knocking Turkey out of the war. In this largest **amphibious** operation of the war, troops from Australia and New Zealand under British command seized the beaches of Gallipoli in late April 1915. Contrary to expectations, however, Turkish troops on bluffs

Verdun French fortress attacked by Germans in 1916, resulting in almost 700,000 casualties.

Henri Pétain (pay-TAN) (1856–1951) French general in World War I who later, during World War II, served as president of Vichy France, the Nazi puppet state.

Somme Battle in 1916 near the Somme River in which the British and French failed to break through German lines, resulting in one million Allied casualties.

Winston Churchill (1874–1965) English politician of aristocratic background who backed the disastrous Gallipoli campaign, nearly destroying his political career; as prime minister during World War II, he inspired British victory.

Gallipoli Peninsula in western Turkey where an Allied attack using Australian and New Zealander troops from April to December 1915 ended in failure.

Imperial War Museum, London/The Bridgeman Art Library

overlooking the beach rained down bullets and shells on the Allied positions. In the end, Churchill could not muster sufficient troops and **materiel** to break the Turkish defenses, and the British and **ANZAC** troops were forced to withdraw. Churchill and Britain were humiliated by the defeat, and Turkey remained in the war. Together the belligerents suffered more than 500,000 casualties.

amphibious Military action using both land and sea troops.

materiel Military hardware such as guns, tanks, and ammunition.

ANZAC Australian and New Zealand army corps, most famous for action at Gallipoli.

Jutland Naval battle in 1916 between Britain and Germany off the coast of Denmark that ended in a draw.

U-boat (from German *Unterseeboot,* "undersea boat") Submarine.

CONNECTIONS: For most of human history, war and advances in technology have gone hand in hand. Some archeologists argue that more effective stone weapons allowed Cro-Magnon men to vanquish the Neanderthals. Ancient Greece carefully guarded its secret formula for "Greek fire," a kind of sticky petroleum product that was shot onto enemy ships to set them ablaze. World War I, too, pushed technology to its limits. In communications, the use of radio to send wireless messages gained in sophistication. Automobiles, airplanes, and explosives were all much more efficient—or deadly—in 1918 than in 1914.

World War II would further the sophistication of radar and end, of course, with the dropping of a new superweapon, the atomic bomb, on two Japanese cities. In the early twenty-first century, computer technology has been used to destroy targets abroad. Will the logical conclusion of this link between war and technology be the total destruction of life on earth?

The Battle of Jutland Despite this setback, the British navy continued to dominate the seas, blockading Germany's North Sea harbors. Given British naval superiority, the German navy preferred caution to bold moves until mid-1916, when the two fleets clashed at the Battle of **Jutland,** off the west coast of Denmark. Although the German fleet was smaller, it inflicted heavy losses on the British. In the end, the battle was indecisive. The British blockade continued, but the German navy still dominated the Baltic, standing between the British navy and its Russian allies.

The U-Boat Vastly more important than this conventional naval battle was what the Germans called the war on commerce, carried out almost entirely by a new type of warship, the submarine, or **U-boat.** The British could be starved into submission, thought the Germans, if their submarines could prevent the delivery of food and raw materials. Germans argued that Britain's naval blockade of Germany, causing considerable hardship and even widespread hunger, justified this measure.

In early 1915, the Germans announced **unrestricted submarine warfare**, warning that any ship entering British waters, including those of neutral countries, could be attacked and sunk. Because of the vulnerability of submarines when on the surface, there would be no warning before an attack. This policy, which violated traditional rules of war for engagements on the high seas, antagonized the United States, which had declared neutrality but traded actively with Britain.

Although millions of tons of Britain-bound shipping fell prey to submarines, it was the sinking of the British passenger liner *Lusitania* on May 7, 1915, with the loss of over a hundred American lives, that intensified anti-German feeling in the United States. For their part, the Germans insisted that the ship had been carrying an illegal cargo of arms, a claim that historians later verified. Rapidly the British developed antisubmarine measures, including mines, aerial surveillance, depth charges, and, most effective of all, the use of armed escorts of naval shipping—the **convoy system**—which was introduced in May 1917.

Airplanes in War While not as effective as U-boats, "flying machines" also played a part in World War I. Airplanes scouted out enemy positions, attacked enemy troops, and dropped bombs and propaganda leaflets. Their pilots were known as aces; perhaps the most famous was Manfred von Richthofen, the "Red Baron." Aces engaged in aerial "dogfights," but in the final year of the war airplanes were also used in mass formation to support ground troops—an actual military advance. Both sides also developed antiaircraft guns. Airplanes were also important in spotting U-boats. The planes themselves changed rapidly in these four years, as tens of thousands were built and destroyed. By 1918 the first all-metal fighters were appearing. German airships, called zeppelins after their inventor, were used to bomb London and military targets in England. Bulky, slow, and inflated with flammable gas, they were extremely vulnerable to attack by aircraft. This bombing of civilian areas blurred the line between the fighting front and the "home front." Every element of society was expected to support the war, and even civilians at home could come under attack by enemy bombs. World War I was the first **total war**.

25-2e A World at War

Many eighteenth- and nineteenth-century European conflicts had taken place far from Europe, but this war in Europe's heartland affected the entire world. At the same time, technological advances, such as the submarine, brought warfare to the high seas. More than anything else, Europe's unprecedented economic and colonial domination brought every continent—directly or indirectly—into the conflict and made it difficult for independent states to remain neutral. Eventually twenty-four states were drawn in on the Allied side—from the African Republic of Liberia to China, Japan, and Siam (Thailand) in Asia; Brazil, Cuba, Guatemala, and Honduras in South and Central America; and, eventually, the United States. Of the total world population of 1.6 billion, some 1.4 billion lived in states officially engaged in the conflict.

Africans and Asians in War Thousands of Asians and Africans from Europe's colonies fought on the western front, where their bravery was noted, challenging Europeans' sense of racial superiority. Young men from Australia and New Zealand fought at Gallipoli; Canadians and South Africans also joined the British war effort. Battles also took place in the colonies. In Africa, the Allies attacked the German colonies of East Africa, Togoland, and Southwest Africa. Fighting was particularly bitter in East Africa, involving British Kenya in the north down to present-day Zambia. Both European and African troops fought in these regions, and many African homes, crops, and herds were destroyed. The defeat of German troops and their African allies during the war presaged the total expulsion of Germany from the continent.

In the Far East, Japan took advantage of the war to extend its dominion over former German colonies in the Pacific and occupying (1914–1922) the Chinese city of Qingdao, which had been a German concession. While Japan did not directly support the Allied war effort, its position in East Asia was considerably strengthened by the war. Chinese laborers were recruited to serve as support workers for the British and French armies; their amazing journey around the world via the Pacific and across Canada shows how desperate the Allies were for manpower.

Nationalism During the War National and ethnic groups took advantage of warfare to press their own ambitions. In Russian Central Asia, Kazakhs revolted in 1916 against

---

unrestricted submarine warfare German policy of attacking without warning any ship entering British waters during World War I.

Lusitania British passenger ship torpedoed by a German submarine off the coast of Ireland in May 1915, drowning more than 1,000 passengers, including 120 Americans.

convoy system Grouping merchant ships together with an escort of armed naval vessels, successfully used to protect shipping from U-boats.

total war Conflict in which all elements of the population, economy, and politics are obliged to serve the military effort.

forced labor and war taxation, venting their anger on recently arrived Russian colonists. The revolt was put down with massive bloodshed. Half a world away in Dublin, on Easter Day 1916, Irish nationalists led a revolt against British rule, demanding an independent Ireland. The **Easter Uprising** was quickly crushed, but the anxiety of the British government over the Irish question increased. Both Allied and Central Powers attempted to incite the minority national groups under enemy rule. The Russian tsar and German Kaiser, for example, each sought to gain Polish loyalty by promising the Poles some kind of resurrected Poland after the war. In the Ottoman Empire, the British encouraged nationalist Arabs to revolt against their Turkish overlords as the young English officer **T. E. Lawrence**—"Lawrence of Arabia"—dressed in Arab garb to lead Arab troops against Turkish positions. Today the military cemetery at Mount Scopus, Jerusalem, bears witness to the thousands of British and Arab troops that died in that conflict.

Even before fighting had ended, the future of the region had been decided. In 1916, the British and French negotiated the **Sykes-Picot Agreement**, dividing up former Ottoman territories in the Middle East between themselves. When it became clear that the British government did not intend to grant the Arabs real independence, Lawrence resigned in disgust. Another appeal to a national minority in the region was the **Balfour Declaration** of November 1917, in which the British government indicated its willingness to set up a Jewish "national home" in Palestine. Support for Zionism, the British thought, would strengthen Jewish sympathy throughout the world for the Allied cause.

The Armenian Massacre
In the eastern region of the Ottoman Empire, along the border region between Russia and Turkey, an unprecedented attack on a civilian population occurred: the **Armenian Massacre**. Relations between Christian Armenians and Muslim Turks and Kurds, never cordial, had become severely strained by accusations that the Armenians had been spying for the Russians. During the winter of 1915–1916, Ottoman authorities gave orders to deport Armenians from their native villages near the front with Russia. In the course of these deportations, Turkish military units and Kurdish locals killed many unarmed Armenians or allowed them to perish in the harsh winter or from lack of food and water. Up to 1.5 million Armenians died in these operations, which nearly wiped out the Armenian community in Turkey. As an instance of genocide, the Armenian Massacre stands as a precursor to even more horrific ethnically based attacks on civilian populations later in the twentieth century.

The participation by colonized people in the European war effort radicalized movements opposing European rule and weakened the legitimacy of imperialism. If Indians, for example, could shed blood for the Allied cause, Indian nationalists argued, why could they not also rule themselves? In Africa, too, the economic effects of the war fueled nationalist and anticolonial sentiments after 1918.

Easter Uprising Nationalist rebellion in Dublin in 1916 that demanded Irish independence and was bloodily suppressed by British authorities.

T. E. Lawrence (1888–1935) English soldier and scholar known as "Lawrence of Arabia" who led the Arabs against Turkish domination during World War I.

Sykes-Picot Agreement Treaty of 1916 dividing up Ottoman territory in the Middle East between Great Britain and France.

Balfour Declaration Official statement by the British government in November 1917 in favor of a Jewish "national home" in Palestine, a major victory for Zionism.

Armenian Massacre Killing of as many as 1.5 million Christian Armenians by the Muslim Turkish military and Muslim Kurds in 1915–1916.

25-3 Total War, 1914–1918

» **How did war influence everyday life and family relationships?**

» **In what ways did governments aim to control their citizens?**

The Great War broke down the distinction between the military and noncombatants. Entire societies were harnessed to the war effort. Governments intruded into the economy and everyday life of their citizens as never before, making this the first total war. The right to free speech was limited. Shortages affected households and diets. Women took up new jobs as millions of men left for the front, unions and employers agreed to avoid conflicts to increase war production, and political parties vowed to work together. Everywhere taxes went up and governments borrowed staggering amounts of money to finance the war effort. Like the mass mobilization during the French Revolution, but far more encompassing, the state demanded that citizens devote full energies to crushing the enemy.

25-3a State Control and Intervention

Within months of the outbreak of war, all governments realized that supplies of foodstuffs and raw materials were threatened. State intervention in the form of rationing, restrictions, and planning aimed to safeguard these precious supplies.

State Intervention in the Economy The German government rapidly set up a Raw Materials Department in the War Ministry to secure raw materials vital to war industries. In Russia, Tsar Nicholas II proclaimed that, for the duration of the war, no vodka would be distilled. This measure, designed to reserve millions of tons of grain to feed Russian soldiers, had the unintended effect of eliminating the government's largest source of income, the tax on vodka.

In Britain, the government negotiated a settlement between unions and big business to assure that war production would not be interrupted by strikes. As the war dragged on, government intervention in the economy became more radical. In 1915, Britain **nationalized** the railroads. In May 1916, the British government moved the clock forward one hour to take advantage of summer daylight—the first daylight savings time.

Food Rationing To prevent hunger, governments stepped in to manage the production and sale of foodstuffs. With overseas food supplies cut off by the British naval blockade, Germany began to ration bread in early 1915. By mid-1916, labor shortages in agriculture and the effect of German submarine attacks forced the French and British governments, also, to introduce food rationing. In France, the beloved baguette was outlawed as wasteful, as were ice cream and most forms of candy. By late 1916, Germans had ration cards not just for bread but also for meat, potatoes, milk, sugar, butter, soap, and eggs. Even so, supply could not keep up with demand. Governments introduced various food substitutes, such as vegetable beefsteaks, artificial eggs, and "war bread," which contained a limited amount of white flour.

Military Conscription and Tax Hikes Government intervention was most direct in military conscription. Compulsory military service, long in force in most countries, was expanded. Britain's 1916 Military Service Act drafted men between eighteen and forty. All across Europe, almost all young men were either serving in the army or working in war industries. Those not serving in the armed forces found themselves scorned or even physically attacked as cowards.

To pay for the costs of the war, governments raised taxes and took out loans, both domestic and international. The domestic loans took the form of "war bonds," which patriotic citizens were urged to purchase. For the Allies, most international loans came from the United States. Even these measures could not cover war costs, however, and everywhere governments printed money, thereby starting an inflationary cycle that would continue into the 1920s.

Buyenlarge / Contributor / Getty Images

Hungarian Beer Advertisement

Propaganda merged with commercial purposes during World War I. This advertisement for a Hungarian brewery suggests that its beer was so delicious that the enemy soldiers would come running—and surrender—just to get a glass.

» *Do you think this is an advertisement from early or late in the war? Why?*

» *Looking at the uniforms, which soldiers belonged to which army?*

25-3b War Propaganda

Throughout Europe, governments attempted to control what citizens could know about the war's progress. The German people did not know that German troops had destroyed the priceless library at Louvain, in Belgium, and the people of England and France did not know that the Allies had bombed civilians in Karlsruhe, Germany. In this period before radio broadcasts, government censorship was particularly effective. Propaganda campaigns sought to keep up morale and convince citizens that right was on their side. The enemy was always characterized as vicious, cunning, and hardly human. The Allies portrayed German troops

nationalization The taking over of private enterprise by a government, sometimes with compensation, sometimes not, often in emergencies.

as "the Hun," murderous creatures bent on looting and destruction. German atrocities in Belgium were said to include bayoneted children and raped nuns. German propaganda countered with stories of German prisoners being tortured by Allied captors, all the while depicting German soldiers as defenders of culture pitted against effeminate French decadence and Russian barbarism.

Culture in the Service of War Politicians' speeches, press editorials, posters, and even songs warned citizens to be ever vigilant, to avoid defeatism, and to work for the war effort. In Germany, the poetic "hit" of the war's first years was Ernst Lissauer's "Song of Hatred Against England," for which the author was awarded the **Iron Cross**, a military decoration. Postcards bore such gruesome rhymed inscriptions as "Jeder Schuss ein Russ" ("Every shot, a Russian") and "Jeder Stoss ein Franzos" ("Every bayonet thrust, a Frenchman"). Similarly, patriotically minded Russians could send New Year's greetings on cards depicting a Cossack lopping off a German soldier's head and bearing the message, "Happy New Year! A successful blow!" French posters called on citizens to save wine for the troops and to support the war effort by buying war bonds.

Films also bolstered spirits, and because one-third or more of the people of Europe—at least those in cities—attended the movies at least once a week, their effect was significant. In Germany, melodramatic war films, such as *How Max Won the Iron Cross*, inspired patriotism. Among audiences in Allied countries, **Charlie Chaplin**'s comedies enjoyed immense popularity, including his rare, unheroic portrayal of a frontline soldier in *Shoulder Arms*, produced in 1918. Moviegoers were also treated to newsreels, which showed a sanitized and upbeat version of the week's military developments.

Iron Cross High military honor awarded for bravery to Prussian and German soldiers from 1813 to 1945.

Charlie Chaplin (1889–1977) British film actor and producer who created the Little Tramp character and whose silent comedies were extremely popular.

DORA Defence of the Realm Act, a law that curtailed civil liberties in Britain during World War I.

Bertrand Russell (1872–1970) British mathematician, philosopher, and pacifist.

Karl Liebknecht (1871–1919) German left-wing socialist who spent most of the war in jail for his socialist and antiwar agitation.

May Day International labor holiday, celebrated since the late nineteenth century throughout the world except in the United States.

Espionage and Sedition Acts Laws in the United States passed in 1917 restricting free speech to prevent antiwar statements ("sedition") and spying ("espionage").

Sanitizing the Reality of War Propaganda everywhere dealt in half-truths and, at times, outright lies. In London one could visit a model trench that, as returning soldiers complained, hardly resembled the real thing. In fact, soldiers found the patriotic falsehoods spread at home to be almost unbearable. Even civilians on the home front grew weary of the emphasis on the positive and upbeat as news of casualties mounted and food in the cities grew scarce. In the end, it is doubtful that the large expenditures on propaganda had any significant effect on the final outcome of the war.

Besides controlling the flow of information, governments restricted civil rights. Fearing civil unrest immediately after the declaration of war, in August 1914 the British Parliament passed the Defence of the Realm Act, known as **DORA**. This act essentially placed Britain under martial law for the duration of the war, allowing police to question and arrest individuals without a warrant and severely restricting freedom of speech. Individuals like the philosopher **Bertrand Russell** who dared to question the wisdom of the war or to advocate pacifism were harassed and even imprisoned. In Germany, when the radical socialists **Karl Liebknecht** (LEEP-knekht) and Rosa Luxemburg denounced the war at a **May Day** rally in 1916, calling for it to be transformed into a class war, they were arrested, tried for treason, and imprisoned. Even in the United States, the declaration of war in 1917 was quickly followed by the **Espionage and Sedition Acts**, which outlawed agitation against the war effort or criticism of the government.

25-3c Domestic and Family Life

In this war, every segment of society fought in one way or another. All were admonished to "do your part." Wealthy and middle-class women were pressured to volunteer as nurses. Retired people put their savings into war bonds to help finance the purchase of weaponry. Schoolteachers instilled patriotic and military virtues in their pupils and encouraged their students to prepare "care packages" to send to soldiers on the front. From the top to the bottom of society, people tried to economize and waste less, with more modest meals for the British royal family setting an example.

Women in War The deterioration in quality and quantity of basic consumer goods and foodstuffs meant that most German women were fully occupied simply obtaining calories for their families and mending clothing that could not be replaced. German women also supplemented their income by taking in work, such as the home production of gas masks, uniform items, and sandbags. Numerous posters called on women to subscribe to war bonds as one way of doing their part to help their men in the trenches.

Women also began to take jobs previously reserved for men. In Britain, female "postmen" and bus conductors startled onlookers at first. In Russia, a famous propaganda poster showed a women working at a lathe. British and German women also worked in armament factories, and everywhere women worked as nurses. With doctors overwhelmingly occupied at the front, nurses took their place at home in treating civilian ailments.

Although no army put women into combat, the British organized auxiliary units, such as the WAACs (Women's Army Auxiliary Corps) and Wrens (British Women's Royal Naval Service), in which women carried out office duties and also served as nurses. In Germany, the military command established the "Women's Home Army" to keep up morale and root out spies. Strikingly, Russia formed and trained a "Women's Battalion of Death," a volunteer unit whose purpose besides serving in combat was to shame male soldiers who were reluctant to attack.

CONNECTIONS: In one of his most hilarious plays, *Lysistrata*, Aristophanes described enraged Athenian women—in the fifth century B.C.E.—coming up with a unique weapon to end war: a sex strike. As long as Athenian husbands continued to fight with Sparta, their wives would turn them a cold shoulder (see Section 3-4c Learning from a Primary Source: Aristophanes Suggests How to End the War). Even though *Lysistrata* was a fiction, Aristophanes, through comedy, was able to deal with real events. Whether fictionalized or real, the theme of between women and pacifism recurs throughout the history of the west. As we saw in Section 22-4d Internationalism in Politics, Baroness Bertha von Suttner dedicated her life to the cause of pacifism, even convincing Swedish tycoon Alfred Nobel to found the Nobel Peace Prize to this end. More recently, in pop culture, the campy Polish science fiction parody, *Seksmisja* (Sex Mission), portrayed a world without war: because all men had been "neutralized" (warning: the film has a surprise ending). Of course, women were not always against war and violence. In ancient Greece, Spartan women undertook military duties (see Section 3-3 Sparta and Athens); in ancient Rome, female gladiators took the arena with stage names that recalled warriors (both real and fictional) from the past (see Section 6-2 The Roman Peace).

Roman Female Gladiators *

Mobilizing the Family Even the most intimate spheres of life were militarized. A French poster showed a newborn baby lamenting, "Alas! I arrived too late." Another showed a soldier surrounded by beaming women proclaiming, "Let's do our part for

* Roman civilization, Relief portraying fight between female gladiators / De Agostini Picture Library / A. Dagli Orti / Bridgeman Images

repopulation." In this way, even the newborn and the not-yet-born were mobilized for the war effort.

Old family patterns were disrupted by the absence of fathers who were at the front. Women assumed new responsibilities that helped break down old stereotypes and encouraged demands for economic and political equality. In Britain, greater numbers of women in wage work outside the home strengthened the arguments of women's suffrage activists. By war's end, British women had gained the vote and by the early 1920s nearly every European country extended suffrage to women. Children, too, became more independent and self-reliant. Men returning from the front were sometimes shocked by the new attitudes of their wives, sisters, and children. Entire societies felt the impact of the new social and economic roles for women that developed during wartime.

25-4 Russia in Revolution, 1917

» **What caused the Russian monarchy to collapse?**

» **What caused the Provisional Government to collapse in November 1917?**

Stalemate, shortages, mounting casualties, and millions of deaths: war stalked all of Europe, but the Russians were most miserable of all. Russia was the largest, poorest, least industrialized, and most politically repressive among major European states. Russia also had the largest army in Europe, a heavy burden on its limited resources. By late 1916, overwhelmed by rising prices and widespread shortages of food and fuel, and facing another cold, dark winter, Russians were desperate. Strikes broke out as workers protested the excessive profits earned by arms manufacturers while their own wages failed to keep up with inflation.

Anger with the tsarist regime mounted with military disasters and the seeming indifference of the tsar and his German-born wife. In March 1917, popular discontent exploded and swept the tsar from power. Suddenly Russia found itself without a tsar but also without a stable government. The new government continued the war effort, to the anger of most Russians. In November, a small band of radical socialists took advantage of political instability and widespread discontent to seize control and impose a new economic, social, and political order. Denouncing the "imperialist war," the new Bolshevik leaders of Russia urged soldiers on all sides to join in a class struggle that would topple corrupt empires and destroy capitalism itself. Exhilarating for some and horrifying for others, the Russian Revolution posed a direct challenge to existing economic, social, and political powers around the world.

25-4a The March Revolution

Repeated military setbacks made the tsar's many subjects heartily sick of war and bitter about the failures of his leadership. They believed that his German wife, Alexandra, sympathized with the enemy. Suspicions of treason at the highest level of government were reinforced by the presence in the imperial palace of a notorious peasant healer and womanizer, **Grigory Rasputin**. The tsar and his wife appreciated Rasputin's ability to ease the bleeding of young Alexis, the heir to the Romanov throne, who suffered from hemophilia. Many Russians, however, falsely and absurdly believed Rasputin to be a German spy and Alexandra's secret lover. Foolishly, Nicholas refused to send Rasputin away.

Failure of Leadership in St. Petersburg Nicholas's refusal to acknowledge ugly facts made him unable to deal effectively with Russia's deteriorating military situation and rising social unrest. A man who hated conflict, the tsar politely banished strong personalities from his presence and simply ignored criticism or advice from public figures or the press. In September 1915, he made a fatal decision when, in direct opposition to his advisers and despite his complete lack of military expertise, he left Petrograd—the new, more Russian-sounding name given to St. Petersburg in 1914—to join the general-staff headquarters near the front lines. As his advisers had feared, the tsar's presence at headquarters both distracted the officers there and meant that the Russian public connected every military defeat directly with the tsar's person. Back in Petrograd, Alexandra and Rasputin, together in the imperial palace, fueled more rumors that the "German woman" and her degenerate peasant lover were the real rulers of Russia. The truth was simpler: Russia lacked any effective leadership.

The March Revolution Every morning in the Russian capital, women lined up before dawn in front of shops that might have some bread and milk to sell, knowing that supplies would soon be sold out. On March 8, 1917, however, many shops had received no food at all, and women were turned away empty handed. As they trudged home, angry, cold, and worrying how they would feed their families, they encountered radical women demonstrating in support of **International Women's Day**. The two groups came together, and soon the entire capital city was in an uproar, with ten thousand women demanding equal rights

Grigory Rasputin (1869–1916) Siberian peasant healer whose ability to ease the suffering of Tsar Nicholas's son Alexis gained him entry to the Russian imperial family.

International Women's Day International holiday celebrating the achievements of women, whose demonstrations for "bread and peace" in Petrograd on March 8, 1917, grew into workers' riots that deposed Tsar Alexander II.

Stock Montage

Satirical Political Cartoon of the "Russian Imperial Family"

This wartime cartoon mocked Tsar Nicholas II and his wife Alexandra as mere pawns in the hands of the sinister bearded Rasputin. In fact the Siberian peasant healer's influence on policy was negligible, despite what many Russians thought. In any case, Rasputin bitterly opposed the war, though few Russians knew that.

》 *How does the artist's technique underscore Rasputin's evil power?*

》 *How are Nicholas and Alexandra portrayed?*

for women, a Russian republic, and an end to the war—demands summed up in the slogan "Bread and Peace." As workers (of both genders) went out on strike and even middle-class professionals took to the streets, the local chief of police telegraphed news of the riots to Nicholas. The president of the Duma sent a similar telegram, begging Nicholas to take notice of the people's demands. Instead, the tsar chose repression, commanding the local authorities to crack down on demonstrators.

Nicholas failed to appreciate how much the power of local authorities had eroded. Any attempt to "reestablish order" by means of violence would have led to armed clashes that the police would probably have lost. Very quickly, control of the city passed over to the rebels. It soon became dangerous for those associated with the tsarist regime to show themselves in public. Policemen were shot and beaten to death. When Nicholas finally decided to return, railway workers sabotaged the route, stranding the emperor outside the capital. Conservative Duma members persuaded the tsar to abdicate to preserve Russia. His patriotism touched, Nicholas signed away his power and thus ended more than three centuries of Romanov rule in Russia.

25-4b The Provisional Government

News of the tsar's abdication was greeted in the streets with shouts of "Long live the Russian republic!" Support for the monarchy seemed to evaporate overnight. Former Duma members of the center and moderate left formed a new government that was quickly recognized by the Allied Powers. This **Provisional Government** was to rule Russia for most of 1917. Its leaders proclaimed a free, liberal, and democratic Russia. They issued a blanket **amnesty** for political prisoners, ended all restrictions on non-Russians (thereby giving Russia's Jews and Muslims equal rights for the first time), and promised to convene an elected constituent assembly to draw up a constitution for the new republic. The Provisional Government also pledged to continue the war effort against Germany, hoping that the Allies would offer significant material support to the new, democratic Russia. Outside of Petrograd, however, the end of tsarist rule brought little change; even local administrators generally remained at their posts.

Dual Power The Provisional Government, representing mainly middle-class Duma members, espoused such liberal ideals as the rule of law, civil liberties, and private property. Almost immediately, it was challenged by the more radical, socialist **Petrograd Soviet**, a council that represented factory workers and soldiers. Issuing Order No. 1 in early March, the Soviet called on each military unit to form committees of elected representatives, demanded that officers show proper respect to the common soldiers, and proclaimed that no military orders were to be honored unless approved by the Petrograd Soviet. The Provisional Government felt unable to oppose this order directly. As unpopular officers were killed or, more frequently, simply warned to disappear, the conservative officer corps found it exceedingly difficult to maintain discipline.

As Order No. 1 vividly demonstrates, after March 1917 there were two centers of power in Russia. The Provisional Government was the internationally recognized government, but it lacked power and legitimacy at home. It saw itself as a caretaker, in place only until a permanent constitution could be drafted and put into effect. The Petrograd Soviet, on the other hand, had little time for such liberal and parliamentary niceties. Inspired by the Petrograd Soviet, workers' councils sprang up in other cities and in the countryside to push through radical solutions to Russia's wartime problems.

Bolsheviks Return Home Soon after the blanket amnesty, political prisoners in Siberia and political exiles around the world began to make their way home. In April, Vladimir Ilyich Lenin, the leader of the radical Bolsheviks, arrived in Petrograd after a complicated journey, supported by the German authorities, from his exile in Switzerland. Quickly he published a fiery article—his so-called "April Theses" (see Learning from a Primary Source: Lenin Proposes His "April Theses")—demanding an end to the war in the Bolshevik newspaper *Pravda*. His clear and radical program appealed to many, and support for the Bolsheviks grew.

The Bolsheviks had two things other political parties in Russia lacked: the dynamic leadership of Lenin and an easily understood program summed up in the slogan "Peace, Land, and Bread." But the Bolsheviks were a small and extreme group, and no one thought they would triumph.

Alexander Kerensky Meanwhile, the Provisional Government was also moving to the left politically. In July, **Alexander Kerensky**, a socialist lawyer and the only man to hold posts in both the Provisional Government and Petrograd Soviet, became prime minister. Kerensky enjoyed great popularity at first. His talents as an orator were considerable, though when he preached to the troops at the front that they had a sacred duty to give their lives for Mother Russia some scorned him as the "persuader-in-chief." Unfortunately for Kerensky, his speeches proved unable to prevent the collapse of the Russian army. A major Russian offensive launched in the summer of 1917 turned into a rout.

As a moderate socialist, Kerensky faced serious enemies on both the right and the left. The military despised him as a windbag lacking political legitimacy, and the Bolsheviks saw him as ineffectual. In a sense, both were correct. But Kerensky was in an impossible situation. Having neutralized the Bolshevik threat after a coup attempt

Provisional Government Temporary Russian government in March–November 1917 that was led by former Duma members and deposed by the Bolshevik Revolution.

amnesty General pardon by government.

Petrograd Soviet Radical council that represented socialist workers and soldiers and shared power with the more moderate Provisional Government.

Alexander Kerensky (1881–1970) Moderate socialist and prime minister of the Provisional Government who was deposed by the Bolsheviks.

Lenin Proposes His "April Theses"

When V. I. Lenin returned to Petrograd in April 1917, the enthusiasm for the democratic revolution of March had not yet worn off. Even socialist parties—including Lenin's own Bolsheviks—had agreed to support the Provisional Government until the war was won. Within days of his return, Lenin shocked his Bolshevik colleagues with his "April Theses," which demanded a far more radical and confrontational course of action. In any other country at war—including the United States—Lenin would have been arrested and silenced for demanding an immediate end to the war and agitating for revolution. The fact that he was able to publish these radical comments openly shows that, indeed, as he himself commented, Russia after the March revolution was "the freest country in the world."

❶ Why did Lenin term the war "predatory?" What did capitalism have to do with that?

❷ Why would overthrowing capitalism bring about a "truly democratic peace?"

❸ Was the Provisional Government conservative or antisocialist? What does Lenin mean by "annexations" here?

[Thesis 1: Against the war]
❶ The war … unquestionably remains on Russia's part a predatory imperialist war owing to the capitalist nature of that government… .
The class-conscious proletariat can give its consent to a revolutionary war… .
❷ It is necessary … to explain the inseparable connection existing between capital and the imperialist war, and to prove that without overthrowing capital it is impossible to end the war by a truly democratic peace… .

[Thesis 3: Against the Provisional Government]
❸ No support for the Provisional Government; the utter falsity of all its promises should be made clear, particularly of those relating to the renunciation of annexations… .

Sputniki

Soldiers Marching in Petrograd for Communism, 1917

The support of war-weary soldiers like these marching in Petrograd under the banner of communism was crucial for the success of the Bolshevik takeover in November 1917. By continuing to push the war effort, the Provisional Government lost support among many workers, soldiers, and peasants.

❯❯ Why would soldiers march through the streets carrying a banner calling for "Communism?"

❯❯ Are soldiers in uniform normally allowed to express political opinions?

4 Why, following Lenin's logic, would a parliamentary republic be "retrograde" for Russia? How realistic was the call for abolition of police, army, and bureaucracy?

5 What social groups might support Lenin in his call for nationalizing large estates?

6 Would peasants welcome the placing of land under the control of local Soviets?

7 Why did Lenin specifically mention that banks should be nationalized (he does not mention any other kind of business or industry)?

[Thesis 5: For revolution]
4 Not a parliamentary republic—to return to a parliamentary republic from the Soviets of Workers' Deputies would be a retrograde step—but a republic of Soviets of Workers', Agricultural Laborers' and Peasants' Deputies throughout the country, from top to bottom… .
Abolition of the police, the army, and the bureaucracy… .

[Thesis 6: Agrarian program]
5 Confiscation of all landed estates.
6 Nationalisation of all lands in the country, the land to be disposed of by the local Soviets of Agricultural Labourers' and Peasants' Deputies… .

[Thesis 7: For the nationalization of banks]
7 The immediate amalgamation of all banks in the country into a single national bank, and the institution of control over it by the Soviet of Workers' Deputies.

Source: From Lenin's April Theses (1917).

---

in July, in early September Kerensky had to fend off a military coup led by the popular Cossack general Lavr Kornilov. To defeat Kornilov, Kerensky released many Bolsheviks from jail, including **Leon Trotsky**, another dynamic leader. The Bolsheviks regrouped, and within weeks Kerensky faced them again, now more dangerous, well organized, and armed.

25-4c The November Revolution

Hiding outside of Petrograd, Lenin pelted his comrades in the capital with enraged letters and instructions. In mid-October he entered Petrograd in disguise to persuade his party comrades that the time had come to seize power. Opposition to Lenin's timetable was considerable, but his powers of persuasion were even stronger. Trotsky's support proved critical. Despite press coverage of the Bolshevik plan to grab power, the Petrograd Soviet refused to believe it could succeed and refused to help Kerensky and the Provisional Government against the Bolshevik threat.

Executing the Revolution On the night of November 6, the Bolsheviks executed a carefully planned takeover of Petrograd. Bridges across the river Neva were occupied, and the Bolshevik party's **Red Guards** surrounded the main railway stations, central post office, and other strategic buildings. The Provisional Government found itself trapped inside the Winter Palace, unable to communicate with the outside world. Except for a few cadets and the ill-trained Women's Battalion of Death, no one defended Kerensky and the legally recognized government of Russia.

Very much like the tsar's regime some eight months earlier, the Provisional Government collapsed. As Lenin put it later, "Power lay on the street; we merely picked it up." The following day, the Bolsheviks broke into the Winter Palace and arrested the members of the Provisional Government except for Kerensky, who, disguised as a woman, escaped in an American Embassy automobile. Though the Bolsheviks faced stiff opposition and street fighting in Moscow, in the countryside peasants were far more concerned with seizing the land they had been promised by the Bolsheviks. By the end of November, Lenin and his party comrades found themselves unexpectedly in control of the world's largest country.

Bolshevik Rule The Bolsheviks themselves did not expect to be long in power.

They did hope, however, that their revolution would spark a worldwide socialist revolution in more advanced industrial countries like Germany and Great Britain. The Bolsheviks hurried to proclaim Russia the first socialist state in history and rapidly issued decrees calling for peace, nationalizing land for peasants, establishing worker control of factories, and affirming equal rights for all religious and national minorities. Alexandra Kollontai became commissar for people's welfare. To the embarrassment of the Allied Powers, the Bolsheviks published secret treaties concerning promises about postwar settlements

Leon Trotsky (1879–1940) Russian revolutionary who along with Lenin helped bring the Bolsheviks to power in 1917.

Red Guards Troops organized by the Bolsheviks that were instrumental in their victory in the Russian Revolution of November 1917.

revealing, among other things, that Russia was to receive territory from Turkey after the war—agreements that the Allies had earlier denied. The long-delayed elections to the constituent assembly were allowed to take place, but when it convened in January 1918, the Bolsheviks shut it down after only one day. Already the Bolsheviks were curtailing the liberal freedoms gained by the March revolution.

The Bolsheviks had never pretended to be liberals. They had never advocated equal rights or toleration for all political views. When they came to power, they were well aware of how weak their position was and how many enemies surrounded them. In December 1917, they established the secret police known as the **Cheka**—the Extraordinary Commission to Combat Counterrevolution, Sabotage, and Speculation. The Cheka and its agents, Chekists, ruthlessly sought out and arrested anyone suspected of opposing Bolshevik power. By mid-1918, all conservative and liberal parties had been shut down, their newspapers confiscated, and their leaders driven underground or into exile. By the summer of 1918, the enemies of the Bolsheviks had organized themselves to fight the new order in Russia. The **Russian Civil War**, between the Reds (Bolsheviks) and the Whites (diverse groups opposed to the Bolsheviks), was to last until 1920. Some of the first victims were Nicholas II and his family, killed in July 1918 on the orders of Lenin, who feared that the ex-tsar might fall into the hands of the Whites.

25-5 The Turning of the Tide, 1917–1918

» **What events led to the defeat of Germany and the Central Powers?**

» **Why did so many Germans refuse to believe that they had been defeated?**

After two and a half years of war, by early 1917 despair and frustration prevailed on all sides. The ideals and enthusiasm of the summer of 1914 had been long forgotten as governments and military leaders desperately tried to find some way of ending the conflict. Two events of 1917 broke this deadlock: the revolutions in Russia and the decision of the United States to enter the war on the Allied side. With the arrival of American finances, troops, and equipment, chances for a victory of the Central Powers faded. The year 1918 began with German victory

Cheka Secret police established in Soviet Russia in December 1917 to eradicate enemies of the Bolshevik regime.

Russian Civil War War between the Bolshevik government ("Reds") and its opponents ("Whites") from 1918 to 1920, ending in victory for the Reds.

on the eastern front but ended with defeat in the west. Few Germans realized at the time how crushing this defeat would be. But even the exhausted Allies had little cause for celebration in 1918.

25-5a War Exhaustion

Based on the military situation in early 1917, it would have been difficult to predict World War I's final outcome. Despite the stalemate in the west, the German army had advanced into Russia. Warsaw was taken in mid-1915, and by late 1916 Germans had taken Wilno (now Vilnius, Lithuania) and occupied much of eastern Ukraine, Belarus, and Lithuania. Austrian armies took back Galicia, which had been occupied by the Russians in the first months of the war and, after unexpectedly fierce fighting, succeeded in neutralizing Serbia.

War Exhaustion in Austria-Hungary The military and domestic situation in multinational Austria-Hungary, however, was unstable. Czech and other Slavic troops often deserted across the Russian lines, and even German-speakers in the empire questioned openly the utility of continuing "Prussia's" war. Early in 1916, Emperor Francis Joseph died after a reign of nearly seventy years, depriving Austria-Hungary of a unifying symbol.

Later that year, a young man entered a Viennese café, approached the Austrian prime minister, cried out, "We want peace," then shot him and waited quietly to be arrested. A Russian offensive in the summer of 1916 had brought the Austro-Hungarian army close to collapse, until German troops intervened. Behind the scenes, the young Austro-Hungarian emperor sent out secret peace feelers to the Allies, only to be found out and severely rebuked by the Kaiser. By 1917, the war enthusiasm of a few years earlier was dead, all sides longed for an end to the bloodletting, but no one could see a way out.

Calls for Peace In such a situation, the peace movement gained momentum. In previous years radical socialists, including Lenin, Kollontai, and Luxemburg, had met in Switzerland to issue a manifesto, drafted by Trotsky, calling for "a peace without annexations or war indemnities." These socialists argued that the war should end without any country gaining new territory or demanding payment from their enemies. They believed that the present war was absurd and immoral, serving the interests of the armaments industries, the imperialist powers, and the rich. They demanded, instead, a war against the existing order, in which the working people of all nations would band together and turn weapons on the hated capitalists and generals. No mainstream socialist party could accept such a radical program, but as the stalemate continued on the battlefronts, and misery on the home fronts deepened, calls for peace were also issued by mainstream leaders, including U.S. President **Woodrow Wilson** and the pope.

Strikes and Mutinies In 1917, in Britain, France, and Germany, hundreds of thousands of workers went out on strike, breaking their no-strike pledges. Even wage increases could not keep up with the steep rise in prices, but strikers were also protesting the unending, senseless war. Influenced by left-wing arguments, they increasingly rejected the idea of shared interests with factory owners. Similarly, soldiers distrusted their generals and had only contempt for the politicians back home. For many, it appeared that incompetent leaders were merely spouting hollow lines about patriotism to mask their inability to end a war that by now nobody wanted. In April 1917, at several places on the western front, French soldiers simply refused to "go over the top." Their disobedience was simply a reasonable unwillingness to carry out unreasonably murderous orders, but these mutinies shook the military leadership, who feared that other soldiers would refuse to fight and might even turn their weapons against their own officers.

Russian soldiers, whose morale and material conditions had been shaken by the March revolution in Petrograd, retreated in disorder in the midst of a summer offensive. Shortly after seizing power in November, the Bolsheviks initiated cease-fire talks with the Germans. Germany had already defeated Romania earlier in 1917 and had exacted very harsh peace terms from that country. At the same time, the Central Powers' Bulgarian and Turkish allies were barely hanging on, plagued by low morale and shortages of food and ammunition. The loss of vast Ottoman Middle Eastern territories to the British by late 1917 created a crisis of confidence in the Turkish leadership.

Battle of Caporetto Amid general war weariness, only the Germans appeared to have some reason for hope. In late September 1917, the combined German and Austrian army inflicted a crushing defeat on the Italians at Caporetto. The Italian army nearly disintegrated, thousands deserted, and three hundred thousand men were taken prisoner by the German and Austrian armies. This decisive victory, combined with the Russian collapse, encouraged many Germans to believe that the war would end favorably in 1918. Such wishful thinking failed to appreciate the decisive turn in the war's fortunes caused by the United States joining the Allies.

25-5b The Entry of the United States

Until 1917, the United States had avoided taking sides in the European conflict. Most Americans could not see how their interests were involved in the European war and preferred to remain neutral. Even after the public outrage over the sinking of the *Lusitania* in May 1915, President Wilson remained unwilling to press for American intervention. His election campaign of the following year was conducted under the slogan "He kept us out of war." But just a month after his second inauguration, Wilson signed a declaration of war against Germany.

CONNECTIONS: In a democracy, candidates for political office are expected to set forth their political program in order to gain support from voters. But even in nondemocratic countries, rulers often promise more than they can deliver. In 1868–1869 Japanese traditionalists fought in support of the Meiji Emperor against foreign influences, only to find after Meiji's victory that he embarked on a far more radical project of westernization than the Tokugawa Shogunate (see Section 24-5 The Far East). Woodrow Wilson campaigned for a second term with the slogan, "He kept us out of war." Mere weeks after Wilson's second inauguration, the United States entered World War I. Adolf Hitler promised Germans that he would create jobs and restore strength to the central government; a decade and a half later the country was in ruins and tens of millions of Europeans were dead. Perhaps the only political party to keep its promises was Monty Python's (fictitious) "Silly Party," which vowed to ruin the economy, raise taxes, and destroy the country. Unfortunately, in the twenty-first century reality sometimes comes close to parody.

The Zimmermann Telegram Two foolish actions by the German government had altered American public opinion. In January 1917, the German foreign minister, Arthur Zimmermann, telegraphed the German ambassador in Mexico, instructing him to offer Mexico the return of lands lost in the 1840s to the United States if Mexico would support Germany against the Americans. The British intercepted the telegram and revealed its contents to the American government. The reaction was predictably furious, and when the telegram was published in the American press in March, anti-German war sentiment ran high.

Resuming Unrestricted Submarine Warfare At the beginning of February, the Germans announced the resumption of unrestricted submarine warfare, disregarding the effect that such a move would have on American public opinion. The sinking of several American merchant ships strengthened calls for intervention. The March revolution in Russia heightened the contrast between the militarist regime in Berlin and democratic governments in Paris, London, and now Petrograd. All these factors came together in Wilson's request on April 2, 1917, for a declaration of war. Wilson stated that world peace was his goal: "The world must be made safe for democracy."

Woodrow Wilson (1856–1924) U.S. president, 1913–1921, who brought the United States into war "to make the world safe for democracy" and authored the Fourteen Points.

The Impact of America's Entry into the War The impact of the American entry into the war was felt first financially. American loans and credits, previously somewhat restrained by considerations of neutrality, opened up fully for the Allied Powers. American factories retooled for war production, and more than 20 million men registered for military service. American soldiers began to arrive in France in June 1917, though it was not until 1918 that American troops actually went into battle. Just as in European countries, the American government intervened in the economy. The War Industries Board in Washington coordinated production and distribution of essential goods. As American troops and manufactured goods streamed across the Atlantic, the Central Powers were reaching their last reserves of men and materiel.

25-5c German Victory over Russia

With the American entry into the war, the Germans knew that their only chance for victory was to crush the Allies before American troops could arrive in significant numbers. That seemed possible when the Bolsheviks pulled Russia out of the war. Lenin recognized that the very survival of his new socialist regime depended on making peace, and the Russian army had essentially ceased to exist. As Lenin put it, peasant soldiers had "voted with their feet" by deserting to head home and obtain their share of agricultural land being seized from the landlords.

Treaty of Brest-Litovsk In the autumn of 1917, the Germans had taken Riga and were threatening the Baltic approaches to Petrograd, with little to stop them. On December 15, 1917, representatives of the Bolsheviks and the Central Powers met in the Belarusian town of Brest-Litovsk and agreed on an **armistice**. Both delegations remained in the city to hammer out details of the peace. The deliberations between Bolsheviks, led by the fiery orator Trotsky, and the German delegation, made up mainly of stiff Prussian generals and sober diplomats, revealed the enormous political differences between the two sides. The Soviet representatives demanded "peace without annexations or war indemnities" and **national self-determination** for Ukrainians, Poles, and other non-Russians under German occupation. The Germans were astounded that the Bolshevik representatives dared to make demands, considering their military weakness. When negotiations broke down, the German army simply advanced farther into Russian territory, encountering almost no resistance.

Back in Petrograd, Lenin was furious. He scolded Trotsky for his arrogance and warned that Germany's conditions for peace would now be even harsher. He was right. In March 1918, the Bolsheviks were forced to accept the **Treaty of Brest-Litovsk**. Russia signed away over a quarter of its prewar population and arable land as well as over half its coal mines and iron manufacturing. This vast region, stretching from the Baltic Sea to Ukraine, was carved into new states dependent on Germany. Even though relatively few ethnic Russians lived in these lands, the loss of this huge territory was a severe blow to the young government, one that no democratic government could have survived. The new border with Finland and Estonia ran threateningly close to Petrograd, and for security reasons the Russian capital was moved to Moscow, where it remains to this day.

25-5d German Defeat

In January 1918, Woodrow Wilson issued his famous **Fourteen Points**—a plan of the future peace based not on revenge but on the liberal principles of freedom, justice, and free trade. Among the most important of the Fourteen Points were the demands for "open covenants of peace, openly arrived at," national self-determination, an independent Polish state, arms reduction, free navigation of the seas, and the creation of a postwar international body—the **League of Nations**—that would regulate international relations and prevent future wars. Through private conversations, many Germans and Austrians learned of the speech despite their governments' efforts to suppress the information. For them, the Fourteen Points appeared to open the possibility of peace negotiations. Others, however, denounced Wilson's speech as mere propaganda. As long as there was a chance for military victory, in any case, the German government expressed no interest in Wilson's proposal.

Germany Seeks Peace Hoping to win the war quickly, the Germans launched major offensives on the western front in the spring of 1918, but they failed, with several hundred thousand casualties only further weakening the German army. By autumn, even the German High Command recognized that the war was lost. Thinking that a civilian government could win milder terms from the Allies, and seeking to evade their own responsibility for the defeat, the military leadership persuaded the Kaiser to abdicate. As strikes and political demonstrations rocked German cities, a new government was formed, dominated by moderate socialists. In this way, the burden of defeat fell not on those responsible for the

armistice Temporary cease-fire reached before the official treaty ending a war.

national self-determination Right of ethnic groups or nations to autonomy, often falsely interpreted to mean the setting up of independent nation-states.

Treaty of Brest-Litovsk Harsh peace imposed on Soviet Russia by Germany in March 1918 that stripped Russia of large territories on its western borders.

Fourteen Points President Woodrow Wilson's blueprint for peace and postwar negotiations based on the principles of freedom, justice, and free trade.

League of Nations Postwar international body proposed by Woodrow Wilson to regulate relations between states with the goal of preventing future wars.

war, the Kaiser and his generals, but on the fledgling democratic government of Germany.

Under the armistice agreement, the Germans promised to withdraw from Belgium, return Alsace-Lorraine to France, surrender submarines and rail stock, and destroy artillery. All Allied prisoners of war were to be released immediately, and the Treaty of Brest-Litovsk was annulled. The Germans agreed to pay for war damages. The Allied naval blockade of Germany would continue until a final peace settlement was reached. Though the provisions were harsh, the German delegation signed, one member taking comfort by observing, "A nation of seventy million suffers, but does not die." At the eleventh minute of the eleventh hour of the eleventh day of the eleventh month of 1918, the guns at last went silent on the western front.

Chaos and Consternation at War's End The fighting was ended, but the final conditions of peace were still to be negotiated. News of the harsh armistice terms stunned the German people. Though the German generals knew well that the war had been lost, propaganda at home had predicted victory. Ordinary Germans had no way of knowing that their army was on the brink of collapse. German troops remained in position in northern France, and no Allied troops had crossed onto German soil. Corporal Adolf Hitler, temporarily blinded in action, heard the news in his hospital bed and wept.

Central and eastern Europe floundered in chaos. The Russian and Austro-Hungarian Empires had ceased to exist. Independence was declared in Poland, Ukraine, Czechoslovakia, Finland, and Lithuania. In Vienna, an Austrian Republic was proclaimed; its parliament asked to be accepted into the German Reich. German sailors mutinied and took over the northern port city of Kiel. In other German cities, from Berlin to Munich, radicalized soldiers and workers set up soviets on the Russian model. Budapest, capital of the newly independent Hungary, also experienced a short-lived soviet government. As workers, soldiers, and sailors took to the streets, the middle classes feared for their property and lives. In Moscow, Lenin hoped this was the dawn of the world revolution. Not just a war had ended, but a world.

25-5e End of the European Era

More than eight million Europeans died in World War I, and about twenty million young men had been wounded, many permanently disabled. In many areas, public order had broken down, and governments were in disarray. Four empires—German, Russian, Ottoman, and Habsburg—had collapsed, millions of people had been uprooted, and class warfare had broken out in many parts of central and eastern Europe.

To make matters worse, a worldwide influenza epidemic broke out in 1918. Before it was over, some forty million people were dead. Terrifyingly, the young and healthy seemed more likely to die of the disease than did the elderly. Early cases of what we

Visual Connection Archive

Jaroslav Hašek's Good Soldier Švejk

Czech writer Jaroslav Hašek's (JAH-roh-slav HAH-shek) literary creation, *The Good Soldier Švejk (shveyk)*, was an ordinary soldier—a kind of Czech "Sad Sack"—in the Austro-Hungarian army during World War I. Good-natured and portly, Švejk has been seen as a reflection of Czech national character, but the effort of this "little man" to survive in an absurd war is a universal theme.

›› *Švejk showed no particular patriotism or eagerness to fight, only a desire to survive. How typical do you think that attitude was during the war?*

›› *Why do you think Hašek's novel became so popular both in Czech and in translations during the 1920s?*

now recognize as flu helped weaken the German army already in spring 1918, but the real brunt of the disease hit later. In the United States, public health agencies collapsed under the strain of dealing with the disease. The disease killed on all continents, from Augsburg to Austin to Australia. Even President Woodrow Wilson was afflicted, and some historians have argued that Wilson's illness made him ineffectual at the postwar peace conference in Paris in 1919.

War's Destruction The war caused widespread destruction. Roads and railroads were destroyed. Entire villages and towns ceased to exist. Factories were breaking down without proper upkeep and investment. The total cost of the war is difficult to calculate, but the famous English economist John Maynard Keynes estimated that it represented Europe's entire industrial output of several years.

From London to Constantinople, from Moscow to Marseilles, Europeans were poorer in 1918 than in 1914. Except for Britain, industrial production contracted. Commercial trade ceased, and the center of international finance shifted from London to New York. Agriculture also suffered, and food shortages were so widespread, especially as the naval blockade continued, pending the peace settlement, that millions faced starvation in the winter of 1918. On the other side of the world, Japan prospered during the war and increased its influence in the region at the expense of China. The American economy also boomed as its capital and goods streamed into Europe, further reducing the European proportion of world economic output. For educated Africans, the European bloodletting encouraged efforts for more autonomy (as in South Africa) or even independence from colonial rule.

Psychological Impact The war had a permanent effect on the European psyche. Trench warfare and total war made optimism about the future—and belief in the past—hollow. The notion of human progress was undone. Disorientation, depression, and rage were the surviving emotions, reflected in the paintings of Paul Nash and George Grosz and in the highly unmilitary figure of Jaroslav Hašek's *The Good Soldier Švejk*. Literary critic Paul Fussell has suggested that World War I even altered European perceptions of the natural world. Sunrise had long been the symbol of a new day, full of hope and possibilities. But for soldiers in the trenches, dawn was the most terrifying time of all—the time of the call to "go over the top." After World War I, nothing, not even the sunrise, would be the same.

CHAPTER Review

Summary

» A major war had long been expected, but the length and ferocity of World War I surprised many Europeans.

» Nobody had predicted the frustrating and murderous trench warfare that even poison gas, massive artillery barrages, and aircraft could not break for three years on the western front.

» The Russian empire collapsed under the strain of the war in March 1917, and the liberal Provisional Government was swept away by the communists (Bolsheviks) in November 1917.

» World War I strengthened the role of state intervention in the economy and in everyday life.

» When the Germans sued for peace in late 1918, every European country was exhausted; the real victor of the conflict was the United States whose influence in the world grew hugely.

Chronology

1904–1905	Japan defeats Russia in Russo-Japanese War [Asia]
1905	Dissatisfaction with tsarist rule sparks empire-wide revolution in Russia [Europe]
1908	Austria-Hungary annexes Bosnia-Herzegovina [Europe]
1912	First Balkan War weakens Ottoman Empire [Europe, Middle East]
1913	Second Balkan War strengthens Serbia [Europe]
1914	Archduke Ferdinand is assassinated (June 28) [Europe]
	Austria presents Serbia with an ultimatum (July 23) [Europe]
	Austria-Hungary declares war on Serbia (July 28) [Europe]
	Germany declares war on Russia (August 1) [Europe]
	Germany declares war on France and invades Belgium (August 3) [Europe]
	Great Britain declares war on Germany (August 4) [Europe]
	World War I begins (August) [Europe]
	Germany defeats Russia at the Battle of Tannenberg (mid-August) [Europe]
	French defeat Germans in the First Battle of the Marne (September) [Europe]
	Japanese seize the city of Qingdao, Shandong province, China [Asia]

1915	Turks defeat Allies at the Battle of Gallipoli [Europe]
	Italy declares war on Austria-Hungary (May 23) [Europe]
1916	Battle of the Somme ends without significant advances (July–November) [Europe]
	Strikes and unrest in all belligerent countries increase [Europe]
1917	Russian Revolution begins [Europe]
	Tsar Nicholas II abdicates (March) [Europe]
	United States enters World War I on Allied side (April) [Americas]
	Bolsheviks attempt coup in Petrograd (July) [Europe]
	Bolsheviks seize power in Petrograd (November) [Europe]
1918	Treaty of Brest-Litovsk ends war for Russia (March) [Europe]
	Civil War begins in Russia (to 1920) [Europe]
	Germans launch offensives on the western front (spring) [Europe]
	Armistice ends World War I (November 11) [Europe]
1918–1919	Worldwide influenza epidemic kills millions [Global]

Critical Thinking Questions

Take time to pull together all the important information from the chapter by answering the following questions:

A New Century, 1900–1914

» Why did nationalism present different difficulties for states in western and eastern Europe?

» How did the shifting alliances between countries help set the stage for general war in 1914?

The Unexpected War, 1914

» Why did so many Europeans greet the war with enthusiasm? What did they hope to get out of the war?

» How did new technologies affect the nature of war in this conflict?

Total War, 1914–1918

» How did propaganda present a one-sided picture of the war? How successful was it?

» How did this war, often called the first "total war," differ from earlier conflicts in its impact on society and everyday life?

Russia in Revolution, 1917

» What mistakes did Nicholas II make that helped bring about his downfall? Could he have retained power, and if so, how?

» What mistakes did the Provisional Government make that weakened their power?

The Turning of the Tide, 1917–1918

» What different forms did war exhaustion take in the years 1916–1918?

» Why could the Central Powers not win against the western Allies, though they did win against Russia?

MindTap® is a fully online personalized learning experience built upon Cengage Learning content. MindTap® combines student learning tools—readings, multimedia, activities, and assessments—into a singular Learning Path that guides students through the course and helps students develop the critical thinking, analysis, and communication skills that are essential to academic and professional success.

CHAPTER

26

A Decade of Revolutionary Experiments, 1918–1929

Chapter Outline

As you read, consider the following questions:

❭ What are the weaknesses and strengths of the postwar treaties?

❭ What challenges did new political movements and economic developments pose to European political stability?

❭ In what ways was the Soviet Union a radically new type of state?

❭ What are the defining elements of fascism?

❭ How did cultural experiments of this decade challenge cultural and social norms?

Isadora Duncan

Isadora Duncan (1877–1927), the British dancer who charmed America and Russia, became a symbol of the experimental spirit of the modernist movement. She performed barefoot, adopting a natural style that rejected the formal and more constrictive aesthetics of classical ballet. Generations of choreographers and dancers since then, such as Josephine Baker and Martha Graham, have been inspired by her philosophy and teachings.   Ullstein Bilderdienst/The Image Works

WITH A RADICALLY ALTERED MAP of Europe as a result of the war, in the decade after 1918 many people, from Europe to North America, Asia, and elsewhere around the globe began to reconsider their social, cultural, and political identities. Some abandoned their allegiance to the nationalist or liberal ideals that had yielded few positive results in the Great War. Others found new hope in nationalism, especially ethnic groups from the newly formed states in Eastern Europe. Still more were caught in the colonial enterprises forged in the peace treaties. Women demanded political and economic power, workers fought for social justice, peasants for property rights, and newly created states struggled for recognition. Artists like Isadora Duncan offered new ways of defining beauty and gender norms.

This period saw both a rush toward creating a brand new world from the ashes of war and a withdrawal aimed at imposing stability on the world that had unraveled. As empires collapsed, new states sprang up, forcing a veritable new order. Europe redrew national borders, reformulated the principles of state sovereignty, and redefined the nature of international relations in which colonialism continued to coexist in tension with the principles of self-determination. Democracy became the new foundation for political legitimacy. The postwar peace conference that mapped these changes pleased no one and left many issues unresolved. Mounting economic problems such as postwar payments and debts plagued much of the continent and helped destabilize the U.S. economy by the end of the decade.

To address these new conditions, Europeans tried a broad range of political experiments, from social democracy in Germany and Scandinavia to fascism in Italy. In Russia, the Bolsheviks won a civil war and embarked on a radically new and untested communist system. State institutions forcefully eliminated any real and potential enemies and tried to transform peasants into workers, women and men into equal participants in the building of communism, and a variety of ethnic groups, from Uzbeks to Ukrainians, into compliant followers of the Soviet order. Avant-garde artists created a new revolutionary style.

New social and intellectual movements flourished all over Europe. Women tried on new public identities in popular culture and new political roles in countries where they won the vote. Some challenged economic, social, sexual, and cultural limits. Philosophers, theologians, and artists reacted against the destruction of the war with a renewed commitment to moral values and hope in Christianity. The 1920s also saw the growth of a pacifist movement.

World War I strenuously tested the notion of progress and exposed the frailty of the human condition. Europeans met these challenges in different ways—some by living in the moment and enjoying the freedoms of popular entertainment and consumption, others by searching for absolutes and moral redemption in politics, philosophy, or art. At the heart of many of these responses was the hope that a brand new world could be forged out of the ashes of the war. Some politicians, reformers, and intellectuals tried to find a middle ground, but their voices were barely heard in the chaotic atmosphere of the 1920s. By 1929, Europe was becoming polarized between two extremist political regimes—fascism and communism—and democracy was losing ground.

26-1 The Search for Stability, 1918–1924

» **What strategies did political leaders use to restore stability in Europe after the war?**

» **How successful were they?**

» **What problems stood in the way of political stability?**

When European leaders met in 1919 to write the peace treaties, the mood was grim. The war was over, but violence continued. Four empires—the Habsburg, German, Ottoman, and Russian—lay in shambles. Revolution had engulfed Russia and spread in Germany and Hungary. The economies of all the combatants were devastated. Cities, factories, and fields lay in ruin; people starved. Yet few leaders were ready to rebuild Europe and secure a lasting peace through democracy. Instead, they focused on immediate objectives, such as increasing their territory and population, reducing war payments, and solidifying their own political position at home. The peace negotiations were driven as much by internal as by international considerations. They also were driven by secret treaties made during the war. As a consequence, the ideal of national self-determination promoted by U.S. President Woodrow Wilson stood little chance of success. In the end, the victors were dissatisfied and the defeated humiliated. Even before the ink dried on the paper of the last peace document (1923), radical movements were undoing the stability of Europe.

26-1a The Peace Treaties

As peace negotiations opened in January 1919 at the old royal palace in Versailles, the representatives of the victorious Allied Powers, who dominated the agenda—all gray-haired men in tails and top hats—embodied the old European order established a century before at the Congress of Vienna. But revolutionary changes were at hand: the map of Europe would be redrawn (see Map 26.1), a new international system would redefine state relations, now with a global reach, and nationalism in the hands of nearly universal male suffrage would replace aristocratic privilege as the fundamental basis for political power.

Self-Determination Wilson arrived in Paris with an idea for a European order based on national self-determination: Poles should govern themselves in an independent Poland and Italians should live in Italy. This principle seemed a rational and just solution to some of the problems that had caused turmoil in Europe since the nineteenth century and contributed to the beginning of World War I. Ethnic minorities had come to see themselves as fundamentally oppressed because they generally did not receive the same benefits of economic development and state support for their education and culture as members of the majority ethnic group. Yet the ethnic map of Europe was so complicated as to make self-determination territorially impossible. Polish nationals lived in areas where there were significant Russian and German populations. Italians and South Slavs were mixed in Istria

Legend:

- Boundaries of German, Russian, Austro-Hungarian, and Ottoman Empires in 1914
- Areas lost by Austro-Hungarian Empire
- Areas lost by Russian Empire
- Areas lost by German Empire
- Areas lost by Bulgaria
- Areas lost by Ottoman Empire
- Demilitarized Zones
- Areas controlled under mandates from the League of Nations, 1920
- Boundaries of 1926

Map 26.1 **Europe following World War I** Europe's political map was greatly altered by the peace settlements following World War I. With four empires wiped off the map, and new, smaller states cobbled out of the territories lost by these former great powers, Europe entered a new era of the nation-state.

1. If you compare the borders of European states after the peace treaties with those of 1914, as shown on Map 25.1 in the previous chapter, who were the winners and who were the losers after the war in terms of territorial changes?

2. Which winning countries seem most vulnerable in terms of borders with countries on the losing side of the war?

3. Which countries seem most stable territorially?

and other areas along the Adriatic Sea. No matter where the national boundaries were set, they were likely to retain significant ethnic minorities. Generally though, the winners in Europe's Great War liked Wilson's ideas and supported them as a basis for peace and stability in Europe as well as a justification for territorial gains. Those who had sided with the Allies—such as the Poles and Romanians—gained, while those aligned with the Central Powers lost. And ethnic groups that were part of the European Empires beyond the borders of Europe were excluded from any consideration.

One outcome of self-determination was an array of new and significantly reshaped countries. Among the winners, France, Greece, Italy, and Romania gained territories and populations. From the losers, new countries were created: Czechoslovakia was carved out of Austria-Hungary; Finland, Estonia, Latvia, and Lithuania emerged from Russia's western borderlands; Poland was re-created from the unification of territories lost by Germany, Russia, and Austria-Hungary; and Yugoslavia was created by uniting Serbia with South Slavic territories lost by Austria-Hungary. The western European states' interest in creating these new countries had a great deal to do with self-determination and also with their fear of Bolshevism. The new countries that bordered the Soviet Union would be a buffer zone against communist contamination from the east.

Problematic Outcomes   By contrast, Austria, Bulgaria, Hungary, Germany, Russia, and Turkey lost territories. Most severely reduced were Germany, held responsible for starting the war, and Russia, whose Bolshevik regime had signed a separate peace with Germany. Neither was represented at the negotiations. For all these countries, save the Soviet Union, revision of the **Versailles Treaty** and the supplemental treaties was an important aim in the internal politics of the next two decades, undermining any quest for stability and democracy (see Table 26.1).

Other wartime arrangements undermined the spirit of reconciliation and justice promoted by Wilson. To convince Italy to enter the war, the Allies had secretly offered it Istria, where the majority of the population were South Slavs. Serbia, also an ally of France and Britain, had been promised the same area. In the end, Italy received a good part of this territory, in flagrant disregard for the principle of self-determination. Another victim of the secret treaties was the Ottoman Empire. The Sykes-Picot Agreement (1916) had promised France and Britain various Ottoman territories in the Middle

Versailles Treaty First peace treaty of World War I; established Germany's guilt in starting the war and punished it through reparations and demilitarization.

Table 26.1	World War I Peace Treaties
1918	Brest-Litovsk: Germany with Russia
1919	Versailles: Allies with Germany
1919	St. Germain: Allies with Austria
1919	Neuilly-sur-Seine: Allies with Bulgaria
1920	Trianon: Allies with Hungary
1920	Sèvres: Allies with Turkey
1921	Riga: Poland with Soviet Union
1924	Lausanne: Allies with Turkey and Greece

East. After the war, contradictory promises made by some British leaders, such as T. E. Lawrence, to Arab nationalist groups, and by other British politicians to Jewish Zionist groups (the Balfour Declaration) produced a conflict over Arab and Jewish homelands in Palestine that remains unresolved to this day.

Thus, a great deal of debate at Versailles focused on what counted more—the promises made by the Allies during the war or the new and popular principle of self-determination. The solutions varied, and though the states involved in these disputes were pacified, they were not necessarily satisfied. The greatest casualty, however, was the very principle of self-determination. If secret treaties counted more than the rights of ethnic groups who inhabited the disputed territories, the new states learned quickly that they were still at the mercy of the Great Powers.

Minorities Protection   The Great Powers tried to address potential interstate conflicts in two ways. First, they made sure the peace treaties protected minorities. The borders of Czechoslovakia, Poland, Romania, Yugoslavia, Greece, and Turkey were recognized only if these states agreed to treat ethnic and religious minorities, especially Jews, as equal citizens. Yet these provisions fostered some instability: they gave rise to protests inside states, especially by ethnic majorities, and from outside—from states that had lost populations. On a personal level, consider the dilemma of an educated ethnic Hungarian, a city employee in Kolozsvár, in the heart of Transylvania. After 1919, when Hungarian Kolozsvár became Romanian Cluj, he lost his job because he did not speak the language of the new administration—Romanian. His identity changed overnight: he lost his economic position, his social standing as a respectable government employee, and his cultural position as a member of an important European nation, Hungary. Though

News from the Outside World

This Pulitzer Prize winning cartoon from 1925, by Rollin Kirby, reflects on the conspicuous absence of the United States, Soviet Union, and Mexico from the League of Nations.

❯❯ *What does this depiction of the three nonmember states suggest about their relationship with the League?*

❯❯ *What do the sartorial choices of the artist invoke in terms of ethnic identities of those countries and their international status?*

❯❯ *What might the inclusion of Mexico in this image suggest about the status of that country in the eyes of the American public in the 1920s?*

the same person living in the same place, he was recast as a member of a powerless ethnic minority. It is not difficult to imagine how those who had been part of Europe's privileged old order felt after 1919 and how quickly they looked to revise the peace treaties. **Revisionism** set the stage for future interethnic conflict.

The League of Nations The Great Powers also tried to maintain peace through the new League of Nations, created in the Versailles settlement. This international organization gave sovereign states the means for communicating and solving problems through open, peaceful negotiations rather than through secret treaties. The League also monitored the protection of minorities and various international humanitarian organizations, such as the Red Cross. But it was weak from the beginning because the United States—fearing European entanglements—refused to join, and Germany, Russia, Mexico, and Turkey were excluded. Other Great Powers wavered between playing a strong role and disengagement. The League was

important in establishing and seeking to monitor the upholding of international principles such as human rights, protection against human trafficking, fair labor practices, and the treatment of displaced persons. But it did not have the strength to enforce its decisions. Its most severe punishment was to expel countries that did not comply.

The League did have an important role regarding the status of colonies, however. Former German colonies in Africa and Asia were transferred to Britain, France, Japan, and the United States as **trust territories** or **mandates**, and large parts of the former Ottoman Empire were also placed under British and French authority. Through its new mandate system, the League monitored the treatment of the native populations by colonial governments and facilitated cooperation among colonial powers, which were now also obligated to report to the League on their colonies. The goal of this system was to prepare native populations for self-government. One prominent example was the role of Britain in facilitating the development of modern political institutions and elites in Iraq, which moved from its **protectorate** position in 1919 to gaining full independence in 1932.

CONNECTIONS: In the case of Egypt, however, the nationalist movement that grew during the war came to resent the position of protectorate under British sovereignty and in 1919 the country declared its independence after a series of massive protests, including an unprecedented march by women of various religious backgrounds through the streets of Cairo. While the protests were generally peaceful, the reprisals were not, and over 800 protesters were killed, with another 1,600 wounded by the British authorities. Because of other independence movements elsewhere (see Section 26-1b Revolutionary Upheavals below to read about Irish Nationalism) and to save face, Britain extended nominal independence to Egypt, though under conditions that in effect retained a great deal of British control over strategic economic and military interests in the country. Self-determination in Africa looked quite different from self-determination in Europe. (See Section 24-1b Domestic Politics and National Rivalries for more on how imperial powers came to identify their own national pride with colonial possessions.)

In most cases, the League found it difficult to enforce its supervisory role without military force. Yet the

revisionism Political aim of revising the World War I peace settlements.

trust territories and **mandates** Former colonies and territories of losing countries given by the League of Nations to the winning countries to oversee.

protectorate Political entity that formally agrees by treaty to enter into an unequal relationship with another, stronger state.

British Mandate in Palestine

In the Middle East, the protectorate regime gave rise to resentments that have come to plague peaceful relations until today, from Syria to Iraq. Already in 1936, local nationalists clashed with the occupying forces.

participation of colonial troops in the war and the promises of the League had awakened the hope of self-rule and greater freedom among native peoples, and the League was ineffective in easing the resulting tensions. Especially in Palestine, another British mandate, clashes between the local Arab population and resolute Jewish settlers continued into the 1930s and beyond.

Still, the League represented a major departure from the system of international relations of the nineteenth century, in which small states had been virtual clients of the Great Powers. Some of these uneven power relations continued after the war, but recognition of all member states as equals allowed small and new states to carve out a more independent position in international relations. This more democratic and inclusive setting helped generate a new culture of diplomacy, in which alliances and negotiations were discussed openly. Even though the League was ultimately unsuccessful in preventing another world war, it did bring about greater stability among its members in the 1920s. It also served as a learning ground for the creation of the United Nations after World War II.

Adolf Hitler (1889–1945)
Leader of the Nazi Party and dictatorial ruler of the Third Reich who initiated World War II by attacking Poland.

Béla Kun (1886–1938)
Leader of a short-lived Bolshevik regime in Hungary crushed by Romanian and Slovak forces.

26-1b Revolutionary Upheavals

The Bolshevik threat also shaped the ultimate outcome of the peace negotiations. With revolution in Russia and millions of armed soldiers on their way home to ruined economies and impoverished families throughout Europe, other states were afraid of revolution. In a few cases, this fear was real. In Germany, with the Communist and Socialist Parties on the rise, several bloody uprisings took place between November 1918 and January 1919. They were crushed relatively quickly and violently, with leaders Rosa Luxemburg and Karl Liebknecht brutally murdered on the spot. A young corporal, **Adolf Hitler**, made himself known in the crushing of the communist uprising in Bavaria.

The Bolshevik Uprising in Hungary In Hungary, a Bolshevik revolution in March 1919 helped bring about a short-lived (133 days) Soviet Republic under the leadership of **Béla Kun** (BELL-ah kun). The Bolshevik success here owed much to the Hungarians' dissatisfaction with the results of the war. As junior partners of the Austrians, they had endured great material and psychological losses. Kun's regime did not alleviate this suffering, focusing instead on brutally suppressing its enemies. In swift reaction, the Great Powers allowed Slovak and Romanian forces to invade the country. The results were disastrous for Hungary. The Kun regime was crushed, but Romania and Czechoslovakia extracted large territorial concessions for their role in "saving" the Hungarian people. The result was the Treaty of Trianon (1920), which reduced Hungary to one-third its prewar size, with large groups of Hungarians living outside its borders. The brief and violent Soviet Republic proved a costly experiment. It rendered Hungary small, landlocked, and vengeful, eager to revise the peace treaties.

Proto-Fascists in Italy Another short-lived revolutionary experiment was the **Republic of Fiume**, the brainchild of Italian poet **Gabriele D'Annunzio**. This small Adriatic port was part of Istria, the area claimed by Italy and Yugoslavia on the basis of secret treaties at the beginning of the war. South Slavs constituted a majority in Istria, but the city of Fiume had an Italian majority. Wilson sided with Yugoslavia. Given the controversy over this city, D'Annunzio decided to take matters into his own hands and seized municipal institutions in September 1919. The poet became a military dictator, revered by his followers and feared by the general public.

Fiume was finally granted to Italy, but its ultimate fate was less important than the style of rule and **charismatic leadership** D'Annunzio modeled for **Benito Mussolini**, the future fascist leader. D'Annunzio's dramatic public speeches swayed huge crowds, more through performance and style than content. His followers marched through the streets in black shirts and leather boots, creating the impression of a highly unified and threatening military force. Adopting a look of youthful vengeance and an aura of absolute obedience, these young men seemed ready to renounce their individuality and devote themselves to their leader. The masterful way in which D'Annunzio reshaped identities impressed Mussolini, who adopted the rhetoric, uniforms, and ideas first experimented in Fiume.

Irish Nationalism Other victors also confronted revolutionary uprisings. The turmoil in Ireland intensified after 1919. Newly elected members of the Irish parliament declared independence and a bitter civil war ensued (1919–1921), claiming many victims and ending in a peace treaty that laid the foundation of the **Irish Free State** (1922–1937). This state comprised all of Ireland except the six counties of Northern Ireland and received **dominion** status identical to that of Canada. There was much debate over the requirement to swear allegiance to the British king and especially over the status of Northern Ireland, which remained under direct British rule. The close final vote to ratify the treaty, 64 to 57, virtually ensured that separatist movements, such as the **Irish Republican Army** (IRA), would continue against the British. Unlike most other movements for national liberation in Europe at that time, in Ireland religion rather than language identity was at issue. In the Irish Free State, Catholicism was

the dominant religion, whereas Catholics were a religious minority in Northern Ireland, where Protestants dominated. Yet despite tensions, Catholics and Protestants in Northern Ireland lived in relative peace for the next forty years.

Political challenges from the left and right thus threatened peace in Europe. Most governments and parties equated stability and democracy with suppressing Bolshevism. Liberals, social democrats, and nationalists united against this common enemy; yet some nationalist parties were also aggressive and potentially destabilizing, especially when they fought against the peace treaties. German nationalists in both Germany and Czechoslovakia, for example, used the principle of self-determination to argue that Czechoslovakia, with its large German minority, did not respect the peace treaties and would therefore be Bolshevik-friendly. Opponents of the peace treaties often used anti-Bolshevism to argue their cause.

26-1c War Reparations and Economic Crisis

While the peace treaties sought political solutions to Europe's turmoil, economic stability proved elusive. The cost of the war had been enormous in financing the military effort and rebuilding destroyed lands and industries. Between the deficits incurred to finance the wars and the overall drop in economic production, all European states emerged from the war with major deficits, looking toward the United States for help.

Paying Off the War Debt The victorious Allies, wanting the Central Powers to pay these costs, imposed **reparations** as part of the peace treaties. By far the

Republic of Fiume Revolutionary experiment led by Gabriele D'Annunzio, whose dictatorship and militarized police state were precursors of fascism.

Gabriele D'Annunzio (1863–1938) Italian writer who led the Republic of Fiume.

charismatic leadership Leadership style that uses emotional appeals to arouse followers and compel loyalty.

Benito Mussolini (1883–1943) Fascist dictator of Italy, the first to successfully challenge democracy in Europe; after 1936, a close ally of Adolf Hitler.

Irish Free State Irish state established in 1922 with dominion status, consisting of all of Ireland except Northern Ireland, which remained under direct British rule.

dominion Status in which former colonies recognize the British monarch as the head of the state but control their internal and foreign affairs.

Irish Republican Army Military organization recognized in 1919 by the parliament of the *Republic of Ireland* as its army, revived in 1970 as a paramilitary terrorist organization.

reparations War payments demanded by the victors from the losers.

largest reparations were demanded of Germany, both as revenge and as a means for the political leaders at Versailles to gain popular support at home. Coupled with the treaty's war guilt clause, in which Germany had to admit responsibility for starting the war, and its demand for disarmament, including demilitarization of the Rhineland, reparations reinforced Germany's humiliation and aimed to prevent it from becoming a major power again. The notion of making losers pay for the costs of armed conflict was not new, but the size of the payments was unprecedented. An international commission set reparations at 132 billion gold marks (today about $331.79 billion), or two years' worth of Germany's gross national product.

The German Crisis The British and French pressed Germany to start payments immediately, as both needed to repay the United States billions of dollars in war loans. The Americans were in a hurry to see the loans repaid, and with weak economic performance and potential political instability at home, Britain and France were relying on war reparations as an important revenue source. The French were particularly inflexible. But after making its first payment of 2.5 billion gold marks in 1921, the German government defaulted. Great Britain was willing to work out a **moratorium** and potential reduction of the payments, but France and Belgium, with much greater material and human losses in the war, stood by the Versailles agreement and proceeded to occupy Germany's heavily industrial Ruhr district in order to extract the debt payment in kind.

The **Ruhr occupation** (1923–1925) had a twofold effect on the young German democracy. First, it unified Germans in their opinion of the Versailles Treaty as unjust and of the victorious powers as abusive. This view fostered the growth of nationalist parties, including the **National Socialist German Workers' Party**—the Nazis. In addition, by extracting from Germany some of its most important economic resources (the Ruhr produced 80 percent of Germany's steel and coal), the occupation helped generate a severe economic crisis.

moratorium Delay in the payment of the war debt.

Ruhr occupation Occupation (1923–1925) by French and Belgian troops of Germany's industrial Ruhr district to enforce the war reparations clause of the Versailles Treaty.

National Socialist German Workers' (Nazi) Party Right-wing party that recruited followers by promoting nationalism-socialism, with a nationalist-racist perspective.

hyperinflation Rapid devaluation of a currency that reduces its buying power overnight.

Dawes Plan Financial agreement concluded by France, Britain, and the United States in 1924 that solved the crisis of war reparations and loans.

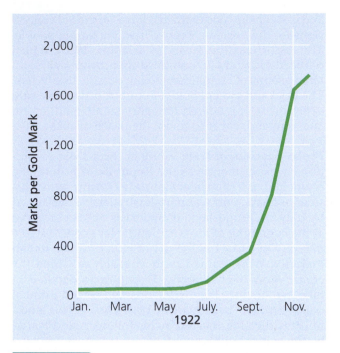

Figure 26.1 **German Hyperinflation in 1922** After 1918 Germany suffered an economic breakdown, due to the punitive war debt payments the state was obligated to assume. It was only after the Dawes Plan came into effect in 1924 that Germany began to recover its economic power.

》 *How was the buying power of an average German citizen affected by the change in the value of the German mark between September and November 1922?*

Source: Wilkinson, James D.; Huges, H. Stuart, *Contemporary Europe: A History*, 9th Edition, © 1998, pp. 136. Reprinted by permission of Pearson Education, Inc., Upper Saddle River, NJ.

The German government only made things worse by printing more money, which led to **hyperinflation** (see Figure 26.1). The buying power of white-collar workers, small business owners, and the lower middle class overall vanished overnight. The hard-won savings of a middle-class professional that once might have paid for a car now barely bought a loaf of bread. Suitcases filled with paper money were not enough for a week's groceries. The professionals and small businessmen who had been the backbone of Germany's social and economic stability were instantly converted into impassioned and desperate critics of the new German Republic.

The Ruhr crisis brought in other mediators, including a commission headed by American statesman and banker Charles G. Dawes. Its recommendations, known as the **Dawes Plan** (1924), set reparation payments at more realistic levels and helped rebuild the economies of other European countries, including Germany's. The United States loaned money to Germany to finance its war debt. Germany then paid installments to France and Britain as part of its reparations. These payments enabled France and Britain to repay their war loans to the United States. By the second half of the 1920s, Europe's economies seemed restabilized.

With inflation under control in Germany and reparations payments steady, a new mood of reconciliation resumed in Franco-German relations. In 1925, they finally accepted their post-1918 common border. The League of Nations, despite the absence of the United States, was active and had a growing membership that after 1926 included Germany. That same year **Aristide Briand** (AR-is-TEED BRAIY-and), the French foreign minister, and **Gustav Stresemann** (SHTRAY-se-mahn), his German counterpart, received the Nobel Peace Prize for their "unprecedented attempt to base politics on the principle of mutual friendship and trust." In 1928, under the leadership of Briand and U.S. Secretary of State Frank B. Kellogg, fifteen countries signed the **Kellogg-Briand Pact**, which "condemned and renounced war as an instrument of national policy." Though the pact suggested greater U.S. involvement in European affairs, it had no means of enforcement; it represented more a hope for peace than a guarantee. Still, international relations were now conducted in a relatively democratic and open fashion, a major shift from the prewar order.

26-2 Postwar Political Experiments, 1924–1929

» **What new forms and responsibilities of government emerged during this period?**

» **Where and in what ways was democracy successful, and what were its failures?**

In the second half of the 1920s, Europe stabilized. Governments rebounded from the disappointments of the peace treaties and hyperinflation. In western Europe, the most successful political parties were conservative and moderate; liberals and social democrats lacked popular trust. New parties tried to take advantage of this vacuum, most prominently the Italian fascists. In eastern Europe, a combination of older liberal and new agrarian parties had the greatest impact on the young states. Only in Scandinavia was there continuity between the prewar and postwar politics. But everywhere, except for Italy, democratic forms of government seemed solidly in place.

26-2a Politics in Western Europe

In the five years after 1918, the politicians of the most powerful European countries—Great Britain, France, and Germany—lost the confidence of their constituents. They had failed to fulfill the promises made before and during the war. Disappointment with the peace treaties and subsequent economic crises further eroded their standing.

Political Contests in Britain and France   In Britain, the most important political casualty of the war was the Liberal Party, which never recovered from the growing division over wartime policies. Though **David Lloyd George** had won at Versailles, his position at the helm of the Liberal Party became weakened, as many politicians and followers were displeased with the economic and political costs of his aggressive wartime policies. He tried to rebuild his popularity and the unity of the party, but allying himself with Conservative politicians cost him dearly, sending many followers toward the growing Labour Party. While the Liberals floundered, between 1920 and 1929 the Conservative and Labour Parties fought for political power. The Conservatives provided an economic platform and an ideology of security that spoke to the older base of this party, the upper classes, and also to many among the middle classes who had lost faith in the Liberals. The newly enfranchised female voters also tended to prefer the Conservatives. For most of the decade, the Conservatives controlled Parliament and pushed stringent measures to protect business interests, often at the expense of the working and lower middle classes. Yet the British economy did not fully recover from its wartime losses.

Leading the anti-Conservative opposition was the Labour Party, which developed rapidly from a marginal, class-based party to a more popular and broad-based party with socialist ideological leanings that attracted workers in the public service sector and lower ranks of the middle class. Though the Labour Party held power for only a brief nine-month period under **Ramsay MacDonald** (1924), it forced the Conservatives to confront workers' concerns such as the length of the workweek and unemployment benefits as mainstream issues. Just as important was the growing union movement, loosely coordinated with the Labour Party but institutionally independent,

Aristide Briand (1862–1932) French foreign minister who orchestrated reconciliation with Germany and the Kellogg-Briand Pact.

Gustav Stresemann (1878–1929) German prime minister and later foreign minister who brought stability to Weimar Germany in the 1920s.

Kellogg-Briand Pact Agreement renouncing war, signed in 1928 by fifteen European countries and the United States and ultimately by sixty-three states.

David Lloyd George (1863–1945) British politician who led Britain through World War I and the postwar settlement as the Liberal Party prime minister, 1916–1922.

Ramsay MacDonald (1866–1937) First leader of Britain's Labour Party to become prime minister.

which in 1926 forced the Conservatives to deal with workers' concerns through a general strike. The strike failed, but the work rights demanded by the strikers entered the vocabulary of both dominant parties.

In France, the disappointment that followed the peace treaties produced a quick succession of governments. No party—centrist, conservative, or left wing—was able to keep power for long. Only after 1926, under the Republican centrist **Raymond Poincaré** (pwon-cah-RAY), did a more secure government emerge. He stabilized the currency and secured prosperity, which gave people hope for the future.

Stability in Weimar Germany Germany faced great political challenges after 1919. All prewar political leaders were compromised by defeat, and following the collapse of the monarchy, a new political system had to be created. The political leaders who drafted the progressive democratic constitution and other political institutions in the city of Weimar—which gave its name to the new regime, **Weimar Republic**—had the difficult task of gaining the trust of an embittered population. Some nationalist leaders were blamed for the outcome of the war, some liberal leaders had been assassinated by radical nationalists, and some on the left had been tainted by the communist uprisings in 1918–1919, so it was unclear who could fill this vacuum.

The key figure turned out to be Gustav Stresemann, a successful businessman and politician with a monarchist conservative background. Before the war he had strongly supported German nationalist aspirations and traditions embodied by the emperor but had looked with some favor upon measures benefiting workers. Above all, he was a realist who knew by 1918 that the old system was bankrupt. For him, democracy was a pragmatic, rather than ideological, choice.

Between 1920 and 1923, when he assumed leadership of the government for one brief year, Stresemann went from opposing the Weimar constitution to supporting it for the sake of stability. After the war, he created the German People's Party to revise the Versailles Treaty, secure economic growth, and offer some support for workers. Stresemann's election as prime minister in 1923 marked a turning point for the Weimar Republic. He stabilized internal politics and, resolving the Ruhr occupation crisis, rebuilt Germany's international stature. Under him, radical right- and left-wing movements were effectively put down, notably the Nazi Party's attempt under Hitler to seize power in Bavaria known as the **Beer Hall Putsch**. Stresemann's successors were able to maintain stability partly because of his achievements. Although the Weimar Republic proved short lived, it was one of the most democratic and progressive states in Europe, with universal suffrage and protections for workers much more comprehensive than in Great Britain or France, from regulation of the workweek to state unemployment insurance.

26-2b Politics in Eastern Europe

After 1918 eastern Europe was responding to dramatic changes in borders and new ethnic compositions and struggling to organize stable governments. Democratic institutions and mass parties were new, so the main concern was order rather than the return to prosperity sought in the west. Some countries—Czechoslovakia, Poland, the Baltic states, Greece, and Turkey—adopted republican governments to foster democracy. The rest—Hungary, Yugoslavia, Romania, Albania, and Bulgaria—opted for more traditional constitutional monarchies. Neither choice brought stability and democratization, however, as both were compromised by corruption.

The Czechoslovak Democratic Model The only new state to demonstrate relative political stability and economic growth was Czechoslovakia. Like all the other new states in eastern Europe, Czechoslovakia experienced interethnic tensions (among Czechs, Slovaks, and Germans) and political weakness. There were so many parties that no single one could capture the majority in parliament. In almost every election, it was necessary to form coalitions among two or three parties, rendering any government unlikely to follow a clear political agenda. But, unlike other eastern European states, Czechoslovakia was fortunate to have a visionary president, **Tomáš G. Masaryk**, who followed a policy of tolerance toward ethnic minorities. Masaryk skillfully negotiated the trust of the population. He also kept his country out of regional conflicts. Just as significant was his faith in the democratic institutions created after 1918.

Stability Through Autocracy Elsewhere in eastern Europe, leaders manipulated the new democratic institutions to maintain power or sometimes disregarded them altogether in the name of stability. These young democracies had little chance to function properly. In Poland, for instance, **Józef Piłsudski** (zho-ZEF peehl-SOOD-ski) used his position as military leader and war hero to undermine the powers of the parliament. Between 1926, when he executed a military coup to replace the government

Raymond Poincaré (1860–1934) French politician, president between 1913 and 1920, then twice premier.

Weimar Republic Name of the German state between 1919 and 1933, taken from the city where its democratic constitution was written.

Beer Hall Putsch (in German, "beer hall riot") Violent failed attempt by Hitler and the Nazi Party to take over the Bavarian local government in 1923.

Tomáš G. Masaryk (1850–1937) First president of Czechoslovakia and a strong supporter of democracy.

Józef Piłsudski (1867–1935) Military leader of Polish liberation forces in World War I and most important political figure between 1926 and 1935.

Tomáš Garrigue Masaryk

Czechoslovakia's first president came to be known as the father of modern Czechoslovak democracy. Many of his ideas about governing through compromise in order to maintain stability came from the years he spent in the United States. He was also a visionary in this part of Europe in his strong feminist convictions.

Mustafa Kemal Leading Turkey (1925)

Mustafa Kemal took on the surname "Atatürk" to fashion himself as the father of modern Turkey. In this poster, he appears on a horse, led by an unveiled female figure symbolizing Turkey. The captions under the two Turkish flags read: "O, beautiful country, we came to you, with feast and rejoicing!" and "Wrap the crescent star around your arms, and love and caress it well."

❱❱ *What political messages does this poster convey?*

❱❱ *What does it communicate about modernization?*

in power with his own, and until his death in 1935 he sought economic stability, international security, and tolerance for minorities—all worthy goals. But he sacrificed any balanced division of power among the branches of government, showing through his actions that democracy could not work in his country. Piłsudski himself never assumed leadership of the country and preferred instead to manipulate policy making through indirect threats and intrigues. Poland's failure to build democracy was typical of most other eastern European states.

In the former Ottoman lands, Greece and Turkey also aimed for stability and prosperity within their new borders, often disregarding democratic aspirations. Greece had been the first constitutional government in the Balkans and by 1920 had almost a century of political experience with modern parliamentary rule. But experience did not improve its chances at establishing a stable democracy. Instead, Greece became embroiled in expansionist dreams at the expense of Turkey. After 1918, it pursued a series of disastrous military campaigns,

only to be defeated and humiliated by **Mustafa Kemal Atatürk's** (ah-tah-TUERK) armies. The territorial losses and repatriation of more than 1.2 million Greeks sent Greek politics into turmoil. In the first half of the 1920s, the king was forced to abdicate, and a new republican system was proclaimed, but it proved ineffective and in 1935 the king returned to the throne. The cradle of democracy proved inauspicious ground for building democratic institutions and practices after 1918.

CONNECTIONS: The use of the female form to represent nationalism became a common trope in the nineteenth century. How does the nearby image of Mustafa Kemal compare with that depicting Bulgaria in Section 22-2 New Nation-States and Nationalist Tensions?

Mustafa Kemal Atatürk (1881–1938) President of Turkey from 1920 to 1938 who pursued modernization and secularization in the name of democracy.

Turkey also failed in its attempt to foster democracy. Atatürk focused his entire career as president of the new republic (1920–1938) on consolidating parliamentary rule, a secular government, and a new type of military, striving to embody this modernizing spirit through his own rejection of traditional garb and even of wearing the fez. He also pursued modernizing social programs, such as compulsory education for all children and many reforms to empower women, such as the removal of the veil. Yet his style of government was not unlike that of Piłsudski, preaching democratization while practicing heavy-handed **authoritarian** tactics. Yet, although substantially diminished in terms of size, during the 1920s Turkey became militarily stronger, more homogeneous, and effectively **secularized**.

26-2c Fascism

While eastern Europe struggled to create democratic institutions, Italy abandoned them altogether. Benito Mussolini established a **fascist** dictatorship, the decade's first successful challenge to democracy. His model was D'Annunzio's police state in Fiume. Born to a blacksmith and a schoolteacher, Mussolini was a talented writer and speaker. In his youth he joined the Socialist Party and edited left-wing publications. His radical pacifism landed him in jail in 1911. Already he was dreaming of organizing a revolutionary mass movement of workers. But in the fall of 1914, he switched to an aggressive prowar position. In 1917, after he was accidentally wounded by a grenade (not on the battlefield), he turned to writing for a nationalist paper and promoting his heroic participation in the war.

The Power of Paramilitary Troops Having once spoken for the workers, Mussolini was skillful at exploiting postwar fears of unemployment with proworker rhetoric. In 1919, when strikes led by communist and socialist unions broke out, Mussolini used the popular anti-Bolshevik rhetoric of the time to cast these actions as a threat to Italy's stability. His call attracted young war veterans and other men looking for a good fight. These recruits were organized in closely knit **paramilitary** groups that operated in a strictly hierarchical fashion, copying the army, and took their orders strictly from their leader. They became the *fasci italiani di combattimento*, or "Italian gangs of combat," the predecessors of the Fascist Party.

Mussolini's fascists terrorized members of opposing parties and by 1921 had become a feared group in Italian politics. In October 1922, Mussolini threatened to march on Rome with his fascist troops and seize power from the weakened parliament unless he was named prime minister. King Victor Emmanuel III gave in. Mussolini moved swiftly to eliminate all political parties and establish a one-party authoritarian state in which he personally controlled all branches of the government and a powerful military. On the surface, he continued to maintain a parliamentary system, but only members of his Fascist Party could be elected, and "debate" meant obedience to the party line set by Mussolini himself.

Mussolini as Dictator Despite the existence of government institutions that suggested a division of power among the executive, legislative, and judicial branches, all power rested in the hands of *Il Duce*—"the leader." At times, Mussolini held as many as seven positions in government ministries, trying to run everything from public works to propaganda and the army. He was obsessed with managing every aspect of government, even hiring decisions about minor personnel. The light in his office was kept on for the entire period of his rule, and little boys and girls would be told that Il Duce was always there, laboring to bring happiness to the Italian people.

Mobilizing the Nation Italian fascism became an important model for other European politicians critical of democratic parliaments who wished to establish strong authoritarian regimes. Mussolini's regime was particularly attractive because its **corporatist** structure combined political and social stability with the promise of economic growth, thus attempting to solve all the dilemmas of postwar Europe. Eliminating political parties and labor unions, which he claimed were destabilizing, Mussolini instead channeled citizens into state-run corporations that would supposedly enable them to express their political views and protect their interests. Corporations would, for example, mediate conflicts between employees and employers without disturbing economic production through strikes. In reality, however, corporations were set up

---

authoritarian Concentrating power in the hands of a ruler.

secularization Change in a society from close identification with religious institutions to a more separated relationship, including transfer of institutions from ecclesiastical to civil control.

fascism Radical-right political movement initiated by Benito Mussolini in Italy that replaced parliamentary democracy with an authoritarian dictatorship emphasizing order.

paramilitary Group of civilians trained and organized in a military fashion.

corporatism System of government that organizes society into industrial, occupational, and professional groups that channel political expression and repress dissent.

United States Holocaust Memorial Museum

mainly to control workers and to disable protests against business leaders and the state.

Special corporations were created for women. These institutions aimed to control women's public activities and at the same time give the illusion that women were actively contributing to the nation's betterment. Mothers' organizations promoted childcare and household management by telling women it was their patriotic duty to be good mothers and wives and giving them a sense of pride in their domestic chores. This propaganda also underscored what was *not* proper for women—to engage in employment outside the home and activities outside the family. Feminist ideas about women's economic and political independence were vilified as antipatriotic and dangerous. Women's corporations were meant as much to shape the identity of women as solely mothers and wives as to allow women a place to come together in public.

Corporations successfully changed social and political institutions, but the fascists had more trouble with religious institutions. Mussolini was an unabashed atheist, and his paramilitary troops often showed little respect for the Catholic Church. Yet for most people being Italian was the same as being Catholic. The church had such a central role that it was really impossible to either ignore or fight it. It took Mussolini many years to come to an agreement over the status of the church, the clergy, and Catholic organizations in Italy, but in 1929 he signed a concordat with the pope that recognized the autonomy of the Vatican and reinforced the dominance of the church in education and marriage law. Relations with the church continued to be rocky in some areas, but most Italians were pleased with this agreement, which greatly increased Mussolini's popularity.

Fascist Economics Finally, the fascist government attempted to solve the problem of economic underdevelopment by increasing agricultural productivity, enlarging the male workforce, and creating public works such as roads and irrigation. There was a program to reclaim land, a program to improve wheat production, a program to promote agricultural self-sufficiency (encouraging purchases exclusively from the internal market), a program to increase the birthrate, and a program to improve transportation and build highways and railways. The economy was still primarily in the hands of private entrepreneurs and farmers, but the state played an important role in regulating business practices (e.g., by eliminating trade unions and dictating priorities in production), communications, and commerce, especially international trade. To some unstable European states, the fascist government's strong grip over both business and labor seemed to have solved the era's political and economic difficulties.

Policing the Nation Yet fascist solutions were neither simply pragmatic nor wholly positive. Workers' rights were reduced for the benefit of industry; farmers' production was closely scrutinized; and women's rights were severely restricted for the benefit of families, their bodies closely monitored for the purpose of reproduction, especially through **pro-natalist** and anti-birth control policies.

Those who were not willing to abide by these restrictions or who were defined as dangerous on account of their convictions, ethnicity, or religion, suffered severe persecutions. To be communist, non-Italian, feminist, or, especially after 1936, Jewish was dangerous. These populations were threatened by economic and social discrimination, subsequently by isolation, and, starting in the late 1930s, by extermination. Thus, in addition to positive definitions of what it meant to be a true Italian, Mussolini imposed categories of unacceptable identities on some.

The Power of Propaganda But in the 1920s, Mussolini was able to hide these negative aspects of his regime through masterful propaganda. Newspapers, films, radio broadcasts, parades, museums, and other state institutions and activities portrayed him as a man of the people and a resolute leader ready to listen and respond to the needs of all Italians. Most people could not imagine their country without Mussolini at the helm: "Italians of my generation carried the portrait of Mussolini within themselves, even before they were of an age to recognize it on the walls," remembered a writer who grew up in the 1920s. Mussolini's image was in every government office and classroom, and his personal style directed fashion trends. Both men and women were attracted to Il Duce—the first political leader to turn his baldness into a symbol of virility and strength. In making himself such a vivid model of the new Italian, Mussolini helped transform the ideals of a whole generation. Marching in the streets by the thousands in their stylish black uniforms, young men experienced power as intoxicating; on the sidewalks, young women swooned. Their emotions rendered them loyal followers in the hands of the charismatic and cunning Duce.

pro-natalism Policy encouraging women to have more children, pursued by most European governments after 1918 to replenish the postwar population.

welfare state State in which the government assumes responsibility for social needs such as public health, education, and unemployment insurance; pioneered in Scandinavia.

26-2d Social Democracy in Scandinavia

A very different approach to the economic and social problems of the postwar period can be seen in the Scandinavian countries, which used the tools of democracy. Here a tradition of charitable work and support for state intervention in matters of employment had existed since the late nineteenth century. Questions regarding the role of government in education, public health, child care, unemployment, and pensions were often the subject of debate in parliament. Social democratic and labor parties had a large presence in Scandinavian parliaments both before and after the war, and they guaranteed that social welfare measures would continue to be on the agenda. In 1923, Norway introduced old-age pensions. Denmark endorsed the principle of full rights for government social services, such as education, health care, and pensions for all citizens, irrespective of class or gender. Sweden launched a system of unemployment benefits, state support for health, and life insurance.

Scandinavian countries were thus at the forefront in establishing the **welfare state**, and their innovative reforms averted both social unrest and state bankruptcy. Yet the Scandinavian context was unique in Europe. With the exception of Finland, Scandinavia had been sheltered from war. The small size and ethnic homogeneity of these countries also helped preserve their stability. Quite simply, the sense of crisis and despair that dominated most of Europe in early 1919 was not present in Scandinavia. Instead, reforms that built on the prewar social welfare agendas proceeded, as the dominant political parties were never discredited by the war. Continuity, rather than upheaval, best describes the political and social development of Scandinavia in the 1920s.

26-3 The New Soviet State

>> How did the Soviet state differ from other European ones in the 1920s?

>> How did the Bolsheviks reshape society and individual identities?

The most radical experiment of the 1920s was the Soviet state. Out of a bloody civil war, the Bolsheviks were able to create a smaller but stronger country in which they reinvented the state and reshaped society according to Marxist-Leninist ideology. The Bolsheviks succeeded because of the unprecedented level of control imposed on every aspect of public life, rendering the Communist Party all-powerful and individuals fearful of the party's every move. The Bolsheviks also tried to attract people to the party by promising a better life for workers and peasants. By 1929, the Soviet Union had consolidated into a stable police state.

26-3a The Civil War

Russia left the Great War in 1918 after the Treaty of Brest-Litovsk, but the country was soon embroiled in a civil war between the Bolsheviks and their supporters, known as the Reds, and an alliance of supporters of the old order, known as the Whites. The Whites included military officers, nobles, and supporters of liberalism and democracy inside Russia and out. In their attempt to stamp out the Bolshevik threat, France, Britain, the United States, and Japan sent troops and financial help to the Whites. In addition, the newly independent Baltic Republics and Poland, which wished to secure their territorial gains, also pursued a war against the Bolsheviks.

Trotsky and the Victory of the Reds Though fighting a desperate war in its borderlands—from the Baltic and Siberia to the Crimea—the Bolsheviks won. What they lacked in experience and military power they made up for in organization and unity of purpose. They had charismatic, driven leaders who inspired great loyalty in their followers. Among them was War Commissar Leon Trotsky, described by an American observer as "the most dramatic character" and the "only great organizer" of the Russian Revolution. Trotsky was a skilled military leader who turned some of the most difficult battles of the civil war into victories. With his wild hair and piercing glare behind wire-rimmed glasses, Trotsky inspired many people, especially among the poor, to join the Reds. Like Mussolini and Atatürk, Trotsky represented a new charismatic style of leader whose ability to project virility, demand action, and use violence made him attractive to the generation that came of age during the war.

By contrast, the Whites were divided in aims and strategies, and the foreign aid they received was half-hearted. By 1922, these supporters were pulling out their war-weary armies and the Reds were winning in the Crimea and Siberia. Poland remained a serious threat, but the new states of eastern Europe did not challenge the Bolshevik regime itself. By 1922, the Reds had won the war by simply giving up some territories in the west, then consolidating their control over the rest of the country (see Map 26.2).

Beginnings of a New Order The civil war set in motion important trends later formalized as components of the Soviet regime. In 1918, the Bolsheviks nationalized almost all industry, legislated the obligation for all adults to work, and placed the government in charge of commercial activities. Another element of the civil war that became permanent was a secret police apparatus, the Cheka, which employed brutal methods to silence enemies. In its first six years, the Cheka killed more than two hundred thousand people. Overall, the human losses in these years, due to military conflict, starvation, and various epidemics, is estimated by some at above 4 million.

In 1919, the Bolsheviks established the Communist International, or **Comintern**, as a means for promoting world revolution, an extension of Trotsky's belief in the mission of the Soviet Union to transform the world into a "workers' paradise." This organization

Snark/Art Resource, NY

Soviet Propaganda

"Workers of the World Unite!" declares this Soviet poster in large red letters. The Soviet propaganda of the 1920s focused on the success of the workers' revolution in crushing the forces of oppression, depicted here through the crown and royal mantle, as well as the shield and broken chains, on which the worker steps with calm confidence.

》 *What relationship between workers and peasants does the poster suggest?*

》 *What role does it depict for women?*

》 *How would you compare its message and imagery to the Kemalist propaganda poster in Section 26-2b Politics in Eastern Europe?*

provided financial support and ideological guidance to communist movements abroad. In exchange, the Soviets demanded that all Communist Parties of the Comintern abandon cooperation with socialist and other left-wing noncommunist organizations; they were to take orders only from Moscow. These developments prefigured the more aggressive policies of

Comintern International organization set up by the Russian Bolsheviks in 1919 to promote communist revolutions all over the world.

Map 26.2 **The Russian Civil War, 1918–1922** The Russian Civil War was a conflict of attrition, engulfing large parts of Russia and lasting almost three years. The victory of the Reds (Bolsheviks) came at a high human and territorial price, as Russia lost many of its western imperial lands.

1. Looking at the shifts in the territory controlled by Bolshevik forces, as well as the 1914 versus 1922 borders, how would you describe the territorial challenges to Russia during this period?

2. Where were lasting changes most radical? What countries had the most to gain from these losses?

political purging and terror, state-controlled economy, and communist imperialism that came to define the Soviet Union in the 1930s.

But in 1922, the Bolsheviks had the more basic tasks of creating a stable political system and reinvigorating the economy. The communist regime of those years was more open to experiments in economic production, propaganda, and social programs than at any other time.

26-3b The Communist Regime

In December 1922, the **Union of Soviet Socialist Republics (USSR)** came into being. The ideological and legal foundations of this state combined the writings of Karl Marx and Friedrich Engels with V. I. Lenin's own ideas.

Ideological Foundations A fundamental principle of the new order was equality, understood very differently from the definition offered in the U.S. Declaration of Independence. Instead of focusing on equal rights for pursuing individual goals, the Soviets focused on economic equality: all people who worked were *equally* entitled to the fruits of their labor. This principle implied that differences in wealth and class were fundamentally unjust, as they were based on the oppression of one class (the workers) by another (the bourgeoisie). The Soviet state set out to eliminate these injustices, first by taking all property and means of production away from the bourgeoisie and nobility and then by enabling workers to gain control over the economy. The proletariat, as the producers of goods, were to control the fruits of their labor. By 1922, most of the means of production were under state control. The system the Bolsheviks imagined was entirely untested. No other country in the world had attempted such a fundamental transformation of the economic and social system overnight.

Strategies for Political Consolidation The Soviet Union also had to address problems of political stability and control. The revolution took place before workers had achieved full "consciousness" of class conflicts, one of the Marxist prerequisites for a communist revolution. Lenin made it an important goal for the Bolshevik regime to consolidate political power both by inclusive means, educating the workers and peasants, and through exclusionary tactics, eliminating enemies of the Bolsheviks. Propaganda and a secret police with an extensive network of informants were essential for this effort; both had been solidified during the civil war. By 1922, they became essential tools in building state institutions and programs.

Finally, the Soviet regime aimed to open opportunities for political participation to people who had lacked a voice before 1917. This goal was also incorporated into Soviet propaganda: the party would listen to the needs and problems of the oppressed and defend their rights; these promises would induce people to join the party and its affiliated organizations. The Women's Section of the Communist Party, or **Zhenotdel** (dze-NUT-del), was one such institution. The Bolsheviks had critiqued the inferior status of women in Russian society and attempted to attract them to the Communist Party through this department. Initially led by Alexandra Kollontai (see the Profiles in Change: Alexandra Kollontai Becomes a Revolutionary), it also served as an advocacy group where women could voice social, economic, and political concerns. Though somewhat democratic and experimental at the beginning, by 1928 it had become centralized and authoritarian and was eventually dissolved.

For all its positive propaganda, the exclusionary policies of the Soviet regime raised questions even among the faithful. Did the ends justify the means? Supposedly, communism was about equality and justice for all. Yet the road to it was paved with violence, and the new state institutions concentrated power in the hands of a small party elite. By the mid-1920s, there were furious debates within the party over centralization, with Trotsky in fierce opposition. In addition, although the party claimed that individuals had choices and that the state was interested in their ideas, most institutions suppressed ideas and actions different from the official party line. Soviet citizens received protection from the state only insofar as they were willing to serve the state with unquestioning loyalty.

26-3c The New Economic Policy and Struggle for Leadership

As the Soviet regime was attempting to deal with enemies at home and in the borderlands, its economy worsened.

Economic Challenges Nationalizing all industry did not lead to economic growth. In 1921 industrial production was just 13 percent of the prewar volume. Many of the best-trained professionals left the country, peasants refused to work for the state, and workers went on strike. Lenin realized that the regime needed to adopt a pragmatic economic policy to win the civil war and consolidate political control. In the spring of 1921 he inaugurated the **New Economic Policy (NEP)**, which allowed for the rebirth of private property and free commerce. The state retained control

Union of Soviet Socialist Republics (USSR) Official name of the Soviet Union, a federation of four, and eventually fifteen, autonomous republics, the largest and most powerful of which was Russia.

Zhenotdel Women's Section of the Soviet Communist Party, which focused on policies and issues such as employment, day care, and domestic work.

New Economic Policy (NEP) Economic plan allowing limited capitalism adopted by Lenin in 1921 to alleviate Russia's deep economic crisis.

Alexandra Kollontai Becomes a Revolutionary

HIP / Art Resource, NY

Aleksandra Kollontai A resolute Bolshevik who also believed that marriage was the root of women's social oppression in the bourgeois order, Aleksandra Kollontai (kol-on-TIE) advocated for free love and women's full independence, economically, legally, and socially.

At age twenty-two, Alexandra Kollontai seemed to have achieved everything expected of a young aristocratic woman. The daughter of a general in Russia's imperial army, she was well educated, privileged, and active in St. Petersburg's high society. She married an army officer and gave him a son. She was obedient and devoted. Then she read August Bebel's *Woman and Socialism*. His ideas that under capitalism women were fundamentally subjugated through the institution of marriage and could achieve full independence only under socialism convinced her that she was enslaved.

She started attending lectures by radical socialists and visiting factories to see the conditions in which the workers, especially women, of St. Petersburg labored. Her

secure and privileged life now seemed nothing more than a gilded cage, and she knew she could never go back to it. At age twenty-five, she abandoned her husband and child, disowned her aristocratic heritage, moved out on her own, and embarked on a remarkable career of revolutionary activism.

Beginning in 1898, she worked with underground Marxist organizations in Russia and abroad. She was an outspoken organizer of women workers, an important opponent of World War I, and leader of the International Women's Day demonstration for bread and peace that triggered the overthrow of the tsar in March 1917. In November 1917, she was at the forefront of the armed Bolshevik uprising.

Though a devoted Bolshevik, Kollontai was never satisfied with just following the party line; she insisted on speaking her mind and following her convictions, regardless of the consequences. Thus, in 1918 she found herself to be the sole opponent of the Treaty of Brest-Litovsk, which she viewed as abandoning the Finnish communist movement, and resigned from her government position as commissar for social welfare. She remained an inconvenience to the Bolshevik leadership throughout the early 1920s, never afraid to stand up to anyone, even V. I. Lenin.

Cleverly, Lenin dealt with Kollontai's radicalism by sending her abroad. In November 1922, she was appointed to the Soviet legation in Norway, then sent to Mexico and to Sweden. Far from Moscow, Kollontai was free to criticize the Bolshevik regime without posing a real threat inside the center of power. Yet she continued to play an important role in the Soviet Union. She was among the first female diplomats in the world to serve at such a high level and was regarded in the diplomatic international community as a very able colleague. Even when sidelined, Kollontai was a trendsetter.

Kollontai's radicalism was most remarkable in her work as the first leader of the Women's Section of the Communist Party (the Zhenotdel). Following Bebel's principles, she advocated ending marriage and the nuclear family in favor of living in free unions and raising children in communal settings, where domestic chores—cleaning, cooking, and child care—would be shared. She lived by her convictions but was unable to inspire others to do the same. Most women were not ready to abandon the satisfaction and security of marriage and motherhood, and men resisted her radical ideas. Yet, Kollontai's choice for freedom and courage to reshape her identity according to her radical beliefs made her a symbol of revolutionary experiments in politics and social relations that marked the decade after the Great War.

over large- and medium-size industries, such as steel and heavy machinery, but small businesses could be privately owned. Under the NEP, three-quarters of retail trade shifted back into private hands. In the countryside, the state allowed peasants to sell their own harvests rather than have the state requisition them at fixed prices. The recovery of the economy was remarkable. By the end of the 1920s, the Soviet Union had reached 1914 levels in agricultural production.

Factionalization and Stalin's Victory But the social and political costs of this recovery seemed too high to many Bolsheviks. The NEP had fostered the rebirth of an entrepreneurial class that was a nuisance to local communist administrators. On the one hand, the regime spoke about the need to eliminate class oppression and give workers control over the means of production. On the other hand, the state allowed for the kind of exploitation it condemned, based on pragmatic considerations. This double standard weakened the control of the Soviet regime and troubled faithful party members.

A struggle over the political costs of the NEP ensued in the **Politburo**, the highest decision-making body of the Communist Party. Lenin's death in January 1924 rendered this debate more complex, as Politburo members became divided over who should succeed him. Trotsky and his leftist supporters wanted to continue the revolutionary struggle in the world at all cost. This group also opposed the NEP as a deviation from communism and was concerned about the growing centralization of the state, which clashed with the democratic foundations of communism. Their strongest opponents were the centrists, led by **Joseph Stalin**, who called for building socialism in the Soviet Union, de-emphasizing the struggle for worldwide revolution. Stalin stressed the principal role to be played by Russia in the USSR and suggested the need to further centralize the state. Communists with nationalist leanings favored this position.

In the end, Stalin won the struggle by working behind the scenes in the Politburo and among his loyal lower party appointees. Few anticipated his victory, as he was less respected than Trotsky. Stalin was, however, a cunning man who advanced his career through power politics. Born in the Georgian Caucasus as Joseph Dzhugashvili, he joined a Marxist group while studying to become a priest and later worked with local Bolsheviks. He undertook dangerous actions on behalf of the movement, ending up in jail and exile, but he was neither a theoretician like Lenin nor an organizer like Trotsky. Instead, he had a good instinct for showing up in the right place at the right time and knowing whom to flatter and whose weaknesses to exploit.

By the early 1920s Stalin had risen to the top of the Bolshevik hierarchy, but neither Lenin nor the other leaders thought he would be Lenin's successor; they assumed that would be Trotsky. Stalin was clever, however, in exploiting Trotsky's criticisms of the NEP and other policies as evidence of disloyalty; eventually Trotsky was eliminated from leadership and sent into exile in Mexico. Stalin then brutally removed all remaining opponents. By 1928 he dominated all institutions of the state in dictatorial fashion, much like Mussolini in Italy, but without the fascist leader's personal allure.

26-3d The New Soviet Man and Woman

The Bolsheviks wanted nothing short of a complete transformation of society. They depicted capitalism as a system that bred greed, narrow-minded materialism, and pettiness among people, and described their own aims in terms of transforming individual and collective identity to foster fairness, selflessness, and dedication to the common good.

Class Enemies To eliminate class differences, supposedly the root of all capitalist problems, the party used brutal policies. In addition to abolishing private property in the early days of the civil war, the Bolsheviks also wished to eliminate all "oppressors," especially the social and economic elites of the tsarist regime—the aristocracy, businessmen, and the professional middle class. In the first phase of this social revolution, the Bolsheviks imprisoned or killed most members of the nobility. The bourgeoisie was also a class enemy, but it was a larger and less clearly defined category. Initially, the Soviet regime eliminated businessmen, easily targeted as exploiters of workers, by nationalizing their wealth and killing many. But if the bourgeoisie included all those who owned private property, it would include peasants as well.

Class enemies also included white-collar workers, professionals, and some educators. Those employed in state institutions, such as bureaucrats and teachers, became targets because of their allegiance to the tsarist regime. Doctors and engineers were viewed as a threat because they belonged to professions with standards independent of the political regime, and the Soviets could not tolerate independence. Architects, scientists, and engineers often had to join the party to maintain their professional standing.

Education and Secularization As large numbers of qualified individuals were removed from professions badly needed in the economy, education, and social services, the party

Politburo Highest decision-making body of the Soviet Communist Party.

Joseph Stalin (1879–1953) Dictatorial leader of the Soviet Union from 1929 to 1953, who transformed the Soviet Union into a police state run by fear and deceit, and into a military and economic superpower.

Alexandra Kollontai Advocates a New Type of Woman

While away from the Soviet Union, Kollontai published several radical writings, including the book from which the following selection is taken, *The Autobiography of a Sexually Emancipated Communist Woman*, first published in Norway in 1926.

1 Kollontai uses the terms "unfit" and "natural selection" to connect capitalism to a certain scientific theory of the nineteenth century. What is she referring to?

2 What does Kollontai imply about marriage?

3 What link does Kollontai draw between prostitution and marriage?

4 How do working women revolt against past "truths?" Does Kollontai criticize or celebrate this challenge?

But who are they, these single new women? The single woman—she is a child of the large-scale capitalist economic system. **1** There is no place in the ranks of those earning their own livelihood for the "unfit," that is to say, the women of the old type. Here, too, therefore, a "natural selection" among the women of the different social strata is discernible: only the stronger, more resistant disciplined natures arrive in the ranks of those "earning their own livelihood." **2 3** The weak, inwardly passive, cling to the family hearth, and when the insecurity of existence tears them away from the protection of the family, to catapult them into the stream of life, supinely, they let themselves be driven by the waves of legal or illegal prostitution: they enter into a marriage of convenience or they walk the streets.

4 The influence of women earning their own livelihood spreads far beyond their own circle. With their criticism, they "poison" the minds of their contemporaries, they smash old idols, they raise the banner of revolt against those "truths" with which women have lived for generations. By liberating themselves, the new, single women, earning their own livelihood, also liberate the passive-backward spirit, as this has been molded down the centuries, of their contemporary sisters.

embarked on its own program of education and training to fill gaps. The government considered eliminating illiteracy (above 50 percent in 1918) an important social goal and created many public schools, but quality was poor. Progress and access to higher education were linked to class background, with priority given to sons and daughters of workers, often at the expense of academic qualifications. The first generation of teachers, doctors, and engineers produced by this system were more likely to be faithful party activists than skilled professionals.

The Soviets used education to promote secularization and a rational understanding of Marxist economy. Though presented as scientific, the Marxist worldview was akin to a religious vision of history. Communists described eliminating class struggle as scientifically predictable. Yet there was no way of proving such developments. Instead, it was through a leap of faith that the Bolsheviks spoke of the certain "withering away of the state" and the inevitable victory of communism throughout the world. Like other religious zealots, revolutionaries such as Trotsky and Kollontai were willing to sacrifice both themselves and all who stood in their way for the fulfillment of this destiny.

Organized religion, however, was seen as irrational and a threat to Soviet ideology. The Orthodox Church, the state religion in tsarist Russia, emphasized faith in the afterlife and accepted the hardships of this life as normal, something to be embraced, not overcome. Social inequality was a fact of life. These beliefs clashed with the staunch atheism of the Bolsheviks. In addition, the Orthodox Church was rich and influential. It owned large estates and economic interests and commanded a great deal of respect, even fear, among the Russian population. From the beginning of their rule, the Bolsheviks persecuted members of this and all other religious institutions, clergy and laypeople alike. These persecutions continued throughout the 1920s, forcing believers to retreat to private places of worship, including homes and forests. Yet the complete elimination of all religious organizations did not become a goal of the Soviet Union until after 1928.

Reshaping Gender Roles In their ambition to transform Russian society, the Soviets also sought to reshape private lives, including family and gender relations. The Bolsheviks were quick to replace religious marriage with civil marriage. Young couples now came to city hall to be married before a judge

5 What does Kollontai imply about bourgeois women's movements?

6 Can the women's movement for liberation remain separate, or does it have to be part of a larger working-class movement? Why?

7 What kind of slavery is Kollontai hinting at here?

5 But whereas with the women of the working class, the struggle for the assertion of their rights, the strengthening of their personality, coincides with the interests of the class, the women of other social strata run into unexpected obstacles: the ideology of their class is hostile to the transformation of the feminine type. In the bourgeois milieu, woman's "rebellion" bears a far sharper character, its forms are set in bolder relief, and here the psychological dramas are far sharper, more variegated, and more complicated. **6** The new type of woman, inwardly self-reliant, independent, and free, corresponds with the morality which the working class is elaborating precisely in the interests of its class. For the working class the accomplishment of its mission does not require that she be a handmaid of the husband, an impersonal domestic creature, endowed with passive, feminine traits. **7** Rather, it requires a personality rising and rebelling against every kind of slavery, an active conscious equal member of the community, of the class.

Source: *The Autobiography of a Sexually Emancipated Communist Woman*, by Alexandra Kollontai (1971, Herder & Herder).

in a ritual that incorporated statements of loyalty to the Soviet regime and the Communist Party. Some party leaders, like Kollontai, believed that marriage itself should be eliminated, as it institutionalized the oppression of one-half of humanity, women, by the other half, men. Only free love, without the constrictions of marriage, would end this oppression. There were some early attempts to create communal housing for those who lived together but were not married and also to give children born out of wedlock full legal rights. The more radical leadership of the party envisioned a future in which children would be brought up in communal housing where domestic chores would be shared by men and women.

But the Communist Party shied away from such radical change. Bolshevik leaders themselves lived in traditional marriages and considered Kollontai's ideas threatening to social stability. By the end of the 1920s, the party had come around to condemning those who were not married and extolling the virtues of the proletarian family. Nuclear families remained the foundation of social stability, yet with more freedom to enter and exit such unions for both partners. In particular, divorce was liberalized, allowing women protection against domestic violence, which had not been recognized as a basis for dissolving marriages under previous divorce laws.

Women also gained more reproductive control. Early on, the Soviet regime legalized abortion and made it inexpensive. The liberalization of abortion would be short lived, however. By the end of the decade, the Communist Party had revised its policies, partly out of fear of depopulation. Under Stalin, abortion was made illegal again.

A lasting change, however, involved the support for and protection of women's employment and education as well as the creation of state child-care institutions for working mothers. These measures helped women become more economically self-sufficient and can thus be viewed as progressive reforms, similar to social welfare measures in Scandinavia during the 1920s. Yet the Soviet regime was interested only in increasing the workforce and fashioning loyal citizens through education. The Soviets looked upon women as an important means for fulfilling these aims rather than as oppressed individuals. Women would not have a choice of motherhood or employment. Rather, they would have to join the workforce and leave child rearing in part to state institutions such as kindergartens and schools.

26-4 Social and Cultural Experiments

> » How did social reformers and intellectuals respond to the aftermath of war?

> » How and with what results did the war and new technologies transform culture and entertainment in this era?

Social reformers, intellectuals, and artists throughout Europe tried to cope with the disruptions of war in radical ways as well. The experience of total war forced both men and women to reexamine many assumptions about their roles in the family and society. This process prompted important changes in gender relations, but fewer than reformers, especially feminists, hoped to achieve. Artists grappled with loss and destruction by fashioning entirely new artistic styles, some democratic and socially engaged and others an escape into dream worlds. Widespread violence had become an everyday experience, and many embraced it as a potentially positive force in art. Others recoiled from the memory of this violence and turned to pacifism and religious faith. Some of these trends had started before 1914 but were greatly reshaped by war's destruction and transformation of European society. These experiments produced some of the most remarkable works of literature and art of the twentieth century as well as important developments in popular entertainment.

26-4a Change and Frustration in Gender Roles

The war had brought upheaval in gender roles, and with the resumption of peace, many wondered if the changes would continue. More than in any previous conflict, the experiences of soldiers had been so vastly different from those of civilians that a great gap opened between husbands and wives, mothers and sons, fathers and daughters.

Pushing Women Out of the Workforce The experience of total war had placed both soldiers and civilians in direct contact with violence, but the physical and psychological burdens of trench warfare often crippled soldiers in unprecedented ways. Returning soldiers suffered from deep trauma and were unable to communicate their suffering to noncombatants. So many soldiers had gruesome injuries that the sight of a maimed body became commonplace. Deep psychological and physical scars forced veterans to question their masculinity and often strained relationships at home; domestic violence increased. These men yearned to have their old jobs and the prestige they had enjoyed before the war, but nothing could go back to the way it had been.

Many women had entered "male" professions and jobs during the war. After 1918, both government and private businesses preferred to rehire men, however, even for positions in which women had been effective and had accepted lower wages. The idea that men were breadwinners and women nurturers remained strong, but not all women returned to the home. Many continued to work, but in jobs that were less secure and poorly paid, including domestic and secretarial work and factory work in the food industry. Women were increasingly important as consumers, as evidenced by the greater diversity in goods available at both the low and high ends of the market. An aggressive fashion industry focused on "working girls" and independent women. The image of the flapper, or "new woman," was plastered all over fashion magazines and movie posters. These changes suggested new identities opening up for women.

Yet little changed for women in the domestic sphere. They were still considered primarily responsible for child care, cooking, and tending to the home. Unlike the Scandinavian welfare experiments and the Bolshevik revolution in women's family responsibilities, governments in the rest of Europe paid little attention to child-care questions. Consequently, women found it difficult to both work and take care of their families, or they did so with enormous effort and little support.

Fighting for Political Rights Still, in the realm of politics women made important gains, achieving voting rights except in France, Italy, Spain, and the Balkans, where they could vote only in local elections. The extent of women's suffrage varied and often included educational, marriage, and age criteria at a time when universal male suffrage was the norm. But even as feminists celebrated this victory, they also wondered how much power women had really gained. Though women could vote, their concerns were not necessarily reflected in party platforms, nor were female politicians successful in the first decade after the war. Traditional parties, even liberal and socialist ones with prowomen platforms, were unwilling to put forth female candidates. Questions about women's rights seemed subordinate to the pressing issues of the Bolshevik threat, war debt, inflation, unemployment, and revisionism.

Feminist activists became somewhat successful in inserting their concerns in the public arena through international networks and participation in the League of Nations. As members of the International Labor Organization (ILO), women pushed for better labor standards and protection against child labor. As members on the commissions established by the League of Nations to study and curb human trafficking, they brought new attention to international prostitution rings. Born out of the antiwar movement during World War I, the Women's International League for Peace and Freedom (WILPF) became a conduit for activism on behalf of peace and women's rights across the world.

Pro-Natalism Politicians appealed to women as mothers and wives, asking them to place family and nation above their individual selves and help rebuild their nation. In France, for instance, a pro-natalist campaign for replenishing the human losses in the war involved a stern government demand that all women of childbearing age, regardless of economic status, produce as many children as possible to regenerate the fighting force. Women were described as patriotic and selfless if they responded to this call and as heartless materialists if they indicated interest in attaining economic independence or limiting their families. There was no comparable campaign to shame men into fatherhood.

of mutual sexual satisfaction, and doctors provided sex advice to husbands. Sex advice columns began to appear in women's magazines. Even though the ideas about what constituted normal sex and pleasure were conventional, removing the taboo on discussing such matters in public and emphasizing women's sexual needs were important and lasting changes.

26-4b Intellectual Responses to the War

The destruction wrought by war prompted the rise of important intellectual movements in the decade after 1918. Among the cries for revenge and revolution, some intellectuals took a stand for peace. The postwar pacifist movement was in part a continuation of prewar pacifism and in part a reflection of Europe's political strategy to keep the peace, but it was no longer linked to particular political ideologies. It was more of an individual reaction to the horrors of war, a conclusion that no ideology—nationalism, liberalism, communism—could justify the enormous human losses. Several women's international networks became important conduits for pacifism.

Pacifism Many pacifists came from socialist or religious backgrounds, but some were completely non-ideological. Among the most prominent figures were the German physicist **Albert Einstein** and British writer **Vera Brittain**, who spent the war as a volunteer nurse and wrote as early as 1914: "The destruction of men seems a crime to the whole march of civilisation." Einstein's strong pacifism was unusual for a prominent scientist. In the following decade, he continued to be an outspoken critic of fascism and anti-Semitism at a time when other scientists were retreating into their labs or committing their research to the service of states with destructive agendas. The impact of the peace movement was small by comparison to the more forceful and well-organized fascist and communist ones. Yet the personal courage of individuals who stood up against the aggressive nationalism of the coming decade represents an important legacy.

Religious Rejuvenation Some intellectuals and artists reacted to the destruction of the war by taking on an overtly atheistic and often Marxist position on religion, whereas others sought spiritual rejuvenation, prompting a revival of Christianity.

Hannah Höch, *Cut with a Kitchen Knife,* 1919
Höch's (Heuch) collage is an example of the Dada movement, which flourished during and right after World War I. Höch's work explored the contradictions of contemporary society in an aggressively ironic feminist vein.

» *What visual elements and symbols does she use in her critique?*

» *What do these depictions suggest about gender and politics in 1919?*

Most European governments were concerned with population growth and hoped to revive the birthrate with positive incentives, such as monetary rewards and patriotic propaganda, and negative measures, such as the criminalization of abortion. Some reformers with similar concerns took a different position on reproduction. They saw sexual satisfaction as key to a couple's desire to reproduce and have a happy family. In the decade after the war, a diverse movement advocating sexual reform emerged. It was a response, in part, to the marital problems many couples were having after years of separation during the war. Husbands who came back with psychological traumas and physical disabilities were often unable to perform sexually; and women, who had gained tremendous self-confidence during the war years, found themselves more interested in an active role in sexual relations. Reformers wrote manuals for couples, encouraging the exploration

Albert Einstein (1879–1955) German-born physicist who developed the theory of relativity, winner of the Nobel Prize in Physics (1921), and active in the pacifist and anti nuclear weapons movements.

Vera Brittain (1893–1970) British author and pacifist who volunteered during World War I as a nurse.

Among these were several prominent thinkers of the time. In Britain, T. S. Eliot and Aldous Huxley turned away from secularization to find spiritual and intellectual solace in religion. The French philosopher and atheist **Gabriel Marcel** converted to Catholicism. Marcel attempted to find a concrete philosophy of being engaged in the modern world through spirituality, and moved away from abstractions such as truth or progress toward a focus on the everyday experience of pain, joy, and other basic human emotions.

26-4c Artistic Experiments

The decade of the 1920s was spectacular in the arts. Writers, painters, dancers, musicians—all types of artists and performers—revolutionized both high culture and popular entertainment. These experiments were connected both to a longer tradition of the avant-garde in the arts, dating from the end of the nineteenth century, and to the war, whose trauma had a direct impact on basic questions about beauty and goodness in the face of overwhelming destruction.

Futurism Several movements in the art world flourished during this period. The Futurists believed in a future marked by technology, power, and even violence. They saw war as a positive tool for cleansing all that was putrid in society and preparing for an era of strength. Futurists became close allies of radical political movements. In Italy, **Filippo Marinetti**, whose paintings depicted movement and speed on canvas, served as Mussolini's minister of the arts. In Russia, poet **Vladimir Mayakovsky** led a generation of Futurist writers who promoted Bolshevism.

Surrealism Even though the Futurists were original, they did not produce the lasting masterpieces created by the **Surrealists**. These visionaries sought alternatives to the "reality" of the visible world in the inner world of dreams and nightmares, the subconscious and suppressed, which they considered more truthful to the human condition and suffering than the decade's obsession with wealth and social stability. Adapting the new interest in psychoanalysis to art, they rebelled against rationality, ignored politics, and explored the mind. The first Surrealist manifesto, authored by the French writer **André Breton**, appeared in Paris in 1924 and declared this movement a revolution, outlining in form and content how Surrealism was to alter human consciousness. Artists, poets, and filmmakers rallied to his call to explore the subconscious and reject immediate reality.

The movement continued to flourish until World War II, with Spanish artist **Salvador Dali** and Belgian painter **René Magritte** as some of its most spectacular practitioners. Dali's haunting work portrayed a dream world, in which distortions of everyday objects were rendered in photographic detail and placed in hallucinatory settings. Dali lived his art, appearing in public in bizarre costumes, sporting a fantastic mustache, immaculate yet always strange. In keeping with Surrealistic principles, he showed no interest in politics. Unlike the colorful Dali, Magritte was far more cerebral and understated, and his paintings reached into dream worlds by a scrupulous, photographic rendition of objects in surprising settings. This paradoxical juxtaposition of the real and unreal, rather than distortion, became Magritte's signature.

Expressionism Other artists more directly engaged with political and social upheavals became affiliated with **Expressionism**. This movement had been developing since the beginning of the twentieth century but took on more social and political tones after the war. German artist **Käthe Kollwitz**, for example, had been a committed socialist and pacifist before the war, depicting the social problems of the working class, especially women and children. The loss of her son in the early days of the war brought on a deep personal crisis. In contrast to the dream world of the Surrealists, her stark woodcuts projected the pain and suffering of people whose emotions were a direct response to the outside world and real events.

Artistic Avant-Garde in the Soviet Union Much more committed to linking artistic experimentation and political engagement were the artists active during the first decade of the Soviet Union. Among the devoted supporters of Bolshevism were writers such

---

Gabriel Marcel (1889–1973) French philosopher of atheist convictions before 1918 who converted to Catholicism after the war.

Filippo Marinetti (1876–1944) Leader of Italian Futurism who served as minister of arts under Mussolini.

Vladimir Mayakovsky (1893–1930) Russian poet, Bolshevik activist, and leading figure of Russian Futurism.

Surrealism Artistic movement of the 1920s and 1930s that explored the realm of dreams and altered reality to find the deeper truth of human experience.

André Breton (1896–1966) French writer and founder of Surrealism.

Salvador Dali (1904–1989) Spanish-born artist who became the most famous Surrealist.

René Magritte (1898–1967) Belgian Surrealist painter famous for his superimposition of photographically depicted objects in unrelated three-dimensional spaces.

Expressionism Artistic movement that aimed to represent the connection between the inner emotional world and outer social reality.

Käthe Kollwitz (1867–1945) German Expressionist artist who portrayed the plight of working-class women and children.

as Mayakovsky and artists such as **Marc Chagall** (sha-GAL). In the early 1920s, Chagall developed his unique dreamlike combination of color and religious imagery. Cinema directors such as **Sergei** (ser-GAY) **Eisenstein** produced remarkable films like *Battleship Potemkin* that revolutionized cinema. His techniques in framing, lighting, and composition were stark and expressive, unlike anything that had been seen on the silver screen before.

Soviet artists were not, however, free of state control. Chagall fell out of favor with the Soviet leadership and had to leave the country in 1923 because of tensions with the party and increased anti-Semitism. Mayakovsky committed suicide in 1930 after his work was severely criticized by party officials. Eisenstein was able to pursue his creative work only by making movies that did not challenge the ideology of the Communist Party. His prominent films from the 1920s were, in fact, powerful propaganda for the Soviet regime. Under Stalin's dictatorship, many writers and artists were silenced, imprisoned, or killed for their art.

26-4d Experiments in Architecture and Design

After the war, some architects and designers sought to redefine the relationship between the practical and the artistic by simplifying architectural and interior design.

A New Focus on Functionality Grouped around Walter Gropius in Germany, these designers, artists, and architects became known as the **Bauhaus** (BAW-house) school, the most influential design movement in the first half of the twentieth century. The motivation of these architects and artists was connected to the horrors of the war. They sought to blend style and functionality, eliminating excesses they identified with the high bourgeois culture before the war and stripping away nationalism in style. Adherents of the Bauhaus school were optimistic: by eliminating the excesses of the past, artists and architects hoped to build a more stable environment accessible to people of different classes.

Another important force in design was **Le Corbusier** (kor-boo-zy-AY), a Swiss-born French engineer and artist—and one of the greatest architects of the twentieth century. Le Corbusier had a vision similar to that of the Bauhaus school—streamlining design, making it affordable and accessible to people of different social classes, and creating a new type of urban environment. Reacting against the cramped and alienating living conditions of the working classes before the war, he envisioned living quarters that were open, transparent, and connected to the community. His aim was to create a new society, and his *Toward a New Architecture* (1923) revolutionized urban planning. The Bauhaus school and Le Corbusier's work helped transform the appearance of old and new cities all over Europe, from Prague to Paris, as well as cities in Brazil, Algeria, and India.

Art Deco The idea that the best in design should be available to people of all incomes generated the movement known as **Art Deco**, which aimed to make everyday objects simple, sleek, and affordable through mass production. Technological advances and assembly-line methods first introduced by Henry Ford in his Detroit automobile plants helped cut production costs. By the end of the 1920s, Art Deco furniture, china, household appliances, and window treatments graced the grand houses of the rich, the homes of the middle classes, and even the bungalows of the working classes. The gap between highbrow and lowbrow culture in the realm of consumer goods was closing up.

26-4e Popular Entertainment

High art joined popular culture in this amazing decade to give new status to entertainment, particularly dance and music.

Popular Music and Modern Dance Cabarets had been popular since the 1910s, but after the war they were transformed by new trends, particularly American **jazz**, which swept working-class music halls and high-class art gatherings from Paris to Bucharest. Jazz was electrifying, showcasing improvisation and defying old classifications in its combinations of African rhythms and slave songs with popular ragtime and the blues. Introduced to Europe by African American soldiers serving in France during World War I, jazz made audiences yearn to know more about American popular culture and entertainment.

Marc Chagall (1887–1985) Russian Jewish painter whose art combined romantic images of lovers, nature, and traditional Jewish symbols with harsh political commentary.

Sergei Eisenstein (1898–1948) One of the greatest film directors of the twentieth century, who used pioneering film techniques as powerful propaganda for the Bolsheviks.

Bauhaus school Innovative German movement of architectural and interior design that sought to make living spaces and furniture designs functional and affordable.

Le Corbusier (1887–1965) Swiss-born French architect whose innovations aiming to eliminate class distinctions influenced city planning throughout the world.

Art Deco Architectural and design style that emphasized simplicity in style and aimed to make quality designs affordable to all through mass production.

jazz Innovative American musical form that combined elements of African rhythm and slave songs with popular music and later avant-garde European influences.

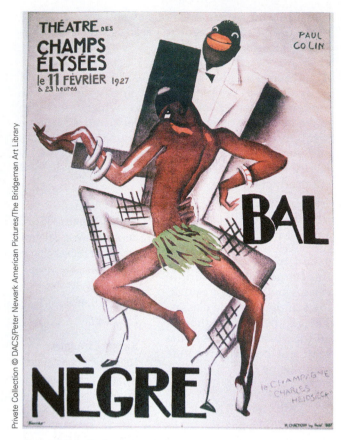

Josephine Baker

The artistic persona of this enormously popular African American jazz dancer in Paris challenged the aesthetic norms of old Europe and reinforced concepts of race in European culture.

❯❯ *How is race depicted in this poster?*

❯❯ *Compare this depiction with the images popular in the nineteenth century, such as this image of an African bushman family. How are they similar and different? In your analysis, consider the gaze of the protagonists in relation to the viewer.*

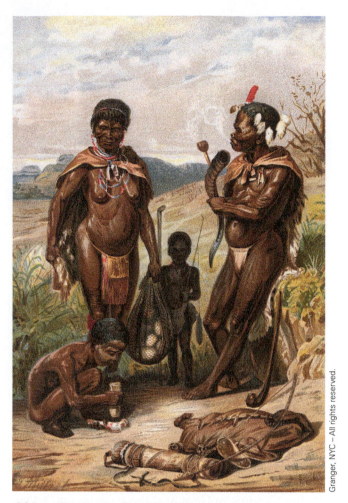

African Bushman Family, 1893

In this lithograph produced by an American artist at the end of the nineteenth century, gender roles are represented as a version of the familiar nuclear family in the United States, while the racial elements of identity are represented as exotic and premodern, suggesting a sharp contrast between western civilization (the artist and voyeuristic viewer) and the "backwards" African one. The lack of specificity in identifying a particular place and society in Africa in the title of the lithograph suggests a superficial knowledge of the culture and customs of the people depicted here.

Soon Europeans were doing the Charleston, with swings and heel kicks said to have originated with black dance styles on the islands off South Carolina. And in 1925, dance was further revolutionized when a U.S. traveling show captivated Paris with wild new jazz rhythms and the sensuous dances of its young African American star, **Josephine Baker**. Baker became an idol overnight, appealing to people of all walks of life who sought to discard the stuffiness of the prewar forms of entertainment for a more democratic and participatory type of dance and music. Baker's freedom and sensuality made her a lasting symbol of American culture in Europe.

At the same time, British dancer **Isadora Duncan** was transforming classical ballet into a new form of performance that emphasized expressive movement and grace rather than virtuosity. Duncan appeared on stage barefoot, in willowy silks instead of the stiff classic tutu; her movements aimed to convey emotions rather than showcase technique. Her new style of modern dance connected the Royal Opera House and rowdy cabarets into one seamless continuum of celebrating human creativity and sensuality.

Josephine Baker (1906–1975) African American dancer who charmed European audiences in 1925 and popularized the music and dance associated with jazz.

Isadora Duncan (1877–1927) British dancer who transformed traditional ballet technique into a more natural and emotion-filled movement style.

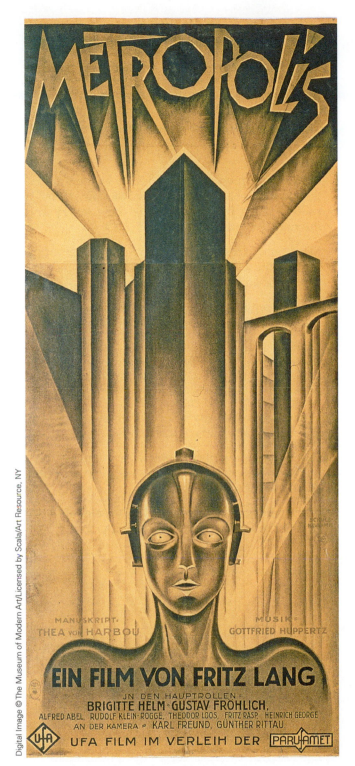

Metropolis

Fritz Lang's *Metropolis* (1927) presented an image of modernity and technological progress that was both alluring and foreboding. The cyborglike figure at the center of the movie was emphatically female.

» *How does the poster connect women and modernity?*

A new invention, the phonograph, also made musical choices more accessible to mass audiences. For a few pennies, anyone could hear the sounds of a favorite band at home, practice trendy new dance steps, and throw a party instead of sitting in the audience at a music hall for an evening's entertainment. Just as revolutionary was the introduction of inexpensive, mass-produced radios, which, starting in the late 1920s, transformed the music industry and news media. Soon the sounds of jazz and other popular music blasted out of windows and courtyards in almost every neighborhood.

Film Film was by far the most important and inexpensive form of entertainment for the masses during the 1920s. German film makers produced some of the most memorable films. The most important directors, such as **Fritz Lang**, were the Expressionists, who used simple plots to exaggerate human emotions, especially suffering, through distorted camera angles, lighting, and creative editing. Lang's best-known movie is *Metropolis* (1927), which examined the relationship between technology and progress by personifying technology as a female with both enticing and ultimately destructive characteristics. The movie also presented the suffering of the lower classes but expressed hope that technology could overcome social problems.

Listening to jazz, dancing the Charleston, and watching movies enabled working people, even the poor, to forget the war and escape the tedium of their hard lives. These forms of popular entertainment also allowed them the freedom to imagine other roles for themselves—as famous dancers, actors, or musicians. The new entertainment styles blurred the distance between the highly educated and privileged elites and the lower masses: fame seemed to be something almost anyone—in the excitement of the 1920s—could achieve.

Fritz Lang (1890–1976) German Expressionist film maker, later active in Hollywood.

CHAPTER Review

Summary

» The end of World War I challenged the old political and social order, relations among states, and the roles of individuals in society.

» Self-determination sowed the seeds of discontent among European states.

» War debt repayments generated economic hardship all over Europe.

» Political leaders, social reformers, intellectuals, artists, workers, and average citizens sought new identities in the new Europe.

» Experiments of the decade offered radically new solutions and ideas, with varied success.

» Established democracies resisted successfully against revolutionary upheaval.

» In newly created countries, democratic institutions had greater difficulty in gaining legitimacy.

» The most radical challenge of the period was the successful establishment of a communist regime in Russia.

» The Soviet Union established itself as the international leader of all communist movements, through radical social programs inside the country and international outreach.

» Mass campaigns for education and secularization showed the will of the Bolshevik regime to reshape the minds and souls of every citizen.

» Fascism represented another important challenge against political and territorial stability.

» Fascism and communism provided important models for radical politicians in Europe in the following decade.

» Women experienced empowering changes but also frustration, especially with regard to family relations, especially in the Soviet Union.

» Lasting experiments in the realm of culture produced many of the century's masterpieces and avant-garde movements.

» Spectacular growth was seen in the realm of popular entertainment, from music to film.

Chronology

1918–1922	Reds and Whites engage in Russian Civil War [Europe]
1919	Comintern is established [Global] Bolshevik revolution in Hungary creates short-lived Soviet Republic [Europe] League of Nations is established [Global] Treaty of Versailles officially ends World War I [Global] Fiume Republic is established [Europe]
1921	Lenin inaugurates the New Economic Policy in Russia [Europe]
1922	Mussolini seizes power in Italy [Europe] Irish Free State is established [Europe] Egypt declares independence from British protectorate [Middle East]
1923	Hitler attempts to seize power in Bavarian Beer Hall Putsch [Europe]

1923–1925	Britain and France occupy Ruhr, precipitate German economic crisis [Europe]
1924	Ramsay MacDonald becomes first Labour Party prime minister of Great Britain [Europe] Dawes Plan resets German reparation payments [Europe, Americas] First Surrealist manifesto is issued in Paris [Europe]
1925	Josephine Baker performs American jazz dances in Paris [Europe, Americas]
1926	Germany is admitted into the League of Nations [Europe]
1928	Kellogg-Briand Pact renounces future war in Europe [Europe] Stalin assumes leadership of Soviet Union [Europe]
1929	U.S. stock market crashes, beginning of Great Depression [Americas]

Critical Thinking Questions

Take time to pull together all the important information from the chapter by answering the following questions:

The Search for Stability, 1918–1924

» What actions did political leaders undertake to restore European order after the war?

» What problems frustrated these efforts?

Postwar Political Experiments, 1924–1929

» What new ideas about the powers of the government emerged during this period?

» Where was democracy successful and where did it fail? Why?

The New Soviet State

» What were the essential elements of the Soviet state?

» What actions did the Bolsheviks undertake to reshape society and individual identities?

Social and Cultural Experiments

» How did social reformers and intellectuals respond to the aftermath of war?

» What were the new directions in culture and entertainment during this era?

 MINDTAP From Cengage

MindTap® is a fully online personalized learning experience built upon Cengage Learning content. MindTap® combines student learning tools—readings, multimedia, activities, and assessments—into a singular Learning Path that guides students through the course and helps students develop the critical thinking, analysis, and communication skills that are essential to academic and professional success.

CHAPTER

27

Democracy Under Siege, 1929–1945

Chapter Outline

As you read, consider the following questions:

❯ How did the challenges to democracy from 1929 to 1945 help transform European civilization and international relations globally?

❯ Were the experiments of Hitler and Stalin an aberration of western civilization or the product of its ideas, science, and technology?

❯ At what price did the Allies win the war?

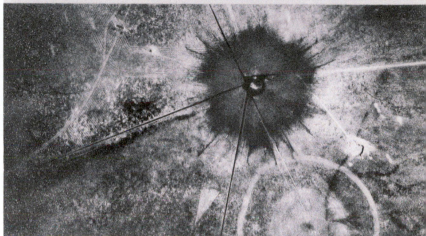

MANY PEOPLE ACROSS THE WORLD WITNESSED with alarm the profound political crisis of the 1930s as the United States' and Europe's democracies plunged into a severe depression. Some became more committed than ever to socialist ideas. Others rejected democracy itself as the problem and turned toward antidemocratic solutions. Colonial territories and protectorates used this crisis to reach greater autonomy from European powers with some success. Of the options taken in the 1930s, the dictatorships in Italy, Germany, and the Soviet Union seemed the most successful in managing the economic crisis, eventually restoring full employment and production growth while democracies struggled. But the success of the Soviets and the Nazis was due largely to their oppressive internal policies, which controlled workers and resources in ways democracies could not. The Nazis' racist ideology and the

First Atomic Bomb Explosion, 1945

The first atomic bomb was detonated in the desert of New Mexico in July 1945. The United States used the unprecedented force of this weapon to force Japan to surrender, bringing World War II to an end. The unleashing of this source of energy and power inaugurated a new age in the world, both in international relations and also in technology and scientific research.

Stalinist paranoid concept of internal enemies institutionalized terror in both countries. Adolf Hitler and Joseph Stalin also aimed to undo the international system that had been developing through the League of Nations. In particular, Hitler's rearmament and expansionist policies challenged the Versailles Treaty, and democratic states stood idle until it was too late.

Still, faced with Hitler's challenge to European international order in 1939, after 1941 the western democracies joined forces with the Soviet Union and by 1945 had defeated Germany and its allies. The conflict became global with the involvement of Japan on the side of Hitler, leading to long-term political changes in Asia. World War II, with its unmatched carnage, involvement of civilians, use of new military technology, and extermination of innocent people, especially the Jews, radically transformed the world order.

27-1 Responses to the Great Depression, 1929–1939

» **What were the causes of the Great Depression?**

» **What were the political consequences of the Great Depression?**

» **What made antidemocratic radical ideologies particularly appealing to so many people during this period?**

In the fall of 1929, the bubble of prosperity burst, bringing on severe economic problems and major political upheaval. After the 1929 stock market crash in the United States, European banks and enterprises lost much of their capital and millions of people lost their jobs. The political impact of the world depression that followed was huge, as most governments lost the trust of the voters, yet starving workers had nowhere to turn. They looked toward the state for solutions, but no one knew how to deal with this economic and social crisis of unprecedented scale. Only in Britain, France, Belgium, Czechoslovakia, and the Scandinavian countries was democracy able to pass this difficult test. Most other countries slid toward regimes that offered security and strength at the price of democracy. With Italy providing an example of successful management of the economic depression, authoritarian regimes rose all over eastern and southern Europe, as well as in Latin America. Germany abandoned its fragile republic under the spell of Adolf Hitler.

27-1a The Great Depression

By the end of World War I, New York had replaced London as the financial capital of the world, and by 1929, European economies had become highly dependent on the U.S. economy. The Dawes Plan for payment of the war debt tied the finances of Britain, France, and Germany to the economic well-being of the United States. During the 1920s, the growing availability of American goods and the lure of American popular culture in Europe also strengthened economic ties across the Atlantic. Thus, when the New York stock market crashed in October 1929, its effects were felt immediately in Europe. American banks and financiers started to call in short-term loans, depleting European banks, especially in Germany and Austria, of sizable resources. By the end of 1930, 1,350 American banks had closed; 2,293 more did so in 1931. Between 1929 and 1934, almost 33 percent of American banks had failed.

Run on the Banks In Europe, panic ensued. As people withdrew cash from banks and closed their accounts, the capital available to business shrank, leading to the collapse of major European banks, including the Kreditanstalt, Austria's largest bank. Unable to pay their workers, these businesses started to fire workers by the thousands. Even the 1931 American moratorium on war debts could not reverse the downward spiral, though it did ease international tensions. Unemployment in Germany reached 3 million in 1930 and skyrocketed to almost 6 million by 1932—almost 40 percent of the workforce. In the United States, 25 percent of the workforce was unemployed. By 1933, economic production had fallen by 50 percent in the United States and by 40 percent in Germany (see Table 27.1).

The consequences of this dramatic collapse were felt across the world, from Australia to China and Brazil. Though less industrialized countries weathered the Great Depression with fewer losses, the slowdown of the world economy meant greater poverty in both colonial territories and countries that depended on western investments and imports. Overall, the problems faced by Britain at home weakened its hold over its protectorates in the Middle East and colonial territories in Africa, leading the way to greater anticolonial opposition.

Economic Theories About the Depression Some economists, such as **John Maynard Keynes** (keenz), believed that the **Great Depression** was connected to the **deflationary** policies of the 1920s, which had followed the hyperinflation scare of the early 1920s. Businesses and individuals had been afraid to borrow, slowing economic growth, and banks had become more conservative, charging higher interest rates. Other scholars have seen the Great Depression as a more acute case of the cyclical process of economic growth and slowdown characteristic of all capitalist economies.

Whatever the causes, the effects of the Great Depression were profound. Many of those who had spent their youth in the trenches of World War I were now middle-aged and had families. When they lost their jobs or businesses, they grew despondent. Some, unable to feed their families or make payments on their homes, slipped into deep depression and abandoned their families. Women's economic status was also badly hurt, though some were able to find part-time work in the service industry—as cooks, servants, and sometimes as sex workers.

27-1b Democracies' Responses

If dependency on American investments and banks along with deflationary policies were the initial causes of economic collapse in Europe, the depth and

John Maynard Keynes (1883–1946) British economist whose theories revolutionized the supply-demand equation and inspired government policies to encourage economic growth.

Great Depression Global economic crisis that began in October 1929 and lasted throughout the 1930s.

deflationary Referring to a fiscal policy aimed at preventing inflation.

Table 27.1 **The Great Depression**

Indices of Industrial Production, 1929–1938, in Major European Countries (1937 = 100)

	1929	1930	1931	1932	1933	1934	1935	1936	1937
France	123	123	105	91	94	92	88	95	100
Germany	79	69	56	48	54	67	79	90	100
Italy	90	85	77	77	82	80	86	86	100
Great Britain	77	74	69	69	73	80	82	94	100

Unemployment (in Thousands)

	1929	1930	1931	1932	1933	1934	1935	1936	1937
France	neglig	13	64	301	305	368	464	470	380
Germany	1,899	3,070	4,520	5,575	4,804	2,718	2,151	1,593	912
Italy	301	425	734	1,006	1,019	964	-	-	874
Great Britain	1,216	1,917	2,630	2,745	2,521	2,159	2,036	1,755	1,484

Source: Stromberg, Roland N., *Europe in the Twentieth Century*, 4th Edition, © 1997. Reprinted by permission of Pearson Education, Inc. Upper Saddle River, NJ.

» *How do the two democracies compare with the two dictatorships in terms of industrial production in the 1930s?*

» *How do these countries compare in terms of unemployment?*

» *What does Germany's performance after 1933 suggest about support for Hitler?*

duration of the Great Depression were also a consequence of the choices various states made after 1929. Politicians tried to balance state budgets and avoid expenditures. Following the lead of the United States, European governments quickly imposed higher tariffs to protect their own industries. The result was a decline in international trade that further reduced production and employment. Keynes argued that economic recovery could be achieved only by abandoning the obsession with balanced budgets and the **gold standard** and by instituting government programs to put people back to work. A larger employed workforce, he pointed out, would increase the tax base, and more taxes would reduce budget deficits. Under President Franklin D. Roosevelt, the United States weathered the Great Depression in part through a broad range of government-supported public works programs that implemented Keynes's ideas.

Toward National Unity in Britain In Britain politicians were not open to these solutions. Labour Prime Minister Ramsay MacDonald, elected in May 1929 on the promise of securing workers' interests, could not cope with the massive unemployment that hit Britain by 1930 (a 60 percent rise just during that year). His government opted for conservative solutions. Hopelessly, it attempted to keep the budget balanced and refrained from setting up the kinds of public works programs developed in America. Instead, MacDonald chose to cut compensation for the unemployed. Such a move by a Labour prime minister seemed so much at odds with that party's ideology that half his ministers resigned.

In an unprecedented move, MacDonald compromised with the Conservatives to create a **National Unity Government**, with himself as prime minister, which he led until 1935, though he was expelled from the Labour Party for betraying workers' interests. Despite political and economic turmoil, the National Unity Government managed two important accomplishments. First, the Conservatives agreed to support issues important to Labour, such as government-regulated health insurance and Housing

gold standard Fiscal policy that pegs national currency to gold reserves.

National Unity Government Coalition government in Britain during the first half of the 1930s, headed by Labour leader Ramsey MacDonald but dominated by the Conservatives.

Library of Congress

Migrant Mother

One of millions of people worldwide left homeless and on the verge of starvation by the Great Depression, this *Migrant Mother* became an iconic image. Florence Thompson was photographed in 1936 in California by the American documentary photographer Dorothea Lange.

》 *What emotions can you see on her face?*

》 *What do the turned away faces of her children suggest?*

Acts that mandated the building of affordable, safe housing. By the late 1930s, politicians of all leanings recognized housing, education, and public health as services for which the state had responsibility, and Britain was on its way to becoming a welfare state. Though private enterprise ran many social services, the government monitored their quality and helped the poor gain access to decent housing and health care.

Such programs and support were not extended to Britain's colonial possessions. In India, the reduction of trade with England resulted in massive economic problems and protests against the British Raj. The Salt March organized in March 1930 in response to taxes imposed by the British on salt production propelled Mohandas Gandhi to national prominence in the independence movement. His leadership in shaping the nonviolent civil disobedience movement of the 1930s had a profound long-term impact on other

anticolonial and civil rights movements across the world, inspiring leaders from Martin Luther King Jr. to Nelson Mandela.

The chief accomplishment of the National Unity Government in Britain was to simply hold on to the principles of democracy. Both communist and fascist movements grew in Britain during the 1930s, gathering strength from the sheer desperation of the economic crisis. But most politicians resisted the temptation to play upon fears in order to increase their following. British politicians followed well-established democratic rules, and average citizens respected this position, although they were often dissatisfied with the results.

Democracy Tested in France   France, too, adopted deflationary measures to cope with the downturn in economic production and rise in unemployment. The French were even more conservative than the British, keeping the franc on the gold standard at a time when every other European country and the United States had abandoned it. By 1935, when most European countries had begun to recover, France was registering its highest unemployment rates (464,000, in contrast to 13,000 in 1930) and its lowest index of industrial production since 1929 (30 percent lower).

Yet France, too, resisted the fascist temptation and defended democratic institutions, weathering a major political scandal in 1934 and a demonstration by 200,000 protesters that was brutally crushed by the police. Though fascist organizations in France had more than 750,000 members, mainstream politicians and average citizens rejected fascist appeals and in 1936 put a strong antifascist coalition in power.

27-1c Authoritarian Solutions

Most of Europe's political elites, however, responded to the Great Depression by undermining or abandoning democratic institutions. Where such institutions were recent, both politicians and ordinary citizens were quick to equate economic problems with a fundamental weakness of democracy and to look for other political solutions.

Catholic Authoritarian Regimes   In Austria, Spain, and Portugal, the response was an alliance between conservative politicians and the Catholic Church. In these countries, the Roman Catholic Church was one of the most stable institutions, shaping not only religious outlook but also political life. In Austria, the Christian Socialists, one of the two largest parties in the country, had a conservative Catholic outlook on moral values and social responsibilities. The party favored government control over education that would be strictly Christian, a traditional social hierarchy with the Catholic aristocracy at the top, and the exclusion of Jews from important positions of public authority. In the early 1930s, both Austria and Portugal replaced democratically elected governments with strong conservative leaders who were devout Catholics. These leaders gave the Catholic Church important educational, propaganda, and social responsibilities. The school curriculum came under the control of the Catholic Church, as did many other social services. Church-controlled censorship of literature and other cultural endeavors were also introduced.

The Spanish Civil War In Spain, the struggle between conservative militarist and Catholic political forces and their secularist left-wing opponents proved more violent and led to a civil war. The **Spanish Civil War** lasted three years (1936–1939) and destroyed trust in democracy in Spain and among many Europeans generally. The country went from a republican government in 1931 to a titular monarchy in 1939, which was headed by the authoritarian general **Francisco Franco**, the leader of the pro-Catholic right-wing forces. The son of a naval postmaster, Franco had, at age thirty-four in 1926, become the youngest general in Europe. Before 1936, he had served under a right-wing nationalist coalition to purge the military of supporters of the left. Through military skill and successful maneuvering among his rivals, he built a reputation as a strong leader and a unifier. Although many regarded Franco as a supporter of fascism, he was in fact a pragmatist who used the support of fascist forces, especially from Italy and Germany, to win the civil war. By 1939, when Franco's Nationalists won against the Republicans, more than one million people had been placed in prison by Franco's victorious dictatorship. The Catholic Church became Franco's right arm in enforcing strict censorship over culture, education, and other public services.

Dictatorship in Eastern Europe In other young democracies, especially in eastern Europe, political leaders and average citizens blamed democratic institutions and ethnic minorities for the economic crisis. Their solution was to dissolve parliaments, suppress the voice of ethnic minorities, and establish authoritarian ethno-nationalist rule. In Romania, for instance, the young king **Carol II** claimed he was the only leader interested in the unity of the country, undermining all political parties. He dealt with the economic crisis by allowing anti-Semitic propaganda and policies to flourish as he militarized the economy, reviving floundering branches of industry by emphasizing the production of armaments. In 1938, he made himself a virtual dictator. By then, **dictatorships** had replaced parliamentary systems in many eastern European states, including Latvia, Poland, Hungary, Greece, and Yugoslavia. Eastern European leaders used the revisionism of ethnic minorities as an excuse to build up the military. The increasing obsession with militarization led to a veritable arms race in the area. Acquiring military equipment from Nazi Germany

in return for agricultural goods that could not find a market in western Europe relieved some of the economic crisis for these countries but also rendered them greatly dependent on Germany for their military needs.

The rhetoric and paramilitary organizations of the authoritarian regimes in eastern Europe resembled those in fascist Italy. Fascist movements were particularly strong in Romania, Hungary, and Yugoslavia. But they did not foment fascist coups like Mussolini's. Instead, the dictators of these countries merely took on a fascist style, with uniformed supporters marching in the streets. Authoritarian regimes in the rest of Europe remained much more conservative in scope and ideology. They were interested in maintaining stability and preventing broad social and political upheaval rather than in generating the kind of changes Mussolini had brought about in 1922.

In Latin America, similar movements challenged the established political system. In Brazil, in 1930 **Getúlio** (zhe-TOO-lee-oh) **Vargas** led a successful coup supported by the military, some economic elites, as well as populist movements on the radical left and right. His corporatist populist policies, resembling those of Mussolini, enabled Vargas to pacify both farmers and the capitalists anxious about their economic losses during the Great Depression. Vargas used the military to put down communist opposition, as Franco did in Spain, and pursued modernization and foreign investment, ramping up trade with Nazi Germany.

27-1d The Rise of Nazism

Between 1930 and 1933 Germany experienced a political and social revolution that brought to power the most radical movement since the Bolsheviks—the Nazis. After the 1929 crash, Germany faced obstacles similar to other young democracies. Political parties had a fluid following, and many people had come to question the democratic institutions of the Weimar Republic set up in the shadow of the much-hated Versailles Treaty. Just months before the crash, Gustav Stresemann—a central figure for the Weimar's

Spanish Civil War (1936–1939) War won by the right-wing Nationalists, supported by the Nazis, over republican left-wing forces, supported by the Soviets.

Francisco Franco (1892–1975) General and leader of the Nationalists in the Spanish Civil War and dictator of Spain from 1939 until his death in 1975.

Carol II (r. 1930–1940) Romanian king who ruled in an authoritarian fashion.

dictatorship Autocratic form of government headed by a single all-powerful ruler, the dictator.

Getúlio Vargas (1882–1954) Brazil's longest ruling president, he helped weather the Great Depression through authoritarian corporatist populist policies.

George Orwell Commits Himself to Socialism

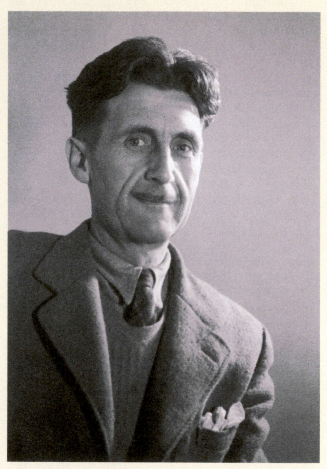

George Orwell Born Eric Arthur Blair, George Orwell became one of the most insightful writers to analyze the authoritarian elements of political regimes in the twentieth century.

In 1930, Eric Arthur Blair became George Orwell. It wasn't just about choosing a pen name but rather about giving up his privileged identity as the son of a respectable servant of the British Raj in India. Instead of following the path to easy security and middle-class respectability opened by his family, at age nineteen Blair turned his back on elite schools to join the imperial police in India for some adventure. At age twenty-four, disgusted with its racist policies, he quit to live among the poor.

Having decided to follow his dream of writing, Orwell aimed high. He wanted nothing less than to become the moral conscience of his country, writing from conviction and experience, unlike many of the pseudo-bohemian writers of the time who enjoyed material privileges while writing about the poor. He didn't want just to move his audiences

but instead aimed to challenge and force them to rethink their identities and act on their beliefs. True to this conviction, Orwell took a job as a dishwasher in Paris and lived in a poorly heated room for many months. It was during these days of self-imposed poverty that he began to understand class inequalities and gain sympathy for socialism as the best direction for democracy.

In his quest to become a good and socially active writer, in 1934 Orwell took on the assignment of writing about the life of coal miners in northern Britain. The result, *The Road to Wigan Pier* (1936), movingly described the appalling conditions of these workers but received mixed reviews from his left-wing editor. Always holding on to his aim of being the moral conscience of his peers, Orwell did not hesitate to criticize British socialists, whom he viewed as armchair critics rather than active reformers.

To demonstrate his own dedication to the cause of democracy through socialism, in 1936 Orwell went to Spain, where a civil war was pitting left-wing forces against a right-wing militarist regime. He arrived as a journalist but couldn't stay away from the action and joined the republican army. His experiences in Spain reinforced his commitment to socialism as profoundly democratic but made him wary of the contribution of the Soviet Union to this cause. Soviet manipulations of the left-wing forces opened his eyes to the controlling and antidemocratic nature of the Soviet regime. These experiences were penned in *Homage to Catalonia* (1938).

Still hungry for action and eager to make a difference, Orwell tried to serve in the British army during World War II but was discharged because of injuries he had received in Spain. Instead, he worked for the British Broadcasting Corporation (BBC) as a reporter, a job that revealed to him the nature of wartime propaganda and the antidemocratic ways in which the British government manipulated information.

Orwell's passionate commitment to "turn political writing into an art" led him to write his last two and most important books, *Animal Farm* (1945) and *1984* (1949). Both reflected his desire to remain the moral conscience of Britain. Exposing the absurdity of sloganeering with expressions such as "war is peace" and "ignorance is strength," he pointed to the deep political corruption, both on the left and on the right, as the root of the tragedies he had witnessed all over Europe in the 1930s and 1940s. These books also represented an impassioned plea on behalf of peace and democracy and against totalitarianism, but they were not exclusively anticommunist, as they came to be depicted later on. Until the end of his life in 1950, Orwell remained committed to his belief in socialism as the most radically democratic ideology of the times, more progressive than liberalism or communism.

Guernica, 1937

Pablo Picasso painted *Guernica* as a political-aesthetic reaction against the mass killings by right-wing forces led by Francisco Franco during the Spanish Civil War. Specifically, Guernica, a small town in northern Spain, was bombed in 1937 by Nazi planes supporting Franco. Through its choice of black and white, the painting became a dramatic symbol of pacifism.

» *What does the image of the mother with the infant in her arms suggest in relation to the war?*

» *What other symbols of pacifism can you identify in the painting?*

» *What images does Picasso use to represent violence?*

stability—died. Moreover, the depression hit Germany harder than any other state in Europe. The Social Democrats, who led the government at the time of the crash, lost power, their presence in parliament shrinking from 30 percent in 1928 to 20 percent in 1932. No other party was strong enough to succeed, so a series of political compromises followed. Various governments tried different approaches, first obtaining a moratorium on war reparations (1931) and then implementing a major land reform. Many politicians were angered by these moves, and average citizens lost faith in the democratic processes that seemed to bring very little stability and even less economic relief to the country. Meanwhile, a political party once marginal and ridiculed by mainstream politicians was growing rapidly. Electoral support for the Nazis increased from 2.5 percent in 1928 to 18 percent in 1930 and 37 percent in July 1932. The reasons for this meteoric growth were many. First and foremost, the Nazis had a charismatic leader unmatched by any other German politician—Adolf Hitler.

The Rise of Adolf Hitler Hitler came from a lower-class Austrian family and had left home at age sixteen to become a bohemian artist in Vienna. Unable to get into the Fine Arts Academy, he became a drifter, living in homeless shelters and eking out a living as a street peddler until 1914, when he volunteered in the German army. Having fought bravely in the war

(he was decorated twice), Hitler was dismayed by Germany's loss and looked for a way to continue his service in a paramilitary organization. His ambitions brought him, in 1919, to the organization that became the Nazi Party a year later. Here Hitler discovered his great talent as a speaker and fundraiser, turning the Nazis into a notable party by 1923. His supporters were a motley crew of disillusioned veterans, drifters like himself, and "little men" who were suffering from the effects of the war and postwar inflation. After the failed 1923 Beer Hall Putsch, Hitler was thrown into jail. The Nazis were made illegal but continued their activities, including the publication of Hitler's *Mein Kampf*, written in prison.

Hitler's Ideology: *Mein Kampf* Hitler was not a great thinker, as *Mein Kampf* shows. The book is a muddled collection of nationalist and racist, primarily anti-Semitic, ideas—the "alt-right" of the time.

CONNECTIONS: During the 2016 election, the terminology "alt-right" was used frequently to distinguish new, radical movements on the right from established right-wing parties, such as the Republicans in the United

Mein Kampf (*My Struggle*) Book written by Hitler in 1925 in which he formulated his ideas of racial purity and his goal of exterminating the Jews.

States and the Tories in Great Britain. Though a neutral self-identification, many believe the formation of the alt-right parallels the ideas made popular almost a century ago by Hitler and his followers, from anti-Semitism to anti-establishment nostalgia and corporatism (See also Section 22-4a Integral Nationalism, Racism, Anti-Semitism, and Zionism for more about the earlier, nineteenth-century phenomenon termed integral nationalism.)

Using the work of racist theorists of the nineteenth century, Hitler developed a genetically determined hierarchy of ethnicities, with the Aryans (Germans, Scandinavians, and Britons) at the top and Slavs and Jews at the bottom, the latter categorized as "subhuman." The book argued for the idea of **Lebensraum**—that because the German nation needed more territory in order to thrive, it ought to expand eastward into Poland, Czechoslovakia, and beyond. Hitler was singularly able to distill the frustrations of many Germans into a few simple messages: Germans had been served poorly by the Weimar Republic, which had been a result of the unfair Versailles Treaty; the enemies of the German people were both outside (especially the Soviets) and inside (communists, Jews, and the capitalists who had profiteered from the postwar economic problems). Eliminating these enemies was the key to bringing Germany back to its former imperial glory.

The Paramilitary Dimensions of the Nazis By the time the Nazis reemerged as an important political party during the Great Depression, Hitler was a seasoned leader and spellbinding speaker, with a loyal paramilitary organization—the Storm Detachment or SA—and a band of personal bodyguards, the **Schutzstaffel**, or SS. His ability to construct a spectacle around the Nazis was another reason for their growing popularity. In a time of growing disaffection and demoralization, Hitler's Brown Shirts marched around as a solid unit—a symbol of Germany's once-great virility and military prowess, now stymied by Versailles and the Social Democrats. Much like Mussolini, whose mastery of ceremony had been a model for the Nazis, Hitler understood well that a powerful show of force sometimes meant more than speeches and ideology. He attracted many students and younger followers simply with the sense of community and strength he seemed to radiate: "Long ago you heard the voice of a man ... and it struck to your hearts, and it awakened you, and you followed his voice…. It is faith in our nation that has made us small people great, that has made us poor people rich, that has made us vacillating, dispirited, anxious people brave and courageous."

The Populist Appeal of the Nazis The appeal of the Nazis rested on posing simple solutions for complicated problems and playing on the fears of a population caught in a deep economic crisis that other parties could not end. It was not just the die-hard anti-Semites who voted for the Nazis. The party attracted educated and uneducated, poor and well-to-do, men and women, workers and entrepreneurs, and religious and secularized Germans. But the largest group of Nazi supporters were those either hurt badly by the depression—small artisans and shopkeepers, some workers, farmers—or those who had come to see in the Weimar government only a betrayal of Germany and defeat by outside forces—soldiers who had fought in the war, men laid off while women still worked, students, and anti-Semites.

By November 1932, the Nazis were the strongest party in the Reichstag. Hitler did not have a mandate to form a single government (the Nazis had received only 33 percent of the vote), but he was not interested in sharing control and no other leaders were willing to give him full powers. Then in January 1933, he became chancellor and embarked on a swift process of undermining all democratic institutions of the Weimar Republic through steps that were technically legal. In February, a mysterious fire in the Reichstag building allowed Hitler to ask for emergency powers to go after the culprits, whom he identified as communists. With the president's approval, Hitler suspended all free speech and asked for new elections, which gave the Nazis 44 percent of the vote. The new parliament moved quickly to outlaw the Communist Party and pass the **Enabling Act**, which gave Hitler extraordinary powers to make executive decisions in all matters of "national security," placing him above accountability to the legal and judicial branches of government. The act enabled Hitler to become a dictator and to begin reshaping Germany according to his vision of a racially pure thousand-year empire—the **Third Reich**.

27-2 The Soviet Union Under Stalin, 1929–1939

» **What were the Soviet Union's successes and failures in the decade of the Great Depression?**

» **What were the new elements added by Stalin to turn the Soviet Union into a totalitarian state?**

As Europe struggled with the Great Depression and political instability, the Soviet Union seemed on an unstoppable track toward modernization,

---

Lebensraum (in German, "living space") Idea that Germany needed to expand eastward to secure the healthy growth of the Aryan race.

Schutzstaffel (SS) (in German, "protective squadron") Hitler's personal bodyguards in the early days of the Nazi Party.

Enabling Act Decree passed by the Reichstag in 1933 that enabled Hitler to legally eliminate all political enemies and assume full dictatorial powers.

Third Reich Title used for the period of Nazi rule in Germany.

industrialization, and full employment. With membership in the League of Nations, it gained international respectability. In the 1930s it was a model for many disillusioned people in the west. As a force in the antifascist struggle, the Soviet Union emerged as a first-rank international power. The reality of Stalin's rule, however, was grim: modernization and stability were accomplished only with much brutality. Stalin's newly powerful country was a ruthless police state.

27-2a Domestic and Foreign Policy

While the rest of Europe was entering a period of economic crisis, the Soviet Union was relatively free of the vagaries of the free market, as it had not been involved in the Dawes Plan or affected by the rise of American banking in the world of international finance. Fully in control of the country's political apparatus, in the late 1920s Stalin turned his attention toward improving the Soviet Union's international standing and developing the economy.

A More Moderate Course in Foreign Policy During the early 1930s, the Soviet Union reversed its policy of fostering world revolution, focusing instead on international security. The most important foreign policy concern was to counter the rise of threats in the west (Nazi Germany) and in the east (Japan). The Soviets pursued this goal with a two-pronged strategy: diplomatic and military. In the realm of diplomacy, foreign commissar **Maxim Litvinov** played the most important role. A skillful diplomat, he projected an image of cosmopolitan sophistication, unlike most other representatives of the Soviet Union. During the 1920s, when the country was still an international **pariah** and had no diplomatic ties with the Great Powers, Litvinov had become involved in disarmament discussions in the League of Nations. Through his relentless efforts, France (1932) and then the United States (1933) finally reestablished diplomatic relations with the Soviet Union, opening the way for its admission into the League in 1934 and for increased international economic ties.

Establishing the Command Economy Another component of the Soviet effort to build international strength was militarization. While Litvinov was praising disarmament in the League of Nations, Stalin was focusing on the armament industry as an important component of economic planning. The military was building new weapons, such as tanks and new types of bombs. The military leadership was fully committed to this program and conducted intensive campaigns for training and diversifying the fighting forces, including the recruitment of women in all areas of military service.

The Five-Year Plans Internally, Stalin's goal was nothing less than to turn an agricultural nation into an industrial powerhouse. In 1929 he proclaimed: "We are becoming a land of metals …, automobiles …, tractors, and when we have put the USSR on an automobile and the peasant on a tractor, let the noble capitalists … attempt to catch up." This ambitious goal needed unprecedented planning and government control. Stalin ended the New Economic Policy (NEP) and called on economic advisers to generate a series of **five-year plans** to set up a **command economy**: all aspects of the economy—from securing natural resources to research and development, employment, and commerce—would be controlled by the state rather than the market. The supply of goods would be determined by ideological goals—industrialization and modernization—rather than consumer needs and wants. The first five-year plan focused obsessively on high production targets in heavy industries, subordinating production in all other areas to this primary goal: it called for an increase of 300 percent in the production of electricity, coal, pig iron, and steel. "There is no fortress that the Bolsheviks cannot storm," boasted the party leadership.

In the first few years, these industries achieved huge levels of growth in part because they were so rudimentary at the start. In addition, Stalin empowered factory managers and directors of heavy industry factories to use any necessary means, often simply reallocating natural resources and transportation from other economic sectors and using forced labor instead of paid workers for some of the most ambitious projects, such as the Volga–White Sea Canal. But by the third year, the rate of growth had slowed down. Without comprehensive planning for the entire economy, the state risked halting production in some sectors, such as agriculture and light industries, to achieve the official quotas in the heavy industry. For instance, if trains were made available only for mining and steel industries, production and delivery in other sectors of the economy became blocked. In the end, the first five-year plan was a failure by its own goals, but it still produced partial outstanding results—a growth of over 100 percent in steel, electricity, and machinery production, although some of these statistics were manipulated. By the end of the third five-year plan, in

Maxim Litvinov (1876–1951) Soviet foreign commissar in the 1930s who orchestrated the admission of the Soviet Union to the League of Nations.

pariah Outcast; a state that is diplomatically shunned, its leadership and actions not recognized as legitimate.

five-year plans Centralized formula for economic planning initiated by Stalin in 1928 to direct and coordinate production in all sectors of the economy.

command economy State-controlled economy in which all aspects of the economy are controlled by the state in a centralized manner.

1939, the Soviet Union was outproducing Britain and France, both still mired in depression, and was, after the United States and Germany, the third-largest industrial power in the world.

Worker Dissatisfaction

The greatest failure of the five-year plans pertained to workers' welfare. To the Soviet leadership, the only thing that mattered was the growth of production; the basic material needs of average people were unimportant. Only work and its products—the finished good—had quantifiable value. In practice, this meant that Soviet industries were built without any regard for worker safety. The Soviet workplace looked a lot more like the filthy capitalist enterprises criticized by Friedrich Engels and Karl Marx a century earlier than the workers' paradise envisioned by V. I. Lenin.

The Soviets used both rewards and coercion to mobilize the labor force and increase productivity, especially in heavy industries. Workers who more than met production goals received higher pay and other benefits, such as better housing. In addition, convict labor continued to be used in mining, lumbering, and building roads and waterways. Most workers put up with these measures, some out of conviction and others out of fear or need.

Collectivization

Peasants, however, resisted more stubbornly as the Soviets converted agriculture into a state-owned sector. The five-year plans called for **collectivization**—the confiscation of private land to create state-owned farms where production targets set by the state dictated the crops to be grown and the quantities to be produced. Peasants became wage-laborers who could keep only small plots of land and a few animals around the house for basic household needs. From the perspective of the state, collectivization was a rational way to consolidate small holdings and increase productivity. Large state farms, with machinery unaffordable to most individual farmers, could produce better crops and larger yields, to everyone's benefit. But collectivization robbed peasants of their identity. To be a peasant in Russia meant to have land, not just live on it. A man's dignity, in particular, was tied to his ability to feed his family from his land. Communist officials who pushed for collectivization were aware of this problem. But they believed the peasants, especially the newly enriched **kulaks** (coo-LAX) from the NEP period, needed to be broken. Collectivization was as much an ideological and social goal—eliminating a class enemy and creating a larger proletariat—as it was an economic aim.

> **collectivization** Soviet policy for turning all agricultural land into state-owned farms and peasants into wage laborers.
>
> **kulaks** Entrepreneurial peasants who enriched themselves during the NEP years.

The Great Famine

Collectivization was accomplished at appalling human costs and failed miserably to reach its economic goals. In the winter of 1932–1933, outrageous production quotas induced a general famine, especially in the Ukraine. Forced by the state to give up even the animals and crops they would have needed to survive through the winter, between 5 and 7 million peasants starved to death. The lucky ones were able to find shelter and food with relatives in the city. Others were reduced to eating tree bark and bugs—and even cannibalism. Young mothers, unable to feed their infants, killed them. By the end of 1933, ruthless methods had forced most peasants to give up their land. By 1940, all agricultural land was in the hands of the state.

This apparent victory masked important failures. First, peasants had been forced to give up their land through imprisonment, torture, exile in Siberia, and, in many cases, execution. The number of victims of this brutal process is still disputed, but it was certainly in the millions—6 to 10 million, according to various scholars. Some of the best working hands were eliminated in the first years of collectivization, and survivors were broken psychologically and physically. Second, the peasants did not go down without a fight. Many burned their crops and killed their livestock rather than see them in the hands of the government. As a result, the cattle population decreased by over 40 percent and the pig population by almost 50 percent between 1928 and 1931. Such violence continued into the late 1930s because peasants simply could not see collective farms as anything other than theft by the state.

The one goal in which collectivization succeeded was ideological. Peasants were forced to become workers, with no other resources for survival. In the next generation, the very notion of taking pride in one's land was wiped out. The communists had eliminated another social enemy from the old regime and reshaped the identity of the rural population into a subservient, if resentful, category of workers. Using brute violence, Stalin was on his way to refashioning the New Soviet Man and Woman.

27-2b Stalin's Totalitarian State

Having subdued the peasantry, Stalin turned toward intimidating other internal enemies—distrusted members of the party. This campaign began in 1936 and lasted until 1939, starting with the party's upper hierarchy and then widening to include family, friends, and other connections. By 1934, there had been significant disagreement among party leaders over industrialization and collectivization. Most in the Politburo leaned toward slowing down the pace and ending the most brutal policies. Unable to persuade or intimidate his opponents, Stalin turned the **NKVD**, the secret police, on them. The terror employed by the NKVD was not new for the Soviet regime, but the scale of the **Great Purges** that followed was unprecedented.

The Great Purges The first victims were high-ranking old Bolsheviks, some in the Politburo, followed by the most prominent army leaders and eventually the very leaders of the NKVD who had engineered the first purges. Stalin's diabolical system ensured that responsibility for the purges would always fall on the shoulders of his henchmen. Most old Bolshevik elites perished or were exiled, 70 percent of the Central Committee was removed, a significant number of officers were exiled or executed, and most of the leadership of the NKVD was also killed. In 1939, less than 2 percent of the delegates who had attended the 1934 party congress remained. By the end of the decade, the purges had produced a new generation of party, army, and secret police leaders personally subservient to Stalin.

The purges were a conscious policy engineered by Stalin to eliminate all opposition through execution and fear. Most people learned not to speak in public. A comment about how crowded the bus was might land one in jail. Criticism of food in a cafeteria might bring an NKVD agent to the table. Individuals disappeared so often in public places, never to be heard of again, that most people came to believe that the secret police were everywhere and that everyone was a potential informer, including children, spouses, and other close family members.

Labor Camps By 1939, several million people had been harassed and arrested by the NKVD in connection with alleged opposition. Many were executed; many more were sent to forced-labor camps, the **gulags**, where a majority perished from the brutality of the guards and the dreadful living conditions. An infamous camp was Solovetsky, an island in the Arctic Circle. Those who survived were used as slave labor, building railroads and hydroelectric stations as well as working in coal, gold, and copper mines.

Purges and the NKVD succeeded in transforming high-ranking communist officials and average citizens alike into fearful, powerless pawns in the hands of the state. They completed Stalin's social revolution. Through relentless and arbitrary brutality, the Soviet Union was now a **totalitarian** police state. The fate of all citizens rested in the hands of the party and on the whims of the Great Leader. The party and the state were one. The state controlled the economy and, through the secret police, intruded itself into everyone's daily life. A member of the Politburo could become a victim of Stalin's rage as easily as a poor peasant. In fact, the closer one was to the center of power in Moscow, the tighter the control exercised by

Stalin's apparatus of fear. His ability to control Soviet society through terror was unmatched by any leader in the twentieth century, save Hitler.

The Cult of Personality Yet Stalin was not content to project the image of a feared tyrant. He wanted to impress Soviet citizens and the world with his great accomplishments. Through a costly and sophisticated propaganda machine, he built a mythical cult of personality that depicted him as a beloved father of the country. One propaganda ode from this period declared: "O great Stalin, O leader of the peoples, / Thou who broughtest man to birth. / Thou who fructifies the earth, / Thou who restorest to centuries …, / O thou, / Sun reflected by millions of hearts." Writers were pressed into composing such poems; to write in opposition to Stalin meant certain death.

CONNECTIONS: Vladimir Putin came to dominate Russian politics starting in 2000 by following many of the same techniques perfected during Stalin's time (see Section 30-1a Russia's Collapse and Reemergence as Superpower). He gained control over most media outlets and continuously flooded all platforms of information dissemination with propaganda that trumpeted his achievements and denigrated all opponents, internal and international. The effectiveness of Putin's propaganda can be gleaned from his approval rating, consistently above 70 percent, an achievement some democratically elected leaders have envied.

But many were in awe of Stalin and honest in their praises. A movie producer who later became a critic of the regime confessed: "The strangest thing to me is that I was absolutely sincere. I thought all this was a necessary part of building communism. And then I believed Stalin." Western intellectuals disillusioned with their weak democracies and inability to fight the fascist threat were also impressed by Soviet accomplishments. The Spanish painter Pablo Picasso, for instance, came to glorify the Soviet Union under Stalin. Engineers and scientists from Europe and the United States were likewise enthusiastic. But many of those who went to the Soviet

NKVD (Russian acronym for "People's Commissariat of Internal Affairs") Soviet secret police under Stalin that organized the massive purges of the 1930s.

Great Purges Campaigns of political repression and persecution in the Soviet Union orchestrated by Joseph Stalin during the late 1930s.

gulag (Russian acronym for "Chief Administration of Corrective Labor Camps") Soviet forced-labor camp system in which political enemies of the state were confined and literally worked to death.

totalitarianism State system in which the ruling party has total control over politics, economic life, and society at large.

Union during the 1930s also disappeared into the gulag. It was safer to admire the Soviet Union from afar than to experience it up close.

27-3 The Third Reich, 1933–1945

» **What methods did the Nazis employ to achieve total control over German society?**

» **How does Stalin's dictatorship compare to Hitler's?**

In Germany, Hitler was also creating a totalitarian state. A pragmatist, he used the economic elites and existing political institutions to gain support and eliminate his enemies. But he was as quick to destroy inconvenient allies, making himself—like Mussolini and Stalin—the supreme leader, the Führer. The Nazis did not come to power with a clear political agenda other than Hitler's concepts of racial purity and the need to revise the Versailles Treaty. But in a few years, violence against internal enemies, in particular Jews, and expansionism became the hallmarks of the Third Reich.

27-3a Hitler's Consolidation of Power

Night of Long Knives First purge of the SA, in which Hitler's personal political enemies and disloyal followers were killed in one night in 1934.

Aryan race Pseudoscientific idea of the racially superior group that made up the German nation.

euthanasia Forceful termination of one's life in a presumably painless way.

Gestapo (German contraction for Geheime Staatspolizei, "secret state police") Nazi secret police that implemented Hitler's policies of total control.

concentration camp Camp for the internment of political prisoners and "undesirables," especially as organized by the Nazi regime.

Hitler won his mandate in 1933 by vowing to do away with internal enemies. First on the list were the communists, the purported villains behind the Reichstag fire. After the Enabling Act, he eliminated all political parties and trade unions. Labeling his moves as security measures, in 1934 he ordered his SS troops to kill all conservative leaders who had opposed him before 1933 as well as leaders of his own storm troopers. This **Night of Long Knives**, Hitler's first internal purge, paved the way for his dictatorial rule by terror, much like Stalin's purges that began during the same period.

Nazi Racism as State Ideology Within six months Hitler had consolidated all political power in his hands. With other political parties

gone, the Nazis moved to control civic and public institutions in the name of national and economic reconstruction. The foundation of this policy was the racist ideology set out in *Mein Kampf*. To ensure the purity and well-being of the **Aryan race**, Jews—whom Hitler considered morally and physically subhuman, materialistic, and physiologically unable to work for the nation's greater good—had to be eliminated. To this end, Hitler used some of the popular ideas at that time, especially eugenics, to suggest swift, "scientific" ways to sort out those who were "desirable" from the rest and to eliminate the biological threat posed by "undesirables." The eugenicist theories adopted by the Nazis considered the health of an individual a function primarily of genetic makeup, implying that it was impossible to cure or rehabilitate the genetically deficient. Eugenicist solutions ranged from preventing intermarriage with the "healthy" population and denying any social services to the genetically inferior to outright sterilization and **euthanasia**. Under the guise of national reinvigoration—"creating a Germany for Germans"—Hitler's goal was to create a racially pure state.

This irrational ideology worked because it was convenient: it offered an easy scapegoat for Germany's ills and did not force non-Jews to take responsibility or look for difficult solutions. In time, Jewishness came to be defined in increasingly complicated ways to include individuals who did not self-identify as Jews. Men and women who were Catholics, for example, and had Aryan blond hair and blue eyes, were considered Jewish if the state could uncover one Jewish grandparent. The Nazis forced all people into trying to conform to racial stereotypes and hide any elements of their identity that might raise the suspicions of the dreaded **Gestapo**, Hitler's secret police.

Hitler's division of people into desirables and undesirables went beyond Aryans and Jews. Based on his racist theories, the category of undesirables broadened throughout the 1930s to include all Jews, Roma (Gypsies), and Slavs (e.g., Poles) as well as socialists and communists (said to have joined with Jews in a "Judeo-Bolshevik plot" against Germany), homosexuals, members of some religious denominations (e.g., Jehovah's Witnesses), feminists, disabled persons, and anyone who supposedly suffered from a genetic disease or from tuberculosis, syphilis, or alcoholism.

Nazi Policies of Extermination The policies for dealing with undesirables aimed to eliminate them. Starting in 1933, the Nazis sterilized Roma and then others deemed "unfit" to reproduce. Doctors and judges, not the Gestapo, were the primary administrators of this policy. In 1933, the first **concentration camp**, meant to advance the elimination of undesirables, was established at Dachau, a town north of Munich. Here initially communist and other left-wing dissidents were taken to perform hard labor in subhuman living conditions intended to starve them

Mary Evans Picture Library/The Image Works

Kristallnacht

Along with many other temples, this Jewish synagogue was vandalized by Nazi party members on the night of November 9–10, 1938, which came to be known as Kristallnacht (Night of Broken Glass).

❯❯ *What message was the Nazi regime communicating to the Jewish population and to non-Jews about Jewish civilization and sacred spaces?*

to death. Later, these "labor" camps were turned into more effective killing factories, where most of Europe's Jews and many other "undesirables" were exterminated.

The Nuremberg Laws The policy of segregating and later eliminating Jews began to take shape in 1935 through the **Nuremberg Laws**. These stripped Jews of citizenship, forbade them to marry non-Jews, and restricted their economic and social activities to the Jewish community. Jewish doctors could treat only Jewish patients; Jews could shop only at Jewish stores. Now Jews who saw themselves as Germans and did not identify with Jewishness in terms of religion, customs, or language were forced to assume a Jewish identity.

Controlling the Aryans The Nazis were equally intent on controlling the desirables. Aryan women had to abide by the regime's pro-natalist policies, which limited their social role to the home and children. Those who bore no children were considered disloyal to the Führer and punished, while unwed mothers of Aryan children were praised as patriotic Germans.

People had to continually show their loyalty to the Nazi state to avoid the terror of the Gestapo, which could at any moment arrest people on the suspicion of treason or for being undesirables. By the late 1930s, the Third Reich had become a totalitarian state under the complete control of the Nazis and their supreme Führer, much like the Soviet Union was under Stalin.

Still, for ethnic Germans there was room for economic and social improvement in Hitler's racist state. During their first five years in power, the Nazis virtually eliminated unemployment, reducing it to less than 1 percent (though that figure did not include more than 1 million noncitizens—Jews and others imprisoned or simply stripped of citizenship). For those who were citizens, incomes were going up, business opportunities were growing due to Hitler's remilitarization of the economy, and housing was becoming more affordable. Industrial production rose by nearly 30 percent between 1932 and 1938, a success similar to Stalin's accomplishments.

Nuremberg Laws Edicts issued by the Nazis in 1935 that deprived Jews of German citizenship and initiated their segregation from German life.

And, like Stalin, Hitler also built these successes on the bodies of those forced to give up their wealth, freedom, and life. But unlike Stalin, Hitler successfully rallied the wealthy business class to engage in his plan of economic recovery. From an economic standpoint, the Nazi regime turned out to be more capitalistic and less socialistic than it had claimed at the beginning.

Anti-Semitic Propaganda Intense anti-Semitic propaganda also worked to justify the actions of the Nazis and gain the cooperation of many average and well-educated Germans. School textbooks were revised to include discussions of racial purity and the threat of marriages with Jews and other "inferior" races. Hitler skillfully used movies and radio as propaganda tools. The Nazis harnessed the talents of outstanding artists such as film director **Leni Riefenstahl** to produce arousing and flawless documentaries and feature films designed to seduce average citizens into identifying with the ideals of the Third Reich. The most notable was *Triumph of the Will*, a cinematic masterpiece in communicating a racist message with eloquence and in revealing how the Nazis hoped to transform the German people into a homogeneous, energized, militarized, and obedient unit. Hitler also encouraged the production of affordable radios so he could reach most Germans on a regular basis. In addition to music, listeners got a daily dose of anti-Semitic propaganda through newscasts, speeches, and even humor.

Finally, the Nazis turned to sports, already an important pastime in Europe, and determined to demonstrate the superiority of the Aryan race in the Berlin Olympics of 1936. Athletes were carefully selected and trained in a grueling regimen that did produce many medal winners. But the Nazis also suffered some embarrassments, especially in the resounding victories of the African American track-and-field athlete Jesse Owens, whose supposed racial inferiority did not prevent him from breaking eleven Olympic records.

Intense propaganda was successful in transforming German society. By the late 1930s, educated people supported the Nazis. Doctors were willing to go along with sterilization programs and to pressure those with a good racial "pedigree" to have children. By the late 1930s, German industrial power was second only to that of the United States.

27-3b The Nazi Challenge to Europe

Hitler's dream of an Aryan state included an essential expansionist component. He was dedicated to revenging the German losses in World War I and wanted to recover all territories in which German populations lived, to save them from oppression by inferior races such as Slavs and Jews. His

Leni Riefenstahl (1902–2003) Famous German film director who made propaganda films for the Nazis.

Hugo Jaeger/Time Life Pictures/Getty Images

Hitler and Mussolini

Adolf Hitler and Benito Mussolini appeared together on many occasions to underscore their strong alliance and personal friendship. In reality, Hitler thought of Mussolini as an inferior, if useful partner in his plans for world domination.

concept of Lebensraum aimed to justify the conquest of Poland and Russia so that Germans could resettle these lands and make them productive by using the native populations as slave labor. Not everyone grasped the extent of Hitler's idea of world domination until the beginning of World War II, but most Germans supported revising the Versailles Treaty and strengthening the military.

Gaining Allies in the East Initially Hitler focused on projecting a nonconfrontational international position. Germany was isolated in Europe, so he worked to increase trade with countries weakened by the Great Depression, especially in eastern Europe. Although these were also territories slated for occupation, where Slavic people he deemed inferior lived, Hitler was pragmatic. His offers to trade guns for grain and natural resources were received with interest by impoverished authoritarian regimes in Bulgaria, Romania, and Hungary. Such international agreements served to rearm these countries and also provide Germany with important resources, especially Romania's oil, for its economy and for a future war.

With new markets for their guns, in clear violation of the Versailles Treaty, the Nazis began to rebuild the armament industry, using the very capitalists whom they had criticized before 1933. Starting in 1935 Hitler built a new air force, the Luftwaffe, and encouraged the creation of new offensive weapons through a vast program of research and development. The draft was introduced (1935), increasing the fighting forces to half a million, in flagrant defiance of the Versailles Treaty. But the first significant violation of the treaty came in March 1936, when German troops marched into the Rhineland, the region on the French border that was supposed to remain demilitarized as a buffer zone. The western democracies failed to respond strongly to this challenge, protesting through the League of Nations but taking no action.

The Axis Alliance This inaction was a vital mistake because it bolstered Hitler's self-confidence, popularity at home, and appeal among similar foreign regimes. Italy also had expansionist ambitions and in 1935 had invaded Ethiopia. By the end of 1936, the **Berlin-Rome Axis** had been formed, an alliance of like-minded states that would later include Japan, a militarist and expansionist power already embarked on conquest in East Asia and the Pacific. The alliance was based on their mutual imperialist interests, their profound disregard for democracy, and their fear of the Soviets.

27-3c Resistance and Appeasement

Hitler's rise to power challenged the Soviet Union. In 1935, the Soviet Union began to focus resolutely on the threat Hitler posed to the stability of Europe. The cornerstone of the new Soviet position in international affairs was collective security. The threat of war in both the west and the east forced the Soviets to consider cooperation with capitalist countries, something unthinkable a decade earlier. But Stalin argued that this position did not contradict the goal of world communist revolution. It simply focused on eliminating the most imminent threat, fascism. This position led to his signing of mutual-aid pacts with France and Czechoslovakia in 1935, directed primarily against Germany.

Establishment of the Popular Fronts The same pragmatic vision led to a reversal of Comintern policies in 1935 from noncooperation to coalition-building with other antifascist parties. This radical change paved the way for the formation of the **Popular Fronts** in Spain and France as well as the coalition in China against the Japanese threat. In France, the Socialist **Léon Blum** was able to talk the Communist, Socialist, and Radical Parties into forming the Popular Front in 1936. Blum was the first Jewish prime minister in France; his victory was an important symbolic challenge to the Nazis

and on behalf of democracy, inclusiveness, and social responsibility of the state toward all citizens.

Blum quickly introduced major changes: the forty-hour workweek, the paid two-week vacation, the right of workers to collective bargaining, and other social programs. Under Blum, the Bank of France and the armaments industry were also nationalized. These changes signaled a major shift in defining government responsibilities but were not endorsed by everyone. Blum was attacked by members of his coalition and by opponents on the right. He resigned in June 1937 but remained an important force in the coalition and resumed leadership briefly in 1938, in strong support of the Spanish Republic's struggle against Franco.

Artists Defend Democracy While politicians tried ineffectively to defend democracy against radical challenges, writers, popular culture stars, and religious leaders tried to address, if not solve, the crises of the day. The art and literature of the 1930s became more engaged with current events than had been the case in the more escapist 1920s. Writers like the German novelist **Thomas Mann** made it a personal quest to salvage the humanist spirit in Germany and the spirit of tolerance toward Jews. In Britain, **Virginia Woolf** confronted women's continued inequalities and militarization in her book *Three Guineas* (1938).

A far more powerful and effective critique of the social problems of the times and the rise of fascism came from an unlikely source, the silver screen. Charlie Chaplin effectively depicted social and economic inequalities while offering an amusing and deeply humane picture of the poor. In *Modern Times* (1936), his famous Little Tramp character became a symbol of humanity's vulnerability in a world run by machines and obsessed with mechanized progress. Similarly, *The Great Dictator* (1940) confronted the racist irrationality of Nazi Germany through comedy and farce involving a Jewish barber (the Little Tramp) standing in for Hitler at a Nazi mass rally.

Berlin-Rome Axis Agreement between Mussolini and Hitler in 1936 to support each other in their expansionist goals.

Popular Fronts Moderate left-wing coalition governments during the 1930s that brought political stability, social reforms, and some economic recovery from the Great Depression.

Léon Blum (1872–1950) First Jewish prime minister of France, a Socialist who led the Popular Front government in 1936.

Thomas Mann (1875–1955) Great German writer of the twentieth century who was persecuted by the Nazis for his staunch criticism of their anti-Semitism.

Virginia Woolf (1882–1941) Pacifist English writer who drew attention to gender inequalities.

Two Boa Constrictors (Hitler and Stalin)

The caption of this British cartoon from 1939 states: "I don't quite know how to help you digest, my dear Adolf . . . but I understand you very well." In the struggle for the hearts and minds of their fellow citizens, European artists and journalists played an important role in exposing Germany's and Russia's expansionist designs at a time when western leaders were unwilling to challenge these moves.

》 *What sort of relationship between the two dictatorships does the cartoon depict?*

》 *What does the imagery of the two leaders as boa constrictors suggest about the threat they pose to other countries?*

Dietrich Bonhoeffer (1906–1945) German Lutheran pastor who openly criticized the Nazis and organized an underground church during the Third Reich.

Pius XII (r. 1939–1958) Pope who failed to take a strong stance against the Nazis under the pretext of neutrality.

Munich Conference Emergency meeting in 1938 in which Britain and France gave in to Hitler's demand for the Czech Sudetenland.

appeasement Policy of giving in to an opponent's requests to prevent further demands.

Reactions of Religious Leaders Some religious leaders, such as the German Lutheran pastor **Dietrich Bonhoeffer**, attempted both to criticize the inhuman policies of the Nazis and to minister to religious communities. Bonhoeffer went so far as to establish the underground pacifist Confessing Church, which remained active throughout World War II, at great peril to its leader and his following. Throughout the 1930s and the war, Bonhoeffer voiced his strong opposition to the Nazis; he was executed in April 1945 for his role in a plot to assassinate Hitler.

Other prelates, such as Eugenio Cardinal Pacelli,

later Pope **Pius XII**, chose a policy of compromise with the Nazis to protect the Catholic Church. Though Pacelli spoke on several occasions against the Nazis and was critical of their anti-Semitic policies in some writings, he also orchestrated a concordat in 1933 that established official relations between the Nazi regime and the Vatican. Critics saw the concordat as condoning the Nazis' dictatorial powers and the Vatican's abandonment of the German Catholics into Hitler's hands. Supporters saw the concordat as a practical means for the Vatican to exercise some pressure on behalf of Catholics in Germany.

Yet many in Europe and America stood idle during this period of increasing tensions and violence. Burdened by their own anti-Semitism and racist policies either at home or in their colonies, many democratic countries refused entry to the Jews who were desperately trying to flee the Third Reich. The governments of both Britain and the United States, where many German (and later Austrian and eastern European) Jews sought refuge, were reluctant to lift immigration quotas. One of the most egregious incidents was the refusal by the American government to grant entry to ten thousand Jewish children, a request made insistently by First Lady Eleanor Roosevelt.

CONNECTIONS: During the recent civil war that tore apart Syria, a similar stance on the part of many citizens and politicians in the United States has led to rejecting many desperate refugees to enter the country. Some European countries, most notably Germany, have been more welcoming, in part because of lessons learned from the horrors of the Nazi regime (See Section 30-2c Nation-States in a New Context.)

Nazi Expansion into Austria and Czechoslovakia

As there were no protests from abroad, Hitler continued his quest for aggrandizement (see Map 27.1). Claiming to respond to the wishes of Austrians—as true Aryans—to be part of the great German nation, in March 1938 he annexed Austria through coercion and manipulation. This action emboldened him to move toward the next target, Czechoslovakia, where a large German minority was concentrated mainly in the western region of the Sudetenland. But Czechoslovakia could not be easily intimidated. Its democratic government had strong military and mutual assistance pacts with France and the Soviet Union. Hitler gambled and requested that the Sudetenland be ceded to Germany, prompting an international crisis.

At the **Munich Conference** in September 1938, the British and French caved in to the German demands, justifying their desertion of Czechoslovakia as a small price to pay for securing peace. This policy of **appeasement** was meant to reduce the German threat under the misguided notion that Hitler's quest for Lebensraum could be satisfied by the Sudetenland. In fact, appeasement signaled to all countries in the east that the European order and frontiers could be violated and that they might be abandoned by the western democracies

Map 27.1 **The Expansion of Germany** Starting in 1938, Nazi Germany aggressively pursued its goals of acquiring Lebensraum for its Aryan population. Its success would prove short-lived, especially as the Axis powers started to overstretch their resources.

1. What happened to Poland, Austria, and Czechoslovakia between 1938 and 1939?
2. How did these changes threaten European international order?
3. What direction did German territorial expansion have? Can you explain that in reference to Nazi ideology?

at any moment. Within six months, Czechoslovakia was divided into annexed (Sudetenland), occupied (Bohemia and Moravia), and independent (Slovakia) territories controlled by the Nazis. Slovakia became a puppet state ruled by the Catholic priest Josef Tiso, whose full cooperation with the Nazi policies of exterminating Jews was never denounced by the Vatican.

The Nazi-Soviet Pact As Hitler was preparing his next step—the invasion of Poland—Britain and France finally determined to stand up to Hitler's challenge by guaranteeing Poland's integrity. But it was not clear whether either of these countries was willing or prepared to

honor that promise or whether they were merely making a gesture. Either way, Hitler had so much confidence by now that he was completely unimpressed. In addition, he now turned cunningly toward another potential ally, the Soviet Union.

On August 23, 1939, the two mortal enemies, Hitler and Stalin, signed a nonaggression agreement known as the **Molotov-Ribbentrop Pact**, for the foreign ministers who

Molotov-Ribbentrop Pact
Nonaggression agreement of 1939 that secretly divided the Baltic countries and Poland between the Soviets and the Germans and allotted part of Romania to the Soviet Union.

negotiated it. Many were surprised about this about-face in Soviet-Nazi relations. The pact went against the Nazi racist idea that the Slavs and Bolsheviks were enemies of the Third Reich; it also contradicted all the antifascist statements and alliances of the Soviet Union since 1935. Instead, the pact was a pragmatic move. Stalin had been excluded from the Munich Conference, and as France and Britain seemed intent on isolating the Soviet Union, he sought another partner in Europe. The Soviets also wanted to recover some of the territories lost in World War I. Thus the pact included several secret clauses that pertained to the division of Poland and the Baltic countries, as well as to the recovery of Bassarabia from Romania. Hitler wished to pursue his drive toward the east but wanted to ensure that the Soviets would not precipitate a two-front war. The solution was to divide Poland. On September 1, 1939, Germany launched a surprise attack on Poland from the west. On September 3, Britain and France honored their commitment to Poland by declaring war on Germany. World War II had begun.

27-4 World War II, 1939–1945

» How did World War II differ from previous wars?

» What military strategies, technological developments, and other factors enabled the Allies to win the war?

World War II was unprecedented in the extent of the destruction it wrought on the entire world, the degree to which it involved civilians, and the depth of the moral questions it raised. New military technologies, fighting strategies, psychological manipulation, and scientific discoveries ensured that this would be a war unlike any other. By the end of the conflict, the entire world had been touched by war; almost 70 million people had perished, most of them in Europe; and democracy had been challenged to the core (see Table 27.2). Although the Allies defeated the Axis, Europe lay in ruin and democracy was not secure. Communism became Europe's next important challenge, as Stalin emerged victorious in eastern Europe.

blitzkrieg (in German, "lightning war") German attack strategy involving massed air force cover and rapid, motorized tank and troop movements that overwhelmed opponents.

27-4a Germany's Early Triumphs

Hitler managed to occupy the western half of Poland in four weeks. Tanks and motorized armored troop carriers raced across the

Table 27.2 Major Events of World War II

September 1939	Poland occupied by Nazis and Soviets
May 1940	Churchill becomes prime minister of Britain
June 1940	Nazis occupy France
Fall 1940	Battle of Britain
March 1941	Lend-Lease Act
April 1941	Nazis occupy Greece and Yugoslavia
June 1941	Operation Barbarossa: Nazis invade Soviet Union
December 1941	Pearl Harbor; United States enters the war
November 1942	Allied invasion of North Africa
February 1943	Germans surrender at Stalingrad
July 1943	Soviet victory at Kursk
September 1943	Allied invasion of Italy
June 1944	Operation Overlord: Allied invasion of Normandy and liberation of France
August 1944	Warsaw Uprising
February 1945	Yalta Conference
May 8, 1945	Soviets liberate Berlin; Germans surrender
August 6 and 9, 1945	United States drops atomic bombs in Japan
August 14, 1945	Japanese surrender

border, supported by air power and paratroopers, introducing the world to a new type of warfare, **blitzkrieg** (BLITZ-kreeg). The Poles fought desperately, but their military strength was inferior to that of the Nazis, and their allies Britain and France offered little help. When the Soviets invaded Poland from the east on September 17, the Poles surrendered within ten days. The Soviets also proceeded to occupy Latvia, Estonia, and Lithuania and to incorporate them as Soviet Republics. Only Finland resisted Soviet demands, fighting back and scoring some victories, but it, too, was ultimately defeated in the winter of 1939–1940.

Nazi Victories in Western Europe In the spring of 1940, Hitler turned west, invading Denmark and Norway and then attacking the Netherlands and Belgium, which fell in two weeks. France was next. In mid-June 1940, German troops marched into Paris and Henri Pétain, the hero of Verdun, signed over to German occupation the northern three-fifths of the country. The south, **Vichy France**, became a German puppet state under Pétain. This defeat was the greatest humiliation France had ever experienced, and it finally awoke the west to the aims and methods of the Third Reich.

Britain Fights Back Britain offered some aid to Belgium in May but had to evacuate its troops to prevent their capture by the Nazis. In response to the fall of Norway, Winston Churchill assumed leadership of the country and radically shifted the British position from uncertain support for its allies to standing fast against Hitler, who now began an intensive bombardment of Britain's industries and cities in preparation for invasion. During those difficult months, Churchill provided what the British people needed—an unbounded energy and faith in the army, air force, civilians, and democracy that proved inspiring. In June 1941, he declared resolutely: "We shall go on to the end. . . . We shall never surrender."

Churchill had been in British politics for a long time, but he had never made more than a temporary mark. As an officer he had first served in India and Africa, then entered politics in 1901. As head of the British navy, he was responsible for the disastrous loss at Gallipoli early in World War I, which discredited him for the next twenty-five years. By the mid-1930s, he was considered a political maverick, always sure to take unpopular positions and often, critics said, too eager to jump into half-baked plans. But Churchill was also a passionate speaker, and his powerful warnings about the threat to democracy posed by the two great evils of fascism and communism captivated the attention of the public and politicians alike. By 1940, he seemed the only leader with the vision and courage to change the course of the British policy of appeasement and the magnetism to carry the country with him: "Let us therefore brace ourselves to our duties, and to bear ourselves that, if the British Empire and Its Commonwealth last for a thousand years, they will say, 'That was their finest hour.'"

Between July and October 1940, Britain and Germany engaged in intensive air combat, known as the **Battle of Britain**. Initially the Nazis pursued a policy of strategically bombing air bases. Their success depended almost exclusively on the strength and versatility of the Luftwaffe, while the British Royal Air Force (RAF) had a sophisticated system of command and coordination among its pilots enhanced by a radar network and good intelligence work in Germany. These advantages gave the RAF great precision in intercepting enemy planes (over 80 percent at times)

and coordinating aerial attacks. By contrast, though the Nazis had excellent planes and pilots, they were often less precise and had to resort to riskier blanket bombing. In September, the Nazis shifted to a strategy of bombing civilian targets, bent on terrorizing the population and killing more than 23,000 civilians. But by October 1940, the RAF had outmaneuvered the Germans. The Battle of Britain was significant because it was the first time since 1939 that the Nazis had suffered defeat and it severely weakened the strength of the Luftwaffe. It also convinced Hitler to shift his attention to other areas, though the Nazis continued their attacks on Britain until June 1941.

U.S. Support for the Allies Churchill also gambled on assistance from the United States and initially received limited help. But the heroic resistance of the British galvanized support from the Roosevelt government, which in March 1941 passed the **Lend-Lease Act**, granting "all aid short of war" to Britain. Later that year, the two leaders met to formulate a statement of war aims, the **Atlantic Charter**, which announced a commitment to restoring democracy in Europe. Finally, Churchill gambled by sending British troops to the Mediterranean to fight Italian forces bent on conquering Egypt and Greece. This strategy left the British Isles vulnerable but created an important diversion in the south, as Hitler had to send German reinforcements to a new battlefront in North Africa and the Balkans. For the first six months of 1941, German forces concentrated on taking Algeria, Morocco, Tunisia, Greece, and Yugoslavia.

The Nazis Invade the Soviet Union By June 1941, the Axis controlled almost all of Europe, from Norway to the Mediterranean and from France to Poland. Britain stood alone, with support from the United States. The blitzkrieg strategies had worked well for Hitler, and he now prepared to turn east again, toward the Soviet Union, to pursue his Lebensraum policy. The about-face against his former ally was anticipated in Britain, where intelligence concerning **Operation Barbarossa** had leaked in May. Churchill tried to

Vichy France Puppet state established by the Nazis in southern France during World War II, named so for its capital in Vichy.

Battle of Britain Nazi air campaign against the British Isles in the fall of 1940 that became Germany's first major defeat.

Lend-Lease Act U.S. Commitment in 1941 to grant massive financial and military support to the Allies.

Atlantic Charter Agreement between Churchill and Roosevelt in 1941 stating Allied goals for the war, including the commitment to restoring democracy in Europe.

Operation Barbarossa Code name for the Nazi invasion of the Soviet Union in June 1941.

warn Stalin, but to no avail. Other signs made it increasingly clear that Hitler was mounting a large-scale operation against the Soviet Union, especially a series of alliances that drew Hungary, Romania, and Bulgaria into the Axis.

Thus, when the Nazis finally embarked on Operation Barbarossa on June 22, 1941, no one except Stalin was surprised. The campaign was unprecedented in size and scope, including more than three million Axis troops, an air force of thousands, and more than three thousand tanks. The Soviets had a formidable army as well, in terms of size and equipment, but they lacked leadership. In addition to the purge of the officer corps, which demoralized the remaining personnel, the military was also paralyzed by Stalin's inability to come to terms with Hitler's betrayal. Quickly, the Germans drove to Kiev, where they took more than six hundred thousand prisoners in just one battle. By the end of October, they were besieging Leningrad and threatening Moscow in the north, while advancing toward oil fields in the south. **Joseph Goebbels** (GOER-bels), Hitler's propaganda minister, announced that the war was over: the Soviets had lost more than two million soldiers, three hundred thousand square miles of land, and thousands of planes and tanks. Germany seemed invincible, but important developments in 1942 turned the tide of the war.

27-4b Allied Victory

The Axis had driven across a large portion of the Russian steppe, but the vast distances, harsh climate, and rudimentary roads proved their greatest obstacles. As winter arrived, the Germans and their allies were unable to get fresh troops and supplies to the front. In addition, the Soviets conducted a scorched-earth policy of burning fields, removing livestock, and disassembling industrial enterprises before retreating east. Blitzkrieg collapsed into a war of attrition. German troops grew demoralized as temperatures plunged to minus 60 degrees Fahrenheit. Many Germans froze to death, while the Russians went into hiding.

The United States Enters the War Meanwhile, the British and the Soviets soon had a new and important ally, the United States, which was compelled to declare war on the Axis following Japan's surprise attack on **Pearl Harbor** on December 7, 1941. Roosevelt sent an important infusion of food, supplies, and armament to the Soviets, helping them rebound from the massive losses incurred in 1941. Thus, when the Germans reopened their offensive in August 1942 by attacking **Stalingrad**, an important industrial center at the edge of European Russia, the Soviets were ready to fight back (see Map 27.2). In addition to Stalingrad's being a gateway to Asian Russia and oil resources in the south, taking the city renamed for the Soviet leader had become an obsession for Hitler.

For Stalin, defending the city that bore his name was also personal, and he used all available propaganda to promote the idea that saving it was the same as saving the Russian soul. The war was no longer between communism and fascism; it had become the Great Patriotic War, in which soldiers and civilians, men and women, parents and children were called on to help Father Stalin and save Mother Russia from the Germanic invasion. Film director Sergei Eisenstein made his masterpiece, *Ivan the Terrible*, in the midst of war, depicting the medieval ruler as both despot and great patriot—the man who saved Russia from foreign threats. Stalin wanted to be seen this way—ruthless against foreigners but an ally of the simple people, who followed him faithfully. The morale of the people proved crucial to the defense of Stalingrad, which withstood months of house-to-house fighting before the Nazis surrendered on February 2, 1943, their troop strength diminished from five hundred thousand to eighty thousand. Stalingrad had been reduced to rubble, and Soviet victory came at the great price of over 1.5 million casualties.

Turning the Tide of the War The crushing defeat at Stalingrad slowed down the Nazis, but it was fighting at **Kursk**, between February and July 1943, that permanently turned the tide of the war in the east. At Stalingrad, Nazi troops had been at a tactical disadvantage because they were engaged in urban warfare, for which they were inadequately prepared; but at Kursk, they could use blitzkrieg techniques. At the same time, the Soviets had learned much about Nazi military strategy and had been able to upgrade their armaments, especially tank power and antitank guns. Defeated by the Soviets at their best game, the Nazis were profoundly demoralized and began to retreat.

In North Africa, German forces had also been pushed back by the British, now joined by American troops. By May 1943, the Germans had withdrawn entirely from the region. With North Africa secured, the Allies were able to launch an invasion of Sicily, a steppingstone to the invasion of Italy in September 1943. Mussolini was forced from power but remained in the hands of the Germans, at the helm of a puppet republic in northern Italy.

Joseph Goebbels (1897–1945) Hitler's propaganda minister who played a central role in the Final Solution.

Pearl Harbor U.S. naval base in Hawaii bombed by Japan on December 7, 1941, drawing the United States into World War II.

Stalingrad (today Volgograd) Soviet city held under siege by the Nazis for six months where the Soviets scored one of the most important victories in 1942.

Kursk Battle in which the Nazis received a crushing defeat through Soviet blitzkrieg tactics.

Map 27.2 **Axis Victories in World War II, 1942** World War II tested the limits of European civilization and democratic legacies. The threat was greatest in the spring of 1942, when Adolf Hitler's Axis alliance controlled most of Europe and North Africa.

1. What European states disappeared during World War II?
2. What might have been the weaknesses of the Nazis at the moment of their greatest victories in World War II?
3. What seem to be the Allies greatest challenges in fighting against the Nazis?

In addition, the Allies pursued a strategy of all-out air attacks on Germany. The policy of strategic bombing—attacking important military, industrial, and transportation centers—failed in its immediate goals of destroying the military capacity of the Nazis, but it did cut production. Night bombing afforded greater protection from antiaircraft guns but also reduced precision in hitting targets and increased civilian losses. Some 300,000 Germans died and 750,000 were maimed in Allied air raids. It became clear that Hitler would be defeated only by an invasion.

The War in Asia The importance of the United States in turning the tide of the war was nowhere greater than in Asia, especially in Japan and the Philippines. Japan's imperial expansionist designs had been developing since the early 1930s, when it invaded Manchuria and subsequently occupied part of China, where they pursued ruthless violent means of subjugating the military and civilian population. During the **Nanjing Massacre**, Japanese troops tortured and killed over 300,000 Chinese soldiers and civilians and raped tens of thousands of women.

After Pearl Harbor, the United States began assisting China and pursued an active policy of fighting the Japanese forces by air and sea. In the ensuing four years, many colonial possessions of European powers fell into Japanese hands, whose occupation policies continued the brutal behavior displayed in Nanjing. With substantial support from Australia and Britain, the United States began to take back some of these territories, especially after the decisive **Battle of Midway** in June 1942. By the end of 1944 the Allies had retaken the Philippines and Burma, but the Japanese held strong in China (see Map 27.3).

Allied Victory On June 6, 1944, **Operation Overlord** began. In one of the most intense military operations of the war, the Allies crossed the English Channel to land more than two million soldiers (Americans, British, Poles, Belgians, Canadians, Norwegians, Dutch, and French) and millions of tons of military equipment in Nazi-occupied France. Securing the first strip of beach involved heavy casualties, but months of careful planning paid off. Now the Germans had to fight a three-front war—east, west, and south—and could do little more than resist while retreating. Paris was liberated by August, Brussels in September, and that month the first Allied troops crossed into Germany.

In the east, the Soviets were also advancing steadily. In January 1945, they liberated the concentration camp at **Auschwitz** (OW-shwitz) and took Warsaw; in April, advance units of the American and Soviet armies met south of Berlin on the Elbe River. Mussolini met his end on April 28, killed by Italian partisans while trying to escape. He was then publicly hung so that crowds could freely abuse his body. Two days later, trying to avoid the humiliation of capture, Hitler committed suicide together with his wife, Eva Braun, in his Berlin bunker. On May 8, the Soviets finally liberated Berlin and brought the war to an end on the European front. Three months later, the United States used a newly developed weapon against Japan, the **atomic bomb**. The Japanese surrendered on August 14, and World War II was over.

The Human Costs The total human toll of the war was as high as 70 million people, by some estimates, with Europe suffering roughly half of the casualties. Approximately 20 million of these were soldiers, and the remaining 50 million were civilians. The astronomic number and ratio of civilian to soldier casualties were unprecedented. Those who suffered the most were in eastern Europe: Yugoslavia lost 4.5 million people, a higher ratio of its population than Germany's 7.7 million casualties, while in Poland, Warsaw alone had more casualties in absolute numbers than Britain and the United States combined. The vast majority of the Jewish population exterminated in the war came from eastern Europe. The extent of material destruction was equally unprecedented, with eastern Europe again experiencing the highest losses as two waves of occupation and destruction—the Nazis and then the Soviets—swept through the area between 1939 and 1945.

Technology and the Allied Victory The Allies won the war by outperforming their enemies in military technology, intelligence gathering, science, diplomacy, and mobilization on the home front. On the eastern front, the Soviets spared no expense and converted more than 50 percent of their industrial production to building tanks that were larger and more powerful than Germany's. The British developed radar technology essential to the RAF success in the Battle of Britain. The Allies also used new technology to break the German and Japanese military codes. And the Americans invested nearly $2 billion and employed more than 130,000 people in the **Manhattan Project**, the vast nuclear engineering complex that worked steadily between 1942 and 1945 to develop the atomic bomb before the Germans did and used it to force Japanese surrender.

Victory and Allied Diplomacy Another key to Allied victory was diplomacy. The ability of Churchill, Stalin, and Roosevelt to work together, despite their fundamental ideological differences and deep distrust between Stalin and his western

---

Nanjing Massacre The torture and killing of over 300,000 Chinese people and rape of tens of thousands of women at the hands of the Japanese forces during their takeover of that city in December 1937—January 1938.

Battle of Midway Decisive Allied victory in the Pacific in June 1942, which helped turn the tide of the war against the Japanese forces.

Operation Overlord Code name for the Allied invasion of France in June 1944.

atomic bomb Bomb powered by nuclear energy, with unprecedented destructive capability, developed first by scientists in the United States.

Manhattan Project Extensive science and development program in the United States in 1942–1945 that produced a nuclear bomb.

Map 27.3 **War in Asia** In the war against Japan in the Pacific, a different configuration of the Axis versus Allies conflict took place.

1. Who bore the brunt of the war effort?
2. What other supporting countries helped in the effort against the Axis?
3. What other features of the conflict that are different from the European theater of war can you discern from this map?

allies, was one of the remarkable successes of the war (see Map 27.4). The three met on two important occasions during the war, in Teheran in 1943 and Yalta in 1945. The **Yalta Conference** was particularly important: it laid the foundation for the creation of the United Nations; determined policies for liberating and dividing Germany; allowed postwar Poland and eastern Europe to fall primarily within the Soviet sphere of influence; and arranged for the Soviet Union's entry into the war against Japan. The last two provisions were the result of an informal exchange between the Americans, who desperately wanted support against Japan, and the Soviets, who sought to control the political future of eastern Europe. The Yalta Conference would play a major role in the political reconfiguration of Europe after the war.

Yalta Conference Meeting of Churchill, Roosevelt, and Stalin in 1945 to discuss postwar peace.

Map 27.4 **Allied Victory in Europe** Soviet, British, and U.S. troops, supported by numerous resistance movements in Axis-occupied territories, turned the tide of war after 1942.

1. How would you describe the position of Nazi Germany in Europe in 1942?
2. What were the obstacles faced by the Allies at that point?
3. By looking at the movement of military forces over this map and the reoccupation of Axis-controlled territories by different Allied forces, which country bore the brunt of the effort?

27-4c Mobilization, Collaboration, and Resistance

The Allies could not have won the war without the unprecedented mobilization of civilians, who worked in war industries and other essential capacities and, in occupied regimes, participated in resistance movements. Women, especially, served in new capacities. They were allowed to join, and in some cases were even drafted into, the military. In the Soviet Union 800,000 women served as combatants, from ambulance drivers to pilots. More important, however, women were mobilized for economic production and auxiliary services, such as medical aid, supplies, and various public service jobs, from secretaries to bus drivers. Their service was significant in Britain and especially the Soviet Union, where women already

constituted almost half of the labor force. During the war, female employment in Soviet industries climbed to an unprecedented 60 percent.

Mobilizing the Home Front In Germany, the mobilization of civilians was carefully weighed against fears of demoralization. Hitler allowed the production of consumer goods as a means of diverting the anxiety of families whose sons and husbands were away at war. The standard of living of Aryan Germans remained close to the prewar levels long after Soviets, Italians, and Romanians were asked to give up their personal comforts. By contrast, in Britain, people were asked to conserve, give up, and buckle down throughout the war. The constant bombings during the Battle of Britain both frightened civilians and helped build their resolve. The tremendous losses incurred by the

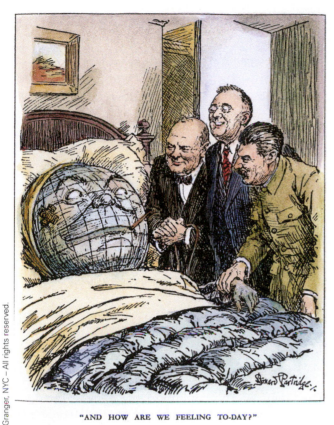

"AND HOW ARE WE FEELING TO-DAY?"

Churchill, Roosevelt, and Stalin after Yalta

In February 1945, Winston Churchill, Franklin Roosevelt, and Joseph Stalin met in the Russian resort town of Yalta, in the Crimea, to map out plans for ending the war in Asia and for establishing order in postwar Europe. Roosevelt was already ailing; he died in April. In July, Churchill was voted out of office. The Yalta Conference was the last time the leaders of the three great powers were able to work together peacefully for more than forty years.

》 *How does this cartoon depict them in relation to the world's well-being?*

Soviets during the first year of combat also worked as powerful propaganda in the hands of the communist government, which used patriotism to recruit the help of civilians and then celebrated their heroism, especially after Stalingrad.

Civilian help was also essential in occupied territories, such as Slovakia, Vichy France, and Croatia, where the Nazis set up puppet governments. To supply the war machine with much-needed armaments and other industrial products, food supplies, and fuel, the Nazis depended heavily on collaboration with native populations. Even in places like Poland, where the official policy was to exterminate all Jews and where more than 2.5 million non-Jewish Poles perished in the war, the Germans needed to work with the Polish population. This policy was also implemented in the Czech lands, France, the Netherlands, Serbia, and Greece. The peoples of occupied countries faced difficult choices—either collaborate with the Nazis or become their victims.

Many learned to work within this harsh system and to play by its methods. In Prague, for example, a Czech man working for the German authorities stopped saluting his Jewish neighbors on the street, fearful that he might be suspected of being a Jew himself. Soon he asked his son not to play with their Jewish neighbor, until one day the Jewish family was gone. Though he was sad and afraid, he was also relieved. Occupation forced most people to spy, lie, and vilify fellow humans in order to survive, corrupting their human dignity.

Resistance Movements Despite fear and violent reprisals, resistance movements developed in all occupied territories and even in Germany, some spectacular in scope and results, others merely symbolic. In Germany, the most remarkable were the efforts of military leaders to assassinate Hitler in 1943 and 1944. These officers were attempting to rescue the German war effort from Hitler's increasingly irrational leadership, but they were not necessarily opposed to either the racist ideology or the expansionist goals of the Third Reich. They all failed, and the officers were executed.

More widespread resistance movements developed in France, Yugoslavia, the Soviet Union, and Poland. In France, the Free French, under the leadership of **Charles de Gaulle**, provided a focus for courage and hope. The Free French military contributions were modest, but they helped de Gaulle establish himself as the liberator of his people.

The most successful partisan movement in occupied Europe was that of the Yugoslav Communists, led by **Josip Broz Tito**. His well-organized guerilla army liberated Yugoslavia with only indirect assistance from the Allies, and largely independent of the Soviets. This movement was more successful because of broad popular support, Tito's tight leadership, and Germany's weak control in Yugoslavia. But Tito accomplished this remarkable feat by also committing atrocities against other partisan movements and civilians.

In Poland, the underground Polish Home Army acted to thwart German operations with great bravery. They were also able to supply important intelligence to the Allies. In the final months of the war, a large part of this resistance force perished in the **Warsaw Uprising**, which attempted the liberation of the city from Nazi occupation in August 1944. Despite

Charles de Gaulle (1890–1970) Leader of the Free French, the partisan movement that worked to liberate France, and first president of postwar France.

Josip Broz Tito (1892–1980) Leader of the Yugoslav Communist Party and of the most successful partisan movement in World War II.

Warsaw Uprising Revolt by the partisan Polish Home Army in the fall of 1944 against the Nazis.

promises to come to the aid of the Poles, Stalin kept the advancing Soviet armies from providing any support to the uprising, which was violently crushed. Though valiant in its efforts to liberate Poland, the Home Army did little to help Polish Jews and was generally reluctant to accept Jews as members.

27-4d The Final Solution

The unprecedented level of brutality against civilians is one of the deepest moral challenges posed by World War II (see Map 27.5). Millions of innocents on both sides of the conflict were imprisoned, placed under siege and starved to death, forced into slave labor, raped, and bombed, initially with conventional artillery and at the very end with nuclear bombs. But by far the most horrifying aspect of World War II was the Nazi policy of destroying the Jews of Europe. Eliminating the Jews from German society had been a fundamental concept of the Nazis since before 1933. And yet the technologies to bring about the **Final Solution**—the physical extermination of all Jews—did not come together until the war. This diabolical policy came into being in a combination of Hitler's irrational theories of racial purity and with the expertise of architects, engineers, doctors, biologists, and other people well grounded in the foundations of science and reason. Many of them subscribed to the assumption that there was a "Jewish problem" in Europe. The progression of the Final Solution is summarized in Table 27.3.

Planning for the Extermination of All Jews The decision to pursue a policy of genocide against all Jews was made official at the **Wannsee Conference** in January 1942, though the specific means by which the estimated 11 million Jews of Europe were to be killed was not yet discussed. Experiments with mass killings through conventional and chemical weapons had already been tried both before the war in Germany and during the eastern campaigns in Poland, Byelorussia, Ukraine, and Russia. The rounding up of the Jews was assigned to special troops, the **Einsatzgruppen** (AYN-zatz-groop-en), small mobile killing units made up of the cruelest SS and Gestapo recruits. The Einsatzgruppen were to eliminate other undesirables also, including communists, Roma, Jehovah's Witnesses, and Slavs.

Final Solution Nazi concept of exterminating all European Jews as a response to the so-called Jewish problem in Europe.

Wannsee Conference Meeting of high-ranking Nazis in early 1942 that officially decided to exterminate all Jews.

Einsatzgruppen (in German, "mission groups") Nazi death squads created at the beginning of the war to round up and execute Jews and other "undesirables."

ghetto Small, sealed-off areas in Nazi-controlled cities where the Jewish population was forced to live.

Table 27.3 The Final Solution

March 1933	Dachau concentration camp opens
September 1935	Nuremberg Laws
October 1939	First Polish ghetto
October 1941	Auschwitz concentration camp is opened for the extermination of Jews
January 1942	Wannsee Conference
January 27, 1945	Soviets liberate Auschwitz and its remaining 7,000 inmates
April 1945	Allies liberate last concentration camps

The Ghettos Another important policy was to place all Jews in occupied territories in **ghettos**, where they were sealed off from the non-Jewish population. In Warsaw, for instance, the European city with the largest Jewish population, several thousand Poles were moved out to make room for around half a million Jews, crowded into a few city blocks. Before being sent to concentration camps, these people were first stripped of all possessions and forced into crowded, unheated, and lice-infested rooms. Jews unable to leave the ghettos were gradually starved to death through inadequate food supplies. Some also perished because of unsanitary and overcrowded conditions, which fostered tuberculosis and other epidemics.

The Nazis used deceit and fear to manage the ghettos. They set up Jewish councils and police, dividing communities by forcing Jews to monitor one another and compete for inadequate food supplies and menial jobs, while Nazi death squads periodically entered the ghettos to kill people at random. Jewish leaders were required to select and round up those who would be sent to concentration camps. Some of these leaders committed suicide; others were killed by their own communities. Upon his arrival at Auschwitz, the leader of the Lódz ghetto was beaten to death by Jewish inmates, who viewed him as the filthy tool of the Germans. The Nazis were clever in setting Jews against Jews, forcing them to victimize each other and question the very core of their identity.

Scientific Genocide In the camps, Nazi engineers and architects designed gas chambers made to look

Map 27.5 **The Holocaust**
Nazi genocidal policies toward European Jewry resulted in the murder of more than six million Jews. Most were from eastern Europe, where all of the death camps were located.

1. What state had the highest losses?
2. Where were most of the camps located?
3. What state had the fewest losses?

Map legend:
- ■ Extermination camp
- ● Concentration camp
- ★ Major ghetto
- **7,680** Estimated Jewish death toll, by country
- Under Axis control
- Allied nations
- Neutral nations

Country death tolls shown on map:
NORWAY 762 · FINLAND 7 · ESTONIA 2,000 · LATVIA 71,500 · LITHUANIA 143,000 · SOVIET UNION 1,000,000 · DENMARK 60 · NETHERLANDS 100,000 · BELGIUM 28,900 · LUX. 0 · GERMANY 141,500 · BOHEMIA & MORAVIA 78,150 · FRANCE 77,320 · AUSTRIA 50,000 · SLOVAKIA 71,000 · HUNGARY 569,000 · POLAND 3,000,000 · ROMANIA 287,000 · CROATIA / SERBIA 60,000 · BULGARIA 0 · ITALY 7,680 · GREECE 67,000

---

like shower rooms, and scientists identified **Zyklon B**, an insecticide, as a cheap and effective lethal gas. Labor camps in Poland were transformed into extermination camps; at Auschwitz alone, 1.5 million Jews perished. By April 1945, when the last camps were liberated, over 6 million Jews had been killed as well as more than 4.6 million other people classified by the Nazis as undesirables.

The Moral Failure of Europe The tragedy of European Jewry is incomprehensible in rational terms and raises questions about what could have been done to save Jews and others and why such efforts failed. Those who committed these crimes against humanity abound. In Germany, they were not only Nazi fanatics but also ordinary citizens who either willingly helped or looked the other way. In occupied territories, non-Jews were under intense pressure to collaborate with the Germans, and some did so more easily than others. The Allies had detailed knowledge of concentration camps and atrocities as early as 1942, but they failed to impede the program by bombing the camps or the railroads that led to them. Pope Pius XII, who was aware of anti-Semitic laws and violence committed by Catholics in Italy, Poland, Germany, and Slovakia did not condemn these actions, failing in his role as moral and spiritual leader of the Roman Catholic Church. The general public in Europe and the United States was more concerned with defeating Hitler than saving the Jews. Anti-Semitism was a mainstream attitude in the western world. Though it did not necessarily translate into support for Hitler's ideas, it meant that sympathy for the Jews was limited,

Zyklon B Type of insecticide used by the Nazis for efficient extermination of the Jews in the death camps.

A Young Jewish Woman's Diary During the Holocaust

Eva Heyman was 13 years old when she started writing her diary. She was brought up in a secular middle class family in Hungary. Eva started her diary in February 1944 and continued until May 1944, when she was deported to Auschwitz. She died on October 17, 1944.

1 As a girl growing up in the 1930s, Márta is subject to the same type of racist thinking that was used against Jews as well. Her unselfconscious reference to Josephine Baker as significantly different from her friend because of being a "Negro" shows how prevalent racism was at the time.

2 How does the reality of the Holocaust become a personal matter to this girl?

3 How does this distinction between various types of Jews force Eva to think about her friend's fate?

February 14, 1944

Dear diary,

I promised to write Márta's story down in you. **1** Márta was two years older than I. Ági said that she was a genius in dance and resembled Josephine Baker, except that she is a Negro and Márta was only dark and glorious. I was always very proud that a genius two classes ahead of me was my friend **2** . . . . We had an afternoon snack, chocolate with whipped cream and strawberries with whipped cream, which Márta loved more than anything else, even more than dancing. Suddenly the bell at the front gate rang five times. It was Márta's nursemaid: "Mártika, come home. The police are there, and you have to go with Papa and Mama." She turned white as the plaster on the walls. I heard Ági tell Grandma that at the Journalists Club the night before they had said that the government was preparing to do something terrible, and Jews who weren't born in Hungary would be taken to Poland where a horrible fate was in store for them.

3 I didn't understand this right away, because Márta was born in Várad, and so was her mother. The tension was awful. Then Ági rushed into town to the journalists, and they told her that tens of thousands of people like Márta and her

The U.S. National Archives and Records Administration

Public Humiliation of Jews

The Nazi troops made it a point of pride to demonstrate their superiority dehumanizing the Jewish population in the ghettos and camps in very public ways. They often photographed themselves proudly in staged poses and kept these images or sent them home to show their "successes."

» *How would you describe the facial expressions of the military personnel in this photograph?*

» *What might be the impact of such photographs on other Jews?*

4 What sort of choice is being forced upon Jews in Hungary?

5 How does Eva convince herself and her friend not to fear deportation?

6 An adolescent girl who did not to know what fascism was at the time—when Mussolini had been in power for over two decades—seems curious. What does this lack of knowledge suggest about what sorts of information children learned at school and home?

7 What techniques are used to pacify the Jewish population against rebelling or fleeing from deportation?

8 Do you believe Eva is deluding herself or is simply naive in her assessment of the deportations?

family had been taken away to Poland in a train, without luggage and without food. **4** They said that if Aunt Münzer hurried up and got a divorce, she and Márta might be allowed to stay. But they didn't want to get divorced. And Márta didn't want to stay here without her father. Ági heard that Grandmother Pásztor went to Pest, the capital, where she tried everything. I think that some Minister by the name of Keresztes-Fisher sent a telegram to the Polish border to have them taken off the train, but the telegram never arrived. Márta's bicycle was left near mine, beside the gate, and we didn't have the heart to send it to Márta's grandmother. Ági cried a lot whenever she saw the two red bicycles standing alongside each other. **5** I even asked her why she always cried, since they wouldn't take us away from here, because my father was born in Budapest. But she only cried more and said they could still take us to Poland in a train just because we were Jews and because there was fascism here. **6** I don't know what fascism is, but one of the things it probably means is deporting Jews to Poland. **7** Márta's grandmother says that Márta and her parents are alive, but they can't write, because the Germans don't allow it. A lot of soldiers have already dropped in on them quite a few times, and after asking her for money they told her that they had seen Márta, and her mother, too, in some Polish town called Kamenetz-Podolsk. I found the place on my map and marked it with red. **8**

Source: *The Diary of Eva Heyman*, Yad Vashem, Jerusalem, 1974, pp. 31–33 (http://www.yadvashem .org/odot_pdf/Microsoft%20Word%20-%203689.pdf).

Courtesy of Dr. Leonid Smilovitsky, The Goldstein-Goren Diaspora Research Center, Tel Aviv University, from *The Holocaust in Belorussia, 1941–1944* (Tel Aviv: 2000).

Jewish Partisans

In Belorussia, as the Nazis and their local collaborators began implementing Nazi genocidal policies, Jewish men and women organized military units that struck back, with the support of the Soviet Union.

❯❯ *Why did these Jewish partisans turn toward the Soviet Union for support?*

and Jews themselves, like the American secretary of the treasury Henry Morgenthau, hesitated to use the example of the Jewish plight to mobilize support for the war.

Yet some individuals and communities also acted courageously to assist Jews and others persecuted by the Nazis. Towns in France helped Jews escape to Switzerland, and several were wiped out by the Nazis as a consequence. The Danes and Bulgarians were notable for their efforts to hide Jews and refusal to hand them over to the Germans. But brave acts were rare, and no effort, it seems, could stop the Nazi intention to exterminate the Jews of Europe.

Finally, the Jews of Europe were themselves in disbelief about the Final Solution. Many German, Hungarian, Polish, and French citizens of Jewish ancestry had become culturally integrated into their national cultures and thought of themselves as part of the nation rather than as a racially defined group. Only under the Nazis were they forced to identify themselves as Jews. Jewish resistance against the Holocaust developed rather slowly and with limited effect, partly because of the dangers involved and partly because Jews were themselves a diverse group.

The failure to stop the Holocaust had significant consequences in Europe after the end of the war.

Although democracy was saved, Europeans and Americans were forced to look within themselves for the source of this profound failure of western civilization. Genocide had succeeded in advanced European countries because the technology was available to implement it, and people were generally willing to use or allow it.

CHAPTER Review

Summary

» From 1929 to 1945, democracy was severely challenged in Europe by radical movements from the right and the left.

» The Great Depression destabilized all European economies, bringing about high unemployment, loss of capital, and political unrest.

» Colonial territories suffered economically as well, especially where new policies were harnessed to help the well-being of European states governing them.

» Two totalitarian dictatorships, Germany and the Soviet Union, were able to address economic problems more successfully than democratic countries.

» Remilitarization and antidemocratic policies were key to their economic recovery.

» Nazi state ideology of racist extermination was made clear in the 1930s, but encountered weak

responses from the European states and the United States.

» The failure of the western democracies to stand up to Hitler's early defiance of the Versailles Treaty played a role in emboldening him.

» World War II brought unprecedented destruction and transformed the relationship between civilian and military involvement in war, encompassing the entire populations of the combatant countries.

» New military technology widened the scope and intensity of destruction and made military operations more complex than ever before.

» The Nazi extermination of entire populations and the atrocities committed by both occupiers and liberators (especially the Soviets) laid bare horrors that belied all concepts of civilization and progress in Europe.

Chronology

1928–1933	Stalin initiates first five-year plan in Soviet Union [Europe]
1929	Great Depression begins [Americas]
1930	Gandhi leads hundreds of thousands in peaceful Salt March against the British Raj [Asia]
	Getúlio Vargas establishes authoritarian rule in Brazil [Europe]
1931	United States initiates moratorium on war debts [Americas]
	Japan invades Manchuria [Asia]
1933	Hitler comes to power in Germany [Europe]
	Dachau labor camp established in Germany [Europe]
1934	Soviet Union is admitted to League of Nations [Europe]
1935	Mussolini invades Ethiopia [Europe, Africa]

1936	Popular Front is formed in France [Europe]
	Spanish Civil War begins [Europe]
	Great Purges begin in Soviet Union [Europe]
1937	Nanjing Massacre [Asia]
1939	Nazis take over Czechoslovakia [Europe]
	Franco wins Spanish Civil War [Europe]
	Hitler and Stalin sign Molotov-Ribbentrop Pact [Europe]
	World War II begins [Western Europe]
1940	Nazis occupy Norway, Denmark, the Netherlands, Belgium, and France [Europe]
	Nazis bomb England in Battle of Britain [Europe]
1941	U.S. Lend-Lease Act grants war aid to Britain [Europe, Americas]
	Nazis invade Soviet Union in Operation Barbarossa [Europe]
	United States enters the war after Japanese bomb Pearl Harbor [Americas, Asia]
1942	Wannsee Conference plans Jewish genocide [Europe]
	Battle of Midway [Americas, Asia]
1943	Soviets win decisive battles at Stalingrad and Kursk [Europe]
1945	Soviets liberate Auschwitz [Europe]
	Churchill, Roosevelt, and Stalin meet at Yalta Conference [Europe, Americas]
	United States drops first atomic bombs in Japan [Americas, Asia]
	World War II ends [Global]

Critical Thinking Questions

Take time to pull together all the important information from the chapter by answering the following questions:

Responses to the Great Depression, 1929–1939

» What were the causes of the Great Depression?

» What were the political consequences of the Great Depression?

The Soviet Union Under Stalin, 1929–1939

» What were the Soviet Union's successes and failures in the 1930s?

» How did Stalin turn the Soviet Union into a totalitarian state?

The Third Reich, 1933–1945

» What were the distinguishing features of the Nazi regime and which ones made it so successful?

» How did Germany manage to challenge the European international order?

World War II, 1939–1945

» How did World War II differ from previous wars?

» What military strategies, technological developments, and other factors enabled the Allies to win the war?

MindTap® is a fully online personalized learning experience built upon Cengage Learning content. MindTap® combines student learning tools—readings, multimedia, activities, and assessments—into a singular Learning Path that guides students through the course and helps students develop the critical thinking, analysis, and communication skills that are essential to academic and professional success.

Chapter Outline

As you read, consider the following questions:

❯ How did the Cold War change the international system?

❯ What differences can you identify in the process of postwar reconstruction in western versus eastern Europe?

❯ What important differences in politics, social developments, and culture emerged between western and eastern Europe during this period?

❯ How did the new world order affect the process of decolonization?

❯ Why did 1968 become a pivotal year in the history of Europe, and what changes did it bring about?

Valentina Tereshkova
During the Cold War, the United States and the Soviet Union fought for global influence on the ground and in space. The Soviets were first both in launching a human-made satellite into space in 1957, and also in putting the first female cosmonaut in space in 1963. Valentina Tereshkova became a symbol of many successes boasted by the USSR, from the space exploration program to gender equality. Her proletarian background made her also a powerful symbol of eliminating class inequality.

ILITARY HOSTILITIES ENDED in August 1945, but peace did not immediately follow. Instead, many Europeans experienced occupation by "liberating" armies and retribution for war crimes. Yet war memories were quickly silenced by new challenges. By 1949, the United States and the Soviet Union were struggling for global power and parceling up the world into zones of influence. Europe became the first and initially most important site for superpower confrontation, as it was divided between East and West, communism and capitalism, and totalitarianism and democracy. Europeans had to realign their identities. For some, the new era meant transforming their societies in the likeness of the Soviet Union. For others, the end of one war was the beginning of a new one to protect democratic values against communism. This war—a cold war—was fought at the highest level of military and diplomatic planning, usually in great secrecy; yet it touched the lives of every person living in Europe and throughout the world.

The end of World War II threw colonial territories into disarray. Some colonial countries tried to hold on to their power, with dire consequences to the native populations, while others decided to slowly pull back from their rule. In this process, emerging elites among the native populations, like Franz Fanon, played a crucial role in providing intellectual and political leadership for the anticolonial struggle, some aligned with the United States, others with the Soviet Union, and a third group seeking a more independent nonaligned status.

By the late 1950s, western Europeans had settled into a comfortable view of themselves as the "real" Europe and their enemies as distant contenders. In France and Germany, in particular, economic reconstruction brought about great hopes that Europe could regain its leading role in the world. In the meantime, eastern Europeans were thrown into the challenges of building communism according to Stalin's vision of it. The communist regimes employed harsh policies but achieved some measure of success in modernizing their economies. By the late 1950s, the separation between East and West was entrenched. It took another generation to challenge this division. In the wake of anticolonial movements and a new antiestablishment youth, Europeans were forced to look across the East–West divide more carefully and to reexamine their values as events during 1968 shook the political establishment.

28-1 The Iron Curtain, 1945–1958

» **What conflicts over Europe's future paved the way for its division?**

» **How did international relations change in the first two postwar decades?**

The end of World War II brought to Europe a tense and precarious stalemate among the winning Allies. There was no comprehensive peace treaty. The United States and Great Britain were at odds with the Soviet Union over the future of the liberated territories and their own role in the process. Initially, each victor had its own methods for dealing with Nazi war crimes. The issue of what to do with the people displaced by the war also posed significant problems. But everything came under the shadow of a growing rift between the United States and the Soviet Union. By 1948, the Soviet Union had given up the pretense of cooperating with the West and forcefully put an end to democratic politics in eastern Europe. The rift became a division, with the United States assuming the role of protector of western European democracy and capitalism. The Soviet Union became the protector of oppressed peoples everywhere and the counterforce, through the spread of communism, against Western imperialism (see Map 28.1). The United Nations added another dimension to the polarized international system.

28-1a Occupation and Denazification

percentages agreement Secret agreement reached by Churchill and Stalin in 1944 regarding the division of eastern Europe.

Nuremberg Trials Postwar trials of Nazi leaders and collaborators, held in Nuremberg, Germany, in 1945–1946.

denazification Destruction of Nazism and its influence.

Hermann Göring (1893–1946) Nazi leader, founder of the Gestapo and head of the Luftwaffe, who was convicted at the Nuremberg Trials.

At the end of World War II, millions of Europeans were homeless and impoverished. Entire cities and economies lay in ruin. The political leadership of many countries had either perished or been thoroughly compromised by collaboration with the Nazis. To ensure a stable transition to postwar peace, the United States, Britain, France, and the Soviet Union occupied and divided the territories formerly controlled by the Third Reich and its allies. Germany, Austria, and the city of Berlin were divided into four occupation zones, while other areas of Europe fell under the control of the liberating ally.

The Percentages Agreement In 1945, Soviet troops had liberated all the countries east of Berlin and were fully in control of them. A 1944 **percentages agreement** between Churchill and Stalin had assigned Romania and Bulgaria to the Soviet sphere of influence, Czechoslovakia and Greece to the West (Britain, France, and the United States), with Yugoslavia and Hungary in a fifty-fifty arrangement. Subsequently, at Yalta (1945), Poland was placed in the hands of the Soviets, while Czechoslovakia's fate remained open.

Denazification To be viewed as liberators, the Americans, aided by the British and French, swiftly rounded up Nazi Party members and collaborators. The **Nuremberg Trials** were the most famous of the **denazification** war crime trials that took place in Europe between 1945 and 1948. These international tribunals brought charges of "crimes against humanity," a new legal concept rooted in Enlightenment notions of human rights, to sit in judgment on Nazi racism and the Final Solution. But many high-ranking Nazi officials involved in the death camps and most rank-and-file party members escaped trial. Many of them now cast themselves as victims or innocent bystanders. During his trial at Nuremberg, **Hermann Göring**, head of the Luftwaffe, rejected the notion of collective guilt. "It is the leaders of the country who determine the policy," he said cynically, "and it is always a simple matter to drag the people along, whether it is a democracy or a fascist dictatorship."

Using the Nuremberg model, in eastern Europe, as the Soviet sphere was increasingly called, the Soviets orchestrated trials against many military and political leaders who had worked with the Nazis or, more recently, opposed the Soviets. Invariably, those tried were found guilty and executed or sent to prison. In eastern Europe, the denazification trials became both a form of intimidation and an attempt to legitimize the communists—the Communist Party being the only political party that appeared untainted by wartime collaboration with the Nazis. With so many experienced politicians removed, the trials paved the way for the future communist takeovers and created a myth that responsibility for war crimes rested exclusively on the shoulders of the Germans and other foreign fascists.

The denazification trials failed to find all Nazi collaborators and punish them. The prosecutors had neither the ability nor the political will for such a vast task, and many collaborators went into hiding or committed suicide. But the trials did enable survivors to achieve a degree of closure on the Nazi past and get on with their lives. In addition, in light of the growing competition with the Soviet Union, the Western Allies found it politically expedient to complete denazification quickly in order to shift focus toward economic reconstruction.

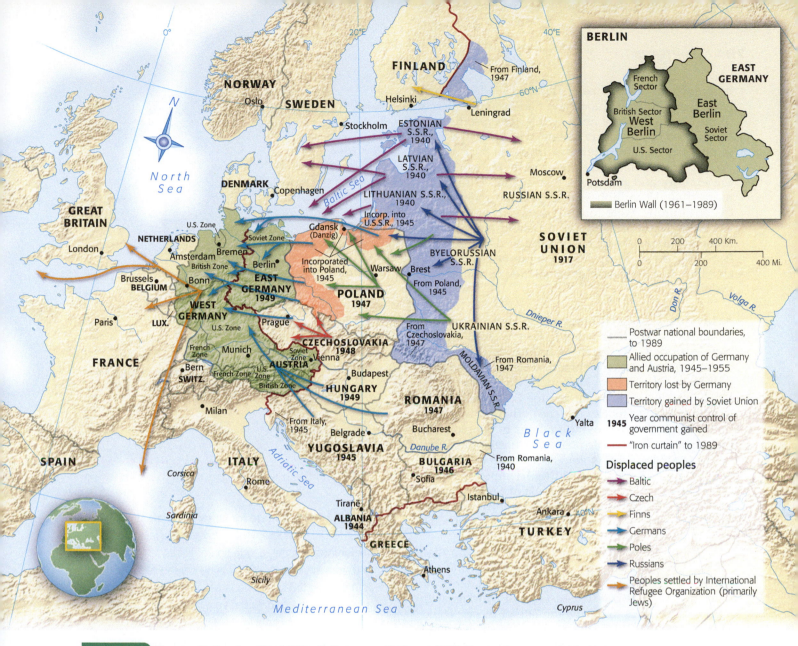

Map 28.1 **Europe Following World War II** Between 1945 and 1989, Europe became divided into two camps struggling for legitimacy in an ideologically polarized world.

1. How do the territorial changes after World War II compare to those after World War I?
2. What countries witnessed the most population displacement?
3. What changes on this map reflect the bitter division between East and West?

28-1b Displaced Persons

To get on with their lives, however, many Europeans first had to try to find a home. Entire cities were in rubble, and many Germans and others had fled west as the Soviet armies advanced. At the end of the war, between 11 and 20 million individuals were displaced persons.

Resettling Germans Moreover, entire populations were resettled. At the **Potsdam Conference** in July 1945, the Western Allies agreed that eastern European governments in Poland and Czechoslovakia could forcibly remove all Germans from their countries. In Poland, hundreds of thousands of ethnic Germans were expelled. A similar policy sent hundreds of thousands of Poles from western Ukraine and Belorussia to Poland. Czechoslovakia also expelled its Germans. There was much debate over who exactly was a German, as there were many ethnically mixed marriages and individuals whose families had long lived in the contested areas. A Czech woman married to a Sudeten German would likely become a candidate for expulsion, even though she and her husband had been

Potsdam Conference
Meeting in July 1945 at which the United States, Britain, and the Soviet Union decided how to administer postwar Germany.

born subjects of Czechoslovakia and his family had lived there for generations and had become subjects of the Nazi state only after 1938. Often resettlement was abused by envious neighbors who wanted a piece of property or simply revenge for some past wrong. The process reinforced the power of the state to decide the identity and fate of its inhabitants. Ultimately, more than 13 million ethnic Germans, mostly in eastern Europe, were forcibly removed. In expelling Germans, Czechoslovakia and Poland enforced the racist definitions of nationality developed by the Nazis. Ironically, the Western defenders of democracy were enabling the elimination of populations promoted by the Nazis.

Achieving Ethnic Homogeneity Those forced out left almost everything behind. They walked or rode bicycles or donkeys; the lucky had horse-driven carts. In the process, children were sometimes separated from parents and wives from husbands. More than 100,000 families ended up living across the East–West divide, unable to keep in touch with each other for a generation. The process of moving millions of people away from their homes and into potentially hostile communities generated psychic wounds that began to heal only later, primarily through forgetting. An important political result was the reshaping of most of eastern Europe into more ethnically homogeneous countries. Poland, for instance, became almost entirely Polish and Catholic, with Jews, Germans, and Ukrainians gone.

Among the displaced persons were more than 250,000 Jews, located primarily in the American zone, where they were placed in camps. Jewish leaders from Palestine, such as **David Ben-Gurion**, worked with the Western Allies to decide the fate of these people. More than 130,000 of them settled in British-controlled Palestine, which became Israel in 1948 (see Map 28.2). Those who stayed in Europe were subjected to anti-Semitic discrimination and even postwar pogroms, which generated additional emigrations to Israel.

28-1c Beginnings of the Cold War

The wartime alliance between the United States and the Soviet Union against a common enemy dissolved into an adversarial relationship, as the victors could not agree on postwar goals for Germany and the rest of Europe. Both countries emerged from the war as superpowers, with enlarged international prestige, and each embarked on a struggle for political, economic, and moral-cultural world supremacy. No other state could match their strength, and most European states owed their survival to one or both of them. In this contest, the engagement of the United States in

David Ben-Gurion (1886–1973) Zionist leader central to the establishment of the state of Israel and its first prime minister.

Map 28.2 **UN Mandate for Israel and Palestine, 1947** The UN Mandate, which created the legal framework for international recognition of Israel, left the status of the Arab inhabitants of Palestine unresolved. The conflict that rages today among Israel, Palestinians, and the Arab states in the Middle East originated with the formation of the state of Israel in 1948.

1. What problems might derive from the shape of the proposed Jewish state?
2. How might problems arise from the borders of the proposed Palestinian state?
3. What does this map suggest about territorial stability in the region, especially looking at the actual borders of 1949 versus the proposed 1947 partition?

European affairs was a greater departure from past behavior than for the Soviet Union. After World War I, the Soviets had aided communist movements in Europe, but the United States had pursued isolationism. After World War II, however, the development of Europe cannot be understood without the essential involvement of the United States.

Constructing the East–West Ideological Divide Europe and European colonies around the world became the playing field in a struggle between the opposing options of the Americans and the Soviets: liberal democracy versus communism, private property versus state ownership, capitalism and free-market economies versus state-controlled ones, and freedom and material comforts versus equality and social justice. Both sides wanted to erase whatever gray areas existed in each European country between these poles. New identities and allegiances were created in connection with the two superpowers, and new enmities developed among old neighbors. The Hungarians, who had been the Austrians' partners in ruling the Habsburg Empire a century earlier, were now to be their enemies by virtue of the barbed wire that separated the two countries. East Germans, under Soviet occupation, were to begin thinking of their West German relatives and friends as imperialist traitors. This division of Europe into East and West came about as a result of the superpower confrontation. In Africa and Asia, colonial territories of imperial powers now allied with the United States were courted by the Soviets as their anti-imperialist protectors.

Soviet Wartime Losses and Strategic Claims In the contest over world domination, the two superpowers gave different explanations and used different methods. The Soviet Union had lost more people (over 30 million by some accounts) and resources than any other war combatant and wanted to recoup the economic resources spent fighting the war. In fact, since Germany had experienced 80 percent of its casualties at the hands of the Soviets, Stalin was not exaggerating when he claimed that Europe owed the Nazi defeat to his country. To rebuild the Soviet economy, he wanted Soviet troops in the occupied zone to oversee the production and subsequent transfer of goods to the Soviet Union. The Soviets also acted out of fear. Having been attacked by Germany twice in the twentieth century, they wanted a buffer zone in eastern Europe, where friendly political regimes and military resources would protect Soviet security (see Map 28.3).

The United States as Defender of Democracy The United States, on the other hand, had an overwhelming interest in bringing back democratic institutions and capitalist markets to the regions it had liberated. One lesson from World War I was that a punishing peace could lead to resentment and revenge. This time, the victors focused on rebuilding a Germany committed to their ideals. In addition, the Great Depression's costly economic and political consequences also pointed toward rebuilding markets as a better strategy than exacting high war payments. Strong capitalist economies would bolster political stability, American strategists concluded. These goals were not entirely altruistic. The American economy had grown during the war, and businesses were looking for new markets. European countries had already become deeply dependent on American goods and dollars, and they were a good investment. Beyond Europe, working with anticolonial independence movements provided opportunities to open other markets and forge new alliances. Yet democratic institutions in most of these areas had to be built from the ground up and demanded resources and a willingness to trust local processes the United States and their European allies were often unwilling to fully extend those societies.

The means by which the Soviets pursued their goals in eastern Europe were in keeping with Stalin's personality. He fundamentally distrusted those not under his control. He sent some of the toughest military leaders and most unquestioning loyalists from the communist parties in eastern Europe, such as Ana Pauker, to oversee postwar regimes. The Soviets manipulated the Western observers and used any legal means available, as well as illegal and violent ones, to eliminate all political enemies and place Soviet pawns in power. Political legitimacy and the well-being of the populations involved were low on Stalin's agenda.

Stalin had a formidable opponent in U.S. President Harry Truman, who, as vice president, had never trusted the Soviet Union. Following President Roosevelt's death in April 1945, the simple man from Missouri brought his common sense to the presidency and his own strong views about the postwar peace. He followed a careful line of encouraging a stable international environment through the **United Nations (UN)** and an increasingly hard line against the Soviets.

The Truman Doctrine In Europe, Truman was committed to prosperity and democracy through positive, though anti-Soviet, incentives. Instead of sending troops to defend American interests, in March 1947, he issued the **Truman Doctrine**, which offered to help countries fighting communist expansion, specifically Turkey and Greece, where communist partisans in a civil war were receiving help from Yugoslavia and the Soviets. Greece was considered key to the political stability in the Mediterranean and American overseas markets. With substantial American support, the military establishment defeated the communists and imposed its own authoritarian rule.

In addition, the 1947 **Marshall Plan** allocated more than $13 billion in grants and loans to rebuild Europe's economies. This money helped rebuild roads,

United Nations (UN) International organization founded in 1945 to facilitate collaboration among nations; replaced the League of Nations.

Truman Doctrine Policy statement issued by U.S. President Harry S. Truman in 1947 announcing the U.S. commitment to fight the spread of communism everywhere in the world.

Marshall Plan Economic recovery plan established by the United States in 1947 that offered grants and low-interest loans to noncommunist European states.

Other NATO members:

U.S.A.
CANADA

U.S. loan of $3.5 billion, 1946
Exploded first atomic bomb, 1952

Berlin blockade, 1948–1949

Uprising, 1956

Exploded first atomic bomb, 1949

Uprising, spring 1968
U.S.S.R. invasion, August 1968

Exploded first atomic bomb, 1960

Joined NATO, 1955

Zones of occupation ended, 1955

Uprising, 1956

Tito-Stalin split, 1948

Left CMEA, 1961
Withdrew from WP, 1968

Truman Doctrine, 1947
Joined NATO, 1952

Truman Doctrine, 1947
Joined NATO, 1952

$ Participant in the Marshall Plan

Members of NATO, formed in 1949

Members of CMEA, formed in 1949, and the Warsaw Pact, organized in 1955

Non-aligned communist country (became a CMEA associate member, 1964)

Member of the European Community, formed in 1958

East European Stalinism
- Prison camp
- Major prison
- Labor camp
- Town renamed after Stalin
- Mountain peak renamed "Stalin"

Map 28.3 **East European Stalinism** Between 1945 and 1953, the Soviet Union consolidated its grip over the political institutions and economies of its eastern European satellites. Yugoslavia alone remained a thorn in Stalin's side. Magocsi, Paul R., *Historical Atlas of East Central Europe*, cartographic design by Geoffrey J. Matthews, Seattle: University of Washington Press, 1993. Reprinted by permission.

1. What elements of political control and violence are highlighted on this map?
2. Where does the grip seem tightest?
3. Why do you think that is the case?

industries, and housing. The plan found unprecedented support among Americans and generated a host of programs that paved the way for the European Union. American aid came at a price, however. The United States encouraged France, Britain, and Germany to hunt down communist sympathizers who might have infiltrated leftist parties and be plotting communist takeovers. The Marshall Plan also served to further separate western from eastern Europe, where countries occupied by Soviet troops were never in a position to accept U.S. aid.

Stalemate over Berlin In Germany, the Soviets dismantled industrial plants in their occupation zone and took no interest in preventing the starvation of German civilians, which drew the criticism of the West. In response, in February 1948, the Soviets set up a blockade to isolate the western zones of Berlin from access by Western powers. To avert military conflict, the United States sent in supplies by means of the **Berlin airlift**, flying in up to 13,000 tons per day. By May 1949, the Soviets had backed down, and Germany became divided into the Federal Republic of Germany, known as West Germany, and the German Democratic Republic, known as East Germany. Berlin itself was divided into East and West Berlin. Though stabilized, Germany remained at the epicenter of the contest between the United States and the Soviet Union for the next forty years—the **Cold War**.

The Cold War Goes Global Developments outside of Europe also shaped the Cold War. After the contentious creation of Israel in 1948, the Middle East became an important ground for competition between the Soviets, generally backing Arab states and insurgents, and the Americans, generally supporting Israel, especially from the late 1960s onward. In addition, in 1949, **Mao Zedong** led a successful communist revolution in China, against nationalist forces that had the backing of Western powers during and after World War II. A protracted **civil war** pegged the communists, who had substantial grassroots backing since the 1930s, against the nationalists. Each side used the two superpowers to secure international backing, as well as financial and military support. Mao proved better skilled at maneuvering this complex landscape and swept into power by October 1949, a development that made the United States more fearful of the spread of communism. Communist China complicated American strategies, as it operated independently of the Soviet Union. Finally, after the Soviets exploded an atomic bomb in 1949, the prospect of nuclear war intensified. Fear of total annihilation kept the Soviets and the Americans at some distance, while their ambitions kept them in uncomfortable proximity and often in indirect military confrontation in the regional struggles they wanted to manipulate.

Nuclear Arms Race The Soviets' development of nuclear weapons after 1949 ushered in an arms race. Starting in the 1950s, both the United States and the Soviet Union expended huge sums on military technology and espionage, as each tried to keep up with the other. In 1953, the United States spent $50 billion, or almost 40 percent of the federal budget, on the military. Spending by the Soviet Union for the same purposes reached 25 percent of its revenues during the same period. This obsession with being militarily prepared for global conflict created a predicament, as neither country had enough intelligence about the other's capacity to make reasoned judgments, and the political leadership was easily persuaded about the need for military spending. Unprecedented levels of military spending only increased the fear of conflict and fed the perceived need to spend more.

28-1d International Security

The piecemeal peace agreements of the first postwar years secured a somewhat stable relationship between the superpowers in Europe. But the most important step for creating a different international order was the establishment of the United Nations (UN) in 1945. Unlike the League of Nations, which it never joined, the United States was a founding member of the UN. This organization was similar to the league in its aim to facilitate collaboration among all states by giving all members the same rights regardless of size, military power, or wealth. But the UN was different from its predecessor in how it achieved these goals. It included a governing body, the **Security Council**, on which China, France, Great Britain, the Soviet Union, and the United States sat as permanent members, along with ten rotating members. The UN also acquired financial resources and a military force to take action when necessary. Its large budget enabled it to manage international programs for public health, child protection, and cultural exchange, giving states large and small, poor and rich, access to new opportunities for peaceful cooperation, such as the successful antimalaria campaigns in Africa and assistance in underdeveloped areas to increase productivity and eradicate poverty.

CONNECTIONS: Since the 1990s, the UN has come under increasing criticism for the behavior of its military forces. While the intent of their establishment was to conduct peacekeeping missions and protect vulnerable populations caught in war zones, UN troops have been found to participate in human trafficking and sexual exploitation of especially women and children. These horrendous crimes have severely hurt the legitimacy of this organization.

Berlin airlift (1948–1949) U.S. shipment of supplies to Western-controlled sectors of Berlin following a Soviet blockade.

Cold War Name by which the 1945–1991 standoff between the superpowers, the United States and the Soviet Union, came to be known.

Mao Zedong (1893–1976) Leader of the communist revolution and, from 1949, the communist regime in China.

Chinese Civil War (1927–1949) Conflict between communist and nationalist forces in China to establish control over the country, in which the communists defeated the nationalists. The war was partly fueled by the interests of various powers, from Japan to the United States and the Soviet Union, in controlling China's government for their own political and economic interests.

Security Council Leading body of the United Nations in matters of international security.

Human Rights The UN's **Universal Declaration of Human Rights** (1948) specified unprecedented rights and freedoms, such as the freedom to move from one location to another, the right to education, and the right to be protected from unemployment. Though not legally binding, the declaration became a powerful means whereby citizens could hold their governments accountable for human rights abuses in an international arena. The autonomous International Criminal Court at The Hague became an important forum for punishing human rights abuses and war crimes. Thus, the UN revolutionized international relations and brought pressure and resources to bear on broad issues from human rights to poverty and health.

NATO However, other international organizations reduced hopes for peaceful solutions to international problems. In 1949, the **North Atlantic Treaty Organization (NATO)**, a military defense alliance aimed primarily against the Soviets' alleged plans for armed global conflict, was created, with collective security as its cardinal principle—an attack on one member was an attack on all, and the security of each individual member depended on the security of all. NATO forced uniform policies on its members and required that each be in a permanent state of military preparedness. The establishment of NATO signaled a formal division of the postwar world between the Western democracies, with the twelve NATO members—the United States, Britain, France, Canada, Italy, the Netherlands, Belgium, Luxembourg, Portugal, Denmark, Norway, and Iceland, later joined by West Germany, Greece, and Turkey—at the forefront, and the Soviet-dominated communist camp on the opposite side.

CONNECTIONS: Throughout the Cold War, NATO remained inactive as a military alliance, serving primarily as a deterrent against violent conflict. Since 1991, NATO has been activated as a military alliance in a number of international military conflicts, from Afghanistan to Iraq and Libya. NATO has become a major point of contention in Russian–U.S. relations after the rise to power of Vladimir Putin. (See Section 30-1a Russia's Collapse and Reemergence as Superpower.)

Universal Declaration of Human Rights Declaration adopted by the United Nations General Assembly in 1948 outlining universal basic human rights.

North Atlantic Treaty Organization (NATO) Defensive alliance established by Britain, France, and the United States in 1949 with Canada and other western European allies.

Committee for Mutual Economic Assistance (CMEA) Soviet organization created in 1949 to coordinate economic production and trade in communist bloc countries.

Warsaw Pact Organization of communist states created in 1955 as a counterpart to NATO.

Soviet Economic and Security Counterparts The Soviet Union retaliated by calling for the creation of a communist alliance. First, the **Committee for Mutual Economic Assistance (CMEA)** was formed in 1949 as a counterpart to the Marshall Plan to increase Soviet control over eastern European economies. Subsequently, the **Warsaw Pact** was created in 1955 as a direct response against the rearming of West Germany and as a counterpart to NATO. But the Warsaw Pact increasingly policed its own communist member states.

In this new international order, European states were pawns rather than major players. Military buildups provide an example. Although NATO presumed that all members would participate actively in military defense, the United States and Britain led in armament production, and when Charles de Gaulle attempted to upgrade France's nuclear program, he was hastily rebutted by the Americans and the British. The power imbalance was even more evident in the Warsaw Pact, with the Soviets supervising the production and sale of armaments, even when the factories were in Czechoslovakia.

28-2 The Revival of Western Europe

» **Why was western Europe so successful in rebuilding its economic power?**

» **What were the political consequences of the commitment to economic recovery?**

Given the magnitude of the material destruction and political disarray at the end of the war, western Europe's record recovery has been rightly called a miracle. By 1950, the region was producing at a level 30 percent higher than before the war (see Figure 28.1). This great achievement owes much to the immense financial resources poured into the economies of western Europe, to international stability (if not without tension), and to the expansion of the welfare state, which secured internal social and political stability.

28-2a The Economic Miracle

Thanks to the Marshall Plan, France and Italy had surpassed their prewar levels of production by 1950, but West Germany had the most impressive success. Between 1945 and 1950, production shot up 25 percent, 15 percent higher than in 1938. Many West German cities destroyed during the war were completely rebuilt to accommodate former inhabitants and to make room for the more than 12 million refugees from the communist East. By the 1960s, West Germany was the undisputed economic leader in western Europe in industrial production, research and development, and

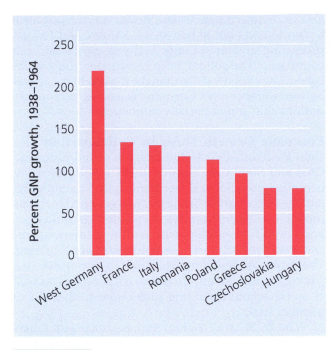

Figure 28.1 **Economic Growth in Europe, 1938–1964** Between 1945 and 1964, western Europe experienced a virtual economic miracle. In part due to the Marshall Plan, and in part due to successful internal political and economic policies, Germany, France, and Britain regained their economic prominence.

≫ *What country had the highest GNP growth? Where did the lowest growth happen?*

≫ *What do these figures suggest about the differences between eastern and western Europe during this period?*

Source: Wilkinson, James D.; Huges, H. Stuart, *Contemporary Europe: A History*, 10th Edition, © 2004, p. 422. Reprinted and electronically reproduced by permission of Pearson Education, Inc., Upper Saddle River, NJ.

ability to put its swelling population to work. Even with a tremendous growth in population, the country had virtually no unemployment until the 1960s, when a majority of West Germans were living in unprecedented comfort, able to fill their apartments and homes with refrigerators, television sets, and automatic washing machines.

Rebuilding the West German Economy It is no wonder, then, that **Konrad Adenauer**, the leader who oversaw this economic miracle, continued to dominate the political scene until the 1960s. The founder of the Christian Democratic Union, he was the first postwar chancellor. Like other successful western political leaders after the war, he had a record of resistance to the Nazis, a commitment to rebuilding capitalist democracy, and a center-right political orientation. An active opponent of Hitler, he had spent part of the war in a concentration camp, but he was not a sympathizer of the left. He used his reputation to push economic

recovery and political distance from East Germany. Under his leadership, the great German industries and private business were rebuilt and workers were guaranteed decent wages and health care. The Old Man, as he came to be known, masterfully developed a new image of Germany that highlighted the nation's industrious and democratic spirit. His politics gave hope to West Germans and attracted their loyalty, discrediting claims by communist East Germany that it also represented the German people. Adenauer's Christian Democrats, committed to economic recovery and social stability, dominated German politics until 1963.

28-2b Recovery in France

In France, economic recovery was also remarkable, but it was not accompanied immediately by political stability. France had largely escaped physical destruction during the war, and its population had suffered smaller losses than had most other countries. However, France had experienced great shame and humiliation. Reconstruction thus had much to do with resurrecting faith in a vigorous France.

Charles de Gaulle Charles de Gaulle overshadowed all other politicians during this period, even though he did not hold office between 1946 and 1958. Raised in a well-educated Catholic family, de Gaulle embodied some of the oldest and proudest French traditions. He grew up among history and philosophy books and in adolescence opted for a military career to live out his patriotic sentiments. He served in the infantry, almost died at Verdun in 1916, and subsequently volunteered to fight against the Bolshevik Russians in 1919–1920. His family's political leanings were monarchist, but de Gaulle became a republican. Still, party divisions were never to his taste, as he preferred either the strict hierarchy of the army or the direct voice of the people at the ballot box. Above all, de Gaulle saw two fundamental traits in his countrymen: "The desire of privilege and the taste of equality are the dominant and contradictory passions of the French of all times."

France had had a vibrant socialist movement since the nineteenth century and was prominent in anti-Nazi resistance. The resistance had also been fertile ground for the communists, yet de Gaulle, who represented the conservative nationalism in European politics, led the liberating French forces in 1945. Until 1958, France was bitterly divided between left and right. The left claimed legitimacy based on its wartime efforts, but the communists became compromised by connections with the Soviet Union. The right, dominated by de Gaulle's party and other nationalist movements, had U.S. support. On colonial

Konrad Adenauer (1876–1967) Christian Democratic conservative opponent of Hitler who was elected the first chancellor of West Germany in 1949.

matters, France saw challenges from its territories in Southeast Asia, where China was becoming an important contender for political patronage in Vietnam, and in Algeria, where the independence movement gained a strong military component starting in 1954. More than nineteen governments rotated in and out of power during this period.

The Price of Stability In 1958, a political crisis fueled by the independence movement in Algeria brought de Gaulle into office and launched the **Fifth Republic** under a new constitution that gave broad powers to the presidency and limited those of the parliament. He was a more difficult ally for the Americans than Adenauer but no friend of the Soviet Union or the communists. As premier, de Gaulle helped restore people's faith in France as a great nation. His victory in French politics had come primarily at the expense of the left, which became increasingly marginalized in the decade after the war, accused of being a tool of Soviet expansionism. The decline of the left in France was like that in other western European countries with strong socialist and communist movements, such as Germany and Italy.

28-2c The European Community

The hardening of the East–West division between 1947 and 1958 served to deepen ties among western European states. These countries began to create stronger internal markets and to cooperate in trade, economic production, and employment policies. Given the nationalist jealousy that had dominated relations between France and Germany since the nineteenth century, this cooperation was remarkable. But European politicians and economists had learned the hard lessons of the Great Depression and were ready to take new directions. In addition, the Marshall Plan stipulated that the recipients were to cooperate in areas of investment, production, and trade.

Ending French–German Enmity The main architect of these bold policies was **Robert Schuman**, an economist and the first premier of postwar France. Together with other French and German economists and politicians, he put forth a plan to end enmity between Germany and France, promising greater stability and prosperity for both countries. "The solidarity in production thus established," he explained, "will make it plain that any war between France and Germany becomes not merely unthinkable, but materially impossible."

Economic Growth Through Collaboration Discussions led in 1951 to the creation of the **European Coal and Steel Community (ECSC)**, with six members—Belgium, France, Germany, Italy, Luxembourg, and the Netherlands. Trade tariffs were lifted for some products, workers from member countries could cross borders to find employment, and investment in coal and steel production across borders was encouraged. The union offered opportunities to entrepreneurs, paving the way for multinational corporations, as well as workers, and extending protections to them in all member states.

The ECSC was a great success, increasing steel and iron production by 75 percent in its first three years, with industrial production rising by 58 percent. It made possible the creation of the European Atomic Energy Community (1957), which oversaw the development of atomic energy for civilian purposes, and finally the European Economic Community (EEC). The 1958 EEC Rome Treaty provided the institutional foundations for four areas of cooperation among members: administrative (Council of the European Union), legislative (European Parliament, largely on paper), economic (European Commission), and judicial (European Court of Justice). The EEC also became known as the **European Community** or the Common Market. This transformation did not mean the end of political independence for the members but ensured cooperation and joint planning to enhance economic growth.

The success of the European Community was also linked to the optimism and self-sacrifice present everywhere in Europe after the war. Most people focused their energies on stability and economic well-being rather than politics. Thus, political leaders could take swift steps toward recovery in the major industries at the expense of consumer goods. The spirit of cooperation also developed among political parties, which began to make connections across borders with others of similar leanings—from left-wing socialists to center-right Christian Democrats. NATO also induced military cooperation among members.

Continued Tensions Yet nationalism continued to pose problems for the European Community. De Gaulle, for example, used France's veto to block Britain's membership in this organization in 1963 and 1967. His opposition was based on his negative view of Britain's postwar subservience to the United States and also on his skepticism about Britain's

---

Fifth Republic Current French political regime established by Charles de Gaulle in 1958 through a presidential coup.

Robert Schuman (1886–1963) First premier of postwar France, instrumental in forming the European Union and the European Coal and Steel Community.

European Coal and Steel Community (ECSC) Organization established in 1951 that created a common customs, production, and labor market for coal and steel.

European Community Precursor of the European Union, founded in 1958 with the creation of the European Economic Community, the European Coal and Steel Community, and the European Atomic Energy Commission.

willingness to accept all EEC responsibilities. De Gaulle's concerns were not groundless: given its success in postwar recovery, Britain was slow to show interest in the European Community.

CONNECTIONS: In 2016, the fears expressed by de Gaulle proved to be correct, when British voters passed a referendum that demanded their country leave the European Union based on fears that immigrant labor was sapping economic opportunities for British citizens. (See Section 30-2c Nation-States in a New Context.)

28-2d Great Britain and the Welfare State

After the war, Britain's political and economic problems forced its leadership to focus inward. Though a wartime hero, Churchill was defeated by Labour Party contender **Clement Attlee** in July 1945. The election outcome reflected a widespread desire among the public to shift away from deep involvement in European and world security. For more than five years, the British public had been told to sacrifice for others, and they did so at great human and material cost. Now they wanted the government to look out for them.

Rise of the Welfare State in Britain The Labour Party interpreted its victory as a mandate for welfare programs. The state established firm control over important areas of the economy and public services, from transportation to utilities. The Bank of England was nationalized, as were the coal and steel industries. The National Health Service Act of 1946 placed health insurance under state control while still allowing for private practice. This pioneering law made health care accessible to all British citizens. A similarly radical reform established government-funded pensions for all working citizens—a social security fund. Britain thus became a leader in welfare policies and a model for other European countries, which were encouraged to adopt similar policies. The sweeping welfare measures worked both because of the conciliatory mood of the Conservatives, who continued the policies of the Labour Party after they came to power in the 1950s, and because of the generous financial help—more than $3 billion—of the Marshall Plan.

Educational Opportunities The state also expanded educational opportunities. The 1944 Education Act made schooling mandatory until age fifteen and increased government funding to create the necessary schools, as well as scholarships for university students. More poor pupils than ever before were able to finish secondary schools and attend college, a development that took place just as rapid modernization escalated the need for educated professionals and skilled workers in the industrial and service sectors. Simultaneously, important shifts in agricultural

production pushed new waves of people into urban areas. The population of the countryside fell by 50 percent as urban growth soared.

Women on the Margins Women, however, lagged behind as beneficiaries of these new social welfare programs. Quotas imposed for access into secondary education, even when state mandated and funded, ensured that the number of girls who attended the best schools was always smaller than the number of boys, despite girls' overall superior academic performance. And though more women than ever before were employed, their wages lagged 30 to 50 percent behind men's. They also received insufficient support for child care and often had to leave the labor force for this reason.

Overall, however, the growth of work opportunities, education, and inexpensive or free public services from the state made it possible for record numbers of workers to partake in the consumer culture and enjoy leisure activities. British workers attended concerts, participated in sports, took paid vacations, and traveled abroad. Tourism took off, with more than 100 million people taking trips every year. The working class was looking like and identifying more with the middle class, and old stereotypes about national characteristics weakened as people traveled in other countries and worked together in Common Market projects.

28-3 The Restructuring of Eastern Europe

》 **What were the important steps in the communist takeovers in eastern Europe?**

》 **What was the effect in the region of Stalin's death?**

By 1948, the communists were in power everywhere in eastern Europe, revolutionizing politics, and in the next two decades internal and external forces solidified these regimes. In some cases, communist leaders preferred to follow Moscow to ensure their own political survival. In other cases, local communists attempted to gain legitimacy by portraying themselves as leaders of their nation. But the Soviets reacted swiftly against all who deviated from the interests of communism as defined in Moscow and put down any important attempts at reform. By 1968, all the communist leaders who had dreamed of reform and autonomy from Moscow were gone, generating broad disillusionment with all communist ideals.

Clement Attlee (1883–1967) British prime minister from 1945 to 1951 and Labour Party leader who oversaw the establishment of the welfare state and the end of British colonialism.

28-3a The Communist Takeovers

In 1945, the communists were a tiny political group in eastern Europe, except for Czechoslovakia and Yugoslavia. Most members of these parties had perished at the hands of the Nazis or their own governments during the war. Some had escaped to Moscow, as Stalin worked hard to recruit European communists who, like Ana Pauker, were fully devoted to Soviet goals for eastern Europe. By 1945, these communists had been returned to their countries to begin organizing mass movements and building political power.

Eliminating Political Contenders The only other potential contenders for political power were the representatives of the governments in exile, especially the Poles and Czechoslovaks, as well as the leaders of parties that had not cooperated with the Nazis. The Soviets were able to eliminate many of these during the denazification trials. And with the Soviet troops on the ground at the end of the war, noncommunist politicians stood virtually no chance of resuming office in the new regimes unless they cooperated with the Soviets.

The noncommunist Czechoslovak leader **Edvard Beneš** (ED-vahrd BEN-esh), for example, had kept channels of communication with Moscow open throughout the war, and after the war his country was not occupied. Instead, the Soviets used Beneš's political and moral authorities to smooth the transition to the postwar regime. Beneš won the 1946 presidential election as head of a coalition government led by communists and socialists, who had been fairly strong in Czechoslovakia in the 1920s and 1930s. In contrast to other eastern European countries under Soviet domination, these elections were not outright rigged. By 1947, however, the Soviets had made it clear that Czechoslovakia was not to accept Marshall Plan aid. The electoral popularity of the Czech Communist Party quickly dropped to 20 percent. In February 1948, the Soviets helped the communists force a political coup. Beneš refused to sign the new constitution, which banned all parties save for the Communist Party, and died soon afterward.

In Romania, where the Communist Party had only about a thousand members, the Soviets played a more direct role in the communist takeover. Under the strict oversight of Soviet generals and their troops, Pauker and a handful of other Moscow protégés imprisoned, exiled, or executed all noncommunist politicians. This loyal leadership also followed Moscow's orders in taking over all newspapers and radio stations, the police, the military, and labor unions. By 1947, the communists controlled the elections and orchestrated the victory of their party. The communist takeovers in Hungary, Poland, East Germany, and Bulgaria were similar.

Communist Victory By 1948, the Communist Parties had outmaneuvered their political opponents everywhere in eastern Europe, often due to the presence of Soviet troops. But the victory of communist regimes was also due to the lack of viable political options and to the collapse of democracy long before the Soviet occupation. In Poland, many saw the Soviet Union as the only power interested in securing the Polish borders against future aggression from the West, and Polish communists cast themselves as patriots protecting their nation from another German invasion.

To oversee relations with Communist Parties abroad and the new governments of the communist bloc, as communist eastern Europe came to be called, the Soviets established the **Cominform**. Under direct Soviet control, it was a ruthless instrument for purging various Communist Parties. As relations with the West worsened, Stalin became convinced that he was surrounded by enemies, that he could not trust even allies, and that his efforts to win the war had gone unappreciated. The Cominform's close control over the affairs of European Communist Parties reflected his increasingly paranoid view.

28-3b Yugoslavia's Independent Course

Yugoslavia was the only country in eastern Europe where the communist victory was due overwhelmingly to internal forces. Communist partisans had effectively struggled against the Nazi occupation and liberated Yugoslavia's territory. To be sure, the Yugoslav communists also abused their power, especially at the expense of populations who had collaborated with the Germans, such as the Croatians. But by 1947, the Yugoslav Communist League was popular and widely viewed as the legitimate political leader.

An Ambitious Leader Josip Broz Tito, the leader of the communist partisans, became the undisputed leader of Yugoslavia, and he stood up against Stalin's designs for eastern Europe. Born to a Slovenian mother and Croat father, Tito embodied a Yugoslav identity devoid of ethnic nationalism. Moreover, he was a veteran communist, initially favored by Moscow. He had fought for the Reds in the Russian Civil War, was trained in Moscow afterward, and ruthlessly followed Stalin's line during World War II. Thus, he considered himself untouchable and after 1945 embarked on an independent plan to industrialize and modernize the economy. He also sought to speed up communist revolution in the Balkans by giving military aid to

Edvard Beneš (1884–1948) President of Czechoslovakia after World War II who resented the communist takeover in 1948 and resigned.

Cominform Postwar international organization, directed from Moscow, that coordinated Communist Parties abroad, including those in western Europe.

communists in Greece and Albania. At a time when all regional relations were subject to Soviet oversight, he sought closer relations with Bulgaria independently of Moscow.

Stalin Reacts Stalin perceived these moves as a direct challenge to his authority, and Tito's insistence on remaining autonomous soon incurred the wrath of the Soviet leader. Increasingly paranoid about the growing strength of his ideological and personal enemies, Stalin was fixated on punishing anyone who disobeyed. After repeated warnings, Stalin summoned Tito to Moscow in 1948. When the Yugoslav leader failed to appear, Stalin denounced him as a capitalist spy and expelled him from the Cominform. Tito stood his ground and survived, due to internal support and significant help from the West. The United States, perceiving him as an important tool in the Cold War, lavished financial aid on Yugoslavia, over $600 million in 1950–1953 alone. In some ways, Yugoslavia became another pawn in the superpower game for world domination.

Tito's Winning Bid Yet Tito also remained independent of both superpowers, challenging the notion that the world had to be divided into two camps. He became a role model for many **Third World** countries emerging from colonial rule and, after 1948, founded the **Nonaligned Movement**. Tito saw a great opportunity among newly liberated colonial territories such as India and Indonesia to create a bloc of states independent of the Soviet and American alliances. This movement focused on increasing trade relations among members to reduce their economic dependency on the two superpowers and lobbying the UN to represent their interests, especially in international crises. For instance, as a supporter of Arab nationalism in the Middle East, Tito used nonalignment to represent the interests of the **Palestine Liberation Organization (PLO)** against Israel.

28-3c Anti-Tito Purges

While Tito purged his internal political enemies and skillfully used his position to advance his interests in the international arena, other Soviet bloc countries bore the brunt of the Tito–Stalin split (see Map 28.3). Stalin took his anger out on the eastern European regimes, as the Soviet Union helped orchestrate vast purges of the communist leadership between 1948 and 1953. Many leaders who had been in Moscow during the war and ruthlessly followed Stalin's orders in the early postwar years were now put on trial for fabricated charges of collaboration with Western "imperialist" forces against their own people. These sham trials were staged to satisfy Stalin's growing fear of imagined enemies and to reinforce the threat that the communist police state could eliminate anyone at any time, even its highest leaders. Ostensibly aimed at all communist leaders who had been friendly to Tito before 1948, the anti-Tito campaign actually proved an opportunity for revenge among Communist Party factions, as exemplified in Romania by the purge of Ana Pauker at the hands of her rival, **Gheorghe Gheorghiu-Dej** (jior-JYUH-DAYZH).

Fear and Violence The years 1948 to 1953 were dominated by fear and violence, similar to the Great Purges in the Soviet Union but with the important difference that these purges came about through both internal rivalries and Soviet interference. For many loyalists, this interference tainted the ideals of communism. Any legitimacy the Communist Parties claimed on the basis of having fought the fascist threat and struggled for social justice now eroded. As leaders fell and were replaced by others, who in turn could fall at any time, people learned to keep their heads down in fear and to distrust party ideology. Those who rose to the top of the party hierarchy were not idealists but opportunists.

Anti-Semitism and the Purges The most bitter disillusionment came in Czechoslovakia in 1951 with the **Slánský** (SLAN-skee) **trial**. Like Pauker, Rudolf Slánský had been a ruthless communist, but now he was accused of having spied for the West and plotting against the Soviet Union. Slánský's Jewish background was used against him, and others who were purged with him were Jewish survivors of concentration camps and idealistic communists. Anti-Semitism had become a feature of Soviet policies in Russia and beyond. In Czechoslovakia, the communist-controlled press identified the Jewish communist leaders alternatively as Zionists and as fascist radicals, once picturing Slánský in an SS uniform. Most troubling, people generally accepted the absurd anti-Semitic accusations not only out of fear but also because they often shared anti-Semitic attitudes. By 1953, most of the top echelon of the communist

Third World Term coined in 1952 to identify the nations that aligned with neither the West (the First World) nor the Soviet bloc (the Second World) during the Cold War.

Nonaligned Movement Grouping of states initiated by Josip Broz Tito in 1948 that did not wish to be caught in the East–West cold War and tried not to choose sides.

Palestine Liberation Organization (PLO) Organization founded in 1964 by Palestinians fighting for an independent Palestinian state in territories claimed by Israel after 1948.

Gheorghe Gheorghiu-Dej (1901–1965) Leader of communist Romania from 1948 to 1965 who carried out a ruthless campaign of collectivization in the 1950s.

Slánský trial Anti-Titoist purge trial in 1951 against Rudolf Slánský, leader of the Czechoslovak Communist Party.

Ana Pauker Submits to the Communist Party

Corbis Historical/Getty Images

Ana Pauker In 1948, *Time* magazine named her "the most powerful woman alive."

In August 1944, Ana Pauker (POW-ker) rode into Bucharest atop a Soviet tank, returning to the city of her troubled youth as a liberator (or conqueror). She had traveled a long and difficult path from her birth to an impoverished Jewish family in northern Romania, at a time and place where anti-Semitism was popular and where women were regarded as second-class citizens. Intelligent and fearless, she worked hard against this double discrimination and the roles traditionally assigned to women like her. She first chose to study Judaism and then went on to join the Communist Party during World War I, having opposed Romania's entry into the war. Though she spent some years abroad after the war, she returned to Romania to lead underground activities against Romania's unstable governments. During the 1920s and 1930s, she served several prison sentences, the last one at the same time that her husband, Marcel Pauker, was imprisoned by the Soviets during the Great Purges.

Pauker denounced her husband at his 1938 trial in Moscow. At that moment, she understood clearly that she had to pick one of her conflicting loyalties—family or the communist revolution. If she questioned the Moscow party line, she would be betraying her ideological convictions. She chose ideology. By betraying her husband, she aligned herself with Moscow and made herself ready to win control in Romania after the war.

After she returned to Romania in 1944, she retained this all-consuming loyalty. She willingly gave up leadership of the Communist Party in recognition that, as a woman and Jew, she was a liability to the party. Only by downplaying these identities could she be a decision maker in the government. As shadow leader of the party in the Politburo, she oversaw the purging of the precommunist political leadership and the

leadership and government officials in the communist bloc had been removed from power, stripped of their party membership, like Pauker, or executed, like Slánský.

28-3d State-Controlled Economies

While implementing these purges, the communist regimes in eastern Europe also began economic reconstruction with direct Soviet support. Initially, the Soviets focused on rebuilding Russia, and they did so by directly extracting resources from the communist bloc, from wheat and cattle to entire factories. The Soviets justified these seizures as war reparations. Thus, there was little economic growth in eastern Europe during the first few years of communist domination.

Soviet Economic Control Moscow sent observers, usually with military personnel, to oversee economic planning in each country. Instead of imposing a Soviet-style command economy, planners required each country to specialize in certain areas so that the region would collectively achieve economic growth. This clever plan ensured that no one state could gain economic autonomy. Thus, East Germany, Poland, and Czechoslovakia, which were already more industrialized, were to focus on industrial goods, while Romania, Bulgaria, and, to some extent, Hungary were to provide raw materials and agricultural goods to support the industries and consumer needs of the other countries. The Soviets provided energy sources for industrial production in exchange for finished industrial products, at prices set by the Soviets. The Committee for Mutual

transformation of the state into one modeled after Stalin's vision. In 1948, *Time* magazine named her "the most powerful woman alive."

Yet by 1951, Pauker had come into conflict with other Romanian communist leaders, as well as Stalin, especially over collectivization. Having given so much of her personal life to the party, Pauker assumed she could independently make the most important decisions in this aspect of economic reform. She wanted to collectivize slowly, to ensure that peasants would not come to resent the party. Though she did not come from a peasant family, she cared about the fate of peasants, and though she felt deep personal loyalty to Stalin, she also cared about Romania. Still, many in Romania perceived her as a "foreigner" because of her Jewish origins. In an atmosphere of growing anti-Semitism, Pauker's competitors in the party used this conflict to accuse her of betraying communism. Only her personal friendship with Stalin saved her life. But in 1953, Pauker was forced to denounce herself as a traitor and renounce her membership in the Communist Party. Once more she sacrificed herself for the sake of the party.

Few people mourned Pauker's departure from the party leadership, as her ruthless style was much feared. But, unlike other communists, Pauker seems to have wanted power not so much for herself but rather in order to carry out her convictions. She passed away two decades later, in anonymity and still much hated by many Romanians.

Economic Assistance coordinated economic exchanges among these countries, with support from the Soviets, but in reality the Soviets controlled all the economic exchanges. For instance, the sale of Czech-produced cars in Poland was subject to Soviet approval.

Economic Growth and Its Price This formula for economic growth had some payoffs: by 1950, some industrial products, such as steel, had surpassed pre-war production. But these successes came at great cost for both agricultural and consumer goods. In addition, just as in the Soviet Union, the performance of the economy was judged by production rather than its value on the open market. For this reason, the quality of goods remained inferior to goods produced in western Europe.

Although the goals of economic restructuring were everywhere the same, the processes varied, depending on the relationship of the local communist leadership with Moscow. For instance, collectivization of agriculture was pursued aggressively in Romania but not in Poland. Polish communists viewed collectivization as potentially destabilizing, while the Romanians were more willing to apply violent means to accomplish it. As a result, by 1958, the Romanian state fully controlled agriculture, and the regime was able to persuade the Soviets to withdraw all troops. The Poles relied on Soviet troops, however, to secure their western borders, which were not recognized by West Germany until the 1960s. Without the incentive of Soviet troop withdrawal, Polish communists allowed most peasants to keep their land but controlled the sale of agricultural products instead.

Changing the Social Landscape of Eastern Europe Economic restructuring produced a social restructuring like that in the Soviet Union in the 1920s and 1930s. Using the Soviet model, each Communist Party attempted to create a larger urban proletariat and eliminate all class enemies, including the old middle classes and rich peasants. In addition, many religious leaders were imprisoned, and writers and artists with a "bourgeois" background were censored or imprisoned to make way for a new atheist communist spirit. Ultimately, the communist regimes in eastern Europe wanted to replicate the total social control achieved by the Soviets in their own country.

Stalin Mania The stamp of Soviet domination was made visible also through the renaming of places after Stalin. The old Romanian city Braşov became Stalin; the highest peak in the Tatra Mountains in Poland was renamed Stalin; and one of the largest squares in Budapest took on Stalin's name as well. But no Poles, Bulgarians, or Romanians rushed to name newborns after the Soviet leader, as many in the Soviet Union had done in the first decade of communist control. Many feared Stalin's close embrace; few admired him in the way Russians had looked up to V. I. Lenin in the 1920s.

28-3e De-Stalinization

In 1953, Stalin suddenly died. Soviet leaders and the population at large were petrified: Stalin's presence had been so overwhelming that virtually nobody knew how to behave in his absence. The funeral became a performance for anticipating Stalin's successor, as he had not given the issue much thought. Thousands crowded to see the corpse, laid beside Lenin's in the mausoleum in downtown Moscow. Party members paid their respects out of loyalty and fear of the unknown future; average people were mostly curious to see the great man dead. The pallbearers and funeral speakers were viewed as the potential successors, especially **Georgy Malenkov**. He was prime minister and assumed the position of party general secretary.

Georgy Malenkov (1902–1988) Soviet communist leader who lost to Nikita Khrushchev in becoming Stalin's successor.

Krushchev's Rise to Power In the following months, a fierce battle took place in the Politburo. Initially, the decision was to revive the principle of collective leadership. At the same time, however, two opponents began to vie for first place: Malenkov and **Nikita Khrushchev** (KROOSH-chef). Khrushchev had been faithful to the party and loyal to Stalin and also cultivated an image as a simple man of the people. Born to an impoverished peasant family, he was the first among them to learn to read and write. He had fought in the Civil War and had worked hard and ruthlessly to become the leader of the Moscow party organization in 1935. At the height of the Great Purges, Khrushchev was one of Stalin's henchmen in Moscow and the Ukraine, where he eliminated opponents of collectivization. By 1953, he had a forceful presence in the Politburo and controlled the main party newspaper, *Pravda*.

The Secret Speech Within a year, Khrushchev's newspaper succeeded in tarnishing Malenkov's attempts to paint himself as a reformer interested in improving living standards. Like Stalin, Khrushchev worked behind the scenes, and he orchestrated Malenkov's resignation. Between 1955 and 1956, he outmaneuvered other contenders for first place in the collective leadership of the party and in February 1956 made a dramatic move that catapulted him to the top. At the Twentieth Party Congress, Khrushchev delivered a **Secret Speech** that denounced the abuses of Stalin's era and called for a reassessment of that legacy, together with punishment for Stalin's henchmen. Declaring himself the true heir of Lenin, he placed himself in opposition to those who had supported Stalin.

The speech became a watershed in Soviet and communist history. It called for reassessment and encouraged internal criticism of the party, overturning the doctrine of infallibility established by Stalin. Khrushchev made good on this promise by freeing some political prisoners of the Stalin regime, in both the Soviet

The Hungarian Uprising of 1956

The Hungarian Uprising of 1956 gained mass support when it shifted from a communist conflict between elites to a national uprising of the Hungarian people against Soviet imperialism.

❯❯ *What does this photograph, taken in the midst of the uprising, suggest about the attitude of the Hungarian rebels in relation to the Soviet Union and the communist regime?*

Erich Lessing/Magnum Photos

Union and eastern Europe. Some labor camps were closed down, and the **KGB**'s powers were reduced. At the same time, purges against Stalin's supporters began all over the eastern bloc.

From De-Stalinization to Rebellion When Khrushchev opened the pages of *Pravda* to criticisms of the party and suggestions for reform, even Poles and Hungarians began reading it, interested in the changes it outlined. But many were aware of Khrushchev's past and realized that his call for reform had limits. That he avoided explanations, but claimed the mantle of Leninist leadership, was a signal to proceed cautiously. The most important test case for **de-Stalinization** came in Hungary in 1956, where two communist factions vied for leadership. One faction, led by **Imre Nagy**, adopted Khrushchev's liberalizing attitude and gained the support of the younger generation and lower-ranking party members, while

Nikita Khrushchev
(1894–1971) Stalin's successor as leader of the Soviet Union and Soviet Communist Party who criticized Stalin's excesses and opened up a period of mild liberalization.

Secret Speech Speech by Khrushchev in 1956 to a closed party meeting that criticized Stalin and marked the beginning of his campaign to purge Stalin's supporters.

KGB The Soviet Union's premier security, secret police, and intelligence agency, from 1954 to 1991.

de-Stalinization Elimination of Stalin's followers from the leadership of Soviet bloc Communist Parties after Stalin's death.

Imre Nagy (1896–1958) Hungarian communist leader who broke with Moscow in 1956 and attempted to establish an independent socialist path for Hungary.

the other wanted to preserve the Stalinist controls over political and economic life.

Initially Khrushchev supported the reformers, who became emboldened. Yet in October 1956, the party conflict gave way to a popular uprising that called for the expulsion of all Soviet forces. Nagy announced Hungary's withdrawal from the Warsaw Pact. The insurgents looked with hope to the West, but the United States was unwilling to risk its stable relations with the Soviets to support the **Hungarian Uprising**. And in western Europe, while the conservative parties took the same approach as the United States, their left-wing counterparts followed the Soviet line. A brief and bloody struggle ensued, with the Soviets prevailing through violence. As Soviet tanks rolled over the border and into Budapest, guns and homemade bombs were not enough to stop them. More than half a million Hungarians were imprisoned as a result, several thousand were killed in the initial clashes and the subsequent purges, and thousands managed to flee the country. Eastern European leaders learned the hard way that de-Stalinization would have to proceed at the speed and in the direction approved by Moscow.

Yet de-Stalinization did bring improvements. As people learned to live by the new rules, the violent purges ended. The state began spending more money on housing, public health, and basic consumer goods. Workers now had paid vacation time and opportunities to travel in other countries of the communist bloc. By the beginning of the 1960s, Stalin's legacy was becoming a distant memory. His name was removed from Soviet encyclopedias and his photograph taken down in public buildings; places named Stalin were renamed once again.

28-4 Superpower Conflicts and Colonial Independence Movements, 1945–1968

» **What role did the American–Soviet conflict play in the colonial struggles for independence?**

» **What were the consequences of the liberation movements?**

Europe's transformation into the two opposing camps of the Cold War coincided with a revolution in the European colonies, most of which gained independence in the two decades after World War II. Yet the degree of actual political and economic autonomy of these postcolonial states varied greatly. Many continued to depend heavily on Europe, now with support from the Americans as well, while others

opted to embrace the Soviet side of the Cold War. Yet some states chose a third way, nonalignment. Overall, the East–West divide became replicated all over the postcolonial world, with the United States and the Soviet Union coming into conflict in Southeast Asia, the Middle East, and Africa.

28-4a Superpower Confrontations

In the 1950s, the United States and the Soviet Union became embroiled in Korea in their first direct military confrontation of the Cold War. A postwar settlement had divided the former Japanese territory into a communist Democratic People's Republic in the north and the Republic of Korea in the south.

The Korean War What started as a war between the two in 1950 quickly became internationalized in the bipolar world of the Cold War. After the Soviets sent military support to the North, the Americans went before the UN Security Council to request a military intervention on behalf of the South. The Security Council agreed, primarily because the Soviets, boycotting the UN at the time, were not present to veto the decision. The United States thus sent in troops under the guise of South Korean requests for help and UN endorsement. In reality, the **Korean War** was a heated conflict unfolding between the Soviets' pursuit of a zone of influence in Korea and the Americans' implementation of the Truman Doctrine to aid those fighting the spread of communism. The new Chinese communist regime also became involved, sending military aid to the North Koreans. A truce in 1953 left Korea divided, with families split across the border and unable to communicate. The Soviets and Chinese celebrated a communist victory, while the United States boasted success in stopping the spread of communism.

Yet the Korean War was an abysmal failure. It brought the two superpowers into a military conflict that left nothing resolved; troops remain poised at the border today. The outcome of this conflict for the world scene was twofold: it established that the two superpowers were willing to use military power in their contest for world domination, and it showed the great military and human costs of such actions. If Korea could be a setting for war among the superpowers, then all political leaders of liberation movements in colonial territories had to think carefully about the choices they made.

The Race for Outer Space In the following decade, the contest between the

---

Hungarian Uprising
Nationwide uprising against the Soviet occupation and communist regime in 1956 that was violently crushed by the Soviets.

Korean War (1950–1953) Military conflict between communist-backed North Korea and U.S.-supported South Korea.

Berlin Wall

In June 1963, U.S. President John F. Kennedy stood on a platform above the Berlin Wall, addressing 12,000 West Berliners and a few East Berliners silently watching on the other side of the wall. Speaking on the themes of freedom and citizenship, he asserted, "Ich bin ein Berliner" (I am a Berliner).

❯❯ *What does this image of Kennedy standing above a crowd in West Berlin and looking over to East Berlin suggest about U.S. policies during the Cold War?*

Soviets and the Americans circled the globe and escalated to outer space. Under President Dwight Eisenhower, the United States expanded its military alliances and placed nuclear missiles around the world, from France to Pakistan and the Philippines. The Soviets also built a missile arsenal. In 1957, they launched **Sputnik 1**, the first space satellite and a scientific achievement that placed them ahead of the Americans in the space race.

Sputnik 1 Soviet satellite that in 1957 was the first to be launched into earth orbit and began the Soviet–American space race.

Berlin Wall Wall built through Berlin by East Germany in 1961 to prevent its citizens from escaping into West Germany.

Cuban Missile Crisis Standoff between the United States and the Soviet Union in 1962 over Soviet equipping of Cuba with nuclear missiles.

Fidel Castro (1926–2016) Leader of Cuban communist revolution in 1956 and president of Cuba between 1959 and 2008.

Dividing Berlin The Soviets attempted to parlay this success by threatening to hand over control of access to West Berlin to the East Germans, hoping to force the Americans out of the city and ending the flow of Germans from East to West. After a three-year standoff, in 1961 East Germany put up the **Berlin Wall**, dividing the city. There was little the Americans could do about it. The wall became a powerful symbol of what the Cold War meant for average people.

Near Nuclear Disaster The most dangerous global confrontation of the Soviets and Americans came in 1962, during the **Cuban Missile Crisis**. After **Fidel Castro** came to power in Cuba in 1959 on a wave of popular anticolonial protest, he was courted by both the Americans and the Soviets. For the United States, Cuba had great economic and strategic interest because of its proximity. For the Soviets, Cuba could be an outpost for nuclear missiles, to counter the American bases in Turkey and Pakistan. After a failed American attempt to depose Castro in 1961, the Soviets offered to bolster the Cuban defenses by bringing in nuclear weapons. For a few days in October 1962, President John F. Kennedy and Khrushchev came close to nuclear war. Each leader called on the other to back down, while both were in fact mobilizing out of fear that the other would strike. Then, when the Americans promised not to invade Cuba and to withdraw their missiles from Turkey, the Soviets removed the missiles from Cuba. The crisis made both powers aware of the need for constant communication. Though boasting its independence from imperial powers, the Castro regime remained dependent on the economic and military supports of the Soviet Union until the demise of the communist regime in 1991.

28-4b Colonial Independence Movements

As American and Soviet economic and military powers expanded, most European countries with colonies realized that their reduced political, military, and economic resources made it impossible for them to maintain control over vast territories outside of Europe. At the same time, indigenous political elites were on the rise in these areas, leading to rebellions and political movements that eventually brought about independence from colonial rule.

Mau Mau Rebellion

In this image taken during the Mau Mau Rebellion, Kenyan rebel soldiers are being held in an improvised pen by the British authorities.

» *What sort of power relations between the colonizing power and the rebels does the image convey?*

» *What are the signs of these power differences?*

British Decolonization In Britain, the Labour Party favored liberating the colonies as a matter of ideology and pragmatic consideration. The British led **decolonization** by offering colonies independence and a new, autonomous relationship with Great Britain through the **Commonwealth of Nations**, which focused on economic relations (see Map 28.4). India was a relatively successful model. Given the large population and great variety of traditions and cultures that existed on the subcontinent, the Indian nationalist movements were remarkably united in their negotiations with the British. Gandhi's leadership gave these movements cohesion and a strategy of peaceful resistance to colonial rule. His protégé **Jawaharlal Nehru** (JA-wa-HAR-lal NAYR-oo) became the first prime minister of independent India. Both resisted the strategy of outright military conflict over India's borders, a serious threat as India was culturally and ethnically divided, most importantly between Hindus and Muslims. In 1947, British India devolved into Muslim-dominated Pakistan and Hindu-dominated India. Border conflicts between the two countries continue today.

The British pursued a similar disengagement policy in their African colonies but proceeded more gradually, as these colonies had not yet developed an indigenous intellectual and economic elite like that in South Asia. In addition, as the white settlers in these African territories were far more numerous than those in Asia and unwilling to give up their homes, the process of decolonization was more contentious and violent. West Africa, Ghana, and Nigeria were the first to gain independence peacefully. By contrast, more conflict occurred in Kenya, where white settlers wished to retain their economic privileges after independence, by force if necessary, while indigenous radical groups such as the **Mau Mau** fought for a radical break from the British. After five years of violence, the British won the war but lost the colony. Having become financially overextended, the British pulled out their troops. Kenya became independent in 1963.

French Decolonization

The French wanted to preserve greater control over colonies in Africa and Asia and chose to repress independence movements. In Asia, de Gaulle attempted to persuade Vietnam to remain part of the French Union. This arrangement allowed colonial territories to gain more autonomy and become more democratic through enfranchisement of the local population. But administration, education, and commerce would remain heavily dominated by French-educated-and-speaking elites, which replicated power relations from the previous regime.

decolonization Process by which European imperialist powers moved to withdraw from colonial holdings and ready colonies for independence.

Commonwealth of Nations Association of independent states, originally former British colonies, that was created in 1947 to enhance economic and cultural cooperation.

Jawaharlal Nehru (1889–1964) Leading figure the Indian independence movement who became the first prime minister of India in 1947.

Mau Mau (in Kikuyu, "burning spear") Pro-independence Kenyan rebels who advocated violent methods against white settlers in order to reclaim land and political power for indigenous Africans.

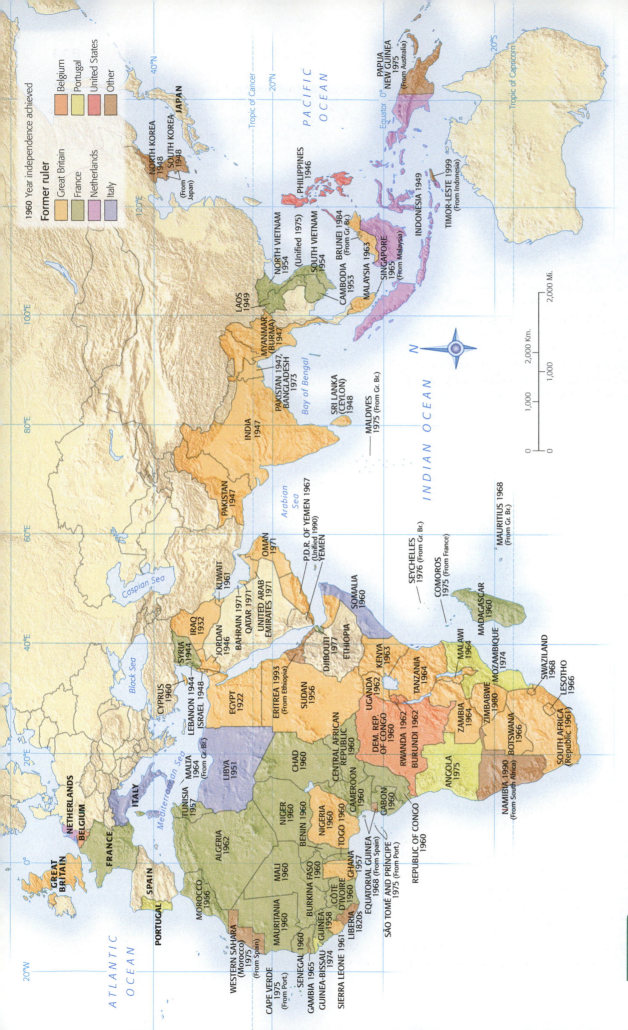

Map 28.4 Decolonization Movements, 1945–1968 Between 1945 and 1968, most European colonies gained independence. For some, like Ghana, the process was peaceful. Others, like Vietnam, fought bloody wars. The United States and the Soviet Union became involved in these struggles as the new world power brokers.

1. If you look at the dates on the map, how would describe the decolonization process of the British colonies?

2. What about the French colonies?

3. What territory was last to be decolonized?

1960 Year independence achieved

Former ruler

Great Britain	Belgium
France	Portugal
Netherlands	United States
Italy	Other

NORTH KOREA 1948
SOUTH KOREA 1948 (From Japan)
JAPAN

PACIFIC OCEAN

PHILIPPINES 1946

PAPUA NEW GUINEA 1975 (From Australia)

Tropic of Cancer
20°N
40°N
120°E
100°E

Equator 0°
Tropic of Capricorn
20°S

NORTH VIETNAM 1954
SOUTH VIETNAM 1954 (Unified 1975)
CAMBODIA 1953
BRUNEI 1984 (From Gr. Br.)
MALAYSIA 1963
SINGAPORE 1965 (From Malaysia)
INDONESIA 1949
TIMOR-LESTE 1999 (From Indonesia)
LAOS 1949
MYANMAR (BURMA) 1947
PAKISTAN 1947, BANGLADESH 1973
INDIA 1947
SRI LANKA (CEYLON) 1948
MALDIVES 1975 (From Gr. Br.)

Bay of Bengal

PAKISTAN 1947

Arabian Sea

INDIAN OCEAN

MAURITIUS 1968 (From Gr. Br.)
SEYCHELLES 1976 (From Gr. Br.)
COMOROS 1975 (From France)
MADAGASCAR 1960

N

0 1,000 2,000 Mi.
0 1,000 2,000 Km.

Caspian Sea

P.D.R. OF YEMEN 1967 (Unified 1990)
YEMEN
OMAN 1971
BAHRAIN 1971
QATAR 1971
UNITED ARAB EMIRATES 1971
KUWAIT 1961
IRAQ 1932
JORDAN 1946
SYRIA 1944
LEBANON 1944
ISRAEL 1948
CYPRUS 1960

Black Sea

SOMALIA 1960
DJIBOUTI 1977
ETHIOPIA
ERITREA 1993 (From Ethiopia)
SUDAN 1956
EGYPT 1922
KENYA 1963
UGANDA 1962
TANZANIA 1964
RWANDA 1962
BURUNDI 1962
DEM. REP. OF CONGO 1960
CENTRAL AFRICAN REPUBLIC 1960
MALAWI 1964
ZAMBIA 1964
MOZAMBIQUE 1974
ZIMBABWE 1980
SWAZILAND 1968
LESOTHO 1966
BOTSWANA 1966
SOUTH AFRICA (Republic 1961)
NAMIBIA 1990 (From South Africa)
ANGOLA 1975
REPUBLIC OF CONGO 1960
GABON 1960
CAMEROON 1960
NIGERIA 1960
TOGO 1960
BENIN 1960
GHANA 1957
CÔTE D'IVOIRE 1958
LIBERIA 1820s
SIERRA LEONE 1961
GUINEA 1958
GUINEA-BISSAU 1974
GAMBIA 1965
SENEGAL 1960
MAURITANIA 1960
EQUATORIAL GUINEA 1968 (From Spain)
SÃO TOMÉ AND PRÍNCIPE 1975 (From Port.)
BURKINA FASO 1960
MALI 1960
NIGER 1960
CHAD 1960
LIBYA 1951
ALGERIA 1962
TUNISIA 1957
MOROCCO 1956
WESTERN SAHARA (Morocco) 1975 (From Spain)
CAPE VERDE 1975 (From Port.)
MALTA 1964 (From Gr. Br.)

Mediterranean Sea

GREAT BRITAIN
FRANCE
SPAIN
PORTUGAL
NETHERLANDS
BELGIUM
ITALY

ATLANTIC OCEAN

0°
20°W
20°E
40°E
60°E
80°E

The postwar Vietnamese political factions proved impossible to control. The communists were a growing pro-independence group that secured help from the new regime in China. In 1954, the communist leader Ho Chi Minh defeated the French, despite massive financial help from the United States. Vietnam was divided between the communist-controlled north and the western-supported south. The loss of Vietnam produced a political crisis in France that eventually brought colonial rule to an end.

Vietnam remained an important battleground in the Cold War. In the early 1960s, the United States sent military advisers and then troops into South Vietnam to forestall what President Lyndon Johnson depicted as the threat of communist revolution everywhere in Asia. The **Vietnam War** became increasingly brutal but did not bring any resolution. In 1973, under pressure from the American public, who watched the atrocities committed by both sides every day on television, President Richard Nixon reached a truce with North Vietnam and pulled out.

Algeria and the Challenge to French Democracy

The French had troubles with their overseas territories in Africa as well, with the costliest conflict in Algeria. More than 1 million European settlers had lived there for generations, and the territory had been formally integrated into France as an administrative region. Therefore, when a revolt broke out in 1954, shortly after the humiliating defeat in Vietnam, the French felt a threat to the homeland, and repression of the rebels became a core political issue. Yet the Muslim rebels were committed to fighting for independence from French rule. The **Algerian War** divided France both at home and in North Africa, bringing down the Fourth Republic in 1958. In this civil war, some white settlers and European French citizens sided with the pro-independence insurgents, while some of the North African indigenous populations sided with the French colonial administration. By and large, however, the division was racial—whites against nonwhites—and the abuses committed during the war only reinforced racism in French society. De Gaulle was able to save the state from the brink of collapse in 1958 through a new constitution that strengthened the power of the president and military establishment against the parliament. Yet he eventually gave up Algeria in 1962.

The rest of French Africa, where the French were less invested politically and culturally and the number of European settlers smaller, gained independence with less strife. After Algeria, the French administration was eager to grant independence to the rest of its colonies. Yet, as the level of indigenous economic development remained low, these countries continued in their economic dependence on France.

Emerging Conflicts over the Middle East

Although disengagement and decolonization dominated the political fate of former colonies in Asia and Africa, the Middle East became a new battleground for the two superpowers, primarily because of its tremendous oil resources. The United States gradually replaced the British in the area, trying to broker between the newly established state of Israel and its hostile Arab neighbors while competing with the Soviet Union for alliances with oil-rich Arab leaders.

The development of Arab nationalism was accelerated by the creation of Israel and the failure of the UN to create a Palestinian Arab state. On the one hand, Israel came to define itself and be viewed increasingly as a promoter of progressive ideas and of Western civilization. After 1967, it was sturdily on the side of U.S. interests in the area. On the other hand, some Arab populations in Palestine and the rest of the Middle East began to look toward the Soviet Union as a better broker for their interests. After 1964, when the PLO established itself as the foremost leader in the Palestinian struggle for statehood, the organization was quickly recognized by and sought the material support of the Soviet Union and other communist states, such as Yugoslavia.

Yet neither communism nor capitalism was the choice of most political leaders of the Middle East. Instead, the region produced a blend of Arab nationalism with strong Muslim influences. Many territories remained kingdoms, and postcolonial states established authoritarian governments with only a thin veneer of parliamentary life. Political institutions in these countries often resembled premodern theocracies, and their oil resources brought great wealth to ruling elites. States like Saudi Arabia could display the trappings of material civilization in step with Europe while its justice system and suppression of women remained violent. Until the 1970s, neither superpower intervened directly in the internal ideological preferences of these states so long as they could benefit from access to the region's oil resources.

28-4c The Nonaligned Movement

By the late 1960s, European colonial rule had come to an end almost everywhere. This process was uneven and very costly in some instances, and it brought about radical change in international relations. The UN General Assembly became dominated numerically by relatively poor postcolonial states. By 1980, the Nonaligned Movement had grown from 25 to 117, becoming the largest bloc in the UN and acting forcefully

Vietnam War (1959–1975) Successful effort by the communist North Vietnamese to take over South Vietnam, which was supported by the Americans and the French.

Algerian War (1954–1962) Civil war in which Algerian nationalists eventually defeated the French colonial administration and established an independent state.

Anticolonialism Before and After Independence

AS EUROPEAN STATES AND THEIR COLONIES WERE EMERGING FROM THE VIOLENCE OF WORLD WAR II, a new generation of indigenous intellectuals and political leaders were becoming active from the Carribean to Africa. Franz Fanon (1925–1961) grew up in French-ruled Martinique and spent part of the war as a volunteer for the Gaullist liberation forces against the Nazis. After the war, he returned home to complete high school and then moved to France, where he completed a medical degree in psychiatry and psychopathology, while remaining in close collaboration with Marxist thinkers that had influenced him since youth. Though he greatly benefitted from educational opportunities in France, after 1954 he joned the Algerian liberation movement and committed himself to violent resistance to colonialism. He was later expelled from France and continued to travel and collaborate with anticolonial movements in North Africa until his death from cancer in 1961. Fanon's work became a strong influence for other anticolonial activists, such as Ernesto Che Guevara, as well as the civil rights movement in the United States, especially the Black Panthers.

Wangari Maathai (MAH-thai) (1940–2011) was raised in Kenya during the last two decades of British colonial rule and became interested in biology, moving to the United States on a scholarship provided by the John F. Kennedy Foundation to complete her undergraduate and master's degrees in science. Subsequently she became one of the first women in her country to achieve a PhD in biological sciences and start teaching at the University of Nairobi. Through her organization, the Green Belt Movement, she became one of the most prominent global leaders in ecological activism and in 2004 received the Nobel Peace Prize for her efforts against deforestation.

As you read, consider how the two authors describe indigenous elites in Africa. What are the sources of inspiration for each of them in terms of their struggle for empowerment? What sort of obstacles against that do the two identify? How are they similar and how do they differ?

❶ Fanon's reference to stages of "social consciousness" suggests he was inspired by and grounded his own writings in Marxist ideas.

❷ The reference to "primitive tribalism" indicates Fanon's unproblematic use of some of the same racist categories of understanding African societies as the people he is criticizing.

❸ The reference to "all citizens" may be interpreted here as either inclusive of women or just of all men.

Franz Fanon

The African people and indeed all underdeveloped peoples, contrary to common belief, very quickly build up a social and political consciousness. What can be dangerous is when they reach the stage of social consciousness before the stage of nationalism.**❶** If this happens, we find in underdeveloped countries fierce demands for social justice, which paradoxically are allied with often primitive tribalism.**❷** The underdeveloped peoples behave like starving creatures; this means that the end is very near for those who are having a good time in Africa. Their government will not be able to prolong its own existence indefinitely. A bourgeoisie that provides nationalism alone as food for the masses fails in its mission and gets caught up in a whole series of mishaps. But if nationalism is not made explicit, if it is not enriched and deepened by a very rapid transformation into a consciousness of social and political needs, in other words into humanism, it leads up a blind alley. The bourgeois leaders of underdeveloped countries imprison national consciousness in sterile formalism. It is only when men and women are included on a vast scale in enlightened and fruitful work that form and body are given to that consciousness. Then the flag and the palace where sits the government cease to be the symbols of the nation. The nation deserts these brightly lit, empty shells and takes shelter in the country, where it is given life and dynamic power. The living expression of the nation is the moving consciousness of the whole of the people; it is the coherent, enlightened action of men and women. The collective building up of a destiny is the assumption of responsibility on the historical scale. Otherwise there is anarchy, repression, and the resurgence of tribal parties and federalism. The

4 Maathai was in the United States during this period. What does this quote suggest about the inspiration she drew from the civil rights movement?

5 At that time, there wasn't a single female faculty in the department of zoology at University of Nairobi.

6 How does Maathai describe tribalism in relationship to gender and ethnic identity?

national government, if it wants to be national, ought to govern by the people and for the people, for the outcasts and by the outcasts. No leader, however valuable he may be, can substitute himself for the popular will; and the national government, before concerning itself about international prestige, ought first to give back their dignity to all citizens, **3** fill their minds and feast their eyes with human things, and create a prospect that is human because conscious and sovereign men dwell therein.

From Franz Fanon, *The Wretched of the Earth*, New York: Grove Widenfeld, 1991 [1961], pp. 203–204.

Wangari Maathai

America transformed me. It taught me not to waste any opportunities and to do what can be done—and that there is a lot to do. The spirit of freedom and possibility that America nurtured in me made me want to foster the same in Kenya, and it was in this spirit that I returned home. . . . I could almost hear myself agree with the concluding words spoken by the great American civil rights leader Dr. Martin Luther King Jr. at the Lincoln Memorial in Washington, D.C., on August 28, 1963: "Free at last! Free at last! Thank God Almighty, we are free at last!" **4** These thoughts dominated my mind in the days and months that followed as I reconnected with my country and my people. . . . With great enthusiasm, I presented myself to the professor of zoology, my new boss. **5** To my dismay, without blinking an eye, he had the audacity to inform me that the job had been offered to someone else. I was shocked. "But you wrote me this letter," I protested, showing him the handwritten letter of appointment on official university letterhead and signed by him. "I've come all the way from the United States of America." . . . I found out that the zoology professor had indeed offered the job to someone else, and that that person was someone from his own ethnic community. To add insult to injury, that person was still in Canada. It was the first time I had encountered that form of discrimination. Was it also because I was a woman? . . . **6** What I did not know then was that tribalism and other forms of corruption were going to become some of the most divisive factors in our society, and they would frustrate the dreams of the Kenyan people after independence.

Wangari Maathai, *Unbowed. A Memoir*. New York: Penguin, 2007, pp. 97–101.

as a faction when important matters came to a vote. Thus, the nonaligned bloc was able to direct financial assistance to underdeveloped areas, such as South Asia and Africa. This bloc regarded Europe sometimes positively, as an important patron in cultural and economic relations, and at other times with bitterness, as the seat of imperialist oppression. Almost half of the presidents of the assembly have come from postcolonial states of the nonaligned bloc.

Postcolonial Realignments in the Cold War Postcolonial regions became a new arena for superpower struggle. The Soviets invested heavily in economic and educational exchanges with the newly independent African states, accompanied by a heavy dose of communist ideology. African rulers often found the Soviet propaganda about Western imperialism appealing.

By contrast, the U.S.-backed regimes supported its economic interests. American oil investments in the Persian Gulf, for example, prompted U.S. support for an authoritarian monarchy in Iran that replaced the nationalist republican independence movement.

States such as Indonesia, Egypt, and India maintained more distance from the two superpowers. One important moment in this process was the **Suez Canal Crisis**. In 1956, during the Hungarian Uprising, Egyptian leader **Gamal Abdel Nasser** (ga-MAHL AB-del

Suez Canal Crisis Military attack on Egypt by Britain, France, and Israel in 1956 after Egypt seized the Suez Canal from British administration.

Gamal Abdel Nasser (1918–1970) President of Egypt from 1956 to 1970 who nationalized the Suez Canal.

Hulton Archives/Getty Images

Three Nonaligned Movement Leaders

These three leaders of the Nonaligned Movement— Egypt's Gamal Abdel Nasser, Yugoslavia's Josip Broz Tito, and India's Jawaharlal Nehru—saw themselves as the advocates of independence for their nations and critics of imperialist oppression.

❯❯ *What does this image convey about the lifestyle of these leaders of oppressed people?*

NA-sir) nationalized the canal. With encouragement from the Soviets, the Egyptians hoped to secure control over this strategic body of water that had been under French, British, and more recently American control. But Khrushchev did not send direct military aid. Thus, in winning the conflict, Nasser established an independence position, able to broker between the superpowers without a direct commitment to either side. Like Tito before him, Nasser also secured hefty financial support for Egypt from both superpowers.

28-5 Cultural Developments and Social Protest

❯❯ **Why was there a moral and spiritual crisis in the 1950s?**

❯❯ **What were the generational divides behind the revolt of the 1960s?**

In the 1950s and 1960s, European culture took many new turns, especially as the very meaning of being European was questioned and redefined. Although a consensus seemed to develop in the 1950s about European identity and culture, a new generation of intellectuals and rebels in the 1960s helped shake it up. Europe became divided between old and young, between conformist and antiestablishment factions.

28-5a Consumption and Conformity

After the war, western Europeans sought to forget the past, work hard, and acquire material goods. Instead of participating in mass political movements, they sought recognition for individual achievements. Initially success measured by material goods meant simply having a job, a place to live, and food on the table. But as the economic miracle began to make consumer goods more affordable, the culture of consumption took off. At first, people wanted refrigerators, radios, and comfortable furniture. By the 1960s, they wanted a television, a car, and the leisure activities that a car made possible. For African Americans engaged in a struggle for civil rights in the United States, equal access to consumer benefits became an important stage on which wider concerns about racism in American society were articulated, from buses to lunch counters.

Consumer Culture in Western Europe The availability of inexpensive consumer goods was closely connected to technological advances made during and after the war. Plastics made everything cheaper— and also created an unprecedented level of dependency on oil. As consumer goods proliferated, their very availability induced people to want to have more of what other people had. The desire to conform increased as the possibility for purchasing the same goods grew. This kind of social pressure was not new, but it had never before been expressed on a massive scale that defied social class divisions. Ironically,

Police Brutality, Alabama, 1963

The civil rights movement became a mass phenomenon in the 1960s, in large part because peaceful protests were met with violent responses on the part of the police and other government institutions. Access to consumer goods such as television, newspapers, and radio amplified the impact of images such as the one shown here, making it increasingly difficult for segregationist officials and voters to justify the policies of excluding African Americans from equal access to the same public spaces and services as whites enjoyed.

›› *Compare the confrontation between this protester and the police with the images on pages 815 and 817. What differences are noticeable?*

while struggling to be individually successful, people now proclaimed their status by fitting in; conformity and anonymity gave a sense of security. This reaction seemed natural after the wartime years, when many had lived the experience of being singled out in painful ways.

Racism, Consumer Goods, and Civil Rights

In the United States, for many African Americans, conformity was a dream out of reach. Though on paper they enjoyed the same rights as white citizens and they paid taxes, had served in the war to defend the principles of democracy, and worked in the paid economy in larger percentages than whites, the African American population in the United States was subjected to systematic forms of institutional racism, from access to education to employment and other economic activities.

Starting in the 1950s, African American students, civil and religious leaders, began organizing peaceful protests to end education segregation, taking the fight all the way to the Supreme Court with the ***Brown vs. Board of Education*** decision in 1954. When the Court sided unanimously with the protesters, public education institutions were obligated to desegregate. Civil rights activists became emboldened, while their opponents, from the Klu Klux Klan to many segregationist elected officials, hardened their resolve to prevent integration. Over the next fifteen years, millions of people joined the civil rights movement, and thousands died at the hands of segregationist mobs and their allies on the police force. Antidiscrimination legislation protecting African Americans became more forceful, culminating with the 1964 **Civil Rights Act**.

Yet the implementation of this legislation was uneven, especially in the South. Some African American organizations, such as the **Black Panthers**, resolved to take matters into their own hands and built self-defense networks that combined military training with community service work founded on Marxist principles. Their Free Breakfast for Children Program became particularly widespread and came to include support for poor children of every background in the neighborhoods where the Black Panthers were active.

Conformity Without Consumption in Eastern Europe

Nothing parallel to consumer culture developed in eastern Europe, but the new communist regimes did place great emphasis on conformity. This conformity was, however, imposed without mercy from above and enforced by manipulating fear. Behavior regarded as deviant was harshly punished, with imprisonment or exile to labor camps. Priests and religious believers were often singled out. Some theological institutes were closed. All denominations were persecuted, but not to the same extent. For instance, members of the Greek Catholic Church, made illegal in Romania in 1948, were harshly punished for any public

Brown vs. Board of Education In 1954, the U.S. Supreme Court heard this case and decided unanimously that racial segregation of public education institutions was unconstitutional, opening the way for many other challenges to racist practices in public policy.

Civil Rights Act The Civil Rights Act was passed in 1964 in response to pressure from African American activists and with support from President Lyndon B. Johnson. It outlawed discrimination based on race, color, religion, sex, or national origin.

Black Panthers African American Revolutionary Party founded in 1966 in Oakland, California, by Huey Newton and Bobby Seale. It embraced both peaceful and violent methods of self-defense and self-help against racism.

religious displays, whereas members of the Roman Catholic Church in the same country were allowed to continue their religious practices in limited ways.

Under the pressure for strict conformity to the party line, people quickly learned to live double lives. A member of an illegal faith might openly abandon his or her religious allegiance but continue religious practice in hiding. Because the communist regimes could not police a person's every action, most eastern Europeans became skilled at shifting between public and hidden identities.

By the beginning of the 1960s, the communist regimes were also using the mass media to enhance conformity and social stability. Radio and television programs, films, and magazines—some glossy and appealingly designed—became effective communist propaganda machines. Starved for information and entertainment, people often embraced these propaganda products as a form of relaxation and escape.

28-5b Moral and Spiritual Crisis

As western European culture became more conformist and consumer oriented, it also became increasingly secular and even unconcerned with questions of morality and spirituality. For many, the war and the Holocaust had unraveled the very concept of civilization. In the first decade after the war, a few intellectuals and spiritual leaders attempted to offer answers to the deep moral questions opened up by the wartime violence, corruption, and utter degradation of the human condition. Yet these answers proved unsatisfactory to the following generation, who challenged the solutions offered by their predecessors.

Ideological Commitment or Moral Alienation

Intellectuals such as **Albert Camus** (cah-MIEW) and **Jean-Paul Sartre** (SAR-treh) tried to claim social relevance for literature through personal engagement against injustice. In the Algerian War, these writers took opposite sides—Sartre for postcolonial independence, Camus for retention of links with France. Sartre's position derived from his ideological commitment to communism, whereas Camus arrived at his stance through direct experience in his native Algeria. Their quarrel became famous in intellectual circles, but, powerful as they were, their writings offered no moral guidance or satisfactory answers to their readers.

RDA/Hulton Archive/Getty Images

Sartre and De Beauvoir

Jean-Paul Sartre and Simone de Beauvoir (bo-VWAR) were the most celebrated couple in postwar France—intellectuals committed to political and social causes. Yet de Beauvoir remained for a long time in the shadow of Sartre, her feminism viewed secondary to his existential philosophy.

❯❯ *How do they appear in this photograph?*

In fact, it was Camus's gradual distancing from the ideological commitment of Sartre that resonated most strongly. The condition of the postwar generation was one of moral alienation.

New Departures Among Religious Institutions

This context provided important opportunities for the Catholic and Protestant churches in western Europe to regain spiritual relevance. But it was not the churches that grew. Instead, the Christian Democratic political parties gained a wider following in France, Germany, and Italy and especially when they demonstrated concern for social justice and progressive measures relating to workers' rights and social welfare. But these parties also represented a social and cultural conservatism that had little appeal to the generation born after the war, which seemed detached from the challenges of the postwar years and unable to find moral and spiritual guidance either in religious parties or in religion itself.

Albert Camus (1913–1960) Algerian-born French writer and philosopher who opposed Algerian independence and was awarded the Nobel Prize in Literature in 1957.

Jean-Paul Sartre (1905–1980) Most famous French philosopher of the twentieth century, an open communist sympathizer.

Beatlemania

The Beatles became a worldwide phenomenon in the mid-1960s. At their concerts, fans crushed each other and had to be held back by the police to prevent further chaos.

» *What does this image suggest about changes in youth culture with regard to music and consumerism by the late 1960s?*

In response to this moral crisis, Pope **John XXIII** attempted to provide a new direction for Catholicism. At the **Second Vatican Council**, he presented a broad agenda for changes in all areas of the church's organization and social engagement while attempting to preserve its fundamental mission. Decisions at this series of meetings, from 1962 to 1965, allowed churches to use local languages, gave reformist bishops more autonomy, and permitted greater involvement in social activism—for instance, on behalf of the poor in Latin America.

If the primary struggle of churches in western Europe was against the moral and spiritual alienation of the population at large, in the communist bloc, churches and religious believers fought for their very survival in the face of political persecution. The communist regimes tolerated and gradually used some churches both to appease religious believers and to inform on them with the help of corrupt priests. In other instances, however, religious institutions became the seat of spiritual survival against communism. In Poland, the Catholic Church preserved a degree of integrity and moral authority unparalleled anywhere else in eastern Europe. In fact, religiosity among Poles grew, and many gravitated to the church as the one institution uncorrupted by communism. Protestant denominations also offered a secure and morally uplifting refuge. But most eastern Europeans became estranged from religious experience through the aggressive antireligious campaigns of the communist regimes.

28-5c Youth and the Counterculture

By the mid-1960s, a new postwar generation was questioning the direction of prosperity and security in western Europe and rejecting the values and lifestyles of their elders. The clash of generations arose from several factors. First, while the direct experience of deprivation and death made the prewar generation overly preoccupied with material comforts, abundance made the postwar generation indifferent to the value of material goods. Those born after 1945 were marked by the culture of conformity and consumption in two ways: on the one hand, they fully enjoyed the fruits of the economic miracle, the availability of cheap material goods, books, records, and other forms of entertainment and information; on the other hand, they wanted more meaning in

John XXIII (r. 1958–1962) Reformist pope who spearheaded changes in language use and liturgical rituals and initiated the Second Vatican Council.

Second Vatican Council Meeting of cardinals and bishops of the Roman Catholic Church between 1962 and 1965 to promote church reform.

their lives than the satisfactions their parents found in material goods. They deplored the conformity and cultural boredom of their elders and wanted to engage in meaningful choices and spread their comforts among others less fortunate. Finally, the postwar generation had much greater access to college education.

Rock 'n' Roll A new pop culture best expressed the mood of this new generation. Rock and roll developed first in America, but by the mid-1960s, European bands such as the Beatles and The Who had taken the new musical form and made it theirs. Rock music anthems like "My Generation" were rebellious and appealing precisely because rock 'n' roll was loud and rough. Young people loved it as much as their parents hated it. Some performers brought broader political and social content to their lyrics. Bob Dylan, the most powerful voice of the postwar generation, wrote verses that resonated with young people all over Europe. Initially a beloved folk hero, he broke the sound barrier from acoustic to electric rock 'n' roll shows that alienated many fans and inspired generations of other musicians to come.

In film, New Wave Cinema merged a social and political critique with a harsh style that echoed the loudness of rock music. The films of French director **Jean-Luc Goddard** confronted materialism, sexuality, and political violence. He and other filmmakers broke free of the conventions and conservative aesthetics of their predecessors. Film, they contended, should not be an escape. It should depict life, and life was neither heroic nor even coherent, but full of violence, breakdown, and loss.

Education and the Youth One unifying element of this new generation was its unprecedented access to education. In France, for instance, university enrollment went up by almost 200 percent in the 1960s, especially among women and working-class people (see Figure 28.2). This dramatic change forced important questions about the quality of education and the political agenda of its content. In the ensuing battles over democratizing university education, both students and teachers became increasingly radicalized and involved in political protest, giving rise to a new wave of left-wing activists and politicians.

Jean-Luc Goddard (1930–) Prominent French New Wave film maker.

Martin Luther King Jr. (1929–1968) African American Baptist minister and nonviolent leader of the American civil rights movement in the 1960s.

Daniel Cohn-Bendit (1945–) German-born charismatic left-wing leader of the student protests in France in May 1968.

28-5d 1968

These generational tensions came to a head in the extraordinary year 1968. In an explosive set of coincidences, the world seemed headed toward a revolution.

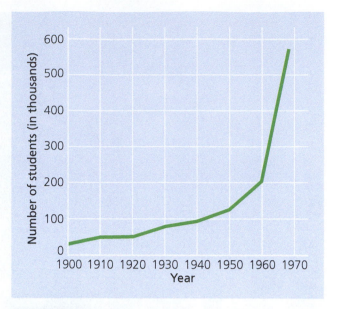

Figure 28.2 Enrollment Figures for French Universities from 1900 to 1968 After World War II, western Europe was fundamentally changed by the great growth in college attendance. The beneficiaries of this growth were especially the poor and women.

❯❯ *What decade saw the highest rate of growth?*

Source: Wilkinson, James D.; Huges H. Stuart, *Contemporary Europe: A History*, 9th Edition, © 1998, p. 425. Reprinted by permission of Pearson Education, Inc., Upper Saddle River, NJ.

In the United States, the charismatic civil rights leader **Martin Luther King Jr.** was assassinated.

From Peaceful Protests to Violent Clashes King's murder signaled the end of the peaceful civil rights movement and the ramping up of more belligerent African American protests. At the same time, protests against the Vietnam War were taking a more radical form. On campuses across America, peaceful marches often ended as violent clashes with the police. Television news reports showing long-haired hippies clobbered by steel-helmeted police made this generational clash real for everyone. To some, the young appeared unruly, self-indulgent, and irresponsible. To others, they were heroic for shaking up the political establishment and addressing large issues such as racism, sexism, postcolonial imperialism, and naked military aggression.

The Student Rebellions in France A similar style of protest emerged in Europe, as student antiwar and anticolonial protests erupted from London to Berlin. But the most powerful student movement was centered in Paris, where, in May 1968, under the inspired leadership of **Daniel Cohn-Bendit**, it made common cause with the French workers. Born in the year the war ended, Cohn-Bendit embodied many of the characteristics of his generation. He came from a German Jewish family that, having fled the Nazis during the war, had returned to West Germany afterward. His background

Bruno Barbey/Magnum Photos

made him painfully aware of the cost of postwar western European reconstruction—the abandonment of moral imperatives for the sake of material well-being. In the impassioned works of Marxist revolutionaries, Cohn-Bendit found inspiration for challenging all that was accepted around him and struggling for social justice in ways that the traditional left seemed to have abandoned. The national strike Cohn-Bendit led put France on hold for almost a month and helped bring down de Gaulle. Similar student protests across Europe evidenced the reengagement of youth in politics, in support of the anticolonial struggle, social justice, the guerrilla fighters in Algeria and Vietnam, and communist leaders such as Mao in China.

Prague Spring The most important political challenge of 1968 came from inside the communist bloc, in Prague. Until the late 1960s, the Czechoslovaks had avoided de-Stalinization because of their success in industrial production. As long as their industrial production worked to the benefit of the Soviet Union, Khrushchev left the Czechoslovaks alone. By the early 1960s, however, the productivity of the Czechoslovak economy was decreasing, and growing numbers of party members called for economic, social, and cultural reforms. **Alexander Dubček** (DOOB-chek), a reformer who had spent the wartime years fighting in the anti-Nazi resistance, convinced the Soviets, responding to pressure from dissidents, to allow him to experiment with liberalizing reforms. For a few brief months during the **Prague Spring**, Dubček attempted to create "socialism with a human face"—abolishing censorship of the press, allowing criticism of the communist leadership, and reviving

workers' councils. He tried to combine social policies that would benefit all citizens with policies that would accelerate economic growth. He even pardoned political prisoners, including religious believers, who had been harshly persecuted in the 1950s.

The reforms in Czechoslovakia proved too radical for the Soviets, who recalled the 1956 Hungarian Uprising, even though the Czechoslovak movement proposed not to end communist rule but to reform it. In August 1968, **Leonid Brezhnev** sent tanks into Czechoslovakia to wipe out all opposition. All Warsaw Pact members save Romania also sent in troops. The military intervention was out of proportion, given the fact that Czechoslovak reformers did not put up armed resistance, and the West came to associate the communist leadership of eastern Europe with this crude military response. The crushing of the Prague Spring brought to a tragic end the era of de-Stalinization and reform. Over the next two decades, while the western European youthful protesters became influential in politics, culture, technology, and commerce, their counterparts in eastern Europe spent years in jail or learned not to challenge the system. A lucky few escaped into the West.

Alexander Dubček (1921–1992) Leader of the Czechoslovak Communist Party during the Prague Spring who initiated liberalizing reforms but was forcibly removed from power.

Prague Spring Short-lived period of liberalization in Czechoslovakia in 1968 that was violently crushed by the Soviets.

Leonid Brezhnev (1906–1982) Soviet leader between 1964 and 1983 who oversaw the reversal of the liberalization efforts of the Khrushchev regime.

CHAPTER Review

Summary

» World War II transformed Europe into a pawn in the struggle between the two superpowers of the Cold War—the United States and the Soviet Union.

» Europe became divided into two camps, East and West.

» The capitalist West became a place for rebuilding democracy and the cradle of the new welfare state.

» In the communist East, dictatorial regimes came to power under Soviet control.

» New multinational organizations such as the UN, NATO, and the Warsaw Pact marked an entirely new international order in which European states were often relegated to the sidelines in the contest between the Soviet Union and the United States.

» European colonial powers engaged in a process of relinquishing power over their non-European territories.

» Decolonization was sometimes peaceful and other times violent, playing a direct role in political stability in Europe.

» The generation born after World War II came to challenge the wisdom of the materialist values of the reconstruction generation, bringing in a new mood of social and political engagement, moral responsibility, and self-sacrifice.

Chronology

1945	Potsdam Conference discusses how to administer postwar Germany [Europe, Americas] Nuremberg Trials begin [Europe]
1946	National Health Service Act ensures health care in Britain [Europe]
1947	India gains independence [Asia] Truman Doctrine commits the United States to fight communism worldwide [Americas] U.S. Marshall Plan offers reconstruction aid to western Europe [Americas, Europe]
1947–1948	Communists take over Romania, Czechoslovakia, Hungary, Poland, East Germany, and Bulgaria [Europe]
1948	Stalin expels Tito from Cominform [Europe] Stalin begins purges of eastern European communist leadership [Europe]
1949	Division of Germany, Konrad Adenauer elected chancellor of West Germany [Europe] Indonesia gains independence [Asia] North Atlantic Treaty Organization (NATO) is founded [Europe, Americas] Committee for Mutual Economic Assistance (CMEA) is founded [Europe] Mao Zedong leads communist takeover in China [Asia]
1950–1953	Korean War ends in stalemate [Asia]
1951	European Coal and Steel Community (ECSC) is established [Europe]
1953	Stalin dies [Europe]
1954	Vietnam gains independence [Asia] Brown vs. Board of Education [Americas]

1954–1962	Algerians win independence from the colonial French government [Africa, Europe]
1955	Warsaw Pact is formed [Europe] West Germany joins NATO [Europe]
1956	Khrushchev delivers Secret Speech criticizing Stalin [Europe] Hungarian Uprising is crushed by Soviets [Europe] Egypt nationalizes the Suez Canal [Africa]
1958	European Economic Community is formed [Europe] French Fourth Republic falls [Europe] De Gaulle succeeds in French presidential coup [Europe]
1961	Soviets construct Berlin Wall [Europe] 1 million Volkswagen Transporters sold [Global]
1962	Second Vatican Council begins [Europe] Cuban Missile Crisis [Americas]
1964	Civil Rights Act [Americas]
1968	Martin Luther King Jr. assassinated [Americas] Prague Spring is crushed by Soviets [Europe] Students and workers create national strike in France [Europe]

Critical Thinking Questions

Take time to pull together all the important information from the chapter by answering the following questions:

The Iron Curtain, 1945–1958

» What international conflicts in the early postwar period paved the way for Europe's division?

» How did international relations change in the first two postwar decades?

The Revival of Western Europe

» By what means was western Europe successful in rebuilding its economic power?

» What were the political consequences of the commitment to economic recovery?

The Restructuring of Eastern Europe

» What were the important steps in the communist takeovers in eastern Europe?

» What was the effect in the region of Stalin's death?

Superpower Conflicts and Colonial Independence Movements, 1945–1968

» What role did the American–Soviet conflict play in the colonial struggles for independence?

» What were the consequences of the liberation movements?

Cultural Developments and Social Protest

» Why was there a moral and spiritual crisis in the 1950s?

» What were the generational divides behind the revolt of the 1960s?

MindTap® is a fully online personalized learning experience built upon Cengage Learning content. MindTap® combines student learning tools—readings, multimedia, activities, and assessments—into a singular Learning Path that guides students through the course and helps students develop the critical thinking, analysis, and communication skills that are essential to academic and professional success.

Chapter Outline

As you read, consider the following questions:

❭ What were the important challenges to democracy in Europe during this period?

❭ What important changes took place in European politics in Europe over this period?

❭ How did relations between Europe and the developing world change during this period?

❭ How did European identities change during this period?

❭ What important new trends in European culture and societies can you identify during this period?

❭ What brought down the communist regimes?

THE 1968 REVOLTS SHOOK the establishment and put traditional political parties on the defensive, forcing them to redefine themselves if they were to speak to the postwar generation. These challenges also pushed governments in the East and West to learn to live with the idea of permanent threat brought about by the Cold War while achieving internal political stability.

Inside western Europe, the political challenges of the 1970s and 1980s came not from traditional political organizations but rather from radical new political formations, such as the Greens, feminists, and antinuclear activists. These groups did not propose choosing between capitalism and communism but rather moving beyond the Cold War divide and recognizing the greater problems that threatened the well-being of all people, from nuclear obliteration to gender inequality.

The Berlin Wall

The wall erected in 1961 to separate West and East Berlin became a symbol of the Cold War. When fearless citizens from communist East Germany climbed on the wall and began to dismantle it in October 1989, everyone around the world and especially in other communist bloc countries understood they were witnessing the end of Soviet hegemony in eastern Europe and possibly the end of the Cold War. Images like this emboldened people in Hungary, Czechoslovakia, Romania, and Bulgaria to speak and act against their own rulers. By January 1990, all communist regimes in eastern Europe, save for Yugoslavia, fell from power. Thomas Kienzie/AP Images

An economic crisis that started with the oil embargo of 1973 and continued into the 1980s complicated the political choices of western Europeans, who had to contend with economic depression, unemployment, inflation, and a severe slowdown of the postwar "economic miracle." The European Community also became involved in unprecedented global economic connections. These changes had a wide-ranging impact beyond Europe's borders in many postcolonial states and especially in the Middle East.

The economic crisis of the 1970s also brought about radical change in eastern Europe and the Soviet Union. Governments looked for new markets and took advantage of a relaxation of tensions to increase trade. People in the communist bloc started to get a taste of consumer goods through popular culture, travel, and even access to coveted Western status symbols, like blue jeans. The same economic crisis finally forced Soviet leader Mikhail Gorbachev to acknowledge that the Soviet Union was financially unable to maintain its hold in eastern Europe and to concede that each state in the bloc should follow its own path. East German citizens were among the first to understand this change and they reacted by dismantling the Berlin Wall, the single most powerful symbol of the East–West divide. Within three years, all eastern European communist regimes had fallen like a house of cards, and the Soviet Union itself had disappeared, ending the communist experiment initiated by revolution in 1917.

29-1 Politics in Western Europe

» What role did the relaxation of international tensions play in western Europe?

» How did political parties change in the 1970s and 1980s?

In the 1970s, tensions between western and eastern Europe relaxed, and governments began to consider issues on which they could cooperate, such as human rights initiatives. At the same time, the West faced important internal challenges, such as an energy crisis after 1973 and the emergence of radical terrorist groups from Northern Ireland to Italy. Leftist parties were less able to deal with these problems than their center-right counterparts, who gained political control in many places by 1980. Yet, especially in southern Europe and in France, left-wing parties held the power throughout the 1980s. The Common Market expanded but was also burdened by the weaker new members that joined in this decade (see Map 29.1).

29-1a Relaxed Tensions and Renewed Cooperation

The 1968 protests challenged western European parties to define a new kind of politics in which people could participate more directly and be counted. At the same time, the dominant presence of the two superpowers raised questions of European autonomy in international relations, especially in Europe. These two concerns combined to produce two new directions in European politics: a focus on internal stability and a stabilization of international relations. Relations with postcolonial states continued to be dominated, however, by the economic superiority of the European powers and clientelism in both political and economic relations, rendering indigenous elites internally weak and dependent on international support.

détente (in French, "release from tension") Easing of political relations between the Soviet Union and the United States in the 1970s.

Antiballistic Missile Treaty Treaty signed in 1972 by the Soviet Union and the United States reducing their nuclear arsenals.

Willy Brandt (1913–1992) West German chancellor from 1969 to 1974, Social Democrat, and architect of détente.

Détente In the United States, the violent protests of 1968 helped secure the victory of a Republican law-and-order presidential candidate, Richard Nixon. Once defeated by the charismatic John F. Kennedy, Nixon returned to politics by casting himself as a representative of stability and reason. With his secretary of state, Henry Kissinger, Nixon engineered a major shift in international politics, the policy of **détente** (DAY-tahnt). From reconsidering the Vietnam War to opening relations with communist China, Nixon led the way toward relaxing the tough stance that had defined relations between the democratic and communist blocs in the previous decades. He also sought to reengage the United States in Europe by building bridges of communication across the East–West divide. Through contributions to the UN and other organizations, such as Planned Parenthood International, the United States supported development policies around the world that favored slowing down demographic growth among nonwhite populations as the price for investing in the modernization of those economies. In places like India, this led to the sterilization of millions of men and women, done with the knowledge of the Indian political elites. Those subjected to these policies were often misinformed about the benefits and costs of this procedure.

By the end of the 1960s, not only Nixon but also his Soviet counterpart Leonid Brezhnev and many politicians in western Europe realized that the Cold War had achieved a balance of power and military escalation was unlikely. An important departure in the 1970s was the decision by Nixon and Brezhnev to limit their military buildups, evident in the **Antiballistic Missile Treaty** (1972). In agreeing to limit their antiballistic missile systems and put a cap on military spending, the Americans and Soviets conceded that military parity was sufficient for both to feel secure and that to continue spending would in fact increase the possibility of conflict, especially nuclear war. This kind of self-limiting thinking was a complete reversal from the military planning of the late 1940s and represented a major step toward a more peaceful international environment.

West Germany's Eastern Politics No longer content to be pawns in the superpower game, European political leaders played an active, even pioneering, role in this process. In West Germany, Chancellor **Willy Brandt** initiated a policy of normalizing relations with East Germany and, years before Nixon and Brezhnev, worked on a policy of reconciliation between the West and the East. His accession to power in 1969 signaled a momentous change in West Germany: It was the first time since the 1920s that the Social Democrats were in power. Brandt had an unimpeachable past. He had been a Social Democrat since the age of seventeen, and in 1933, when the Gestapo tried to arrest him, he fled to Scandinavia, where he became an outspoken journalist and antifascist activist until the end of the Third Reich. He saw these years not as a cowardly flight but rather as "a chance to serve the 'Other Germany,' which did not resign itself submissively to enslavement."

Expansion of European Community

- Original members, 1967
- New members, 1973
- New member, 1981
- New members, 1986
- Members of CMEA

Map 29.1 **From European Community to European Union** In the 1970s and 1980s, the European Community became a source for European integration in economic matters and a springboard for cultural change toward a shared European identity that stood for democratic values, greater tolerance, and decreased nationalist tensions.

1. Who were the original members of the Common Market?
2. How much did it grow before 1989?
3. How large a part of the European continent did the Common Market represent in comparison to countries in the CMEA?
4. How does the change in the map of the Common Market suggest changes in the actions and sense of identity of the European Community?

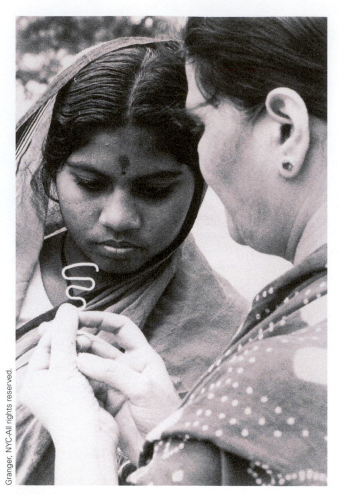

Birth Control in India

With financial support from the UN and Planned Parenthood International, millions of Indian men and women received access to birth control. The Intrauterine Device (IUD) depicted here was offered less frequently than vasectomies for men and tubal ligation for women. Many of those individuals were not properly educated about the effects of the procedures and were bribed to accept them through gifts such as transistor radios.

In the Bundestag, which had replaced the Reichstag as West Germany's parliament, Brandt made his mark as a defender of democracy and socialism against communist dictatorship. He was the mayor of West Berlin when the first bricks in the Berlin Wall went up in August 1961. Finding that the contest between the superpowers made him powerless to attend to the well-being of ordinary Germans, he took on a pragmatic view of Cold War politics. By 1969, when he was elected chancellor, he had become the foremost

Ostpolitik (in German, "eastern politics") West German policy of reconciliation with the communist East.

Conference on Security and Cooperation in Europe Meeting of all European states, the United States, and Canada in 1972–1975 to rethink East–West relations.

spokesman of **Ostpolitik**, the policy of taking small, steady steps toward normalizing relations with East Germany and, by extension, serving as a model for better relations between the East and West in Europe. He was a pioneer in the détente shift in international relations.

Brandt successfully cultivated an international image acceptable to both the United States and the Soviet Union and, at the same time, independent of their whims. Though his politics were far to the left of those of the Christian Democrat Konrad Adenauer, Brandt appeared to Nixon as a peaceful and loyal ally and to Brezhnev as a reasonable representative of socialism.

Brandt proceeded to make good on his promise to open up relations with the East by traveling to Moscow and signing an important nonaggression pact with the Soviets, which paved the way to recognizing the border between East and West Germany in 1972. This action of legitimating the post–1945 rearrangement of European states was, in fact, the final peace treaty of World War II. And this time Europeans themselves acted on their own behalf rather than at the beckoning of the superpowers, as had been the case in 1945. Brandt also normalized relations with other eastern European countries, most prominently Poland. Possibly the most famous of his gestures of reconciliation was his visit to Warsaw in 1970, where he knelt before the memorial to the Warsaw Ghetto heroes and begged the forgiveness of the Polish nation for the horrors committed by the Third Reich. Brandt's public career was crowned by the Nobel Peace Prize, which he received in 1971 for his leadership role in East–West relations.

If Ostpolitik and détente meant relaxation, tolerance, and the willingness to sit down at the negotiating table, they also encouraged greater scrutiny and manipulation of the flow of information between East and West. It was a gamble on both sides, and it proved very costly for Brandt. A few dramatic cases of Soviet agents in West Germany caught with important German secrets encouraged the perception that western leaders who promoted détente were not watchful and tough enough on communist threats from over the wall. Brandt became the victim of one such scandal. Although he had not been personally responsible for the actions of a Soviet spy who had infiltrated his administration, Brandt lost legitimacy at home and finally resigned in 1974. But the policy of détente continued in the hands of other European leaders and with the support of U.S. Presidents Gerald Ford and Jimmy Carter.

Stability and Human Rights Brandt's policy of opening up trade with the East in order to improve the quality of life under communism provided an important starting point for a broader international process of European cooperation, and this gave birth to the **Conference on Security and Cooperation in Europe**. The conference represented the first attempt

Willy Brandt

In a symbolic gesture, in December 1970 West German Chancellor Willy Brandt knelt before the Warsaw Ghetto Uprising memorial, asking forgiveness from the Polish people for the violence of the Nazi regime. The gesture greatly improved West German–Polish relations and helped decrease East–West tensions generally in the 1970s.

» *What does his demeanor and facial expressions in this photograph communicate?*

to broadly rethink European international relations not only in terms of the Cold War superpower contest, but also in terms of the interests and needs of the European states. All European states participated, as well as the United States and Canada. The process itself, together with the **Helsinki Final Act** (1975) it generated, created a new forum for collaboration between East and West, especially in the area of human rights. All signatories recognized existing European borders and committed themselves to protecting their citizens' human rights, including freedom of religion, free speech, freedom to move or travel, and the right to due process. The Final Act became a guiding principle for the Carter administration's foreign policy not just in Europe, but throughout the world. For Europeans, it represented a new basis for international relations that went beyond the political interests and ideologies of the United States and the Soviet Union.

The conference also gave rise to institutions for implementing these agreements. **Helsinki Watch** became one of the important **nongovernmental organizations (NGOs)** reporting on human rights violations throughout the world. As Helsinki Watch and other NGOs worked with western governments to guide the implementation of the Final Act, they became new players in international relations. Often lobbying on behalf of the powerless, they also worked with western governments to expose abuses by regimes that did not acknowledge their violations of basic human rights and brought international pressure on them. The United States, for instance, offered reduced tariffs to eastern European countries that abided by the provisions of Helsinki and threatened to cut off economic benefits to regimes with human rights abuses.

29-1b Security and Economic Challenges from the Middle East

As tensions across the East–West divide relaxed, European countries faced new security and economic challenges from the Middle East. In October 1973, in alliance with Syria, Egyptian President **Anwar el-Sadat** attacked Israel, to regain territories lost in the **Six-Day War** (1967). The **Yom Kippur War** grew in complexity as Arab states lent support and troops to Egypt, while Israel enlisted the support of the United States and western Europe.

Helsinki Final Act Accord signed in 1975 by all European states that introduced human rights as a principle in international relations.

Helsinki Watch Nongovernmental organization created to oversee the implementation of the Helsinki Final Act's human rights provisions.

nongovernmental organization (NGO) Voluntary nonprofit organization often focused on humanitarian issues.

Anwar el-Sadat (1918–1981) President of Egypt who contributed to the rise of Arab nationalism in the 1970s.

Six-Day War War fought in 1967 between Israel and its Arab neighbors Egypt, Jordan, and Syria; won by Israel.

Yom Kippur War War in 1973 between Egypt and Israel over the Sinai Peninsula and Golan Heights, which had been conquered by Israel in 1967; won by Israel.

CONNECTIONS: The territorial disputes that rose out of these wars have continued to plague peace in the Middle East until today. In what has become known as the "occupied territories," Israel continues to expand settlements even as the Palestinian population and international community, including the UN, protests. Arab nationalism has incorporated hatred of Israel and anti-Semitism as core features since that period. (See Map 30.3 Israel-Palestine since 1948.)

The Oil Crisis Arab states, viewing western support of Israel as a conspiracy against Egypt's legitimate reconquest of territories Israel had seized in 1967, retaliated through an **oil embargo** that lasted until March 1974. The embargo sent the world economy into a decade-long crisis. The immediate effect was soaring oil prices, which generated a rise in the price of virtually all products. In addition, most European states were unable to provide sufficient energy resources for their economies. Some went so far as to ration the use of oil and other energy resources. In the United States, the government introduced unprecedented supply and price regulations.

The energy crisis signaled two important long-term trends in Europe and elsewhere. Economic processes were becoming increasingly **globalized**, so it was no longer possible for the West to be economically self-sufficient. And western Europeans, with only meager internal oil resources, resolved to deal with the crisis by looking into alternative energy resources, from hydroelectric to wind and nuclear. Overall, the energy crisis induced greater cooperation among members of the Common Market in finding alternative fuels and markets that would buffer them from fluctuations in the global economy. During the oil crisis, the Common Market provided important benefits to its members, such as access to nuclear power and coal, but its success was also measured by its general prosperity and growth, as Brandt had been able to reconcile the French to the idea of allowing Great Britain to join in the very year of the oil embargo.

oil embargo (1973–1974) Refusal by Arab petroleum-exporting countries to ship petroleum to countries that had supported Israel in the Yom Kippur War.

globalization Increasing global connections among national and international economic and cultural forces, starting in the 1970s.

European Monetary Union Unification in 1990–1999 of the fiscal policies of European community members, with the goal of creating a single currency.

Iranian Revolution Nationalist uprising in 1977 that ousted the Iranian monarchy and destabilized the global oil supply.

Afghanistan invasion Military invasion by Soviet Union in 1979 to prevent the spread of Muslim fundamentalism to the Soviet republics in Central Asia.

Member countries continued to negotiate and move forward toward a **European Monetary Union**. But in 1979, a second oil crisis brought about by the 1977 **Iranian Revolution**, together with a spike in the value of the dollar, made European currencies more vulnerable on the international markets. As European economies slowed down, further discussions of the monetary union ended. The strongest western European economies—the German and the British—turned inward to solve their problems with rising unemployment and low economic performance instead of pursuing further collaboration with the Common Market.

The End of Détente Overall, by 1979, the era of détente was ending. There were some important changes—the stabilization of European borders and recognition of human rights as an important component of international politics. Yet, trust did not catch hold, and ideologues on both sides of the Cold War skillfully exploited the fears of average voters about loss of stability. In addition, the Soviets changed their international stance significantly. On Christmas Eve 1979, they invaded Afghanistan. The reason for this intervention seems to have been the fear of the spread of Islamic fundamentalism from Afghanistan into Soviet-controlled Central Asian territories. But the United States read the **Afghanistan invasion** as a challenge to the balance of power in the Persian Gulf, a region to which it had become vulnerable since the 1973 oil embargo. The Soviet occupation also threatened the regional interests of Pakistan, a U.S. ally. The Americans reacted swiftly and sent military help to the Islamic Afghan rebels who opposed the Soviets.

CONNECTIONS: The rebels the United States funded saw themselves engaged in a jihad against the modernizing, secularizing regime imposed by the Soviets. The military and financial support they continued to receive from the United States for over a decade helped sustain their ambitions and fueled greater factionalization in the Afghan Civil War (1996–2001). When the Taliban took over in 2000, it was against the warring factions that the United States had sustained.

Thus, a significant change in U.S. relations with the Soviet Union and western Europe took place in the 1980s. American voters viewed Carter's stance on human rights and his response to the Iranian Revolution as weak, and they put Ronald Reagan, an unabashed hawk in international relations, in the White House. The United States shifted toward a renewed military buildup against the Soviet Union, which responded with similar moves. Until 1985, relations between the two superpowers remained extremely tense. NATO became an important institution for rallying western Europe support behind Reagan's vision of military buildup as the guarantee for peace, with Britain as the most outspoken ally. Other Europeans saw themselves cast again as second-tier participants in the superpower contest.

Yet, despite such challenges, western European states moved along toward European integration. The major successes of the 1980s were Greece, Portugal, and Spain, which quietly abandoned authoritarian rule between 1970 and 1975 and in the 1980s were welcomed into the Common Market. By this time, vestiges of the old dictatorships were largely gone in the politics of these countries, while their economies began to flourish and a culture of **pluralism** also developed. Their Common Market membership enhanced political stability in the face of continued challenges from extremist movements.

29-1c The Transformation of the Left

In the 1970s and 1980s, domestic politics in western Europe saw an ebb and flow among traditional parties, but two trends were about to transform them. First, traditional politics seemed to draw less voter support. As 1968 had shown, average citizens were less interested in what politicians had to offer through the regular channels of political platforms and elections. Second, new types of movements—grassroots politics and radical, secret terrorist organizations—attracted more followers.

Crisis in Northern Ireland In Britain, where the Labour Party had come to power in 1973, the oil crisis of that same year undermined economic prosperity. Unemployment stayed high, the economy did not bounce back, and the pound remained weak. When the party proved incapable of effective solutions, it lost power in 1979.

The Labour Party also lost support because of its inability to deal with the rise of protests in Northern Ireland. In the late 1960s, the **Northern Ireland Civil Rights** Association sponsored peaceful street protests and began documenting the abuses of the **Unionist** government against Catholics. The government's violent crackdown led to actions by the Irish Republican Army (IRA) that brought the level of violence to unprecedented heights. Car bombings in Protestant communities and assassinations of government loyalists became staple activities of this group. The situation in Ireland soon became a permanent crisis in British politics, with both British and Irish nationalists unwilling to compromise. Instead, violence and terrorism became a way of life for the next generation—both Protestants and Catholics.

In an era of rapid secularization elsewhere in Europe, the people of Ireland went in a different direction, with religious identity as a rallying point. Religious spaces, rituals, and practices became nationalist and overtly political. The voice of religious authorities on these divisions mattered less than the use of religious language by politicians and terrorists. Friendships across this harsh divide became dangerous, shunned by both communities, even though children grew up speaking the same language and playing the same games.

Communism and Terrorism in Italy In Italy, the communists made important gains in the early 1970s. The recovery of the Communist Party after the 1956 and 1968 uprisings in Hungary and Czechoslovakia was due to the ability of the Italian communists to represent their party as humane. Under **Palmiro Togliatti**, Italian communism succeeded in becoming both a nationalist movement, highlighting the "Italian way," and also a party consistently committed to social justice. For most of the 1970s, the Communists and Christian Democrats shared power and succeeded in preserving stability and prosperity.

Yet, a parallel development, prompted by grassroots dissatisfaction with these political compromises, gave rise to terrorist movements on both the left and right. By 1978, the **Red Brigades**, a radical left-wing communist terrorist organization, regularly staged kidnappings and other terrorist attacks, such as bombings. Their most prominent action was the 1978 murder of **Aldo Moro**, who had been instrumental in the left-center-right compromise. Eager to blame each other for the violence, the left and right broke off their alliance.

The nationalist terrorist movement in Northern Ireland and the communist terrorist movement in Italy were but two examples of a more general trend in Europe. 1968 had opened a new era of grassroots politics, of taking ideas to the streets and using new technologies, especially television, to force action and change outside parliamentary debate, legislation, and election. These terrorist movements were not widespread; most were small, secret organizations that could not operate on a large scale. But, in the

pluralism State of society in which diverse groups can participate while maintaining their interests and traditions.

Northern Ireland Civil Rights Association Organization started in the late 1960s by Northern Ireland Catholics to record abuses by the Unionist government.

Unionists Representatives of the British government in Northern Ireland who favored preserving the union with Great Britain.

Palmiro Togliatti (1893–1964) Italian Communist Party leader who devised a compromise with the Christian Democrats that brought stability to the government.

Red Brigades Radical communist group in Italy that led a campaign of terrorist actions from street and car bombings to kidnappings.

Aldo Moro (1916–1978) Italian Christian Democratic politician who was instrumental in the compromise with the Italian Communist Party.

beginning at least, they did resonate with a broader population. The IRA specifically used dissatisfaction among the Irish in general to strike against established political institutions.

Stability in France In France, however, traditional left-wing governments dominated the 1980s. In 1983, **François Mitterrand** gained power and remained president of France for two terms, the first socialist head of government since Léon Blum in 1936. But Mitterrand was moderate and continued many policies of his center-right predecessor, **Valéry Giscard d'Estaing** (val-er-EE zhis-CAR de-STAHNG). After attempting to nationalize important financial institutions and initiate an increase in wages and social benefits, Mitterrand found such policies ineffective in addressing larger problems such as trade deficits and the devaluation of the franc. Within a year, his government returned to many of the previous center-right policies. Yet, Mitterrand improved some social services and welfare measures, such as shorter working hours and increased pension benefits.

Spain and Greece also saw the emergence of socialist governments. The Spanish Socialist Workers' Party secured both stability and steady economic growth, despite repeated challenges from the right. King **Juan Carlos I** played an important role in restraining the military establishment against the democratic left. The financial commitment of the European Community was also important in this process.

29.1d The Antinuclear and Environmental Movements

The 1968 protests expressed opposition to the colonial wars, and as the Vietnam War continued into the 1970s, the peace movement also grew. Many involved in these movements saw themselves standing outside the division between capitalism and communism; they viewed themselves as advocates of a world free of the threat of war and of the arms race that dominated U.S.-Soviet relations. They hailed the Antiballistic Missile Treaty of 1972 as a victory and committed themselves to continuing reductions of the

François Mitterrand (1916–1996) French president from 1982 to 1994, first socialist French president of the postwar era.

Valéry Giscard d'Estaing (1926–) French president from 1974 until 1982 who pursued centrist policies supporting business interests and social welfare services.

Juan Carlos I (r. 1975–) King of Spain who helped smooth the transition from the authoritarian Franco regime to a democratic pluralist government.

Campaign for Nuclear Disarmament Antinuclear British organization founded in the 1950s that became a leader in the peace movement of the 1970s and 1980s.

Table 29.1	Antinuclear Protests
1971	Demonstrations against nuclear power plants in France and Germany
1972	Antiballistic Missile Treaty
1978	UN first special session on disarmament
1981	Millions of western Europeans participate in antinuclear street protests
1981–1991	Women's protest at Greenham Common military base in England
1983	Antinuclear Green Party wins twenty-seven seats in West German parliament
March 1983	U.S. Strategic Defense Initiative announced; Relations with Soviet Union reach all-time low
October 1983	Protests of millions in western Europe against U.S. intermediate-range nuclear force (INF) deployments
1983–1984	Over forty thousand women resume protests at Greenham
1987	Reagan and Gorbachev sign intermediate-range nuclear force treaty
May 1991	Last U.S. cruise missile leaves Greenham Common military base, site of a decade of antinuclear protests organized by women

nuclear arsenal. Yet, even as the energy crisis of the early 1970s made nuclear power attractive to some, fears of a nuclear disaster gained new dimensions. Table 29.1 summarizes antinuclear protests during this period.

The antiwar and antinuclear/environmental movements were closely connected and drew support from a wide range of scientists, student activists, housewives, and people of any or no political persuasion. In Britain, the **Campaign for Nuclear Disarmament**, founded in the 1950s, became the leading organization of the antinuclear movement. It served as a political lobbying force and also a link for people beyond national boundaries, ideologies, and religious beliefs. Other environmental NGOs built communities on an ethic of caring that crossed national borders and promoted a new global identity.

The Press Association (PA Photos)

Women's Peace Camp

For ten years, thousands of women kept a continuous presence at the Greenham Common military base west of London. They camped, held vigils, and engaged in various other forms of protest to signal their commitment to creating a nuclear-free Britain.

❯❯ *What does this image suggest about the attitudes and relationships of these protesters?*

Free from the adversities of the ballot box, these NGOs often acted swiftly and also across borders, especially in moments of crisis.

Rise of Environmental Parties The same concern for environmental issues gave birth to a new left-wing party in Germany, the **Green Party**. The party grew from small local groups that lobbied on behalf of ecological concerns starting in the early 1970s and attracted voters dissatisfied with the social and environmental policies of the traditional left. This trend was not exclusive to West Germany, but it developed faster and had broader appeal there, in part because of the committed sense of citizenship that was particular to post-1945 German political culture. In the 1980s, the Greens remained a marginal presence in the Bundestag but made steady gains in local politics. Throughout this period, they continued to work closely with local environmental NGOs in a new blend of community activism and parliamentary politics.

Popular Protests Against Nuclear Weapons After 1981, as the Reagan administration resumed its military buildup in Europe, the antinuclear movement offered increased resistance. Though the British government welcomed the American missiles, the popular support of the generation who had welcomed the Americans as liberators during World War II was almost gone. Their sons and daughters, taking security and prosperity as a given, opposed nuclear threat of any sort—from West or East. Thus, when the Reagan administration announced the deployment of new Pershing II intermediate-range missiles on U.S. bases in western Europe, almost one million people marched in Bonn, London, and Rome in opposition; a month later, half a million protesters gathered in Amsterdam. These protests continued throughout the 1980s, most famously at the **Greenham Common** military base, where an all-woman camp established in 1981 continued until 1991,

Green Party West German party founded by antinuclear and environmental activists in 1979.

Greenham Common Military air base in England that became the site of a long-standing antinuclear protest from 1981 to 1991.

when the last nuclear missiles were removed from the site.

Nuclear Disaster and Its Consequences In April 1986, an explosion at a nuclear power station in **Chernobyl**, in Soviet Ukraine, forced all Europeans to face the reality of environmental nuclear disaster. Though the details were at first suppressed by the Soviet leader, **Mikhail Gorbachev** (mi-KYLE gore-bah-TCHYOV), the effects were so severe and widespread that Chernobyl became an instant symbol of the dangers of nuclear power. More than thirty thousand square miles of land were contaminated and, according to a 1994 study, almost five million people in the region were affected. In western Europe, environmental pressure groups forced the closing of nuclear power plants: France, which had been a leading producer of nuclear energy, had to retool its energy sources. By the end of the 1980s, concerns over the possibility of nuclear disaster had breached political divisions between East and West to become a common cause across Europe.

29-1e The New Conservatism

In the 1980s, with the traditional left losing support and new grassroots movements still politically underdeveloped, West German and British parliaments were dominated by conservative regimes. In West Germany, the Christian Democrats, led by **Helmut Kohl**, assumed control in 1982. As chancellor, Kohl continued the policies of Ostpolitik and the effort to change political culture in Germany. German laws, culture, and educational policies openly acknowledged and discussed the atrocities of the Third Reich and worked to prevent any recurrence. More than any other European state, Germany was quick to condemn extremism and avoid aggression. Kohl also oversaw a tremendous economic recovery of the country that made Germany the backbone of the Common Market, producing one-third of its exports in the 1980s.

The Iron Lady In Britain, the electorate brought back the Conservatives in 1979 under the leadership of **Margaret Thatcher**, the first woman prime minister of

Reagan Presidential Library

Reagan and Thatcher

British Prime Minister Margaret Thatcher and U.S. President Ronald Reagan, here at the presidential retreat Camp David in 1986, are generally considered the two staunchest defenders of a tough policy of nonnegotiation with the Soviet Union during the 1980s.

» *How would you describe the relationship between the two leaders, as depicted here?*

Britain. She dominated politics throughout the 1980s, orchestrating a decisive shift in foreign and domestic politics. Thatcher came to be known as the Iron Lady for her resolute support for the Reagan administration's rearmament policies and for her stiff refusal to consider the social welfare costs of her government's support for business and industry. Whether people admired or despised her, Thatcher articulated a clear new path for conservative politics. Her years in power and her policies have reshaped the relationship between the traditional left and right, making Thatcherism an important force in contemporary politics even today. The focus on individual freedoms rather than social programs and on encouraging business rather than favoring labor unions became the trademarks of this movement.

As a woman, Thatcher was an improbable leader of the Conservatives, a party in which women were

---

Chernobyl City in Soviet Ukraine where the greatest nuclear disaster to date occurred in April 1986, resulting in widespread nuclear contamination.

Mikhail Gorbachev (1931–) Soviet leader between 1985 and 1991 whose reforms paved the way to the fall of communism in 1991.

Helmut Kohl (1930–) Christian Democratic chancellor of West Germany from 1982 to 1998 who continued Ostpolitik.

Margaret Thatcher (1925–2013) First female British prime minister who led the Conservative government between 1980 and 1992.

underrepresented and that generally lined up with areas of political and economic life that were dominated by men—from the armaments industry to the landed aristocracy. Most western European women who entered politics after World War II gravitated to left-wing parties, which tended to have woman-friendly positions on issues such as child care, health care, education, and birth control. But Thatcher was not one to fit any particular cliché of a female politician, and she followed her own path. Born in 1925, she became interested in politics as a chemistry student at Oxford. In 1953, as a brand-new mother of twins, she also passed the bar and soon returned to work as a tax specialist. After she won a seat in Parliament at age thirty-four, she fully dedicated her public life to working for the Conservatives. She served in several cabinets in the 1960s and in the 1970s drew attention as a leader of the Conservative opposition by condemning détente and supporting rearmament: "The men in the Soviet Politburo put guns before butter," she quipped, "while we put just about everything before guns."

Thatcher and Militarism These policy stands won her the "Iron Lady" nickname, and she proceeded to make good on it in the 1980s. In foreign policy, she reinvented the "special friendship" with the United States that still defines the relationship between the two countries. She vocally supported Reagan's nuclear rearmament policies and gladly offered British military bases for stationing U.S. nuclear missiles. No other European state took such a friendly view of Reagan's policies toward the Soviet Union; her aim was to restore Britain's international position as a partner with the United States in the Cold War.

Thatcher was unapologetically imperialistic, opposing nationalist movements in Wales and Scotland, and offered symbolic victories that drew even the working classes to support her government. Britain's easy victory in the 1982 **Falklands War** helped solidify her reputation. The British Navy came out in full force to confront Argentina's takeover of the tiny Falkland/Malvinas Islands. The conflict lasted only a few weeks, but it inflicted serious casualties on the Argentineans while yielding a victory for Britain that stirred those nostalgic for empire. For many in Britain, disaffected by dull leaders and ineffective government, Thatcher seemed to have commanded respect, regardless of party.

Lessening Government Role in the Economy In domestic politics, Thatcher deregulated communications and energy industries and refused to bow to trade unions. The new climate helped generate economic growth, but also brought higher unemployment rates and diminished spending on social programs. Thatcher favored limiting state interference in social services provided by private businesses. Thus, while she retained national health care, she allowed private providers greater freedom. The aim was no longer to serve all populations, especially the poorest, but to harmonize the well-being of private businesses with access to these services.

Although Thatcher did continue funding for public education, her careful pulling back from the universal commitments to social welfare of postwar governments represented an important and permanent departure. She had her share of opponents among British politicians and the public, but her policies of favoring the free market and diminishing state services were never fully reversed after she lost power. Thatcherism became a political hallmark of the late twentieth century.

29-2 Social Change in the West

» **How did western European societies change during this period?**

» **How did western European identities alter?**

Despite growing prosperity and opportunities for social advancement in western Europe, the years after 1968 saw challenges from various groups. Women demanded greater social, political, and economic power. Demographic change spurred social change as birthrates decreased and working populations aged. Newly arrived immigrants and guest workers tested the ability of western governments to deliver the same social services to all those who lived and worked in their countries.

29-2a The Feminist Revolution

By 1970, European women had made dramatic gains in many areas. More women were employed outside the home and received college degrees than ever before. Yet, their economic opportunities were more limited than those of men, their wages were significantly lower (by about one-third), and they were still expected to be primarily wives and mothers. A woman with a college degree in business would more likely become a secretary than a manager. Left-wing parties, which advocated economic and social equality, remained unsympathetic to glaring gender inequalities in politics and the workplace. They were willing to offer social assistance to workers but not to consider housework as labor that was entitled to respect and protection.

Falklands War (1982) Conflict won by Great Britain against Argentina over a small archipelago off Argentina, the Falkland/Malvinas Islands.

The Personal Is Political Even in left-wing movements, women were relegated to secondary roles—making signs, typing, and making coffee—behind the masculine façade of the protests. Disillusioned, many women left these movements and formed their own, vowing to promote gender equality in structures that rejected the male patriarchal model. "The personal is political" was the motto of this feminist movement, which focused primarily on the social and economic empowerment of women rather than their relationship to men. Celebrating women's identities as women and defining them as worthy of public concern was at the heart of this new movement. Thus, giving birth was viewed not as a personal and private event but as a unique female experience with deep social, emotional, and political implications for the whole community. Feminists also addressed the problem of "compulsory heterosexuality." Lesbian activism developed during this period as a form of celebrating women's identities unencumbered by relations with men.

Difference and Equality The most prominent intellectual figure of the women's movement in Europe, **Simone de Beauvoir**, defined the struggle for women's liberation as an individual quest to gain respect for differences. Her study of women's cultural and psychological conditioning, *The Second Sex* (1949), became an important manifesto for European feminists, who focused especially on family issues. They sought the right to divorce, access to birth control (including abortion), and childcare for working mothers. This emphasis was in contrast to American feminists, who also embraced these issues but who generally focused less on difference and complementarity than on equality in economic power and in politics. American feminists, for example, demanded "equal pay for equal work" and full representation in government, business, sports, and education.

New Social Rights: Divorce and Birth Control De Beauvoir herself had not been interested in taking a public stance on women's issues until 1971, when she signed the **Manifesto of the 343**, acknowledging that she had had an abortion. Since abortion was a crime in France, signing this document was an act of civil disobedience and became a springboard for securing women's access to birth control. Abortion was legalized three years later, one year after it was also decriminalized in the United States. Other Catholic countries followed suit—Italy in 1978 and Spain in 1985—with women's groups applying the pressure. In 1990, Belgium became the last western European country to decriminalize abortion.

Catholic countries also eventually legalized divorce. Left-wing governments in Italy (1974) and Spain (1981) gave in to grassroots pressure in which women played a major role. Women were only loosely organized in informal networks that focused mostly on coping with women's burdens. But as more women became educated and understood their burdens as discriminatory treatment that could be changed, they started to act differently in their daily lives. They applied pressure to the Italian government by marching in the streets, a traditional form of protest; but they also withheld household "services" such as cooking and cleaning. These methods made the point, as 60 percent of Italians came to support legalization of divorce in this most Catholic of western European states.

Women's actions on behalf of abortion and divorce had broad effects throughout society. The birthrate dropped significantly, and marriage patterns changed. Couples married later and became more committed to long-term monogamous relationships than in the past. Overall, women were now able to lead freer lives, with more economic and social choices than ever before.

Finding Their Own Political Parties But in traditional politics, women remained marginal. The percentage of women in elected national offices remained disproportionately low, at 5 to 10 percent, with a slightly higher level in local government. Women tended to be appointed to "feminized" government positions—in social services, education, public health, or the arts. At the same time, however, Thatcher's position in Britain, though she represented a conservative party and did not encourage female participation in politics, proved an important milestone toward redefining women's politics.

In leftist parties, women did assume leadership positions. **Petra Kelly**, of West Germany's Green Party, was elected to a seat in the Bundestag in 1983, and she set new directions. At age thirty-six, she was younger than most other members. She focused on environmental safety and antinuclear activism as unifying concerns, "beyond left and right." She was a feminist without making feminism the center of her political struggle. Her strong belief in the need for women's equality was shaped by her experience of growing up in the United States in the 1960s, and she was quick to point out gender biases in the Green movement itself. Kelly was part of a generation that

---

Simone de Beauvoir (1908–1986) French philosopher and author of *The Second Sex* (1949), a central text of the second-wave feminist movement.

Manifesto of the 343 Manifesto in support of legalizing abortion in France, signed in 1971 by 343 Frenchwomen who acknowledged they had had illegal abortions.

Petra Kelly (1947–1992) West German feminist who helped found the Green Party and became the first Green Party member to serve in the West German Bundestag.

Udo Weitz/AP Photo

Petra Kelly

Petra Kelly, the first Green Party candidate elected to the West German Bundestag, combined street activism and legislative work on behalf of her deeply held ecologist, pacifist, and feminist beliefs.

》 *How does Kelly appear in comparison to Margaret Thatcher?*

took gender equality as a given and simply acted accordingly.

29-2b New Populations

Between 1960 and 1990, the natural population growth in European Community states declined by three-quarters. The birthrate decreased dramatically everywhere in western Europe but most remarkably in Catholic countries that legalized abortion during this period. In Spain, for example, the birthrate dropped from 21.5 per thousand in 1960 to 10.3 per thousand in 1990. The downturn in the birthrate raised concerns about a shrinking workforce. At the same time, the number of elderly people entitled to retirement benefits was growing. The average age expectancy for western European men in 1980 was 71 and for women 77, while retirement ages averaged 60 for men and 55 for women. Thus, western European states needed to provide retirement and health care benefits for an average of twelve years for each retired person. Overall, it seemed that the number of people contributing to the workforce was going down while the number of those entitled to social services was rising.

Guest Workers To fill needs in the labor force, western European governments opened up their borders to **guest workers** and immigrants. People with skills for critical economic needs were permitted to live temporarily in European Community states as guest workers. The needs most often cited were for low-paying, menial jobs, such as domestic service and janitorial work, and for hard labor in dangerous settings. The migrants had the right to work. They had to pay taxes, but they did not have the right to apply for permanent residency, nor did they have the same social rights as citizens. Health care, education, pensions, and vacations were not guaranteed to guest workers. Nor was there any attempt to acculturate them to the language and customs of the host country. Guest workers remained on the margins of their host societies.

New Muslim Populations Yet, foreign nationals reshaped the demographic profile of western Europe. Policies encouraged immigration from the old colonies in Asia, Africa, and the West Indies, and large numbers of Muslims came to work in Germany, the Netherlands, Denmark, Spain, France, and Britain. At first, guest workers seemed largely invisible, but as their populations grew, cultural differences with the host societies were exposed. Western European governments were largely unprepared for the presence of large groups of unassimilated migrants. Moreover, just as Italians, Danes, and

guest workers Citizens of foreign countries temporarily allowed to live and work in western European countries.

Germans were starting to identify themselves as Europeans, there were new populations to define themselves against—new people of color and adherents of different religions. New tensions arose over what it meant to be European.

Tensions also arose as guest workers lived in poverty while they worked in prosperous settings. A Turkish worker cleaning toilets in the Frankfurt International Airport, for example, saw the lifestyle available to Germans and knew it would never be possible for him. The loneliness and resentment of guest workers was compounded as they observed ethnic Germans repatriated from eastern Europe gaining citizenship and access to full social services. The significance of race in eligibility for citizenship was clear. The race line was a particular problem for children born to guest workers in the host country: Were they to be "tolerated," or could they become citizens with full rights? As temporary workers lived in host countries for decades, a new generation of children was exposed to the possibility of losing their rights if their parents were deported. And, because they attended European schools and spoke European languages, they began to identify themselves as Europeans. Thousands of families struggled with divided identities.

29-3 Growing Crisis in the Communist East

> » **What impact did détente have for the people of the communist bloc?**
>
> » **How did the Soviet Union change from the 1970s to the late 1980s?**

For most eastern Europeans, 1968 represented the end of hope. Yet, by the late 1970s, Ostpolitik and détente had increased the availability of consumer goods, allowed people to travel more freely inside the bloc and beyond, and made room for dissidents to express their criticisms. The 1973 economic crisis did not hit eastern Europe as hard as it did the West, in part because of the lesser dependency on oil and in part because of the continued heavy subsidy of various consumer goods. But by the beginning of the 1980s, severe inflation and underproduction were forcing the Soviet Union to rethink its economic and foreign policy. At the same time, popular protests and strikes in Czechoslovakia and Poland forced communist regimes there to use increasingly brutal repressive measures. Communism was weakening.

Brezhnev Doctrine Policy of Soviet military intervention to secure the interest of communism in Soviet bloc countries, established by Leonid Brezhnev in 1968.

29-3a Détente and False Prosperity

When Brezhnev pulled Soviet bloc troops from Czechoslovakia in 1969, the hope of reform—so strong during the Prague Spring on 1968—seemed dead. The leaders of the dissident movement had been imprisoned or purged. By directly participating in the invasion, eastern European communist regimes had also signed on to the **Brezhnev Doctrine**, a commitment to crush dissent.

Consumer Goods and Political Stability The communist leaders understood that military force and fear alone were not sufficient to suppress opposition. The era of détente made possible a shift in economic planning from heavy industries toward consumer goods. For the first time, radios and television sets became widely available. New countries began to produce their own cars. Only a generation earlier, most transportation had been either by horse and cart or on foot; in contrast, this new emphasis in economic policy was breathtaking. Items formerly considered luxuries were now mass-produced, and western consumer goods began to be imported.

For many eastern Europeans, the early 1970s was an age of prosperity. For the first time, a factory worker could get in his car and take his family on a trip to another country. A Bulgarian teenager could wear jeans and makeup. Polish students spent their summer vacations camping in Romania, sipping Cuban rum and Pepsi at dance clubs that played the latest tunes from the Swedish pop band ABBA. Workers from nonaligned Yugoslavia went to West Germany to work and returned home with western cars, whiskey, or plain cash. Though salaries were relatively low, many people now dreamed less of life in the free West than of vacations and new furniture.

The communist regimes shifted economic priorities partly because oil from the Soviet Union was available at a time when the rest of the world was suffering from the oil crisis and partly because cheap loans were a stimulus. West Germany had been the first to extend cheap loans to East Germany, but soon Poland, Yugoslavia, Romania, and others benefited. After the Helsinki Act, the United States and western European countries extended special loans and lower tariff rates to eastern European countries that agreed to protect human rights and allow the freedom of religion.

This deal afforded the communist regimes new means of "buying off" the loyalty of their citizens. But it also compelled these regimes to conceal their human rights abuses, if not to curb them. And the availability of western goods, especially movies, VCRs, and books, also made many increasingly aware of the prosperous lifestyle of the noncommunist West. People did not regard the new goods as proof of the success of the communist regimes but rather as proof of the West's ability to offer superior products.

The Return of Dissent By the end of the 1970s, the veneer of economic well-being was wearing off. Because they were not producing goods that could be sold abroad, most eastern European states could repay foreign loans only by raising prices for basic goods, such as bread and milk, which had long been subsidized. But wages were not raised, and in 1976–1977 strikes erupted from the Jiu Valley in Romania to Gdańsk, Poland. At the Lenin shipyards in Gdańsk, violent clashes between workers and police were followed by a crackdown. The government canceled the price hikes but avoided dealing with the underlying economic issues. People went back home, bruised and fearful, but it was clear that the consumerist policies of the early 1970s had backfired.

By the mid-1970s, even the Soviet Union was experiencing economic troubles. There was a sense of stagnation—that things were not getting any better during a period when people expected more. Voices from inside the Soviet Union rose to criticize Brezhnev. **Andrei Sakharov** (an-DRAY sah-KHA-rov), a brilliant physicist who had helped develop the Soviet hydrogen bomb, gave up his privileges when he openly discussed Soviet treatment of dissenters and put his life in danger by speaking out on behalf of human rights. For these efforts, he received the Nobel Peace Prize in 1975, but he was unable to collect it. Placed under house arrest, he continued his activities from his tiny apartment in Gorky and remained one of the important leaders of the movement for peace and human rights until his death in 1989.

29-3b Charter 77 and Solidarity

By 1977, it was becoming clear that the governments of eastern Europe had failed in their attempt to win loyalty through consumerism. Centralized economic planning could not sustain the growing demand for consumer goods at the low prices people had come to expect. And with increased expectations about consumer goods, those inside communist countries were more likely to become dissatisfied when such goods disappeared or became too expensive. The strikes were the most visible sign that the workers' states were facing the revolt of the workers. In Gdańsk, the strikes gave birth to an underground organization, the **Workers' Defense Committee**, which offered assistance to those who lost their jobs in the strikes. This network provided the foundation for an alliance of workers, lawyers, and intellectuals that was a first in the communist bloc.

Dissent and Human Rights The Czechoslovaks followed the Polish example with **Charter 77**, which called on the government to abide by the Helsinki Final Act. It listed actions taken by the government, such as imprisoning citizens without due process, which contravened the agreement signed by the Czechoslovak government in 1975. This petition was signed by more than a thousand people, including prominent writers such as **Václav Havel** but also engineers, workers, and other average people. The petition refused to define itself as a political movement; it simply stood as a grassroots act. Thus, it became the foundation for a new type of **civil society** that tried to change political culture and government policies outside traditional political channels. Like citizens in the West, but for different reasons, eastern Europeans were tired of traditional politics and turned toward grassroots activism to express their criticism. For those living under a dictatorship, the price of such actions was high. Predictably, the leaders of Charter 77 were imprisoned and stripped of their rights. But the crackdown did not match the purges of the early 1950s (see also Profiles in Change: Václav Havel Chooses Dissent).

The Workers' Rebellion

The most devastating challenge to a communist regime came in 1980, when another wave of strikes swept through Poland following a government announcement that it would raise the price of basic foods. The deep economic problems that lay behind the previous round of strikes had not been solved. Poland was defaulting on its international loans, and its economy collapsed. People were forced to wait in line for everything from bread to shoes, as the state became unable to deliver even basic goods.

The strikes in the Gdańsk shipyards were led by **Anna Walentynowicz** (vah-lehn-TEE-no-vitch), a feisty union organizer, and **Lech Wałęsa** (va-WEN-sah), a young worker with boundless energy, great charisma, and an unshaken belief in the Catholic Church. Walentynowicz was universally

Andrei Sakharov (1921–1989) Soviet physicist who was the most prominent human rights and antinuclear activist during the Brezhnev era.

Workers' Defense Committee Polish underground organization founded after the 1976 Gdańsk labor strikes to provide assistance to the participants.

Charter 77 Document signed by Czechoslovak citizens in 1977 protesting the communist government's noncompliance with the Helsinki Final Act.

Václav Havel (1936–2011) Czech playwright and dissident who became the first president of postcommunist Czechoslovakia.

civil society Nongovernmental institutions and social networks that help negotiate civil rights, social justice, and a public space outside of direct state control.

Anna Walentynowicz (1929–2010) Labor activist at the Gdańsk shipyard, whose opposition activities and subsequent firing by the communist management led to a national strike and the founding of Solidarity.

Lech Wałęsa (1943–) Shipyard worker who led 1980 labor strikes in Gdańsk, Poland, and leader of the Solidarity union and movement, who has recently been accused of having been an informer for the Polish secret police.

Václav Havel Chooses Dissent

Václav Havel Vaclav Havel became the face of democratic resistance to totalitarianism in the 1980s and was one of the few dissidents to successfully transition from speaking "truth to power" to responsible political leadership of his country. Like Nelson Mandela, Havel remained uncorrupted by the power he gained after he became president.

To live in truth: this is the deceptively simple choice Václav Havel, the first president of postcommunist Czechoslovakia, made most of his life. In a brave letter to the communist leadership, he stated that acting truthfully from a moral perspective is important not necessarily in the short run, but rather as a commitment that can garner political weight over time. This strong faith in the power of each individual to make a difference in the world by living a moral life guided the famous playwright in his own life and imposed on him costly personal choices—from social isolation to imprisonment—but it also made him an inspiration to people throughout the communist bloc.

During the short-lived Prague Spring, from January to August 1968, Havel was at the forefront of the reform movement that sought full freedom of the press, religion, and assembly in addition to important social and economic changes advocated by the reformist party leadership. Thirty-two at that time, and thus older than most of the students who stood beside him, Havel publicly criticized the injustices of the communist regime even though, as a prominent playwright, he had much to lose. But he believed in truth telling, and in an open letter to the communist leadership, he laid out the major abuses of the regime.

These actions made him a target of the repression that came in 1969, after the Soviets rolled their tanks through Prague. Havel was blacklisted, his plays removed from all theaters: he was forced to choose between being a playwright without a stage or abandoning his political principles. Havel chose neither. He remained an unconcealed opponent of the regime, but as he was not allowed to publish or stage his plays, he created an underground publishing house and arranged to have his plays staged in unlikely places, from

respected by her co-workers and when she was fired for her opposition activities in August 1980, the whole shipyard went on strike. Throughout Poland, most factory workers, teachers, rural workers, and even some party members struck in sympathy with the Gdańsk workers. Poland's economy came to a standstill.

Solidarity First noncommunist workers' union of any communist regime in eastern Europe, founded in August 1980 in Poland.

flying university Underground Polish educational network that was a training ground for dissidents in the 1980s.

The Violent Crush of Solidarity With other dedicated workers, Walentynowicz and Wałęsa established **Solidarity** to negotiate better working conditions and wages. The organization was independent of communist control and at its height had more than ten million members. This organization gave hope to most

Poles that they could organize themselves and function independently of the communist regime. Entire communities gave everything they had to make this effort work, from Catholic priests, who described the actions of Solidarity in their sermons, to housewives, who turned their apartments into miniature publishing houses, hostels, and cafeterias. By December 1981, the communist regime regarded Solidarity as enough of a threat to send tanks into the streets of Warsaw. For a year, Poland was under martial law. Solidarity leaders were imprisoned, and the state imposed harsh control over all media. But the organization was too strong to be eliminated.

Opposition Underground In the following years, Solidarity supporters formed an underground network known as the **flying university**. The government tried to shut it down but had neither the will nor the resources to succeed, as many Poles were no

barns to restaurants. As he could not make a living as a playwright, he took on a day job stocking barrels in a brewery. In this way, he continued to provide an inspiring example of how one could not only survive but also live in truth under a regime of lies, exposing it for what it really was. His underground press published many texts that opposed the regime, contributing to the development and recognition of an important body of work. Many of these publications were smuggled abroad, making Havel, his cohort of writers, and, more broadly, Czechoslovakia a place to which western Europeans and Americans looked for signs of a crack in the Soviet bloc.

Havel's best-known act of opposition was his central role in co-writing and publicizing a petition against the Czechoslovak government in 1977. Charter 77, as it became known, pointed out real but undisclosed facts about the abuses of the communist regime, which in 1975 had signed the famous Helsinki Final Act that guaranteed citizens' basic human rights. Charter 77 became the foundation for a new movement for rehumanizing social relations, restoring human dignity, and reenergizing moral conviction. In its most public challenge, the petition asked the government to release the members of a rock band who had been imprisoned for their lyrics and for loud aesthetics—supposedly "unbecoming" of a musical group in a communist state. Charter 77, and Havel in particular, challenged the regime to show how it could claim to support freedom of speech and personal movement while treating people as subjects of a tyranny. For his role in Charter 77, Havel was imprisoned in 1979 and suffered great abuses. In 1983 he almost died from an untreated case of pneumonia, and only under great international pressure was he finally released to recover in a regular hospital. By now he had become a larger-than-life hero of the underground intellectual and civil rights reform movement in the communist world. In 1989, he emerged as leader of the anticommunist opposition and was soon elected as president of a democratic Czechoslovakia. After Slovakia declared its independence in 1991, he remained the president of the Czech Republic until his retirement in February 2003.

_____

Source: From a letter written by Václav Havel (1936–2011).

longer afraid. Writers expelled from official publications immediately found employment as teachers and editors in the underground classes set up in churches and farmhouses. Those who still had official jobs used their economic resources to help people in the underground. Virtually everyone in Poland, including party members, either knew someone who was an underground activist or helped in such activities. An underground gray economy began to flourish.

The Polish Pope The Polish dissident movement was unique in eastern Europe for its long-term worker activism and the organizational structure of the Workers' Defense Committee and also because of the role of the Catholic Church, which opened its doors to the flying university and Solidarity activists after 1981. In addition, in 1978, the Catholic Poles gained one of their most important spokesmen in the international community through the election of Karol Cardinal Wojtyła as Pope **John Paul II**. The first Polish pope, John Paul was an inspiration for Catholics in Poland and gave them renewed faith. The pope himself became an outspoken, if diplomatic, critic of the communist bloc. Even though there were large groups of Catholics in Slovakia, Hungary, Romania, and Croatia, nowhere else did the Catholic Church provide such a catalyst for mass dissent in the last decade of communism.

29-3c Reform in the Soviet Union

In 1985, Mikhail Gorbachev became the new Soviet leader, turning out to be the right man at the right time, as many in the party and the general population had come to see the necessity for change. With the old generation of party activists from World War II passing away, younger people, who had not lived under unconstrained Stalinist terror, came to expect reform to be possible. Gorbachev exemplified this new generation of leaders. He had been just eight years old when Germany invaded the Soviet Union, and when Stalin died he was pursuing a law degree in Moscow. In some ways, Gorbachev was typical: An ambitious, hardworking, and talented party activist, rising through the ranks very quickly to become, at age forty-nine, the youngest member of the Politburo. His relative youth made him attractive to those desiring reform.

A New Openness Once in power, Gorbachev moved swiftly to eliminate most of the upper and midlevel old party leadership, replacing them with younger men he personally trusted. Such a change might have appeared autocratic, but he followed this power consolidation with a much more radical change. Starting in 1986, he introduced the policy of **glasnost**, or openness, which was an invitation to both party members and the media at large to discuss domestic problems honestly. Initially, the policy was not intended as full freedom of speech. Gorbachev hoped to control reform by positioning trusted party members

John Paul II (r. 1978–2005) Pope who inspired Polish Catholics and encouraged their opposition to the communist regime.

glasnost (in Russian, "openness") Policy of encouraging constructive criticism of the Communist Party that was introduced by Mikhail Gorbachev in 1985.

as critics of the status quo and the advocates of change. He anticipated criticisms of Joseph Stalin and Leonid Brezhnev but also a positive reevaluation of some Leninist legacies, especially the NEP years, as well as of Nikita Khrushchev, all intended to reinforce commitment to the central ideals of communism.

The Price of Glasnost

The gamble was fundamentally wrongheaded: Gorbachev believed openness would strengthen communist rule and restore the faith of satellite regimes. But reform was too little, too late. Both inside the Soviet Union and elsewhere, many took glasnost to mean openness *not* to choose communism and tested Gorbachev's willingness to deliver on his promise. Within three years the Soviet Union was falling apart.

Still, glasnost led to important accomplishments, especially the growth of independent organizations that became the kernel of a new civil society, much like Solidarity in Poland. Gorbachev himself oversaw the restoration of civil rights to many political prisoners, including Sakharov, and a new respect for human rights. The new openness also had an intolerant underside. For instance, the organization **Pamiat'**, dedicated to the victims of communism, had openly anti-Semitic overtones and encouraged new forms of **xenophobia**.

Restructuring Economic and Political Processes

Gorbachev saw glasnost as part of a broader agenda, which also included **perestroika**, or restructuring. In 1988, he introduced open elections and set new time limitations to political office. In effect, he was institutionalizing a more democratic process that prized change, rather than stability, as the key to healthy politics.

In the economy, perestroika proved more challenging, as some reformers called for decentralizing planning and production, which would have meant a system-wide overhaul. Previous economic reform had focused on fighting corruption, reviving worker control on the factory floor, and replacing political leaders with able technocrats. Gorbachev himself gained popularity by firing corrupt factory managers and giving speeches about making peasants the new masters of the land. But the Soviet economy was too large and sluggish to be changed just by introducing new laws and vague possibilities for freer market relations. All signs pointed toward the need to let the market, rather than the party, set prices and production priorities. But neither the party leadership nor the population at large was ready for such a radical change.

Resistance to Change

After several generations of workers raised in a top-down command economy, the very culture of work needed to be transformed so as to encourage personal incentive and creativity. But neither the manager of a textile factory nor the workingwoman on the floor could make such a switch in thinking overnight. The communist regime had so successfully reshaped the identity of the New Soviet Man and Woman that workers identified more closely with the fixed paycheck they took home every month than with productivity or creativity at work. The security of access to free public health, education, and a meager pension rendered workers as supporters of this status quo. Similarly, the communist regime had successfully directed factory managers to respond to party directives: They were not used to having to make decisions about what the factory would produce, for whom, and at what cost. These decisions were made in Moscow, and the manager's job was to simply implement them.

So, when Gorbachev's reforms allowed the opening of small individual enterprises and gave more power to factory managers, the response was mixed. Most managers were unwilling to really change: Their choice was most often to maintain things as they had been. Workers were no less conservative. And allowing prices to reflect the true market value of products brought inflation, which devalued the savings most people had gathered for years under their mattresses. By the end of the 1980s, the Soviet gross domestic production figures had declined by 17 percent and retail prices had increased by 140 percent. The communist system was collapsing, though the speed with which it unraveled caught the whole world by surprise.

29-4 Cultural Leaps over the Wall

> » How did cultural concerns shared by people on both sides of the Iron Curtain transform European identities?

> » What role did these cultural trends play in challenging the division between West and East?

In the 1970s and 1980s, cultural divisions between East and West became muted. People on both sides of the Iron Curtain had similar cultural concerns. In increasingly secularized societies, they embraced sexuality as a part of their identity. Intellectuals challenged faith in progress, and many people turned to new spiritual practices. In eastern Europe, these shifts did not directly challenge communism, but they did

Pamiat' Nongovernmental Soviet organization that fostered anti-Semitic, radical-right nationalism.

xenophobia Intense fear of foreigners.

perestroika (in Russian, "restructuring") Failed economic reforms aimed at decentralizing state control of the economy, initiated under Mikhail Gorbachev.

show the extent to which people no longer believed in government propaganda and tried to create alternative identities.

29-4a Whose Sexual Revolution?

The four decades after World War II saw a virtual revolution in sexual identities. Men and women became more open about sex as integral to their identity. New technologies for birth control made it easier to separate reproduction from sexual intercourse. And with methods that allowed both partners to control the process, men and women both became generally more sexually active—earlier and with more partners. And heteronormativity was challenged by growing communities of same-sex couples.

Sexual Inequalities This new openness did not necessarily bring about greater sexual equality between men and women. In the West, feminists lobbied for greater access to birth control, especially the contraceptive pill, as a means for women to eliminate unplanned pregnancies. Yet the pill, first available in Europe in the late 1960s, and other contraceptives increased pressure for women to become sexually active. By the early 1980s, the average age when a girl became sexually active in Sweden was fifteen years and two months and for a boy, two months later. For almost half of these young women, their first sexual encounter was not consensual.

Women Workers and Birth Control in Eastern Europe In communist Europe, with abortion having become legal after World War II and with methods of birth control available, especially IUDs, there was a revolution in sexuality. But here the revolution was directed from the top down, as the communist regimes wanted to separate production from reproduction to facilitate the entry of a maximum number of women into the workforce. Indeed, in some eastern European countries, almost 40 percent of women worked, but usually in low-level, poorly paid jobs. More women entered technical professions than in the West (engineering was especially popular), though, as elsewhere, women were less likely to rise to the top of their professional ranks than men.

Pro-natalism Under Communism By the late 1960s, concerns for women as active workers were replaced by fears of depopulation. Everywhere in Europe, the birthrate was decreasing dramatically, and the total population of many countries was going down. In western Europe, the solution was to bring in guest workers. But communist bloc governments looked to other methods. The most dramatic solution was found in Romania, where, in 1967, on the advice of sociologists and doctors, the government of **Nicolae Ceauşescu** (nee-ko-LAH-eh tcha-oo-SHES-koo)

recriminalized abortion and eliminated all forms of birth control. Women went overnight from being free to choose any form of birth control to being forced to undergo monthly gynecological examinations to monitor any pregnancy. Women's identity shifted from being partners in the labor force and public life to becoming birthing vessels. Yet, mothers were given little assistance by the state, and the quality of health care and childcare indicated that the regime was interested primarily in the number of children born.

The Slow Acceptance of Homosexuality Another important aspect of the sexual revolution was the emerging acceptability of homosexuality as an identity. Underground gay communities and culture had existed for a long time, but in the late 1960s and early 1970s politicians began to consider decriminalizing homosexual acts. Sweden had led the way in 1944. In the 1970s and 1980s, gay rights activists in the West largely achieved decriminalization and a degree of cultural tolerance. Sexual equality was added to the list of human rights that most western European governments protected by law. By contrast, in the communist East homosexuality remained criminalized, and many gay persons were placed in abusive psychiatric wards.

Then, in 1983, the AIDS (acquired immune deficiency syndrome) crisis reignited worldwide fears of sexual promiscuity, especially regarding male homosexuals. Despite medical research indicating that heterosexuals were often as likely as homosexuals to become infected with the AIDS virus and that the source of infection could be blood transfusions rather than sexual contact, the myth that AIDS was a homosexual illness or punishment for sexual deviants persists in many places.

CONNECTIONS: In the last few decades, the spread of HIV in Russia has become rampant, reaching over 1 percent of the population according to UNAIDS estimates. Though this epidemic is largely due to the use of infected needles among intravenous drug users and the lack of use of condoms among heterosexual couples, the Russian state and Orthodox Church continue to proclaim this is a problem linked to the presumed moral failings of homosexuals.

These important changes in how sexuality was defined had much to do with social practices, medical advances, and public policy. But equally important was the role of popular culture. The emergence of rock'n'roll and youth culture as a product that could be easily marketed, together with the growth of television, helped popularize sexual freedom. Rock stars openly flaunted their sexuality, and their fans imitated these trends.

Nicolae Ceauşescu (1918–1989) Dictatorial leader of communist Romania from 1965 to 1989.

Movies, television programs, billboards, and newspaper advertisements promoted sexually explicit images, reinforcing the notion that people's sexual desires and actions were not shameful taboos but integral components of their identity.

Sexuality in Pop Culture Popular culture generally did little to challenge traditional gender and sexual identities. James Bond movies celebrated masculine sexual promiscuity and the ideal of the sexually submissive woman. Later in the 1970s, the lifestyles of rock stars such as David Bowie and Elton John challenged the staunchly heterosexual aggressive masculine ideal, but most people in western Europe were not ready to accept their sexual choices as anything more than eccentric. In eastern Europe, attitudes changed even more slowly, though by the 1980s infatuation with Western pop culture introduced important aspects of the sexual revolution in the communist bloc. As men traveled abroad, they brought back copies of pornographic magazines and sexually explicit movies. Yet, untouched by feminism, many women in eastern Europe came to equate freedom from communist oppression with the freedom to be erotically provocative in ways that Western feminists might decry as turning themselves into sexual objects for the enjoyment of men.

29-4b Religious Revival

In both West and East, the generation coming of age in the 1970s and 1980s turned away from established religious traditions. In the West, those who rejected the increasingly consumerist and materialist society sought a new spirituality. In the East, many who were alienated from the ideas of communism and from the religious institutions that had not opposed communism also became interested in nontraditional religions. Buddhist and Hindu practices, particularly yoga, offered spiritual fulfillment for some. Following the trend set by famous stars such as the Beatles, some Westerners traveled to Asia to immerse themselves in local traditions. People retreated into either private or highly informal ways of expressing their religious beliefs rather than supporting established religious institutions. Church attendance declined even as interest in spirituality grew.

Islamic Revolution Revolution by Islamic fundamentalist forces that brought down the Iranian monarchy in 1977 and instituted a republican government under the authority of a supreme leader, the Ayatollah Ruhollah Khomeini (ko-MAY-nee).

Catholicism and Resistance to Oppression Ireland and Poland were exceptions, however, as in both the Catholic Church became a focus of national resistance to oppression—imperial in Ireland and communist in Poland. In Northern Ireland, the Catholic population, whether they supported the IRA or not, found in the Catholic Church a space in which to cultivate Irish national identity as separate from Protestant English nationalism. In Poland, there was an upsurge of religious attendance as young people found the church a refuge from their bleak political and economic life.

The Persistence of Anti-Semitism Other developments revived affiliation with traditional religions. In the case of Judaism, anti-Semitic policies in eastern Europe and the Soviet Union prompted Jews to reassert their religious identity and request permission to emigrate to Israel. In Poland, the turning point was 1968, when Jewish students and intellectuals were targeted in the crackdown against the protest movements. In the Soviet Union, the Jewish population began to demand the implementation of the Helsinki Final Act, but only after Gorbachev came to power were a considerable number of emigration requests granted. With a significant influx of eastern European Jewry in the 1980s, the population of Israel changed dramatically. Many immigrants arrived in Israel barely familiar with the religious and cultural traditions of their new home and had to make a radical transition to assume their role as citizens.

Growth of Islam As eastern European Jews were leaving Europe, another religious group was growing—Muslims, who arrived as guest workers. Because of their poverty and cultural marginalization by the larger community, most guest workers remained conservative in their religious practices. Their children were often raised in the spirit of strict Muslim traditions in the midst of larger secular communities often intolerant of Islam. These economic and cultural factors combined to reinforce the marginalization of Muslims in their host countries, even in France, where this group had become the second-largest religious denomination by the beginning of the twenty-first century.

In many Islamic countries, growing secularization in the previous decades saw a backlash. In Iran, which had embraced a secular monarchy and celebrated links with the West, an **Islamic Revolution** brought to power a regime that sough to erase any cultural signs of Western influence. While many secular intellectuals and rich individuals fled, most people stayed behind and suffered atrocities at the hands of the Revolutionary Guard. In Egypt, the state had embraced secularization since the 1950s and in the 1970s saw the growth of radical left-wing groups that opposed the government. The government encouraged the revival of Islamic fundamentalist organizations, which became an increasingly vocal presence in

Egyptian politics. By the mid-1980s the **Muslim Brotherhood** was active in parliament and fundamentalist imams were calling for reinstating sharia as the basic law of the country. Still, more moderate intellectuals and politicians sought a middle way between secularization, modernization, and their Western trappings, on the one hand, and upholding the principles of Islam, on the other. Feminists such as **Fatema Mernissi** provided nuanced interpretations of the Quran that sought to preserve rights women had recently won in many Muslim countries (see Learning from a Primary Source: Fatema Mernissi's Islamic Feminism).

29-4c Postmodernism

Some Europeans experienced new or renewed religious affiliations, but others questioned the essence of faith in progress and Western civilization itself. In the formulations of French philosopher **Michel Foucault**, the most important thinker of the postmodern movement, these two critiques were closely intertwined. Born in 1926, Foucault was active in the 1968 political protests. Yet, as a homosexual, he was a closet minority even within that progressive vanguard. In the 1970s, he published a series of studies that questioned the concepts of "knowledge" and "truth," arguing that both were products of specific ways of thinking and thus fundamentally subjective.

Power and Positionality In the postmodernist universe, action was part of a complex web of relations, and individual ideas and deeds did not have meaning outside that web. Postmodernists suggested it was foolish to believe that any political or social system could be reformed from within. The fundamental injustices were in the imbalances of power between those who had economic and other resources and those who started from marginal positions. Thus it was impossible to pinpoint the causes and consequences of any action. The theory generated a fundamental dilemma: If there was no way of establishing a clear relationship between any two actions of even one individual, then knowledge was nothing more than an illusion. To "know" was to insert one's own beliefs into the interpretation of facts. This critique did not point to any way out. The only response was irony and skepticism.

An Age of Contradictions For many intellectuals in both the West and East, postmodernism expressed the contradictions of their age—the promises of plenty and the persistence of poverty, access to education and growing ignorance, the ideals of freedom and the shackles of consumerism. In particular, the ironic stance proposed by postmodernists was a survival tool for many writers behind the Iron Curtain. They were themselves caught in a web of powerlessness vis-à-vis the political leadership, for political repression made it impossible to be true to one's calling as a writer and at the same time the calling compelled them to try to express their ideas. It is no wonder, then, that some of the most original and sophisticated thinkers of the postmodern movement came from eastern Europe. For example, the Slovenian philosopher **Slavoj Žižek's** (slah-VOY ZHEE-zhek) preoccupation with the ways in which language is shaped by power, and power by language, was an extension of his experience growing up with a regime in which lies were the norm.

29-4d The Americanization of European Popular Culture

While some intellectuals worried about the meaning of postmodernism, most Europeans became addicted to American television. Comedy shows such as *Married with Children* and *Roseanne* became popular in Britain and Germany. At seven o'clock in the evening, families across the continent could watch the evening news in their native language or broadcasts of American sitcoms. Late-night shows that tried to replicate David Letterman's format sprang up everywhere. There were local alternatives, but the popularity of American programs was undeniable.

American musicians from Willie Nelson to Madonna regularly sold out their European performances. American fast-food franchises such as McDonald's opened everywhere in Europe, including Budapest and Moscow. Some worried that eating Big Macs and watching reruns of *Roseanne* would make European culture bland. In fact, Europeans still read more and watch less television than Americans, and they are less likely to eat fast food. It is not clear whether economic reasons or cultural preferences are behind these differences. But it seems that Europeans have self-consciously attempted to preserve some distance between their consumption of American popular culture and material goods, on the one hand, and their identification with their local and regional European culture, on the other.

Muslim Brotherhood Sunni Islamic organization founded in Egypt in 1929, it became politically active in opposing secularizing measures starting in the 1980s.

Fatema Mernissi (mer-NEE-see) (1940–2015) One of the most prominent Muslim feminist intellectuals and activists of the late twentieth century, she wrote passionately about the feminist aspects of the Quran and sought to combine Western feminist ideas with Islamic traditions and values.

Michel Foucault (mi-SHELL foo-COHLT) (1926–1984) French philosopher and prominent postmodernist author.

Slavoj Žižek (1949–) Postmodernist Slovenian philosopher and literary critic.

Fatema Mernissi's Islamic Feminism

Born in Fez into a traditional Islamic family, Fatema Mernissi was raised in a harem at the home of her affluent grandmother. Later in life, she wrote an evocative and powerful memoir about this period, *Dreams of Trespass* (1994). Though both her mother and grandmother were illiterate, she was encouraged to pursue an education and attended a number of schools in Morocco and later France (the Sorbonne) and the United States (Brandeis). In 1974, having obtained a PhD in sociology from Brandeis, she returned to Rabat to teach at Mohammed V University.

Mernissi became intensely interested in the relationship

Fatema Mernissi

Sueddeutsche Zeitung Photo / Alamy Stock Photo

between Islam and women's rights and did extensive field work in Morocco on this topic. She also chose a historicist approach to understanding Islam, bringing to light aspects of the Quran linked to women's position in Islamic society that had been either buried or interpreted in an overly misogynistic way in the modern period. Fellow Moroccan sociologist Sumaya Naaman Guesus has stated that Mernissi was "the first woman to have the great courage to take up various themes considered taboo around the interpretation of the Koran and the texts of the Islamic tradition". Mernissi's first book, *Beyond the Veil* (1975) became a classic for anyone seeking to understand Islam from a feminist perspective and paved the way for the rise of feminist scholarship among many other Islamic scholars.

Mernissi worked for a number of Moroccan and international organizations on women's issues. She prepared reports and did analyses of gender issues for UNESCO, and worked for the International Labor Organization to analyze work issues for women living in Islamic societies. She published eighteen books on these topics and garnered many international awards. In 2003 she was awarded the Prince of Asturias Award in Spain. In the 1993 "Fresh Air" interview excerpted below, she speaks about the sources of her feminism, her love of her home country, and her commitment to Islam as a feminist.

❶ What does this suggest about the role of new media in the circulation of ideas?

❷ What role did the older generation of women play in Mernissi's feminism?

Teri Gross: When I spoke with Mernissi in 1993, I asked if her mother felt like a prisoner in the harem.

Fatema Mernissi: Oh, she hated it, of course. She hated it, mostly because already the Arab world then was completely, completely entranced with the idea of progress. And the nationalist songs, you know, about freedom and self-fulfillment and all that - she would hear it on Radio.**❶** Cairo was then the center of an incredibly powerful feminist movement. And so she could just compare how sad was her confinement.**❷**

3 What do you make of this analogy in terms of protest through clothing?

4 How does she describe her relationship to Moroccan society?

5 What does this terminology suggest about the role of tradition in Mernissi's life?

6 Why is history such an important site for women to reclaim?

7 How does she situate herself in relationship to secularizing Western influences?

TG: Did your mother try to not wear a veil when she went out?

FM: She fought in the limits which were granted to her. What she did was, instead of wearing the haik, for example, which is this seven meters long piece of white cloth, she wanted to take men's djellaba, the long robe with trimmed sleeves which give much more freedom to the movements. And that was a huge battle because it was like when the French women or the American women took the liberty to wear men's pants. It was the same thing. **3**

TG: You studied in the West in college. You returned to Morocco. What has kept you there?

FM: Oh, my God, I think if you know Morocco (laughter), you'll understand my situation. Morocco is such a beautiful place… And also it is captivating place because for a writer, you feel that you make impact. I mean, when I write something in the press, the day after in the fish market, people will be discussing it. Either they're attacking me or they like what I've written, and then two men will get into a fight with each other. One is for me and the other against me. **4** You are umbilically linked **5** and rooted in this society which has its own, of course, worries and fears about modernity.

TG: I take it you've remained a Muslim even though you've challenged a lot of people's beliefs about Islam.

FM: Absolutely. And you see one of the frontiers I crossed is actually the act of analyzing the memoir and the religious text and the historical text and how history is made and framed and produced and packaged…I discovered, first of all, that the Prophet is a wonderful person and any Muslim woman could claim it as an inspiring model…On the other hand, that I showed that the real mistake of women was to let the memoir, the collective, the history, space of producing history in the hands of men. **6** No one can mutilate me by telling me I cannot have the mosque or the Koran. Someone else is going to read for me or go at my place to the mosque, and/ or to tell me you shouldn't take anything from the West because the West is the enemy and so on. It is to me to decide. I am intelligent enough to be critical towards the West and take what I need and reject what is bad for me. **7**

29-5 The Collapse of the Soviet System, 1989–1991

> » What were the immediate causes of the collapse of communism in eastern Europe?

> » How was the fall of communism different among the communist bloc countries?

By 1989, Gorbachev's attempts at reform in the Soviet Union were failing. Talk of perestroika was not followed by spectacular results at a time when most people were expecting a dramatic rise in their quality of life. Yet the final blow to Gorbachev's reforms resulted from his unwillingness to hold back the new nationalist wave sweeping through both the Soviet Union and its eastern European clients. Even as he was struggling to revive the Soviet Union's viability, his actions prompted dissident movements in eastern Europe to overthrow the communist regimes. With no hope of support from Moscow, most of these regimes gave up without a struggle. Romania, however, experienced a bloody revolution that brought the end of communism at a much higher price. By the end of 1991, the communist bloc had ceased to exist. The fall of communism is summarized in Table 29.2.

29-5a The Velvet Revolution

Under glasnost, many informal groups with an openly non-Russian national character developed in various Soviet republics. They were more outspoken and well organized in the Baltic republics, where massive rallies in 1988 showed popular

Table 29.2	The Fall of Communism
1976–1977	Massive strikes in Poland and Romania
1977	Charter 77 movement in Czechoslovakia
1978	Polish cardinal becomes Pope John Paul II
1980–1981	Solidarity movement in Poland
1985	Mikhail Gorbachev becomes leader of the Soviet Union
1988	Anti-Soviet demonstrations in Lithuania
April 1989	Roundtable talks between Solidarity and Polish communist regime
June 1989	Anticommunist protests in Tiananmen Square, Beijing
September 1989	Hungary opens border with Austria
September 11, 1989	125,000 East Germans cross into Austria via Hungary
November 9, 1989	Berlin Wall comes down
November 10, 1989	Bulgarian communist leader Todor Zhivkov deposed
November 17–December 29, 1989	Peaceful street demonstrations and deposition of communist regime in Czechoslovakia
December 16–21, 1989	Massive street protests in Romania; thousands killed
December 22, 1989	Romanian communist dictator Nicolae Ceaușescu flees
March 1991	Baltic republics gain independence from Soviet rule
August 19–21, 1991	Failed coup by authoritarian communist group in Moscow
December 1, 1991	Ukraine declares independence from the Soviet Union
December 8, 1991	Commonwealth of Independent States is established
December 25, 1991	Soviet flag lowered for last time from Kremlin

support for economic independence from Moscow. Perestroika was interpreted there in a nationalist-separatist direction. In addition, by 1988 Gorbachev was speaking clearly about the need to let European nations follow their own paths. This policy reversed the interventionist Brezhnev Doctrine and signaled the beginning of Soviet disengagement from its imperialism in eastern Europe. Though Thatcher and Reagan took credit for pressuring the Soviet leader into making such statements, Gorbachev's position was, in fact, an extension of the glasnost and perestroika policies he had promoted since his arrival in the Kremlin in 1985.

Ending the Brezhnev Doctrine In eastern Europe, the reversal of the Brezhnev Doctrine was perceived by most of the older party leaders as a personal threat to their authority. Reformers moved quickly to secure a peaceful transition to a younger and more dynamic party leadership. In Poland, Solidarity was the first noncommunist organization to become the engine of change. In early 1989, it held roundtable talks with communist officials who hoped to secure a peaceful transition to a regime that would allow the party to retain some political power. But free elections resulted in a complete victory for Solidarity and in the peaceful ousting of the communists (see Map 29.2).

Peaceful Protests and Departures A wave of activism followed. In the summer of 1989, Estonians, Latvians, and Lithuanians formed a peaceful

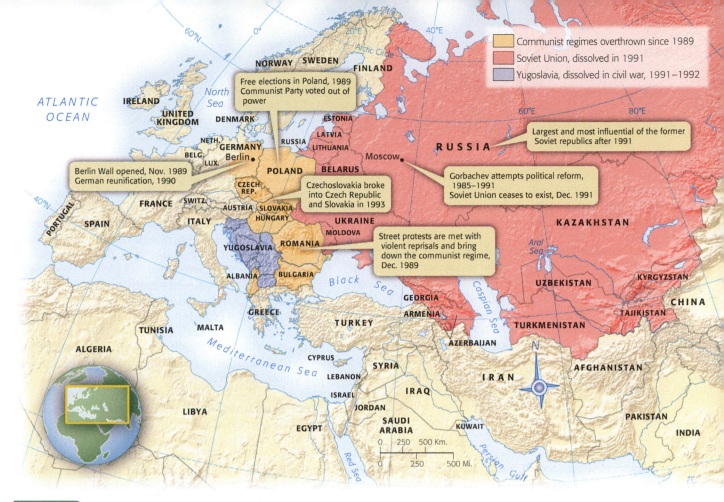

Map 29.2 The Fall of Communism, 1989–1991 Between 1989 and 1991 most of the communist states in Europe collapsed, bringing the Cold War to an end.

1. How would you describe these changes in comparison with those after World War I, in terms of borders?
2. How would you describe the changes in comparison with those after World War II in terms of level of violence?
3. Similarly, how would you compare post–World War II and post–1989 changes in borders?

human chain more than four hundred miles long in opposition to Soviet rule. The rest of eastern Europe awaited Moscow's reaction to these political challenges. Yet nothing happened—no troops crossed into Poland, no tanks entered the streets of Riga. This lack of response prompted the Hungarian government to open up its border with Austria. In a few days, the East Germans started to leave in droves for West Germany through Czechoslovakia, Hungary, and Austria. The road was tortuous, the lines at the border were long, but nobody could stop the exodus. Driving beat-up Trabants, riding old motorcycles, or walking, people camped out on the side of the road, sharing food, music, and their strong hope that they were finally getting out.

Bringing Down the Wall By October 1989, the East German leadership had acknowledged defeat and opened up the border with West Germany. In a frenzy of youthful hope and pent-up hate for the regime,

people took axes, hammers, and household knives to the Berlin Wall and tore it down. News of what was happening in Berlin was flashed instantly by Radio Free Europe and Voice of America throughout the communist bloc. From Warsaw to Tirana, people celebrated in the streets or rejoiced quietly at home.

In November–December, the **Velvet Revolution** brought down the Czechoslovak government. Although massive student demonstrations in Prague on November 17 were brutally suppressed by the police, peaceful street marches continued. Almost half a million Czechoslovaks joined the protests after the first signs of repression. Unlike in 1968, the government had neither the force nor the political will to continue. Instead, the communists retreated. On December 29, Václav Havel was elected as president by the "power of the powerless."

Velvet Revolution The peaceful fall of communism in most of eastern Europe in 1989.

29-5b Violent Struggle in Romania

In two countries, however, the fall of communism proved more violent. In Yugoslavia, a bloody civil war set the country on a path of self-destruction that would last a decade. In Romania, a much shorter violent popular uprising became the means by which communist dictatorship was forced out. Ceauşescu was alone in disregarding Moscow's encouragements for reform.

The Costs of Romania's Independent Road Since the 1960s Ceauşescu had acted independently, securing good relations with China when the Soviets were in conflict with that country and, in the 1970s, emulating North Korea by breaking all links with the outside world to show that Romania needed no economic assistance from the West or the East. In reality, the Romanian economy suffered from the same problems of soaring prices and lack of energy resources as the rest of the continent.

By 1989, basic goods such as bread, milk, and toilet paper were unavailable, and Romanians were simply struggling to survive. On December 16, people took to the streets of Timişoara to protest the imprisonment of a prominent local Hungarian clergyman. Despite the climate of terror that had increased in the 1980s, thousands joined the crowd. Then the police attacked, killing some civilians. The street uprising seemed to calm down by evening.

A Violent End A few days later, on December 21, Ceauşescu decided to demonstrate his power by holding a public gathering in Bucharest. The plan backfired. Within minutes there was loud booing, and the dictator fled the scene. A few hours later he and his wife were seized by a group of secret police, military, and political leaders. By the end of the year, the **National Salvation Front** was in charge. Ceauşescu and his wife had been executed after a sham trial, and some top communist leaders were in prison. But many midlevel communists were part of this new government, led by an old party activist who had known Gorbachev since his youth, **Ion Iliescu**. The Romanians had rid themselves of the most horrible aspects of communism, but they had not achieved a democratic regime. Still, the year 1990 began with great optimism in eastern Europe. The Iron Curtain had been lifted.

29-5c The End of the Soviet Union

1990 began with the recognition that the communist experiment had failed to achieve a viable workers' state. The Soviet political and military establishment realized that Gorbachev's reformist talk had permitted the lawful and peaceful exit of the eastern European communist bloc states and that even Soviet republics no longer wished to be part of the Union. The Baltic states had already made that clear, and after Gorbachev pulled troops out of Afghanistan in 1989, a growing wave of independence movements swept the republics of Central Asia. Nationalism, whether secular or strongly Muslim in orientation, was challenging the authority of communism and the Russian party elites everywhere.

The Communist Leadership Divided By August 1991, the party had become sharply divided into two factions: one led by **Boris Yeltsin**, the president of the Russian Republic and a young former supporter of Gorbachev, now disappointed with perestroika's lack of success; the other, a conservative faction, now led by Gorbachev, which tried to undo many of the reforms of the 1980s. The unforeseen consequences of his reforms had pushed Gorbachev to retreat. He was fundamentally still a supporter of the communist project and could not embrace the disintegration of the Soviet Union even though he had provided the means for it. Thus, for a brief period of time, Gorbachev attempted to rein in the nationalist independence movements, with strong support from the military establishment and older party leaders.

Crisis in the Kremlin Yet Gorbachev was also troubled by his abandonment of the principles of glasnost and perestroika. By early 1991, he returned to his reformist stance and, under strong international pressure, allowed the independence of Latvia, Lithuania, and Estonia. By August, together with Yeltsin, he had prepared a new treaty for a looser union with the remaining Soviet republics. This treaty set the stage for the creation of a **Commonwealth of Independent States (CIS)**, which offered its members autonomy in the management of internal affairs while the CIS would coordinate foreign affairs, security, and some economic policies, such as trade.

In a last-ditch effort to save the status quo, a group of eight conservative party leaders tried to seize power and establish a hard-line authoritarian regime. Working with the KGB, they detained Gorbachev at his summer home on August 19. But

National Salvation Front
Emergency government that came to power in Romania in 1989 after dictator Nicolae Ceauşescu fled.

Ion Iliescu (1930–) Communist leader of the National Salvation Front in postcommunist Romania who became the first president of the country after elections in 1990.

Boris Yeltsin (1931–2007) First president of postcommunist Russia, 1991–1999, who oversaw the dismemberment of the Soviet Union and privatization of the economy.

Commonwealth of Independent States (CIS) Alliance of former Soviet republics that oversees some trade, economic reform, and defense issues.

Boris Yeltsin

In August 1991 Boris Yeltsin became an instant symbol of revolt against the old Soviet system as he stood with civilians and soldiers on the top of this tank, demanding the resignation of the Soviet leadership. Shortly after these events he outlawed the Communist Party in the Russian Soviet Socialist Republic.

❯❯ *How is this image of transition in political power different from that of the Berlin Wall in October 1989? (see the chapter opener image)*

Yeltsin remained in Moscow, where he appeared in public, made statements broadcast in the state-controlled media, and rallied around him the support of the people and even many military troops. The most defiant moment of Yeltsin's opposition to the **August coup** came when he stood atop a tank that was supposed to separate the Duma from the population and spoke on live television surrounded by large crowds of supporters. Russians everywhere instantly realized that the army was divided, the coup was a sham, and Yeltsin was the man of the hour. Within three days, the conservative coup collapsed and Gorbachev returned to Moscow.

From Reform to Breakup But the real winner was Yeltsin, who had stood up to the hard-liners and confronted the army through an act of passive resistance. Instead of operating behind closed doors to outmaneuver his opponents, as the conservatives had done, Yeltsin had instead stood with the people to protest the abuses of the government. Earlier, when Soviet troops had threatened to intervene in the Baltic republics, he had flown to Riga to stand by protesters. Now, when the party threatened to take over the government, he called on the people and the lower army ranks to stand by him as a Russian patriot.

Yeltsin thus became the face of democratic Russia. As president of the Russian Republic, he shortly outlawed the Communist Party there, closed down communist newspapers, and transferred most state authority from the Soviet Union's federal level of government to his own Russian Republic. On December 1, Ukraine, the second most populous republic of the Soviet Union, proclaimed its independence. By Christmas Day 1991, the Soviet Union had ceased to exist. The hammer and sickle flag in Red Square was lowered, and the Russian flag raised. The seventy-year communist experiment had ended, and Russian nationalism was restored.

The collapse of the Soviet Union was surprisingly more peaceful than its beginnings and signaled the end of the Cold War. Arguments remain over the most important causes for this collapse: the strong military stance of Reagan and Thatcher, Gorbachev's reforms, or dissent movements in eastern Europe. Although the West had won the Cold War, the meaning of this victory for Europeans at large was still to be determined because the communist bloc states remained weak economically and politically. Beyond Europe, the end of the Cold War led to realignments in which nationalism, secularism, religious fundamentalism, liberalism, and corrupt opportunism became increasingly strong forces.

August coup Attempt in August 1991 by communist hard-liners to bring an end to the reforms of Yeltsin and Gorbachev that was crushed by a popular uprising.

CHAPTER Review

Summary

» Between 1968 and 1991, Europe went from being divided to becoming open to the flow of people, ideas, and goods from all regions.

» During détente, the actions of western and eastern political leaders helped increase the exchange of ideas and goods across the Cold War divide.

» In eastern Europe, dissidents bravely challenged their governments to honor human rights.

» Tensions between the superpowers increased after the Soviet invasion of Afghanistan, yet in the mid-1980s Gorbachev reversed the Soviet position in eastern Europe.

» By the end of 1991, the communists had lost power everywhere in eastern Europe except Yugoslavia.

» In western Europe, traditional parties were confronted with new types of activism, from the Greens to radical nationalist and terrorist movements.

» The decade-long economic crisis that began in 1973 created new challenges for political stability, as Europe became more vulnerable to shifts in the global economy.

» Western European governments achieved renewed prosperity and stability in the 1980s by scaling back welfare programs and privatizing some economic sectors.

» While people in the East looked to the West, some western Europeans questioned the faith in progress in their societies.

» Religion remained an important site for political opposition in some areas.

» The feminist, environmental, and antinuclear movements created new alliances and forms of grassroots activism.

» Demographic shifts brought important changes, from an aging population and lower birthrate to a more ethnically, religiously, and sexually diverse mix of people.

» The fall of communism was overall a bloodless transition.

Chronology

1972	West Germany recognizes the East German border [Europe] United States and Soviet Union sign the Antiballistic Missile Treaty [Americas, Europe]
1973	Great Britain, Ireland, and Denmark join the Common Market [Europe] Egypt and Israel engage in the Yom Kippur War [Middle East] Arab oil embargo begins [MIddle East]
1974	Abortion is decriminalized in France [Europe]
1975	European states sign the Helsinki Final Act [Europe]
1976–1977	Massive strikes erupt in Poland and Romania [Europe]
1977	Charter 77 movement in Czechoslovakia begins [Europe] Islamic Revolution [Middle East]
1978	Polish cardinal Karol Wojtyła becomes Pope John Paul II [Europe]
1979	Soviets invade Afghanistan [Europe, MIddle East] Margaret Thatcher becomes British prime minister [Europe]

1980	Solidarity movement begins in Poland [Europe]
1981	Greece joins the Common Market [Europe] Spain legalizes divorce [Europe] Millions march in antinuclear protests in western Europe [Europe]
1982	Britain defeats Argentina in Falklands War [Europe, Americas]
1983	François Mitterrand becomes president of France [Europe] Petra Kelly, first Green Party representative, is elected to the West German parliament [Europe] AIDS crisis begins [Global]
1985	Mikhail Gorbachev becomes leader of the Soviet Union [Europe]
1986	Explosion at the Chernobyl nuclear power plant spreads contamination [Europe]
1989	Berlin Wall is taken down [Europe] Communism falls in eastern Europe [Europe]
1991	Soviet Union collapses [Europe]

Critical Thinking Questions

Take time to pull together all the important information in the chapter by answering the following questions:

Politics in Western Europe

» What role did the relaxation of international tensions in the 1970s play in Europe, East and West?

» How did political parties in western Europe change in the 1970s and 1980s?

Social Change in the West

» How did western European societies change during this period?

» How did the feminist movement change western European society?

Growing Crisis in the Communist East

» What impact did détente have for the people of the communist bloc?

» How did the Soviet Union change from the 1970s to the late 1980s?

Cultural Leaps over the Wall

» How did cultural concerns shared by people on both sides of the Iron Curtain transform European identities?

» What role did these cultural trends play in challenging the division between West and East?

The Collapse of the Soviet System, 1989–1991

» What were the immediate causes of the collapse of communism in eastern Europe?

» How was the fall of communism different among the communist bloc countries?

 **MINDTAP** From Cengage

MindTap® is a fully online personalized learning experience built upon Cengage Learning content. MindTap® combines student learning tools—readings, multimedia, activities, and assessments—into a singular Learning Path that guides students through the course and helps students develop the critical thinking, analysis, and communication skills that are essential to academic and professional success.

Europe in a Globalizing World, 1991 to the Present

Chapter Outline

As you read, consider the following questions:

❭ What has the end of the Cold War meant for Europe?

❭ How has the European Union reshaped the European political and economic scene?

❭ What are the most important changes in international security and cooperation since the end of the Cold War?

❭ How successful has Europe been in retaining a powerful role in the process of economic globalization?

❭ What role have European states played in the War on Terrorism in relation to the United States?

❭ What important changes since 1991 have reshaped European identity today?

❭ What challenges does Europe face in the near future?

IN 1991 EUROPE found itself confronting new challenges, the first of which was to undo the economic and political legacies of the Cold War. Liberal democracies won the war, and the postcommunist European states now took on new significance for western Europe as trading partners, a source of labor, and simply as neighbors. The creation of the European Union (EU) and its enlargement eastward have been important steps toward European integration.

Arab Spring?

For a few months in 2010–2011, the youthful faces of Egyptian men and women brandishing the national flag in Tahrir Square, Cairo, became a symbol of hope for a democratic future in the Middle East. The repression that followed hardened both autocratic rule and radical sectarian Islamic movements from Egypt to Yemen.   Khalil Hamra/AP Images

Overall, democracy has been secured in Europe, and Europeans now live in greater stability and prosperity, with tolerance toward each other's differences. Where such tolerance remains challenging is in accepting growing Muslim influences in European societies. Although Muslim workers and their families are allowed to live in Europe, they generally have been treated as outsiders, even when local Islamic traditions go back hundreds of years.

Europeans have once again become strong players on the international scene as a leading force in the global economy. Though far from united, Europeans have also been active in international conflicts, from the Yugoslav Wars of the 1990s to the War on Terrorism since 2001 and the Arab Spring, supporting efforts by especially young protesters to develop democratic institutions and practices. More recently, the Syrian civil war has become a source of great concern for European governments and societies, from questions of international security and terrorism to welcoming the hundreds of thousands of refugees displaced by the war.

Internally, the greatest challenges have been preserving democratic principles in the EU while stretching its boundaries to include countries of the postcommunist bloc and more recently, negotiating Great Britain's vote to leave the EU. Externally, the most important challenge has been how to negotiate with the United States their collective position as winners in the Cold War in economic and international security matters. Who has paid the cost of this victory and who is reaping the benefits have remained subjects of contention in American-European relations. Many have tried to preserve the particular character of European culture in this era of increasing homogenization and the dominance of global economic and political concerns. More recently, the impact of globalization on everything from population movement to economic development and climate change has been the most important set of new problems faced by Europeans.

30-1 Eastern Europe After Communism

» **How did the collapse of communism affect Russia's role as a superpower?**

» **How has Vladimir Putin refashioned Russia's position in the world?**

» **What impact did the postcommunist transition have on eastern European states and societies?**

» **To what extent have these countries become more democratic?**

The West won the Cold War. By the end of 1991, the Soviet Union was defunct and all but one eastern European country had renounced communism. Within a few years, Russia became a friendly competitor and sometimes ally of liberal western Europe, the most remarkable achievement in international relations until 2000. Yugoslavia, however, remained a vestige of the old communist order, transformed into an ethnonationalist dictatorship. As the postcommunist states claimed a place in the larger European "home," new challenges arose for countries embarking on democratization. The only politicians with experience were the communists, and the most popular ideas uniting the citizenry were nationalist and often nondemocratic. Eastern European politicians had to deal with internal political and social problems while also responding to outside pressures from the West for transparency, increased economic freedoms, and reduced corruption. For Romania and Bulgaria, these challenges were initially difficult to meet, but Poland, Hungary, the Czech Republic, and Slovakia managed the 1990s effectively. The postcommunist transitions led in different directions, and democratization did not always bring economic betterment, nor was international investment a guarantee for democratization.

30-1a Russia's Collapse and Reemergence as Superpower

Russians woke up on Christmas Day 1991 to a brand-new state: a noncommunist Russia and its Commonwealth of Independent States (CIS). At the helm was Boris Yeltsin, the jovial and forceful politician who had stood up to the fearful Gorbachev and staunch communist old-timers to demand reform and democratization. Yeltsin was hugely popular in the days of the August 1991 coup, when he stood atop a tank and asked the Russian people to protect him and the reformist politicians from the abuses of the communist leadership. He sounded and looked like a man of the people, and his wild stunt worked in rousing the population.

From Rebel to Reformer Yet Yeltsin was not an outsider to Communist Party politics. He had been hand-picked by Gorbachev to pursue perestroika in the mid-1980s as party chief in the Moscow region. But dutifully following the rules was not Yeltsin's way. He was ambitious and wanted to rise high in the party. But he had been a thrill seeker since childhood, when he pursued many sports competitively, from volleyball to boxing. As a teenager, he learned the skills of the construction trade and then in college became an engineer and joined the party. By 1985, he catapulted into the Politburo, becoming the youngest member and Moscow party chief, where he was broadly popular for his tough stand against corruption.

Unceremoniously fired in 1987 for daring reforms that pushed perestroika and glasnost too far, Yeltsin returned to a humble job in construction. But in 1989, Gorbachev's reforms in electoral law enabled the people of Moscow to bring Yeltsin back to the Duma. With broad popular support, Yeltsin quickly rose to become the most outspoken and trusted reformist of the communist elite, in 1990 creating a Democratic Platform group that demanded radical change in the party's leading role, as well as decentralization of the state structure.

By August 1991, when conservatives attempted a coup, Yeltsin was the popularly elected president of Russia. This victory emboldened him to contest the power of the Soviet federal authorities. He swiftly dissolved the Communist Party in Russia and proceeded to fire officials appointed on the basis of party loyalty. In all these radical changes, Yeltsin risked a great deal of personal and professional safety, but it was in his nature to gamble and think big.

By early 1992, Yeltsin commanded the admiration of the entire world: the amazingly sudden and peaceful transformation of the Soviet Union from the "evil empire" of U.S. President Ronald Reagan's rhetoric into multiparty Russia was one of the most important developments of the post–Cold War period. Politicians in the West celebrated the victory of the United States over the Soviet Union. The Soviet people themselves celebrated the end of communist rule as though waking from a bad dream. But these celebrations were short-lived. Within months, the reality of the aftermath of political, social, and economic collapse set in.

Russia's Difficult Transition Yeltsin continued to rule Russia throughout the decade, but his popularity and success were never as high as in 1992. Politically the country became democratic in that the communist monopoly was replaced by a multitude of political parties, but many, and eventually most of them were undemocratic. Measures to transform the state-controlled economy into a market-driven one benefited a narrow stratum of people who controlled the infrastructure and markets of power in the enormous country, while most Russians became impoverished.

And in matters of national unity and international security, Yeltsin satisfied neither die-hard nationalists nor progressive reformers.

In 1992 the only Russian politicians with experience were communists, and most people who were not already involved in the party had no desire to participate in politics. Therefore, even though Yeltsin's regime introduced full political freedoms, most political parties represented small groups interested in political gains rather than voters' interests. Most prominent among these groups were newly enriched businessmen, who were able to gain control over important economic resources illegally and wanted to protect their businesses. The natural gas industry became a particularly powerful force in several parties.

CONNECTIONS: The development of the political class in Russia after the fall of the Soviet Union resembles the capture of state institutions and resources that characterized the development of the plutocracy in Great Britain in the eighteenth century. (See Section 18-3d The Social Order).

Other groups were motivated by the nationalist desire to make sure the new Russia served Russians above other nationalities. These groups grew in the early 1990s because they spoke to the electorate in terms people understood. They blamed poverty and personal insecurity on outsiders—the West or enemies within the CIS, such as Ukraine and Georgia, former Soviet republics now seeking independence from the Russians. Though these parties acknowledged social and economic problems, their solutions, such as increasing military spending to alleviate poverty, were ineffective. Yeltsin tried to balance these new factions and the communists but could not manage to create a popular, reform-minded party of his own.

Economic Corruption and Collapse Given the lack of parties that offered solid solutions to the economic and social problems of the broad electorate, most people did not fare better in these early years of Russian democratization. The economy was swiftly **privatized**, with the state selling or simply giving up its previous control over most economic enterprises, from factories to beauty salons. By 1995, over half of all economic activity was in private hands. It was in these private enterprises that almost 90 percent of the industrial workforce was employed. New service sectors developed, while large public enterprises and services, such as health care, social services, and education, remained largely in the hands of the state. State employees such as coal miners and teachers sometimes did not get paid for months, and inflation reduced the buying power of the ruble. Thus, even when the checks arrived, many public employees could not support their families. In 1993, more than 30 percent of the population was living in poverty.

During the same period, there was a marked increase in criminal groups, who took advantage of irregularities and took over many services and state enterprises. The state did not have enough reliable law enforcement agents to deal with corruption. Thus, while some of the signs of privatization looked encouraging, the overall welfare of the population declined. For a majority of Russians, the benefits of democracy were not apparent, and many began celebrating the old national holiday of the Soviet Union (November 7) with parades and even mourning Joseph Stalin.

In August 1998, the Russian stock market collapsed. Under pressure from international financial organizations such as the **World Bank** and the **International Monetary Fund (IMF)**, which had loaned Russia billions of dollars for economic reform, the government devalued the ruble, a completely unexpected measure that went against Yeltsin's repeated promises never to do that. Many lost their life savings and trust in the banking system. The ruble slowly recovered some of its value, but faith in the stock market and in Yeltsin's brand of reform was never fully restored.

Irredentist Challenges Yeltsin's decade in power was also plagued by crises in former Soviet territories. **Chechnya** (chech-nee-YAH), where the native Islamic majority had never accepted the Russian takeover of 1859, made a bid for independence in the early days of postcommunism. In 1994, Yeltsin sought to regain control through military invasion. After three years of military conflict his popularity plummeted when he signed a shaky truce with the Chechen rebels in 1997. By 1999, Chechnya had become a haven for traffic in illegal weapons and drugs, as well as a training ground for Islamic radicals. In the following decade and a half, relations between the Russian-installed Chechen leader and Moscow improved, and the region became also a recruiting area for military personnel sent with Russian consent to places such as Eastern Ukraine and Syria to foment war.

Among the former Soviet states that initially remained in the CIS, the Ukraine quickly resigned

privatization Replacement of state ownership of property with private ownership in the postcommunist states.

World Bank International financial organization controlled by developed countries in the West that offers discounted loans for economic reform to developing countries.

International Monetary Fund (IMF) International financial organization started in 1946 that is responsible for managing the global financial system.

Chechnya Region in Central Asia controlled by Russia since 1859, with a predominantly Islamic population and ruled by an authoritarian government backed by Moscow.

Euromaidan

Between November 2013 and March 2014 Kiev was engulfed in a massive street protest that had as its nexus this square, renamed by participants as "Euromaidan," or the pro-EU open space.

Vasyl Molchan / Alamy Stock Photo

Viktor Yanukovich (1950–) Ukrainian president (2010–2014) deposed by a popular uprising that criticized his close links with Russia and lack of support for EU integration.

Donbas Region embroiled in a civil war (2014–) between pro-Russian separatist forces and pro-Ukrainian government forces, where Russia has sent substantial military support for the rebels.

Vladimir Putin (1952–) President of Russia, 2000–2008 and since 2012, and prime minister between 2008 and 2012, popular because of his nationalist credentials and forceful display as a strong leader in international affairs.

United Russia Party Formed in 2001 out of two movements supporting Vladimir Putin, this political party has gained the largest presence in the Russian Parliament, controlling over 76 percent of the seats.

from full membership and began to negotiate closer relations with the European Union, the United States, and NATO. The country was marred in corruption and further roiled by massive protests surrounding the presidential elections of 2004. These events laid bare a deep division between the western and eastern parts of the country in terms of political interests and loyalties, which worsened over the next decade. Then, after ten years of further corruption and greater fragmentation among the population in their view of Russia and the European Union, in November 2013 Ukrainians took to the streets of Kiev. They began by protesting president **Viktor Yanukovich's** refusal to continue the process of EU integration and eventually succeeded in deposing him and exposing the Russian influence in Ukrainian affairs. By the end of February Russia had invaded Crimea and claimed it as its own, and the **Donbas** (don-BAHS) eastern region

of Ukraine began a Civil War against national Ukrainian authorities, seeking self-rule. Since 2014, Ukraine has remained embroiled in a violent civil war, with little hope for moving ahead toward a stable and transparent government and sustained economic development.

Putin Comes to Power After a decade of political, economic, and international challenges, Yeltsin finally decided to step down. Suffering from severe health problems and battling alcoholism, he had taken steps to secure his successor in the summer of 1999, when he appointed **Vladimir Putin** (vlad-EH-meer POO-tin) as premier. On December 31, Yeltsin called Putin into his office and handed over the presidency to him. This choice of a successor has proven to be Yeltsin's most troubled legacy.

With a professional background as a KGB officer, Putin swiftly directed his efforts toward recovering Russia's international prestige and power. Using the skills learned in an institution known for its violence and relentless fear tactics, he has worked to eliminate any serious political contenders through trials held in courts controlled by loyal allies and through severe economic punishments against any oligarchs who would not comply with Putin's rules on how to divide and control economic assets. Putin also developed a very successful grassroots mass organization through the **United Russia Party**, an unabashedly nationalist corporatist group that came to dominate Russian politics and the economy with populist slogans about making Russia great again.

Russia's Growing Global Influence In the following fifteen years, Russia managed to grab attention around the world through bold and violent shows of its ambitions and military power. The government imprisoned a pop group for criticizing the Orthodox Church and leaders of social media protest movements for criticizing Putin. Any nongovernmental organizations with international funding became suspect of spying. In 2014, Putin sent troops into Ukraine-ruled Crimea to claim the peninsula for Russia. Swift condemnation of this military aggression and economic sanctions followed in the European Union and the United States. Undeterred, Russia started to send substantial military support to the pro-Russian rebels in eastern Ukraine.

During the same period, Putin began aggressively developing new forms of espionage and interference in the affairs of other states, from seeking out ties with antiglobalization and anti-EU parties and movements in Europe, to hacking into government and other systems and providing safe harbor for **Edward Snowden**, the whistle-blower fugitive from the United States. In 2007, Russian hackers took down all Internet services in Estonia, a NATO and EU country with a strong anti-Russian record and significant Russian ethnic minority. In 2016, Russian hackers got into the email servers of the Democratic Party in the United States in the midst of one of the most contentious elections in the history of the country.

Russia has flexed its muscles also through more traditional ways of demonstrating its prowess. It has provided direct substantial military support for the **Bashar al-Assad** regime in Syria during its long and bloody civil war (2011–present), inclusive of targeting UN humanitarian relief convoys. It has developed new economic ties with China in a partnership of self-interest against the United States. Putin has warmly welcomed maverick European leaders such as Hungarian Premier **Victor Orbán** and Turkish president **Recep Erdoğan**, (REE-tsep ER-doh-ghan), steadily encouraging disunity inside NATO and in other international institutions that have long acted to keep Russia in check. Though it continues to face huge internal problems in terms of quality of life, employment, and freedom of speech, under Putin Russia has regained the international reputation of a superpower to be feared and watched carefully, increasing security concerns in Europe considerably.

30-1b The Dismemberment of Yugoslavia

In the 1990s, Yugoslavia plunged into a bloody civil war that destroyed the country, brought appalling human losses, and prompted the first major military intervention by NATO. The political and economic troubles that destroyed Yugoslavia had begun as early as 1968, when a new wave of nationalism became apparent in various regions of the country. Yugoslavia had been created after World War I, primarily as an extension of Serbia's ambitions for unifying all the South Slavs; Croats, Bosnians, and Slovenes were brought into this union as unequal

partners. World War II further antagonized various ethnic groups, as Serbs massacred Croats and Croats massacred Serbs under the watchful eye of the Nazi occupiers. After 1945, Josip Broz Tito had attempted to create "brotherhood and unity" among these embattled ethnic groups (see Map 30.1).

From Yugoslavism to Ethnic Cleansing When Tito died in 1980, hope for brotherhood and unity vanished. Politicians began to depict inflation and other economic problems in ethnocentric terms. As president of Serbia, **Slobodan Milošević** (mi-LOH-seh-vitch) attracted attention by laying blame for the Serbians' economic problems on the Croats, Bosnians, and Kosovar Albanians. With the state fully in control of politics, the media, and the army, Milošević embarked on a campaign to discredit non-Serbians and liberal economic and political reformers.

Slovenes and Croats reacted by declaring independence in June 1991. The Slovenes walked away from the Yugoslav union without contest, but Croatia and then Bosnia, which declared independence in 1992, became engulfed in civil war. Between 1991 and 1995, Serbs, Croats, and Muslim Bosnians engaged in **ethnic cleansing**, killing each other relentlessly on the basis of ethnic identity. Most of the fighting took place outside Serbia proper, but Milošević's actions as supreme commander of the Yugoslav army and in helping Serbian paramilitary groups

Map 30.1 **The Breakup of Yugoslavia** Between 1991 and 2006 the federal, multiethnic Yugoslavia fragmented into small and relatively poor independent states. Slovenia became a success, but Montenegro is still struggling to become an economically viable state.

1. What does the ethnic map of Bosnia–Herzegovina suggest about the internal challenges of this state?
2. What advantages does Slovenia have in relation to other former Yugoslav countries in terms of location and ethnic makeup?

Geneva Conventions Four international treaties that forbid the mistreatment of civilians and prisoners of war during wartime.

sanctions Punitive measures adopted by a country or group of countries against another state for political reasons.

Dayton Agreement Peace agreement signed in 1995 that ended the Bosnian civil war and established the grounds for an independent Bosnia and a Serbian Republic.

in Croatia and Bosnia played a central role in the atrocities committed by the Serbian forces. The exiling, killing, raping, and seizure and destruction of property had the sole purpose of eliminating the presence of these other ethnicities. More than twenty thousand women, most of them Muslim, were systematically raped in Bosnia as part of the Serbian and Croatian ethnic cleansing campaigns. The egregious nature of these crimes led to eventually designating rape as a war crime in international law.

Peace Through Compromise By 1994, enraged world opinion prompted belated action against these outrageous crimes. The internationally sanctioned **Geneva Conventions** forbade the mistreatment of civilians and prisoners of war, and the UN attempted to impose **sanctions** and sent in observers, but these measures had little effect. After the publication of evidence about several massacres, the UN finally approved air strikes by NATO, its first military intervention ever. By December 1995, the war was over, and all parties signed the **Dayton Agreement**, which recognized both an independent Muslim-Croat federation and a Serbian Republic in Bosnia, with a UN peacekeeping force to oversee the postwar transition. This peaceful resolution created important longer-term problems. It implicitly endorsed the right of the Milošević government to fight any future pro-independence movements, creating the legal justification for military intervention in Kosovo, and it generated a political system that has prevented war but also slowed down progress toward economic development and political stability.

"Rejoining" Europe: Economic Recovery Most post-Yugoslav countries pursued economic and political reconstruction with the aim of "rejoining" Europe. Slovenia quickly developed a free market while maintaining important components of the communist welfare system. By 2010, this country had a per capita Gross Domestic Product of over $28,000 and was a EU member. Croatia had more problems, especially given the staunchly nationalist and sometimes illiberal bent of its government in the early 1990s. With much of the economy trying to reinvent itself outside the Yugoslav markets, and with many of its resources having been diverted to civil war, Croatia moved slower toward a democratic system and a free-market economy. Yet, by the end of the 1990s, nationalist excesses were diminishing, trade with western Europe was picking up, and the economy was growing so fast that in 2013 Croatia became an EU member.

The Kosovo War Milošević tried to pull together Yugoslavia's remaining resources. His corrupt regime controlled the media, military, and political parties with support from abroad, especially Russia. To revive his popularity, he turned to Kosovo, where tensions between the overwhelmingly Albanian majority (80 percent) and the powerful Serbian minority had long festered. Tensions increased as Kosovars suffered increasingly from economic problems and political oppression. In the summer of 1998, as many as three hundred thousand Kosovo Albanians were forced to flee their homes, going elsewhere inside Yugoslavia or across the border to Albania, Macedonia, and Greece. This mass exodus raised international concern.

In February 1999, with one civilian massacre by the Serb forces confirmed, American, British, and Russian negotiators attempted a settlement between the Kosovo Albanians and Serbs. Serbians and their Russian supporters walked out of the talks, and on March 24, NATO began air strikes against Serbia. The **Kosovo** (KO-so-vo) **War** lasted just a few months. Its most spectacular features—the American bombing of the Chinese Embassy and Serbian hospitals—received much media attention, while the number of casualties was disputed because few independent observers were allowed on the ground. The number of Kosovo Albanian refugees skyrocketed to more than one million. When the NATO bombing ended, it was not clear who had won. Inside Serbia, Milošević declared victory and saw a rise in his popularity. The NATO campaign had the adverse result of mobilizing more Serbs, who cast themselves as patriots defending their country against a foreign invasion.

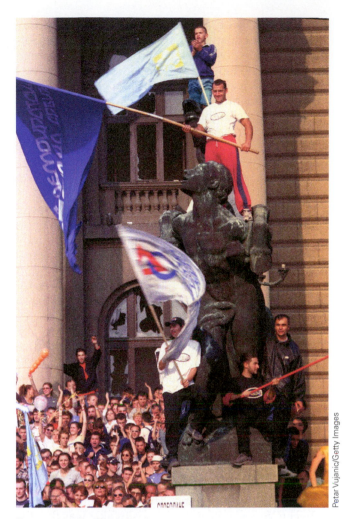

Petar Vujanic/Getty Images

Power to the People

In October 2002, Slobodan Milošević was brought down by a popular uprising in which young people and Internet communication played an important role. Serbia has struggled since then to fashion an international image of a viable democracy. How does this image compare to the collapse of the Berlin Wall (see the opening of Chapter 29) and fall of the communist regime in Moscow (see Section 29-5c The End of the Soviet Union)?

Toward a Precarious Peace The massive abuses in Kosovo ended, though instances of ethnic hatred have erupted periodically since 1999. The area's stability still depends on the continued presence of UN troops. Kosovo declared independence in 2008 and has been recognized as an autonomous state by 114 states (and 24 of the 28 EU members). Most refugees (eight hundred thousand) returned, and autonomous government institutions were set up to represent the Albanian population.

The Kosovo War did not bring down Milošević, but in October 2002 a popular revolt, with street protests all over Belgrade, removed

Kosovo War (March–June 1999) Military conflict between NATO forces and Serbia over abuses against Kosovo Albanians.

him from power. His replacement was Vojislav Koštunica, a constitutional lawyer with strong Serbian nationalist credentials and a more internationally acceptable reputation. The Milošević regime was brought down by its own massive corruption, the impoverishment of the population, general fatigue after a decade of fighting, and the growing sense that Serbia had become an outcast in Europe.

30-1c Postcommunist Transitions in Eastern Europe

The transformation of the other eastern European countries from members of the communist bloc to members of the European international community has been more successful. They developed constitutional, pluralist governments, with free elections, multiple parties, freedom of the press, and free-market economies. But each has faced specific problems, and their solutions have differed widely.

The Visegrád Four and European Integration Like Yugoslavia, Czechoslovakia was created after World War I. And like Yugoslavia, Czechoslovakia was dismembered in the early postcommunist years under the weight of nationalist pressures. But rather than starting a civil war, the Czechs and Slovaks went their separate ways on the basis of national referenda. At the end of 1992, the population simply voted to split up the country in two. Václav Havel, the playwright president, oversaw this peaceful democratic process and accepted its outcome. The important difference between Yugoslavia and Czechoslovakia was that the political leadership of the latter refused to pursue a violent path even though nationalist enmities existed. Instead, leaders trusted the newly developed democratic institutions, even when these institutions turned them out of power.

Coming together as the **Visegrád** (vee-sheh-GRAHD) **Four** in 1991, the Czech Republic, Slovakia, Hungary, and Poland agreed to coordinate internal reforms from education to the environment, with the goal of joining the European Union. By building regional trade, the four countries turned their communist economies into competitive capitalist ones. The keys to their success were three factors: agreement among the political leadership, public support, and economic and administrative infrastructures compatible with reform. In addition, long-standing personal links forged in the communist era among the underground oppositions in Poland, Czechoslovakia, and to some extent Hungary fostered institutional cooperation. Moreover, both the European Union and the United States regarded the economies of these four countries as the most advanced of the former communist states and invested in them both political hopes and financial resources.

Nationalism Returns to Eastern Europe Hungary embraced democratic politics, albeit with a strong nationalist element. Some popular politicians of the 1990s openly espoused anti-Semitism and pushed for special protection for ethnic Hungarians living in other countries. Yet such ethnocentric issues did not play any role in the economic policies pursued by either center-right or left-wing governments in the next decade. Overall, Hungary was successful in maintaining a talented labor force, attracting foreign investments, and improving the quality of life of its citizens until the late 2000s. In the aftermath of the global recession of those years, Viktor Orbán was elected for a second time as prime minister and used his strong victory to rewrite the constitution with a focus on restricting the independence of the courts, the freedom of the press, and gay rights. A vociferous Eurosceptic, Orbán has also developed a cozy relationship with Moscow, including criticism of the sanctions imposed on Russia for the annexation of Crimea.

After 1989, Poland saw the return and then departure of Solidarity leader Lech Wałęsa. In 1980, Wałęsa had been a charismatic unifier of opponents to communism, but after 1989 he was ill prepared to assume the responsibilities of governing a democratic regime. He had neither the vision nor the skills to offer good solutions to the challenges of privatization and to the increasing activism of the Catholic Church. Still, though Solidarity lost its initial appeal, it did give rise to numerous other parties and provided the groundwork for a generation of democratic politicians, the most talented of whom has been **Donald Tusk**. He became active in politics also through Solidarity in the 1980s, but after 1989 formed his own political party, the Civic Platform, with a platform similar to other Christian Democratic parties, such as the one led by Angela Merkel in Germany. Tusk went on to serve in parliament continuously after 1991, with two terms as prime minister and subsequently appointment as president of the European Council in 2014. Poland was also fortunate in that it proceeded quickly with privatization and implemented tough reforms that brought healthy economic growth by the end of the decade.

In social and cultural policies, however, Poland seemed to cling strongly to the past. Having been a main force of opposition under communism, the Catholic Church, with the direct support of Pope John Paul II, proceeded to create its own political following.

Visegrád Four Group formed in the early 1990s by Hungary, Poland, the Czech Republic, and Slovakia to coordinate internal reforms toward joining the European Union.

Donald Tusk (1957–) Polish politician who got started as a dissident activist during the Solidarity strikes of 1980 and went on to found the Civic Platform Party after 1989, serving in parliament and subsequently as premier (2007–2014) until he was appointed as president of the European Council.

Since then, the church has cultivated socially conservative politicians who wanted to make abortion illegal and advocated Catholic "family values," pursuing antigay propaganda campaigns. The public presence of the church grew, from television programs to educational institutions. In the late 2000s, the Catholic Church came to dominate the opposition to the rapid transformation of Polish society and culture after the country's accession to the European Union, especially on matters of birth control and same-sex rights. By 2015, with Tusk out of Polish politics, the Law and Justice Party led by Jarosław Kaczyński, with the full endorsement of the Catholic Church, won elections and proceeded to veer Poland's internal politics toward a radicalized nationalist direction. The new government acted fast to begin restricting the freedom of the press and attempting to criminalize abortion. The country remains deeply divided between this party and those who see adherence to the values and institutions of the European Union as a guarantee for individual rights and prosperity for the Polish people.

The Baltics Look West Latvia, Lithuania, and Estonia traveled a different road from direct Soviet control to successful democratization. Here, the legacies of communist politics and state economies were more difficult to undo. In Estonia, where a large Russian population had been brought in by the Soviets, the ethnic antagonism between the two groups ran deep, especially since Russians had been predominant in positions of power. While Latvians found it relatively easy to tolerate the presence of the Russians without fear of further russification, the Estonians (and to some extent the Lithuanians) saw ethnic Russians as agents of imperialism even after the dissolution of the Soviet Union. Indeed, Russia remained vocally concerned about the large Russian minority in Estonia but had little power to act on its behalf. Under the influence of growing nationalism, the Estonians have implemented some policies to diminish the public presence of the Russian minority, such as mandating a majority of classroom hours in Estonian, even in towns where only ethnic Russians live. Overall, however, with unemployment relatively low and new economic opportunities opening up, the people of the Baltic states remained relatively content in the 1990s and enthusiastically supported EU accession. All three countries have stable democracies, though fear of Russia's meddling in their affairs has grown considerably since the 2007 cyberattacks in Estonia and the more recent Russian annexation of Crimea.

Slow Reform in Romania and Bulgaria In the first decade and a half after 1989 Romania and Bulgaria failed to become fully functioning democracies. They held free elections in which a multitude of parties competed. But these parties were closer to the kinds of factions that developed in Russia under Yeltsin, led by old

Communist Party activists and interested in protecting narrow interests. Political corruption continued to dominate the electoral process, with few checks and balances. Corrupt judges protected corrupt legislators, and local law enforcement agencies worked with administrators to protect each other's interests.

In Romania, Ion Iliescu, a disgruntled protégé of Nicolae Ceaușescu, won the first presidential election and then proceeded to win again after a four-year interregnum by a more reform-minded coalition. Most successful Romanian politicians of this decade espoused some form of nationalism, from mild to radical. There was a short revival of a neofascist party, and one openly anti-Semitic and anti-Hungarian party won 20 percent of the vote in the 2000 presidential elections.

Romania's most debilitating problem was that no government in the 1990s pursued a thorough policy of privatizing large state enterprises and encouraging investments in competitive new businesses. Instead, political clients won investment bids through bribery and squandered many of the state and private resources for personal gain. Foreign investment was also discouraged by Romania's inability to protect private property. By 2000, the Romanian economy lagged behind that of every country in Europe save Albania.

Bulgaria fared marginally better. Though plagued by political corruption, its service and tourism industries outperformed those in Romania. Nor did nationalism play a strong rallying role, although small Muslim enclaves remained relatively impoverished and received inadequate support from the government. The country was also relatively less affected by organized crime than Romania and Russia, whose economies were sapped of important revenue resources by these criminal organizations.

Overall, economic growth in Romania and Bulgaria has been impeded by the harsh political and economic legacies of the communist period as well as a lack of investment incentives or interest from western countries. By the time these regimes achieved internal political stability, curbed corruption, and created legislation friendly to foreign investment, the initial enthusiasm of the West to invest in the postcommunist countries had vanished.

30-2 European Integration

» How has the European Union transformed European politics and economies?

» What impact has the European Union had on European security matters?

Due to these remarkable changes among the postcommunist states, eastern Europe both transformed and was transformed by the European Union. With the Soviet threat removed, western Europe perceived

Table 30.1 **Development of the European Union**

1951	European Coal and Steel Community (ECSC) is established
1957	Treaty of Rome establishes the European Economic Community (EEC), made up of Belgium, France, Italy, Luxembourg, the Netherlands, and West Germany
1973	Britain, Denmark, and Ireland join the EEC
1981	Greece joins the EEC
1985	Portugal and Spain join the EEC
1992	Maastricht treaty creates the European Union (EU); European Economic Community is renamed the European Community (EC) as part of the EU
1995	Austria, Finland, and Sweden join the EU; Schengen Agreement goes into effect
2002	The euro becomes EU currency
2003	First EU constitution is drafted
2004	Cyprus, the Czech Republic, Estonia, Hungary, Latvia, Lithuania, Malta, Poland, Slovenia, and Slovakia join the EU
2007	Bulgaria and Romania join the EU
2009	Slovakia becomes the sixteenth member of the Eurozone; Lisbon Treaty is ratified by all members
2010–2012	Financial bailout of Greece by the EU, IMF, and World Bank
2016	United Kingdom votes to withdraw from the EU

the future differently. The former communist countries became participants in a larger framework of European integration. This process of challenging established divisions and offering new ways of connecting European states and people created unprecedented opportunities to redefine Europe as a political, economic, and cultural community. In the 1990s, the Common Market underwent important institutional changes from a loose economic union to a fiscal unit, a political institution, and a cluster of cultural and social institutions that today are truly multinational and reach into every corner of the continent. Europeans tackled international security challenges on the basis of cooperation. Yet, internal political contests and nationalism have continued to test the boundaries of international collaboration. Table 30.1 summarizes the development of the European Union.

30-2a From Community to Union

After 1985, when Jacques Delors became the president of the **European Commission**, the highest executive authority of the Common Market, the European Community embarked more forcefully on a plan to create a single-market entity. Euro enthusiasts pointed to the outstanding track record of the participating countries since the inception of the Common Market in terms of economic growth, employment, and per capita income, suggesting that greater institutional cooperation among members would increasingly benefit them.

The growing complexity of economic globalization since the 1970s also suggested that greater political cooperation would be needed to sustain the well-being of member countries. To enable the workforce to move across borders in order to effectively match skills and needs, states would have to work out better policies regarding migration, labor rights, and social welfare. Coordinating taxation, interest rates, and other fiscal measures would also help businesses operate across borders. For example, for an enterprise such as Airbus, with capital and profits in France, to expand its foreign operations meant depending on the willingness of Spain and Britain to protect its business interests and accept its practices. Since the inception of the Common Market, such arrangements had developed through bilateral agreements. By the 1980s,

European Commission
Executive branch of the European Union, responsible for drafting legislation and enforcing regulations.

many believed that an international political institution would improve cooperation and serve the interests of both employers and employees.

Obstacles and Opposition The unification of institutions and standardization of economic regulations, from taxation to the labeling of agricultural products, was to take place between 1985 and 1992. The process of ratification was cumbersome, as Common Market members had to individually ratify all changes. This arrangement respected the sovereignty of each member state but rendered the process vulnerable to political change in any member country.

At the beginning there was a great deal of enthusiasm for the idea of a single market, increased opportunities for investment, and the unrestricted movement of workers and goods across borders. But by 1990 the enthusiasm was largely gone, as politicians, corporations, and consumers began to see that regulations meant to free up access to markets and goods also had a restrictive impact. For instance, agricultural producers were to test, package, and label their goods in accordance with new Common Market regulations. Smaller organic farmers suffered in the process because their costs of production and shipping increased significantly. If they passed these costs on to consumers through higher prices, they would make themselves less competitive than multinational corporations, such as McDonald's, which could produce certified genetically modified products more cheaply.

Monetary Unification At a series of intergovernmental meetings in 1991, member countries addressed such issues. Achieving a European Monetary Union demanded a complex plan of coordinating fiscal policies among members. And since such a massive fiscal restructuring had never before been attempted, policy makers and ordinary people alike worried about potential negative consequences. A policy of moving to one single currency, the **euro (€)**, was outlined, with the ultimate goal of having one European Bank and the euro in circulation by 1999. That change actually occurred in 2002.

Cooperation and Sovereignty The question of political integration raised nationalist fears about the expanded powers of the European Commission and European Parliament at the expense of national governments. By 1992, members worked out the formula of a loose federation. No one country could dominate either of these bodies. Any legislative measures by the European Parliament would have to be approved by a broad international margin, and the most important measures, such as a European constitution, would have to be ratified by each member. Furthermore, the European Parliament would have the power to check the executive powers of the European Commission.

Another thorny issue was the growth of the German share of the Common Market, especially with the unification of the two Germanies in 1990. Suddenly, this country counted for a quarter of the total population and 27 percent of the European Community's production. Concerns that a strong and ambitious Germany might again threaten the stability of Europe were allayed only when well-respected politicians, in particular French President François Mitterrand and German Chancellor Helmut Kohl, pursued a campaign for European integration: "We consider it necessary to accelerate the political construction of the Europe of the Twelve. We believe that it is time to transform relations as a whole among the member states into a European Union . . . and invest this union with the necessary means of action."

Free Movement Across Borders The idea of free movement of people across borders became vastly more complicated with the opening of borders in eastern Europe after the fall of communism and the incoming flood of eastern Europeans. A unified EU policy on immigration initially reconstructed the East–West divide. In 1995, most EU members began implementing the **Schengen Agreement**, which eliminated the need for citizens of signatory states to obtain visas to travel and work inside the Schengen space. Citizens of most other countries still had to apply for entry, but once they obtained a visa from one of the signatory states, they could travel without additional visas elsewhere in the Schengen space. In practice, it became more difficult for most people outside the Schengen territory to obtain work or permanent residence visas in any of the signatory countries, but it was easier to obtain travel visas. For people from postcommunist eastern Europe, still having to apply for a visa was a humiliating reminder of their outsider status in Europe.

Birth of the European Union In February 1992, the Common Market foreign ministers signed the **Maastricht** (MAHS-trikt) **treaty**, which created the European Union, the most important milestone toward European integration since the creation of the European Coal and Steel Community in 1951. Though member countries were expected to ratify the treaty, there was opposition in Denmark and Britain, where politicians and the populace at large preferred national policies in certain crucial areas.

euro (€) Currency introduced in most EU member countries starting in 2002.

Schengen Agreement Treaty signed by seven members of the Common Market in 1985 allowing the free passage of people and goods across their borders, which went into effect in 1995.

Maastricht treaty Treaty signed in 1992 and ratified by all members of the Common Market in 1993 that brought the European Union into being.

In Britain, the Conservatives retained the policy of deregulating industries and upholding the strength of the pound. In Denmark, the vote went narrowly against the treaty in order to retain environmental and other public policy standards higher than those of the European Union; the Danes also feared German domination. In both cases, however, opposition stemmed less from nationalist pride and anxieties than from concern about specific economic and social policies. After a year of negotiations with both countries, the Maastricht treaty went into effect in November 1993 and the European Union came into being.

30-2b The European Union in Operation

The European Union consists of a set of existing institutions, now with expanded powers, as well as some new bodies.

Executive Powers The highest executive body is the **European Council**, composed of heads of state or government and the president of the European Commission. Since 1993, the European Council has met several times a year to discuss issues of interest at the national and international level and on occasion to iron out tensions among member states. This body does not deal with the specific implementation of day-to-day measures passed by the European Parliament but only with broad issues, such as the balance between national political autonomy and international cooperation.

The **Council of Ministers** is charged with implementing EU goals on a practical level. A cross between an executive and legislative body, the Council of Ministers attempts to find a balance in unifying everything from energy to taxation policies so as not to run counter to national prerogatives and to maintain cooperation. For instance, the use of nuclear power for the energy needs of a particular state has to be reconciled with the environmental regulations of the European Union as a whole. The ability of this body to work well has been greatly tested by the financial crisis of the late 2000s and more recently by the influx of refugees into the European Union starting especially in 2015.

The European Commission, whose president also sits on the European Council, mediates between national and EU interests but works solely as an elected body of the European Union. Before 1993, the European Commission was the primary initiator of legislation and also served as the executive power in dealing with the Council of Ministers and the European Council. After 1993, the European Commission lost some of its legislative authority to the European Parliament, especially in matters of the EU budget. The EU Parliament has also helped restrain the executive powers of the European Commission, especially those of its president.

Legislative Powers The development of the **European Parliament** from a symbolic body to a legislative assembly with EU-wide powers from taxation to education is one of the most important political developments in Europe since Maastricht, and it has started to reshape European political parties. The number of seats assigned to each country varies but is not strictly proportional, so smaller countries have disproportionate influence. These smaller countries can form coalitions to block passage of laws they view as harmful to their interests. Representatives in the EU Parliament tend to act not only according to their national flags but also according to their ideological platforms, and the body divides more consistently along ideological than national lines. French delegates are as likely to be at odds with each other over environmental concerns, such as the use of genetically modified organisms in agriculture, as they are to be at odds with their German colleagues. Delegates who are members of Green parties, for example, tend to vote as an international bloc on environmental matters, regardless of what other representatives from their home countries think.

Expanding the Union In the 1990s, the European Union began to consider inviting countries from the former communist bloc to join (see Map 30.2). When the Visegrád Four began to lobby for admission, the European Union had to consider the impact of such a change on its economic strength and also the very criteria for admission. Greece, Portugal, and Spain had all been accepted as members in the 1980s on the premise that they had potential for democratic politics rather than a proven record. Yet to many EU leaders, the admission of Greece, because of its weak economy in the 1980s, set an unfortunate precedent.

Still, members such as France, Germany, and Italy supported rewarding the stable postcommunist democracies with EU membership. Supporters of enlargement eastward pointed to the larger markets and increased stability in Europe as advantages. Ultimately, market expansion and European stability became the criteria for enlargement in the next phase. Yet how these criteria were applied in some cases raised questions. For instance, many argued that having Estonia, Latvia, and Lithuania, with their sizable Russian minorities, in the European Union would, in

European Council EU advisory body composed of the heads of state or government of member countries and the president of the European Commission.

Council of Ministers Main legislative body of the European Union, composed of ministers from each country, that carries out EU goals in legal measures and policy making.

European Parliament The directly elected parliamentary body of the European Union.

Map 30.2 **The European Union in 2017** Since 1993, the European Union has been a powerful force in refashioning European identities. Originally an international economic organization, it has gained political and cultural dimensions.

1. What proportion of the European Union do the original members represent at the present time?
2. What does this change suggest about the relationship between western and eastern Europe?
3. How do you view the nonmember status of various countries in Europe in relation to the development and specific features of the European Union?
4. Looking at the members of the Schengen space and at the fences EU members have erected inside that space and on borders with other countries, what countries seem to display greater openness to people from other countries, such as refugees?

fact, create new tensions between the European Union and Russia, reducing European stability. Starting in 2015, these fears came to haunt NATO and the European Union.

By February 2003, eight of the postcommunist countries (the Czech Republic, Estonia, Hungary, Latvia, Lithuania, Poland, Slovakia, and Slovenia) became members along with two other applicants (Cyprus and Malta). In January 2007, they were joined by two additional postcommunist states, Romania and Bulgaria, followed by Croatia in 2013, bringing the total number of members to 28, of which nearly half (12) had been in the communist bloc. Britain's vote to leave the European Union in 2016 has further altered this proportion and balance of influence.

The EU Constitution and the Lisbon Treaty With so many new members in the European Union, discussions about changing its legal framework resulted in a new constitution, which was initially signed in October 2004 but had to be ratified by each member state before going into effect. In 2005, France and the Netherlands failed to ratify it, bringing the process to an impasse. Discussion resumed through a series of negotiations among member states and resulted in the **Lisbon Treaty**, which was ratified by all members and went into effect in December 2009. The treaty fundamentally altered the executive and legislative powers of the European Union, generally making individual members and their citizens accountable to new fiscal, judicial, and human rights standards. Individual citizens are now able to hold their national governments to higher standards in terms of human rights, from gender and sexuality issues to racial discrimination. (These same human rights provisions have brought about a backlash against the European Union from nationalist parties.) The Lisbon Treaty has made it possible to demand greater fiscal accountability from individual members, a change that has played a major role in Europe's recovery during the current economic crisis. In Greece, in particular, EU laws have greatly shaped the response to the economic crisis that started in 2010, when the government debt came to overwhelm the country's ability to function. The policies of austerity imposed by the European Union together with the World Bank and IMF have become a powerful example of the tension between national sovereignty and EU membership in times of crisis.

Lisbon Treaty Treaty signed by all EU members in 2007 that became the new constitution of the union in 2009; it gives the European Union additional legislative, executive, and judicial powers, including protection of individual citizens against human rights abuses by national governments.

Tony Blair (1953–) Labour Party prime minister of Britain from 1997 to 2007, credited with creating a more centrist position for the British left.

30-2c Nation-States in a New Context

The European Union has not meant European unity, even among the older member countries. Between the early 1990s and the late 2000s, in Britain, Germany, and Spain, right-wing governments were replaced by left-wing ones, though not necessarily for the same reasons. Starting during the global recession of the late 2000s, radical parties on the left and right have been more successful in national elections. Nationalist eurosceptics from Britain to Denmark have come to criticize, sometimes very effectively, the deleterious effects of open borders on national prosperity and security. Marxist coalitions from Spain to Greece have also won successive elections by criticizing the fiscal neoliberal policies of the European Union, strangely resonating with criticisms leveled by radical nationalists that the union was leaving the interests of workers in their countries unaddressed.

Leftist Coalitions In Britain in 1997, the Labour Party returned to power with **Tony Blair** as prime minister when the public reacted against the Conservative government's aggressive policies of privatizing national industries and reducing social programs. Blair pursued business-friendly internal policies and a commitment to the European Union. To Conservative skepticism about the impact of the European Union on the British pound and industries, Blair responded with enthusiasm for the EU's social and political components. Still, he was careful to continue his support for the pound, even as the rest of the European Union was adopting the euro.

After Britain came to accept large numbers of migrant workers from especially eastern Europe, a backlash against open borders grew, and with the global recession impacting the economic wellbeing of especially the lower middle class, a wave of euroscepticism swept through the country. In 2016, to the consternation of the world and many British citizens, 52 percent of voters in the referendum about leaving the European Union approved the measure. Still, just one year later, in June 2017 the ruling conservatives lost their majority in Parliament after early elections called by Prime Minister Theresa May to bolster the support for Brexit. The Labor Party, though still in opposition, gained nearly 10 percent.

The shift toward the left in Germany was both a product of EU integration and the condition for it. Helmut Kohl was a central player in promoting Maastricht and EU enlargement, but he faced problems at home connected to reunification, including fluctuating unemployment, the democratization and privatization of the former East Germany, and important disparities in the standard of living. The socially conservative chancellor lost some of his popularity during this period, as voters in both parts of reunified Germany began to identify the Christian Democrats with the economic and social problems of reunification.

AP Photo/Paul White, Files

Madrid Bombings

In March 2004, a series of related bombings on commuter trains in Madrid killed 191 and wounded more than 2,050 people. The heavily used commuter system of the Spanish capital came to a standstill. Though horrified by these events, Spanish politicians and the Spanish public only grew increasingly critical of U.S. President George W. Bush's so-called War on Terror.

» *How would you describe the scene in this attack?*

As a result, the Social Democrats came to power in 1998, with the younger **Gerhard Schroeder** as the first German chancellor to have grown up after the war and also the first to rule in a coalition with the Greens. Schroeder was a disappointment to the more left-leaning Social Democrats and the Greens, as he increased German military involvement in NATO and was unable to reduce unemployment. Still, he secured a second term in 2002. Among his important achievements were the lowering of taxes, preservation of government funding for education, and recognition of same-sex civil unions.

In 2005 he lost power to **Angela Merkel**, who became the most powerful supporter of the European Union in the face of increasing criticism and a series of crises (see Profiles in Change: Angela Merkel Completes Unification). She was reelected twice, serving for 12 years. Merkel has overseen a period of growth and stability in Germany's economic performance at a time of crisis in other parts of the European Union. Her position on keeping Germany's borders open to refugees from especially the Syrian civil war first won her great respect and subsequently growing criticism in terms of reshaping Germany's values and threatening its social stability.

In Spain, a centrist government dominated politics after 1996, overseeing the country's full integration into the European Union and a healthy economic growth after 2000. But it lost popularity by 2004 because of Spain's active role in the **Iraq War**. After **al-Qaeda** engineered a series of bombings in Madrid in March of that year, killing and injuring hundreds of people, the Socialist Workers' Party under the leadership of **José Luis Rodríguez Zapatero** won a close victory. From a staunchly Catholic conservative country under Franco, Spain became a leader in political reforms that surpassed the most ambitious EU civil rights policies. In 2005, the Socialist Workers' Party government passed a law recognizing same-sex marriages and engineered a reconciliation with terrorist Basque separatist groups. Reelected in 2008 at the beginning of the global economic crisis, Zapatero struggled to reform taxation, social welfare, and various fiscal policies to enable Spain to return to fiscal solvency. After 2012, the country has struggled to form and retain stable governments, with the electorate divided among several increasingly radical parties, some on the left and others on the right.

Center-Right Governments
By contrast, in France and Italy left-wing parties became weakened, creating electoral opportunities for center and increasingly staunchly right-wing parties. In France, **Jacques Chirac**, leader of the center-right Rally for the Republic, won the presidential election in 1995 in a close contest with the socialists. Chirac had built a career as a successor of the Gaullist tradition and after several unsuccessful

Gerhard Schroeder (1944–) Social Democratic chancellor of Germany from 1998 to 2005 who led a coalition government with the Greens.

Angela Merkel (1954–) Leader of the Christian Democratic party in Germany, the first woman and also first East German to be elected chancellor (2005–).

Iraq War War begun in March 2003 when a U.S.-led coalition overthrew Iraqi President Saddam Hussein in an attempt to establish a new, democratic regime.

al-Qaeda Islamic terrorist organization established by Saudi Arabs in 1988 to fight against the Soviet Union in Afghanistan.

José Luis Rodríguez Zapatero (1960–) Social-Democrat politician who served as prime minister of Spain for two terms (2004–2012), overseeing government reforms in response to the economic crisis, the eruption of terrorist al-Qaeda attacks, and reconciliation with the Basque separatists.

Jacques Chirac (1932–) French president from 1995 to 2007, leader of the center-right party Rally for the Republic, and outspoken critic of American policy in Iraq.

bids emerged as president in the middle of a decade of slow economic growth and high unemployment. Despite his promise of opposing further EU integration, he became an advocate of the euro. Though he was implicated in several high-level corruption scandals, he managed to distance himself from former close allies who were prosecuted. Chirac also maintained his popularity in France because of his staunchly anti-American position on the Iraq War.

In 2007, the center-right **Nicholas Sarkozy**, who proved tough on Muslim rioters two years earlier as minister of the interior, won a resounding victory as Chirac's successor. Sarkozy made a mark through critical views of EU expansion and his pro-American stance, which set him apart from his predecessor. During his term, he was criticized by both the left and the right in France, the former for racist remarks and actions against Muslim and Roma immigrants, and the latter for his inconsistency in terms of government deregulation of economic life. In the 2012 elections, Sarkozy lost to **Francois Hollande**, the Socialist candidate.

Though Hollande signaled for many the return of the left, the economic policies pursued by his government aligned more closely with the neoliberal position advocated by more conservative counterparts elsewhere. In addition, with public opinion deeply divided over questions of national security and multiculturalism, his presidency was not effective in sustaining popular support. After the Paris and Nice attacks from 2015–2016, the public came to see Hollande as either too soft or too harsh in pursuing the terrorists. Similarly, on questions of how to engage with religious values that depart from the staunchly secular mainstream, the Hollande presidency satisfied very few French citizens.

When in 2016 several cities passed ordinances disallowing women from wearing the modest burkini on French beaches and police began to arrest women who refused to comply, the public became aggressively divided over the issue of the freedom of religious expression via the veil. The debate over veiling was not new, but the extent of the issue's divisiveness between those who see multiculturalism as a democratic value and those who see such expressions of religiousness as a major departure from French republican values was unprecedented. The ban was overturned later that year.

Among those who supported the ban was the National Front, an ultraright nationalist party led by **Marine le Pen**, who in early 2017 became a rising popular contender for the next French presidential elections. A radical eurosceptic, le Pen brought the National Front from a marginal extremist faction to a mainstream organization with a huge following. Established by her father in the 1970s, the party reached enough public support (11 percent) to secure representation in parliament in the 1980s. By early 2017 the National Front commanded 23 percent of the public support in the presidential polls, ahead of other contenders. Le Pen's strength has been bolstered by anti-Muslim feelings, the weak performance of the Hollande government, as well as considerable funding by Putin's business allies.

During the 2017 Presidential elections, the National Front received nearly 40 percent of the vote, a remarkable and worrisome rise in popularity. **Emmanuel Macron**, an independent investment banker with very little experience in public service, won the presidency as the head of a newly formed party, becoming the youngest person to serve in this position in France. The Socialists suffered the greatest loss. Macron promised a fresh departure from traditional politics, which he has a chance to deliver with the newly inaugurated government, composed of conservatives, centrists, and socialists. Notable elements in the membership of this cabinet are the inclusion of a number of civil society leaders, as well as gender parity.

In the 2000s, Italian politics were likewise dominated by a center-right government led by **Silvio Berlusconi**, a media mogul turned politician. Having made millions of dollars in the entertainment industry, especially television, in the 1990s Berlusconi developed a party devoted to defeating the communists with a nationalist, business-friendly platform. Like Chirac, Berlusconi was involved in several high-profile corruption scandals that eventually led to his resignation in 2011.

Eurosceptics and Right-Wing Electoral Victories

By 2004, the rightward shifts in some national elections combined with negative reactions to the effects of EU integration produced a general shift to the right in the European Parliament elections, in which various right-wing parties and coalitions garnered more than 60 percent of the vote. Almost one-quarter of these representatives were outright opponents of the European Union. Yet the financial troubles that have plagued individual EU economies

---

Nicholas Sarkozy (1955–) President of the French Republic (2007–2012), led a center-right government that attempted to deregulate government control in the economy and limit the powers of the presidency while enhancing those of the parliament.

Francois Hollande (1954–) Socialist French politician who served as president between 2012 and 2018 and failed to retain the support of the citizenry.

Silvio Berlusconi (1936–) Television mogul, leader of a center-right coalition, and prime minister of Italy (2001–2006 and 2008–2011).

Marine le Pen (1968–) Ultranationalist French politician and leader of the National Front, whose presidential platform for 2017 was to make France great again by criticizing EU policies of open borders and free trade. She was soundly defeated by newcomer Emmanuel Macron.

Emmanuel Macron (1977–) Newly elected president of France, defeated the Socialist candidate in the first round, as well as the ultra-nationalist National Front in the second round. He was a member of the Socialist Party between 2006 and 2009 and served briefly as Minister of the Economy and Finances before declaring his bid for the presidency and founding his own party. He is the youngest president in the history of France.

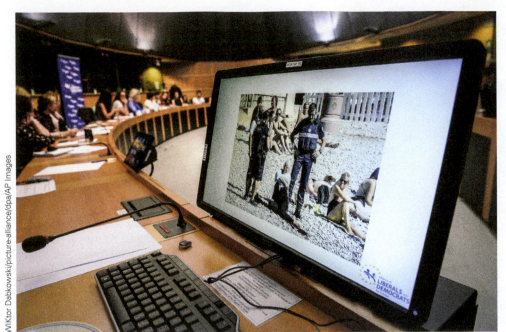

WIKtor Dabkowski/picture-alliance/dpa/AP Images

The Burkini Ban

In the summer of 2016 several French cities passed ordinances banning women from wearing body-covering outfits at the beach, as seen in this image. The ban divided the French citizenry, with some defending individual freedom to dress modestly at the beach, and others supporting the ban as reflecting French secular values and a symbol of religious fundamentalism among Muslims.

since then resulted in very different electoral results by 2009, when right-wing parties and eurosceptics counted for less than 12 percent of the vote.

By 2017, however, both national and EU-wide elections showed a decided shift toward antiglobalization and curtailing individual freedom of movement across borders. With Britain leaving the European Union over fears of immigrants, Poland and Hungary in the hands of ultranationalist governments, and France with a rising extreme right-wing party, the stability of the European Union has come to depend on Germany and newcomers such as Estonia and Romania, who still consider the cost of membership a worthwhile investment into their countries' stability and well-being. Debates over the EU's future are guaranteed to remain wide-ranging, from questions about enlargement to specific economic, social, and cultural policies. The most intractable of these are how to confront the Russian security threat, how to engage with the refugee crisis generated by the Syrian War, and how to respond to the "America first" platform of newly elected U.S. President **Donald Trump**.

30-2d European Security and International Organizations

The greatest challenges for the European Union have been international security matters, where the changing roles of the UN and NATO have also impacted EU states' potential for representing their interests as a bloc. Although during the Cold War the UN had been influential in the postcolonial world in security matters and had tried to mediate between the two superpowers and other states, it did not play an important security role in Europe. The ethnic-cleansing atrocities and utter chaos of the Yugoslav civil wars, however, convinced the UN to send a peacekeeping force. EU members generally supported this idea, and British, French, and Italian troops figured prominently among the peacekeepers. The UN intervention was framed as a globally significant means of halting human rights abuses and the European Union remained marginal in decision making.

NATO's Military Role in Europe The ineffectiveness of UN troops forced the international community to consider more drastic measures, and NATO stepped in to oversee a military intervention against the rebel Serbs in Bosnia. Traditionally, NATO had focused on securing western Europe against threats from the communist East. In the 1990s it transformed itself, partly through this intervention, into a broader alliance to secure democratic Europe, east and west, against external or internal threats. Russia, no longer the main enemy, played a sometimes friendly, if passive, role. Under Yeltsin, though aligned with Milošević, it never challenged NATO militarily.

As part of its expanded mandate of preserving security and democracy in Europe, NATO also embarked upon a process of eastward enlargement, building **Partnerships for Peace** with postcommunist countries as a bridge toward their full membership in the alliance. Partnerships with thirty countries allowed for increased cooperation in matters of military training, ground operations, and logistical links for future strategy planning. NATO requirements forced reforms, including civilian leadership at the top of the armed services administration and

Donald Trump (1946–) Real estate tycoon who became president of the United States in 2017 on the populist ultranationalist platform of "making America great again."

Partnerships for Peace NATO project to increase cooperation in military matters between its members and postcommunist states.

Angela Merkel Completes Unification

Angela Merkel The most effective political leader in Germany after World War II, Angela Merkel has successfully managed internal political and social challenges while becoming the voice of the EU during the economic crisis of the past decade and a staunch defender of the union on international strategic and security matters.

In 1989, when Germany was searching for a new identity and path in Europe, nobody in the East or West would have predicted the daughter of a Lutheran pastor from East Germany would become the most powerful woman in the world by 2009, according to *Forbes* magazine. How Angela Merkel rose from her station in life to this remarkable position of power illustrates the important opportunities that opened up for many in Europe after the end of the Cold War, and suggests the boundless possibilities for change on the continent in the future, both internally and globally.

Merkel was born Angela Dorothea Kasner in Hamburg (then West Germany) in 1954. Her father was a Lutheran pastor and her mother a member of the Social Democratic Party. When she was a few months old, her father was called to head a parish in East Germany, so Merkel grew up under the communist regime. She was gifted in the sciences and went on to obtain a doctorate in physics in 1978, and later worked as a researcher at the Central Institute for Physical Chemistry of the Academy of Sciences in East Berlin. She only became interested in political issues in 1989 as part of the "Democratic Awakening," when prodemocracy street protests took place in many East German cities in the months before the fall of the Berlin Wall. As a spokeswoman for this movement and for the speedy reunification of Germany, she was elected to parliament in the first East German free elections in 1990, and subsequently joined the Christian Democratic Union (CDU).

She slowly rose through the ranks of that party, which dominated the process of reunification under then chancellor Helmut Kohl. When he was ousted from party leadership because of murky financial dealings, Merkel was elected the first chairwoman of the CDU. Merkel was unusual in many regards: she was the first woman to lead the party, as well as the first non-Catholic to do so, and the first politician from the former communist regime. For a party that stood for family values, as a divorcee without children she also hardly fit the ideal German woman. She was also the first person

increased expenditures on armaments, equipment, and personnel. In 1996, the Czech Republic, Poland, and Hungary were admitted to NATO, paving the way for admission of most other postcommunist eastern European states in the next decade. Thus, NATO became the broadest military alliance representing the security interests of Europe.

After Putin became president, he harshly criticized NATO as a direct threat to Russian security interests, starting with the Baltics' entry into NATO in 2004. Subsequent gestures to other post–Soviet republics, especially Ukraine, to apply for NATO membership resulted in more drastic measures on the part of Moscow, culminating with the annexation of Crimea in 2014. NATO came under further criticism from the

United States after Trump became president, primarily in terms of the lack of financial commitment on the part of most European members. With the exception of Greece, Poland, and Estonia, no other EU member spends the required 2 percent of their GDP on defense.

The United States and European Security The U.S. role in NATO has remained central, as its largest and most important funding and armament source. Some European states, such as France, urged a more European-centered framework for solving international conflicts on the continent, but most others, especially the postcommunist countries of eastern Europe, were happy to have American troops and military support in their countries, as they were still

with such an outstanding academic background. In fact, it is likely that her impeccable academic credentials, together with her reputation for hard work and personal integrity, enabled her to overcome any questions of inadequacy that other elements of her biography might have invited.

From 2000 on she ably rebuilt the reputation of the CDU and won the 2005 elections, becoming the first woman top political officer in the history of Germany. Due to her rising popularity, she was reelected by a wide majority in 2009. Merkel was one of the main architects and an active lobbyist for the Treaty of Lisbon, pressuring less enthusiastic EU members to sign on. As chancellor of the strongest economic power in the European Union during a period of global recession, Merkel has successfully brought Germany to a position of strong economic growth and fiscal solvency.

Under her leadership, Germany has come to embody a balance of probusiness and prowelfare policies that, combined with fiscal self-restraint in terms of government spending and debt accumulation, have established new standards for all EU members.

Merkel's bid on strengthening Germany by opening its borders to refugees has seen more mixed reactions. Some initially complained that Merkel's policies were too unwelcoming to certain categories of refugees. Others, especially after a public debacle surrounding incidents of sexual assault during New Year's Eve 2016 in Cologne, have come to view Merkel as too soft on Muslim refugees. Overall, however, Merkel remained the staunchest defender of EU institutions and goals amid a growing trend of criticisms from within and outside Europe.

---

concerned about Russia's interests in the area. The Kosovo War became the first test of the new members' and partners' commitment to upholding their military obligations, and Poles, Czechs, and Romanians all gave significant help. Between 2000 and 2014 NATO operations in Europe remained minimal, while the bulk of operations shifted to the Middle East and Central Asia. However, with the Russian annexation of Crimea NATO has turned its focus on greater military preparedness and defending its eastern members in Europe.

30-3 Europe and Globalization

>> **How has globalization transformed the economic power of Europe in the world?**

>> **What have been the great international challenges since 1991?**

Since the early 1990s, a combination of technological, political, and market forces have transformed the world economy into a dynamic, close-knit web of processes. The growth of the European Union played a central part in this change, securing a privileged role in globalization as the largest economy in the world. As the speed of global communication has increased, Europeans have become increasingly involved in world affairs and culture while non-Europeans have remained interested in Europe. But the international security problems that emerged after the Cold War have been challenging, and Europeans have often been divided over crises in the Middle East and international terrorism. The greatest challenge faced by the European Union since the mid-2010s has been how to respond to the growing waves of refugees seeking safety or a better life in the European Union, in the midst of rising antiglobalization movements in every

EU member state. This growing crisis has tested the limits of the democratic values at the core of the union.

30-3a Economic Globalization

In the 1990s, economic production and trade became more closely interwoven on an unprecedented global scale, owing to several developments. New technologies, such as accurate and instant communication of information, computerized assembly lines, and new types of large trucks and refrigerated crates, made it easier to produce and transport more goods anywhere from the United States to Taiwan. Support for free trade among the most powerful countries in the world facilitated the exchange of goods across borders. An already high standard of living in the developed countries meant that people expected access to cheap consumer goods. To feed this process, many American and European businesses, such as Unilever, started to look for production sites with low costs, loose labor and environmental protections, and high product quality. Postcommunist eastern Europe fit this profile, as did China, Vietnam, and other places in the developing world. Evian and Nissan production facilities sprouted from Hungary to Taiwan.

New International Structures and Economic Power
The most important institutional supporter of globalization has been the **World Trade Organization (WTO)**, created in 1995 to oversee the **General Agreement on Tariffs and Trade (GATT)**. First signed in 1947, this agreement encouraged free trade in order to generate economic prosperity in the early postwar years. There was no institution to oversee the agreement, which remained

World Trade Organization (WTO) International organization created by GATT in 1995 to implement GATT's free-trade principles.

General Agreement on Tariffs and Trade (GATT) International agreement promoting free trade, first signed in 1947, and most recently signed by 123 countries in 1993.

loosely enforced by individual countries. For instance, the countries of the Common Market abided by GATT, but countries in eastern Europe and Latin America were less inclined to allow cheaper western goods to be introduced in their markets. Instead, most developing countries pursued policies that protected internal production so as to reduce their dependency on imports. Equally important were the ideological considerations of countries like China, which feared that the impact of western goods might destabilize communism.

But with the end of the Cold War, many of these considerations became obsolete. Beginning in 1995, the WTO allowed countries to become members on the basis of stable trade policies and governments. The 164 member countries benefit from reduced tariffs, preferential trade agreements, and access to international loans through connections with the International Monetary Fund (IMF) and the World Bank. Entry into this group and policy making are both accomplished through consensus, an arrangement that has tended to give the wealthiest economies greater power than members with weaker economies. It has also facilitated the operation of large multinational corporations in foreign markets, to the detriment of small producers everywhere, especially in less developed countries. And since most multinational corporations are still overwhelmingly controlled by investors in the United States, European Union, and Japan, the WTO has enhanced the economic power of these areas at the expense of the rest of the world.

During the economic recession of the late 2000s the IMF played an aggressive role in demanding austerity measures on the part of debtor countries like Greece and Spain, provoking harsh responses, especially when welfare measures were eliminated in the process. However, since the appointment of **Christine Lagarde** as managing director of the IMF, the institution has begun to measure and address the effects of economic policies more carefully, especially regarding economic inequality between men and women. By carefully measuring development in terms of alleviating gender economic inequality, the IMF has become an important institution to address some of the most intractable economic and social problems in the world in recent times.

European Union's Economic Competitiveness

Individually, European countries and corporations might have been at a disadvantage against the greater economic power of the United States or, more recently, China and Russia. But the EU framework has enhanced their competitiveness in the scramble for new markets and cheap labor in the developing world. In the early 1990s, the markets in eastern Europe were flooded with chickens from the Netherlands, milk from

Christine Lagarde

In 2011 Christine Lagarde became the first woman to head the IMF, bringing unprecedented sustained attention to the gender aspects of economic inequality and poverty in the world.

Italy, and shoes from Spain. These products were often partially manufactured in eastern Europe, but still under western brand names. The flow of goods was overwhelmingly west to east for the first decade after 1989. But western producers then set up shop in many eastern European locations and shipped their goods, for example, from Budapest to Paris. For the postcommunist countries now in the European Union, this process has reached near-parity, with the newer members having achieved greater buying and production power. By 2016, the European Union was the largest economic power in the world. The European Union has also used members' links with former colonies, forging strong relations with developing economies from Indonesia to Nigeria. British Petroleum, for example, works in South Korea to develop technologies to be used in Cameroon and Nigeria to extract oil and natural gas.

The Global Economic Recession

The spectacular growth of interdependency in economic processes, from foreign trade to stock trade, prices, and availability of capital, bore bitter fruit in the second half of the 2000s. The collapse of several important banks and

Christine Lagarde (1956–) French politician and labor lawyer who in 2011 became the first woman to head the IMF, directing the organization to begin paying closer attention to the sources of economic gender inequality in the world.

international companies, due initially to the deregulation of the mortgage industry, has led to a worldwide recession that has affected entire countries, private individuals, and multinational corporations. Iceland became the first such victim in 2008, when three of its main banks folded and the currency collapsed. The severe problems faced by its economy became a warning for the European Union, which assumed a more aggressive role in terms of limiting access to loans and other financial assistance to other members, such as Greece, Portugal, and Spain. Countries facing major debt and currency devaluation have been pressured to drastically reduce welfare programs and establish new banking and business regulations to prevent future disasters for the European Union.

Multinationals based in the European Union have generally done better, given the continuing strength of the euro, though individual citizens have fared worse, with rising taxes, decreasing salaries, and vanishing benefits. Some countries, such as Germany, have managed to retain more of their social welfare programs and even sustain economic growth. But the possibility to predict future economic problems in the European Union remains limited, given the linkages of all aspects of European economies with markets and resources that are well beyond the control of the European Union.

Antiglobalization Activism Producers have successfully used the WTO and other international organizations like the IMF to secure business interests, but human rights, environmental, and consumer activists have not been as effective in curbing the deleterious effects of globalization. Questions about product safety, abusive labor practices such as child labor and sweatshops, and environmental damage have not received much attention in private corporations' business practices. Even when states have tried to increase legal regulations against such abuses, multinational corporations such as Shell or Nike, with higher annual revenues than some European countries, have used the WTO effectively to lobby on behalf of deregulation in the name of free trade. More recently, however, Amnesty International and other human rights groups have forced the question of human rights abuses by member countries or members-to-be. A precondition for China's admission to the WTO, for example, was the reduction of abuses in labor practices.

The antiglobalization movement has gained other supporters since the early 2010s. From Britain to the United States, from Poland to France, populist nationalist movements started decrying globalization as the source of unemployment, secularization, and the demise of traditional family values. After seven years of intense negotiations, the Trans-Pacific Partnership was signed in 2016 to bring eleven countries into a preferential trade agreement, but without the United States as a member, despite the strong support of President **Barack Obama**. This turnaround suggests a major shift in how the United States engages with trade issues. Britain's exit from the European Union was also prompted by the antiglobalization attitude of citizens in that country.

It remains to be seen how far this opposition will go and to what extent the worldwide interconnectedness of economic processes can be impacted globally by such unilateral shifts in attitude and policy.

International organizations made slow progress toward dealing with other global problems, such as **global warming**, world poverty, and the AIDS epidemic. Scientists have linked the **greenhouse effect** to rapid industrialization and have urged governments to come to a global agreement over basic regulations that would prevent further erosion of the earth's atmosphere. In 1997, representatives from 160 countries met in Kyoto and signed an agreement to cut greenhouse gas emissions by 10 percent, but the United States, the world's larger industrial producer of greenhouse gases, declined to ratify it. By 2015, 195 UN members gathered in France and signed the **Paris Agreement**, the first global agreement to reduce pollution substantially (see Learning from a Primary Source: The Paris Agreement on Climate Change). By November 2016, 132 members, including the United States, ratified the agreement, bringing its provisions into force. The agreement asks the main producers of greenhouse gases (the United States, China, and the European Union) to both curb pollution and also provide financial support to other countries to alleviate the effects of pollution. Alas, on June 1, 2017, President Trump announced that the United States would withdraw from the agreement. Even so, the agreement establishes an unprecedented form of accountability for the effects of globalization, and may substantially change the ecological well being of the planet even without the contribution of the United States in the near future.

World Health Issues The UN has worked to bring economic help to the world's poorest areas, such as Africa and South Asia, but even as farmers produce more than enough to feed the world's population, the UN's direct aid policies and the WTO's advocacy for free trade have not eliminated starvation as a cause of premature death. The continuing waves of refugees from underdeveloped to developed economies speaks to these unmet goals.

global warming Increase in the average temperature of the air and oceans in recent decades and its projected continuation.

greenhouse effect Effect of gases emitted by human activities, especially pollution.

Paris Agreement Agreement signed in 2015 by 195 states to reduce greenhouse gas emissions, went into effect in November 2016.

Barack Obama (1977–) First African American President of the United States (2008–16), managed the withdrawal of U.S. forces from Iraq and Afghanistan, oversaw the economic recovery after the 2008 Great Recession, passed the first comprehensive national healthcare act, and supported substantial investments in the research and practical solution to reducing climate change.

The Paris Agreement on Climate Change

At the end of the twenty-first conference of the United Nations Framework Convention on Climate Change, on December 12, 2015, representatives of 195 states agreed to the language in the following agreement, which by December 2016 was signed by 194 of the represented states and ratified by 132 of them, including the United States and China. The agreement went into effect on 4 November 2016. On June 1, 2017, U.S. President Trump announced that the United States would withdraw from the agreement.

What principles undergird the climate agreement? How does the agreement understand "climate justice". How do the agreement's provisions define the relationship between developed and developing countries? What is necessary for the agreement to fulfill its aspirations?

❶ What "special situations" might the agreement be referencing?

❷ How does the document define the eradication of poverty in relation to addressing climate change?

❸ What does it mean for the agreement to single out these categories of people as deserving special attention?

Recognizing the need for an effective and progressive response to the urgent threat of climate change on the basis of the best available scientific knowledge.

Recognizing the specific needs and special circumstances of developing country Parties.

Taking full account of the specific needs and special situations of the least developed countries with regard to funding and transfer of technology. **❶**

Emphasizing the intrinsic relationship that climate change actions, responses and impacts have with equitable access to sustainable development and eradication of poverty. **❷**

Recognizing the fundamental priority of safeguarding food security and ending hunger, and the particular vulnerabilities of food production systems to the adverse impacts of climate change.

Taking into account the imperatives of a just transition of the workforce and the creation of decent work and quality jobs in accordance with nationally defined development priorities.

Acknowledging that climate change is a common concern of humankind, Parties should, when taking action to address climate change, respect, promote and consider their respective obligations on human rights, the right to health, the rights of indigenous peoples, local communities, migrants, children, persons with disabilities and people in vulnerable situations and the right to development, as well as gender equality, empowerment of women and intergenerational equity. **❸**

Noting the importance of ensuring the integrity of all ecosystems, including oceans, and the protection of biodiversity, recognized by some cultures as Mother Earth,

Since the 1990s, another significant global concern has been the persistence of malaria and the spread of the AIDS virus, especially in sub-Saharan Africa, where 71 percent of the world's cases of HIV were found in 2013. In the 2010s, significant progress was recorded in combating this epidemic, with 39 percent of adults on the antiretroviral treatment due to efforts by the World Health Organization (WHO), national governments, and private funding sources.

Likewise, malaria, for which preventive vaccines have existed for more than a generation, still kills millions of people each year in the poorest areas of the world, with 89 percent of those infected living in sub-Saharan Africa. The most effective programs for containing these two epidemics have been international philanthropic nongovernmental organizations working with the WHO. Since 2000, through the efforts of especially the Bill and Melinda Gates Foundation, billions of dollars have gone to programs to eradicate this deadly disease, an initiative that has encouraged further fundraising toward this goal. There is hope that by 2040 malaria will be eradicated.

30-3b International Security and Terrorism

Since the 1990s, a sweeping transformation has occurred in international relations. Though the Americans and western Europeans were partners in winning the Cold War, the United States largely determined the international agenda in the first two decades after 1991.

4 How would you define a "sustainable lifestyle and pattern of consumption and production"

and noting the importance for some of the concept of "climate justice", when taking action to ad-dress climate change.

Recognizing that sustainable lifestyles and sustainable patterns of consumption and production, with developed country Parties taking the lead, play an important role in addressing climate change. **4**

This Agreement aims to strengthen the global response to the threat of climate change by: Holding the increase in the global average temperature to well below 2°C above pre-industrial levels and pursuing efforts to limit the temperature increase to 1.5°C above pre-industrial levels, recognizing that this would significantly reduce the risks and impacts of climate change; increasing the ability to adapt to the adverse impacts of climate change and foster climate resilience and low greenhouse gas emissions development, in a manner that does not threaten food production; and making finance flows consistent with a pathway towards low greenhouse gas emissions and climate-resilient development.

Developed country Parties should continue taking the lead by undertaking economy-wide absolute emission reduction targets. Developing country Parties are encouraged to move over time towards economy-wide emission reduction or limitation targets in the light of different national circumstances.

Developed country Parties shall provide financial resources to assist developing country Parties with respect to both mitigation and adaptation in continuation of their existing obligations under the Convention.

Accelerating, encouraging and enabling innovation is critical for an effective, long term global response to climate change and promoting economic growth and sustainable development.

At any time after three years from the date on which this Agreement has entered into force for a Party, that Party may withdraw from this Agreement by giving written notification to the Depositary.

Source: United Nations Framework Convention on Climate Change (http://unfccc.int/paris_agreement/items/9485.php)

Security concerns in the West changed from the contained fears about relatively stable communist states to a vague terrorist threat, largely located in the Middle East and in Muslim communities, but often without a state sponsor that could be held accountable through the conventional means of international relations. Overall, this change has reduced the effectiveness of the UN as a means for peacefully alleviating security threats. Its function has shifted instead to poverty, AIDS, climate change, and other human rights issues. Though peacekeeping remains one of its functions, the UN has not used its troops to great effect anywhere in the world since the 1990s, from Bosnia to Haiti. Instead, the United States has come to rely primarily on NATO and other bilateral and broader agreements to further its security interests. Europeans have participated in this process either as members of NATO or more recently as individual allies of the United States in the **War on Terrorism**.

Conflicts in the Middle East The most intense site of conflict has remained the Middle East. In 1991 Iraq, under the leadership of **Saddam Hussein** (sah-DAHM hoo-SAIN), invaded Kuwait, a country rich in oil and with close economic ties to the United States. The noncompliance of the Iraqi leader with the UN resolution demanding his withdrawal prompted an international military response. In the **Gulf War**, the United States led a coalition of more than thirty states that included significant forces from Britain, France, and Egypt. East European countries sent in specialists to lend logistical support.

This conflict signaled an intensification of tensions that had been building up in the Middle East since World

War on Terrorism Term used by the George W. Bush administration to refer to military, political, and legal actions taken to curb the spread of terrorism since 2001.

Saddam Hussein (1937–2006) Iraqi president from 1979 to 2003 who fought against the United States in the 1991 Gulf War and was deposed during the Iraq War.

Gulf War (1991) War between an international coalition led by the United States against Iraq in response to Iraq's invasion of Kuwait.

War II. Since the inception of Israel in 1948, the United States, Britain, and other western countries have been committed to its security as an outpost of democratic rule and western civilization. Arab countries in the Middle East came to view the West with mistrust and Israel as a symbol of western imperialism in the area. While Jordan remained relatively friendly to the West, since the mid-1950s, Egypt, Syria, and later Iran and Iraq became open supporters of Arab nationalist claims at the expense of Israel, on occasion testing the strength of this state through military campaigns at its borders (see Map 30.3).

The Rise of International Terrorism The fate of the Muslim and Christian Palestinians in Israeli territories has remained a point of contention between Arab nationalists and Israel. By the 1970s, as peaceful negotiations had not yielded much success for the Palestinian cause, a new method of struggle emerged—**terrorism**. At the 1976 Olympics in Munich, Israeli athletes were taken hostage and killed by Arab nationalist terrorists. After that globally publicized incident, the Palestine Liberation Organization and other such groups continued to pursue terrorist actions against Jewish citizens of Israel and other states. Anti-Semitism was an important component of these terrorist groups' agenda.

In Iraq, Saddam Hussein managed to fashion himself as a regional protector of Arab nationalism against the West. Hussein had come to power in 1979 as a secularizing popular nationalist, and the United States had assisted his regime because he seemed to offer a counterbalance to the radical Islamic regime in power in Iran since 1977. From the beginning, Hussein played American concerns and Soviet regional interests to his advantage, securing financial help from both superpowers during the Cold War. Content to have him in power and as a supplier of oil for western needs, the United States overlooked the regime's abuses against religious and ethnic minorities. But when Hussein refashioned himself as a paragon of Arab nationalism against Israel and the West and attacked Kuwait in 1991,

the West reacted with military intervention. During the Gulf War, Hussein launched missile attacks against Israel. This anti-Israeli and more broadly anti-Semitic agenda continued during the 1990s, when Iraq offered cash to the families of **suicide bombers** who attacked Israelis.

Growing Tensions The American-led coalition scored a sweeping victory, but the Gulf War left complicated legacies that came to haunt the UN, the European Union, and the international community in general. Inside Iraq, Hussein became solidly entrenched. The country's Shi'ite and Kurdish peoples suffered harsh reprisals, including the use of chemical and biological weapons, and the traumatic environmental and psychological effects of the war on both civilians and soldiers are still unfolding. During the 1990s, the European allies in the war remained convinced that UN sanctions and inspection teams could curb Hussein's abuses, but the American leadership began to lose faith in such methods.

An important consequence of the Gulf War was the destabilization of the Middle East, with Israel enlisting the support of the United States and European governments while some Arab states began to see themselves as more in conflict with the West than as allies of the Americans in putting down Hussein's bullying actions in the region. European countries that had supported the United States in the 1991 war resisted drawing the same clear lines as the Americans between supporting Israel and vilifying its Arab foes, including the Palestine Liberation Organization. In 1993, when President Bill Clinton hosted Israeli and Palestinian leaders and orchestrated the **Oslo Agreements** as a step toward a peaceful resolution of their conflict, Europe remained in the background. Many in Europe viewed the United States as unfairly favoring Israel, though Britain steadily supported the American role.

The War on Terrorism Terrorist attacks continued in the 1990s in Africa, Southeast Asia, and Europe, but an unprecedented challenge to the international order came on **September 11, 2001**, when an al-Qaeda attack brought down the World Trade Center in New York and destroyed part of the Pentagon in Washington, D.C. The 9/11 attacks killed more than three thousand people from more than sixty countries and were the most severe attacks on American soil since Pearl Harbor. They prompted a major foreign policy shift by the George W. Bush administration.

Within days, president Bush declared a War on Terrorism and embarked on an aggressive policy of employing all American intelligence, diplomatic, and military resources to respond to this grave terrorist threat. Although a significant number of European nationals were killed during the 9/11 attacks, European countries responded to the American call

terrorism Violence or other harmful acts against civilians, often by disempowered groups trying to force political change.

suicide bombers Individuals who carry out terrorist attacks by setting off explosive devices that also kill themselves.

Oslo Agreements Agreements signed by Israel and the PLO in 1993 to establish an independent Palestinian state and subsequently repudiated by both sides.

September 11, 2001 Day on which al-Qaeda terrorists crashed hijacked passenger planes into the World Trade Center in New York, the Pentagon in Washington, D.C., and in a field in Pennsylvania (a plane headed for the White House).

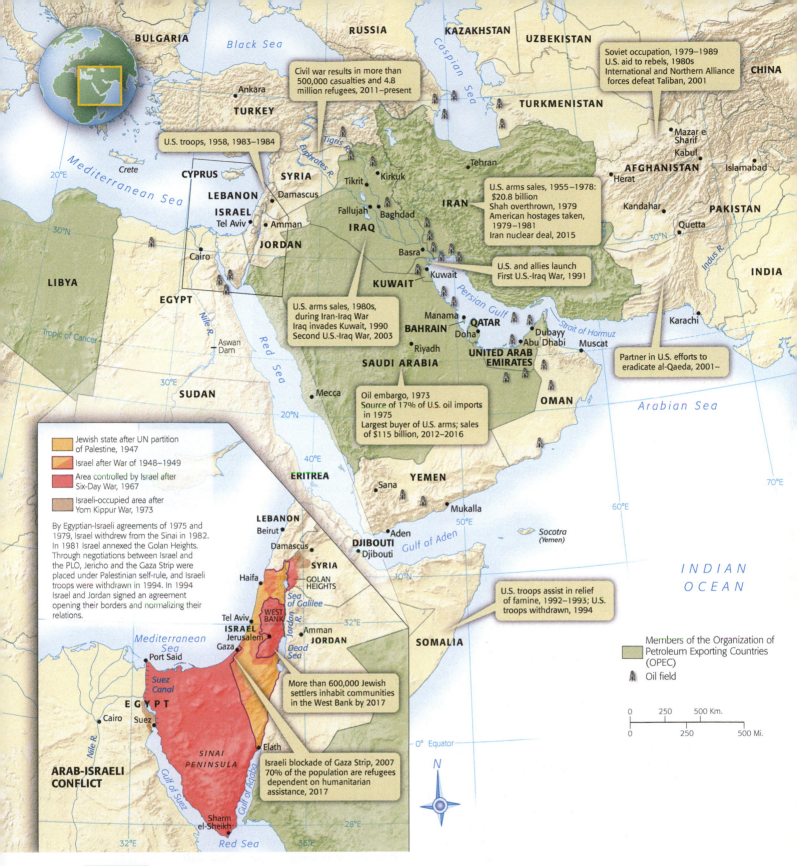

Map 30.3 **Israel-Palestine since 1948** The state of Israel and the stateless Palestinians have been at the heart of struggles in the Middle East for economic resources, political legitimacy, and international support.

The map includes the following annotations:

- Civil war results in more than 500,000 casualties and 4.8 million refugees, 2011–present
- U.S. troops, 1958, 1983–1984
- Soviet occupation, 1979–1989 U.S. aid to rebels, 1980s International and Northern Alliance forces defeat Taliban, 2001
- U.S. arms sales, 1955–1978: $20.8 billion Shah overthrown, 1979 American hostages taken, 1979–1981 Iran nuclear deal, 2015
- U.S. and allies launch First U.S.-Iraq War, 1991
- U.S. arms sales, 1980s, during Iran-Iraq War Iraq invades Kuwait, 1990 Second U.S.-Iraq War, 2003
- Partner in U.S. efforts to eradicate al-Qaeda, 2001–
- Oil embargo, 1973 Source of 17% of U.S. oil imports in 1975 Largest buyer of U.S. arms; sales of $115 billion, 2012–2016
- U.S. troops assist in relief of famine, 1992–1993; U.S. troops withdrawn, 1994
- More than 600,000 Jewish settlers inhabit communities in the West Bank by 2017
- Israeli blockade of Gaza Strip, 2007 70% of the population are refugees dependent on humanitarian assistance, 2017

Legend (ARAB-ISRAELI CONFLICT):
- Jewish state after UN partition of Palestine, 1947
- Israel after War of 1948–1949
- Area controlled by Israel after Six-Day War, 1967
- Israeli-occupied area after Yom Kippur War, 1973

By Egyptian-Israeli agreements of 1975 and 1979, Israel withdrew from the Sinai in 1982. In 1981 Israel annexed the Golan Heights. Through negotiations between Israel and the PLO, Jericho and the Gaza Strip were placed under Palestinian self-rule, and Israeli troops were withdrawn in 1994. In 1994 Israel and Jordan signed an agreement opening their borders and normalizing their relations.

- Members of the Organization of Petroleum Exporting Countries (OPEC)
- Oil field

1. Can you estimate how much Israel has expanded the territories it controls since its founding in 1947?

2. What are the states with which Israel has ongoing border tensions?

3. What percentage, roughly speaking, of the border of the state of Israel is or has been recently contested?

Elise Amandola/AP Images

Chemical Weapons

In February 2003, U.S. Secretary of State Colin Powell went before the UN General Assembly to convince the international community that Saddam Hussein was concealing chemical and biological weapons, and request the approval of the Security Council to commence military action against Iraq. Here he holds up a vial of anthrax, a life-threatening infectious disease reputed to be in the terrorist arsenal.

❯❯ *How is Colin Powell making use of his position to drive home the argument for war?*

to action in different ways. The initial military campaign in Afghanistan, one of whose goals was to find and capture **Osama bin Laden**, the al-Qaeda leader and mastermind behind the 9/11 attacks, was broadly supported by governments in Europe. NATO members sent military, logistical, and humanitarian support. The European public was less eager to support these actions, however, and massive antiwar protests took place all over western Europe. The protests generally identified the United States as the sole country engaged in military and economic imperialism. Though the war officially ended in 2014, U.S. troops continued to participate in various military operations into 2017.

The Iraq War When President George W. Bush shifted his focus in the War on Terrorism from Afghanistan to Iraq, European political leaders responded in an increasingly negative manner. The UN was at that time involved in overseeing economic sanctions and inspections to make sure Iraq was destroying its military capabilities, as Saddam Hussein had agreed to do after the Gulf War. Starting in 2002, reports about Iraq's nuclear and chemical capabilities in defiance of the 1991 agreements and UN resolutions led the Bush administration to contemplate military action against Iraq. In late 2002, the European countries on the UN Security Council (Great Britain, France, Russia, and Spain) made it clear that they would not support

Osama bin Laden (1957–2011) Militant Saudi Arabian Islamist who founded al-Qaeda in 1988 and organized the 9/11 attacks on the United States; spent the next decade in hiding in Afghanistan and Pakistan, where he was finally ambushed and killed by American forces.

military action by the United States until all peaceful options, especially international inspections, had been exhausted. In 2003, the inspectors openly stated that there were no weapons of mass destruction left in Iraq.

In a last attempt to convince the UN that collective military action was necessary, in February 2003 U.S. Secretary of State Colin Powell presented an impassioned report on Iraq's severe violations of the UN resolutions. Some, such as Britain and Spain, were convinced, but most other countries were not. The United States went to war against Iraq a month later, its preemptive strike justified as intended to destroy nuclear and biochemical weapons capabilities, but these capabilities proved to be an illusion, as Powell later acknowledged.

The Iraq War split the European political leadership and population, but not along Cold War lines. The French, Russians, and Germans vehemently opposed the war, and the British, Dutch, Italians, and Spaniards supported it. These different responses were based on different fears regarding terrorist actions; different views about the U.S. disregard for the UN as well as U.S. policies on the Middle East, especially the Israeli-Palestinian conflict; and pragmatic assessments of economic benefits and costs in the aftermath of the war. For instance, the Spanish were concerned about terrorism at home and supported the Americans as a deterrent to their own internal enemies, whereas the Russians opposed the intervention because they did not want to invite terrorist activities in volatile places like Chechnya. The French and Germans resented the American disregard of the UN. The postcommunist countries generally identified Hussein with the kind of tyrannical government that had dominated their region for fifty years and so were eager for a direct military alliance with the United States that would stand against Russia. Romania and Bulgaria welcomed American bases that would deploy troops to Iraq. Yet the level of anti-Americanism in Europe had never been so high among both politicians and the general public.

Iraq emerged out of this conflict a bruised and unstable country. Though a new constitution and free parliamentary elections took place, the country soon became embroiled in a civil war caused by friction among various religious and ethnic factions. The rise of the **Islamic State of Iraq and Syria (ISIS)** in 2014 provoked a new wave of instability and fear in the area, with global repercussions. The Jihadist terrorist group was successful in tapping into antiwestern frustrations after the end of the Iraq War, together with antiglobalization feelings exacerbated by the economic recession staring in 2008. Control by ISIS of significant parts of Iraq and Syria into 2017 has prompted repeated discussions of international military action and eventually the participation of Russia on the side of the Assad regime in Syria.

30-3c Instant Communication and the Internet

Even as they remain divided over international politics, Europeans and Americans have become more closely connected than ever through new means of communication, information exchange, and entertainment. The end of the twentieth century brought communications revolutions that have made distances insignificant and provided instant access almost anywhere on earth. The new technologies brought people greater freedom to relate to each other and to become "virtually" anyone; they also brought greater power to those who create and implement these technologies, from generating "fake news" to organizing simultaneous protests of millions of people around the world.

CONNECTIONS: Just as the development of the printing press in the fifteenth century revolutionized the production and especially circulation of ideas (see Section 12-3c Printing, a New Medium), the Internet altered how we think and communicate with each other since the late twentieth century.

Connected Through TV Cable television, first introduced in the United States in the 1970s, became wildly popular across Europe in the 1990s. Many people in the postcommunist countries went from having access to one or two government-controlled channels to having twenty or more public and private channels through inexpensive cable packages. Overnight, a person sitting in his living room in Sofia, Bulgaria, went from watching the daily dose of communist speeches to being able to choose everything from Scooby-Doo cartoons to the *Daily Show with Jon Stewart*. The impact of the diversity of mostly American programs and channels was tremendous all over the globe.

The Internet Revolution Another component of the communications revolution was the **Internet**, which, since its inception in 1992, has become the most important means for information gathering and exchange in today's world. Ubiquitous in Europe, it has proved to be an equalizer, as differences in access arise largely from differences in education and technical know-how rather than from economic status. Young people have come to assume they can always be connected to others anywhere in the world, and they share ideas and music with people they have never met. But the spread of the Internet has not necessarily encouraged communication across cultures or languages. It has become more of a resource for creating parallel communities of people with similar tastes and interests. Fans of Lady Gaga, for example, create websites to communicate about her; they rarely explore other types of music. White supremacist groups, too, have found niches where their biases are reinforced by all participants rather than challenged by those who oppose their racist ideologies.

Above all, the Internet has facilitated the possibility of imagining multiple identities, of turning the concept of the self in a community into a more fluid and less concretely bound thing. Fact and fiction blend together in the virtual space, making it easy to converse across national borders and to imagine being anyone or anywhere. The free flow of ideas challenges national allegiances, and authoritarian regimes, such as China, have censored the Internet. But users have ways of getting around such controls.

The Twitter Generation and Political Protest The most spectacular events to date in terms of the political uses of the Internet and instant telecommunications have involved the use of cell phones, YouTube, Facebook, and Twitter to document egregious political abuses by authoritarian regimes in countries such as Iran, Moldova, and Kyrgyzstan, as well as abuses by law enforcement in democratic countries. In all these places,

Communication Revolution Just as the development of the printing press in the fifteenth century revolutionized the production and especially circulation of ideas (see chapter fifteen), the Internet altered how we think and communicate with each other since the late twentieth century.

Islamic State of Iraq and Syria (ISIS) Jihadist terrorist group also known as ISIL and Daesh that, beginning in 2014, has seized control of significant parts of Iraq and Syria.

Internet Global computer network created in 1992 that makes it possible to instantly connect to people and information around the world.

Mario Ionescu.

Anticorruption Protests

In February 2017, over half a million Romanian citizens took to the streets to protest against measures taken by the recently elected Social Democratic government to protect corrupt politicians. The measures were retracted and the minister of justice resigned after a week of massive gatherings.

popular street uprisings and government violence against the protesters have become instantly broadcast all over the world, in many instances when no independent media had access to the events.

In the early 2010s, in Tunisia, Egypt, and Libya, protesters made successful use of the new technologies to get organized, publicize their views, and expose the abuses of the regimes against which they were fighting. The **Arab Spring**, as these series of protests came to be known, brought hope and trepidation in the world about internal and international trajectories of the countries in the Middle East. While a more democratic regime came about in Tunisia, the protests in Syria brought about a swift and brutal response from the Assad regime, and contributed to the regional instability that eventually gave rise to ISIS.

By early 2017, the revolution in social media enabled waves of street protest without precedent in size and diversity of participation. Starting from a post on Facebook by three women, the Women's March on January 21, the day after President Trump was inaugurated, brought into the street between 3.3 and 4.6 million people in 550 cities in the United States and another 100 cities around the world. Billed as a loose coalition of opponents to Trump and supporters of women's issues, this protest became the largest in U.S. history and the world, and it came about in an entirely grassroots fashion. The long-term impact of this historic event remains to be seen, but in the short term it seems to have generated hope and motivation in

participating in such street protests, as seen on campuses and at airports in the United States shortly after.

In February 2017, drawing inspiration from such protests and using the social media, the citizens of Romania went into the street to show their opposition to measures by the newly elected government to undermine a popular anticorruption campaign. The protests continued for over two weeks and inspired similar gatherings in France, Albania, and Bulgaria. More recently, these protests have inspired other young people to organize anti-corruption pro-EU mass gatherings in Hungary and Slovakia. Most notable among all of these events has been their peaceful character, with both the protesters and law enforcement personnel treating each other with respect and a clear understanding of the rule of law. It remains to be seen how much this sort of street pressure becomes a recurrent part of politics and what sorts of long-term changes it can elicit.

30-4 The Future of the West

» **What important challenges are likely to reshape the West in the near future?**

» **What is the meaning of western civilization in the global future?**

The face of the West is likely to become less specifically "western" in the twenty-first century. Even as Europeans are holding on to old institutions, from politics to social relations and culture, they are debating the meaning of these institutions both inside Europe and beyond. Demographically, with migration on the

Arab Spring Series of uprisings that began in December 2010 in Islamic countries in North Africa and the Middle East that have resulted in important reforms by the existing regimes, the overturn of some regimes, as well as brutal reprisals by others.

rise and large birthrate differentials among various social categories of Europeans, the face of the West is also likely to change significantly in the next generation. In the short run, the most important challenges and frictions remain between Christian and Muslim populations. In the long run, it is not clear whether the primacy of western civilization, as asserted in the past few thousand years, is likely to endure.

30-4a Old Institutions, New Directions

In the twenty-first century, the West seems to have retained important institutions, but their future is somewhat uncertain. Nation-states are still the basic political units of government. Nationalism remains an important rallying force for politicians and average citizens, from Washington to Moscow. But the multinational EU has created a new model for international political organization and peaceful cooperation among states. Whether the European Union can retain this healthy balance remains to be seen after Britain completes its departure from the EU.

New Economic Competitors In the global economy, most traditional economic institutions have taken on new elements. Small businesses continue to exist, but they are rarely able to operate without some direct or indirect assistance from multinational companies. With oil controlled by the **Organization of Petroleum Exporting Countries (OPEC)** and in the hands of a tiny group of multinational corporations, no one government can dictate the use of these resources, and small businesses are very much at the mercy of rising oil prices. A weaver in Bloomington, Indiana, may succeed or fail in selling her product not only on the basis of its quality or the demand for weavings but ultimately also on the basis of competitive pricing. Yet the costs for producing those weavings—from paying for yarn transported from elsewhere to paying for the electricity and other utilities in the workshop—are controlled by global market forces, especially the rising cost of energy. The until recently undisputed economic leadership of the United States in the world has recently been surpassed by the European Union and is being further challenged by China's spectacular rise since the 2000s.

Changing Social Institutions Even basic social and cultural institutions and traditions are likely to be greatly transformed. The traditional definition of marriage as a social institution, initially sanctioned by religious authorities in the Middle Ages and in the twentieth century identified as a secular institution, has recently been challenged. Gay couples all over the world have succeeded in challenging legal restrictions against same-sex marriage. This challenge is testing the boundaries of secularization in the West, and

evangelical organizations have reacted with heavy criticism against these changes as a threat to the stability of the family.

The Future of Organized Religion Religious institutions are also being challenged from within the ranks of the clergy. With the decrease in young men's willingness to join the Catholic priesthood, religious reformers have suggested the need to reconsider clerical celibacy. Others have suggested that women should also be allowed into the priesthood. Christian denominations such as the Episcopalians and Methodists have undertaken reforms toward greater gender and even sexual inclusion, but the Catholic Church has refused to consider any such reforms.

30-4b Who Is a European?

Even though an Argentinian became the first non-European pope in 2013, Catholic institutions remain essentially tied to Europe, while Muslim institutions remain defined as largely nonwestern. The growth of Muslim populations in many European states, such as Holland, Denmark, Spain, Britain, France, and Germany, is forcing non-Muslims to ask themselves about their relationship with these often deeply religious communities that uphold seemingly non-European traditions and cultural values. For instance, a video that depicts the culture of Holland for its immigrant populations includes images of topless women and gay couples kissing as examples of the tolerance and liberal tradition that the Dutch government is proud of. But the video does not also include images of Muslim women in traditional veils, suggesting the limits of what liberal democratic Europe is willing to embrace.

Overall, the decreasing birthrate among secular and Christian Europeans, and the parallel rising birthrate among Muslim Europeans, is posing a serious question about what being a European might mean a generation from now. Israel faces a particularly perplexing dilemma, as the sharp differences in birthrates between Jews and Arabs in that state indicate that in the next generation Muslims will constitute more than a quarter of the Israeli population.

Democracy and Europeanness Politically, democratic forms of government have become an important marker of Europeanness. EU enlargement has been tied to how well applicants can demonstrate potential (Greece, Portugal, and Spain) or success (the postcommunist applicants) in creating a democracy. Yet radical antidemocratic movements are still present everywhere in Europe,

Organization of Petroleum Exporting Countries (OPEC) International organization that oversees price and supply fluctuations in the production and sales of oil.

both as political parties and as militant terrorist cells. One thing is certain: the clear-cut East–West divide between those who belong to the European core and those who are at the margins is vanishing. Not everyone wants to welcome every country, from Iceland to the Ukraine, into the new European home, but it is becoming increasingly difficult to justify any divisions along these lines.

Education and Urbanization Europeanness has also become identified more closely with highly urbanized and well-educated societies that are secular yet tolerant of religious difference. The vast majority of Europeans live in cities, yet some are choosing to reject the overcrowded, traffic-jammed, polluted urban setting for the simpler country life. This choice has been a response to the excesses of globalization and an embrace of the local resources it endangers. Yet this "simple life" is facilitated by new communication technologies, such as cell phones, luxuries many cannot afford.

Most Europeans have graduated from high school and have attended institutions of higher education. Education has been an important tool in providing greater equality to all people, regardless of gender, class, ethnicity, or religion—one of the great successes of the post–1945 welfare state. Yet the cost of these state services has become so burdensome as to endanger the quality of public education. As a result, private institutions are proliferating, creating new levels of competition and possibly inequality in terms of access to high-quality education.

Religiousness and Secularism Even though secularism and religious tolerance have remained important components of Europeanness, since the 1990s, debates over the acceptance of religious differences, especially with regard to Judaism and Islam, have grown. Anti-Semitism and anti-Muslim attitudes are on the rise, especially since 9/11. The ban in French schools against the headscarves that all observant Muslim girls must wear calls into question the level of religious tolerance in the cradle of modern European democracy.

Even though European people like to represent their identity and culture as very different from the American identity and culture, the lifestyle of the average person in Europe is increasingly similar to that of the average person in the United States. The European past, long a mark of European distinctiveness, is becoming more difficult to discern in the face of a shared popular culture. A Polish college student in Warsaw is much closer in her fashion preferences, job options, and hobbies to an American college student in Chicago than she is to her Polish parents who grew up under communism. It is increasingly the past, rather than the future, that is likely to define the West as somehow unique in the world.

CHAPTER Review

Summary

» Since 1991, Europe has become increasingly democratized.

» States have had to cut back welfare programs, but overall public services from health care to education remain important benefits.

» Since the mid-1990s, European companies have become serious competitors of U.S. companies in the world market.

» The European Union has been an economic success, even in countries hit most seriously by the global recession.

» Europe has not been able to act as a unit in international affairs, especially after the terrorist attacks of 9/11.

» There has been a growth in popular anti-American attitudes.

» There is increasing homogeneity across Europe in terms of markers for social advancement, consumer tastes, and the tendency of people to identify themselves as European along with their other national and regional identities.

» Europeanness has become tied to a past culture, something significantly unique to their continent, rather than to the current and future aspirations of people living in Europe.

Chronology

1991	Gulf War begins [Middle East, Americas, Europe] Soviet Union is dissolved [Europe]
1991–1995	Serbs, Croats, and Bosnians fight ethnic-based civil wars in Yugoslavia [Europe]
1992	Internet society is chartered [Global]
1993	Israel and the Palestine Liberation Organization sign Oslo Agreements [Middle East] European Union comes into being after ratification of the Maastricht treaty [Europe]
1995	World Trade Organization is created [Global] Dayton Agreement ends Bosnian War, establishes an independent Bosnia and Serbian Republic of Bosnia [Europe] Schengen agreement goes into effect [Europe]
1996	Poland, Czech Republic, and Hungary join NATO [Europe]
1997	Tony Blair is elected prime minister of Great Britain [Europe]
1998	Russian stock market collapses [Europe]
1999	NATO begins Kosovo War against Serbia [Europe]
2000	Vladimir Putin is elected president of Russia [Europe] Fall of Miloševic government [Europe]
2001	Al-Qaeda hijacks passenger planes to attack the World Trade Center in New York and the Pentagon in Washington, D.C. [Americas]
2002	Euro becomes European currency [Europe]
2003	Iraq War begins [Middle East, Americas, Europe]
2004	Al-Qaeda terrorists bomb commuter trains in Madrid [Europe] Ten new members, mostly postcommunist countries, join the European Union [Europe] Russians reinvade Chechnya [Europe]
2005	Same-sex marriage is legalized in Spain [Europe] Angela Merkel becomes the first woman chancellor of Germany [Europe]
2007	Romania and Bulgaria join the European Union [Europe] Russian cyberattack brings down all Internet services in Estonia [Europe]
2008	Iceland's currency collapses at beginning of global recession, European Union orchestrates a bailout [Europe] Kosovo declares independence [Europe] Barack Obama becomes the first African American to serve as President of the United States [Americas]

2009	Ratification of Lisbon Treaty [Europe] Great Britain withdraws troops from Iraq [Middle East, Europe]
2010	Beginning of the Arab Spring [Middle East]
2011	Osama Bin Laden captured and killed [Middle East] Christine Lagarde appointed first woman to lead the IMF [Global] Syrian civil war begins [Middle East]
2013	Ukrainian street protests begin [Europe]
2014	Official end of War in Iraq [Middle East, Americas] rise of ISIS [Global] Russia annexes Crimea [Europe] beginning of civil war in Ukraine [Europe]
2015	Paris terrorist attacks, killing 130 people [Europe]
2016	Paris agreement on climate change begins to be enforced [Global] Britain votes to leave the European Union [Europe]
2017	Over 3 million people in 650 cities around the United States and the world join the Women's March opposing newly elected U.S. President Trump [Global] United States announces it will leave the Paris Climate Accord [Global]

Critical Thinking Questions

Take time to pull together all the important information in the chapter by answering the following questions.

Eastern Europe After Communism

» What impact did the postcommunist transition have on eastern European states and societies?

» To what extent have these countries become more democratic?

European Integration

» How has the European Union transformed European politics and economies?

» What impact has the European Union had on European security matters?

Europe and Globalization

» How has globalization transformed the economic power of Europe in the world?

» What have been the great international challenges since 1991?

The Future of the West

» What important challenges are likely to reshape the West in the near future?

» What is the meaning of western civilization in the global future?

MindTap® is a fully online personalized learning experience built upon Cengage Learning content. MindTap® combines student learning tools—readings, multimedia, activities, and assessments—into a singular Learning Path that guides students through the course and helps students develop the critical thinking, analysis, and communication skills that are essential to academic and professional success.

Index